DATE DUE

DE 7 '97			

DEMCO 38-296

ELIZABETH GASKELL

by the same author

Documentary and Imaginative Literature 1880–1920
Elizabeth Gaskell: A Portrait in Letters
Science and Literature in the Nineteenth Century

R

ELIZABETH GASKELL

THE EARLY YEARS

JOHN CHAPPLE

Manchester University Press

MANCHESTER AND NEW YORK

distributed exclusively in the USA by St. Martin's Press

University Press
r M13 3NR,UK
New York, NY 10010, USA

in the USA
ifth Avenue, New York,
JSA

In-Publication Data
A catalogue record is available from the British Library

Library of Congress Cataloging-in-Publication Data applied for

ISBN 0 7190 2550 8 hardback

First published 1997

01 00 99 98 97   10 9 8 7 6 5 4 3 2 1

Typeset in Galliard
by Koinonia, Manchester

Printed in Great Britain
by Redwood Books, Trowbridge

To Joan Leach & John Geoffrey Sharps

William James to Henry James:
'You haven't to forge every sentence in the teeth
of irreducible and stubborn facts as I do.
It is like walking through the densest brushwood.'

Contents

Appendices

Illustrations

Sandlebridge Farm
By permission of the Cheshire County Council Archives and Local Studies

Old kitchen fireplace in Sandlebridge Farm
Courtesy of Manchester Central Library

Old Lindsey Row and Beaufort Row, Chelsea
By permission of The Royal Borough of Kensington and Chelsea
Libraries and Arts Service

Uncle Peter Holland
Dr Henry Holland
Mrs Lumb's house, Knutsford
Courtesy of Manchester Central Library

The Byerleys' School for Young Ladies
Courtesy of the Shakespeare Birthplace Trust

Elizabeth Stevenson's first music book
Courtesy of Manchester Central Library

Avonbank from the river
Courtesy of the Shakespeare Birthplace Trust

Cousin Samuel Holland
***The Slate Mine*, Stadtler after de Loutherbourg**
Courtesy of The National Library of Wales

William Gaskell
Courtesy of Manchester Central Library

Bust of Elizabeth Stevenson by David Dunbar

the illustrations are placed between pp. 174-5

Acknowledgements

I must acknowledge the generosity of those who have allowed me to use letters, diaries and papers, especially Mrs Rosemary Trevor Dabbs, Mrs Portia Holland and Mr David Holland, the help of scholar-collectors like John Geoffrey Sharps and Mrs Joan Leach, Secretary of the Gaskell Society, the pains taken on my behalf by archivists, librarians and curators in several countries and the assistance of hundreds of individuals whom I am forced to thank here collectively but nonetheless very sincerely. I am grateful to the Trustees, Fellows and others who have permitted me to quote from documents in their care. (Private and institutional owners are recorded in the list of abbreviations below.) I am also indebted to the Master and Fellows of Corpus Christi College, Cambridge, for a visiting fellowship in the first half of 1992, to the Leverhulme Trust, which awarded me one of its emeritus research grants, and to my wife and children for their infinite patience – to date.

The rewards of actually working with letters and documents in collections at Berwick, Edinburgh, Knutsford, Leigh, Halifax, Wakefield, Warrington, Stratford, Chelsea and a number of other places have in practice complemented the advantages of access to the vast resources of the British Library, the Public Record Office, Manchester Central Library, John Rylands University Library of Manchester, the Brotherton Collection of Leeds University Library and Cambridge University Library. Dr Williams's Library in Bedford Square, London, Manchester College Oxford, and the Literary and Philosophical Society of Newcastle upon Tyne also deserve special mention, together with my own libraries in the University and City of Hull.

I am also indebted to Arthur Pollard, who invited me to edit the letters of Mrs Gaskell with him over thirty years ago, to Janet Allan, John Bennett, Bill Chaloner, Wendy Craik, Angus Easson, John Jump, Angela Leighton, Christine Lingard, Francesco Marroni, Bill Ruddick, Marion Shaw, Alan Shelston, Patsy Stoneman, Margaret Smith, Anna Unsworth, Frank Whitehead, Philip Yarrow and members of the Gaskell Society for help and stimulating discussions over many years, to my sons John and James for solving my many computer problems, to Stephen Gill for generously presenting the results of his own research in America and to Jenny Uglow for passing on to me the new information brought to light by the publication of her most stimulating biography of Elizabeth Gaskell in 1993. My wife Kathleen, Linda Bankier, Francis Cowe, Owen Knowles, Joan Leach, Michael Lewis, Frank Whitehead, Lewis Hill and Philip Yarrow have made valuable comments upon sections of my text.

Note on sources

The great diversity of sources has suggested that the most significant manuscripts and books used in this study should be grouped by subjects in a bibliographical appendix (pp. 462-76 below), the order of which will be found to correspond pretty closely to the order of chapters. Appendixes A, B and C provide condensed information about the Stevenson, Holland and Turner families in particular.

Notes after each chapter provide short references to works listed in the bibliographical appendix and full descriptions of incidental sources where they first occur. Important manuscripts have been faithfully transcribed with their characteristic spellings – such as possessive 'it's' – but I have lowered all superscript letters and, occasionally, corrected minor slips or ignored alterations that seemed insignificant.

Abbreviations and short titles

LRO	Leicestershire Record Office
LSE	London School of Economics
LUBL	Leeds University, Brotherton Library
MCL	Manchester Central Library
MCO	Manchester College Oxford
NLI	National Library of Ireland
NLS	National Library of Scotland
NLPS	Literary and Philosophical Society of Newcastle upon Tyne
NLW	National Library of Wales
NPG	National Portrait Gallery
NYPL	New York Public Library
PCC	Prerogative Court of Canterbury
PCY	Prerogative Court of York
PML	Pierpont Morgan Library, New York
PRO	Public Record Office, Chancery Lane and Kew
PSUL	Pennsylvania State University Libraries
PUL	Princeton University Library
RL	Rochdale Library
RTD	Collection of Mrs Rosemary Trevor Dabbs (LUBL)
RUL	Rutgers University Library
SCA	Sheffield City Archives
SRO	Scottish Record Office
SSBT	Stratford-upon-Avon, Shakespeare Birthplace Trust
TCC	Trinity College, Cambridge
TWA	Tyne and Wear Archives, Newcastle
UCL	University College London
WAL	Wigan Archives, Leigh
WCL	Warrington Central Library
WRO1	Warwickshire Record Office
WRO2	St Helen's Record Office, Worcester
WYA	West Yorkshire Archives, Bradford
YHA	York Health Archives

SHORT TITLES

Bicentenary Lectures   *The Literary and Philosophical Society of Newcastle upon Tyne: Bicentenary Lectures*, intro. John Philipson, Newcastle upon Tyne, 1994

Boase   Frederic Boase, *Modern English Biography*, 6 vols, repr. London 1965

Brontë Letters   *The Letters of Charlotte Brontë With a Selection of Letters by Family and Friends*, ed. Margaret Smith, I (1829–47), Oxford, 1995

Carlyle Letters   *The Collected Letters of Thomas and Jane Welsh Carlyle*, ed. Charles Richard Sanders *et al.*, 24 vols, Durham, N.C., 1970–cont.

Chadwick, 1910   Mrs Ellis H. Chadwick, *Mrs. Gaskell: Haunts, Homes, and Stories*, London, 1910

Chadwick, 1913   *Mrs. Gaskell: Haunts, Homes, and Stories*, new and rev. edn, London, 1913

CH Gaskell   *Elizabeth Gaskell: The Critical Heritage*, ed. Angus Easson, London and New York, 1991

Coleridge Letters   *Collected Letters of Samuel Taylor Coleridge*, ed. Earl Leslie Griggs, I, Oxford, 1956

Darwin Correspondence   *The Correspondence of Charles Darwin*, ed. Frederick Burkhardt, Sydney Smith *et al.*, Cambridge, etc., 1985– [vol. VII, 1991, Supplement' 1821–57]

Easson   Angus Easson, *Elizabeth Gaskell*, London, Boston and Henley, 1979

Edgeworth Letters   *Maria Edgeworth: Letters from England 1813–1844*, ed. Christina Colvin, Oxford, 1971

Fryckstedt   Monica Correa Fryckstedt, *Elizabeth Gaskell's 'Mary Barton' and 'Ruth': A Challenge to Christian England*, Studia Anglistica Upsaliensia 43, Uppsala, 1982

Gérin   Winifred Gérin, *Elizabeth Gaskell: A Biography*, Oxford, 1976

Green   Henry Green, *Knutsford, Its Traditions and History with Reminiscences, Anecdotes, and Notices of the Neighbourhood*, 1859, repr. E. L. Burney, Didsbury, 1969

Greville Journal   C. C. F. Greville, *The Greville Memoirs: A Journal of the Reigns of King George IV. King William IV. and Queen Victoria*, ed. Henry Reeve, new edn, 8 vols, London, etc. 1896

Haldane   Elizabeth Haldane, *Mrs. Gaskell and Her Friends*, London, 3rd imp., 1931

Hall   Edward Hall, TS, '*Cranford* again: the Knutsford letters, 1809–1824' (MCL)

Hopkins   A. B. Hopkins, *Elizabeth Gaskell: Her Life and Work*, London, 1952

Hunter   Joseph Hunter, *Familiae Minorum Gentium*, Harleian society XXXVII, London, 1894

Irvine   Wm Fergusson Irvine, ed. *A History of the Family of Holland of Mobberley and Knutsford in the County of Chester ... from Materials Collected by the Late Edgar Swinton Holland*, pr. pr. Edinburgh, 1902

Jewsbury Letters   *Selections from the Letters of Geraldine Jewsbury to Jane Welsh Carlyle*, ed. Mrs Alexander Ireland, London, 1892

Knutsford Edn   A. W. Ward, ed. *The Works of Mrs. Gaskell*, 8 vols, London, 1906 (The Knutsford Edition)

Letters   *The Letters of Mrs Gaskell*, ed. J. A. V. Chapple and Arthur Pollard, Manchester, 1966; Cambridge, Mass., 1967

Letters and Memorials   *Letters and Memorials of Catherine Winkworth*, ed. [Susanna Winkworth and Margaret J. Shaen], 2 vols, pr. pr. Clifton, 1883–86

Losh Diaries   *The Diaries and Correspondence of James Losh*, ed. Edward Hughes, Surtees Society CLXXI, CLXXIV, Durham and London, 1962–63

Macaulay Letters   *The Letters of Thomas Babington Macaulay*, ed. Thomas Pinney, Cambridge, 1974

McLachlan   Herbert McLachlan, *English Education Under the Test Acts, Being the History of the Nonconformist Academies 1662–1820*, Manchester, 1931

Parish   Charles Parish, *The History of the Literary and Philosophical Society of Newcastle upon Tyne*, II, Newcastle upon Tyne, 1990

Payne   George A. Payne, *Mrs. Gaskell and Knutsford*, 2nd edn, Manchester and London, [1906]

Payne Biog.   George A. Payne, *Mrs. Gaskell: A Brief Biography*, Manchester, 1929

Pollard   *Mrs Gaskell: Novelist and Biographer*, Manchester, 1965

Portrait   J. A. V. Chapple, *Elizabeth Gaskell: A Portrait in Letters*, Manchester, 1980

Priestley Works   *The Theological and Miscellaneous Works of Joseph Priestley*, ed. John
    Towill Rutt, London 1817–32, 26 vols
Rubenius   Aina Rubenius, *The Woman Question in Mrs. Gaskell's Life and Works*,
    Upsala [*sic*] Essays and Studies on English Language and Literature, 1950, repr.
    New York, 1973
Sanders   Gerald DeWitt Sanders, Cornell Studies in English, *Elizabeth Gaskell*, New
    Haven, etc., 1929
Scott Letters   *The Letters of Sir Walter Scott 1787–1807*, ed. H. J. C. Grierson *et al.*,
    London, 1932–37
Sharps   John Geoffrey Sharps, *Mrs. Gaskell's Observation and Invention: A Study of
    Her Non-Biographic Works*, Fontwell, Sussex, 1970
Smith   Barbara Smith, ed. *Truth, Liberty, Religion: Essays Celebrating Two Hundred
    Years of Manchester College*, Oxford, 1986
Stoneman   Patsy Stoneman, *Elizabeth Gaskell*, Brighton, 1987
Uglow   Jenny Uglow, *Elizabeth Gaskell: A Habit of Stories*, London and Boston, 1993
Waller   Ross D. Waller, 'Letters addressed to Mrs Gaskell by celebrated contem-
    poraries', *BJRL*, XIX, 1935
Ward Notebook   Adophus William Ward, MS notebook at Peterhouse, Cambridge
Wellesley Index   *The Wellesley Index to Victorian Periodicals*, ed. W. G. Houghton and
    B. Slingerland, 5 vols, 1966–89
Wordsworth Letters   *The Letters of William and Dorothy Wordsworth*, ed. Ernest de
    Selincourt, 2nd edn, rev. Chester L. Shaver, I, Oxford, 1967; II, rev. Mary
    Moorman, Oxford, 1969; III, Part 1, ed. de Selincourt, 2nd edn, rev. Alan G. Hill,
    Oxford, 1978
Wright   Edgar Wright, *Mrs. Gaskell: The Basis for Reassessment*, London, New York
    and Toronto, 1965

OTHER ABBREVIATIONS

ECS or ECG	Elizabeth Cleghorn Gaskell (née Stevenson)
frag., conj., wmk	fragmentary, conjugate, watermark
MS, TS, MF	manuscript, typescript, microfilm

Initials are used in notes where full names are clear from the main text.

ABO	*The Annual Biography and Obituary*
AHR	*American Historical Review*
AR	*Annual Register*
AS	*Annals of Science*
BJIM	*British Journal of Industrial Medicine*
BJRL	*Bulletin of the John Rylands University Library of Manchester*
BJS	*British Journal of Sociology*
BSL	*Transactions of the Bibliographical Society: The Library*
BST	*Brontë Society Transactions*
CF	*The Christian Freeman*
CHJ	*Cambridge Historical Journal*

CR	*The Christian Reformer*
CRAL	*Critical Review; or, Annals of Literature*
CSR	*Chetham Society Remains*
CT	*The Christian Teacher*
DAB	*Dictionary of American Biography*
DAJ	*Derbyshire Archaeological Journal*
DNB	*Dictionary of National Biography*
DR	*Dalhousie Review*
EA	*Etudes Anglaises*
EconHR	*Economic History Review*
EHR	*English Historical Review*
ELN	*English Language Notes*
ER	*The Edinburgh Review*
ESTC	*Eighteenth Century Short Title Catalogue*
FF	*Faith and Freedom*
GE	*Gender and Education*
GM	*Gentleman's Magazine*
GSJ	*Gaskell Society Journal*
GSN	*Gaskell Society Newsletter*
HS	*History of Science*
HSLCOS	*Historic Society of Lancashire and Cheshire Occasional Series*
HSLCPP	*Historic Society of Lancashire and Cheshire Proceedings and Papers*
IGI	*International Genealogical Index, Utah, U. S. A.*
JHI	*Journal of the History of Ideas*
JKHAA	*Journal of the Knutsford Historical and Archaeological Association*
JMHRS	*Journal of the Merioneth Historical and Record Society*
JMS	*Journal of Mental Science*
JPHS	*Journal of the Presbyterian Historical Society*
JRSS	*Journal of the Royal Statistical Society*
LH	*Library History*
MG	*The Guardian (Manchester)*
MH	*Medical History*
MM	*Monthly Magazine*
MR	*The Monthly Repository*
N&Q	*Notes & Queries*
NCL	*Nineteenth-Century Literature*
NHJ	*Nathaniel Hawthorne Journal*
NMMLJ	*New Monthly Magazine and Literary Journal*
NSTC	*Nineteenth Century Short Title Catalogue (I.i: 1801-1815)*
OED	*Oxford English Dictionary*
PDM	*Protestant Dissenter's Magazine*
PH	*Publishing History*
PMLA	*Proceedings of the Modern Language Association of America*
PMLC	*Papers of the Manchester Literary Club*
QR	*Quarterly Review*
SEL	*Studies in English Literature 1500-1900, 19th Century*
SH	*Social History*
SJPE	*Scottish Journal of Political Economy*

SSF	*Studies in Short Fiction*
SSQ	*Sunday School Quarterly*
TAPS	*Transactions of the American Philosophical Society*
TEAA	*Transactions of the Edinburgh Architectural Association*
THSLC	*Transactions of the Historic Society of Lancashire and Cheshire*
TLCAS	*Transactions of the Lancashire and Cheshire Antiquarian Society*
TUHS	*Transactions of the Unitarian Historical Society*
VCH	*Victoria County History*
VS	*Victorian Studies*

Introduction

THE EARLY WRITINGS of Elizabeth Gaskell have never been found, though we know from letters by her father and brother that she was composing amusing accounts of her travels when she was nearly seventeen and had begun to keep a journal. Apart from this, there are only some words and music by others that she copied into song books now in Manchester Central Library and a single banal phrase jokingly repeated in a letter from her brother. The earliest of her letters that has so far been discovered was sent to Anne Burnett in the early summer of 1831; it was written just a few months before her twenty-first birthday. A great deal has been lost or destroyed. We can only feel grateful that five letters to her friend Harriet Carr in 1831-32 have recently turned up and that Mrs Gaskell's oldest daughter, Marianne, disobeyed her mother's occasional orders to burn the hasty missives she received or was given.

The letters written from 1831, especially those gathered in the 1966 edition of *The Letters of Mrs Gaskell* and in *The Gaskell Society Journal* for 1990, have been joyously exploited for their own lively sake and in the service of a far more detailed account of her mature career. But they contain few memories of her youth. There is a copy of a fragment containing a striking allusion to her unhappiness when she stayed in Chelsea with her father and stepmother at some indeterminate time or times, perhaps during the last few years of her father's life. She also communicates a very deliberate and positive sense of 'the little, clean, kindly country town' of Knutsford in which she had mostly been brought up, and the 'solemnly poetical places' around it in Cheshire, as she put it in a letter of May 1838 to William and Mary Howitt. But these glimpses of past existence are Wordsworthian, as much creations as recollections. They compose the beginning of a flowing self-portrait, a prelude to her imaginative life, the earliest in a series of brilliant epistolary self-projections that in some ways challenge her published fiction for value and interest.

Standard sources for her background and life up to her marriage in 1832 are not always adequate. The dates of birth of her mother and of aunt Hannah Lumb, who brought up the motherless child from babyhood, have never been discovered. They are not even given in the substantial *History of the Family of Holland of Mobberley and Knutsford* on which we have all been accustomed to rely. But relatively trivial omissions are not as serious as repeated errors. If an opinion is no longer doubted, Samuel Johnson maintained, the evidence ceases to be examined. Was Elizabeth's father William Stevenson born in 1772, as all printed sources proclaim? Was he the son of a Post-Captain in the Royal Navy? No confirmation can be found in the Admiralty papers at Kew and the records of William's birthplace, Berwick-upon-Tweed, which happen to be unusually comprehensive. They tell quite another story.

By and large, the publications of William Stevenson during an age of profound change over the turn of the century have not been authenticated and read. Besides these, even the essays he composed as a student for the ministry (some in shorthand) still exist amongst the dissenting records that abound in Dr Williams's library in London. These have lain undiscovered, and even known collections of letters by William, his sister Dorothy and his son John have not been explored in any depth. William's later handwriting is difficult to read, however, and wet-press copies of replies can be fearsome. Some documents are beautifully written. William Turner of Newcastle's well-formed hand springs to mind, as do the finely kept minutes of the committee set up in Chelsea in 1823 'for the better assessing and collecting the parish rates' and those of the Manchester Board of Health during the cholera epidemic of 1832. But very few private letter writers of the time sat down with perfect sheets of writing paper and newly sharpened quills. They scribbled so fast that their hands degenerated; they attempted to save paper by squeezing in words, writing at right angles across existing lines or even at distinctly odd angles – 'Read the corner crossings first', one enjoins. Few missives possess an address and a complete date.

Family trees can be a nightmare. Elizabeth's grandfather Samuel Holland married a daughter of Peter Swinton by a first wife before Samuel's widowed older sister Elizabeth married Peter as his second wife. Quite apart from the complications caused by cousin marriages, or the union of two brothers with two sisters, pedigrees never seem to agree with each other and guesswork is recorded as fact. There is good excuse, of course. Human behaviour is infinitely various, and baffling in practice even for the heroic few who strive to keep or construct impeccable records, with the result that biographical, histor-ical and genealogical research often resembles unsuccessful archaeology – endless digging and scraping for trivial rewards, sites only partially opened and left for later researchers to develop, not to mention total failure to find anything.

Why was so little written about the actual lives of women? One would think that their main purpose in life was to become 'relicts' of more fleeting males. No wonder Mrs Gaskell's biography of Charlotte Brontë had such an impact: a new and female voice was heard at length. Many of the central private documents relating to Elizabeth Gaskell's early life have disappeared. In 1892

L. B. Walford claimed that 'a charming little simple letter ... penned at the age of sixteen' had been recently been shown to her, probably by a relation of Elizabeth. It is not known now. Where are the 'long and amusing letters' from her old pupil that Miss Jane Byerley thanked her for in 1829? Where is the 'great deal of correspondence between Mrs Gaskell's grandfather and grandmother' Clement Shorter stated early in this century that her daughter had given him? All this correspondence is yet to be found if it has not been destroyed.[1] But no one should be reluctant to rummage when the rewards of discovery are so great. Research is neither an abstract nor a romantic process; places, books, manuscripts actually exist and can be seen, felt, consulted.

A large collection of manuscript letters by Mrs Gaskell's cousin Henry, son of her mother's brother Peter, has survived in the hands of a generous descendant. They are preserved with three travel journals of the 1820s written by Peter's daughters, Mary, Bessy and Lucy, the famous ladies of Knutsford. The secretary of the Gaskell Society, Mrs Joan Leach, drew to my attention the diary of Edward Herford, who knew Elizabeth Stevenson in Manchester at the very time she was being courted by William Gaskell. Family wills, almost all of them carefully preserved in the usual places, provide fresh and often surprising evidence. A number of documents in the remarkable John Goodchild loan collection at Wakefield, hitherto unknown to biographers of Elizabeth Gaskell and often of a kind that do not survive, allow us to reconstruct the sad features of Hannah Lumb's marriage and its aftermath – a story quite as strange as the approximate narratives that have been handed down about the aunt mainly responsible for Elizabeth's upbringing.

Biographical myths are fatally easy to create or reshape. The two daughters who lived on in Plymouth Grove with their father after Mrs Gaskell's death, Margaret Emily (Meta) and Julia Bradford, did not really know much that was accurate about their mother's childhood. Notwithstanding the annoyance Meta expressed to the editor of *Good Words* at Margaret Howitt's publication of private letters by Mrs Gaskell in its September 1895 issue, they were prepared to help with biography and criticism, notably A. W. Ward's entry in the volume of the *Dictionary of National Biography*, first published in 1890, and Thomas Seccombe's edition of *Sylvia's Lovers* in 1910. Ward's working notebook at Peterhouse, Cambridge, consulted by kind permission of the Master and Fellows, proved to be illuminating. It is extremely miscellaneous, containing long quotations in his neat, scholarly hand from such authors as Mme Louise Swanton Belloc (grandmother of Hilaire Belloc), whose thirty pages on 'Elisabeth Gaskell et ses ouvrages' of 1867 was one of the earliest accounts of Elizabeth Gaskell's life and writings and even now is hardly known in this country, let alone used. Ward's *DNB* article and introductions to the eight-volume Knutsford edition of the *Works* in 1906, which, Edgar Wright reminds us, he was reluctant to undertake because of pressure of other work, were valuable and have been highly influential.

But not everything is carefully set down in his notebook. He must have sat somewhere (perhaps in 'the stately and rather sombre drawing room' that a Brontë centenary address of 1916 tells us was hardly changed between the death of Mrs Gaskell in 1865 and Meta's in 1913) with notebook on knee – to judge by the hasty, sometimes illegible pencil scrawls in the first half of the little volume. Though a historian, he seems to have accepted much of what Meta and Julia told him about their family history at 'Christmas 1887/8', more than a century after some of the facts, without question. The aunt who brought Elizabeth up in Knutsford was hardly poor. Mrs Gaskell knew her brother far better than her daughters seem to have realised, and so on. But Ward is not alone in failing to check all that has been asserted. Was Elizabeth the second or the eighth child of her parents? Did her mother die in 1811? Was her father fifty-seven, fifty-eight or sixty-three when he died in 1829? Briefly and respectively: we can't be sure; almost certainly; he was fifty-eight, notwithstanding the statements in his obituary. One oddity in this connection is that Ward's notebook, with all its honey of daughterly invention, seems to be the only place where William Stevenson's year of birth is given correctly as 1770 rather than 1772.

Mrs. Gaskell: Haunts, Homes, and Stories, published by Mrs Ellis H. Chadwick in 1910, is a fascinating book: not a formal biography, it is both admirable and amateurish. Clement Shorter in *The Daily Chronicle* of 15 September 1910 recognised that she had collected more material about the family background and Elizabeth Gaskell's youth than ever before, but went on to note a number of errors. Other reviewers made valid criticisms of its poor organisation and literary naiveté. There was also a good deal of sniping. Meta Gaskell herself wrote to *The Guardian* on 30 September to deny that she had given her co-operation to Mrs Chadwick, saying that she had been unguarded in her private conversation because she thought that she would respect her 'mother's wish that no biography should be written of her'. A tough reviewer in *The Manchester Guardian* of 26 September 1910 corrected or denied a number of details, including the statement that Thackeray's daughters had told Mrs Gaskell and her daughters that her own father had decided long before his death that there should be no biography, and that Mrs Gaskell had thereupon expressed the same wish. There was a wounded reply to this by Mrs Chadwick on 30 September, but the editor then reiterated his stern judgement that the book was 'too faulty to be of value, or even to be harmless'.

This is too severe, and the changes she made for a second edition of *Haunts, Homes, and Stories* in 1913 have been surprisingly neglected ever since, though it is often illuminating to read the revised text against the first and speculate – there are no notes – about the sources of new material. On the very first page of the 1910 edition she informed us that Elizabeth was the second child of her parents; by 1913 she was the eighth. In her preface Chadwick states that she had revisited many places, met people who knew Mrs Gaskell and received useful information from a number of correspondents. In the interval she had discovered Elizabeth's birth certificate and published two important articles in *The Bookman* for January and December 1912, giving the evidence for the identification of her birthplace and the dating of her mother's death. These articles are listed in Robert Selig's standard reference bibliography, but Chadwick's 'new and revised edition' of 1913 is not separately listed. It is always easy to correct and supplement a pioneer, but it is done in this study with a true sense of indebtedness for what she discovered and preserved. As Matthew Prior wrote (even if he had his tongue in his cheek),

> Be to her virtues very kind;
> Be to her faults a little blind.

For all the basic research that has been carried out in the last thirty or so years, by J. G. Sharps in particular, Elizabeth Stevenson in her youth has proved as elusive as the blue rose or the green mouse sought by those for whom nature has not been prodigal enough. What would one not give for a diary like that of Cecily Cardew in Wilde's *The Importance of Being Earnest* – 'simply a very young girl's record of her own thoughts and impressions, and consequently meant for publication'! Casting flies over reluctant waters has landed many new facts about friends and relations, but not a great deal that is derived from Elizabeth herself. In this context, the letters of her brother John from 1819 and the three travel journals Mary, Bessy and Lucy Holland composed in the mid-1820s are especially rewarding. John nourished her literary interests at an early stage, by example as well as by precept. The journals are perhaps the closest parallels that could have been found to Elizabeth Stevenson's lost early writings. In addition, they reveal, consciously and unconsciously, the characters of her older cousins when they were young women of Knutsford – so often we hear about Mary and Lucy as old maids, 'characters' in a quaint little Cheshire town – and prove beyond any doubt the strong literary culture of these close relations in the 1820s.

I have therefore chosen to write a composite history of the circles in which she was brought up, a rich tapestry of friendship and association in which, for example, relations like her uncle Samuel Holland were automatically sustained in a great network of support when economic individualism failed. By the family, at least initially, her own father was assisted. This book is an attempt to recreate the interrelated lives of her family and friends, and the life she lived amongst them up to the time when she dwindled into the wife of the Reverend William Gaskell of Manchester. It is a study of *race, milieu* and *moment* that begins back in the eighteenth century and moves between Berwick and Saughton Mills and Edinburgh, Chelsea and Knutsford, Calcutta and Rangoon, the Vale of Ffestiniog, Stratford-upon-Avon and Newcastle. Material has been found on visits to most of these. (The sites of a Burmese river war and naval actions in the Adriatic are understandable exceptions.) Whenever possible, strictly relevant documentary sources have been examined. To cite a polemical title like her father William Stevenson's *Remarks on the Very*

Inferior Utility of Classical Learning is informative enough for a broad-brush portrait, but the true gleam of particularity is only achieved by reading and analysing the work itself. 'Contexts' are secondary. Biographies, histories and more general works have been consulted, frequently, but only to provide a series of specific comparisons and perspectives. As for Elizabeth Gaskell's creative works, I have deliberately refrained from using them.

Flora Masson's workmanlike and neglected account of Mrs Gaskell for the ninth edition of the *Encyclopaedia Britannica* (volume X, 1879) provided a good model in its day. There are some biographical errors, but alone till very recently she knew that Mrs Gaskell had seven rather than six children, only four of whom survived infancy. Moreover, her account of the writings was kept neatly distinct from the life. She did rather better than her father. Soon after Mrs Gaskell's death David Masson declared in *Macmillan's Magazine* for December 1865, 'Of her private life it would not only be unbefitting to speak, but I believe that its record, even if it could be fully told by those to whom it is known, would throw but little light on the literary aspect of her character.' He also claimed that *Ruth* and *Sylvia's Lovers* 'rested on a delineation of passions with which the writer was either unable or, as I rather believe, unwilling to grapple firmly'. He avoided the trap of using fiction as uncomplicated biography but thought her too sensitive and delicate-minded. We might think him too smoothly elegant, and suspect that he was intent upon a harmonious, snag-free tale.

Older writings are just as frictionless, their authors gliding almost imperceptibly from life to art and back again, or hanging fictional pearls in biographical cowslips' ears in much too simple a manner. Recent books on Elizabeth Gaskell, such as those by Aina Rubenius (1950), A. B. Hopkins (1952), Arthur Pollard (1965), Edgar Wright (1965), Margaret Ganz (1969), J. G. Sharps (1970), Wendy Craik (1975), Coral Lansbury (1975), Angus Easson (1979), Patsy Stoneman (1987), Hilary M. Shor (1992), Jane Spencer (1993), Jenny Uglow (1993) and Terence Wright (1995) are more sophisticated, though what has till recently been the standard biography, by Winifred Gérin for the Clarendon Press in 1976, is disappointing from a scholarly point of view. The complex approach of a modern critic, Felicia Bonaparte's in *The Gipsy-Bachelor of Manchester* (1992), is based on a belief that Gérin's work was definitive. This is simply too shaky a premise to support Bonaparte's otherwise stimulating interpretation of Elizabeth Gaskell's life and art combined as if they had been a single imaginative enterprise.

Origins assume great importance in a scheme of that kind, but even now certain glaring gaps in our knowledge of the early life and background mean that some things remain uncertain. Jenny Uglow claimed at the outset of her *Elizabeth Gaskell: A Habit of Stories* that 'the story of her parents and their families bears directly on her life and work; when she came to write fiction, she returned again and again to the times they lived through, the movements they took part in, the ideas they were stirred by.' This, I believe, is true. Given

Uglow's success in providing both relevant information and controlled, subtle analyses of Elizabeth Gaskell's creative works over an entire writing career, I have been able to concentrate on extending our biographical and historical knowledge of those early years where our factual knowledge is most flimsily based.

NOTE

1 C. Shorter, 'A literary letter. The late Miss "Meta" Gaskell', *The Sphere*, (*London*), LV, 8 November 1913, p. 154; Mrs L[ucy] B[ethia] Walford, *Twelve English Authoresses*, London, 1892, p. 155; Collection of J. G. Sharps: TS, JCB to ECS, n. p., 4 November 1829. See also Shorter, 'Mrs. Gaskell and Charlotte Brontë', *BST*, V, 1916, pp. 144-9, and *Brontë Letters*, I, p. 52 et seq.

1

Berwick and the Stevensons

THE OLD BORDER town of Berwick-upon-Tweed within its massive walls stands on a great hill that slopes towards England, to which it was finally surrendered in the fifteenth century, leaving little Duns a few miles away in Scotland to be the county town of Berwickshire. The surrounding hills, the river and the sea can be seen from most parts of the town, but visitors who climb to the top of its fortified walls and Elizabethan bastions, strengthened in the 1760s but now softly grassed over, will realise the full extent of the Scottish hills to the north, the 'British Ocean' stretched out to the east and the broad, slow curve of the estuary of the Tweed which marks the town's boundary to the south and west. A sharply engraved plan of it forms an austerely attractive frontispiece to John Fuller's *The History of Berwick upon Tweed*, published in Edinburgh in 1799.[1]

It is only too easy to imagine Berwick in the last decades of the eighteenth century, so much has survived from those days within its mile and a quarter of walls. There were a few streets of mostly plain two- and three-storey houses faced with neat ashlar stone, a central high street with a strangely narrow Georgian town hall and steeple dividing its southern lower end, a rare if not unique church without a tower built during the Commonwealth period to the north-east on the more open, seaward side and, across a parade ground, the first purpose-built barracks in the country, dating from the early eighteenth century. Many of the streets are almost unchanged, though one or two have lost their older names – the pleasant Ravensdowne of today was known to Fuller as Back Way and before that, unattractively, as Ratten Raw, the street infested by rats. The legend of Fuller's map indicates the special nature of Berwick – names like Meg's mount, saluting battery, shore gate, governor's house, hospital and magazine all speak of one of the better fortified towns in the Europe of its time. His chapters on manners and customs are usefully descriptive, and his engravings of characteristic scenes bring the town to a carefully posed kind of representative life.

The inner town is much like what it was two hundred or more years ago – if one can ignore the high rail and road bridges of later centuries that drive disastrously into its north-west corner and dwarf the beautiful red sandstone bridge down river, spanning with its fifteen arches the broad waters of the Tweed as it makes its last curve to the sea. All that seems needed to complete an earlier scene is the main sea-fishing fleet on the water and the small cobles of the men spreading their nets in the Tweed for the thousands of salmon that ran every year as their ancestors had done for centuries. Berwick salmon were famous – sent out fresh for short distances, exported live to London in ships' wells or salted in barrels, and, after 1788, packed in ice 'pounded to be like salt in appearance', five or six to a box. The trade was carried on by merchants called coopers, who either owned vessels themselves or chartered them from others.

In the latter part of the eighteenth century the population increased rapidly but was still estimated in Fuller as no more than ten thousand by 1799. The 1801 census gave the population of Berwick itself as just over seven thousand, but the communities of Tweedmouth, Spittal and Ord to the south made it up to about ten and a half thousand in all. Berwick was more than a fortified border town. There were shipyards with a good reputation, each building ships of a few hundred tons, together with an extensive and regular coasting trade. 'Berwick smacks', small vessels that could carry cargo and a dozen or so passengers, sailed for London every week, the journey taking three or four days. 'Safe, cheap, and generally expeditious', they also sailed from Edinburgh's port of Leith down the east coast of Britain and took a great deal of the ordinary passenger traffic of the time. Walter Scott thought they might, together with mail-coaches, have done more than the Union to alter Scottish national character, 'sometimes for the better and sometimes for the worse'.[2]

There was also a certain amount of trade with Norway and the Baltic, but many of the townsfolk must have been dependent upon the permanent garrison of soldiers in the barracks built to hold more than six hundred officers and men. It now houses a military museum. Amongst the English Heritage displays celebrating the triumph of British arms at Malplaquet, Waterloo and the like is a simple barrack room, stripped of its later additions to show sad graffiti and the far less glorious domestic life of common soldiers. The room contains eight rough wooden bunks, with a table and benches in the centre. Everything in the room is simple and crudely functional, no more than the necessities of a very basic existence. The poignant wax figure of a woman nursing a baby is placed on the table and one corner of the room is curtained off. An illustration of the inner quadrangle of the barracks in Fuller's *History* appropriately shows three soldiers in the foreground – but also two lively dogs and a woman holding a small child by the hand. Berwick, it appears, was not garrisoned by sturdy country lads called or pressed to the colours but by older men broken down by wounds, disease and general debility after years of service in tropical climates abroad.

The burgesses or freemen of this most independent of towns might welcome the custom of these prematurely aged men as they finished their hard careers, but must have regretted the fact that they so often took healthy young wives and fathered children before they died, leaving the town to support their numerous offspring. The children of men lost at sea would cast a similar charge upon the townsfolk. Both the episcopalians of the parish church and the dissenters belonging to the various meeting houses placed inconspicuously up side alleys (the numbers estimated to be in the proportion of one to two and a half by about the end of the century) would regard this as an inescapable religious duty, but the civic burden was not always lightly borne.

Joseph Rumney, vicar of Holy Trinity parish church and grammar school master, stressed to Fuller the humanity of private individuals when there was dearth and scarcity: 'Nay, our ladies too on many occasions dance to relieve the distrest; and tax their own pleasures to supply the poor with necessaries; many reduced families having been timely relieved by charity.' Berwick must have displayed the extraordinary contrasts of eighteenth-century life even when times were good: the filth and stench of cattle killed in the very centre of town, with blood running in open gutters from the shambles to the river and getting into private water pipes 'on the great killing days'; and evening assemblies in the Town Hall, like the one in which the ladies wore white hats with white feathers, 'decorated with the present prevailing fashionable tartan ribbon', whilst the band of the Royal Welsh fusiliers played until past two o'clock – 'when the whole concluded with the greatest harmony, joy and loyalty.' A splendid illustration in *The Berwick Museum, or, Monthly Literary Intelligencer*, which contains this account of the King's birthday celebrations on 4 June 1787, shows the Genius of the magazine, assisted by Piety, arranging the arts, sciences, amusements &c. for public approbation. Rumney himself published *Berwick Beauties*, occasional poetry in the eighteenth-century manner – 'Tremble, ye beaus; shun Circe's face; / Ye belles, a rival fear!' This was from a poem addressed to Miss Hester Lauder, daughter of 'an excellent surgeon of Berwick', then in her charming sixteenth year. The old border town obviously had a elegant provincial culture as well as unpaved, unlit streets and other degradations.[3]

Elizabeth Gaskell's paternal grandfather, Joseph Steavenson or Stevenson, was baptised in Berwick parish church on 11 September 1719.[4] He became a freeman of Berwick in 1748, but is not recorded as the eldest son of a freeman in the roll of its burgesses, who from the early thirteenth century until 1835 exercised the functions of a town council. He qualified by an alternative route, as apprentice to a freeman for a period of seven years from the age of sixteen – one Gabriel Stevenson in this instance.[5] Joseph, however, did not apply for his freedom when he was twenty-three in 1742, perhaps because he was away at sea. His son William's obituary makes him a 'Captain in the Royal Navy'. Descendants even called him a post-captain, which strictly speaking means the officer commanding the largest ships of all. But as a satirist of the time wickedly remarked, this title 'bestowed on the elevated rank of the commander of a post ship, descends by prostitution, or courtesy, which you will, to the *commander of an oyster boat'*. It is possible that he acted as a captain in the ordinary sense of the word, but on a small vessel only.[6]

Joseph Stevenson was certainly in the royal navy from the summer of 1744, not long after Tobias Smollett, who drew upon his own experience as surgeon's mate on a disastrous naval expedition to the West Indies at the beginning of the decade for the blackly comic chapters describing naval life afloat in *Roderick Random*, published anonymously in 1748. Joseph served as able seaman and as midshipman in the *Mermaid, Vigilant, Berwick* and *Fougueux* for varying periods, and finally as master's mate for over four years in the *Seahorse*, a total of more than eight years. Royal navy regulations demanded that future officers should have served six years at sea, two of them in the ratings of midshipman or master's mate. There was also an oral examination in seamanship, which Joseph Stevenson passed on 6 June 1753, having produced his journals in the usual way. He was actually promoted lieutenant[7] with seniority dating from 15 June 1757 during the years of an expanding service after the outbreak of the Seven Years' War in 1756, when a great French fleet gathered at Brest and invasion was threatened. He would probably have been a man like Smollett's lieutenant Bowling, 'a brave fellow as ever cracked biscuit – none of your guinea pigs, nor your fresh-water, wishy-washy, fair weather fowls' (chapter 24). But promotion depended mainly upon patronage and success in action. Joseph never went beyond the rank of lieutenant.[8]

He did not get married until he was nearly fifty years of age, to a rather younger bride, Isabel, the daughter of a Joseph Thomson. They were married by licence on her twenty-eighth birthday in Holy Trinity parish church, Berwick, on 2 August 1769. The witnesses were Joseph Thomson and John Stevenson. Elizabeth Gaskell believed that 'Isabella Thomson' was '1st cousin once removed to the Poet', that is, James Thomson, who had been born in 1700, the son of the minister of Ednam, a village about twenty miles south-west of Berwick. Perhaps James Thomson was Joseph's first cousin. Five children were born to Joseph Stevenson and Isabel between 1770 and 1780, four boys and a girl. After this year the rate books show him dwelling in the Hide Hill quarter of the town, just below the town hall.[9]

Their eldest son William was christened in Holy Trinity parish church on 26 November 1770.[10] His parents sent him to be educated in Greek and Latin at the local grammar school run by Joseph Rumney, 'under whom it was a seminary of great repute', writes Stevenson's obituarist, rather glibly. However, Rumney certainly won it under competitive conditions in 1750 when the master's post was advertised in London, Newcastle and Edinburgh. A few years later a number of houses were rebuilt on the corner of the High Street and Golden Square ('neither golden nor a square' but a large yard entered through an arch) in order to provide better accommodation for the school.

The garrulous memoirs and anecdotes of an early student, Percival Stockdale, are very informative, though one soon realises that old scores are being paid off.[11] He claims that his master was glaringly partial to the rich and powerful. He also characterises him as 'naturally a mild, candid, and liberal man', ruined over the years by his wife, 'a narrow-spirited, vulgar creature; and very little deserving of the husband, whom she entangled, and obtained.' Stockdale was a boarder with them in the new school for a few months in 1754 and obviously found the change from an earlier, soft-hearted landlady too bracing.

The feel of the place, and an escape from what he termed 'scholastick drudgery', comes over strongly in one of his anecdotes:

> At the upper end of the school, and opening into the garden, there was an apartment, which, at that time, contained a publick library. To this apartment, our master often used to retire; and through *it*, he used to pass from his house, into the school. We had bought some bottles of wine; and, by what infatuation I know not, had lodged them in this room; where we had resolved to empty them. ... It happened, however, unexpectedly, and to our 'severe amazement', that he bolted in upon us, when we were wrapped in elysium; when we had mounted to the felicity of Ariadne.

Rumney and his brother, who taught at Alnwick for fifty-five years, were efficient teachers of Greek and Latin, working in a strong northern tradition that sent a supply of students to university. Classical allusions ornament Stockdale's prose to a remarkable degree, but this does not prevent him from claiming that the Rumneys neglected 'the constantly careful and elegant cultivation of the *english* tongue; in which our countrymen will always express their thoughts with more freedom, energy, and grace, than in *any* other'. Joseph Rumney, he asserted, had a correct literary taste and a talent for writing true poetry – 'which, perhaps, very sensibly, and prudently, he neglected to cultivate'. Rumney later took orders, becoming vicar of Berwick in 1767 and Sunday lecturer to the corporation in 1778, which suggests that his early reputation was good. He did not resign his teaching post until 1801, by which time the grammar school is said to have declined. The reports of the Charity Commissioners in the next century show that this state of decline was far from untypical of old grammar schools if not as downright scandalous as some, where endowments left to educate deserving children supported quite undeserving masters in careless ease.[12]

Stevenson's obituarist, who obviously had access to private information, was able to quote from a letter written by his mother to her husband Joseph, then stationed at sea off Cork: 'The children are all well, and give me no trouble, except William, who hardly ever attends school, and is constantly running about the walls.' William was then about nine or ten (rather than eight) years old. He must have been running with the urchins, many fatherless, who played about the shambles and dodged among the carriages and horses as well as swarming over the fortifications. Walter Scott, too, was 'a desperate climber' about the walls of the old city of Edinburgh and the cliffs of its castle and park at about the same time, bored by the pace of schoolwork in the High school and the rote learning of Latin technicalities in the early classes, and only 'indifferently well beaten'. But Scott's resistance to pedagogues took its origin in the impression made upon him by old tales of love and magic and battles. 'Feelings, rous'd in life's first day / Glow in the line and prompt the lay', he acknowledged in *Marmion*.[13]

In comparison, Stevenson showed no signs in later life of such romantic attitudes. Rather the reverse, in fact. He would ignore books he 'had proved from his researches to be inaccurate, or considered as frivolous', even if this on one occasion gave offence to an intimate friend (quite possibly John Galt). 'Contrary to the practice too prevalent in these days', Stevenson's obituary reads, he 'dived into original sources of information; and with the true spirit of a faithful historian, consulted the interests of truth rather than the amusement of his readers'. We might speculate that his later precision, even pedantry, stemmed from the powerful attempt he must have made at some point to buckle down to scholarly pursuits, rather than fling his bonnet over the windmill and follow his father into the navy.

Two out of his three younger brothers went to sea in the French wars over the turn of the century. Joseph Thomson Stevenson, born in 1772, became a freeman on 7 November 1794 and is recorded in the printed burgess roll of Berwick-upon-Tweed as a 'ship master' in 1796. In merchant ships it was the master who commanded the ship and usually owned shares in it. In the royal navy he was the navigator, the most senior of all the warrant officers, a man with hopes of attaining full commissioned rank. Descendants believed that Joseph was a lieutenant in the royal navy and died a prisoner of war at Dunkirk, but his name is not found in the navy lists. Ward records in his notebook information apparently conveyed to Meta Gaskell by her mother's first cousin, a Mrs Robina Robertson: 'Joseph died in a French prison during the war'. The 1806 burgess roll certainly has 'Dead' against his name, and Napoleon's threat of invasion during the year 1805 had made the French coast the scene of innumerable naval engagements and skirmishes. On 5 July, for instance, the gun-brigs *Plumper* and *Teazer* were becalmed off Granville, and later attacked by French gun-vessels propelled by sweeps. After a hard fight, both were defeated. No exact account of their casualties can be found. Joseph might have been captured in a similar way. The only other fact known about him comes from the will his brother Robert, the father of Mrs Robertson, made in 1809, which contains a proviso that if all his children were to die before the age of twenty-one without issue whilst his wife was living, half his personal estate was to go to her and the other half to 'William Stevenson the natural son of my late brother Joseph Thompson Stevenson' as well as to his other nephews and nieces.[14]

Ward was also informed that the youngest son, 'John Camfield Turner', was a lieutenant 'in the Royal Navy, & drowned in attempting to make his escape in an open boat from France with two other Berwick men'. 'You will see', added Mrs Robertson for the benefit of future commentators, 'that a strong love of the sea ran in the family; & the Joseph Thompson Stevenson who died in a French prison must have suggested the part in *Sylvia's Lovers* about Philip's being detained in a French prison.' Once again, it is difficult to prove the facts. John Thomson Turner Stevenson, born in 1780, did not become a freeman like his father and brothers. If he was a lieutenant in the royal navy called John Stephenson, a man whose seniority dated from 19 February 1800, Mrs Robertson's information is correct in this respect, but he was not drowned in the Napoleonic war period. This John's passing certificate, which is often accompanied by a baptismal record and other details, has not yet been found, so he cannot be conclusively pegged within the knotty entrails of oaken fact as William's youngest brother. A return of service in 1817, signed with no more than 'John Stephenson', records a typical career pattern. He went to sea in his early teens and served as able seaman, midshipman and master's mate. On the *Audacious* from 17 March 1793 to 11 December 1799, he patrolled mainly in the Channel and the Mediterranean. When Nelson ordered the bombardment of Cadiz in July 1797 he was wounded, but he might have recovered in time for the battle of the Nile in 1798.

For a short two months at the turn of the century, from 11 December 1799 to 19 February 1800, he was on the *Foudroyant* as a midshipman with rear-admiral Nelson and then commissioned as a lieutenant on the *El Corso*, sailing in the Mediterranean and the Adriatic. This is described as 'a small, under-gunned brig', on which one Captain (not John Stephenson's) managed in eighteen months to pay off his debts and gain £25,000 by the capture of many small prizes. John held this post until the summer of 1802. He next spent some time ashore with the Sea-Fencibles at Westhaven and on 26 June 1805 joined the *Zealous*, which was stationed off Cadiz. This was his last post. He records it as finishing on 26 December 1807, but an official annotation in faint red ink appears to read 'Dismissed by Court Martial'.[15]

Great squadrons of ships had been assembled on the outbreak of war with France in 1793. A string of naval victories followed, and on 21 October 1805 at Trafalgar, a Spanish cape south of Cadiz, Nelson set the seal upon his unique reputation. John Stephenson's ship seems to have been detached before this took place, but there is not much doubt that both of Elizabeth Gaskell's uncles followed sea careers and were caught up in the stirring events of a nation at war. Their sister Dorothy, born in 1774, and their brother Robert, born in 1776, seem to have stayed in Berwick. Robert became a surgeon, sometimes as much a trade as a profession in the rough and ready days of surgery without anaesthesia. By contrast, their oldest brother William settled to his books and despite his carefree youth running about the walls, ended as head of his grammar school class.[16]

When he reached the age of sixteen, it was decided that he should continue his education elsewhere. Although William and all his siblings had been christened in the episcopal parish church, he left Berwick to begin a five-year preparation for the dissenting ministry at Daventry Academy in the Midlands. One of his father's neighbours is said in Stockdale's memoirs to have been 'candid, and liberal in religion; for he was half a churchman, half a presbyterian'. The vicar of Bray had many spiritual descendants. Something like this was probably true of the Stevenson family. Dissenting academies generally provided for younger students a significant alternative to English universities, and Daventry, then in its most flourishing period, was open to lay as well as divinity students. William was not the first to go all the way there from Berwick-upon-Tweed. A Christopher Michelson had registered in 1784, later having to give up his course on account of ill health. No connection, however, is known between him and William Stevenson, who registered in 1787.[17]

Oxford and Cambridge degrees were just not available to conscientious dissenters, since at some point they would have to subscribe to the thirty-nine articles of the Church of England. Though Daventry was small, with about fifty students in all, it was often regarded as giving the equivalent of a university education – in its own way. As the most famous of eighteenth-century Unitarians, the scientist Joseph Priestley, wrote to Theophilus Lindsey about his own student days there, 'It had many disadvantages; but certainly afforded little opportunity of dissipation, and, on that account, was favourable to study.' By today's standards its course was incredibly overstuffed: classics, divinity, ethics, ecclesiastical history, Hebrew, New Testament, Rich's shorthand (Philip Doddridge's version, taught 'immediately on coming'), mathematics, 'doctrine of the human mind', government and several natural sciences, not to mention a 'set of lectures against Popery', some lectures on Anatomy and a course on Oratory. Students intended for 'the learned professions' had to deliver orations. A letter from Timothy Kentish, a student in the 1770s, shows that the paper syllabus was followed in practice. Time as well as opportunity for dissipation must have been lacking.[18]

Intellectually, it was a golden age for English dissenters and their academies. Also, the last decades of the eighteenth century were a time when they believed they were on the verge of obtaining complete freedom to practise their religion without penalties. The discriminatory test and corporation acts still forced all political and economic office holders to take the sacrament in the Church of England, though the practice of occasional conformity ('playing bo-peep with God Almighty', Defoe called it) was common enough in practice amongst some denominations, Presbyterians and Congregationalists if not the Baptists. In late 1786 renewed efforts were made to secure complete repeal of the acts. In 1789 a motion was lost by only twenty votes in the Commons. Two months later the Bastille was stormed.

Hostility to dissenters no doubt had its origins in many local causes, but when Charles James Fox introduced another bill in March 1790, in a totally different political climate, it was rejected by 294 votes to 105. It was a decisive and divisive moment in English social history. Sucessive defeats 'added the bitterness of recent discontent to the tumultuous emotions aroused by the Revolution in France', comments Anthony Lincoln, and led to a definite decline in the customary loyalty of dissenters to the crown. 'I profess myself not the man of a party but the servant of the Dissenting Interest' was the ringing assertion of the Reverend Thomas Belsham, who had been a temporary tutor in classics at Daventry Academy whilst still a student, then its tutor in mathematics, logic and metaphysics from 1771 and finally, in 1781, its principal and theological tutor.[19]

For men like Belsham, whose strength of mind had impressed James Boswell even as he regretted his heresies and 'his not having been fortunate enough to be educated a member of our excellent national establishment', independence was of primary importance – in thought and religious belief as well as in political allegiance. Belsham was one of several leaders moving away from the older orthodoxies of Presbyterianism and re-defining the nature of dissent itself as well as its political allegiance. In philosophical terms he is said to have been the first to teach what he rapturously called 'the great and glorious doctrine of Necessity' in a dissenting academy, denying the traditional mind-body distinction and subjecting all human actions and choices to the play of material causes. Men like Priestley and Belsham had carefully studied David Hartley's *Observations on Man, His Frame, His Duty, and His Expectations*, published in 1749, a 'strange fusion' of Christianity and necessitarianism. The causal chain binding all human responses and impulses was declared to lead inexorably back to God, the first cause. This doctrine of necessity is somewhat paradoxically associated with the powerful individuals in the Unitarian tradition who proclaimed it so vigorously. They took full advantage of their liberty to think and act, even if ultimately they might be considered by their own theory mere vehicles, automatons. For orthodox men like James Boswell they were simply propagators of 'pernicious doctrines'. Samuel Johnson rather more cautiously took an intermediate position: 'all theory is against the freedom of the will; all experience for it.'[20]

Belsham's divinity lectures were unusual in a religious establishment, though perfectly consistent with the principle of 'free discussion of any question of importance' enunciated by Joseph Priestley in the 1780s. One can imagine Priestley as he lived, acted and inspired others: a man of middle stature, slenderly made (quite unlike Belsham), modest and courteous, pouring out his thoughts to young men and women who were encouraged to ask questions during as well as after the lecture. Dissenting tutors in this pedagogic tradition strove to cover every system of belief. Arguments for and against were carefully stated and students left to judge for themselves. Such men 'employed themselves in what they called free inquiry, converting the academy into a gymnasium to try the strength of their speculative powers', wrote hostile Trinitarian witnesses. In later years William Turner of Newcastle was inclined to suspect that this even-handedness encouraged either a sceptical or a disputatious spirit.[21]

It certainly made for change. Their attitude was regarded in the dominant culture of England as politically subversive and theologically heretical, both then and well into the next century. 'Above all things, be careful to improve and make use of the *reason* which God has given you', Priestley advised the young, 'have nothing to do with a parliamentary religion, or a parliamentary God'. Unitarians especially were 'a sect everywhere spoken against', yet more and more dissenting ministers and congregations, especially Presbyterian ones, became Unitarian as the century drew to its close. By the 1770s twelve of the Cheshire congregations had done so, leaving only six orthodox, weak and struggling.[22]

Two old words were revived in the eighteenth century to label those who denied the doctrine of the Trinity maintained by most Christian churches – Arian and Socinian. Both groups thought the Bible proved that Christ was a lesser being than the Father, but eighteenth-century Arians believed that he had existed in some way before his human birth whilst radical Socinians (unlike Faustus Socinius) denied both his divinity and 'pre-existence'. Belsham's own 'summary' is more complicated. It encompassed simple humanity, the Sociananian scheme rejecting original sin, eternal punishment and the atonement, the low Arian scheme (Christ's soul was pre-existent, but he was definitely inferior to God the Father), the proper or high Arian hypothesis (though inferior, he was usually thought to be the instrument of Creation and the administrator of Divine Providence), the semi-Arian scheme (equal to the Father in all respects except self-creation), and so on through the indwelling scheme, the Sabellian and Swedenborgian doctrines, Tritheism and Trinitarian beliefs.[23]

Logically, Arians were able to retain the doctrine of Christ's atonement for human sin, but most orthodox Trinitarians would deny all kinds of Unitarian the right to call themselves Christian at all. At the very least their faith was said to be devoid of feeling: 'It has been asserted that Unitarianism is the frozen zone of Christianity, wherein the sun of Divine love and mercy never shines, in whose ungenial clime the fairest blossoms of religion wither, and its choicest fruits fall blighted from the tree.' The author of this passage went on to claim that such an 'uncharitable theory' (held by Wordsworth and Coleridge in later years) was disproved by the fervent life of the lady whose obituary he was writing. But his defensive rhetorical strategy is unmistakable.[24]

Priestley, who moved from Arian beliefs to a very positive Socinianism, claimed that in 1770 he did not know more than a half a dozen dissenting ministers who were Socinian. By the time a Unitarian society for promoting Christian knowledge was set up in 1791 its rules went so far as to reject the worship of Christ as 'idolatrous'. Historically speaking, this is what Donald Davie has described as 'the precipitate dissolution of English Presbyterianism into Unitarianism, either avowed or (more often) unavowed.' Belsham himself tells us that he had been 'a firm believer in the pre-existence of Christ', but in Daventry he could not content himself with using Philip Doddridge's standard text-book and 'going over the old lectures in a slovenly way'. As he engaged in deeper investigations, he was mortified to find that many of his best students began to believe in the simple humanity of Christ before he did. He wrote to a friend about Unitarian beliefs, 'I feel myself so fixed in these sentiments, that I begin almost to wonder that I could ever be an *Arian*. ... I hope that you will never see, what I think that I clearly see, viz. that your sentiments very nearly correspond with my own, except in the trifling circumstance of the pre-existence of the human soul of Christ.'

In January 1789, after elaborate self-examination, he confessed his changed beliefs to Daventry's governing body of Independent ministers and laymen, the Coward trustees, and sent in his resignation for the end of the session, this despite the fact that the academy was becoming very successful. There was 'the prospect of twelve or fourteen new Students' for the following session, more than he had ever known before at that point. But at the age of forty Belsham gave up everything he had created at Daventry and went to join the staff of the short-lived Hackney college as theological tutor.[25]

He was destined to be one of the leaders in his communion. When in 1830 W. J. Fox confidently began to determine the major phases of recent Unitarian history, he proclaimed that Priestley had been the original mental adventurer. (Coleridge at one time had regarded every experiment Priestley made in chemistry 'as giving *wings* to his more sublime theological works'.) Belsham in comparison was for Fox no more than a superlatively diligent consolidator and controversialist, rather too insistent upon the simple humanity of Christ.

'In fact, it matters but little which link be first broken from the chain of corruption', Fox announced grandly. 'Original Sin, Total Depravity, Vicarious Suffering, Eternal Torments; any one of these will, if the inquirer persist in his course, be as sure to drag all the rest after it as the doctrine of the Godhead of Christ.' He characterised Belsham as lacking in originality, feeling and imagination but also unfailingly diligent, with great powers of assimilation and force of mind, peculiarly suited to the times in which he lived. Eventually, Fox decided, men of 'more lively fancy and more fervid feeling', like the famous American divine, Dr William Ellery Channing, proved themselves able to cultivate 'the *love* of that truth which they discovered and demonstrated' and to extend 'the dominion of pure religion from the head to the heart'. By then, of course, a second generation of Romantic poets were Fox's contemporaries, and he himself was aspiring to leadership in a new era.[26]

Owen Chadwick employs crisp oppositions: older rationalists thought the doctrine of the Trinity unreasonable, the scriptures irrelevant; fervent new believers thought it unscriptural, its reasonableness unimportant.[27]

Stevenson had been for two years in close touch with a remarkable man at a time of great personal and institutional crisis, a man willing in the last analysis to sacrifice his position at Daventry for conscience sake. Of eleven or twelve students in Daventry Academy's senior year, the great majority became avowed Unitarians and left altogether. The Coward trustees acted vigorously, closing Daventry after the long vacation and opening a new institution not far off at Northampton, where the academy had originally been established under Philip Doddridge. About a dozen students altogether seem to have transferred, including William Stevenson. Their Daventry tutors, William Broadbent and Robert Forsaith, went too. Broadbent, always a close friend of Belsham, was still theologically 'a moderate Arian', only becoming a radical Unitarian after some years as pastor at Warrington, where he brought over the great majority of the congregation to his belief. Broadbent – 'though formerly a practical he is now ... a doctrinal preacher', wrote a contemporary in 1812 – was to baptise William Gaskell in the next century. When he died his funeral discourse was given by his successor, the Reverend Edward Dimock, who became William Gaskell's stepfather.[28]

At Daventry Stevenson would have begun his classical course under a distinguished scholar, Eliezer Cogan, whose boarding school at Walthamstow later became famous, but after one year he was taught by Forsaith, said 'as a classic' to have had 'few superiors, in regard either to critical knowledge, or facility of communicating it'. The new foundation at Northampton was now confined to students for the ministry and placed under the Reverend John Horsey, pastor there for fifty-two years – who nevertheless believed in intellectual freedom as much as Belsham and was so anxious not to give an undue bias in his lectures that it was difficult to discover his precise views on any controversial subject, according to a student who boarded with his family. Horsey agreed with Priestley: 'Freedom of enquiry on all subjects', he expansively declared in his opening address, 'is the birthright and glory of a rational being.'[29]

'At first the students, who were probably all sympathizers more or less with Mr. Belsham, did not take kindly to the new arrangements,' wrote Samuel Newth in his memorials of academies supported by the Coward trust, 'but after a while when the Seniors had left a different feeling sprang up'. In Stevenson's year, the 1787 entry at Daventry, there had been eleven students, only two of whom transferred with him to Northampton in the autumn of 1789, Benjamin Davis and Thomas Warwick. Presumably, the three were Trinitarians in belief, at least at the time of the transfer. A fellow student who met him two or three years into his course wrote that he associated with those 'who were most distinguished for their knowledge and ability in metaphysical and theological discussions', then 'much in vogue'.[30]

He disliked sports, we are told in his obituary, preferring to read rapidly through long novels by Fielding or Smollett and active enough to take long and energetic walks. Academically,

> in appearance his studies were below par in point of laboriousness; but they were
> equally above it in efficiency. It may be a dangerous example to hold up; but

certainly, in his case, hours apparently unoccupied were employed in meditating on and arranging the knowledge which he had almost intuitively acquired; and of which he then and throughout life, availed himself with such singular correctness and advantage. When it came to his turn to deliver an oration, however it might seem to have been deferred and neglected, and however rapidly it was eventually written, its excellence always demonstrated the skill and care with which it had been digested.

It seems clear that although a harum-scarum youth had produced a true bookworm, Stevenson was accustomed to rely upon his powers of rapid reading and assimilation to make up for a natural reluctance to buckle down to continuous study and composition.

Surprisingly, some of his essays survive. He wrote six between 28 March 1788 and 30 March 1791, dated at irregular intervals, the last four in the shorthand always taught to students in dissenting academies. The two in longhand, on Fortitude and Ambition, are cogent but unremarkable in argument and style.[31] More tantalisingly, some numbers of a manuscript magazine called *The Academical Repository* also survive; it contains anonymous articles written out neatly and passed round amongst the students, with a small fine to be paid if they were not circulated quickly. The number for April 1787 shows the degree of unrest that must have existed in the year when Stevenson went up to Daventry, not only over questions of fundamental belief but also about such professional matters as praying extempore, strongly recommended in these circles to men training for the dissenting ministry. The rhetoric of 'An Address to those Students who prefer forms of prayer' shows that one of his fellows had forsworn thin potations: 'Your Tutors reasoning on this head is absurd.' Or more heroically, reinforced by a pointing finger in the margin, 'Inform then your Tutors & your Trustees, that no force, no laws, no men or body of men shall compel you to act contrary to your principles.' Sweeping statements of principle seem to have been endemic.

Given the fragmented history of Daventry and Northampton, it is perhaps inevitable that only an incomplete run of the *Academical Repository* can be found. An unbound issue exists for November 1788 and next comes a Northampton one for March 1792. 'An interval of more than two years is elapsed since the last number of the Repository was circulated in the Family', it blandly proclaims. The most interesting item of all, however, is an anonymous article of some twelve small pages in volume 11 for May 1792, entitled 'On the Value of Classical Learning'. Its inadequacy was to be the subject of Stevenson's *Remarks on the Very Inferior Utility of Classical Learning* (1796).[32]

Some fifty years before, Dr Philip Doddridge had for practical purposes changed the language of lectures in his dissenting academy at Northampton from Latin to English. This was acceptable enough, but many tutors, including Joseph Priestley, who had begun his career at Warrington Academy in 1761 teaching, amongst other things, languages, oratory and belles lettres before he went on to become scientist and a Fellow of the Royal Society, resisted any general devaluation of classical studies as such. The writer of the anonymous article began very cautiously, though his opening praise of them was probably tactical. He conceded that classical studies should not be allowed to fall into neglect, but maintained that they hardly deserved the time and attention they were still receiving in an age of growing enlightenment; 'if the performances of Antiquity are cultivated to the prejudice of real science & substantial knowledge, they will with justice, I imagine fall under the imputation of pompous trifles.' In particular, he claimed, the knowledge of the ancients was defective from a scientific and utilitarian point of view. A key argument is that classical authors might be superior in imagination, taste and elegance of style, but they lacked the 'information' to bring about human happiness and progress. He did not even think it possible to demonstrate in practice the necessity and utility of classical studies for theologians interpreting the scriptures.

Not unexpectedly, the neat, featureless hand of the student composition bears no resemblance to the extant examples of William Stevenson's hardpressed later hand – which is reminiscent of the scrawls 'in desp'rate charcoal upon dark'ning walls' in Pope's *Epistle to Dr Arbuthnot*. Nor does its content seem sophisticated enough to be the work of a final-year student. Education is a brief afterthought in the student piece – study of the dead languages is best for the young, when the memory is strong and the intellect weak – but it is central to Stevenson's *Remarks*. The exponential growth of old and new sciences was to exert increasing pressure as the decades rolled by, despite eminently successful counter-attacks and metamorphoses in the content of classical studies. But Charles Darwin asserted that nothing could have been worse for the development of his mind than the strictly classical education he had received at Shrewsbury school.[33]

Apart from the essays, the rest of Stevenson's career in Northampton Academy is obscure. A little more evidence is provided in the obituary of William Winstanley, M.D., who went there in the spring of 1790 and formed a close intimacy with him. Stevenson is flatteringly described as 'a student for the ministry, of superior talents and attainments'. We gather from this obituary that 'the freedom of inquiry permitted, and the impartiality of reference encouraged' at Northampton led 'its most intelligent and promising students generally' to rest 'in the theological views known as Unitarian.' Winstanley himself served as a Unitarian minister for almost ten years, before becoming an honorary physician at the Manchester Infirmary in 1808, but there is no certain evidence that Stevenson's religious views changed at this time. In secular terms, 'the sentiment of humanity and the love of freedom' then fired most students' imaginations. They were inspired by two questions of international significance, the French revolution and the struggle for abolition of the slave trade.[34]

According to Stevenson's obituary, he did not complete 'the usual course of studies', which would have finished for him in the summer of 1792. He perhaps left his Northampton course as early as March 1791, the date of his sixth essay, or he might have given up at some point during the next session, officially his fifth and last. On 27 January 1792 we know that he appeared in person – it was mandatory – before the Berwick guild of freemen to be admitted to their number, having just a few months before attained the necessary age of twenty-one as the son of a freeman. His signature appears in the guild book amongst the 'Names of the Burgesses admitted in the time of the Right Worshipful David Stow Esquire Mayor from Michaelmas 1791 to Michaelmas 1792'. The fee paid was £1 10s, but to be a burgess brought certain advantages, such as a free education for one's children. Was he possibly thinking of returning to Berwick and perhaps finding another profession? The life of a dissenting minister might not have been overwhelmingly attractive to him, yet he had not felt called to an active life at sea like his brothers Joseph and John. Nor did he fancy the medical career his younger brother Robert had embarked upon at Berwick and his friend Winstanley was eventually to adopt. Yet there would have been few other careers open to him.[35]

His obituarist states that he accepted an invitation to become a private tutor in the family of a 'Mr. Edwards of Bruges, with whom he lived some time'. Edwards, who has not yet been identified with any certainty, might have been the William Edwards who met Thomas Paine in Bruges in 1800, Librarian of the Ecole Centrale there. He had two sons, the eldest 'something of a pedant but very clever', who piqued himself on telling characters by their handwriting according to Maria Edgeworth, who said that Edwards was 'a Jamaica-man' who had once lived at Warrington. It was at his house, she noted, that 'Mr. Barbauld paid his addresses to Mrs B.' These were Presbyterian circles. Mrs B. was the famous Anna Letitia, daughter of John Aikin D.D., tutor at Warrington academy.[36]

At about the same time William Wordsworth was looking for ways in which to evade the prospect of 'a paltry curacy' in the Church of England which his relations' interest might have obtained for him, and had set off late in 1791 for a winter in the Loire valley in order to learn French and Spanish well enough 'to qualify him for the office of travelling Companion to some young Gentleman if he can get recommended', wrote his sister Dorothy naively. For him, and for many other exulting liberals, France after the storming of the Bastille was a land 'standing on the top of golden hours, / And human nature seeming born again.'[37]

Indeed, one of Stevenson's cohort at Daventry, Priestley's second son William, said to be highly strung and impatient of discipline, applied for French naturalisation in 1792 and was introduced to the national assembly in June. *The Times* found in this episode a perfect opportunity of attacking his father and other radicals:

> It is asserted that the reception of the Birmingham hero in the national Assembly, has determined his Reverend Sire to follow him to that land of liberty – and in

order to render himself the more acceptable, he has chartered a vessel to be freighted with his own writings, Tom Paine's *Rights of Man*, &c. &c. – which he means to present to that August Body for the purpose of making cartridges for the use of the troops. This is well considered – as their combustible quality, no doubt, will prove a prodigious saving in the article of gunpowder.[38]

Stevenson is said in his obituary to have 'returned to England at the breaking out of war'. France declared war on Austria on 20 April 1792. Prussian forces invaded French territory in August. Panic led to the September massacre of suspected royalists in Paris and the estabishment of a French republic. The Prussians were forced to turn back at Valmy and French forces began to advance on several fronts. The Austrian Netherlands were easily subdued, Brussels falling on 13 November and Ostend on the 16th. Though the French republic did not actually declare war on England until the beginning of February in the following year, Wordsworth had returned before this, in late 1792 when the French Royal family was arrested and the guillotine again began its dread work. ('The earthquake is not satisfied at once.') He was still looking for a post two summers later. France's invasion of modern Belgium in November 1792 would seem a likely date for Stevenson's return. Edwards was less fortunate, being 'imprisoned in France during the Revolution'. If William Stevenson responded with Wordsworthian exhilaration to political and social events that were changing the course of European and world history, there is no evidence. Given Edwards's fate his return to England was only sensible; to have taken up his freedom at Berwick merely prudent.[39]

All this time Winstanley was steadily preparing himself for the ministry. He left Northampton for a while because of the death of his father, and then chose to finish his studies at a newly established academy in Manchester, where the admired William Stevenson had arrived as a classical tutor. 'In no slight degree influenced by the inducement of his residence there', Winstanley entered the new Manchester institution in September 1793 and remained for two sessions.[40] Stevenson's obituary, perhaps because of the source of its information for this early period, gives the impression that he was now, if not committed to some form of Unitarianism, at least closely associated with men who very definitely were. Its author makes a point of noticing that two friends who had studied with Stevenson were settled in the neighbourhood of Manchester, the Reverend George Wiche at Monton and the Reverend John Holland at Bolton.[41]

Both Wiche and John Holland were firmly Socinian in belief. Wiche, who had transferred to Daventry from Hoxton, began his ministry in 1788. He was to play a very significant part in Stevenson's life. John Holland, 'ardent in his feelings, and glowing with sentiments of civil and religious liberty', intrepid in preaching the doctrines of Unitarianism against all opposition, succeeded his uncle Philip Holland as minister at Bank Street chapel, Bolton, in 1789. He immediately formed a vestry library with 'a large grant of books set aside for that purpose by his uncle', added other works and began a successful Sunday school. But his 'utter disregard to all opposition' when he thought 'truth and justice required him to speak and act' proved inflammatory in the next decade, during which he became related to Stevenson by marriage.[42]

NOTES

1 Fuller is an important source; see also the bibliographical appendix.

2 *The Farington Diary* [for 17 September 1801], ed. James Greig, 4th edn, London, 1923, I, p. 321; John Stoddart, *Remarks on Local Scenery & Manners in Scotland During the Years 1799 and 1800*, [1801], II, p. 3; *Scott Letters*, I, p. 285.

3 Fuller, *History*, pp. 267, 441, 575-6; *Berwick Museum*, I, Berwick 1785, frontispiece; III, 1787, p. 225; *Memoirs of Stockdale*, pp. 123-6.

4 See appendix A for sources and genealogical details.

5 The baptisms at Berwick of five of Gabriel's children between 1714 and 1732 are recorded in the *IGI* for Northumberland. Christian names are not very distinctive: William, Margaret, Esther, Jane and Joseph.

6 *ABO, 1830*, XIV, 1830, p. 208; Lewis, *Social History of the Navy*, pp. 186-92; qu. from Rodger, *Wooden World*, p. 18. Ward Notebook, f. 7 verso: 'Captain Stevenson RN' (said to be an 'exact copy' of ECG notes on her father's family). Ward was told of a Joseph Stevenson, 'Commander R. N.', 1734-78, who 'married Isabel Thompson' (f. 1 verso); and another, 1734-99, who 'married Isoble Thompson' (f. 108).

7 PRO: ADM 107/4, p. 254 (he appeared more than thirty-three years of age); [David Bonner-Smith and M. A. Lewis], *The Commissioned Sea Officers of the Royal Navy 1660-1815*, 3 vols, 1954 (TS).

8 Clowes, *The Royal Navy: A History*, III, p. 145; Rodger, *Wooden World*, pp. 263, 297. There are a number of references to Stevenson's ships in Clowes, and a reference to Nelson at the age of fifteen on the frigate *Seahorse* in Lewis, *Social History of the Navy*, pp. 141, 157; Carola Oman, *Nelson*, London (1947), 1954, pp. 19, 22.

9 Ward Notebook, f. 7v (cf. A. W. Ward, *Collected Papers*, Cambridge, 1921, IV, p. 416n.); James Sambrook, *James Thomson 1700-1748: A Life*, Oxford, 1991, p. 2; BRO: rate books and registers (see Appendix A).

10 Cp. born 26 November 1772 in *ABO*, the basic source. Other obits in the *AR*, for 1829 (1830, p. 225), *GM* (1829, p. 644), *NMMLJ* (1829, part III, Historical Register, pp. 272-3) and John Sykes, *Local Records* [for Newcastle, 22 March 1829] are merely derivative. The 'Treasury Memoir' (Hopkins, p. 341, *et al.*) in LUBL is a TS copy of *ABO*.

11 See Cowe, *Berwick upon Tweed*, p. 19, and *Memoirs of Stockdale*, I, pp. 44-8, 98-9, 123-38; Janet D. Cowe, 'The development of education in Berwick upon Tweed to 1902', M.Ed. thesis, Durham University, 1969. I am grateful to Mr Francis Cowe for considerable assistance.

12 Scott, *Berwick-upon-Tweed*, p. 367 [dates correct]; Douglas, *Berwick Grammar School*, pp. 20-4; Lamont-Brown, *Life and Times*, p. 188.

13 *Scott Letters*, I, p. 343; Arthur Melville Clark, *Sir Walter Scott: The Formative Years*, Edinburgh and London, 1969, pp. 18-19, 24, 50. Cp. John Sutherland, *The Life of Walter Scott: A Critical Biography*, Oxford UK and Cambridge USA, 1995, pp. 22-4.

14 Rodger, *Wooden World*, pp. 20, 264-5; Clowes, *The Royal Navy: A History*, V, pp. 175-81; Sharps, p. 376n.; Ward Notebook, ff. 107 verso-108 (all in his hand); infm about will from F. Cowe. Mrs Robertson's genealogical details are often inaccurate, though (uniquely?) she gives the year 1770 for William Stevenson's birth.

15 PRO: ADM 9/7, f. 2186; Clowes, *The Royal Navy: A History*, IV, pp. 32, 357, 369; V,

p. 126; Lewis, *Social History of the Navy*, pp. 329-30. ADM 6/118 (passing certificates from overseas 1788-1813) and ADM 107/64-5 (examination records 1795-5 March 1800) have also been combed; his name continues to appear in the quarterly Navy Lists until 1827. Further research at Kew is possible: see Stella Colwell, *Dictionary of Genealogical Sources in the PRO*, London, 1992.

16 David Mathew, *The Naval Heritage*, London, 1945, pp. xvi, 105, 117; W. J. Reader, *Professional Men: The Rise of the Professional Classes in Nineteenth-Century England*, London, 1966, pp. 16, 33; *ABO*, p. 208.

17 *Memoirs of Stockdale*, I, p. 36; DWL: MS 24. 56, and T[homas] B[elsham], 'A list of students educated at the academy at Daventry', *MR*, XVII, 1822, p. 286.

18 Williams, *Belsham*, pp. 224-6, 231, 234-6; McLachlan, pp. 157-63; *Priestley Works*, I. ii, p. 78; TK to Samuel Kenrick, Daventry, 24 December 1774, 'The Kenrick Letters', *TUHS*, III, pp. 255-7. The building is now marked by a plaque in honour of Priestley (P. O'Brien, *Warrington Academy 1757-86: Its Predecessors and Successors*, Wigan, 1989, p. 33).

19 Watts, *Dissenters*, pp. 482-6; Davis, *Dissent in Politics*, pp. 46-9, 59-61; Lincoln, *Social and Political Ideas*, pp. 12, 24, 26-7, 239; Ditchfield, 'The campaign in Lancashire and Cheshire', *passim*.

20 McLachlan, pp. 162, 251, 279; *Boswell: Life of Johnson*, ed. R. W. Chapman, corr. J. D. Fleeman, London, Oxford, New York, 1970, pp. 276n., 947, 1247n. See also Thomas McFarland, *Coleridge and the Pantheist Tradition*, Oxford, 1969, pp. 169-71 and his extensive note, 'The religious heterodoxy of Hartley, Priestley, and Godwin', pp. 311-14.

21 *Priestley Works*, I. ii, p. 162; Mineka, *Dissidence of Dissent*, pp. 41-2; Williams, *Belsham*, pp. 226, 328, 426; McLachlan, p. 162; Bogue and Bennett, *History*, II, p. 573; Turner, *Warrington Academy*, intro. Carter, pp. 12, 19; McLachlan, *Warrington Academy*, pp. 52-7.

22 Gibbs, *Priestley*, p. 39; *VCH Cheshire*, III, p. 108. For literary consequences see Valentine Cunningham, *Everywhere Spoken Against: Dissent in the Victorian Novel*, Oxford, 1975.

23 T. Belsham, *A Calm Inquiry into the Scripture Doctrine Concerning the Person of Christ ... and A Summary of the Various Opinions Entertained by Christians Upon the Subject*, London, 1811, Part II (summary). See also Mineka, *Dissidence of Dissent*, pp. 3-20.

24 *CR*, XVII, 1822, pp. 770-1 (obituary of Mrs Pilkington, née Ormerod); Mineka, *Dissidence of Dissent*, pp. 122-3.

25 Belsham, *Calm Inquiry*, Preface; Seed, 'The role of Unitarianism', pp. 37-40; Watts, *Dissenters*, pp. 371, 474-6; Davie, *Dissentient Voice*, pp. 26, 105-6, and *A Gathered Church*, *passim*; [W. J. Fox], 'On the character and writings of the Rev. T. Belsham', *MR*, n. s. IV, 1830, pp. 79-80.

26 [Fox], 'Belsham', pp. 244-51; C. Lawrence, 'Humphry Davy and Romanticism', *Romanticism and the Sciences*, ed. A. Cunningham and N. Jardine, Cambridge, etc., 1990, p. 214; Mineka, *Dissidence of Dissent*, pp. 216-17. Mineka devotes a chapter to Fox, who was the father of one of ECG's best friends. See also Daniel Walker Howe, *The Unitarian Conscience: Harvard Moral Philosophy, 1805-1861*, Cambridge, Mass., 1970, ch. VI, 'The Religion of the Heart'.

27 Owen Chadwick, *The Victorian Church*, Part 1, 3rd edn, London, 1971, p. 397 ('Presbyterians', pp. 391-8).

28 Williams, *Belsham*, pp. 376-84; Malcolm Deacon, *Philip Doddridge of Northampton 1702-51*, Northampton, 1980, p. 172; DWL: New College MSS L54/3/53 (transfers); McLachlan, pp. 163-7; *MR*, n. s. II, 1828, p. 59 (Broadbent); SCA: SLPS 52/12, T. A. Ward to Joseph Hunter, Sheffield, 9 March 1812; Barbara Brill, *William Gaskell 1805-1884: A Portrait*, Manchester, 1984, p. 13.

29 Henry Solly, *'These Eighty Years' or, The Story of an Unfinished Life*, London, 1893, I, chapter 3 (Cogan's school); *PDM*, V, 1797, p. 280 (Forsaith); *MR*, n. s. I, 1827, pp. 609-10 (Horsey).

30 Newth, 'Memorials', p. 105 (Daventry names listed in DWL: MS 24. 56, and TB, 'A list of students at Daventry', pp. 286-7). See also Appendix G.

31 The essays are neatly boxed, DWL: New College MS L12/15. (I have not attempted to decipher the shorthand.) Cp. McLachlan, p. 297.

32 DWL: MS 69/8-11*. See especially 69/10, pp. 51, 53; 69/11, pp. 1, 154-66.

33 McLachlan, p. 21; Lincoln, *Social and Political Ideas*, p. 77; Edward C. Mack, *Public Schools and British Opinion 1780-1860*, London, 1938, pp. 147-50; Richard Jenkyns, *The Victorians and Ancient Greece*, Oxford, 1980, pp. 60-7, 274-9; *Charles Darwin, Thomas Henry Huxley: Autobiographies*, ed. Gavin de Beer, London, New York, Toronto, 1974, p. 12. See also p. 38 below for Stevenson's *Remarks*.

34 'Winstanley obit., *CR*, n. s. VIII, 1852, pp. 637-8; Charles Webster and Jonathan Barry, 'The Manchester medical revolution', in Smith, p. 176.

35 BRO: B. 1/21, 143 (with no indication of his profession). The rule that new freemen had to sign in the year they were admitted was not relaxed until wartime in this century.

36 See Keane, *Tom Paine*, p. 444; *Maria Edgeworth in France and Switzerland: Selections From the Edgeworth Family Letters*, ed. Christina Colvin, Oxford, 1979, pp. 6-7, 'Colonel' (index). See further *The Poems of Anna Letitia Barbauld*, ed. William McCarthy and Elizabeth Kraft, Athens and London, 1994, p. 262, and Keane's Belgian sources, p. 607, n. 147.

37 *Wordsworth Letters*, I, pp. 59, 66; *The Prelude*, 1805, VI. ll. 353-4.

38 DWL: MS 24. 56, and TB, 'A list of students at Daventry', p. 286; Gibbs, *Priestley*, pp. 194, 214-15; *Priestley Works*, I. ii, p. 185.

39 Jeremy Black, *European Warfare 1660-1815*, London, 1994, pp. 169-71; *Wordsworth Letters*, I, p. 95; *The Prelude*, 1805, X. 74; *Edgeworth in France and Switzerland*, ed. Colvin, index. See Stephen Gill's subtle analysis of Wordsworth's French experiences in his *William Wordsworth: A Life*, Oxford, 1989, pp. 44-67.

40 *Roll of Students Entered at The Manchester Academy, 1786-1803, ... With A List of the Professors and Principal Officers*, Manchester, 1868; Winstanley obit., *CR*, n. s. VIII, 1852, p. 638.

41 *ABO*, p. 210: the 'Rev. George Wicke [*sic*] of Morton [*sic*] near Manchester' and the 'Rev. John Hallard [*sic*] of Bolton'. Holland entered in 1783, Wiche in 1786 (TB, 'A list of students at Daventry', pp. 285-6).

42 For Wiche, see p. 36 below; for Holland see *DNB*, *MR*, XXI, 1826, p. 430, and Franklin Baker, *The Rise and Progress of Nonconformity in Bolton: An Historical Sketch*, London, 1854, pp. 64-70, 112-13.

2

Dissent and politics in Manchester in the 1790s

IN 1790 the Honourable John Byng suffered a culture shock. He travelled from Knutsford, 'a clean, well-built, well-placed town where the cotton trade brings plenty', along to a 'great, nasty, manufactoring town', Manchester. In Knutsford comfortable cottages were decorated with geraniums in pots, his large inn had provided good food ('as spitchcock'd eel, cold fowl, cold lamb, tarts, and custards') and the church was attended by a well dressed company arriving in their own coaches and even by a sedan chair. In Manchester he was horrified by the clangour and bustle of his hotel, and the narrow, crowded streets in particular – 'such a hole', he called it, 'this great *Hot-Hell*'. Old Manchester round the ancient collegiate church by the river Irwell was 'built of wood, clay and plaister', with dreadful cellar dwellings and sordid lodgings that survived for many decades.

But improvements were being made, as Byng reluctantly recognised; 'opulence and increasing trade' were creating a new town away from the congested centre. A 'neat theatre, an elegant and capacious concert room, and large and commodious assembly rooms' were added to the great Infirmary in Piccadilly. 'The famous chorus-singers of Lancashire' continually sang in churches 'the most effective parts' of Handel's chief oratorios, De Quincey tells us, remembering the time when he lived a mile or so further out in the country at a house called 'Greenhay' and attended the old Manchester grammar school in the town by Chetham's library. By the end of the century new streets of brick had nearly doubled the town in size. Richer citizens, however, were already escaping to outer suburbs like Ardwick Green, then semi-rural and resembling London's west end, according to that voluminous author John Aikin, M.D., in 1795.[1]

More significantly, Manchester was fast becoming one of the most impor-tant cities in England, a centre for men who knew they were either replacing or growing well beyond the old order of rank and power in society, possessing independent sources of knowledge and creating new ones of their own. Its famous Literary and Philosophical Society, founded in 1781, had strong links with the new academy. Dr Thomas Percival, M.D., a powerful figure in the intellectual life of Manchester and beyond, author of a book on medical ethics that was standard for many years, was at some time president of both institutions. The college principal, the Reverend Dr Thomas Barnes, had been educated in Philip Holland's 'very respectable boarding-school at Bolton' between 1761 and 1764, then at Warrington academy under John Aikin, D.D., and Joseph Priestley. Barnes and Percival were liberals in politics, prominent in anti-slave trade agitation and members of the Manchester abolitionist committee of 1792 with Thomas Walker, the barrister George Lloyd, Dr Thomas Henry and Dr John Ferriar. Barnes had also chaired the first of a series of public meetings on 15 May 1789 in the renewed campaign against the test and corporation acts, which did not receive anything like the Anglican and Evangelical support enjoyed by the anti-slavery campaigns. Unitarians in particular, ever conscious of the social and political discrimination they laboured under, tended to regard themselves as 'theological negroes'. The culture of reform was part of their being.

Barnes became one of two secretaries of the Manchester Literary and Philosophical Society. Stevenson's name, however, unlike the names of all his academic colleagues, does not appear in the 1793 and 1797 printed lists of members of the Literary and Philosophical Society, by this time very successful. Barnes's papers published in volume 2 of the society's *Memoirs* show us his temper, especially 'A Plan for the improvement and extension of liberal education in Manchester', which he gave in April 1783. Dr Percival and other friends obtained for him a D.D. from the University of Edinburgh in 1784. He played a leading part two years later when the academy Stevenson and Winstanley were to join was first established in Manchester to provide religious and commercial education open to all, 'from whom no test, or confession of faith, will be required'.[2]

The new academy had been established in a fine new building on the west side of Dawson (later Mosley) Street near St Peter's church, 'in an airy and pleasant part' where a relatively small Manchester was beginning to extend towards the south and Cheshire. In William Green's truly magnificent 'Plan of Manchester and Salford', engraved by J. Thornton in 1794, it is labelled 'Academy', but it was also known as Manchester New College. Barnes became professor of divinity and the Reverend Ralph Harrison professor of classics and 'polite literature'. In 1789, Francis Nicholls was added as tutor for mathematics, and when in the following year Harrison resigned for reasons of health, Barnes appointed the Reverend Lewis Loyd (his spelling) as assistant tutor for classics. Loyd later married Sarah Jones, the sister of Samuel Jones, a banker and a stalwart of Cross Street chapel, leaving the ministry to become a banker himself. Stevenson filled the vacancy. When Nicholls left, he was succeeded by a young scientist who was to become nationally famous, John Dalton.[3]

Though there were no religious tests, the new college was Unitarian in many respects, 'by sympathy if not by formal profession'. After its move to York in 1803 it was to train many of the leading Unitarian ministers of the next century, colleagues of William Gaskell in Manchester and its twin town Salford like John Gooch Robberds, James Martineau, John Relly Beard and John James Tayler. On the other hand, of 142 students educated at Manchester between 1786 and 1803 only about twenty entered as divinity students. Most students, who began aged about thirteen to sixteen, came to study commerce. Turnover was fairly rapid. Those destined for business sometimes stayed a year or less; students for professions and the ministry stayed longer. The academy avoided 'the dangerous experiment of collegiate residence', which was held largely responsible for the demise of Warrington academy. They lived in boarding houses – '*divide,* in order to *govern*' was the watchword. They had to be in by 10 p. m., were not allowed to ride out of town or frequent taverns and inns without special leave.[4]

Science and utility were not neglected. The Bishop of Llandaff, Harrison noted approvingly in his inaugural, had even suggested that lectures on agriculture and commerce should be introduced into the older universities. Nevertheless, in Manchester's new academy Harrison was at first responsible for Latin and Greek, 'observations on the History, Mythology, Manners and Philosophy of the Ancients' and a course of lectures on 'Polite Literature; namely, the theory of language, particularly the English; Oratory; Criticism; Composition; History; and Geography'. Examinations were held in February and June; a mark scheme runs from 20 (perfect) down to 3 (very idle) and 0 (very bad). Loyd and his successor William Stevenson must have taken over much of this when Harrison's health gave way.[5]

The soaring optimism of all these educated liberals towards the end of the century is manifest in a paper of March 1784 by an honorary member of the Literary and Philosophical Society, the young William Turner of Newcastle, an 'Essay on crimes and punishments' printed in the same volume as Dr Barnes's papers. In this essay Turner hymns 'the progress of that humanity of spirit, which, happily for mankind, has been making such rapid advances in our part of the world' – progress towards 'that perfection of universal charity, which ought to be the governing principle of the human mind'. The Unitarian minister was here at one with the Quaker John Dalton, who, soon after coming in 1793 from his remote Cumbrian home to join the staff at Manchester, walked to nearby Warrington and saw on the outskirts an unfamiliar, indeed quite unknown sight to him: 'namely, a man gibbetted by the road-side, on a post as high as a steeple, his hat on his head and shoes on his feet, and completely dressed; it is a wonder that so shocking a spectacle, which everybody exclaims against, should still be continued in any civilized country', he exclaimed in a letter of May 1794. It was in fact the last execution of this kind in the district and is now the subject of a grim display in the Warrington museum, together with the fearsome man-traps that were soon to be abolished by act of parliament.[6]

The best account of everyday life in Manchester Academy is to be found in a long letter written on 20 February 1794 by Dalton (his head 'too full of

triangles, chymical processes, & electrical experiments, &c. to think much of
marriage') to his cousin and early patron, Elihu Robinson of Eaglesfield near
Cockermouth:

> I need not inform thee that Manchester *was* a large & flourishing place. – Our
> Academy is a large & elegant building in the most elegant & retired street of the
> place; it consists of a front & two wings; the first floor of the front is the hall
> where most of the business is done; over it is a Library with about 3000 Volumes;
> over this are two rooms, one of which is mine; it is about 8 yards by 6, & above
> 3 high, has two windows & a fireplace, is handsomely papered, light airy &
> retired; whether it is that philosophers like to approach as near to the stars as they
> can, or that they choose to soar above the vulgar into a purer region of the atmos-
> phere, I know not; but my apartment is full 10 yards above the surface of the
> earth.
>
> One of the wings is occupied by Dr. Barne's [*sic*] family, he is one of the
> tutors, & superintendant of the seminary; the other is occupied by a family who
> manage the boarding, & 17 In-students with 2 tutors, each individual having a
> separate room, &c. – Our out-students from the town & neighbourhood, at
> present amount to 9, which is as great a number as has been since the institution;
> they are of all religious professions; one friend's son from the town has entered
> since I came: The tutors are all Dissenters.
>
> Terms for In-students, 40 Guineas per Session (10 months); Out-students,
> 12 Guineas. Two Tutors and the In-students all dine, &c. together in a room on
> purpose: we breakfast on tea at 8½, dine at 1½, drink tea at 5, & sup at 8½; we
> fare as well as it is possible for anyone to do. At a small extra expence we can have
> any friend to dine, &c. with us in our respective rooms. My official department
> of tutor only requires my attendance upon the Students 21 hours in the week;
> but I find it often expedient to prepare my lectures previously.
>
> There is in this town a large library [Chetham's]; furnished with the best
> books in every art, science & language, which is open to all, gratis; when thou
> art apprized of this & such like circumstances, when thou considerest me in my
> private apartment, undisturbed, having a good fire, & a philosophical apparatus
> around me, thou wilt be able to form an opinion whether I spend my time in
> slothful inactivity of body & mind.[7]

Life there sounds industrious but far from strenuous in Dalton's lengthy
letter – a pleasant new building, decent library, experiments and limited
teaching duties, the opportunity to lead a private life as well as a social one. But
the teaching of Greek and Latin was everywhere under attack. Far away in
America the versatile Dr Benjamin Rush, physician, humanitarian (he objected
to public and capital punishment) and patriot (he encouraged Thomas Paine
to write in favour of republican government and signed the American declaration of independence), had in 1789 published anonymously in the *American
Museum* 'An enquiry into the utility of a knowledge of the Latin and Greek
languages, as a branch of a liberal education'. Rush thought the ascendancy of
classics was as undesirable as British political domination of America; young
men would do better if they learnt to speak Indian languages in a republic of

the new world. He immediately sent his essay to John Adams, whose defence of classical studies had inspired this rebuttal, but Adams and most of his correspondents still disagreed. Benjamin Franklin was a notable exception.[8]

This essay also came into the hands of James Currie, a Scottish doctor with literary interests settled in Liverpool, who brought it to the attention of his circle of friends.[9] One of these was Thomas Percival, a good friend of Currie and an important overseas correspondent of Rush for some fifteen years, from 1786 to 1801. Percival had seen to it that an essay by Rush, 'A letter to Thomas Percival: an account of the progress of population, agriculture, manners, and government in Pennsylvania', was read at a 1786 meeting of the Manchester Literary and Philosophical Society and printed in the 1790 volume of its *Memoirs*, but Rush's article attacking the utility of classical education inspired profound disagreement. One of Currie's friends responded in 'A vindication of classical learning, being an answer to Dr Rush's Enquiry into the utility of the knowledge of the Greek and Latin languages, in a letter to James Currie M.D.' The clear hand of the opening pages soon degenerates and becomes a more hurried script. Deletions are frequent and after about thirty pages whole sections are crossed out. Its author must have run out of steam.[10]

But this international flurry was not allowed to subside. A year or two before Stevenson actually took up his post at Manchester College, Percival had called upon Dr George Gregory, a learned translator and voluminous author – he was the first biographer of Thomas Chatterton – for a paper entitled 'On the uses of classical learning'. Dated 9 April 1791, it is a lucid and balanced defence of its value and was printed in the 1793 volume of the Manchester Literary and Philosophical Society's *Memoirs*. It could be regarded as a kind of manifesto for classics in the new college, a subject that was very definitely taught in the institution of which Percival was the president, under a sympathetic principal, for Barnes himself was a good classical scholar. Classical studies were to them every bit as valuable as the mathematics and 'experimental philosophy' taught by Dalton.

The college was afflicted with persistent financial problems, despite the financial support of leading families in Manchester and men like Richard Milnes of Fryston Hall, his cousin James Milnes and Daniel Gaskell, both of Wakefield, James Milnes junior of Thornes House, Dr James Currie and the Reverend John Yates of Liverpool, Samuel Gaskell of Warrington and Josiah Wedgwood of Etruria – but not at this time the Hollands of Knutsford. Lack of support, especially from outside the Manchester area, exhausted the building fund in five years, bringing a period of severe financial retrenchment. The subscription income would not even pay the tutors' salaries. As a professedly secular college, it was ineligible for support from such bodies as the Congregational fund, the Presbyterian fund and the William Coward trust.

The manuscript minutes of the Academy's main committee suggest that more than financial troubles were involved. Lewis Loyd was paid fifteen guineas on 30 September 1790 for his assistance to Barnes, who had also been empowered on 24 February to appoint him as assistant classical tutor for the coming session. On 4 October 1792, however, a committee meeting thanked Loyd for his past services; he was going in to a banking partnership with his brothers-in-law, Samuel and William Jones. Another meeting on 29 November was told that 'at present' Barnes had authority to appoint an assistant classical tutor in Loyd's place, but this was followed by a meeting on 26 December 1792 at which a letter of resignation by Barnes was read. A special committee had apparently decided that he did not possess the 'authority' he had been accustomed to exercise, which caused him 'painful embarrassment'. He would have deferred his resignation, he wrote, 'but reflecting that Mr. Lloyd's [sic] department would remain so long vacant, and that perhaps the opportunity of uniting it with the pastorship of Dobb Lane might hereby be lost', he gave immediate notice.

It looks as if the committee had been trying to save money by failing to appoint a classical tutor for the session. The trustees responded by noting their lack of funding for the 'professors as originally intended', asked him to continue for a period of five years with 'general superintendency' and 'the whole responsibility', and finally asked him to provide an 'Assistant Classical Tutor' in place of Loyd. A private letter from Dr James Currie to Dr Percival makes it fairly certain that Barnes had sent in his resignation for reasons of common sense and 'utility' against the abstract principles of control urged by his opponents amongst the trustees.[11]

The printed records and the official history of Manchester College state that William Stevenson followed Lewis Loyd as 'Assistant Classical Tutor' in 1792, but this is too early and cannot be correct. Unfortunately, the manuscript minutes of the main committee almost break down after the power struggle in late 1792 and are uninformative for several years. In fact, no contemporary official record of the college has survived to prove that William Stevenson was ever there. Even a cash book for these years, which contains far more details, is silent. Amongst payments to plasterers, plumbers and a singing teacher, regular disbursements for chief rent, a seat in St John's church and poor rate, coals and candles and the like, we find the salaries of Dr Barnes, Nicholls and Dalton noted (but not Loyd's). At the beginning of the 1792-93 session, according to the minutes, Nicholls was appointed Librarian and given £20 a year extra, but when Dalton took over as tutor from Nicholls he did not receive the £20 a year. There are also for the years 1792-96 payments of five guineas a year for a librarian, who perhaps issued and received the actual books. This does not seem to have been Stevenson, for the recipient of the five guineas is named in one year, 1793, as a Mr Davis. Later, the college minutes of May 1798 speak of reviving the office of Librarian to go with the Classical Tutorship.

There is, however, a clear statement in Stevenson's obituary that on his return from Bruges 'he was engaged as classical tutor at the academy at

Manchester'. Winstanley's obituary is more equivocal on this point: 'Not improbably, Mr. Stephenson for a time superintended the classical department in this institution, which he was eminently qualified to do.' Dalton's letter certainly suggests that there was at least one other tutor besides himself, but gives no name. Barnes did not gain his point until Boxing Day 1792, so we could assume that Stevenson might have appeared in early 1793 and was in post when his friend Winstanley, several years older than most divinity students at the age of twenty, appeared in September for the new session. But if Stevenson was any kind of tutor in classics at Manchester Academy, he cannot be shown to have been formally appointed and any payments to him (and to Lewis Loyd) must have been funded in some special manner.[12]

Stevenson had come a long way from his days running with the street urchins of Berwick. He had been soundly educated at a good dissenting academy and must have been thought well qualified for the teaching post he obtained in his early twenties. His colleagues and associates were remarkable men. John Dalton was a true original, a genius (a term he himself would have rejected), destined to achieve a European reputation within a few years and a place in the history of science for his atomic theory, problematic in content but serviceable in practice, and his pioneering descriptions of colour-blindness, from which he himself suffered. He was not only the author of *A New System of Chemical Philosophy* (1808), but had also composed, like Priestley, a useful pedagogic work, *Elements of English Grammar* (1801). It was 'respectfully inscribed, as a testimony to his merit', to a radical figure of the age, John Horne Tooke.[13] The principal of Manchester New College, Thomas Barnes, 'had an uncommonly fertile mind; great quickness of conception, as well as readiness of expression', and though he could not be persuaded to publish very much, 'composed with wonderful facility; so that writing was rather a pleasure than a work of labour to him'. He was reputed to be cheerful, lively and actively benevolent, with a good 'general knowledge of what is called polite literature'. He was not only capable of encouraging Stevenson as an academic tutor of classics but also of guiding his first steps in the world of letters. Such men were leaders in a vibrant intellectual life of the provinces that was beginning to rival the dominant culture of London and the English universities. In career terms Stevenson had fallen on his feet.

A career in teaching was not thought to be incompatible with a religious one in such dissenting circles – far from it. Their ideal was a learned ministry; a phrase like 'going to preach a lecture' was regularly used. Thomas Barnes and Ralph Harrison were ministers of the most famous Unitarian chapel in the north of England at Cross Street in Manchester, where the very first meetings of the Literary and Philosophical Society were held. It is said that Dr Barnes, whose charismatic preaching had attracted a huge congregation to the chapel, converted Stevenson to Arianism, which survived at Cross Street in a rising sea of Socinianism until Barnes's death in 1810. No less than sixty-four gentlemen, 'with hat-bands and mourning provided at their own expense', walked before his hearse, which was also accompanied by another funerary sign of social success – many carriages.[14]

During the years Stevenson was in Manchester he too practised as a minister. There is no record of his ordination, which is not unusual, though his friend John Holland had been ordained a few years before in 1789, by Dr Barnes himself and William Turner of Wakefield.[15] However, not only was he characterised as a clergyman in Manchester when the Berwick roll of burgesses was printed in 1796, his obituary informs us that he preached 'for a short time' at Dob Lane chapel near Manchester. This was a tiny dissenting chapel without a settled minister but able to call upon staff and students from Manchester college between 1790 and 1803. Six men are known to have helped the congregation in this way.[16]

Dob Lane chapel lay to the north-east in the direction of Oldham and was 'only reached by a bridle-path through the fields'. The chapel was secluded amongst trees, and a very narrow, hedged lane ran on up to Watchcote, Failsworth. Stevenson's immediate predecessor, Lewis Loyd, used to ride a white Welsh pony to get there.[17] The congregation was diminutive, so small that those who preached to it received help from the Presbyterian board. Lewis Loyd was given a £4 annual exhibition in May 1792, backdated to Christmas 1790, but there does not seem to be another entry for Dob Lane in the minutes until October 1796. This records the annual exhibition of £4 allotted to W. Marshall 'from Midsummer last', Dr Barnes 'stating that the people do not raise £40 a year'. The omission is curious and perhaps significant. William Stevenson might not have wished to accept any money for preaching.[18]

Dob Lane chapel's size and rustic seclusion did not shelter its members from the political battles raging all over the country, in the provincial centres of the north where religious dissent was strongly established as well as in London. After their two recent failures in parliament to achieve civil liberties, the second more stunning than the first, dissenters became more and more identified with subversion. John Holland of Bolton was burnt in effigy, and on another occasion 'represented riding on an ass, as chief mourner, in a procession intended as a mock celebration of the funeral' of the loyalists' bogeyman, Thomas Paine. A great Unitarian manufacturer, Holbrook Gaskell of Prospect Hill, a large house in the country just south of Warrington that William and Elizabeth Gaskell often used to visit in the early years of their marriage, became 'a marked man' for supporting the principles of the French revolution, and 'had not for several years an associate or companion out of the bosom of his own family'. The Gaskells were a numerous and rather self-sufficient tribe, one might add. Holbrook married Ann, William Gaskell's aunt on his father's side.

The Reverend Harry Toulmin, minister of Chowbent to the west of Manchester from 1788 to 1792, was a popular clergyman with a congregation often eight hundred strong, but his aggressive defence of a Warrington resolution against the test and combination acts in March 1790 (a Samuel Gaskell

was present) caused him to be attacked as a dangerous radical even by some
fellow dissenters. In the west country his father Joshua Toulmin, minister at
Taunton, had an effigy of Thomas Paine burnt before his door and his
windows broken in 1791. Harry Toulmin received threats of violence, had his
chapel attacked when he was preaching and on another occasion had to hasten
home to disperse a mob that had gathered round his house. 'Various reasons
concurred', we are told, to persuade him in 1793 to emigrate with his family
to America. In England men like Percival and Currie became more and more
circumspect, aware of government spies and loyalist vigilantes.[19]

The forces of reaction were strong. Reformers of all kinds were lumped
together, sometimes imprisoned by the authorities and always in danger of
violence from loyalist mobs. A notorious instance in Manchester was the attack
on Thomas Walker's house. There were also arrests for treason in 1794.
Manchester College made sure it 'kept a low political profile after the early
1790s', writes a modern historian.[20] In Dob Lane, however, Stevenson
preached to a strongly radical congregation. Like Dryden's Shaftesbury, for a
calm unfit, it sought the storms. In early 1793 petitions in favour of the war
with France were 'signed by all the inhabitants of Failsworth, except twenty
heads of families, nearly all of whom attended Dob Lane Chapel'. For this the
house of a prominent member of the congregation was attacked by a vocif-
erous mob: 'You are Jacobins, Painites and Presbyterians; you are enemies to
your king and country, and deserve to be killed!' The members of Dob Lane
chapel were bold enough to meet after service to talk Jacobin politics – this in
a district where on 1 January 1793 an effigy of Paine had been taken in a
church-and-king procession with a band of music half-a-mile long to be hung
and ritually burnt. We can assume that Stevenson did not find such politics
uncongenial, whilst recognising that we have as little direct evidence of his
political views in these years as of his theological.

A dim sidelight on the latter is provided in Alexander Gordon's history of
the chapel at Dukinfield, just to the east of Manchester. Thomas Smith, originally a Methodist preacher, was introduced to its congregation by Stevenson,
who wrote on 25 November 1794 that Smith was attached to 'the real principles of Dissent', and described his opinions as 'neither what are deemed
extremely orthodox nor extremely heretical'. This perhaps means that he was
not, like Wesley and many other Methodists at that period, a reluctant nonconformist. Wesley himself was far from pleased with Smith's defection at the time.
This 'gifted, artistic and delightfully eccentric man', Ian Sellers writes, also
published *Original Miscellaneous Poems* (Stockport, 1790) and *Poems*
(Manchester, 1797), which display 'a deep love of liberty, a passionate hatred
of both despots and anarchists' and 'a generous humanitarian concern for the
poor'. He also founded a literary society at Dukinfield to which all could
contribute poems – not at all Stevenson's line, however much he may have
shared Smith's other values.[21]

After about three years at Dob Lane William Stevenson gave up preaching. His obituary implies (if only by juxtaposition) that the influence of a man who had been a fellow student with him at Daventry was critical. The 'most amiable and disinterested' George Wiche, it states, 'published a pamphlet against the employment of any person as a hired teacher of religion, and practically enforced his own doctrines by resigning his ministerial office, to the great regret of all friends. Mr. Stevenson did the same at Doblane ...'

A native of Taunton, Wiche had migrated to Daventry from Hoxton academy in 1786, the year before Stevenson entered. As minister for some seven or eight years at a village near Manchester, Monton, Wiche was successful and 'universally beloved' by his congregation, according to a friend from Daventry days, the Reverend John Kentish. Like many of his generation in the Manchester area, Wiche was a staunch Unitarian. He wrote defending Unitarian beliefs in the so-called 'Wigan Controversy' of 1791, as did the Reverend Lewis Loyd (described later as 'the very distinguished owner and occupier of Overstone Park, near London'), the Reverend John Holland of Bolton and the Reverend Harry Toulmin, Wiche's predecessor at Monton. But when Wiche came to believe that he could not in conscience continue to be a pastor, he left, in the spring of 1796.[22]

The Declaration of George Wiche, on Resigning the Office of an Hired Preacher, a pamphlet dated Monton, 17 December 1795, was published at Manchester in 1796. He clearly felt in an age of extreme views that attack was the best form of defence. 'The truths of Revelation would have double sway', he wrote in this short pamphlet, 'if the simplicity and benevolence of the preacher were beyond all doubt'. He criticised ministers not only for the fact that they received a salary for preaching but for the way in which they were accustomed to demand a rank for themselves in society and toadied to the rich. Any advance in spiritual knowledge, he claimed, inevitably divides a minister from his congregation; he must nevertheless 'flatter the prejudices of the old, the wealthy and the dull' and 'too much consult the vitiated tastes, and prevailing, though dangerous, desires, of his pampered employers'. (It becomes difficult to believe with Kentish that he was 'universally beloved' by his congregation.) Most striking of all is Wiche's assertion that he lived in 'times like the present, when convictions force themselves upon the mind, with a power not recorded to have taken place, since the day of the Revelation of God to man by Jesus Christ.' This is a revolutionary, millenarian statement.

After his resignation he found a position with difficulty in the warehouse of a silversmith, under a 'vulgar, brutal foreman', and eventually, after more experience in trade, sailed for New York as the agent of a Manchester commercial house. There, not unexpectedly, 'he saw, he abhorred, and instantly refused to encourage, the commercial spirit and practices of the merchants in that part of the United States'. He hastened to join his fellow Unitarian, Harry Toulmin, who had by now arrived in Lexington, Kentucky. In 1792 Toulmin had published three pamphlets favouring emigration to America; by February

1794 he had been elected president of Transylvania University. (It was 'hardly more than a grammar school', he told Priestley.) But Wiche never reached him, dying on 23 August 1799 of the yellow fever raging in Philadelphia, where Priestley had inspired 'the first permanently established Unitarian congregation in the New World' a few years before and it had been hoped Harry Toulmin would become its minister. Toulmin, forceful and intelligent, went on to have a distinguished career as a judge in America.[23]

Wiche's death brought to an end a life that was uncompromising in both social and religious terms. From his mercantile experience 'it became his fixed persuasion', John Kentish wrote, 'that till extensive commerce and great capitalists are unknown, man can make no progress in virtue and happiness'. He had progressed to the position of a famous Unitarian thinker of an earlier generation, Richard Price, who advised the Americans in his *Observations on the Importance of the American Revolution* in 1784 that they should discourage commerce and foster instead 'the innocent and fraternal art of agriculture', thereby creating a virtuous and free society. Price made it explicit that he was objecting to a system. Ideologically speaking, he attacked an age of capitalism, when as so often in the century to come, 'enormous money-making' was associated with 'intense religiosity'.[24]

But Wiche's immediate concerns when at Monton in 1795 were more down-to-earth, focused for us especially by his assertion that the 'readiness which preachers discover to move from a less to a more lucrative situation, is so common, that the first question on a removal, is, "what is his salary?"' Stevenson's experience at Dob Lane chapel must have brought him into contact with the same kind of worldliness.[25] One of the congregation at this time was a Mr Taylor, 'whose chief talk was of making money'. He it was who helped persuade Lewis Loyd to change his minister's black dress for 'a coat almost white' and begin his banking career. Stevenson must have reacted like his friend Wiche rather than his predecessor Loyd, who continued to support Unitarian causes and institutions from the fortune he went on to make. As so often, too, the consequences of such an individual choice echoed for years to come: Loyd's deeply religious son exercised considerable influence over Sir Robert Peel and his successors and was raised to the peerage as Baron Overstone. He died in 1883, one of the richest men in England, with a personal estate of under £2,100,000, owning land that had cost £1,500,000 to purchase.[26]

Yet Stevenson resigned from a congregation with some members at least whose thoughts went well beyond money-making. Dob Lane chapel trustees in 1804 were Samuel, James and William Taylor and Jonathan Hobson (from Moston), John and Samuel Hobson, John, William and Thomas Barrett, John Hobson and Thomas Moffett (from Failsworth) and James Darbishire, 'now or late of Failsworth, merchant'. They were mostly manufacturers and merchants, though Samuel Taylor was described as esquire. He, presumably, was the man who talked money. James Darbishire, on the other hand, founded a chapel library in April 1796 which contained books selected for the young as well as for the improvement of older readers, and continued to support it year after year. For a long time it was the only lending library in the district, with as many as eighty-five subscribers in 1819. A printed catalogue of 1803, which like an early manuscript history of the chapel cannot now be found, is reported to have contained details of over 200 volumes – works by thinkers like Voltaire and Mirabeau, plays by Shakespeare and early English poetry. Stevenson had not been amongst the philistines. Nevertheless, despite the difficulties of earning a living in any other way, he abandoned the ministry and relinquished his academic career as well.[27]

In that year, 1796, appeared his first publication, entitled *Remarks on the Very Inferior Utility of Classical Learning*. Stevenson's printers served him well. The type of his title-page is well laid out and weighted, and – a nice touch – 'very inferior utility' is set in light, individually spaced roman caps whilst 'classical learning' materialises densely in the dark caps and lower case letters of a Gothic font. His radicalism reminds us of George Wiche in a general way, but for Stevenson classical learning 'occupies a niche in the temple of science'. Though he mentions the 'will and authority of the Deity', and, briefly, the education of divines, his argument hardly goes beyond an earthly value that for a time achieved the status of an alternative, quasi-religious principle, utility. Jeremy Bentham, who had read David Hume's essay 'Why Utility Pleases', tells us he cried *Eureka,* 'as it were in an inward ecstacy', when he came across the phrase 'the greatest happiness of the greatest number' in Priestley's writings. As with Stevenson, only more so, his secular understanding of 'happiness' is very different from Priestley's religious frame of reference and belief in an ultimately Divine moral order.[28]

A great friend of George Gregory, Gilbert Wakefield, reported that classical literature was said to be 'imperfectly known or valued amongst the dissenters', though both the student at Northampton Academy and William Stevenson give a strong impression that they were arguing against their institutional authorities. Did earlier views current amongst the Northampton students harden, or did some three years as classical tutor at Manchester College bring disillusionment to William Stevenson? Nobody knows, but he was bold enough to publish at his own expense this thirty-six page booklet, with what must have been in his situation a highly provocative title. It was printed at Manchester for the author at the office of G. Nicholson, and sold for a shilling by H. D. Symonds of 20 Paternoster-row, London. Stevenson's name is on the title-page. At least he did not flaunt the teaching post he had held at Manchester College.[29]

The arguments he brings forward are at first calm, rational and pragmatic. No kind of knowledge is absolutely useless, but the science of the classical past is quite superseded by 'the number and variety of facts' available to modern thinkers. Classical 'works of taste' may retain their value, but 'if imagery apposite, beautiful, and bold, constitute the essence of Poetry, modern times may boast of productions more truly poetic'. This sounds promising, but is immediately dropped; instead, he makes the usual reductive claim that the classics 'afford but a momentary pleasure' and 'weaken the mind, whilst they interest and strengthen the imagination'. Language, in this view, should be a smoothly efficient surgical tool: 'an Englishman will improve his style with more ease, and to a higher degree of correctness, purity, precision, elegance, and force, by studying the best authors in his own language' – here echoing the views of his old schoolfellow at Berwick, Percival Stockdale, though these had not yet appeared in print.

Stevenson's reader is left in no doubt about one of the best authors – a dangerous one, too – for he quotes approvingly from the first part of Thomas Paine's *The Age of Reason*. In his *Rights of Man* (1791-92) Paine had savaged the hereditary system of government, been indicted for seditious libel in 1792 and fled to France, burning his boats with a letter to the attorney-general in which he asked, 'Is it possible that you or I can believe, or that reason can make any other man believe, that the capacity of such a man as Mr Guelph, or any of his profligate sons, is necessary to the government of a nation?' Eventually, he fell out of favour with the Jacobin faction in France as well and spent many months in the Luxembourg prison under the shadow of the guillotine, during which time his *Age of Reason* was published, initially in Paris in the year of terror, 1794, and afterwards circulated widely in cheap English editions. Both Joseph Priestley and John Prior Estlin published rebuttals of this work.[30]

Paine rejected the Bible, divine revelation and all forms of ecclesiastical authority, because in his view ordinary human reason could find enlightenment in nature itself. 'The Almighty lecturer', he wrote craftily, 'by displaying the principles of science in the structure of the universe, has invited men to study and to imitation'. (Blake was appalled by this kind of deism – 'The Divine Vision dimly appeared in clouds of blood, weeping'.) As for the study of languages, Paine contended that it had no place in modern times; it had simply 'nothing to do with the *creation* of knowledge'. Another author Stevenson cites, the combative and eccentric John Horne Tooke, insisted in his Socratic *Diversions of Purley* (1786 and 1805) – neither a novel nor a work on games but a lengthy marriage of philosophy and philology admired by Belsham, James Mill, Henry Brougham and Hazlitt as well as Dalton – that truth 'has been improperly imagined at the bottom of a well: it lies much nearer to the surface; though buried indeed at present under mountains of learned rubbish'. Stevenson's position is the same. He also goes out of his way to praise Paine's 'pertinent and judicious' observations and his 'concise energy' of style.[31]

Paine democratised language – though he was, paradoxically, a great rhetorician. He found a style for literate but not necessarily classically educated readers and, crucially, helped create a new political force – public opinion. What had been defensive efforts of older radicals and dissenters to preserve their liberty of opinion were turning into positive assertions of equality. Stevenson touched on some of the concerns of contemporary intellectuals who, though only loosely connected, were regarded as a dangerous and thoroughly subversive group. Tooke, for instance, was a man of swift eloquence, shrewd, self-possessed and attractive in society; in priest's orders, he was also said to swear, drink a good deal of claret and live happily with his illegitimate daughters in a villa at Wimbledon. He was 'the heart of the reform movement', an important link between progressive societies in London and the country at large. He was one of those tried for treason in 1794.

There is no evidence that Stevenson was a political extremist. Nor did he display Paine's contempt for almost everything found in the Bible and Christian teaching, or agree with the radicalism that John Adams had called 'Paine's yellow fever'. But his tone and choice of words must have irritated Percival and Barnes:

> Surely it is improper and criminal to devote several years to a study, whence the mind receives no knowledge, and the imagination but little pleasure. It cannot improve, because it does not exercise, the judgment. – Classical literature, therefore, is not an effectual mean to the most important ends of education, – the knowledge of facts, and the deduction of simple and useful truths. ...
>
> The bad effects which, generally, result from the present system of education are the following: an overgrown memory, and a weak and puny judgment: a blind and bigotted attachment to authorities, names and antiquity: disputes merely verbal: and, consequently, the continuance of error and prejudice.

It is noticeable that in a long footnote of the *Remarks* running over pages 21-2 he disagreed openly with the views on language of two prominent Unitarian leaders of the older generation, Philip Holland and Joseph Priestley. One can imagine him being solemnly referred to these authorities by his academic seniors at Manchester, for he quotes specifically from Priestley's *Lectures on the Theory of Language* and Holland's *The Importance of Learning: A Sermon*, published at Warrington in 1762 and 1760 respectively.[32]

Philip Holland (an uncle of Stevenson's wife-to-be) was until his death in 1789 the Unitarian minister of Bank Street chapel, Bolton. The radical credentials of Holland as well as Priestley were beyond question. Holland had drawn up Bolton's petition against the government at the time of the American war of independence, convinced that 'on the side of Britain such a contest was peculiarly unnatural, cruel and unjust'. Priestley, whose house, library and scientific apparatus in Birmingham had been destroyed by a church-and-king mob in 1791, had recently given his farewell sermon to his congregation at the Gravel Pit Meeting, Hackney, on 30 March 1794 before his emigration to America. The treason trials of that year proved abortive, but 'gagging acts' were introduced and the counter-revolution took the form of 'a profound suspicion of ideas and the of the type of man who holds them'. A letter of March 1795 spoke of five American vessels filled with families fleeing the country 'as in the Laudean times'.[33]

Stevenson flaunted ultra-radical names, but in a narrow context; his gaze was fixed on the inutility of classical learning. Yet if not politically subversive, his stance was professionally suicidal. He denied that intensive classical study was necessary for law, medicine or divinity, but only gave a very superficial list of what should replace classics – mechanics, instruments, chemistry, anatomy, medicine, geometry and natural history. His little book approaches its conclusion in passionate (though hardly demotic) advocacy of science and utility:

> let the human mind be studied: let the progress of intellect be marked: let these grand truths be rooted in the memory, that man is the necessary creature of original formation and external circumstances; that the laws of the intellectual and moral world are as fixed and regular as those of the natural; that, therefore, knowledge alone is necessary to render the actions of intelligent beings as certainly subservient to the general good, as are, in many instances, the powers of matter.

This is ironic. Priestley was a famous necessitarian; a believer in the perfectibility of the human race and, in addition, an influential educational reformer. Humankind was for Priestley as much a part of nature as matter, subject to and moulded by circumstances. Rational, scientific observation and experiment were quite adequate to discover the laws that governed education. Children's experiences could then be organised in appropriate ways by applying the associationist psychology of David Hartley ('the universal pick-lock of all metaphysical difficulties', Walter Scott once sarcastically called it) to the practical business of teaching. This model for human progress within a Divine scheme was based on an optimistic view of human potential, but Stevenson, though classical tutor in a new college at Manchester, could not accept Priestley's belief in classical studies.[34]

The leading periodical of the day, the *Monthly Review*, which could call upon the services of a first-rate scholar like Charles Burney the younger or those of the classicist Thomas Burgess, ignored Stevenson's *Remarks* altogether. A brief review in the December issue of the *Gentleman's Magazine* was curtly dismissive: 'A trifling attack on classical learning, by one very superficially acquainted with classical writers', who 'has substituted nothing in their stead'. The *Critical Review*, competitor of the *Monthly* and often favourable to progressive ideas, referred to 'the modern rage of innovation' and unkindly proposed that Stevenson might have wished 'to explode those pursuits with which he is unacquainted', but went on to support the basic educational thesis that classical studies took too much attention from philosophy and science. Dr George Gregory, the scholar who had defended classical learning for the Manchester Literary and Philosophical Society, is known to have been assistant or co-editor of the *Critical* at this time.[35]

Stevenson had no reason to hide from the mob or to leave the country. His distinctly unvisionary career at Manchester College has left hardly any trace. *Remarks on the Very Inferior Utility of Classical Learning*, a copy of which he presented to his colleague John Dalton, did not attract much attention in its time and has been little more than a title until very recently.[36] After he had resigned or been dismissed from his post in 1796, the college committee minutes of 31 May 1797 show that Dr Barnes again raised the matter of his own retirement. On 12 July a long special meeting asked him to keep going whilst funds were obtained and a successor or successors willing to receive boarders were sought. Two thousand copies of an analytical report, which was also printed in the *Monthly Magazine* for August 1797, were circulated. In this it was stated that Dr Barnes had lately taught 'Greek and Roman Classics, with other parts of Polite Literature'. However, the report continued, 'a distinct professorship of these essential branches of instruction formed the original constitution of the New College' and it was hoped that it would be speedily revived. William Turner of Newcastle was approached first to follow Barnes and told that a classical tutor would be appointed when new annual subscriptions reached 70 guineas. He refused, as did Belsham, who was also invited to recommend a classical tutor. Then a succession of distinguished dissenting scholars were invited to take Barnes's post. The Reverend George Walker, F.R.S., finally accepted on 4 May 1798, undertaking to provide classical instruction in addition till a tutor could be found. This all seems a strong affirmation of the college's original position and, obliquely, a public disavowal of the recalcitrant pamphlet published by a former junior member of staff.[37]

Such a closing parenthesis to Stevenson's career at the new college in Manchester pairs neatly, if frustratingly, with the opening defence of classical learning George Gregory had provided for Dr Percival in 1791. Gregory's career shows what could be attained by pliant assiduity. From humble beginnings he became domestic chaplain to the bishop of Llandaff, a prebendary of St Paul's, vicar of West Ham, lecturer of St Giles, Cripplegate and preacher at the foundling hospital. This was in the established church, but some dissenting equivalent would have been possible for Stevenson.[38]

Indeed, the obituary of an important Unitarian minister in the *Christian Reformer* for 1848 might almost suggest that his very presence at Manchester College was being silently dropped from the record:

> At the commencement of the session 1794-95, Robert Smethurst was entered a pupil at Manchester New College, an institution then in the ninth year of its existence, and enjoying the superintendence of Rev. Thos. Barnes, D.D., the very popular minister of Cross Street chapel. Previous to 1792, Dr. Barnes had been successively assisted in the College by Rev. Ralph Harrison and Mr. Lewis Loyd, as classical tutor; but during Mr. Smethurst's studies this office was held by Mr. Charles Saunders, B.A., of Queen's College, Cambridge. The tutor in Mathematics and Natural Philosophy was Mr., afterwards the celebrated Dr. Dalton.

It is easy to see why Dalton, a hero of the British Association for the Advancement of Science, and Loyd, by this time rich, famous and influential amongst Unitarians, should be mentioned by the obituarist, but Saunders, who had been a young Church of England clergyman recommended by

Walker for the classical post at Manchester, was not appointed till 25 July 1798 and left a year later. Smethurst was number ninety-eight on the manuscript roll of students, which records that he entered the academy in September 1794 and left in June of 1798. He would never have encountered Saunders as a student. One wonders if Elizabeth Gaskell, or her husband, noticed the omission of her father's name. Was it just accidental?[39]

When he was a young man in his twenties, William Stevenson was unsettled, perhaps even self-destructive, in the sense that he felt impelled to reject what the ordinary world would call his own best interests – though hardly to the same extent as Coleridge, who gave up his university career at Cambridge in late 1793 to become a private in the 15th Light Dragoons ('a very indocile Equestrian'), then turned radical poet, propagandist, pamphleteer, journalist, charismatic lecturer, tutor and visionary cottager with calloused hands and innocent household mice, falling paradoxically 'plump, ten thousand fathoms down (but his wings saved him harmless) into the *hortus siccus* of dissent', as Hazlitt caustically put it in *The Spirit of the Age*, 'where he pared religion down to the standard of reason, and stripped faith of mystery', preached at Unitarian chapels in Bridgewater and Taunton, and finally accepted the house and post of Unitarian minister at Shrewsbury in January 1798 with a salary of £120 a year ('a permanent income not inconsistent with my religious or political creeds') and a house worth £30 per annum. But not for long.[40]

Coleridge might have seen or heard of Wiche's pamphlet, though its ideas and ideals were widespread. At some date Wiche's father, who died in 1794, had been the director of a workhouse at Ottery St Mary, where Coleridge's father was vicar. Coleridge's early dissenting connections were amongst the Unitarians of Bristol and the Midlands rather than further north, however, though in the course of a brilliant speaking tour he did pay one brief visit to Manchester in February 1796.[41] Wiche's pamphlet was printed in Manchester by Cowdroy and Boden, and sold in London by Joseph Johnson, whose hospitable establishment in St Paul's churchyard was even more of an extra-mural class for radicals than Dob Lane chapel. He published Priestley, Price, the Edgeworths, Belsham, Anna Barbauld and her brother, John Aikin M.D., Blake, Paine, Horne Tooke, Wollstonecraft, Wordsworth, Coleridge and many others in the 1790s, ultimately being sentenced to six months' prison in 1798 for publishing a pamphlet that libelled the bishop of Llandaff. Once incarcerated, he is said to have exchanged open hospitality for a close study of his ledger and realised a large amount of money by sending out bills to debtors. The author, Gilbert Wakefield, was sentenced to two much less profitable years in Dorchester gaol.[42]

It is curious to consider Wiche's blunt public rhetoric alongside the emotional struggles and contortions of Coleridge's private letters. In a letter of 5 May 1796 Coleridge insisted that preaching for hire was not right for him. He was only too well aware that his 'shaping and disquisitive mind' might lead to a change of heart and loss of faith. 'Shall I not be an Agriculturalist, an Husband, a Father, and a *Priest* after the order of Peace? an *hireless* Priest?', he urgently asked one friend. On another occasion he expressed his 'active zeal for Unitarian Christianity'. His special friend and adviser in this context was the Unitarian minister at Bristol, John Prior Estlin. Driven by what he evasively if humorously called those 'two Giants yclept BREAD & CHEESE', and encouraged by the breadth of belief found amongst Unitarians of the time, he temporarily concluded that he could after all become one of their ministers.

The letters he wrote after his call from Shrewsbury in December 1797, full of interlaced and subtle arguments, sometimes 'disarming, and yet machiavellian', as Richard Holmes comments, show far more 'fluctuation of mind' than a disillusioned Hazlitt was later to allow. But one passage, in letter to Josiah Wedgwood, is perfectly straightforward:

> To the *ministry* I adduced the following objections at the time that I decided against entering into it. – It makes one's livelihood hang upon the profession of *particular opinions*: and tends therefore to warp the intellectual faculty; to fasten convictions on the mind by the agency of it's wishes; and if Reason should at length dissever them, it presents strong Motives to Falsehood or Simulation. – Secondly, as the subscriptions of the Congregation form the revenue, the minister is under an inducement to adapt his moral exhortations to their wishes rather than to their needs. (Poor Pilkington of Derby was, I believe, obliged to resign on account of his sermons respecting Riches & Rich Men.)[43]

A full statement of reasons for Coleridge's rejection of the form of Unitarianism he had once espoused would range from its essential pantheism ('God becomes a mere power in darkness, even as Gravitation') to its failure to satisfy the complex emotional and visionary sides of his nature ('Socinianism Moonlight – Methodism &c A Stove! O for some Sun that shall unite Light & Warmth'). In personal terms, he later told De Quincey, 'it grieved him to grieve' John Estlin. But the reference to the fate of the Reverend James Pilkington, Unitarian minister at Friar Gate chapel in Derby from 1779 to 1797, is another indication of the social pressures in prosperous dissenting congregations that both Coleridge and George Wiche, and probably William Stevenson, found intolerable.[44]

Pilkington's congregation was hardly lacking in intellectual distinction; it included members of the 'infant philosophical Society at Derby', begun by the great Erasmus Darwin, who then lived there. Darwin would not compare its members with the 'well-grown gigantic philosophers at Birmingham', where Joseph Priestley at the height of his scientific powers had settled for a time, but its library in particular was thriving and contained Pilkington's book on the state and antiquities of Derbyshire, published in 1789. Darwin obviously approved, contributing to it at Pilkington's request a fine scientific paper proving that 'subterranean fires deep in the Earth' rather than chemical actions were the cause of the hot springs at Buxton and Matlock. Another member of the Society, Dr William B. Johnson, wrote for him on plants. Pilkington received a prize of twenty-five guineas for this book from the Society for the encouragement of arts, manufactures and commerce, according to the *Derby Mercury* for 27 May 1790. The congregation could be proud of its learned minister.

But his next book, *The Doctrine of Equality of Rank and Condition, Examined and Supported on the Authority of the New Testament and on the Principles of Reason and Benevolence* (1795), gave such offence that he felt bound to send in his resignation. The immediate consequence was remarkable: his resignation was refused by a special meeting of the chapel on the grounds 'that persecution or punishment for speculative opinions would be inconsistent with the principles of the friends of truth and free inquiry, and therefore that the objections urged do not appear sufficient for an acquiescence in Mr. Pilkington's resignation'. He only continued as minister for a short time after this, however, and on his resignation Stevenson's friend William Winstanley took over this 'most agreeable circle of highly cultivated society', in 1798.[45]

It seems likely that Stevenson's resignation from Dob Lane was as much social and political as religious in nature. What he says about a preacher of Christianity in *Remarks* is slight and very basic. It is not at all certain that he ever moved from some kind of Arianism to become a fully-fledged Socinian like Priestley or Belsham, whose views were definitely not represented at Cross Street chapel. Indeed, Barnes was regarded by Priestley as a theological opponent. In late 1789 Priestley had joined with William Turner of Wakefield to found a specifically Unitarian rather than merely Presbyterian chapel at Mosley Street in Manchester. Barnes, Priestley claimed, could not 'conceal his jealousy of Mr. Hawkes's Unitarian chapel', which seems to have flourished, perhaps because whilst 'Unitarian' was actually included in the deed, it was agreed that it should be loosely interpreted in practice and eventually led to a more harmonious relationship with Cross Street chapel. In April 1791 Priestley came to stay with Dr Percival at Manchester and preached for Hawkes to a crowded congregation. The young ministers Toulmin and Loyd seem to have been present on this occasion. Dob Lane chapel, with its keen but diminutive congregation, was guided by Hawkes, though George Walker, who is described as a 'tempered Arian', preached there from 1801 to 1803.[46]

It cannot be shown on the evidence available that Stevenson displayed, in this decade torn by intellectual and spiritual conflicts, the ideological assurance of Paine, Wiche and Coleridge, let alone the latter's myriad-mindedness and visionary intensity. He does, however, seem to have responded to the *Zeitgeist* of an unstable and restless age – as did the ill-disciplined and difficult students who in their own boisterous way played their part in Dr Barnes's final resignation as principal in 1798. The letter from John Dalton to his old friend shows that the life of a tutor at the new college in Manchester could be very snug; he positively bloomed in personal and professional terms. Stevenson could not have been such an easy-going, conscientious and comfortable colleague. When Charles Saunders was appointed tutor in classics, with a proviso that he should not interfere with the instructions of the professor of theology, a special meeting of the college's academic committee on 18 June 1798 passed a resolution, to the effect that although they were liberal and unbiased, 'in these critical and turbulent times' they were also 'anxious to pay scrupulous regard, not only to [a classical tutor's] talents, taste and erudition, but to the moderation of his mind, to the discretion of his conduct, and to his exemption from polemic zeal, either as it relates to government or to theology'.[47] It could hardly be more comprehensive. The stable door was firmly closed.

Their political and religious caution as the century began to draw towards its reactionary close was understandable. No longer could the 'friends of freedom, and writers in its defence' behold the light they had 'struck out, after setting AMERICA free, reflected to FRANCE, and there kindled into a blaze that lays despotism in ashes, and warms and illuminates EUROPE!' This triumphant passage is taken from Richard Price's historic discourse of 4 November 1789 to the London revolution society, the speech that occasioned Edmund Burke's famous reply, *Reflections on the Revolution in France*, which marks the beginning of conservative reaction throughout Britain.

Men like Priestley and Price were seen as spiritual descendants of the Puritans who had overthrown both church and state, indissolubly joined, in the middle of the seventeenth century. James Darbishire was amongst those who signed an address on the evils of war in 1792, but when Britain went to war with revolutionary France in 1793 it became progressively more dangerous even to claim to be in the tradition of the 'glorious' British revolution of 1688. Animosities, violence, bankruptcies, riots and epidemics abounded in Manchester at this period. A 'Church and King Club' stood in opposition to the 'Manchester Constitutional Society', founded to promote representative government and freedom of opinion. The chapel in the quiet and residential Mosley Street had its doors battered with trees uprooted from St Ann's Square by a church and king mob on the King's birthday, 4 June 1792. (The doors held.)[48]

The columns of the *Manchester Herald* for 29 December 1792 contain, amongst advertisements for schools, warehouses to let, a performance of *Othello* at the Theatre-Royal and Dr Huntor's pill as the cheapest cure for venereal disease ('Beware of counterfeits'), an effusive declaration of loyalty by the Protestant dissenters of Manchester and Salford, 'steadily and affectionately attached to the British Constitution, consisting of King, Lords, and Commons, as wisely framed for the Promotion and Security of the true Happiness and Liberty of the People'. It is probably too early for William Stevenson's name to appear in the long list of prudent signatories, but those of Percival, Barnes and Harrison are very near its head, together with chapel stalwarts – Thomas Bayley, William Kennedy, Samuel Jones, John Potter and the like.[49]

Dissenters had serious internal subversion to fear as well. Gilbert Wakefield, a dynamic and highly successful classical tutor – for one year – at the sumptuously established Hackney Unitarian College, published in late 1791 an

Inquiry into the Expediency and Propriety of Public or Social Worship, in which, McLachlan nicely comments, 'he proved to his own satisfaction that it was neither expedient nor proper'. Not unexpectedly, students there developed conscientious objections. One of them delivered an oration before 'the assembled tutors, committee and supporters of the institution' against attendance at compulsory religious services. Thereafter several students were sent down and others withdrew, claiming they had lost their religious faith. The young William Hazlitt, who by an extraordinary coincidence was to hear Coleridge's first sermon on the opposition between the spirit of the world and the spirit of Christianity at Shrewsbury, is said to have been 'one of the first students who left that college an avowed infidel', as several undoubtedly did. Some eighteen or nineteen were even unwise enough to hold 'a Republican supper' with Tom Paine as a guest. Paine was no atheist, but gestures like this led to the ignominious closure of the college in the midsummer of 1796.[50]

Some years later William Turner of Newcastle wrote of the need to avoid 'that promiscuous admission of West Indians, wild Irish, and forlorn hopes from other seminaries who were the destruction and ruin of discipline both at Warrington and Hackney'. As for Hackney, 'The spirit of the times was against it; It fell – and the birds of night, ignorance and envy, bigotry and rancour screamed their ungenerous triumph over the ruins of this stately edifice; whilst virtue, truth and learning mourned in secret over the disappointment of their fond hopes and of their too highly elevated expectation', cried Belsham with truly majestic displeasure. (One is relieved to learn that he did not neglect to pay great attention to the fatting of his pigs in ordinary life.) Northampton academy, the successor to Daventry, soon turned out to be too subversive in practice for the Coward trustees, who dissolved it in 1798.

The intellectual independence characteristic of all these academies in the eighteenth century is notable. Constant controversy and failure were its dark shadows. The new college at Manchester, an anomaly, has after various migrations to York, London and Oxford survived until the present day, saved in troubled and revolutionary times by prudence, slow caution and the closing of ranks. The members of its academic committee surely felt they had burnt their fingers with William Stevenson.[51]

NOTES

1 John Byng, *The Torrington Diaries*, London, 1934-38, II, pp. 172, 205-9; Aikin, *Description of the Country*, pp. 192-6, 201, 205-6 (Thomas Percival and Thomas Barnes were subscribers); De Quincey, 'Autobiographical sketches 1790-1803', *Works*, repr. Edinburgh, 1883, XIV, p. 98. For Byng see *DNB Missing Persons*. •

2 Barnes obit., *MR*, V, 1810, pp. 408-12; Ian Inkster, *Science and Technology in History: An Approach to Industrial Development*, London, 1991, pp. 71-2; Baker, *Nonconformity in Bolton*, pp. 60-1; Davis, *Manchester College*, pp. 56-7; E. M. Hunt, 'The anti-slave trade agitation in Manchester', pp. 50, 53, 65; Ditchfield, 'The campaign in Lancashire and

Cheshire', p. 117; David Turley, *The Culture of English Anti-Slavery 1780-1860*, London and New York, 1991, pp. 88-9, 118-21.

3 There is something about Loyd but nothing about Stevenson, in Moore, 'Recollections', pp. 237-41. See also Baker, *Dissenting Chapel*, pp. 95-6; *DNB*, 'Samuel Jones Loyd'; G. M. Ditchfield, 'Manchester College and anti-slavery', in Smith, p. 189 and n.

4 McLachlan, pp. 268-9; Ditchfield, 'Early history', pp. 93-5, and Wykes, 'Sons & subscribers, 1786-1840', in Smith, p. 51; Harrison – next note.

5 MCO copy: R. Harrison, *A Sermon Preached at the Dissenting Chapel in Cross Street Manchester, Together with a Discourse [on] Manchester Academy*, Warrington, [1786], pp. 25, 33; 8, 12-13, 17 (appendixes).

6 Henry, *John Dalton*, pp. 41-2.

7 Portions of this letter have been used in Lonsdale's *John Dalton* and elsewhere, but the MCO Librarian kindly supplied a photocopy of the original MS.

8 *DAB; Letters of Benjamin Rush*, ed. L. H. Butterfield, Princeton, 1951, I, pp. lxvii, 96, 400-6, 517-18, 607; Donald J. D'Elia, *Benjamin Rush: Philosopher of the American Revolution, TAPS*, n. s. LXIV, v, 1974, pp. 42, 76.

9 *Memoir of the Life, Writings, and Correspondence of James Currie of Liverpool*, ed. W. W. Currie, Liverpool, 1831, I, p. 365; II, pp. 47-96.

10 LPL: MS, Roscoe papers, 1110, catalogued as 'Drafts of a letter from Wm. Roscoe' but attributed to Percival in Robert D. Thornton, *James Currie: The Entire Stranger & Robert Burns*, Edinburgh and London, 1963, pp. 144, 411. The handwriting suggests that Roscoe was the author.

11 MCO: MS, Minutes of the Committee, pp. 35, 38, 47-51; Wykes, 'Sons & subscribers', pp. 38-43; Harrison, *Sermon at Cross Street*, p. 17 (appendix); Ditchfield, 'Early history', pp. 86-7; JC to TP, Liverpool, 26 December 1792, *Memoir of Currie*, ed. Currie, II, pp. 88-9.

12 MCO: MS, 'Students admitted', and MS, cash book, ff. 37, 40 (Davis), 44, 47, 50; Paul Morgan, 'Manchester College and its books', in Smith, pp. 115 (cf. pp. 198, 210). See also appendix G. I am grateful to Manchester College's Librarian, Mrs Margaret Sarosi, for considerable assistance.

13 David Knight, *The Age of Science: The Scientific World-View in the Nineteenth Century*, Oxford, 1986, pp. 152-3; Lonsdale, *John Dalton, passim*. I am grateful to Alan Shelston for examining Dalton's *Grammar*, which has no reference to Stevenson.

14 Barnes obit., *MR*, V, 1810, pp. 410-11; *DNB*.

15 TB, 'A list of students at Daventry', p. 284; Baker, *Nonconformity in Bolton*, p. 64. Stevenson does not figure in the Reverend Andrew M. Hill's private index of known ordinations (letter of 6 March 1992). See also his 'The death of ordination in the [British] Unitarian tradition', *TUHS*, XIV, 1967-70, pp. 190-208.

16 Watts, *Dissenters*, pp. 476-7; Gordon, *Dob Lane Chapel*, pp. 44-52 (illustr.); Slugg, *Manchester*, p. 171. The first mention of Stevenson's Arianism appears to be in the *DNB*, an article by E. Irving Carlyle, which provides no specific reference; nor does Davis, *Manchester College*, p. 65. *ABO* is silent on the subject.

17 R. P. Wright's report on the chapel's early history, *Inquirer*, 14 March 1891, p. 174; Gordon, *Dob Lane Chapel*, p. 45.

18 DWL: MS, Minutes, VII, 7 May 1792; VIII, 3 October 1796. This is not consistent with Stevenson's dates of 1792-96 and Marshall's of 1800-01 in Gordon, *Dob Lane Chapel*, pp. 46, 51.

19 Baker, *Nonconformity in Bolton*, p. 68; HG (1771-1842) obit., *CP*, n. s. VIII, 1842, p. 140; Willard C. Frank, jr, '"I shall never be intimidated": Harry Toulmin and William Christie in Virginia 1793-91', *TUHS*, XIX, 1987-90, pp. 24-9; HT obit., *MR*, XIX, 1824, p. 180; HT in *DAB*; JT in *DNB*; Ditchfield, 'The campaign in Lancashire and Cheshire', pp. 118-21; Lincoln, *Political & Social Ideas*, pp. 28, 247, 264. For Samuel,

possibly the grandfather of William Gaskell, see Turner, *Warrington Academy*, intro. Carter, p. 76 ('a respectable merchant, and zealous supporter of the Unitarian doctrine') and p. 402 below.

20 Frida Knight, *The Strange Case of Thomas Walker: Ten Years in the Life of a Manchester Radical*, London, 1957; Ditchfield, 'Manchester College and anti-slavery', in Smith, pp. 204-7.

21 Gordon, *Dob Lane Chapel*, pp. 46-9; Shaw, *Annals of Oldham*, III, pp. 179-80; Gordon, *Dukinfield Chapel*, p. 60; McLachlan, *Essays and Addresses*, pp. 124-5; Ian Sellers, 'The Risley case', *TUHS*, XVI, 1975-78, pp. 178-9. For the Jacobin Club of Failsworth see Percival, *Failsworth Folk*, p. 18.

22 J. Kentish [1799] and anon., [Biographical notices of the late Rev. George Wiche], repr. T. Broadhurst, *Memoir of the Late Rev. Robert Smethurst*, Bath, 1847, pp. 3-4, 11n. (MCL); JH obit., *MR*, XXI, 1826, p. 496; Baker, *Nonconformity in Bolton*, p. 114.

23 *Declaration*, pp. 7, 15-16; Kentish, [Biographical notices], pp. 5-6; McLachlan, p. 124; *Priestley Works*, I. ii, pp. 295, 314; Gibbs, *Priestley*, p. 231; *DAB*.

24 'Kentish, [Biographical notices], p. 8; Thomas, *Richard Price*, p. 278; Hilton, *Age of Atonement*, p. 115. Cp. Paine, *Rights of Man*, ed. Foner, pp. 12-13.

25 Meta Gaskell, in some corrections sent to Thomas Seccombe c. September 1910 for his introduction to *Sylvia's Lovers*, p. xiii, suggested 'conscientious scruples as to receiving payment for religious work' (JGS: MS, 5 pp. 8vo, Plymouth Grove, dated by note MEG to TS, The Sheiling, Silverdale, 9 September [1910]).

26 *Declaration*, p. 8n.; J. Moore, 'Recollections', *CSR*, LXXII, pp. 237-8; Hilton, *Age of Atonement*, pp. 133-6; W. D. Rubinstein, *Elites and the Wealthy in Modern British History: Essays*, Brighton and New York, 1987, pp. 30, 147; *DNB*. Seed, 'The role of Unitarianism', p. 292, gives a table of early nineteenth-century ministerial salaries, which includes Wakefield £120, Mosley Street, Manchester £200, Salford £120, Rivington £67 and Huddersfield £60.

27 *Inquirer*, 14 March 1891, p. 174; Gordon, *Dob Lane Chapel*, pp. 49, 78; Percival, *Failsworth Folk*, p. 18.

28 WS, *Remarks*, pp. 4, 7, 24; Mary P. Mack, *Jeremy Bentham: An Odyssey of Ideas 1748-1792*, London, Melbourne, Toronto, 1962, pp. 102-3; Hole, *Pulpits, Politics and Public Order*, p. 203; Margaret Canovan, 'The un-Benthamite utilitarianism of Joseph Priestley', *JHI*, XLV, 1984, pp. 435-7.

29 *ESTC* 4360S1; *Memoirs of the Life of Gilbert Wakefield* [1792], ed. John Towill Rutt and Arnold Wainewright, London, 1804, I, pp. 178, 347.

30 WS, *Remarks*, pp. 5-9, 15; Turner, *Warrington Academy*, pp. 59-60; Aldridge, *Thomas Paine*, pp. 208-9, 230-5; Keane, *Tom Paine*, pp. 343-4, 389-96, 398 (Estlin not a Methodist); Quinlan, *Victorian Prelude*, pp. 78-82; Brown, *French Revolution*, p. 87 (Paine qu.).

31 WS, *Remarks*, p. 17n.; Payne, *The Age of Reason*, I, Paris, 1794, pp. 30, 32; Blake, *Complete Works*, ed. G. Keynes, London, New York, Toronto, 1966, pp. 685, 737-8. See Hans Aarsleff. *The Study of Language in England, 1780-1860*, Minneapolis and London, 1983, pp. 43-5, 73.

32 *Remarks*, pp. 14, 30; Butler, *Burke, Paine, Godwin*, pp. 6-7, 14, 21; *Losh Diaries*, I, p. 10; Bonwick, *English Radicals and the American Revolution*, pp. 218-31; Brown, *French Revolution*, pp. 51-3; *Rights of Man*, ed. Foner, pp. 7, 16-17.

33 Gibbs, *Priestley*, pp. 19, 201, 222; P. Holland, *Sermons on Practical Subjects*, ed. John Holland and William Turner, jr [of Newcastle], Warrington, 1792, I, pp. vi-vii; Gilmour, *Riot, Risings and Revolution*, pp. 393-5; Seed, 'Joyce and radical intelligensia', p. 103; Butler, *Romantics, Rebels and Reactionaries*, p. 55.

34 Hole, *Pulpits, Politics and Social Order*, pp. 63, 89-90, 142; Clark, *Scott*, p. 192, citing *Letters*, III, p. 211.

35 *GM*, LXVI. ii, 1796, p. 1023; *CRAL*, XVIII, 1796, pp. 355-6; Mineka, *Dissidence of Dissent*, p. 54; Derek Roper, *Reviewing Before the 'Edinburgh' 1788-1802*, London, 1978, pp. 20-2, 177, 292-3.

36 A. L. Smyth, *John Dalton 1766-1844: A Bibliography*, Manchester, 1966, p. 53 ('The author to John Dalton'); Stoneman, p. 184; Uglow, pp. 9-10.

37 MCO: MS, Minutes of the Committee, pp. 65-74, 80-97. See also John Kenrick, *A Biographical Memoir of the Late Rev. Charles Wellbeloved*, London, 1860, pp. 49-50.

38 *DNB*; obit., *GM*, LXXVIII, 1808, p. 277. Gregory also had wider interests, in science and the work of the royal humane society.

39 MCO: MS, Minutes of the Committee, pp. 104-6; Smethurst obit., *CR*, 1848, p. 57; Broadhurst, *Memoir of Smethurst*, p. 4; Davis, *Manchester College*, p. 67; cp. McLachlan, p. 258. See p. 135, n. 10 below.

40 About a fortnight. See Richard Holmes, *Coleridge: Early Visions*, London [1989], 1990, pp. 53-4, 96n., 174-81 especially; Hazlitt, *The Spirit of the Age*, ed. E. D. Mackerness, London and Glasgow, 1969, pp. 59-60. (*Hortus siccus*: a collection of dried and classified plants.)

41 Anon, [Biographical notices of GW], p. 13; Holmes, *Coleridge*, pp. 108-9. See also appendix G.

42 Rees, *Literary London*, pp. 78-9; Butler, *Romantics, Rebels & Reactionaries*, p. 43; Roper, *Reviewing Before the 'Edinburgh'*, p. 178. Standard biography (not seen): Gerald P. Tyson, *Joseph Johnson: A Liberal Publisher*, Iowa City, 1979.

43 *Coleridge Letters*, pp. 171, 210, 222, 255, 361-77; Holmes, *Coleridge*, p. 177.

44 J. B. Beer, *Coleridge the Visionary*, London, 1959, pp. 76-98, 321, n. 72 (variant qu.); McFarland, *Coleridge and the Pantheist Tradition*, pp. 177-84; De Quincey, *Recollections of the Lakes and the Lake Poets*, ed. David Wright, Harmondsworth, 1970, p. 50.

45 Turner, *Warrington Academy*, intro. Carter, p. 65; John Birks, *Memorials of Friar Gate Chapel*, Derby, [c. 1893], p. 10; DCL: QA 376, notes; Eric Robinson, 'The Derby philosophical society', *AS*, IX, 1962, p. 365; *The Letters of Erasmus Darwin*, ed. Desmond King-Hele, Cambridge, etc., 1981, pp. 176-7, 225, 270n.; King-Hele, *Erasmus Darwin and the Romantic Poets*, London, 1986, pp. 11-12; *CR*, n. s. VIII, 1852, p. 638 (Winstanley). For background see E. Fearn, 'The Derbyshire reform societies 1791-1793', *DAJ*, LXXXVIII, 1868, pp. 47-59.

46 *Priestley Works*, I. ii, pp. 23, 35, 109-10; Gordon, *Dob Lane Chapel*, pp. 41-2, 51-2; Seed, 'The role of Unitarianism', pp. 21-2; Ditchfield, 'Early history', p. 94. I am grateful to John Seed for permission to use his Hull Ph.D. thesis, valuable to me in several contexts.

47 MCO: MS, Minutes of the Committee, p. 104; McLachlan, pp. 258-60; Davis, *Manchester College*, p. 67 and n.

48 Thomas, *Richard Price*, pp. 301-9; Brown, *French Revolution*, pp. 30, 61, 76-7; E. R. Norman, *Church and Society in England 1770-1970: A Historical Study*, Oxford, 1976, p. 31; Baines, *Lancaster*, II, pp. 141-2; Prentice, *Manchester*, pp. 5, 9; Kidd, *Manchester*, p. 65.

49 It also appeared in the *Manchester Mercury* for 1 January 1793 (Thomson, *Manchester to 1852*, p. 247). See also Knight, *Thomas Walker*, p. 110.

50 McLachlan, pp. 246-55; *Memoirs of Gilbert Wakefield*, I, pp. 356-7; Kenrick, *Wellbeloved*, pp. 22-5, 28; Lucy Aikin, *Memoir of John Aikin*, London, 1823, II, pp. 355-6 (JA's memoir of GW); Ralph M. Wardle, *Hazlitt*, Lincoln, Nebraska, 1971, pp. 45, 50. For more detail, especially about the influence of Belsham, see H. W. Stephenson, 'Hackney College and William Hazlitt', *TUHS*, IV, 1927-30, pp. 376-411.

51 Turner, *Warrington Academy*, intro. Carter, p. 36; McLachlan, pp. 165-9, 254 (Belsham qu.), and 'The old Hackney College 1786-1796', *TUHS*, III, 1923-26, pp. 185-205; *Memoirs, Miscellanies and Letters of the Late Lucy Aikin*, ed. Philip Hemery le Breton, London, 1864, p. 82; Williams, *Belsham*, p. 384; *CR*, n. s. IX, 1853, p. 270 (Kentish obit.); Lovegrove, *Established Church*, pp. 68, 107-8.

3

Vacillations of a father

A FTER LEAVING MANCHESTER College and Dob Lane chapel, William Stevenson did not attempt to combine hireless preaching with a trade or profession other than teaching. He turned instead to a flourishing applied science, agriculture. According to his obituary he went 'as a pupil to a very eminent farmer in East Lothian', where he 'devoted considerable attention to agricultural pursuits, so as to fix the theory of agriculture indelibly in his mind'. The age of improvement had begun, especially in Scotland. The first professor of agricultural science, a Dr Coventry, had been appointed at Edinburgh University a few years before, in 1790; it was a chair in agriculture and rural economy, for which Sir William Pulteney had given the university the substantial sum of £1,250.[1]

The man who actually instructed Stevenson in farming has never been identified, but many years later Elizabeth Gaskell was sent seven of her mother's letters by George Hope of Fenton Barns, a farm about six miles from Haddington, a little way to the east of the Scottish capital. His grandfather, Robert, had in 1796 taken over both Fenton and Fenton Barns, two completely uncultivated farms on difficult clay and barren sand that resisted his best efforts. Conditions in East Lothian were primitive. Four horses were needed to pull heavy loads; and they had to be accompanied by two men, equipped with a hedge-bill and a spade for cutting whins to fill the larger holes. If Robert Hope was William Stevenson's instructor, he had taken one of his last pupils, for he died heart-broken at the age of fifty-two in 1801. His grandson George became an enthusiastic convert to Unitarianism and was admitted to membership of Edinburgh's chapel in 1836. He succeeded in agriculture, too, his farm becoming known as a model of its kind. A 'passionate free trader', the part he played in national affairs at the time of the corn-law agitation brought him to Manchester, where he visited the Gaskells. Hope speaks explicitly of seven letters from Elizabeth Gaskell's mother to his own – 'one of them written within a week or two before her death'. His mother, Christian, who had married in 1809, might well have written to Mrs Stevenson about George's birth on 2 January 1811.[2]

According to Mrs Chadwick, James Cleghorn of Duns in the nearby Scottish county of Berwickshire 'fostered Stevenson's love of agriculture, for he was a farmer who worked on scientific lines, and, like William Stevenson, wrote articles based on his own practical experience for the agricultural magazines.' (Duns is about fifteen miles to the west of Berwick itself.) James Cleghorn was far from unique in this respect. Men of all ranks had turned their minds to practical, experimental farming at that time. Moreover, there was an 'outpouring of agricultural literature' in Scotland that has hardly been equalled since. A product of the dissenting academies like Stevenson would have been able to master it rapidly.[3]

His apprenticeship could not have lasted long, for by October 1797 he was able to begin farming at Saughton Mills on the other side of Edinburgh from Haddington, about two miles to the south-west, by a road towards Motherwell and Glasgow that leaves the broad and crowded Grassmarket below the castle on its high escarpment.[4] It is now part of the modern city, but an engraving of Alexander Nasmyth's painting of Edinburgh from the Glasgow road shows just how rural the scene was in the early nineteenth century. A light coach is seen, speeding past a static group of men and horses and a heavy farm cart. Roads were being improved; communication was becoming faster and easier. The time for the stagecoach journey between these two major towns of lowland Scotland, little more than forty miles apart, had been cut from a painful day and a half to six hours by 1799.

Edinburgh's classical new town, planned in the 1760s, had by the end of the eighteenth century proceeded westwards as far as its greatest achievement, Charlotte Square. By that square, Cockburn tells us in his *Memorials*, was an open field of 'as green turf as Scotland could boast of', and then a valley followed the thickly wooded banks of the Water of Leith towards Corstorphine and Saughton. 'I have stood in Queen Street, or the opening at the north-west corner of Charlotte Square, and listened to the ceaseless rural corn-craiks, nestling happily in the dewy grass', he wrote in lyrical remembrance. Titled people and professional men, especially lawyers, still lived in the closes and wynds of the old town. But though a prominent Scottish peer like Lord Lauderdale had once had an old-town address in Meal-market stairs, Edinburgh directories show that he had moved to 64 Queen Street by the early years of the nineteenth century. Increasingly, those who could afford it migrated to the new town, where they were joined by a number of wealthy county families, and even English families who could not afford to live as well in London nor travel abroad during the period of the French wars. At Saughton Mills Stevenson was not far from the centre of Scottish life in its golden age.[5] There, too, used to live a farmer called Robert Cleghorn.[6]

A little later William Stevenson returned to England in order to marry a farmer and land agent's daughter, Elizabeth Holland. Born on 19 April 1771, she was the daughter of Samuel and Ann Holland of Sandlebridge in the township of

Marthall cum Little Warford, a few miles to the east of Over and Nether Knutsford. The 'ingenious' Peter Burdett's map of Cheshire in 1777, one of the two before 1800 based on a fresh survey, shows Sandlebridge farm rather nearer Warford than Marthall, close to an old forge on a lane edged by large oaks and elms. Down the lane there was a corn mill turned by a water wheel on a little river. Three quarters of the Little Warford estate was owned by Samuel Holland by inheritance from the Colthurst family. The beautifully lettered tombstone of Peter Colthurst ('In His Mind were assembled all the Virtues ...') and his wife Elizabeth of Sandlebridge is at one side of Knutsford's ancient dissenting chapel. Close by lies their son John ('gent'), who died in his seventy-seventh year on 31 October 1774. The property then came by bequest to Elizabeth's father Samuel, whose father had married their daughter Mary. The other quarter was owned by Sir J. T. Stanley.[7]

The large farmhouse at Sandlebridge was demolished in this century. Photographs of its facade make it appear at least mid-Victorian, but a large chimney stack at the back suggests that part of it might have been built much earlier. It is said by Alan Dale, who used to live in the smithy, that a stone above its front door bore the date 1704. Samuel's oldest daughter Ann adds:

> It seems as if the Colthursts were not over good economists – my Grandfather sold, to enable him to build the present house at Sandlebridge – the old house stood at the top of the back garden. I recollect hearing my grandmother say that the spot in the Churchyard at Mobberley which had long been the burial place of the Hollands was distinguished by the name of 'the honest man's nook'.[8]

It ended as a large house, with a wide double front. There were thirteen windows in front, and tall chimneys to each side; the two gable ends of the facade carried plain barge-boards. The photograph usually reproduced, taken through trees and slightly to one side, does not give such a clear impression of its size as a photograph in Irvine taken from a distance across a field, and amongst other illustrations Dale reproduces a rare photograph of the house before it was obscured by trees.[9]

What life was like at Sandlebridge just a few years after William Stevenson's marriage is disclosed in the manuscript recollections of Mary Robberds.[10] Born on 24 February 1786, elder daughter of the Reverend William Turner of Newcastle, she had been sent to live at Newcastle-under-Lyme for a year, very probably staying with the widow and two unmarried daughters of the Reverend William Willets, who had been Unitarian minister there. One of their daughters, Mary, married Dr Peter Holland, eldest son of Samuel and Ann Holland. Then, in 1794, at eight years of age, little Mary Robberds went to spend two years at a boarding school at Manchester, where she was taught 'Geography & History & Arithmetic' by a blind, clever uncle. This must have been yet another Holland, Thomas, the brother of the Reverend John Holland of Bolton.[11]

Not surprisingly, her school holidays were often spent at Sandlebridge, 'a fine large old house covered in front with a vine', she wrote. It had a flower garden, and in front was a grass court sloping down to a lane in which stood great oaks and elms. Behind was a kitchen garden, at the side a little garden with bee hives. A sand heap where children could play without making frocks dirty was a favourite place. 'In the yard there was a pump and poultry & a pigsty'; beyond these were the dairy for butter and cheese and a farm yard, where they could see calves being fed and cows milked. Sometimes they would hide in the hayfield, or go down the lane to see the great water wheel turning; next to it was the old smithy, where they watched fire blown to brightness with large bellows whilst the smith forged horseshoes and metal tyres for cart wheels.

In her simple way she confirms the brilliant description of Sandlebridge farm in Elizabeth Gaskell's famous letter of 1836 when she sat writing in its old fashioned parlour, casement window opening wide upon a sunny, fragrant court and baby daughter 'wanting to be *bathed* in the golden bushes of wall-flowers'. 'Oh! that Life would make a stand-still in this happy place', she cried. Mary Robberds's recollections are proof that it had already done so. For generations of children it was a paradise:

> When it rained there was plenty of amusement in the house. Besides playing at 'I spy' there was a game called shuffleboard in the dining room or houseplace, where we generally sat. ... Then as I said the old house was a capital place for playing hide & seek, for there were two staircases and different ways into the rooms, to hide in. There were two clocks one in the house place, which struck the hours very quickly, the other on the stair case which struck so slowly that it was said that a man might go to sleep and have a dream between the first & last stroke of twelve. Out of doors there was no end of amusement, besides cows & pigs & horses there were chickens & pigeons and a large barn where we could cover ourselves with hay & there was a pond in which we sometimes saw the sheep washing.

The house was described after it was ultimately given up to a simple farmer by Anne Ritchie, daughter of Thackeray and a close friend of Mrs Gaskell's daughters. She spent two days in and about Knutsford late in the last century. She found a flagged path leading up to a great front door, and inside, a wide hall 'covered with well-worn, diamond-shaped flags'. To the right was a parlour with narrow casement windows and fine wooden chimney-pieces, one within the other; to the left was the house place. It must have contained the two black basalt jugs Samuel had been given by Josiah Wedgwood, which were inherited by his granddaughter Elizabeth, and perhaps the 'funny old Wedgwood drinking cups', a blue 'Monster' on white pattern, that had originally been made for the Wedgwood family breakfast table at Maer Hall. The long oak shuffle-board was seen by Anne Ritchie but had gone by the time Mrs Chadwick arrived early in this century; she was told it was kept as an heirloom in another family home. Shallow oaken stairs led to no less than fourteen bedrooms, some opening into each other, and at the top was 'a large room, littered with straw, used at times as a storehouse for late apples' – Alain-Fournier's *greniers* in the village school of Epineuil-le-Fleuriel come to mind.[12]

It is not known exactly how William and Elizabeth met, but Knutsford is only about sixteen miles from Manchester. The Hollands had long supported one of the old dissenting chapels common in this part of Cheshire, situated in Brook Street on the very edge of Nether Knutsford, as the main town used to be known. At this time (1795-1809) its own 'much esteemed' minister was a Welshman called Philip George Davis, but ministers were accustomed to interchange pulpits and their congregations welcomed visiting lecturers. Meta Gaskell thought this was the most likely connection, but very candidly admitted that she really had no idea. John Holland of Bolton, however, was both a friend of William in Manchester and a relation of the Sandlebridge Hollands, the son of Samuel's sister Ann and therefore Elizabeth's first cousin. In 1812 Samuel named him as a trustee of his will.[13]

William Stevenson and Elizabeth Holland obtained a marriage licence, a common device amongst dissenters in order to avoid having their banns called in the Anglican parish church, though by a law of the 1750s the ceremony had to take place there. The wedding was performed on 1 December 1797 by Peter Wright, and witnessed by Elizabeth's father Samuel and William Winstanley, Stevenson's college friend. It took place at Over Peover parochial chapel deep in the gently rolling Cheshire countryside, not far across fields and parkland from Sandlebridge, in the grounds of Peover Hall, which had been the home of the Mainwaring family for several centuries.[14] On the death of Sir Henry Mainwaring in 1797, the estate passed to his half-brother, who took the family name; his son was created baronet in 1804. The nave and chancel of the ancient little chapel where the marriage was celebrated were rebuilt in brick in 1811, but the numerous arms and sculptured monuments of this family still survive.[15]

Did William Stevenson take up farming because he had met a farmer's daughter? If so, why did he not take up farming in Cheshire, even at Sandlebridge itself? Elizabeth's father, Samuel Holland, was then over sixty years of age, but not one of his three adult sons, Peter, Samuel and Swinton, seems to have been interested in agriculture, though the Sandlebridge estate remained very definitely in the family and they were very willing to purchase land. In fact, the sons were set for considerable success in medicine, commerce and banking, and it is noticeable that their father was described as 'Gentleman' on the marriage bond.[16] Some farming was continued after Samuel's death by the employment of 'a farming man'.

Perhaps the estate had been sufficiently improved and intensive farming was being relaxed, leaving Elizabeth's father what his grandson Henry Holland remembered, or mythologised, as 'an admirable example of old age rendered venerable by all the gentler qualities of human nature' and 'the most perfect practical optimist', either 'walking cheerfully over his fields, or tranquilly smoking his pipe in an arm-chair co-eval with himself.' His wife, 'a person of extraordinary energy and will', sharp and 'excessively particular' with the servants, would have provided all the dynamism needed. William Stevenson's career to date was uninspiring, and he could not have been thought suitable to take over the farming at Sandlebridge. It is also likely that as a native of Berwick on the Scottish border he felt more at home in what was then called North Britain and had friends there to assist him. So he took the high road that led towards Scotland – or, just as likely, went by sea.[17]

Saughton Mills is shown on a rather worn estate map of the property of Charles Watson Esquire in 1795 as a small group of buildings in the parish of Corstorphine, Midlothian, just by an old road bridge with three arches and massive piers over the water of Leith – less than a river and more than a burn – as it made its way in a deep channel fringed with trees and bushes along to Edinburgh and the firth of Forth.[18]

The water was once 'a clear running stream, with plenty of roaches and eels'. Brilliant kingfishers darted through long green tunnels over its peaty-brown water. Numerous working mills marked its short course as it wound though its broad and fertile valley towards the sea, which it met at Edinburgh's port of Leith. Corstorphine hill, like the shore of the firth from Leith all the way along to Queensferry, was open and free, either by the indulgence of private owners or through long usage. Corstorphine village and its old church were a little to the north of Saughton Mills, reached by a lesser road that ran past Saughton Mains farm on a gentle ascent through open fields, the hill hiding the firth beyond. On its southern slopes were some fine villas – Belmont and Beechwood, then owned by Major General David Dundas, and Corstorphine Hill House, the property of William Keith, an Edinburgh accountant. 'For the sake of strangers, however, and even of many of the negligent and indolent natives', wrote Robert Forsyth in 1805, 'one position ought not to pass unnoticed.' At the summit of a ridge of the hills were placed two walls crossing each other, with seats in the angles that gave separate views of 'the City of Edinburgh and its mountainous precincts; of the Frith [*sic*] of Forth and its islands; of an irregular and beautifully wooded country; and, lastly, of the rich cultivated valley which stretches to the westward of Edinburgh Castle.' A little further south lay the romantic Pentland hills, green or blue-grey or shrouded in mist as the weather changed.[19]

Saughton Mills in this rich cultivated valley became a mere suburb in the 1920s, but it was then well out in the country. On the left bank of Leith water below the bridge stood Saughton Hall, an early eighteenth-century house, and its gardens. In the 1780s it was the home of Lady Maxwell, a wealthy philanthropist and friend of John Wesley, who once gave a discourse on the parable of Dives and Lazarus to some of her poor neighbours and inspected the school she had set up for their children.[20] A little up-stream, on a pleasant and open site just to the south of the old bridge, stood an old laird's house constructed of rubble with dressed quoins and window surrounds, 'gable-ended, with crowsteps, dormer windows, steep roofs, and massive chimneys', surrounded by farm and mill buildings. This house, known variously as Saughton, Stenhope and Stenhouse Mills, has an armorial panel bearing the initials P. E. and the date 1623 over its entrance doorway, dating from a time when the house was enlarged.

A stone-vaulted ground floor in the northern wing is the oldest part. Outside, piercing the roughly squared stones towards the bottom of its gable, can be seen a bee-bole and triangular openings. The unusual provision of the latter is thought to be for hens to reach stone nesting boxes that still survive within – though a modern visitor might well speculate about the rabbits, ducks and other small creatures that are regularly dragged in by cats through cat-flaps. Well moulded Renaissance architraves, a turnpike staircase, great fireplace and ogee-headed aumbry on the first floor, ornamental plaster ceilings and the like show that it was once the fine residence of an Edinburgh merchant, Patrick Ellis, but by 1845 the area of what had come to be known as 'Stanhope-Mills village' contained the homes of a score of families. The house had become a 'forlorn neighbour' of Saughton Hall, neglected, 'cut up into small houses for labourers' and 'parcelled out among poor tenants'. Extending from it to a mill lade or water channel were other buildings, 'latterly occupied as dwelling houses', it was stated in the first volume of the *Transactions of the Edinburgh Architectural Association* in 1891, but by that time demolished.[21]

Early in this century the main house was still inhabited but ruinous and heavily vandalised. By great good fortune this fine example of a laird's house was rescued by the National Trust for Scotland and restored as nearly as possible to its former state. It is the only ancient building in this area to have survived, its stern elegance throwing into relief the miscellaneous urban archi-tecture of its surroundings. Some of its former companions must have been working mills, but part of the text of a 1797 advertisement in the *Edinburgh Evening Courant* for the 'Farms of Saughton Mills and Parkhead, the property of Charles Watson, Esq.' makes it probable that Patrick Ellis's old mansion, not yet carved up into tenements, was once ocupied by the Stevensons: 'There is a large and excellent house, with a suitable garden, on the farm of Saughton Mills, together with proper barns, stables, threshing machine, &c.' Only one building, this one, appears to have a garden on the 1795 estate map. The Stevensons were able to live in some style.[22]

Much of the valley's farming land was in tillage or pasturage – fertile soil that had been cultivated to an exceptional degree for many years in farms about two or three hundred acres in size. Saughton Mills farm, to be let 'for nineteen years, and entered into at Martinmas 1797', contained according to the advertisement 'above 144 Scots acres, of which about 8 pasture, rest arable.' The lands were 'in excellent condition ... inclosed with hedge and ditch, and properly subdivided.' Land rents generally were high, £2 or more an acre, given all the advantages of closeness to the city and its markets. An old

Scottish proverb is far from polite about its bucolic inhabitants: 'Ye breed o' Saughton swine, ye're neb is ne'er oot o' an ill turn.'

In the sometimes inaptly named *The Beauties of Scotland* Robert Forsyth described the nature of farming in the neighbourhood of a city of some eighty thousand population which could provide plenty of carriage-horse manure and other 'unsightly sources of fertility'. At ten every evening except Sunday in the old town the day's slops were tossed into the streets from the tall buildings and gathered by scavengers at seven the next morning. The roads out from Edinburgh were filled with a constant procession of their carts in all weathers. Also, winds from the west were said by Forsyth to 'sweep along an uninter-rupted plain of almost 14 miles in length, hemmed in by the Pentland Hills on the south, and by high grounds on the north', and rage in Edinburgh 'with incredible fury'. (They still do.) The state of the lesser roads about the city must have been deplorable, but it meant that fewer cattle needed to be kept on the farmland itself. Beans, peas, clover and rye grass were common. Grain crops were reaped by hand with the sickle, large numbers of men and women arriving every year 'from remote corners of the Highlands' for the purpose. Extensive fields of potatoes were especially profitable, since they could be sold in Edinburgh or used as a preparation for growing wheat. They were cultivated with small ploughs pulled by two horses, regularly hoed and finally harvested by great gangs of women and children, to be kept over winter in pits where the soil was dry or covered with a mound of earth on which a corn stack was sometimes placed.[23]

Letters written from 'Saughton Mills' by Stevenson's sister Dorothy to her brother Robert, surgeon of Berwick, then at 'No 21 St Thomas' Street, Borough, London' (just south of London Bridge and close by Guy's Hospital), belong to this once obscure period of William Stevenson's life.[24] In October 1798 she sent word that she had married Mr Landles (George Landles of Berwick) whilst at Saughton, a Mr Smith, who was staying just on the other side of Edinburgh at Musselburgh, performing the ceremony. She was given away by her brother, who, she said, liked 'the forms of a Scotch wedding better then those of an English'. She also reports that he was very busy taking up his potatoes and that his farmyard makes 'a very good appearance now all his corn is in'. His wife Elizabeth was pregnant and Dorothy had promised to stay with her, though her own new husband was 'very unwilling' to leave her behind.[25]

In the same letter she writes, 'Sister returns you many thanks for the Fan which I brought her this time and thinks she must keep it for a curiosity'. It is a desperately trivial remark, but nothing whatsoever has been known about Elizabeth Stevenson's mother till now. It is a pity the letter is so uninformative – 'there is but one pen in the whole house and I can hardly get it to make a stroke – William is out with the pen knife. Eliza and he send their kind loves and old Friends here send their Compts'. At least William Stevenson was far away from Manchester, its academy, writing, hired preaching and political agitation, living a sophisticated pastoral existence in a Scottish valley, delighting in the waves of light as the wind swept over his corn on sunny days, striding out into the fields to watch the gangs of women and children as they bent their backs to harvest his potatoes, or at home planning his work in the light of the most up-to-date agricultural science whilst his wife and sister made timeless preparations for the birth of a child.

By the end of December Dorothy Landles was back in Berwick. She reported the good news that William was 'the Father of a fine boy', born on 27 November 1798 according to the 'Appendix List of irregular insertions of Baptisms' of Corstorphine church. A fair copy of this entry reads, 'John son of William Stevenson, Farmer Saughton Mills and his Spouse Elizabeth Born 27th Novr and Bapd '.[26] The gap at this point might indicate some form of dissent, though this seems unlikely in the circumstances. The established church in Scotland had been Presbyterian from 1690, so that even 'episcopals were but *dissenters*', Boswell had pointed out to Dr Johnson. Moreover, the Presbyterian minister of the parish, the Reverend James Oliver, made a point of writing in the *Statistical Account of Scotland* about the 'liberality of sentiment' found towards 'dissenters' in his parish during the 1790s. For this lamentable slackness, and for his old-fashioned belief that agriculture was in all ways preferable to manufacturing for his people, he was later sarcastically characterised as 'a sounder politician than a divine'.[27]

The December letter again provides a scrap of information about Mrs Stevenson: the mother of the fine boy was 'not nursing', Dorothy reported. 'She has no milk it seems – they have a Nurse in the House'. No other children of William and Elizabeth Stevenson are recorded in this register, although Mrs Chadwick came to believe that there were six born after John in 1798 and before Elizabeth in 1810. A note by Ward reads '*One* brother who survived ... other children died early'. He does not seem to have used this information, but it is possible that Mrs Chadwick heard about it. No records of the six have so far been found in Corstorphine, Edinburgh, Berwick or London. (Central registration did not begin until 1837.) Frequent pregnancies were a woman's lot at all levels of society in an age when abstinence or separation were for many the usual methods of birth control. It is also sadly true that many children did not survive infancy. Six children of Walter Scott's mother, born either in Edinburgh's Anchor Close or in the steep and gloomy wynd that led up from the Cowgate to the richly decorated gateway of the old college, are known to have died very young.[28]

Mrs Landles gives the earliest hint in this letter about the financial problems that were to afflict William for most of his life. Both her older brothers were behaving badly in their sister's eyes:

Dear Brother,
    Mr Smith sent by young Nesbit yesterday – 2 Geese – which I hope you will get good as they have been kept since last Thursday waiting for a ship to sail –

you will also get a letter for Joe to take out to Mr Addison at Demerara [by wartime convoy] – I sent it to you in case Joe had left London ... I have never heard from him about William's affairs – I wonder William does not apply to his Wifes Brother at Liverpool for money when he wants it – and not Plague mother as he does – I know it hurts her very much – do you know if Joe ever got Mr Hollands letter – about getting him a Ship – they wonder much he has never answered it –

William, having given up two possible careers, could not have been much of a catch as a son-in-law to the older Samuel Holland of Sandlebridge, and his wife must have felt the change from the easy and prosperous life at her father's Cheshire home. Her brother Samuel, then a rich merchant in Liverpool, would have been a likely source of funds. Dorothy's letter ends with a reminder of how coastal towns like Berwick were affected by the French Revolutionary and Napoleonic wars: 'I suppose you have heard that Antony Froster is taking [sic] by a French privateer of[f] Berwick on his Passage home. They have carried him to France.' The existence of 'Lloyd's Patriotic Fund' and 'The Committee for Encouraging the Capture of French Privateers, Armed Vessels and etcetera' is another sign of the heavy losses and the dangers of a career at sea for William's two brothers.[29]

In a letter of early January 1799 Dorothy writes that 'Mother is very agreeable to sell out Joes £100 in 4-P[er]Cents', so that Robert could have whatever the sale of these public securities might produce – not to mention the bag of potatoes, leg of mutton and trunk full of clothes sent by another ship from Berwick. The letter continues, 'I had a letter from Eliza the other day[;] she says William is talking of coming to Berwick – and young Truels is coming with him – Mother does not want to be Plagued with the young mans Company'. Mrs Landles might here be giving an early intimation that her brother was already thinking of giving up farming and returning to his home town if this was not a mere visit.[30]

But then came a carefully written letter of 15 February 1799 from a James Smith of Berwick to tell of the peaceful death of Joseph Stevenson senior 'on Wednesday last', about midnight, a death that had been 'daily to be looked for'. In all probability this was written by the man who had married Dorothy and George Landles in Scotland, a D.D. of the University of Edinburgh and an accomplished Greek scholar, who had evidently become a family friend. At Berwick he was minister of the Presbyterian 'Low Meeting', a church established at the beginning of the century with forms of worship 'the same as in the church of Scotland, with which it has always been in close connexion'.[31] As for the episcopal church in Scotland, it had seriously declined during the eighteenth century, and was described by Walter Scott as 'but the shadow of a shade'.[32]

The news of old lieutenant Joseph Stevenson's death was confirmed in a letter of 26 February 1799 from Dorothy, telling Robert that William had arrived just a few hours late for their father's funeral because of a storm that had delayed or cancelled coaches, and that Joe had not even written home even though he must have heard by then. John was far away at sea in the Mediterranean or the Channel. Mr Stevenson was buried in the graveyard of the episcopal parish church on 20 February 1799; his wife's name is found in the rate books for Hide Hill thereafter. Robert was told that his mother intended to let her house and live with him in Bridge Street, in 'the House belonging to Mr Landles – that goes with the shop'. Robert Stevenson purchased 44 Bridge Street in 1807, according to its title deeds. He was asked to see how his mother was 'to act with regard to getting her pension' and pressed to return to Berwick – 'particularly as your health is not so good'. Amidst all these trials was one irrepressible sign of life: 'I must really leave off writing for Mrs Todd is in the room and her tongue is going at such a rate that I dont know what I write'.[33]

But Dorothy Landles was to die not long afterwards, aged thirty-one on 23 February 1805; an infant daughter was buried with her in the same grave. She was survived by a daughter called Margaret. Her husband George Landles lived on until the age of sixty-four in 1826. Her brother Robert married an Elizabeth Wilson in 1805. Old Mrs Stevenson died, palsy-twitched, early in the following year and was buried alongside her husband. Robert himself died in 1818, but seven of his children were still living in 1842 and the house in Bridge Street was not given up until 1857. Berwick remained the home of many of William Stevenson's relations well into the nineteenth century. Robert's wife, in fact, did not die until 1875, when she was about ninety-six.[34]

The French war had led to the emergence of tenant farmers with capital in times generally propitious for such men. There were nevertheless enormous fluctuations in prices, especially in the so-called 'dear years' of 1799-1800. The Mid-Lothian quarterly report for 1801 in the Archibald Constable's *Farmer's Magazine,* edited at first by Robert Brown, a farmer of Markle, gloomily described 'two defective crops in succession', but went on to say that there were 'at least grounds to hope, that a third year of famine will not be added to the doleful list'. Farmers, it was confidently asserted by Robert Forsyth, who was an Edinburgh advocate himself, should be gentlemen, 'well-educated men, in affluent circumstances', able to withstand instability and one or two bad seasons. A 'very active spirit of improvement' was not enough. He knew it was unpopular to proclaim that small farms should be united, but in his opinion it was an 'absolute necessity' – a view he put foward with the authority of 'that enlightened agriculturist', Arthur Young.[35]

The letter from William Stevenson's sister proves that he was short of money as early as 1798. 'This speculation, however, did not answer', is the dry comment of the unknown obituarist on his farming career, 'and after four or five years Mr. Stevenson relinquished it.' The turn of phrase strongly suggests that he did not have enough capital to withstand the 'dear years'. His father does not appear to have made a will, an expense quite legally avoided before 1815 whenever there was no special need to draw one up and potential heirs were able to agree privately amongst themselves.[36] Anything William earned, and any inheritance he might have received, must have been insufficient if lack of money was the prime reason for his failure. Or was he more like Robert Burns in temperament? Burns's career as a farmer at Ellisland near Dumfries a decade before had ended disastrously. He was not one of the 'grave, geometrical minds', he cried. His farm was 'a bad bargain', he complained to his friend Robert Cleghorn of Saughton Mills in 1791; and then exploded: 'It is a devilish different affair, managing money matters where I care not a damn whether the money is paid or not; from the long faces made to a haughty Laird or still more haughty Factor, when rents are demanded, & money, Alas! is not to be had!'[37]

Stevenson abandoned his farming career at Saughton Mills, just as he had given up his ministry at Dob Lane and his post as classical tutor at Manchester College. But nearby was the grand city of Edinburgh, offering new possibilities of earning a living – not 'stringing blethers up in rhyme / For fools to sing', to be sure, but a return to the classics and tutoring was very feasible if the old voice of conscience could be stilled. Did he take his wife and family there with him? According to his obituary it was *Mr* Stevenson 'about this trying time' who 'kept a boarding-house for students in Drummond Street, Edinburgh'.[38]

His obituarist also reports that Stevenson's problems were compounded by illness in the first years of the new century – 'in consequence, as it was supposed, of his having too frequently eaten at Berwick of salmon out of season, he was attacked by a severe leprous complaint, approaching almost to elephantiasis, the violent operation and long continuance of which completely disfigured a countenance previously handsome.' Eating salmon, whether in or out of date, is probably irrelevant. A doctor might say that an allergy to salmon or some other foodstuff would have given him urticaria, rapid and alarming in its effects. But any consequent swelling would have been short-lived. 'Elephantiasis', or a great swelling that continued, might possibly indicate heart or kidney problems. If the word 'leprous' suggests lumpy swellings here and there, a chronic skin disorder like scleroderma causes the skin to become thickened and tough and swollen, though such swelling is not usually so extreme as to justify the description elephantiasis. But diagnosis in retrospect is very speculative. The general impression given by the obituary, somewhat deceptively, is that this was the lowest level he ever reached. It was not, as far as we know, but there is little doubt that his life in Edinburgh was difficult, problematic and changeable.

Four- and five-storey tenements had been built about 1790 in Drummond Street by taking down a stretch of the old city wall where it ran just south of William Adam's Royal Infirmary and the High School. It was but a step away from the new front of the university, then in the throes of its own seemingly interminable reconstruction. Shortage of money had led to stops and starts in the work. Petitions about the turn of the century complain that part-finished buildings had beams and joists exposed to all weathers, sheds and materials scattered all over the site and, most shocking of all, professors' houses pulled down before new accommodation had been provided for them. To add to the chaos there were 'dangerous and disgraceful bickerings between a number of the High School boys and a body of the younger Arts Students', all of whom were accustomed to playing games of football and shinty amongst the unfinished new buildings. It must have reminded Stevenson of his own wilder days in Berwick. But he could also call in the shop William Blackwood had opened at 64 South Bridge Street in 1804 to deal on his own account in rare books. People were easy, colloquial and familiar with each other, even if distinctions of rank were strong. Famously, as one Englishman stated, 'Here I stand at what is called the *Cross of Edinburgh*, and can, in a few minutes, take fifty men of genius and learning by the hand'. Women could 'pass from street to street singly, as at Bath', and did not 'require a companion, while paying their visits'. Until the establishment of an unarmed police force in 1805 there was only a city guard of veteran soldiers with Lochaber axes (spear, axe and hook combined) patrolling the cobbled streets. Merchants did their business in the open air, and if the boats were late, fisherwomen from Inveresk would run the five miles to Edinburgh in under forty-five minutes; they did it in relays, each carrying a basket for a hundred yards, 'to get the fish to market in time for dinner'.[39]

There is no external evidence that Stevenson lived in Drummond Street, but he paid for entries in the Edinburgh directories that record him as a 'teacher' elsewhere, at no less than three places within easy walking distance of each other. He lived first in the old town, amongst 'those who have moved since Whitsunday 1801', in High School Yards, where he could look down on the handsome English episcopal chapel in the Cowgate attended by the genteel, or over at the plain stone building of the High School in its large enclosure and William Adam's Royal Infirmary, or up to the newly built Robert Adam front of the university in South Bridge Street. An 1874 painting of the Yards by John Le Conte shows a curious mixture of buildings, some very old, leading at its eastern end to Surgeon's Square, where the anatomist Dr Knox was provided with a supply of corpses for dissection by the infamous Burke and Hare. The older structures in this area have now been demolished, but the school building of 1777 became part of the university's geography department.[40]

Stevenson very soon moved a little further south to 6 Nicolson Square, not too far from the larger, more fashionable George Square; to a part of the town built about the middle of the eighteenth century and said to display 'a considerable degree of the substantial elegance which appears in the modern architecture of the city' – a reference to the classical 'new town' with its broad, smooth pavements of hewn stone built a little later across the north bridge. Edinburgh was fast becoming the 'Athens of the north'. But by Whitsunday 1805 he had moved back into the crowded, precipitous and irregular old town, where cellars and upper storeys were inhabited by the poor whilst the nobility and gentry were accustomed to live on the floors between. At least he went to one of the first examples of Edinburgh town planning, Milne's Square, built in the seventeenth century to a design by the King's master-mason Robert Mylne in an attempt 'to give a little more light and air, a little escape from the congested, narrow closes and the lofty, crowded, often dilapidated tenements with their dark and dirty common stairs'. It has now been demolished in pursuit of yet more improvements, but was then just across the High Street from the Tron church.[41]

Students of the university either stayed with relations or lived in lodgings during the session from November to April, with some extension for medical students. Professors did not necessarily have any personal knowedge of the young men they lectured to in large classes. The level of teaching may have been higher but was quite similar to the instruction given to the hundred or so schoolboys forming a class in the High School. In effect students taught themselves. If they were anything like Thomas Carlyle, who went to the University of Edinburgh in 1809, they survived by their own force of character and intellectual powers. Otherwise they were lost among 'eleven hundred Christian striplings', allowed 'to tumble about as they listed, from three to seven years; certain persons, under the title of Professors, being stationed at the gates, to declare aloud that it was a University, and exact considerable admission-fees'. Actually, these amounted to a few guineas a year.

For the rest, there were many 'men of distinguished talents' living in Edinburgh, who advertised themselves as private lecturers in the more popular fields of study. Indeed, richer students could obtain 'at a moderate price, well-informed men who attend them in their apartments, and assist them in their studies, and particularly in preparing them to undergo the examination in the Latin tongue' which was needed before a medical degree. Stevenson is also recorded as a teacher in Edinburgh in the 1806 roll of Edinburgh burgesses and his obituary states that 'he gave instructions to private pupils in the various branches of general education' at his boarding house. He had in effect reverted to his previous way of life. Whatever his fundamental opinion about the utility of classical learning, he lived in a culture and a city that contained 'an assemblage of well-informed persons of all ranks, who respect those literary pursuits to which, at some period of life, most of them have devoted their attention and their time in a less or greater degree.'[42]

One of the most succinct physical descriptions of old Edinburgh at this time is to be found in Charles Dibdin's quaintly named *Observations on a Tour Through Almost the Whole of England, and a Considerable Part of Scotland*. His syntax briefly but successfully mimics the experience of living in this city of steep slopes and turns: 'we gradually ascended in winding directions from among that throng of streets, where loaves, stockings, pitchers, hats, cabbages, and numbers of other incongrous particulars were painted against the houses, to denote the occupations of their inhabitants, who live up stairs into one street, and down stairs into another, burrowing like so many rabbits in a warren ... '. In much of the old city, 'the important convenience of common sewers was neglected', wrote Forsyth with urbane disdain. At their worst, streets were like Fish Market-Close, 'a steep, narrow, stinking ravine', exclaimed Henry Cockburn with more colloquial energy. 'The fish were generally thrown out on the street at the head of the close, whence they were dragged down by dirty boys or dirtier women; and then sold unwashed'. Fruit and vegetables 'were in the hands of a college of old gin-drinking women, who congregated with stools and tables round the Tron Church', he reported, and no water supply to be found in either place.[43]

But when the Chambers brothers arrived in 1813 to begin their remarkable careers in printing and publishing, they found numerous book stalls 'stuck about the College and High School Winds'. A lantern with panes of white calico inscribed 'Auction of Books' showed where sales were held in the evenings. Carfrae's in Drummond Street was 'more genteel and dignified' than Peter Cairns's opposite the university, but Cairns with his warm auction room (or reading room for the impecunious) was easily the more popular auctioneer. His 'caustic jocularities' were greatly appreciated. Over the door of his bookshop in South College Street was displayed 'a huge sham copy of Virgil' as a trade sign. Here at last, after all his earlier failures, Stevenson found his 'capability' before having to shift into his 'last enterprise, that of getting buried', as Carlyle was to write of such setbacks in the 'Getting Under Way' chapter of *Sartor Resartus*. Trained as he had been in the scholarship of dissenting academies with good libraries, Stevenson was able to plunge into article and book-writing with as much ease as his simpler fellow-citizens traded and burrowed away in Edinburgh's stony warrens. Teaching – not necessarily classics – and boarding old friends like William Winstanley, who had given up the ministry and was now studying for the degree of doctor of medicine at Edinburgh between 1804 and 1806, were presumably no more than temporary resorts. We can be fairly sure that Mrs Stevenson was with him by this time, for she achieves a bare mention in Winstanley's obituary.[44]

Now William Stevenson could fairly launch himself into the tide of literary journalism. All the conditions of Edinburgh life at that time, from the physical, economic and institutional to the social, intellectual and ideological, were propitious. Henry Holland, who was a young student in Edinburgh in 1807, describes the easy style of the evening parties that were held in large, elegant and well lighted rooms. Ladies and gentlemen would walk up and down, he told his father, 'collecting themselves into *conversational nuclei* (if you will allow me the expression)'. At ten o'clock tables were spread with cold meat, poultry, desserts, wine and cakes. There was no ceremony; everything favoured conversation and social mingling. The literati produced by Scotland in this era were perhaps unique in European culture; definitely not revolutionary, alienated, or marginal figures. Many of the best played a remarkable part in the central life of Great Britain. Less fortunate men found they had taken their first steps into a publishing maze.[45]

NOTES

1 Richard Hindle Fowler, *Robert Burns*, London, 1988, p. 142.

2 *Letters*, pp. 796-7 (transcr. error: add 'been' before 'touched'); *DNB; George Hope of Fenton Barns: A Sketch of His Life Compiled by His Daughter* [Charlotte Hope], Edinburgh, 1881, pp. 2-3, 105, 177; Andrew M. Hill, 'The successors of the remnant: a bicentenary account of St. Mark's Unitarian church, Edinburgh', *TUHS*, XVI, 1975-78, pp. 158-9.

3 Chadwick, 1910, p. 2 (without evidence); Handley, *Agricultural Revolution*, p. 170.

4 'Saughton Mills' is adopted (called 'Stenhouse Mills' on Robert Kirkwood's *A Map of the Environs of Edinburgh*, 1817). *ABO*, pp. 210-11, reads 'at Laughton, near Edinburgh' – a mistake often repeated, by the *DNB* especially.

5 Cockburn, *Memorials*, ed. Miller, p. 377; Youngson, *Classical Edinburgh*, pp. 29, 97, 228-30.

6 See for Joan Leach's discovery of his name, *GSN,* III, Spring 1987, pp. 9-10, with ref. to *Burns Chronicle* for 1962; also p. 85 below. In her 2nd edn Chadwick changes 'Laughton' (1910, p. 6) to 'Saughton Mills' (1913, p. 4), adding that it was rented from Mr (sc. James) Cleghorn.

7 Burdett, *Survey of Chester*, pp. 1, 18, XI; Lysons, *Magna Britannia: Chester,* [1810], p. 753; Chadwick, 1910, pp. 81-6.

8 Irvine, pp. 56-8, 70; KPL: TS, Alan Dale, *Cheshire Tales*, n. p., 1972. See Appendix B for DCLH: MS, copy of old letter (recipient unknown) and family bible.

9 I am grateful to Dr David Iredale for advice about houses at Sandlebridge and Knutsford.

10 Her 'Recollections of a long life' [c. 1866] will soon appear by kind permission of Miss Barbara Hartas Jackson, in an edn of the MS diaries of Elizabeth Gaskell and Sophia Holland prepared by Anita Wilson and J. A. V. Chapple. See also my 'Unofficial lives: Elizabeth Gaskell and the Turner family', in Parish, pp. 106-20.

11 TH, 1760-1829. See p. 351 below and Appendix B.

12 MR, MS 'Recollections', pp. 1-3 (minor alterations ignored); *Letters*, pp. 5-8; *Cranford*, with preface by Anne Thackeray Ritchie (1891), London, 1911, pp. xiii-xiv, and 'Blackstick papers no. 11', *Cornhill*, n. s. XXI, 1906, p. 784; Payne, p. 62; Marion Leslie, 'Mrs Gaskell's house and its memories', *The Woman at Home*, June 1897, p. 764; Chadwick, 1910, pp. 84-5; Kathleen Tillotson, 'Anne Thackeray Ritchie and *Mary Barton*', *GSJ*, IX, 1995, p. 71; A-F, *Le Grand Meaulnes*, ch. 7. The estate was sold after the death of the first Viscount Knutsford in 1914.

13 Payne, *An Ancient Chapel*, p. 60; Hopkins, p. 17; Hunter, pp. 175, 178. For the will see p. 100 below. John Turner, merchant of Bolton, brother of William Turner of Newcastle, was the other trustee.

14 Marriage licence allegation and bond, 25 November 1797 (CRO: EDC 8, 1797); marriage register (CRO: P 77/3/1). Cp. *ABO*, p. 214: 'Miss Eliza Halland'.

15 For map and descriptions see Lysons, *Magna Britannia: Chester*, pp. 750-1; also Ormerod, *History of the County Palatine*, pp. 485-6; Richards, *Old Cheshire Churches*, pp. 267-73; 'Fletcher Moss', *Pilgrimages in Cheshire & Shropshire*, Didsbury, 1901, pp. 96-8.

16 He was termed gentleman on 12 May 1780 (JRULM: Leycester of Toft muniments 609), but grazier in 1789. See p. 92 below.

17 Hall, p. 79; Chadwick, 1910, p. 71; Henry Holland, *Recollections of Past Life* [pr. pr. c. 1868], London, 1872, pp. 6-7; Irvine, pp. 69-70 (using 'papers of the late Mr. Edgar [Swinton] Holland').

18 Surveyed by John Johnston, 1795 (SRO: RHP 11151). I owe thanks to Jane Brown for ensuring that no key is preserved with this map.

19 Youngson, *Classical Edinburgh*, p. 208; Alan Bell, ed. *Lord Cockburn: A Bicentenary Commemoration 1779-1979*, Edinburgh, 1979, p. 55; *The New Statistical Account of Scotland*, Edinburgh and London, I, 1845, pp. 206-20; Forsyth, *Beauties of Scotland*, I, p. 26.

20 Geddie, *Fringes of Edinburgh*, p. 57; *The Journal of John Wesley*, ed. Nehemiah Curnock (1915), London, 1938, VI, p. 354.

21 See *New Statistical Account*, I, p. 222; Grant, *Old and New Edinburgh*, III, pp. 319-20 (illustr.); *TEAS*, I, Edinburgh, 1891, pp. 116-18; *Book of Old Edinburgh Club*, III, pp. 190-9 (the panel illustr.); VIII, p. 190; *Royal Commission on Ancient and Historical Monuments of Scotland*, 10th report, Edinburgh, 1929, pp. 25-6 (with plan).

22 *Edinburgh Evening Courant*, no. 12,282, 28 January 1797; J. A. V. Chapple, 'William Stevenson and the Edinburgh literary scene', *GSJ*, VIII, 1994, p. 52 (error: read 'hedge and' for 'large'). The house, now the Stenhouse conservation centre, is under the control of the Scottish office. I am very grateful to Robert L. Snowden, principal conservator, for his courtesy in showing me the house and for expert advice, and to Brenda Moon, Edinburgh University Librarian, for valuable assistance.

23 Handley, *Agricultural Revolution*, p. 213; Smout, ed. *Statistical Account, 1791-1799*, II, p. 148; Cleghorn, 'Edinburghshire', IV; Forsyth, *Beauties of Scotland*, I, pp. 27, 251-7; Young, *Edinburgh*, pp. 32-3.

24 See the bibliographical appendix and Sharps, p. 377n., for these letters addressed to 'Mr Stevenson'. John or Robert are both possible, but a reference to dressing a leg suggests the latter.

25 JGS: MS, two conj. 4to leaves (wmk, posthorn in crowned shield over GR), DL to [RS], Saughton Mills, 12 October [1798]. She was perhaps married in Costorphine church; its marriage registers are blank, 1762-99. [Good's] *Directory of Berwick, etc., 1806*, lists a James Landels as Master Cooper, Bridge Street end, but George Landles (also a Berwick cooper in the BRO poll book of the 8 March 1820 election) is identified from his monumental inscription.

26 JGS: MS, two conj. 4to leaves (wmk as before), DL to [RS], Berwick, 29 December 1798; GROS: old parish registers 678/2 (see also Sharps, p. 377n.). The church is illustr. in the 10th report of the royal commission.

27 Young, *Edinburgh*, pp. 15, 45; *New Statistical Account of Scotland*, 1845, I, p. 236n., alluding to the 1795 edition, XIV, pp. 461, 463 (see rev. ed. C. Smout, p. 159).

28 Ward Notebook, ff. 2 verso, 9; Edgar Johnson, *Sir Walter Scott: the Great Unknown*, London, I, 1970, pp. 3-6. In Chadwick, 1910, pp. 1, 19, ECS was the second child; by the 2nd edn of 1913, pp. 1, 12, she was the eighth.

29 Cf. Colin Elliot, 'Some transactions of a Dartmouth privateer during the French wars at the end of the eighteenth century', *Studies in British Privateering, Trading Enterprise and Seamen's Welfare, 1775-1900*, ed. Stephen Fisher, Exeter, 1987, p. 19.

30 JGS: MS, two conj. 4to leaves (wmk as before), DL to [RS], Berwick, 18 January 1799. 'Mr Truels farm is not let yet … Miss B. Truels is still the same' occurs in DL's letter of October 1798.

31 JGS: MS, two conj. 4to leaves (similar wmk), JS to [RS], Berwick-upon-Tweed, 15 February 1799; H. Scott, *Fasti Ecclesiae Scoticanae*, II, p. 46; Thomas Johnstone [minister of the Low Meeting],*The History of Berwick-upon-Tweed*, Berwick, 1817, p. 94. No records of the Low Meeting before 1836 have survived (see K. G. White, 'The disruption of Berwick Low Meeting [c. 1846]', *JPHS*, XII, pp. 170-8).

32 Quoted from Walter Scott's *Guy Mannering* in Andrew L. Drummond and James Bullough, *The Scottish Church 1688-1843: The Age of the Moderates*, Edinburgh, 1973, p. 30.

33 JGS: two conj. 4to leaves (address torn off; wmk as before), DL to [RS], Berwick, 26 February [1799]; p. 14 above. Joseph senior died on 14 February [a Thursday], according to the burial register.

34 Hanson, *Monumental Inscriptions*, chest 385. I am grateful to Mrs Linda Bankier for information about rate books, and to Francis Cowe for details of house documents. See also *Letters*, pp. 272, 863.

35 Symon, *Scottish Farming*, pp. 154-8; *FM*, II, 3rd edn, Edinburgh, 1802, p. 97; Couper, *Edinburgh Periodical Press*, II, p. 262; Forsyth, *Beauties of Scotland*, I, pp. 262-4.

36 No probate record has been found at Durham, York, London, Northumberland or Berwick record offices. See Jane Cox, *Wills, Inventories and Death Duties ... A Provisional Guide*, PRO, London, 1988, p. 1.

37 *The Letters of Robert Burns*, 2nd edn, ed. G. Ross Roy, Oxford, 1985, I, p. 257; II, p. 113.

38 *ABO*, p. 211; in 1801 (Chadwick, 1910, p. 7); in 1802 (1913, p. 5).

39 Fraser, *Building of Old College*, pp. 82, 114-22; Grant, *University of Edinburgh*, II, p. 481; Young, *Edinburgh*, pp. 144-53; *Farington Diary*, ed. Greig, I, p. 325; Tredrey, *House of Blackwood*, p. 9.

40 See *Edinburgh University: An Illustrated Memoir*, comp. Ray Footman and Bruce Young, Edinburgh, 1983, etc.

41 Thomas Aitchison, *Directory to July 1802*, p. 6; *Directory for the Year 1803*, p. 156; *Supplement to the Post Office Directory, 2 September 1805*; Youngson, *Classical Edinburgh*, p. 14; Robert Kirkwood, *Plan of the City of Edinburgh*, 1817; Forsyth, *Beauties of Scotland*, I, p. 21; Watson, *Closes and Wynds*, pp. 38-9. I owe particular thanks here to the most efficient and helpful staff of ECL.

42 Thomas Carlyle, *Sartor Resartus* (1833-34), ed. Kerry McSweeney and Peter Sabor, Oxford and New York, 1987, p. 85; Forsyth, *Beauties of Scotland*, I, pp. 50, 54-5.

43 Dibdin, *Observations*, London (1801, 02), I, p. 329; Forsyth, *Beauties of Scotland*, I, p. 27; Cockburn, *Memorials*, ed. Miller, pp. 405-6.

44 *Robert Chambers with ... William Chambers*, pp. 76-7; Carlyle, *Sartor*, ed. McSweeney and Sabor, p. 93; WW obit., *CR*, VIII, 1852, p. 638.

45 HH to PH, [Edinburgh, January 1807] (DCLH); Sher, *Moderate Literati*, p. 10.

4

Authorship in Edinburgh and London

STEVENSON IS SAID in his obituary to have been the editor – a rather indefinite term at this period – of the *Scots Magazine, or General Repository of Literature, History, and Politics*. This journal, which had been taken over by Archibald Constable, was hardly distinguished if the great Henry Cockburn is to be believed. He called it 'the doited *Scots Magazine*'. The early files are set in double columns of unattractive small print and are very miscellaneous in content, despite the essays on 'some subject of taste, literature, or science' that Stevenson is supposed to have contributed to almost every number about this time. Articles are not fully signed and his contributions have not been identified.[1] One in the issue for 1801 by 'An Observer', however, might well have some bearing on his career as a farmer. It lists a succession of bad seasons, blight and blast destroying peas and vetches, wheat sown in wet land rotting, frost and wireworm, not to mention 'many false paragraphs published in the newspapers' about crops, which affected prices. Then comes a defence of farmers against their landlords, especially in cases where leases were only 'renewed upon the abominable and ruinous principle of secret proposals' and small farms often gathered into one large managed unit.[2]

It has also been claimed that Stevenson contributed to the *Farmer's Journal*, 'of which his friend James Cleghorn was the editor', and to the *Gentleman's Magazine*. The former title is unknown from this period, though a *Farmer's Magazine* was edited by James Cleghorn after 1814.[3] No evidence exists to show that he wrote for the latter – by the early nineteenth century a distinctly old-fashioned production for which mischievous analogies were only too easy to find: 'a repertory of all things lost or mislaid between the Flood and the Conquest, – a strange museum of obsolete knick-knacks, – a withered flower, which may have graced the bosom of my great-grandmother, a feather from the wing of Old Time, worn to the stump by inditing a hundred volumes ...'[4] More impressively, Stevenson became one of the earliest contributors to the publishing event of the new century, the *Edinburgh Review*, a quarterly begun in 1802. Highly talented Scots (with the collaboration of that scintillating English clergyman Sydney Smith) altered the whole basis and style of reviewing. It had till then tended towards lengthy quotation and dull summary. Instead, they produced, anonymously, articles of critical and intellectual distinction on a range of topics. Their ethos was not formed by the Church of England, Oxford or Cambridge, but by powerful Scottish traditions of empirical science, theoretical history of society and Whiggish thought – a confident alternative culture very like that fostered by the liberal English dissenting academies, themselves cut off by their religious beliefs from the dominant intellectual culture south of the border.

An Edinburgh hostess of the time, Mrs Eliza Fletcher, described 'the electrical effects' of the *Edinburgh*'s publication in her autobiography, maintaining that Edinburgh society was transformed by the appearance of this new quarterly on the literary scene. She would have been a typical reader. Her circle of acquaintance, 'with occasional *gleams* of more literary and distinguished persons', was unashamedly liberal: 'a Whig coterie of her own'. Many years later, a friend brought her a copy of Elizabeth Gaskell's *Mary Barton*, published in 1848. She was 'at once struck with its power and pathos', she wrote, and discovered that it was 'by the daughter of one whom I both loved and reverenced in my early married life in Edinburgh'. The tone is a little effusive. William Stevenson is just not mentioned in the pages of her autobiography devoted to her Edinburgh *salon* and those who made a figure in it, but it is pleasant to think of him at Mrs Fletcher's supper table, gazing admiringly at her 'blue gown and brilliant look' and hearing the conversation that so impressed young men destined for worldly success, such as James Mackintosh and Henry Brougham, both of whom were to become 'spirits of the age' for Hazlitt. She was certainly a warm friend of Elizabeth Gaskell in later years.[5]

Stevenson might have written or had a hand in more than a dozen articles in the *Edinburgh*, pieces assigned to him in the *Wellesley Index to Victorian Periodicals* because of the interest shown in farming, etymology and classics, together with a knowledge of obscure sources.[6] He was one of the more obviously learned contributors, beginning in April 1803 with a sober review of a work by the enthusiast who had revived Greek studies at the University of Edinburgh, *Collecteana Graeca Majora* by Professor Andrew Dalzel. Any reservations about the utility of classical learning have vanished without trace. In the July number Stevenson's major analysis of *A Vindication of the Celts* includes 'a succinct and accurate detail of all that is really known upon the subject'. He claims to have examined 'every authority', and shows himself alert to intellectual movements in the sciences, writing easily about the 'origin and destinies of nations, the filiation of distant races, and the affinities of remote establishments' – key terms of the new biology and anthropology at the turn of the century. The antiquary, he proclaims, now takes his station 'where history terminates, and theory begins'. Natural history was leaping clear of mere classification. Stevenson the scholar is in touch.

After a review of John Pinkerton's *Modern Geography* in October 1803, he is thought to have collaborated in the January 1804 issue of the *Edinburgh* with the editor himself, Francis Jeffrey. G. S. Faber's *Mysteries of the Cabiri* is scornfully dismissed, Jeffrey deploying his 'characteristic irony' and Stevenson a more ponderous 'expertise in classical and Hebrew etymology'. Carlyle wonderfully revives for us Jeffrey's slight, nimble figure, bright black eyes and 'oval face full of rapid expression', maintaining that he could tell by certain signs, 'even if behind him, that his brow was then puckered, and his eyes looking archly, half-contemptuously out, in conformity to some conclusive little cut his tongue was giving.' Stevenson's contributions, in comparison, are serious, learned, lucid and balanced. It later years he more truly came up to Sydney Smith's most spirited expectations of *Edinburgh* reviewers, who were expected 'to barbecue a poet or two, or strangle a metaphysician, or do any other act of cruelty to the dull men of the earth'.[7]

There were four more reviews for the *Edinburgh* in 1804, the year in which both Stevenson and his relation by marriage, the Reverend John Holland of Bolton, were elected honorary members of the Newcastle Literary and Philosophical Society, as men who would, it was hoped, keep the Society in touch with a wider intellectual and critical world. Stevenson set out to demolish the second part of Sharon Turner's pioneering if faulty *History of the Anglo Saxons* in January and his *Vindication of the Welsh Bards* in April.[8] In July he was even more scathing about the deficiencies of Edward Davies's *Celtic Researches, on the Origin, Traditions and Language of the Ancient Britons*. But a review of *Prize Essays and Transactions of the Highland Society* in April 1804 is rather different, in that the scholarly tone is lightened by unexpectedly personal touches. He could 'positively affirm' that bees were 'unprofitable in a climate much more favourable than that of the Highlands' – even, presumably, when their Midlothian bee-bole was protected by a building. He also insisted that creatures destructive to the salmon should not have been ignored, for the porpoise 'is often seen *cruizing* across the mouth of the Tweed, and not only destroying the salmon, but preventing them from entering the mouth of the river', whilst the seal 'sometimes pursues the salmon a considerable way up the river: they are also equally inveterate and destructive enemies of the herring.' Stevenson was evidently remembering Berwick days. Similarly, the naturalist and wood-engraver Thomas Bewick wrote about the great shoals of porpoises off Tynemouth he had seen, speeding through the water abreast of each other and preventing salmon from entering the river.[9]

But Stevenson's general thesis in this review is more chilling. (It would not have suited the minister of Corstorphine parish.) Sheep, he argued, should take the place of cattle in the Highlands, and manufacturing ought to be introduced. Not only this. He declared that the Gaelic language, poetry and music should be discouraged, as inhibiting 'useful knowledge' and tending 'to perpetuate those prejudices which it is absolutely necessary to destroy, before any general or permanent improvement can take place.' He is deliberately making a distinction quite alien to the Highlands Society, founded with the practical objects of 'inquiring into the means of their improvement' but also of giving 'a proper attention to the preservation of the language, poetry, and music of the Highlands'.[10]

The first volume of its *Prize Essays and Transactions*, 1799, was edited by the novelist of sensibility, Henry Mackenzie, a very different kind of man from Elizabeth Stevenson's father. Unlike Mackenzie and Samuel Johnson, or, later, Walter Scott, Stevenson seems to care nothing for the language, poetry and music of the Highlands. On his visit to Raasay in the western isles in 1773, Johnson had listened to ladies singing Erse songs as if he had been an English audience at an Italian opera – 'delighted with the sound of words which I did not understand.' Also, as Mary Lascelles finely notes, he 'exposed his full powers of apprehension' to the changing state of the Highlands, to such a degree that his *Journey to the Western Isles* is unparalleled in his writings. Intellectually as just and as balanced as them, it is yet 'unlike, in the intensity of concern as to the outcome, and also in the fact of his own presence, however unobtrusively conveyed. The ideas burn, as in the heart of a fire, and are communicated in a manner he uses nowhere else.'

In comparison Stevenson was sympathetic, but in an abstract, rational kind of way. Economic improvement could at least be achieved without emigration, he thought, so that 'the Highlands, instead of being peopled thinly with an indolent and wretched race, would become the abode of industry and comfort, and support an increased population, not only in its own mountainous districts, but over every part of the empire.' Adam Smith's *Wealth of Nations* (1776), the bible of the Highland improvers, gave intellectual authority for such attitudes. 'Thus the estate perhaps is improved', was Samuel Johnson's blunt summary of the case, 'but the clan is broken.'[11]

In the 1790s Sir John Sinclair in Caithness had carried out crucial experiments to demonstrate to a deputation from the British wool society the superiority of the Cheviot breed of sheep in the Highlands. He too was convinced that a balance could be achieved: sheep-walks were necessary in the national interest but tenants would be better off in crofts on the coast with two acres of arable, a house and garden on a long lease. 'Clearances', whether barbarous and sudden or gradual and benevolent, accelerated in the nineteenth century. The propaganda war began to burn fiercely. There is no doubt that Stevenson was on the side of the improvement ideologues at the turn of the century. His are remarks on the very inferior utility of highland culture – humane, cool and rational, but in essence as righteously contemptuous as those of Patrick Sellar, notorious factor of the Sutherland family:

> Ask Sir William Grant what his Grandfather was – a removed tenant! But for the *just* views of the proprietor this great man would have been now in a place like Scottany and at a rent of £5 – following two or three Highland poneys with a cocked bonnet on his head and a Red top to it, and a ragged philiby reaching half way down his leg, afflicted I doubt not by a hereditary itch which all the brimstone in Scotland would be tardy to cure.[12]

The urban and mentally energetic middle classes of Scotland could be almost as critical of Lowland aristocrats. The July 1804 issue of the *Edinburgh* carried Henry Brougham's swingeing review of a book by James Maitland, 8th Earl of Lauderdale, *An Inquiry into the Nature and Origin of Public Wealth*. Brougham was all that Stevenson was not. Though Dr James Currie thought him 'a scatterbrained fellow' and this review in 'every way unfair and foul', he was a prodigy. He contributed nearly sixty articles to the *Edinburgh* between 1802 and 1807 on subjects as diverse as the slave trade, astronomy and Latin syntax, dismissing Lauderdale's economic theories with as much hard cogency as he turned to ridicule Byron's poetry or Young's undulatory theory of light – mistakenly, in this last instance.[13] In his youth Lauderdale's lean, thrusting features had been the index of his active, stirring character, but now he was one of the conservative leaders of the older Scottish Whigs, 'the seniors', mostly ill at ease with Francis Jeffrey and his circle of ambitious young lawyers like Brougham. They in return thought little of the older men, who, Cockburn believed, suffered from 'considerable jealousy' of their bright and lively juniors. Brougham was to move on in 1803 to a career in British politics and law, managing always to turn 'professional business to political account'. A great public dinner with Cockburn in the chair was given for him in Edinburgh on 5 April 1825 to symbolise his astonishingly successful career.[14]

The paths of both Lauderdale and Brougham crossed that of Stevenson, the former's not long afterwards. In October 1805 Stevenson wrote for the *Edinburgh* a brief and favourable note on Sir Joseph Banks's *Short Account of the Disease in Corn, Called by Farmers the Blight, the Mildew and the Rust*. Then came a pause in his occasional reviewing – and a permanent revolution in his career. In about 1806, after 'happening to be introduced' to the Earl of Lauderdale, according to his obituary, he was fortunate enough to be employed as Lauderdale's private secretary. Later biographers make the earl impressed with his writings, with some plausibility, for Lauderdale could undoubtedly have seen the *Edinburgh Review* at the relevant time.

James Maitland had become the eighth earl in 1789. A clever man, it was said, but notorious in the House of Lords for his behaviour in 'that grave & dignified Assembly: His red handkerchief abt. His neck, or wiping his face with one exhibited an appearance which was new & highly improper.' He had been one of Charles James Fox's supporters during the long years of Whig opposition in the House of Commons. They were good friends. Fox sent choice vines ('Sweetwater' and 'St Peter's') to Lauderdale, who reciprocated with ale and salmon from his Scottish estates. Lauderdale's ancient castle of Thirlestane, brilliantly remodelled by Sir William Bruce after the Restoration of Charles II and provided with splendid ceilings in deep plaster relief to rival the famous ones in Holyrood Palace, lies in a gentle valley overlooking Leader Water to the south-east of Edinburgh. The earl had another castle at the end of the

₊principal street of Dunbar on the north-east coast, just half-way between
Berwick and Edinburgh.[15] The English politician had once been Lauderdale's
second in a duel, and sought his advice about historical sources and problems
of attribution, though his affection did not extend as far as approval of his
prose style. Shrewd, bustling, eccentric and fluent in both speech (with a
strong Scottish accent) and writing, he had been made Baron Lauderdale of
Thirlestane in the county of Berwick in 1806, when after decades in opposition the Whigs at length came into power with their 'ministry of all the
talents'. Fox had already promised him 'the Scotch patronage'. Walter Scott, a
Tory inclined to stress Lauderdale's violent temper, 'irritated by long disappointed ambition and ancient feud with all his brother nobles', thought this
deplorable.[16]

In March it was leaked that the government were going to appoint
Lauderdale governor general of India, but the directors of the East India
Company objected strongly. They remembered too vividly his support of Fox's
India bills and his radicalism at the time of the French revolution, when he was
said to have 'stiled Himself Citizen Lauderdale'. Now the gossip maintained
that he was behaving as if the appointment was a mere formality and, worse
still, was determined to take 'many of His Countrymen with Him'. For some
months Fox and the directors were at loggerheads; the 'flame in the City was
prodigious against Lord Lauderdale and the Government', it was reported.
Lord Grenville eventually advised Fox, whose health was failing rapidly – he
had only a few months to live – that he must compromise. By 24 June 1806
the proposal to make Lauderdale governor general was finally dropped. He
became instead Lord High Keeper of the great seal of Scotland and a privy
counsellor, resigning when Grenville and the Whigs fell from power in March
1807. The cartoons of Gillray kept such matters in the public view, culmin-
ating in 'Bruin in his Boat – or – the Manager in Distress', which shows
Lauderdale in the water vainly trying to reach a floating cask of 'East India
Roupees'.[17]

During this critical period Stevenson had left Edinburgh, perhaps with his
wife and family, to live near the earl's house in Mayfair and make preparations
for the voyage to India and its *lakhs* of rupees. He came, almost certainly by
sea, to a city that dwarfed all others in Britain. From the outer galleries of St
Paul's cathedral, 'the huge dim capital of the world' could be seen spreading
far and wide, 'a province of brick' stretching in the north to 'dim outlines of
the hills, which seem scarce more than a part of the murky atmosphere'; then
'westward to that other realm of houses, outstripping the gaze, and encircling
other distant towers, and stretching away to the seats of government and legislation'; and in the south to a 'wilderness of human habitations' and to
something we do not see today but which was then of supreme importance,
'the wide and gleaming river' with its 'port that raises against the sky its trellis-
work of innumerable masts'. And over all was 'one hue of smoke, and one
unextinguishable hum of activity.'

Stevenson was not left stranded when Lauderdale was forced to withdraw from the glorious position he had thought was his. The new Lord's patronage obtained for him the office of Keeper of the Papers at the Treasury. He was to officiate in a building that was 'very extensive, but by no means handsome, with the exception of the front towards the park, and certainly very inconvenient'. His predecessor had been paid £400 a year as a reward for former services, so he had not felt obliged to attend in person and instead paid £40 a year to a deputy, a stipend made up to £100 by the Treasury. The consequent inefficiencies determined the Treasury Lords to appoint 'an intelligent and efficient Officer, who should be in daily and constant Attendance during the Hours of Business'. Stevenson was appointed on 20 May 1806, with duties beginning on 5 July at a salary of £200 a year paid quarterly, rising after 1812 to £350 in the course of the next fifteen years. (His brother John would have received something over £100 a year as a naval lieutenant, and not much less on half-pay.) The existing deputy keeper at the Treasury, Mr Blake, was to continue. The happy predecessor was with perfect logic allowed a pension of £360 a year.[18]

A brisk and efficient letter dated 10 July 1806 from Lauderdale to Lord Grenville may indicate an attempt at something even better that did not succeed:

> Lord Holland mentioned to me yesterday, when I was talking of my great desire immediately to get a Situation for Mr Stevenson, that there was an Office Mr Allen had declined which would suit him perfectly.
>
> Your Lordship will recollect that I told you he was one of those for whom I was anxious to provide, having taken him out of the line in which he was, at the time I was led to think I had a certainty of going to India. – It is that anxiety, and the conviction that your Lordship could not find a person more capable of fulfilling the duties of the Office, which make me intrude upon you on this occasion.[19]

John Allen is a wonderful illustration of the close relationship that could exist between a noble patron and a dependent intellectual in those days. He was originally a clever young man lecturing on physiology at Edinburgh, and was recommended to Fox's nephew, Lord Holland, by Sydney Smith. Lauderdale wrote with incontrovertible logic that Allen's chosen profession was thoroughly unsuitable: he was 'extremely short-sighted, which is bad for operating'; otherwise he thought him a man of 'genius and talents' – an opinion shared by Henry Cockburn, who thought he might have become the best medical lecturer in Europe. In 1802, Lauderdale introduced this eager, awkward and energetic young Scot with 'enormous round silver spectacles on his nose' to the grand house in rural Kensington that was a centre for the best political and literary society of the opposition during the early nineteenth century. Allen became indispensable. Without 'that species of politness which consists in attitudes and flexibilities', wrote Sydney Smith, 'civil, unaffected and good-natured' to all, he travelled everywhere with the family and became its librarian. A solid, dependable figure in C. R. Leslie's painting, he stands with book in hand between the plump, amiable Lord and the stylish Lady Holland in the long gallery of their library, which extended the length of the west wing. He also became warden of Dulwich college in 1811. 'The duties are not much to your taste but they are not very severe', commented a friend at the time.

'Blest be the banquets spread at Holland House / Where Scotchmen feed, and Critics may carouse', Byron sang in *English Bards and Scotch Reviewers*. Though Allen became master of Dulwich college in 1820, he mostly lived with his patron and his wife, the clever, imperious, moody and unpredictable Lady Holland, satirised in Lady Caroline Lamb's *Glenarvon* as the Princess of Madagascar, who presided over a motley crowd of poets, reviewers and politicians in an ancient Gothic buiding called Barbary House. Macaulay rather despised Allen for allowing himself to be ordered about like a footman in real life, but 'her Ladyship's Atheist in ordinary' issued the invitations, carved at the famous dinners and allocated rooms to those staying overnight. 'Sitting always at the bottom of the table, before carving had been transferred to the sideboard', Henry Holland commented, 'he yet mixed largely in the conversation as an expounder of facts, and a sharp commentator on the words and opinions of others.' Lord Lauderdale was always welcome to Lady Holland, 'notwithstanding his political economy, which she abhorred, and a racy dialect of Lothian Scotch, which sounded somewhat incongruously at her table.' Allen was, too, always at hand to help his patron Lord Holland 'in his political and literary researches, and prepared to push the fortunes of the Whig party with the aid of his facile pen.'[20]

Stevenson had never been a member of the inner circle of those who had a taste for literature and agreeable manners, the utterly informal 'Friday Club' of Edinburgh, which used to meet for supper at Bayle's tavern in Shakespeare Square, where Henry Brougham used to prepare a 'very pleasant but somewhat dangerous beverage, of Rum, Sugar, Lemons, Marmalade, Calves foot jelly, and hot water – a sort of warm shrub'. The list of about thirty convivial souls of all political complexions who met together in the early years of the century contains Dugald Stewart, Francis Jeffrey, Sydney Smith, William Erskine, Walter Scott, Henry Mackenzie, Francis Horner, Thomas Campbell and Andrew Dalzel – all famous men in their day. It also includes the young John Allen. Was Stevenson too hard pressed for money to join, fathoms deep in domestic difficulties – one thinks of the premature deaths of infants – teaching and writing, or just not the joining sort?

Eventually, like many of his fellow Edinburgh Reviewers in the first decade of the new century, he 'thrived by emigration', if not to the same degree. Sydney Smith, Horner, Allen, Thomas Campbell, John Leyden and John Richardson were all 'devoured by hungry London', Cockburn wrote in his *Memorials*. He did not see fit to mention William Stevenson. The success rate of Scottish patronage was exceptional in those days. It was in 1806 that the most famous patron of them all, the Tory Henry Dundas, whose statue now stands high on a column above St Andrew's Square in the new town, helped another who had been by his own account a heedless, climbing boy, Walter Scott, to obtain the clerkship of session in Edinburgh – a useful employment, Scott told Wordsworth, that would 'not unreasonably incroach' upon his time.[21] This was an important consideration for anyone capable of increasing, even vastly increasing, his income by writing. Scott stayed in Edinburgh, but Stevenson came south to a city of a million people that exercised a dominance in books and periodicals only marginally threatened by the early success of Edinburgh in this field and soon to spring back with the brilliant success of De Quincey's *Confessions of an English Opium Eater,* Hazlitt's *Table Talk* and Lamb's *Essays of Elia.* Literary London was reinventing itself by the 1820s.[22]

There is said to have been one chance to travel yet further afield that Stevenson rejected. After his death 'a very complimentary letter' from M. Rizsky, the rector of the University of Charkov, was found. It had been forwarded to him soon after his Treasury appointment by Baron Nicolay, the chargé d'affaires of the emperor of Russia, to declare that the emperor had created him professor of technology at Charkov and that 'bills of exchange to the amount of between three and four thousand rubles were waiting his acceptance, for the purpose of defraying his expenses, besides a much larger sum for the purchase of apparatus.' Stevenson modestly and secretly declined the honour, perhaps because he was ignorant of anything more than simple agricultural technology – though the absence of any previous knowledge whatsoever of chemistry had not prevented the 'joyous, jovial, and cordial' Richard Watson from becoming a professor of the subject at Cambridge. Watson next became the regius professor of divinity and then bishop of Llandaff, whereupon he paid a deputy to perform his duties in Cambridge and settled in the Lake District. Russia might not have been so accommodating, if we may judge from the fact that John Bowring discovered in 1819 that many senior naval and military commanders, diplomatists and ministers there were foreigners, and that 'the most eminent professors of of the universities were strangers, settled in the country'.[23]

Politics and patronage combined to confirm Stevenson's final choices in life. The comfortable connection once made with Lauderdale was never dropped. He must have been as civil, serviceable and accommodating as John Allen. Lauderdale, like Lord Holland, had a facile pen, his magnum opus being the *Enquiry into the Nature and Origin of Public Wealth* of 1804, in which he asserted that agriculture rather than commerce was the basis of public wealth. Brougham's patronising review stung him to produce further writings on finance, public wealth, currency, and the like: *Observations by the Earl of Lauderdale on the Review of His Enquiry* in 1804; *Hints to the Manufacturers of Great Britain* and *Thoughts on the Alarming State of the Circulation and on the Means of Redressing the Pecuniary Grievances of Ireland*, both in 1805. All were published in Edinburgh and are elaborate productions, with figures and footnotes. There is no overt sign that Stevenson lent a hand, but he would have been eminently qualified to do so if he had met Lauderdale somewhat earlier than is known.

Stevenson's contributions to the *Edinburgh* certainly fell off in 1806, though in April 1807 there appeared a distinctly negative review of John Pinkerton, who had brought out a new edition in three volumes of his *Modern Geography*.[24] Pinkerton was an eccentric and unpopular man. 'His home,' according to an angry London neighbour, 'was frequently a place of popular disturbance, by females whom he had married, or lived with, and deserted'. Despite all these diversions and distractions, he brought out numerous antiquarian and historical works, including a *General Collection* of voyages and travels in seventeen volumes between 1807 and 1814. The nature of his literary hackwork, if not his rackety life-style, was very like Stevenson's. It is also said in Stevenson's obituary that he contributed to 'a short-lived Review established by Sir Richard Phillips', entitled the *Oxford Review*. This must have been the one published at Oxford in 1807-8, of which three volumes appeared.[25]

In April 1809 appeared Stevenson's last review in the *Edinburgh* for many years, attributed to him with some certainty. In it he rightly gave the two volumes of John Jamieson's *Etymological Dictionary of the Scottish Language* high praise, noticed how Jamieson helped us read 'our favourite authors' and concluded in his usual manner with corrections and additions. Once again, personal touches can be found. His comments itemise words like *vowbet*, common in Berwickshire, and Newcastle terms like *billies, catters, chares* and *fisher-logges*. Brand's *History of Newcastle* and the Newcastle Slaters' Book are also cited. We can assume that he was in touch, if only by correspondence, with the Unitarian minister of Newcastle upon Tyne, eldest son and namesake of the Reverend William Turner of Wakefield, a man related to William Stevenson's wife in several ways and destined to offer hospitality to their daughter, who was herself to praise Charlotte Brontë's unerring choice of words from any register of language. That Turner was interested in etymology is shown by a reference to his interleaved copy of the first edition of John Trotter Brockett's *A Glossary of North Country Words* in the preface to a new edition of this 'ancient and energetic dialect of the North'.[26]

In 1809, aroused by a new East India Company situation, Lauderdale was induced 'to employ his leisure hours, in the course of the summer, in endeavouring to supply what was deficient in his own information on these affairs'. Stevenson would as far as we can tell have been free to help Lauderdale with an elaborate 'short tract' of some 260 pages octavo entitled *An Inquiry into the Practical Merits of the System for the Government of India*. The *Edinburgh* reviewer of this in January 1810 (possibly Robert Grant) was, or affected to be, agreeably surprised. He began by noting that Lauderdale was popularly known to be rash, violent and unsafe in political affairs, and that even his friends would admit that he was sometimes more zealous than discreet, prejudiced rather than wise; nevertheless, he went on to say, the *Inquiry* was clear, simple and concise in style, temperate, fairly reasoned and well researched in matter. Only the word 'concise' seems inappropriate for William Stevenson.[27]

He appears to have taken no part in the assault on 'the safe and elegant imbecility of classical learning' in schools and universities that Sidney Smith and others mounted in the *Edinburgh Review* between January 1808 and April 1810, but his obituarist makes the rather breath-taking statement that 'for several years he wrote and compiled the greater part' of the *Annual Register,* and immediately adds that 'he completed' Campbell's *Lives of the British Admirals.* The new edition of Dr John Campbell's *Lives,* published in eight volumes 1812-17, is still a standard reference work, but it was brought to completion by another William Stevenson (1741-1821), a fellow of the society of antiquaries, who took over from H. R. Yorke (himself assisted by John Galt, the novelist) at volume 6.[28]

As for one of the *Annual Registers* of the time, a volume for 1806 contains a strongly partisan account of the East India affair, calling the directors of the company 'as obstinate as they were refractory', praising 'the moderation of Lord Lauderdale and the forbearance of ministers' and eulogising Fox. That the volume was some months late, because of the editor's 'anxiety to render the historical part of the work as full and complete as possible', according to the preface, sounds very like Stevenson's dilatory and meticulous caution, which would become even more evident in the years to come. But perhaps it should be regarded a general fault of North Britons, since the Holland's eldest son noted that John Allen, as well as contributing to the *Edinburgh Review,* wrote the historical portion of the *Annual Register* of 1806-7.[29]

The bustling Sir John Sinclair's influence on Stevenson's life at this stage was considerable. 'Agricultural Sir John', a Scot who had begun in 1794 the famous series of *General Views of Agriculture* in England and Wales, with wide margins for farmers' comments (scholarly and practical), must have approved the invitations extended to the hyperactive Henry Holland of Knutsford and, later, his aunt's husband William Stevenson, to help revise the volumes between 1805 and 1817.[30] Henry's name had been suggested by an influential friend and neighbour, another honorary member of the Newcastle Literary and Philosophical Society, Sir John Stanley, afterwards Lord Stanley of Alderley Park. At about this time Henry's father Peter Holland was writing to Josiah Wedgwood on Stanley's behalf, to ask his opinion on the cobalt found at Alderley Edge. Young Henry completed the task in six months, with efficient help from others. In January 1806 he was able to leave the Report with the great Sir Joseph Banks, yet another honorary member of the Newcastle Society, and receive his compliments. *A General View of the Agriculture of Cheshire* actually appeared in 1808 when Holland was about nineteen or twenty. The preface, which mentions his father and grandfather, is dated from Knutsford, 27 October 1806. Peter Holland told Josiah

Wedgwood that his son had received double the original offer of one hundred pounds for this work, 'for it was full of sound and well-prepared material'.[31]

Sir John Sinclair, to whom the first number of the *Farmer's Magazine* had been dedicated in 1800, might have noticed Stevenson's review of the *Transactions of the Highland Society,* or perhaps Henry Holland introduced the two men. There were also Berwick connections. R. H. Kerr was responsible for the *General View of the Agriculture of Berwick* in 1809. Stevenson was later to contribute an introductory volume to Kerr's collection of voyages and travels; it was to be his magnum opus, and incubus. In addition, John Fuller's *History of Berwick upon Tweed* of 1799 had been the first attempt to continue for England Sir John's *Statistical Account of Scotland*. Stevenson would have seen the opportunity here for honest paid work in a field for which he was reasonably well qualified, but he would have taken a very canny view of Fuller's preliminary remarks, full as they were of a quasi-religious enthusiasm and exhortations to abandon 'the old beaten unsystematized tracks' of agriculture, to 'reduce to practice the culture of the earth, on scientific principles'. Fuller's praise for the county reports was more than lyrical: 'Surely a more natural and rational plan, leading to the improvement of a country in every respect, than the one adopted by the Board of Agriculture, could scarcely be devised by human wisdom.'[32]

In 1809 Stevenson brought out a more down-to-earth *General View of the Agriculture of Surrey*, which was reprinted in 1813 'with the additional Communications that have been received since the Original reports were circulated'. He also undertook the *Agriculture of Dorset*. Lauderdale begged Lord Grenville in July 1811 for letters of introduction, and asked if as a property-owner there he knew of any intelligent adviser: 'W. Stevenson a particular friend of mine has undertaken to write the Agricultural Report of the County & he is going to make a tour in it for the purpose of procuring information.'[33] The Dorset volume appeared in the following year. Stevenson's preface, dated Chelsea, 12 August 1812, confessed that it was 'but just' to declare there had not been 'much necessity to add to, or alter, the substance' of a Mr Batchelor's 1810 report on Dorset, which had been rejected. His own business was 'to make it fit for publication'. A third volume, R. W. Dickson's *Agriculture of Lancashire*, 'revised and prepared for the press by William Stevenson', appeared in 1815.[34] Whatever Stevenson's commitment to up-to-date agriculture and his knowledge of the science of the day, his practical experience had been relatively brief and unfortunate. But the 'authors' of the revised *Views* were not necessarily successful farmers; they were in many respects reporters, editors and compilers – a much more suitable trade. It is not likely, however, that he was the author of a *System of Land Surveying*, with editions in 1805 and 1810.[35]

Stevenson's post at the Treasury was not what it had been before his appointment in 1806, a sinecure with all duties performed by deputy; but he had a deputy, 'Blake, an Extra Clerk', until 1813 and the office of assistant keeper, which had lapsed in 1810, was revived in 1820. Like other office holders in those days – James Mill, Lamb, Peacock and Macaulay are famous cases in point – he had plenty of time for writing. Nothing remarkable, however, came from his pen. Sir John Sinclair evidently trusted him to revise and improve the work of others, but utility is perhaps the most that could be claimed for his *General Views*. Though employed by the *Edinburgh*, he was not in the same class for spirit and reformist vigour with reviewers like Francis Jeffrey, Sydney Smith and Henry Brougham. More and more as the years went by he turned into a slave of the insatiable press, attempting to straddle the almost impossible divide between journalism and recondite scholarship for the rest of his days, harassed by tasks he could not perform in the time allotted and seemingly ever behindhand in his finances.

He clearly remained in touch with the Earl of Lauderdale, but it is not known exactly where he and his family lived when they followed him to London in 1806. Then, in 1809, the Stevensons are found living in Chelsea.[36]

NOTES

1 *ABO*, p. 211; Cockburn, *Memorials*, ed. Miller, p. 80. Couper, *Edinburgh Periodical Press*, II, p. 78, gives John Leyden and Alexander Murray as its first editors when Archibald Constable acquired it in September 1801.

2 LXIII, 1801, pp. 822-6.

3 Cp. Chadwick, 1910, p. 2; Gérin, pp. 4, 6; *DNB*, 'James Cleghorn'; Couper, *Edinburgh Periodical Press*, II, p. 262.

4 Julius Charles Hare, *Essays and Tales, by John Sterling, Collected and Edited, with a Memoir of his Life*, London, 1848, repr. Farnborough, 1971, II, pp. 54-5. The *GM* assignment in 1814 that Gérin indicates is improbable.

5 *Autobiography of Mrs. Fletcher*, pp. 82-3, 270-1, 333; George Ticknor, *Life, Letters and Journals*, ed. G. S. Hilliard, 1876, I, p. 279; John G. Peters, 'An unpublished letter from Maria Edgeworth to Eliza Fletcher', *ELN*, XXX, 1992-93, pp. 47-8; Uglow, pp. 64, 623.

6 Fifteen reviews are associated with Stevenson in *Wellesley Index*, I. In III, p. 985, they were reassessed; one (106) was removed and several other attributions made firmer. See also IV, p. 779. I must thank Wilma R. Slaight, archivist at Wellesley College, for her generous help.

7 *Wellesley Index*, IV, p. 779; Carlyle, *Reminiscences* (1887), ed. C. E. Norton, intro. Ian Campbell, London, 1972, pp. 313-14; Bell, *Sydney Smith*, pp. 35-6; J. A. V. Chapple, 'William Stevenson and Elizabeth Gaskell', *GSJ*, I, 1987, p. 2.

8 For Turner see Aarsleff, *Study of Language in England*, pp. 167-9.

9 *Memoir of Thomas Bewick Written by Himself*, ed. Iain Bain, London, New York, Toronto, 1975, p. 175n. For honorary membership see Parish, p. 121.

10 See Harold William Thompson, *A Scottish Man of Feeling: Some Account of Henry Mackenzie, Esq. of Edinburgh and of the Golden Age of Burns and Scott*, London and New York, 1931, pp. 295-6.

11 *Journey to the Western Islands of Scotland*, ed. Mary Lascelles, New Haven and London, 1971, pp. xv, 59, 94.

12 Eric Richards, *A History of the Highland Clearances: Agrarian Transformation and the Evictions 1746-1886*, I, London and Canberra, 1982, pp. 199-204, 252-4; II, *Emigration, Protest, Reasons*, London, etc., 1985, pp. 3-31, 371.

13 Aspinall, *Brougham*, pp. 5-6; Trowbridge H. Ford, *Henry Brougham and His World: A Biography*, Chichester, 1995, pp. 41, 60-1, 402-3; *The Creevey Papers: A Selection from the Correspondence and Diaries of the Late Thomas Creevey*, ed. Sir Herbert Maxwell, London, 1912, p. 30. With plate of Lauderdale opp. p. 172.

14 Clive, *Scotch Reviewers*, pp. 62, 84; Aspinall, *Brougham*, pp. 10, 35-7; Cockburn, *Memorials*, ed. Miller, pp. 200, 398.

15 *Farington Diary*, ed. Greig, II, 2nd edn, p. 256; BL: Add. MS 47564, ff. 132, 252; *Thirlestane Castle*, illustr. guidebook; Walter L. Spiers, *Catalogue of the Drawings and Designs of Robert and James Adam in Sir John Soane's Museum*, Cambridge and Teaneck, N.J., 1979, pp. 10, 30, 78.

16 See *DNB; Complete Peerage;* Reid, *Charles James Fox*, pp. 285, 339-40, 369, 411-12; CJF to L, 30 September 1805 (BL: Add. MS 47564, f. 247v); *Scott Letters*, I, p. 279.

17 Brown, *French Revolution*, p. 54; C. H. Philips, *The East India Company 1784-1834*, Manchester, 1940, pp. 145-9; *Farington Diary*, ed. Greig, III, 1924, pp. 246, 252; A. Aspinall, *The Later Correspondence of George III*, IV, Cambridge, 1968, pp. 445-6 (long n.); George, *English Political Caricature*, pp. 10, 13-14, 38-9, 92-3, 99.

18 'Fragments from the Travels of Theodore Elbert – London' [1828], in *Sterling*, ed. Hare, II, p. 4; William Stevenson, 'London', *Brewster's Edinburgh Encyclopaedia*, XIII. 1, 1819, p. 159; *Farington Diary*, ed. Greig, III, p. 205; Lewis, *Social History of the Navy*, pp. 298-315. Appointment in Treasury minutes, PRO: T 29/87, 20 May 1806, pp. 33-4 ; J. C. Sainty, *Treasury Officials 1660-1870*, London, 1972, p. 39 (the versions of Hopkins, pp. 15, 341-2, and Gérin, pp. 5, 37, 309, are misleading).

19 L to G, Queen Street, 10 July 1806 (BL: Add. MS 58941, ff. 106-7).

20 B. Frere to JA, 1 May [1811] (BL: Add MS 52194, f. 1); Cockburn, *Memorials*, ed. Miller, pp. 170-2; Bell, *Smith*, pp. 47-9; Ilchester, *Journal of Henry Fox*, p. 18 and *Home of the Hollands*, pp. 176-81, 271; *Holland House Diaries*, ed. Kriegel, p. xiv; *Glenarvon (1816) by Lady Caroline Lamb*, facs. ed. James L. Ruff, Delmar and New York, 1972, pp. vi, 64; *Macaulay Letters*, II, pp. 76-7; HH, *Recollections*, p. 233; HH to Maria Edgeworth, 16 June [1814] (DCLH); *Regency Portraits*, ed. Richard Walker, London, 1985, I, p. 258; II, no. 595.

21 Alan Bell, 'Cockburn's "Account of the Friday Club", in Bell, ed. *Cockburn*, pp. 184-9; Cockburn, *Memorials*, ed. Miller, p. 174; John M. Bourne, *Patronage and Society in Nineteenth-Century England*, London, 1986, pp. 128-9; *Wordsworth Letters*, II, p. 40 and n.

22 Sheppard, *Infernal Wen*, p. 22; Marilyn Butler, 'Hidden metropolis: London in sentimental and romantic writing', *London – World City 1800-1840*, ed. Celina Fox, London and New Haven, 1992, pp. 187-8.

23 *ABO*, pp. 211-12 (story not yet investigated); Seed, 'The role of Unitarianism', p. 33; De Quincey, *Lake Poets*, pp. 83-7; Gill, *Wordsworth*, p. 430n.; *Anecdotes of the Life of Richard Watson*, ed. Richard Watson [son], London, 1817, pp. 257-63; *Autobiographical Recollections*, ed. Bowring, p. 124. Watson, convinced of the injustice of the test and corporation acts, gave dissenters his support.

24 *Wellesley Index*, III, p. 985. This review displays expertise in Spanish, however. The *Index* also gives Stevenson a possible review of *Transactions from the Greek Anthology* in January 1807. If this too is his, he has unexpectedly developed an urbane and flowing style.

25 Ford, *Henry Brougham*, pp. 69-71; *DNB* (a lengthy article on JP); Rees, *Literary London*, p. 60. *OR* not seen.

26 *Wellesley Index*, III, p. 985; Aarsleff, *Study of Language in England*, p. 164; Brockett, *Glossary*, Newcastle upon Tyne, 1829, dedication and preface.

27 Lauderdale, *An Inquiry*, Edinburgh, 1809, pp. vi, viii.

28 Simon, *Two Nations*, pp. 87-90; *NSTC*: S3810 (*GM*, LXXXIV, 1814, is not relevant: cp. Gérin, p. 6.); *DNB*, 'Seth William Stevenson'; Ian A. Gordon, *John Galt: The Life of a Writer*, Edinburgh, 1972, p. 17.

29 *AR*, 1806, pp. 256-7; Ilchester, *Home of the Hollands*, p. 180. See W. B. Todd, 'A bibli-ographical account of the *Annual Register*, 1758-1825', *BSL*, 5th s., XVI, 1961, pp. 105, 119.

30 John Barrell, *The Idea of Landscape and the Sense of Place 1730-1840: an Approach to the Poetry of John Clare*, Cambridge, 1972, pp. 64, 68-9, 220-1; Mitchison, *Agricultural Sir John*, pp. 153, 205, and 'The old Board of Agriculture', *EHR*, LXXIV, 1959, pp. 50-1.

31 DCLH: HH to PH, London, 30 January [1806]; HH, *Recollections*, pp. 20-1; KUL: Wedgwood 2-270, PH to JW, Knutsford, 11 October 1806, 25 October 1806, 27 July 1807; Chadwick, 1913, pp. 5-6. Peter Holland had married a niece of Josiah Wedgwood (1730-1795). All Wedgwood letters are quoted courtesy of the Trustees of The Wedgwood Museum, Barlaston, Staffs. I am grateful to KUL's Curator, Martin Phillips, and Helen Burton for their help.

32 *NSTC:* K447-8; Fuller, *History*, pp. 10, 12, 27-9. See below, p. 267.

33 BL: Add. MS 58943, ff. 25-6, L to G, 19 July [1811]. There may well be other passing references to Stevenson in this extensive correspondence.

34 *NSTC:* S3813-15 (the 1813 reprint of *Surrey* is not listed; copies in NLS and BL).

35 *DNB et al.* But see Robert Watt, *Bibliotheca Britannica*, Edinburgh, 1825, in which William Stephenson is given *A System* and *Surrey*, whilst in a later entry W. Stevenson is given the *Remarks* of 1796 and *Surrey*. *A System of Land Surveying* is given a separate entry in *NSTC:* S3722, under William Stephenson, Land Surveyor; I have not seen a copy.

36 Sainty, *Treasury Officials*, p. 39; Sarah A. Tooley, 'The centenary of Mrs. Gaskell', *CM*, n. s. XXIX, 1910, p. 315, and *The Graphic* (London), 1 October 1910, Supplement with illustrs. See also C. K. Shorter, *The Sphere*, 10 September 1910, for the part played by Mrs Chadwick in discovering the house.

5

Mother and 'More than mother'

WILLIAM AND ELIZABETH Stevenson's daughter was born at 'Bell vue' in Chelsea on 29 September 1810 when her mother, herself born on 19 April 1771, was thirty-nine years of age. They recorded their daughter's name as Elizabeth Cleghorn Stevenson some six weeks later at Dr Williams's Library in London, where a register of births had been maintained ever since 1743 for nonconformists living anywhere in this country or even abroad. This non-parochial register entry, now in the public record office, shows that Anthony Todd Thomson of 92 Sloane Street, surgeon (a general practitioner who had qualified at the Royal College of Surgeons), and a midwife, Ann Brewer, were present at the birth.[1] Although this was some twelve years after the birth of John Stevenson, no other children of William and Elizabeth Stevenson are recorded, certainly not the six that are supposed to make Elizabeth the eighth child; nor is John's name in the register for that matter. Yet multiple entries of a family, which could date back as far as twenty years, were common. A London couple with the same surname, George and Alice Stevenson, regis-tered seven children born between 1790 and 1809 on 1 February 1811, for example, and Swinton Colthurst Holland took care on 3 October 1811 to register the births of his children abroad during the previous decade, Edward and Caroline in Trieste and Charlotte and Louisa in Malta.[2]

Elizabeth Cleghorn Stevenson is usually said to have been named after her mother and James Cleghorn of Duns, a Scottish farmer and author who was associated with William Stevenson in literary enterprises in the early decades of the century. No more evidence than this has ever been adduced. Meta Gaskell told Charles Eliot Norton that her mother was called after the baby of a widowed Mrs Cleghorn who had been very good to Mrs Stevenson and whose only daughter had died just as Elizabeth was born. This is quite possible, though it is suspiciously well shaped as an anecdote – one daughter's ending was another's beginning: a perfect circle. Ward was told by the Gaskell daugh-ters that Mrs Cleghorn was 'a kind Edinburgh lady friend of her parents', and some of this information seems to have reached Flora Masson, who wrote in 1910 that a Mrs Cleghorn (mother or wife of James Cleghorn) had been kind to Elizabeth's parents in Saughton and in Edinburgh.[3] The reference might be to James Cleghorn's mother, as he remained a bachelor, but the wife of a friend of Robert Burns, Robert Cleghorn of Saughton near Edinburgh, has stronger claims. This was Beatrix, a widow (née Wight) of James Allen; she married Robert Cleghorn at Corstorphine about 1783. A daughter Elizabeth was born to them in 1784 and a son James a few years later. Both of these, it is stated, died without issue, but no more has yet been discovered.[4]

The first of a number of letters to Robert from Burns is addressed 'To Mr. Cleghorn, farmer. God bless the trade!' It was probably sent in 1787, the year after Burns had first come to Edinburgh to meet with a remarkable reception from the 'noblesse and literati' of the city. The Edinburgh edition of his *Poems, Chiefly in the Scottish Dialect* of that year contains a massive list of subscribers, printed in a small typeface. Robert Cleghorn of Saughton Mills appears amongst the many hundreds of names, which include the Earl of Lauderdale at the head of the L's. On 29 August 1790 Burns ended a letter with unctuous compliments 'to Mrs Cleghorn, the Miss Cleghorns, & Miss Cleghorn of Saughton Mills. – I should like much to see the little Angel.' But beneath this sentimental surface were male confidences that Mrs Robert Cleghorn was not allowed to glimpse. 'I believe the Good Women in general take a freedom to break up or peep into their husbands' letters', Burns wrote cautiously to his 'dear Friend' some time in 1791, at a time when he was being pressed to support two unofficial babies who had the fortune or misfortune to make him a father, 'contrary to the laws of our most excellent constitution, in our holy Presbyterian heirarchy.'[5]

There were other reasons for secrecy. Both men belonged to an Edinburgh group that used to meet in Dawney Douglas's tavern in Edinburgh's narrow Anchor Close and satirically named themselves the 'Crochallan Fencibles'. It had been founded by the man Burns called 'old sinfull Smellie', actually the the learned printer William Smellie, who, beginning in 1768, had edited and written much of the first, three-volume edition of the *Encyclopaedia Britannica*. Its 'Colonel' was William Dunbar, who presided over a catholic mixture of convivial spirits, including Peter Hill the bookseller, the splendidly eccentric Lord Monboddo, William Nicol, a harsh, proud, irascible classical master in the High School, the genial Dean of the law faculty, Henry Erskine, and others to whom Burns carelessly supplied, often through Cleghorn, versions of old 'Cloaciniad' songs – bawdy ballads about twa witty wives, braw, bonie, fodgel hizzies frae the English-side and the like. These only appeared in privately published editions of *The Merry Muses of Caledonia: A Collection of Favourite Scots Songs, Ancient and Modern; Selected for the Use of the Crochallan Fencibles* (1799), and were not openly published until this fortunate half-century.[6]

Byron, however, was shown 'a quantity' of his 'unpublished, and never-to-be-published, Letters' by John Allen of Holland House, who of all people, it turns out, was very probably the stepson of Robert Cleghorn. 'What an antithetical mind!' Byron then famously exclaimed, for Burns's letters to his folk-singing friend contained lyrical as well as bawdy verses – 'tenderness, roughness – delicacy, coarseness – sentiment, sensuality – soaring and grovelling, dirt and deity – all mixed up in that one compound of inspired clay!'[7]

A letter Robert Cleghorn wrote about 'The Chevalier's Lament' shows what a close and congenial a companion he must have been, much more than an acquaintance who could give Burns advice upon farming. Burns sent him some words he had composed when Robert's favourite tune, 'Captain Okean', came into his head, asking him to see if they fitted the music. Cleghorn replied that the words 'fit the tune to a hair', and he suggested the addition of a verse of two more in the Jacobite style, supposed to be sung by Prince Charles after the battle of Culloden. 'Tenducci personates the lovely Mary Stewart in the song *Queen Mary's Lamentation'*, he urges. 'Why may not I sing in the person of her great-great-great grandson?' Robert was one of the few who remained loyal to the poet in his last decline and his name appears in the list of the subscribers to the fund raised after Burns's death in July 1796 for his widow and children. Cleghorn himself was probably forced to give up farming not long afterwards. The *Edinburgh Evening Courant* advertisement of 28 January 1797 stated that the lands of the two farms would be shown 'on applying to the house at Saughton Mills; and proposals for the farms, in writing, may be addressed to Mrs Cleghorn at Saughton Mills, or to Mr Inglis, W.S. [Writer to the Signet].' Robert Cleghorn is a less dignified source than James Cleghorn for Elizabeth's middle name, but his lively, outgoing, pertinacious nature is beyond dispute.[8]

The road running along the north bank of the Thames from central London to Chelsea passes by the parish church of St Luke, known as Chelsea Old Church after the erection in 1824 of a splendid new church in the Gothic style nearer the King's Road.[9] A little further along, the road used to meet the end of a wooden bridge across the Thames from Battersea, which had been erected at the expense of fifteen proprietors subscribing £1500 each, under the supervision of another Henry Holland in 1771-72. (This Henry Holland was the architect responsible for the development of the Hans Town estate in Chelsea.) On the up-stream side of the bridge were stairs leading down to the water, at which boats could be hired, and across the road was situated a handsome building with splendidly decorative doorway, windows and interior features.

Belle Vue House, built by 1771, is reputed to have been designed by Robert Adam, and has a centre portion with imposing bay windows, which stretch the full, three-storey height of the building at back and front, and two lesser wings. For all its size, it is not a detached dwelling, being contiguous with a Lodge on the city side, another handsome building. A weeping willow had been planted just across the road on the river bank in 1776; in the following year two plain, tall and narrow-fronted houses were attached to the other side of the main house. By midsummer 1809 William Stevenson's family had taken up residence in the inner house of these two.[10] In the early nineteenth century Belle Vue House contained a fine collection of paintings belonging to a fellow of the Royal Society, Charles Hatchett. He had been made an honorary member of the Newcastle Literary and Philosophical Society in 1801, just before Stevenson in 1804, and might have been involved in the Stevensons' move to Chelsea. Later he followed Dr Charles Burney as the treasurer of the Literary Club.[11]

The whole complex of houses, then part of Lindsey Row, looked out over the garden opposite and through the tree that partly veiled the old wooden bridge. This great willow was still shown and named on F. P. Thompson's fine 1836 map of Chelsea. The bridge, the moving water and river traffic of Chelsea Reach composed a scene picturesque enough to attract a succession of major artists – Girtin, de Wint, Turner and many more. Steam boats took pleasure parties up the Thames to view the banks above Battersea bridge, which were 'uncommonly rich and beautiful', William Stevenson himself wrote for Brewster's *Edinburgh Encyclopaedia*, 'adorned with a great many tasteful seats'. Where the famous willow once stood is now the end of the Victoria embankment; the bridge has long since been replaced.

The house in Lindsey Row, now part of Cheyne Walk, still survives. It is here, if family legend can be trusted, that Elizabeth proved to be a 'remarkably strong' child, who 'could walk almost unaided at ten months old'. But by midsummer 1811 rate books show that the family had moved round the corner to 3 Beaufort Row, a terrace on the west side of the road running from Battersea bridge and Belle Vue Lodge up to the King's Road.[12] Beaufort Row had also been built in the 1770s; its houses were rated at £24 each. A later picture by W. W. Burgess of 'Old Lindsey Row, Chelsea' is often reproduced; it shows the houses and the road in front, on which can be seen not only a horse and cart but a wherry being carried to the water-stairs, with a little grove of masts higher up at Lindsey wharf. Another picture Mrs Chadwick discovered, entitled 'Corner of Old Lindsey Row, Chelsea', is a better illustration in one sense, in that it shows the first few houses in Beaufort Row as well. These, long since torn down, would have been more familiar to Elizabeth than the house in which she had been born.[13]

The Stevensons' home was by no means grand, but it was in one of the most pleasant residential parts of London. The whole area had long before been the site of a famous mansion, Sir Thomas More's home for fourteen years, his refuge from London and the court. It later belonged to the duke of Beaufort, but was ruthlessly demolished by Sir Hans Sloane in the first part of the eighteenth century. Yet if Beaufort House with its lodges, forecourts, orchards and gardens had been destroyed and built over, just to the west there still survived great houses like Ashburnham and Cremorne, together with their gardens and extensive grounds. Cremorne later became a famous pleasure garden for London. In and around the whole of Chelsea were fields, popular nurseries and market gardens, and at its centre by the river was the historical parish church, crowded with sepulchral monuments and containing a More chapel with stone capitals said to have been designed by Holbein.[14]

Houses in Beaufort Row, none of them far from the Thames, had relatively open views in front – even in 1836 Thompson's map shows there were hardly any buildings across the road on the London side. They looked across vacant ground towards the splendid rectory and its elaborate gardens. William Stevenson lived in Beaufort Row until his death in 1829, neighbour at various times of John Galt the novelist and Ralph Wedgwood, for the famous firm had a Chelsea branch. At 4 Cheyne Walk lived a rich philanthropist, James Neild, who had been born in Knutsford. After great success as a London jeweller, he retired to Chelsea, where he devoted himself to the cause of prisoners and debtors until his death in 1814. As a subscriber to the second edition of Thomas Faulkner's *An Historical and Topographical Description of Chelsea and Its Environs,* published in 1829, Stevenson was due to receive a book that described famous neighbours like this. Chelsea was a 'village of palaces' gradually turning into a suburb, proudly conscious of itself and its inhabitants, home over the years to artists like John Varley the watercolourist and the authors Carlyle and Leigh Hunt.[15]

In the latter part of the year 1811, when Elizabeth was about a year old, Mrs Stevenson's widowed sister, Mrs Hannah Lumb, born on 29 July 1767 and therefore in her early forties, was visiting the capital. Family tradition transmits a story that she had married a wealthy man, Samuel Lumb of Wakefield, a prosperous wool town in the West Riding of Yorkshire, and then run away from him because she discovered that he was mad. Also, even more dramatically, that their only daughter Marianne (her own spelling) was a cripple, because as a baby she had injured herself by jumping from her nurse's arms in joy at seeing her mother. As Ward was told,

> Mrs Lumb only found out after her marriage that *he was out of his* wits. She then ran away from him – he lived at Wakefield in Yorks. One child Marianne of Mrs Lumb had jumped out of window seeing her mother come up – and become a cripple – It was to amuse and please this child that the baby E. S. was sent for to Knutsford.
> She looked upon Mrs Lumb as her mother.[16]

Mrs Lumb's importance as the aunt who brought Elizabeth up in Knutsford, her 'more than mother' as she called her in later years, can hardly be overestimated. Very little indeed, however, has been known about her marriage and early life. How was it that she married a man from a distant town? Who was he, and what kind of life awaited her over the Pennines? How long did she live with Samuel Lumb? What happened after she left Wakefield? Did wife and daughter maintain any kind of connection with him or his family? When Mrs Lumb came back to Sandlebridge and Knutsford, what kind of society did she move in and who were her friends? Was she well off, or dependent upon her parents once more?

Back in the eighteenth century Mrs Lumb's aunt Mary Holland, daughter of John Holland of Dam Head House, Mobberley, had married William Turner, son of a dissenting minister at Knutsford. William himself became minister of Knutsford's little associated chapel of Allostock for a time. His health failing, he settled in Congleton, where he kept a school and became acquainted with Priestley, and in 1761 was appointed to the beautiful Georgian presbyterian chapel in Westgate, Wakefield, built some ten years before at a cost of over £1000. Here he served for over thirty years, preaching from a seventeenth-century oak pulpit rescued from the older chapel, beneath the massive beams of Baltic pine spanning the full width of the building. It was a congregation with a proud history, which became Unitarian under Turner.[17]

Some of his basic values appear in the early pages of a sermon he published at Wakefield in 1785, *A Caution Against Sinful Compliances in a Discourse Addressed to the Younger Part of the Congregation of Protestant Dissenters*: 'Every intelligent and virtuous person ... Every sensible Friend to his country ... Every prudent and careful parent ... Every thoughtful and well-disposed aged person ... '. Such exemplary common sense, however, is a little deceptive.[18] Like many English Presbyterians, William had been at first an Arian, but some years after settling at Wakefield he threw in his lot with the Socinians and became a great friend of their leader, Joseph Priestley, minister at nearby Leeds for six years. Like Priestley and Philip Holland of Bolton, Turner was a radical in politics. All three had condemned the British government's actions at the time of the American war of independence. But it was not a popular stance: Turner confessed to Priestley in 1790 that his chapel's congregation was thin – like the chapels at Halifax and Bradford 'reduced almost to nothing, while the Methodists, &c., increase wonderfully'. Unpopular politics and a belief that Unitarians lacked truly religious fervour was a combination that also affected Unitarians in Knutsford and Cheshire in the later eighteenth century.

He was undoubtedly a learned and very sociable man. He was a friend of 'that eminent confessor for conscience sake', Theophilus Lindsey, who is regarded as a founding father of modern British Unitarianism. Turner's grandson was also able to quote from a poem John Aikin's daughter, Mrs Barbauld, wrote for his father in the leaves of an ivory pocket book after a visit to Wakefield:

> Accept, my dear, this toy, and let me say,
> The leaves an emblem of your mind display -
> Your youthful mind, uncoloured, fair, and white,
> Like crystal leaves, transparent to the sight ...

After this charming beginning, the seven-year-old William is told that should heaven bless him with every science and all the virtues,

'Tis no original, the world can tell,
And all your praise is but – *to copy well.*

In his *Lives of Eminent Unitarians* William Turner III quoted letters his grandfather had written to his two sons when they were young; they are very nicely
targeted at his namesake William, later the long-standing Unitarian minister at
Newcastle, and John, who turned to commerce and became a merchant at
Bolton near Manchester. Their mother had died when they were in their teens,
in October 1784.

For all his radical values, William of Wakefield was a bit like Polonius. When
his son went to study for the ministry at Warrington Academy in the late
1770s, he was advised to 'be polite and respectful to everybody, but intimate
only with a few'; this was 'the wisest plan for a youth of inferior rank and
fortune'. A copy has survived of a letter Turner of Wakefield wrote to his infant
grandchild, Mary Turner of Newcastle, born in 1786, in which he warned her
to copy her mother's pronunciation rather than that of 'servants or common
people', so that she could converse with southerners without singularity.
'Learn everything amiable from thy friends at Newcastle', he advised, 'but
avoid the *burr.* Of all the Alphabet prononounce the r, & the s, softly, the one
is the dog's letter, the other the goose's'. John Scott, son of a merchant and
coal-fitter in Newcastle, who became Chief Justice of the court of Common
Pleas and an Earl (Lord Eldon), is said to have 'had the "burr" in perfection'.
It is often today one of our more musical dialects.[19]

Turner's congregation was small, but it was composed, he told Belsham
with a touch of pride – it would have upset George Wiche – 'for a considerable
part, of persons of fortune and genteel life'. When his *Sermons on Various
Subjects* were published at London in 1793, the list of twenty-six sponsors
included many of Wakefield's most substantial citizens: H. and S. Lumb, John
Lumb, Pemberton Milnes, James Milnes (senior and junior), Esther Milnes,
Thomas Johnstone and W. I. Kendall. Considering the intricate family, social
and business networks that existed across the north of England in particular,
his marriage might not have been the first such connection between Knutsford
and Wakefield. It would have been in every way characteristic of Unitarian
congregations of the time, which, with the exception of a few in London, were
middle-class and often very successful in the world – but isolated to some
degree by their religious beliefs and dependent upon each other. On her marriage
in 1789 Mrs Lumb joined a flourishing, wealthy and select social group.

Wakefield was not large, but it was only surpassed by Leeds as a cloth-
exporting centre and far more than a simple northern working place. John
Aikin wrote in 1795 that it was 'considered as one of the handsomest and most
opulent' of the clothing towns. It was like a superior Knutsford. Many of its
rich citizens kept fine houses in the town itself rather than in the surrounding
countryside. There was a 'season' in September for gentry from far and near,

during which splendidly dressed ladies with hair well powdered were carried about in sedan chairs, the chairman in front bearing a lighted lantern in the evenings. Races were held until the 1790s. It had its own pleasure-garden, assemblies (a Mistress Hannah Lumb was Queen in 1759) and a Theatre Royal in Westgate, where 'a stranger, even from London, would be astonished at beholding the number of Gentlemen's elegant carriages attending that Theatre, to convey their wealthy and spirited owners'.[20]

The Unitarian merchants of the Milnes family, from whom a friend of Elizabeth Gaskell (the incredible Richard Monckton Milnes) was descended, were typical. Generations of rich trading with Russia – they had a contract to clothe the whole Russian army – allowed them to operate on a county and national level, though they did not fail to establish their three-storey town houses on the broad Westgate near the chapel. Pemberton House, built for Pemberton Milnes, still stands, a listed building. Knutsford had nothing to equal this handsome town street and its various mansions. An exceptionally fine one was built by John Milnes in 1750 and finished by his son, another John (1751-1810). When William Turner of Newcastle visited it in 1797 he saw a number of paintings by Joseph Wright of Derby, the most impressive being the eruption of Vesuvius, works at Rome, the destruction of the Spanish floating batteries at Gibraltar in 1782 (an enormous canvas praised by Erasmus Darwin), Dr Beattie's Edwin, Sterne's Captive and Count Ugolino – a collection that encompassed literary and prison scenes, landscapes and celebrations of British power.[21] The son was known as 'Jack Milnes the Democrat'. He had visited France after the Revolution and, with a lady called Catherine Carr, produced a boy, born in Paris in 1792 and given the remarkable names of Alfred Mirabeau Washington Milnes. Later on, Jack did the decent thing and married Miss Carr, and their son sensibly disguised himself as Alfred Shore Milnes.

Some of the Milneses were strong radicals, others far more prudent. By 1779 James Milnes was rich enough to employ the York architect John Carr to design Thornes House on the edge of Wakefield. Its symmetrical facade was over two hundred feet in width and the surrounding estate covered more than a hundred acres. The mansion stood above the river Calder with views over open countryside. Its remarkable hot-houses provided rare fruits when his son James gave a dinner for two hundred people in London to celebrate George III's birthday in 1801. James Milnes junior was childless, and Thornes House eventually came to Benjamin Gaskell, M.P., father of James Milnes Gaskell. Families like this ran the town.[22]

The Lumbs, too, were rich and prominent citizens of Wakefield, though not as splendid as the Milneses. The senior branch lived at Silcoates House or Hall, built about 1748 for John Lumb on an estate near Alverthorpe church with bricks made on Pemberton Milnes's estate in the Ossett Road. (It became the residence of the headmaster of Silcoates school, on the edge of Wakefield.) By his wife Sarah Milnes of Wakefield John Lumb had two sons; the older, also called John, inherited Silcoates House when his father died in 1768.[23]

Richard Lumb of Wakefield and Ackton or Aikton Hall, Featherstone, was the younger son. His wife Sarah had died back in 1763, but she was survived by two sons and five daughters. The second boy, Samuel, was described as a woolstapler on 7 April 1783, when he became a freemason in Wakefield at the age of twenty-one.[24] He was independently rich as an heir of his uncle Robert, who died unmarried in the summer of 1789 leaving property in trust for his sisters and nephew Samuel. Samuel must by this time have met Hannah Holland, for a formal marriage settlement was drawn up late in August. She is described at this date as the daughter of a grazier of Marthall cum Little Warford, Cheshire, rather than gentleman, as he had been in an earlier document. Men who fattened cattle for market were not always regarded as gentlefolk, but could be very wealthy. Hannah's agreement was for a fairly considerable sum, £2000, in consideration of 'the Fortune which the said Samuel Lumb will receive or become intitled to with the said Hannah Holland' under the will of her grandfather, Peter Swinton of Nether Knutsford, deceased.[25]

The actual marriage was not long delayed. On 6 October 1789 Samuel came over from Wakefield to apply for a marriage licence and together with Peter Holland, surgeon of Knutsford and Hannah's older brother, entered into a bond for one thousand pounds before the surrogate of the Chester diocese. He married Hannah on the following day in her own parish of Over Peover, in the chapel where her sister Elizabeth would marry William Stevenson some eight years later. The marriage was witnessed by her father Samuel Holland and William Turner.[26] In December Samuel Lumb made a will, the drafts of which in the Goodchild Loan Collection have a letter attached stating that if there were no children of his marriage, he wished a particular sum of £300 to be shared amongst Hannah's brothers and sisters, who are all named. It forged yet another link between the Lumbs of Wakefield and the Hollands of Sandlebridge.

This marriage between Hannah Holland and Samuel Lumb, so eminently satisfactory from a family, religious and financial point of view, did not last for very long. The consequences and sequence of events that can at last be described in some detail are occasionally problematic and never easy to interpret in their human dimensions. By their very nature formal documents cannot record what is known and left unsaid, let alone what is thought and felt but deliberately suppressed.

There is no doubt, however, that poor Samuel Lumb was of unsound mind. Many of the early records of the Bootham asylum at York have been destroyed, but the admissions registers survive from the time when it opened in 1777. Patient number 311 was Samuel Lumb of Wakefield, 'melancholy', admitted on 19 November 1785 – nearly four years before his marriage in October 1789. The petitioner and surety was his father, Richard. (Certification was waived in the 1780s for 'opulent patients'.) It is stated in the registers that

Samuel was discharged cured, but no date is given for this. In addition, Samuel's older brother John was admitted on 26 May 1789 – just a few months before Samuel's marriage – and was not released for some time. John is described as 'flighty', the commonest category, the third and rarest being most serious – 'wild and flighty'. At least Samuel and John were rich. They were not likely to have suffered from the drastic physical methods so often used upon the unfortunate poor who found themselves immured.[27]

The earliest British biographical account of any substance, by Flora Masson, states that Mrs Lumb discovered her husband was insane and fled from him only a few months after her marriage and before the birth of their child. An only child of the marriage between Samuel and Hannah Lumb, Marianne, was in fact born a year later at Sandlebridge on 17 October 1790 – but baptised by William Turner in the chapel at Wakefield on 21 May 1791.[28] Had Hannah returned to live with her husband in Wakefield despite going home to her parents, as many do, for the birth of her first child? It is inconceivable that William Turner, Hannah's uncle by marriage and minister to the Lumb family, did not know everything about Samuel's mental history, and it seems highly unlikely that it would have been concealed from Hannah and her parents, considering that either he (or just posssibly his son William) was a witness to her marriage at Over Peover in 1789. However, the Wakefield minister was now growing old and weak. His wife had died five years before, and in 1790 his increasing infirmity necessitated the assistance of a former student of Daventry academy recommended by Belsham, Thomas Johnstone, who took over completely at Westgate chapel in July 1792. It was a time of 'rapid decline' for Turner before his death at the age of almost eighty in 1794. He could have misjudged the situation.[29]

Uncle Robert Lumb's will of July 1789 contains express permission for Samuel to leave the family partnership as long as John Lumb of Silcoates and his son Thomas could use and keep in repair the shops, warehouses and premises in Wakefield at a clear yearly rent of fifty pounds. Samuel was therefore specifically permitted to 'decline woolstapling jointly' in the very year of his marriage. He did precisely that. In November 1790, shortly after the birth of his daughter but before her baptism, he sold out his share in the family business.[30] One might speculate that Hannah had brought her child back to Wakefield on the condition that Samuel retired from woolstapling and led the quiet life he could well afford and was positively indicated by his mental history. And if Marianne was crippled as a baby, although not a particle of supporting evidence has yet been found for this assertion, both parents must have felt a considerable degree of stress on this account alone.

Moreover, Samuel's older brother John was discharged from Bootham on 15 March 1791, 'taken away by his friends'. He was not recorded as discharged cured, however, and two other brief, ambiguous entries in the Bootham admissions book might be relevant: a Mr Lumb of Wakefield was admitted on 15 April 1792 and discharged cured on 5 October 1793; a Mr

Lumb, 'flighty', was admitted 21 May 1794 and discharged cured on 25 June 1794, little more than a month later. The brevity of these entries suggests that a patient or patients well known to the asylum are meant. 'Flighty' in the second entry sounds more like John than his 'melancholy' brother, but it is possible that the first entry refers to Samuel and shorter periods of depression.[31] These two unhappy young men were Richard Lumb's only sons, which is why he came to rely upon William Kershaw, who had married his daughter Hannah in August 1787 and was later to be a trustee of his will. Kershaw was a merchant of Halifax, recorded in trade directories of the early nineteenth century at Warley House and at Union Street, a trustee of Northgate-end presbyterian chapel there between 1782 and 1822.[32]

There is better external evidence about the next stage of Samuel's unfortunate life, which sometimes seems like a cross between a Wilkie Collins novel and a play by Ibsen. By the summer of 1795 he was not living with Hannah. He was in Leicester under medical care. His money and property had been transferred by a deed of conveyance in trust to his father Richard Lumb and his cousin Thomas Lumb. A sum of £120 a year (produced from a capital of £2000) was settled on Mrs Lumb, to be paid quarterly from 10 July 1795 'for her seperate maintenance and support so long as she shall remain and live seperate and apart from him'. It would be increased to £150 a year when the residue of her fortune, £700, was received. The document also states that the trustees could revoke the deed if they thought it expedient or necessary, taking advice from any physician 'or other skilful person' they might think 'proper to consult in this behalf' – and at this point in the great parchment document of the original deed there is a curious and intriguing insertion over a caret mark: '(Doctor Hunter of York excepted)'.[33]

The name recalls one of the great scandals of the age.[34] Alexander Hunter was the first and sole physician of the Bootham lunatic asylum at York when after five years of raising subscriptions it opened in 1777, situated on low-lying, ill-drained land but housed in an elegant, three-storey building surmounted by a colonnaded turret, a building designed by that distinguished local architect, John Carr. Bootham asylum also had a illustrious board of governors, headed by the Archbishop of York. It was all too symbolic. Originally intended for paupers, from the county as well as the city, there were soon disputes about 'patients in affluent circumstances', well able to pay fees and said to be more profitable to the sole physician than the institution. Hunter believed that patients 'of middling rank and in low circumstances' should have priority over 'the lowest and meanest of the poor'. He also opened his own private madhouse at Acomb near York in 1793, 'for persons of condition only', a source of considerable extra profit.

His publications show a dilettante interest in cookery. 'Professional men have an undoubted right to their hours of relaxation', he proclaimed in his *Culinary Famulatrix, or Receipts in Modern Cookery with a Medical Commentary*, 'for as Aesop observes, "If the bow be kept continually bent, it will in time lose its elasticity".' He was a medical graduate of Edinburgh University, but his professional publications were *Essays on the Nature and Virtues of the Buxton Waters* (1765) and *The Waters of Harrogate* (1806) rather than anything to do with insanity. Were it not so serious a matter for his disturbed patients, he might have played a part in the novel Jane Austen left unfinished in 1817, *Sanditon*, with its ridicule of the cult of the spa and fashionable hypochondria – 'She can only speak in a whisper and fainted away twice this morning on poor Arthur's trying to suppress a cough.'[35]

Hunter's treatment methods for the mentally ill were, as far as can be ascertained, simple and traditional: 'secret insane powders, green and grey' – powerful emetics and purges. Cruel methods of restraint and punishment were commonplace, especially for paupers. Existing acts of parliament and even the concern aroused by the madness of George III (which first became generally known in 1788 and which could hardly be attributed to divine punishment of sin) were ineffectual in preventing tough treatment of the insane. The King himself was sometimes placed under physical restraint, in a strait jacket or retaining chair. The very brevity of a Mr Lumb's stay at Bootham in 1794 and the discriminatory insertion in the deed of 1795 could be significant. But whatever the Lumb family might have discovered, Dr Hunter and his successor managed to prevent close enquiries right up until 1813, when Godfrey Higgins, a justice of the peace, made what investigations he could and published a damning statement in the *York Herald*. It then took two more years to put things right.

Although the full truth about this suspect asylum was not revealed until 1815, the death of a young woman there in 1790 had impelled the Quakers of York, rallied by a tea and coffee merchant, William Tuke, to establish an establishment that became famous, called The Retreat. Neither hospital nor asylum, it was one of the earliest institutions to provide humane conditions and treat its inmates as rational beings. This new moral and psychological management of the mentally ill, European in scope, has been called a French revolution in psychiatry. It was contemporary with but in the next few decades more successful than William Stevenson's propaganda designed to strike off the mind-forged manacles of classical education in the academies.[36]

In the next century Elizabeth Gaskell's favourite brother-in-law, Samuel Gaskell, became noted at the Manchester Royal Infirmary and Lunatic Asylum for 'his gentle and enlightened views as to the degree of restraint which is requisite even for the worst cases of Lunacy'. In 1840 he was elected medical superintendent at Lancaster, one of England's largest asylums, and was not only in the forefront of the 'non-restraint movement' with John Conolly but ready to try all kinds of positive ideas. The Earl of Shaftesbury on a visit to Gaskell's asylum thought one of them 'a stroke of inspiration'. He found a number of women each with a child in her arms: 'Here are several women wanting recuperation, and there are several children wanting care', Gaskell explained. Shaftesbury was so impressed that he nominated him for the next vacancy as a national Commissioner in Lunacy, in 1849 the first that had ever been taken from the ranks of practical men.[37]

If the Lumbs of Wakefield subscribed to old-fashioned values, Samuel's difficulties with his wife and child, and perhaps his conduct towards them, might have seemed wrong and indefensible. But in advanced circles the principles inspiring The Retreat were associated with a strong hope that the deranged could be cured and returned to normal life. The possibility of Samuel's recovery is certainly envisaged in the 1795 deed; we also find that Richard and Thomas Lumb advanced sums amounting to £1350 from the trust monies 'over & above what the nett annual am[oun]t or Income'.[38] The trusts established by the deed were completely released in 1801. By then Samuel was living at Birstall near Leicester. But not with his wife and child. An associated set of documents make it clear that he and his wife had been living apart 'for some years last past' – it is no more precise, unfortunately – '& have mutually agreed to continue to do so', Hannah receiving her annuity regularly. The trustees were in these circumstances prepared to reconvey his money and property to Samuel, 'by & with the Advice & Cou[n]sel of George Peake of Leicester aforesaid Surgeon and Apothecary and other skilful persons'.[39]

On 19 November 1804 Samuel was sane enough to make a new and valid will. This is a startling document. It provided that after payment of debts his real estate in Birstall and elsewhere, together with his personal property of under £200, was to go to his 'Housekeeper' Esther Scrimsher if she was still living with him at the time of his death. If not, it was all to be divided equally between their four surviving 'Children or reputed Children by the said Esther Scrimsher, Sophia Lumb Scrimsher, Harriet Lumb, Selina Lumb and Samuel Lumb'. As for the sum of £2000 that provided Hannah Lumb's income, it was on the deaths of Samuel and Hannah Lumb to be the inheritance of Esther Scrimsher and her children on similar conditions. George Peake surgeon and John Edward Carter gentleman of Scraptoft in the county of Leicester were appointed trustees and guardians of the four children.[40]

They had been baptised at Birstall between September 1796 and June 1804, according to a note the vicar of Birstall church sent to Mr Thomas Lumb at Wakefield. Samuel had not only separated from his wife some time in the 1790s but begun a second family not too long after July 1795, the date when his money and property were removed from his control. His first child was a short-lived infant called Samuel, buried at Birstall on 11 February 1798.[41] Moreover, in a new place and with Mrs Scrimsher's help Samuel seems to have been able by 1801 to convince Dr Peake, and other skilful persons, that he had recovered and could manage his own affairs – for the few more years that were left to him. Samuel Lumb was totally committed to this new family. Whatever might have been the original causes of the separation from his wife and daughter, there was no reconciliation. Mrs Lumb and Marianne were definitely displaced.

His father Richard Lumb made his own will on 4 December 1804. He left

Samuel one shilling, his 'late Uncle having sufficiently provided for him'. To
be cut off with a shilling, as the saying goes, was in these circumstances quite
usual and probably not intended to be a comment on Samuel's behaviour. The
'older brother John was also cut off with a shilling, though the reason in this
instance was less common. Just over ten thousand pounds were left in trust for
John, because he was 'not at present in the capacity of using and disposing his
property with prudence and discretion'. Sadder still, a codicil of 1806 left six
thousand pounds in trust for their sister Ann, 'at present supposed to be not
of sound mind and understanding'. In this instance, if not in John's, the terms
of Richard Lumb's will envisaged at least the possibility of her recovery.
Fortunately, she did so.[42]

Samuel Lumb died only a few months after he had made his will. The unfortunate man was buried at Birstall on 29 March 1805, according to the
Reverend G. Oliver's letter to Thomas Lumb. A little later Mrs Skrimsher (or
Skrimshaw) was forced by circumstances to let the snug Birstall property, with
its house, yard, garden, orchard, plantation, fish ponds, outbuildings and
stables (less a small cottage and cowshed), for £25 a year. Soon after, Richard
Lumb died at the respectable age of eighty, on 24 January 1807, and was
buried where so many of his family and the two wives who had died before him
lay, in an east-side vault of Westgate chapel.[43]

The children of Samuel's second family were by no means abandoned. They
were looked after by their guardian George Peake, under the general protection
of William Kershaw and Samuel's ummarried sisters, Sarah, Anne and Elizabeth
Lumb. Young Samuel was sent to J. Watson's school at Cotherstone near Barnard
Castle (a Mr Briggs was paid £2 18s 6d for conveying him there by coach),
where he stayed for several years at about five guineas a quarter and gained
good reports. The two older daughters were placed with a milliner at York, and
the youngest in a good situation locally. They all had expectations under
Samuel Lumb's will, but, it was rightly said in 1816, his widow (Mrs Hannah
Lumb) was 'very well & likely to live for many years'. Mrs Scrimsher, by now
Mrs Burton, fell dangerously ill in May of that same year. 'From the nature of
her connection with the late Mr S. Lumb', William Kershaw wrote stiffly to his
informant, 'she cannot possibly have any claim or really expect any assistance
from his friends'. But he had the grace to add that they might help financially
if Dr George Peake would confirm her state. His next letter followed swiftly,
for he had heard of her decease soon afterwards. He was 'glad to learn she was
such a penitent before her death'. He sent £5 towards the funeral expenses.[44]

Not long afterwards, in June 1818, her son died at Cotherstone, despite a
letter written in a flourishing hand from his master that reported him to be
considerably better at the end of May, 'in consequence of which, by the
Doctor's Advice, we have not had the opinion of a Physician.'[45] 'No Vacations'
was usually specified in the advertisements for Yorkshire schools. Southey had
once met a happy boy in what he sarcastically called 'the great grazing country
for children' beginning at Bowes, but was also told that he had been there for

four years without interruption in a school run 'upon the most economical plan'. The flying visit of Dickens to Yorkshire to gather material for *Nicholas Nickleby* is well known. Squeers and Dotheboys Hall raised, inevitably, a controversy that continued for decades, in which the manuscript *Life and Work of James Abernathy* describing his terrible life at Cotherston from 1829 to 1831 has been regarded as one of the most striking pieces of relevant evidence since its belated publication in 1897. This school of fifty boys, housed in a former nunnery built round a gloomy square, with one small stove in its schoolroom, no chairs on which to sit when eating the coarse, cheap food and beds in what could only be called 'granaries', was a fitting setting for the quiet exploitation of a captive and luckless market.[46]

The deaths of both Mrs Scrimsher and her son raised a number of problems and a flurry of correspondence. William Kershaw was looking for a £2000 bond from T. Lumb and partners that he thought might have been left amongst Samuel Lumb's papers. He also wanted the deeds of the Birstall property for a new tenant – the existing tenants were quarrelling – hoping to sell it on behalf of the children by the time the youngest girl came of age. Samuel Lumb's older brother John was thought to be the heir-at law 'in consequence of the Son's Death, being an illegitimate Child', but was bluntly said to be a lunatic, 'who of course cannot give any Title'.[47] Kershaw used a Leicester solicitor as his agent, who found the whole business so troublesome and unprofitable that he eventually resigned.[48]

William Kershaw continued to correspond with George Peake, who eventually signed in the shaky hand of a sick man a cross letter he had dictated to his daughter about old debts of his friend Samuel Lumb still outstanding and accounts left unsettled. He was promised money from the rent of the property at Birstall as it came in, but Kershaw was not really happy with this rather indefinite arrangement. The property was finally sold, 'abt June 1821', for £375. Various sums had been disbursed, including the repayment of loans to the Miss Scrimshers from Samuel's unmarried sisters amounting to £30. The remaining £327 6s 0d was divided into three and 'actually paid' to his daughters – improperly, because it included the dead boy's share.[49]

How much of all these extra-marital and legal entanglements was known to Hannah Lumb is uncertain. Ann, Samuel's sister, who in 1806 had not been of sound mind and understanding, was able to make her will at Acomb in 1812. One wonders just where she was living. Dr Hunter's successor had taken over the private asylum there; a far more competent physician, he was no less interested in profit. Ann Lumb left legacies to her unmarried sisters and a great array of nephews and nieces of the Grimshaw and Kershaw families, but nothing to Hannah Lumb.[50] On the other hand Mrs Lumb was not entirely ignored after the marriage breakdown. When Samuel's sister Sarah drew up her will as late as 1818, she left her brother's widow £100. There were three later codicils, reaffirming this legacy with others. Mrs Lumb presumably received it when Sarah died in March 1828.[51]

On 1 May 1837 Mrs Lumb died at Knutsford. A legal document in the Goodchild Collection at Wakefield makes it clear that the original capital sum of £2000 settled on her had been invested in 'the new Four per cent annuities (since reduced to $3\frac{1}{2}$ per cent annuities)' and the dividends regularly paid. All this time, therefore, it had been unavailable to Samuel's three surviving natural children. The £2000 at length reverted to trustees, who protected the interests of Samuel's second family according to the provisions of his 1804 will. Counsel advised that the state would not take the share of the deceased natural son. Harriet Carris, née 'Crimsher' or Lumb, had not been patient enough to wait for the rest of her inheritance, however. She had sold her reversionary interest for £100 in 1832, the year in which her cousin Elizabeth married William Gaskell.[52]

Baines and Weston's directory of the West Riding shows Aikton Hall inhabited by another family in 1823, and Silcoates House occupied by the Yorkshire Dissenters' Grammar School. There were no direct male decendants of Richard Lumb. Thomas Lumb of Silcoates died without children in 1813 and his widow, 'Lucy Lumb, gentlewoman', née Kendall, lived in Westgate. So, too, did those other Amazons, the Misses Sarah and Elizabeth Lumb. Samuel's sister Elizabeth was the most fortunate member of the family. She ended by living in Jack Milnes's house, still separated from Westgate by a large courtyard and a carriage drive but divided into two by 1830. It had been a true mansion, enhanced by a well proportioned assembly room 66 feet long and about half that in breadth and height, with ceilings painted by Italian artists, two drawing rooms, fifteen bedrooms, a great staircase and a handsome library. In 1831 she married as his second wife the successor of William Turner at Westgate chapel, the Reverend Thomas Johnstone, but did not live with him at the parsonage. He was allowed to call and take tea with her.[53]

It is possible that Hannah Lumb went with her little daughter Marianne back to Cheshire in the year 1791. The will of the oldest child of the Sandlebridge Hollands, Ann, leaves her 'dear Sister Hannah Lumb the sum of Three hundred pounds, as a very insufficient testimony of my affectionate gratitude for the kindness, and support, I have received from her, during the last seventeen years.' As the will was signed from Higher (Over) Knutsford on 16 November 1808, it suggests that Hannah had been living in the area since 1791 and might even have been sharing a house with her. The chance survival of a Legh family rent book shows that Mrs Lumb was renting one of their houses in Over Knutsford in 1799, though she was still thought in Wakefield to be of Little Warford when Samuel Lumb's property was reconveyed to him in 1801. The rent book also proves that from 1807 she was paying fourteen guineas a year rent (in cash and by property tax collector's certificate) for the house and land until Michaelmas 1809, when Willoughby Legh received several articles left there in lieu of half a year's rent. The Reverend Harry Grey then took over the tenancy of the house and its garden. It is likely that Hannah moved to the well known house at Heathside on the edge of Nether Knutsford after Ann's death on 24 January 1809, aged forty-three.[54]

Mrs Lumb's separation settlement shows that she was far from poor by ordinary standards. Coleridge, as we have seen, was offered £120 a year when he accepted the invitation to be a Unitarian minister at Shrewsbury, admittedly with a house worth £30 in rent. £150 a year was thought to be the desirable minimum for a Church of England living, but in 1816 more than half the benefices in Cheshire were valued at less than this and the average annual stipend of a curate was £71. A whole family could live well on £200 to £300 a year. Nor is there any indication that the balance of Hannah's wedding settlement was ever paid to Samuel Lumb.[55] Hannah did not have to rely upon her quarterly income to keep herself and her daughter in some style. As well as the £300 Hannah received from Ann Holland's will, Marianne received twenty-five guineas – 'to purchase a Watch which I request she will keep as a slight memento of my sincere regard', wrote her aunt, who also left Mrs Elizabeth Stevenson at Chelsea 'the sum of Ten pounds along with an account of my decease'. Most of the rest of her estate Ann left to her three brothers, Peter, Samuel and Swinton, in trust for the benefit of her sisters as long as they remained unmarried, 'share, and share alike.' There were several complicated provisos, but in the upshot this meant Mary, Catharine and Abigail.

When Samuel Holland died at the age of eighty-two on 20 May 1816, his daughter Hannah came into yet more money. Peter, surgeon of Knutsford, was the heir, but Samuel arranged for his wife to receive an annuity of £120 a year – it seems to have been a standard figure in these circles – 'in lieu and satisfaction of her dower'. The original will also directed that well over £5000 should be raised and added to his residuary personal estate. After allowing for the dowries of £300 each formerly given to Hannah and Elizabeth, the money was to be divided into equal sevenths for all the younger sons and daughters, that is, Samuel, Swinton, Hannah, Mary, Catharine, Abigail, and (jointly) John and Elizabeth Stevenson; the money was 'at their absolute disposal'. Samuel's trustees were John Turner, second son of William Turner of Wakefield and a manufacturer of Mayfield, Bolton, and the Reverend John Holland of the same town.[56]

But could money and material possessions make up for the complete failure of a marriage? Given the Holland and Turner connections, Mrs Lumb was surely aware of her husband's recovery of mental health and property at the turn of the century. She very probably knew of his second family and the way in which they were being cared for by the Lumbs after Samuel's death. It was not out-of-the-way to do so, judging from the fact that Erasmus Darwin's two natural daughters, brought up with his legitimate family, were to be left £500 each, 'part in money and part in annuities – which last I design to prevent their coming to absolute poverty in case of unhappy marriage'. He did even better: in 1793 he bought a pew in the parish church for £5 and set them up in their own school at Ashbourne, which they ran successfully for more than twenty years for the daughters of leading Midlands families, and provided for their guidance *A Plan for the Conduct of Female Education in Boarding Schools,* not forgetting to suggest science and mathematics in the curriculum. It was only to be expected from the man who had asked James Watt for '*gentlemanlike* facts' about his steam-engine, and showed the Miss Strutts of Derby 'several entertaining experiments adapted to the capacities of young women' when they were somewhat unwilling hostesses at a meeting of the local philosopical society.[57]

Hannah Lumb had in the eighteenth century only briefly shared in the more glittering life offered by Samuel's family and relations in and around Wakefield. As far as we know, she had very little contact thereafter with the Lumbs and the Kershaws. She was certainly in a financial position to take advantage of the growing independence of middle-class women, even those who were not legitimate, and was able to fall back upon all that her own family had to offer in the gentle county of Cheshire, especially her brother Peter in Knutsford. They were all very well off in comparison with most of the inhabitants – but Hannah Lumb had to bring up her daughter without the husband who might have accompanied her. If she was in the church at Over Peover on the occasion of the marriage of her sister Elizabeth to William Stevenson in 1797, she must have been painfully reminded of what might have been. Did it embitter her, or was she only too relieved to be separated from the melancholy Samuel, safe on her own side of the Pennines?

NOTES

1 PRO: RG4/4661/3237, registered on 14 November 1810. The associated parchment certificate (RG5/43) was repr. in Ellis H. Chadwick, 'Mrs Gaskell's birthplace', *Bookman*, December 1912, p. 161, and Chadwick, 1913, opp. p. 2. The signature 'Ann Brewer' is all but illegible.

2 No child of George and Alice Stevenson was called John. Swinton's witnesses were Catherine and Ann Holland, probably his wife and sister (PRO: RG4/4661/3927-30).

3 HUL: MEG to CEN, 5 July 1866, qu. J. A. V. Chapple, 'Cleghorn again', *GSN*, VIII, August 1989, p. 10; Ward Notebook, f. 2; FM, 'The Gaskell centenary. The novelist's career', *Manchester Guardian*, 29 September 1910, p. 12. Chadwick thought James Cleghorn probable in 1910 (p. 2) and certain in 1913 (p. 1).

4 Charles Rodgers, *The Book of Robert Burns: Genealogical and Historical Memorials of the Poet and His Associates and Those Celebrated in His Writings*, Edinburgh, 1889, I, pp. 125-9; ECL: TS, Richard Alan Gilbert, *The Cleghorn Saga*, 13 May 1991, under 'Edinburgh Cleghorns' (spelling 'Wright' given). See also Chapple, 'William Stevenson and the Edinburgh literary scene', p. 43.

5 *Letters of Burns*, ed. Roy, I, pp. 72, 103; II, pp. 48, 113, 122; Fowler, *Burns*, pp. 12, 192-6. Cleghorn was probably dead by 1799. See Alan Bold, *A Burns Companion*, London, 1991, p. 31; *Letters of Burns*, ed. Roy, II, pp. 380 (May 1796: RC apparently ill), 446.

6 'Antiquary', Old clubs no. 5, *Illustrated Edinburgh News*, 5 February 1898; *Letters of Burns*, ed. Roy, II, p. 278, appx II; Robert T. Fitzhugh, *Robert Burns: The Man and the Poet*, London and New York, 1971, pp. 138-9; J. De Lancey Ferguson, *Pride and Passion:*

Robert Burns 1759-1796, New York, 1964, pp. 109-10; James Mackay, *A Biography of Robert Burns*, Edinburgh, 1992, pp. 415, 471.

7 Leslie A. Marchand, ed. *Byron's Letters and Journals*, III, London, 1974, p. 239. In 1827 Allen was the executor of the will of a William Cleghorn (BL: Add MS 52195, f. 210, Comptroller of legacy duties to JA, 24 November 1827). I have not seen this will, which might give more information about the family. Allen himself bequeathed £2500 to a descendant of his mother's second marriage named Cleghorn (obit., *GM*, XX, 1843, pp. 96-7).

8 RB to RC, Mauchline, 31 March 1788 (*Letters of Burns*, ed. Roy, I, pp. 269-70); RC to RB, 27 April 1788 (*The Works of Robert Burns; with An Account of his Life and A Criticism on His Writings*, ed. James Currie, Liverpool, 1800, II, p. 144).

9 For what follows see Faulkner, *Chelsea*, I, p. 89, II, pp. 155-6; Stevenson, 'London', p. 171; *Survey of London*, IV. ii, pp. 28-34, plates 24-31, 35; H. M. Colvin, *Biographical Dictionary of English Architects 1660-1840*, London, 1954, pp. 291-2; Lysons, *Environs of London*, I, p. 33.

10 Tooley, in 'The centenary of Mrs. Gaskell', [1910], p. 315, first pr. an identification of the house. Rate books in CPL have 'Wm Stephens' (in pencil, midsummer 1809, and in ink, Lady Day 1810), then 'Wm Stephenson' (Lady Day 1811). Next door, a Mary Smith paid rates 'for Gardn opposite'.

11 *DNB; Boswell's Life of Samuel Johnson*, ed. J. W. Croker, London, 1891, I, pp. 528-31.

12 Anon. review, *The Guardian*, 26 September 1910. William's surname, sometimes spelt with a *ph* or cut to 'Stephens' (a curt pronunciation?) occurs in the rate books every year until April 1829, when 'Wm' is altered in pencil to 'Mrs'. See also Chadwick, 'Mrs Gaskell's birthplace' [1912], p. 162, which modifies Chadwick, 1910, pp. 17-18.

13 'Old Lindsey Row' in Chadwick, 1910, opp. p. 16, but cp. 'Corner of Old Lindsey Row' in Chadwick, 'The mother of the author of *Cranford*', *The Bookman*, January 1912, p. 198. (CPL: W. L. Walton, lithograph, *c*. 1840). I must thank J. L. Bolton for his help.

14 *Survey of London*, IV. ii, pp. 18-27; VII. iii, pp. 2-3; 1836 map; Sheppard *Infernal Wen*, pp. 357-8.

15 Beaver, *Old Chelsea*, pp. 70, 140-1; Faulkner, *Chelsea*, I, p. 403; Green, pp. 137-8.

16 Ward Notebook, ff. 4-5 ('*he* ... wits' and 'Marianne' inserted words); Sharps, pp. 302-3n. I am grateful for the help of the Ward Librarian at Peterhouse, M. S. Golding.

17 Payne, *An Ancient Chapel*, pp. 66-7; WT (1714-94) obit., *PDM*, II, 1795, pp. 123-5; *Memoirs of the Revd Joseph Priestley ... Reprinted*, Birmingham, 1833, pp. 41, 48; Bass, *Westgate Chapel*, pp. 11-12; Taylor, *Wakefield District Heritage*, pp. 96-7 (illustr.). A good engraving of WT I is in Philip Holland, *A Sermon*, Wakefield, 1782 (TWA copy: 1787/113). See also Appendix C below.

18 What follows is largely based on Wood, *Sermon*, [and W. Turner II], *Memoirs of Turner*, pp. 33-4, 44, 56; W. Turner III, *Lives of Eminent Unitarians*, II, pp. 345-6; WT II obit., *CR*, n. s. XV, 1859, p. 354; *Priestley Works*, I. ii, pp. 85, 201; *VCH Cheshire*, III, p. 10; Lupton, *Wakefield Worthies*, pp. 164-5.

19 *Poems of Anna Barbauld*, ed. McCarthy and Kraft, pp. 27-8, 235-6; Bruce, *Newcastle*, p. 95; NLPS: MS copy (probably by Mary Robberds, née Turner), deposited in 1994; courtesy of the Librarian; Daniel Defoe noted this uvular *r* in his *Tour*.

20 See Aikin, *Description of the Country*, p. 579; Rae, *Turtle at Mr. Humble's*, pp. 26-9; Clarkson, *Merry Wakefield*, pp. 13, 16, 43, 201; Walker, *Wakefield*, II, pp. 509-11 (qu. from the actor-manager, Tate Wilkinson).

21 NLPS: WT II, MS 'Observations on a tour through parts of York and Lancashire', read 8 August 1797 ('Papers read at the monthly meetings, 1794-1814', no. 59); Seed, 'The role of Unitarianism', pp. 74-7; Benedict Nicolson, *Joseph Wright of Derby, Painter of Light*, London and New York, 1968, I, pp. 131, 159, 241-2, 246, 248, 279-80.

22 Walker, *Wakefield*, II, pp. 645-6; Wilson, 'The Denisons and Milneses', pp. 162-5; Mark Girouard, *The English Town*, New Haven and London, 1990, p. 108. For buildings see

Taylor, *Wakefield District Heritage*, pp. 74-5, 78-9, 96-7. Thornes House, illustr. *Vitruvius Britannicus*, 1802, was destroyed by fire in 1951 (Taylor, p. 140).

23 Walker, *Wakefield*, II, pp. 379-81; Hunter, pp. 80-1. I have in what follows benefited immeasurably from the assistance of the Wakefield Archivist, Mr John Goodchild, and the many documents he has personally preserved from destruction.

24 J. R. Rylands, 'Early freemasonry in Wakefield', *Transactions of the Quatuor Coronati Lodge*, p. 259. Richard Slater Milnes became provincial grand master for Yorkshire (p. 258).

25 BIHRY: 133, f. 565, RL's will, dated 3 July 1789, proved at York in September 1789; JGLCW: Copy marriage settlement, 28 August 1789 (cp. p. 66, n. 16 above). Peter Swinton died 6 December 1788 (Irvine, p. 157); CRO: will proved, 23 March 1789. See p. 2 above.

26 Register entry (CRO: MF 264/93); allegation and bond (CRO: mf 243/76). Samuel was 'twenty-eight Years, and upwards'.

27 YHA: BOO 6/2/1/1-2, Admissions books, nos 331, 556. I am most grateful to the archivist, Dr Katherine Webb, for sending me this and other information.

28 *Encyclopædia Britannica*, 9th edn, X, Edinburgh 1879, p. 104; JGLCW: birth record and copy of chapel registers. Flora Masson had some special knowledge, but she is is not error-free.

29 See Wood, *William Turner*, pp. 49, 52; TB, 'A list of students at Daventry', p. 285; *Priestley Works*, I. ii, p. 85.

30 SL to J and TL, Kendall and others, 1790: draft deeds for transfer of stock in trade, & settlement of the purchase price of it, to uses; SL to R and TL, William Jones Kendall: draft indenture; draft articles of agreement on dissolving partnership (all JGLCW).

31 YHA: BOO 6/2/1/2, Admissions books, nos 734 and 880.

32 Hunter, p. 81 (annot. copy at Wakefield); F. E. Millson, *A Bicentenary Memorial. Two Hundred Years of the Northgate-end Chapel, Halifax, A. D. 1696, 1896*, Halifax, 1896, p. 38; infm kindly provided by M. E. Corbett, Central Librarian, HCL.

33 JGLCW: Deed of conveyance in trust, SL to R & TL, dated 3 July 1795.

34 This account is based on works by Higgins, Milnes Gaskell, Digby, 1986 (especially) and K. Jones. See the bibliographical appendix, 8.

35 *BL Cat.;* Austen, *Sanditon*, ch. 5; Alistair M. Duckworth, *The Improvement of the Estate: A Study of Jane Austen's Novels*, Baltimore and London, 1971, pp. 211, 218-19.

36 Anne Digby, *Madness, Morality and Medicine: A Study of the York Retreat, 1796-1914*, Cambridge, etc., 1985, *passim;* Roy Porter, *A Social History of Madness: Stories of the Insane*, London, 1987, pp. 18-19, 42-7.

37 JS&PH, LUBL: *Testimonials of Mr. Samuel Gaskell, Member of the Royal Colleges of Surgeons, London and Edinburgh; Licentiate of the Society of Apothecaries, London, etc.* [1840]; John Conolly, *Treatment of the Insane Without Mechanical Restraints* (1856), intro. Richard Hunter and Ida MacAlpine, Folkestone and London, 1973, pp. 295-6; report of Shaftesbury's speech, *JMS*, XXVII, 1881, pp. 444-5.

38 JGLCW: SL to R & TL, deed to indemnify for advancing £1350, 26 February 1800.

39 JGLCW: Deed dated 26 August 1801; copy grant of a rent charge for separate mainte-nance; draft release of a reconveyance to SL.

40 Found in LRO: will proved archdeaconry of Leicester, 16 April 1806. Dr Peake is listed in trade directories as a surgeon in Peacock Lane, Leicester in 1794; in 1805 and 1815 his name appears with partners in Belgrave Gate (infm kindly provided by M. D. Rafterey).

41 JGLCW: Reverend G. [?R.] Oliver to TL, Birstall, 26 May 1806; annotated, 'Mr S. Lumb's natural Children – as relations will protect'.

42 Will and later codicil, PCC 17 October 1807; PCY 3 December 1807, under £30,000 (BIHRY: vol. 151, sede vacante). The trustees were William Kershaw and Sarah Lumb.

43 JGLCW: Articles of agreement, ES and William Tompson, 28 July 1805. Sarah, died 9

September 1763, aged thirty-seven; Martha, died 17 October 1797, aged seventy-three (JGLCW: Copy of Westgate chapel registers and inscriptions); Hunter, p. 80.

44 JGLCW: G. Peake to WK, Leicester, 30 April 1814, and 16 December 1816; WK to Henry Cooke [auctioneer of Silver Street, Leicester], Warley House, 9 and 13 May 1816.

45 JGLCW: J. Watson to WK, Cotherstone, 29 May 1818; doctor's bill, 20 July 1818; list of quarterly and other payments, 1814-18.

46 V. C. Clinton-Baddeley, 'Benevolent teachers of youth', CM, CLCIX, 1956-7, p. 370; Philip Collins, Dickens and Education, London and New York, 1964, pp. 100-5.

47 JGLCW: WK to HC, Warley house, 9 May, 29 August 1816; WK to Thomas Kershaw [son] – undated, but it repeats WK to George Peake, 20 December 1818.

48 JGLCW: J. S. Cardall to WK, Leicester, 26 February 1817, 13 June 1818, 9 December 1818, 14 January 1819.

49 JGLCW: GP to WK, Birstall, 9 December 1818; copy letter WK to GP, 20 December 1818; undated memo.

50 Digby, York Lunatic Asylum, pp. 15, 21-4. BIHRY: AL's will, dated 24 September 1812, proved at York 11 April 1829, under £14,000; annotated, died 15 December 1828 (copy in JGLCW).

51 Sarah died 10 March 1828, aged seventy-two (Westgate chapel, east vault). BIHRY: SL's will, dated 24 October 1818, proved at York, 17 June 1828, under £16,000 (JGLCW copy annotated, PCC 14 July 1828).

52 JGLCW: Copy indenture of 20 October 1832, sent to Richard Kershaw [son of William], Saville Green, Halifax; Huxby & Scholey, Wakefield, Case upon the will of the late SL, for Mr [Joseph] Burrell's opinion. Goodchild documents also contain a note, 'Samuel Lumb Gentleman Buried March 29th 1805', extracted from the Birstall register by the vicar in 1842; dates of death for William Jones Kendall (18 December 1818, aged fifty), Lucy Lumb, widow of Thomas of Silcoats (30 September 1835) and Sarah Lumb, spinster (10 March 1828); also, Marianne Lumb details, for which see below.

53 Taylor, Wakefield District Heritage, pp. 78-9 (with plan from Goodchild MSS); Walker, Wakefield, II, p. 464. Married at St John's church, March 1831, she died 31 July 1844; administration at York, 12 November 1844, under £1000.

54 CRO: WS 1811, AH's will proved at Chester 2 January 1811, above £1000 and below £1500; 'Rent-book from 1799-1812', pp. 17, 129-32 (MS in possession of Mrs Joan Leach); W. R. Strachan', TS, 'Record of graves and inscriptions', Knutsford, 1971, rev. 1988, no. 90.

55 VCH Cheshire, ed. B. E. Harris, III, 1980, pp. 57-8; Coleridge Letters, I, pp. 366-7; Leonore Davidoff and Catherine Hall, Family Fortunes: Men and Women of the English Middle Class, 1780-1850, Chicago, 1987, p. 23.

56 Strachan, TS, 'Record of graves and inscriptions', no. 116 (also wife Ann and Hannah Lumb); CRO: WS 1816, SH's will dated 12 June 1812, with codicils 29 August 1813 and 31 January 1815; probate Chester 22 July 1816, above £5000 and under £6000. Mary's share fell to the other heirs when she died unmarried in 1812; John Turner died aged fifty-one on 14 December 1816 (Newcastle Courant, 23 November 1816). For codicils see p. 159 below.

57 Desmond King-Hele, Doctor of Revolution: The Life and Genius of Erasmus Darwin, London, 1977, pp. 234-7; ed. Letters of Erasmus Darwin, pp. 78, 209-10; Davidoff and Hall, Family Fortunes, p. 290; Robinson, 'The Derby Philosophical Society', p. 361.

6

Refuge in Knutsford

WHEN ELIZABETH STEVENSON was born in 1810, Hannah Lumb was a comfortably placed widow with a lively daughter of twenty years of age. She had left her 'pretty Cottage in the higher town' of Over Knutsford at Goose Green, to live on the road called Heathside, or The Heath, which ran out to the west of Nether Knutsford. The topographer Samuel Lewis considered the houses of Knutsford 'in general indifferently built and of mean appearance', yet, he added, 'in the immediate neighbourhood' were 'several handsome villas'. The house now known as Mrs Lumb's was one of these, amongst the best available, looking out over the extensive heathland in front. It had been built about the middle of the eighteenth century: a large house of three storeys in warm red brick with a five-bay front, the central bay projecting slightly and surmounted by a small pediment. In those days it was customary to rent; with £120 a year Hannah would have been able to afford this with ease. She would also be able to take her place in the best society of the little town, especially as her brothers Peter, Samuel and Swinton were prospering so well in the careers they had chosen.[1]

Her brief married life must after a time have seemed like a bad dream. She was living near her parents at Sandlebridge and surrounded in Knutsford by numerous friends and relations who had not left the neighbourhood or who maintained strong connections with it. Many of them worshipped at the old dissenting chapel at the bottom of Adam's Hill. Two letters from her daughter, Marianne Lumb, reveal a great deal about their way of life. One of them, written from Knutsford late in 1811, is addressed to her 'very dear Mother' at Messrs Holland & Riggins, London.[2] Mrs Lumb had therefore gone to stay with or by her younger brother Swinton Colthurst Holland, not long returned to England and an energetic man of affairs who would have brought more than a breath of the wider world to the peaceful life of a woman who lived in a little rural town.

Swinton had begun in business at Liverpool, gone to the United States for two years in 1800, travelled extensively in Italy, attempted to set up his own business in Venice and finally entered into a partnership with the American consul at Trieste, a Mr Riggin, in April 1803. There he was able to represent his brother Samuel's firm, Holland and Humble, when one of their ships, the brig Endeavour of Liverpool, got into difficulties at Venice. At one point Samuel had, perhaps unwisely in the event, 'not less than ten vessels of various burden either in the Mediterranean, or making the voyage to or from there.' Swinton was an able second: he was already on his way to becoming very rich in his own right, a partner in the once great financial firm of Baring Brothers, a man able to give advice on a national level.[3]

He returned to the little provincial Cheshire town, nevertheless, in order to marry a lady to whom he had been engaged for many years, Anne Willets. Her brother and married sister Mary, wife of Peter Holland, had died in the early years of the new century, and their widowed mother not long after, at the age of seventy-eight in 1804. Swinton's wedding took place in Knutsford parish church on 9 May 1805. Anne and her surviving sister Jane were the daughters of the Reverend William Willets, Unitarian Minister of Newcastle-under-Lyme in Staffordshire, a man of 'great mechanical ingenuity' and a friend of Priestley and William Turner of Wakefield. The Newcastle-under-Lyme congregation had faltered badly for many years after his death in 1778, till it was rescued in 1819 by the heroic efforts of Miss Mary Byerley and two Trustees, Josiah Wedgwood and Samuel Parkes, a rich and ardent Unitarian who lived in Hackney but who had once run a business in Stoke-on-Trent. The interdependence of these families was profound, and would continue to be so.[4]

After a few days at Sandlebridge and Knutsford, Swinton swept Anne and his own sister Catharine ('Kitty') off on a long journey to Trieste – first by chaise to Hull at a total cost of £11 8s 5d, where they lived well for a week in the Neptune (a 'good dinner and a bottle of Port each day'), and then in a single-masted sailing vessel, a Mecklenburger hoy called the *Hoffnung*, Captain Henrich Voss, from the Humber to modern Tönning in Schleswig-Holstein, through boisterous seas and with the ladies sea-sick most of the time. At Hamburg they took a carriage, and with three horses, or sometimes four, which annoyed the prudent Swinton, they set off on the long journey overland to Berlin, Dresden, Prague, Linz (the approach 'superbly beautiful' with the Danube 'flowing in a Majestic stream by the town') and finally over the mountains via Graz to Trieste at the head of the Adriatic.[5]

It took from 23 May to 13 July and cost £140 17s 4d, including the sea passage. Every distance, stage and expense was detailed in his meticulous fair-copy diary, with comments on the roads and the scenery, the behaviour of postilions, customs officers and landlords. 'Posting in Austria', he concluded, 'is much better than either in Prussia or Saxony; the roads are in general better, and the postmasters much more civil, and less imposing, seldom attempting to put on the carriage more horses than necessary … '. Not that the sea voyage would have been preferable. Spain had declared war on Britain in 1804, and their clothes and furniture were captured by Spanish gunboats off Gibraltar, Peter Holland told Josiah Wedgwood.[6]

At Trieste Swinton and his wife were caught up in the war between Austria and France when the city was left defenceless:

On the 19th November, they made their entrance – a troop consisting of 500 Infantry and 100 Cavalry – about 200 of these soldiers were Negroes, which the French had picked up in their St Domingo expedition – quite a new sight *here* – the Colonel of this troop was also a *Black* and wore the Legion of Honour. The Generals were no sooner arrived at their Inn than the Magistrates were called and told they must immediately procure a contribution of *Six Millions* of *francs*, with daily rations and quarters for the Army following them.

Swinton was arrested in December by a trick and imprisoned for four days with other merchants. He was only released after payment of a large fine, fortunately by a bill of exchange payable in three months, which he was able to repudiate when peace was declared. His opinion of French behaviour was sulphurous: 'In fact, from the highest officer to the lowest soldier, they showed themselves whilst here, in every transaction a mere band of legalized Robbers – plundering without shame and their superior Officers devoted to theft.'

Swinton was bold and adventurous, but clearly liked everything to be under more than just financial control. He soon had some £3000 to invest and wished to leave Trieste and its political uncertainties. He was prepared to come back to England as director and investor in a brewery, or an iron foundry or some such business. The Adriatic was then constantly patrolled by royal navy ships: 'scarcely a single vessel could pass us without our examining them, especially those bound for Trieste', boasted one of the crew of the 40-gun *Unité* in 1807, 'which made our favour courted and our sway dreaded.'[7] Swinton took the opportunity of moving to Malta in the following year, but that did not prove to be satisfactory for long. After two years the little family, now increased by four children and a servant, Mrs Vincent, set sail for Falmouth on 13 March 1810 in the *Diana* packet, Captain John Parsons. Children and men servants, who could 'stow anywhere', were half-price; for women servants, who had to have a berth, the full price of £63 was charged. This springtime voyage, which Swinton describes with more narrative detail than his overland journey five years before, took nearly two months. Their goat 'died in a fit & was thrown overboard', causing Caroline to cry because she had no milk for her supper; all the good bread and the 'Childs Semola', or bran, was finished by 6 May. Fortunately, they were able to land at Falmouth on 9 May. The voyage, with everything found and a good table, cost altogether £366 19s 9d. The fourteen or fifteen packet sailors were only paid twenty-seven shillings a month each and, Swinton guessed, 'make it out by adventures & smuggling'. 'Captains of Ships all Tyrants,' he wrote with dry humour. No good ever came of arguing with them; they had to be humoured and their stories endured. The customs officers were civil and obliging. They ignored a trunk of household linen, and though they charged duty on half-bound foreign books, treated them as unbound – £1 5s for 27 lbs weight.

At Falmouth he engaged two chaises and they all set off through Cornwall and the most beautiful of English counties, Devon, to Bridgewater in Somerset ('charged 7/6. for the same dinner as charged 20/- at Exeter'), Bristol, Worcester, Birmingham, Stafford and Newcastle-under-Lyme, with a stop of four hours at Linley Wood. Here lived a family friend, James Caldwell, staunchly Unitarian son of a successful Scottish tradesman of Nantwich, another friend of Joseph Priestley and William Turner of Newcastle. James was accustomed to read a service of his own composition to the assembled servants and family in the three-windowed bow of his dining room. Wife, children above five or six, guests and relations were all ranged on chairs opposite 'the priest of his family and household' at the large dining table, whilst at the lower end of the room stood a circle of chairs for household and farm servants. At their head was a rich aunt's maid, 'always a rather fine lady'. The cook and kitchen maid were sensibly allowed to come 'Sunday & Sunday by turns, so did the nurse & housemaid as long as there were little ones.' The big house and its life about 1800 is affectionately recreated in the early recollections of his daughter, the prolific novelist Anne Marsh, who conveys the spiritual strength of dissent before what she claims was its later decay, when the fiercely independent presbyterians of former days 'went to Church, & loved to be genteel, they vulgarised, & were left only with their insignificance'.[8]

After this visit to a family into which his nephew Henry Holland was later to marry, Swinton went on to Congleton and eventually, Sandlebridge. This journey took ten days and cost just over one hundred pounds. He then took his family to settle first in Newington Green and afterwards in London Fields near Hackney, which is probably where he was living (until about 1816) when his sister Hannah Lumb came on her visit to London. Many influential Unitarians lived in this area, or not too far from it. Swinton most likely attended the Gravel pit chapel with its remarkably distinguished congregation, where Robert Aspland was the successor of Priestley and Belsham as pastor. Mrs Lumb was visiting her relations in heroic days. Unitarianism was then strong in faith if not in numbers, both in Cheshire and in London.[9]

Marianne's first letter to her mother is a long, crossed one, flowingly written in a mature, spidery hand.[10] Its concerns are parochial in comparison with what Mrs Lumb would have heard from Swinton and his wife in London, but it is animated and even has a touch of exoticism. Marianne gave a lively and detailed account of Knutsford gaieties during a 'long expected, and longest wished for Evening' in 1811 at a Miss Stanley's, who might then have lived in the next house along at Heathside after an empty space, judging by a reference in the letter to 'planting' between her house and Mrs Lumb's. Records show that Isabella Elizabeth Stanley of Nether Alderley paid just under £150 pounds a year in 1810 to rent the larger Heath House with its gardens, orchard, parcels of land and other buildings from Colonel William Handfield. This was another eighteenth-century house, a little further out; the Honourable Mrs

Grey, the widow of Booth Grey, was renting it in 1813 and Charles Cholmondeley in 1824, according to the land tax assessments.[11] Isabella Stanley was a relation of Edward Stanley, a latitudinarian Whig Lord Melbourne was to appoint Bishop of Norwich in 1837, but at that time incumbent of Alderley. His wife Catherine, to whom he had become engaged in 1808 when she was only sixteen, was the daughter of Oswald Leycester of Toft Hall, vicar of Knutsford till 1809 and then of Stoke-upon-Tern in Shropshire. She was a favourite of Sydney Smith, who used to speak of her 'porcelain understanding'.[12]

Knutsford Unitarians might have been most closely associated with their co-religionists, but they were certainly able to socialise with Cheshire gentry in the neighbourhood and with other local families who were members of the established church. This is very evident from Marianne's letter. At this time and place, early in the century, relations with dissenters were generally characterised by politeness and friendly ease, though they later deteriorated. She recites names that represent some of the best society in the district:

To begin then I went at seven, and found the room tolerably full, tho not formidably so. Mrs Edward Stanley, the moment I entered, came up to me, in the most friendly manner possible, and continued talking a considerable time. After Tea, Miss S. made up a Wist table, and we had Music, as before. I was in the midst of playing a Duett, with Miss Wheeler, and the Company all standing round the instrument, when suddenly the Door burst open, and nine Figures stalked into the room whose appearance caused all the Party, to scamper off where they could. The fact was this, Miss D. Leigh, and Miss Dumbleton, who are staying at Toft [Hall], wished to surprize Miss Stanley, by having a Masquerade; they accordingly enlisted Miss Bamford, Miss Mainwaring, Miss Grey, Mr Dumbleton, Mrs Sharpe and Henry, it was to be a profound secret, and they did indeed contrive to keep it so ...

Miss Mainwaring painted all the Masques, and the dresses were borrowed from the neighbouring families, under various pretexts; they equipped themselves at Mrs Greys, and then came in Chaises, to Miss Stanley's who as you may suppose was not a little surprised. ... Mrs Sharpe was Lady Durable, and Miss Bamford was Miss Lucretia, her Grandaughter – Mr D[umbleton] was an *old lady*, Henry [Holland] was an Islander, who could just speak a bit of broken English – it was very fortunate he had such a nice dress I think. ... Miss D. Leigh was a Sailor's Wife, just come from Portsmouth, she acted her part *by far* the best, the Spectators were two or three times in a roar of laughter at her. ... She was much the most conspicuous figure, and attracted all the attention; her Mask, was a frightful one; the Skin, was shrivelled, and her Nose evidently bore the marks of drinking; though she assured the Company, 'She never tasted no sort of Liquor, no not she, though she did like a drop, or a supe of summot, nows and thens'.

The festive occasion can be dated from a letter of 1 November 1811 written by a young visitor, Sarah Whittaker: 'They have been very Gay Masquerading at Knutsford among the Toft family', she told her brother, 'Stanleys Bamfords

&c.' Standards must have changed from the days when students at Warrington Academy, Lucy Aikin and John Rigby's irresistible daughters had been forbidden to get up 'private theatricals'. Those in *Mansfield Park*, which Jane Austen was writing at this time, are a special case, though the dramatic appearance of Miss Leigh as a sailor's wife from Portsmouth brings Fanny Price's slatternly mother and swearing, drinking father to mind. Henry Holland, Sarah tells us, 'exhibited as an Icelander in a real dress of the Country'. Marianne's first cousin must have obtained this on his visit to Iceland in the summer of 1810. He became an inveterate and speedy traveller in the world at large, requiring no more than five grains of calomel and a pair of black stockings for luggage, acccording to Sydney Smith.[13]

A letter from Henry to Maria Edgeworth, a family friend, in the following summer mentioned that he was going to Knutsford for two or three months. He stressed its smallness and lack of intelligent, informed society. 'New fashions of dress travel with vastly more rapidity into our provincial towns, than do the new books & new discoveries of the day', he had written to Lucy Aikin just before this time; it was fortunate, he proclaimed, that papers from Humphry Davy in London and occasional visits to the son of a Knutsford chemist, Dr Thomas Henry at Manchester, kept him in intellectual touch. A little later he told Maria incidentally that his sister Bessy was coming to see London for the first time. This was in 1814, when she was about eighteen.[14]

Marianne's long letter to her mother in London eventually drew to a close:

Miss Stanley, the following day sent a *brace of Partridges* for my Aunt Mary, who she said as an invalid should have a little something nice. Miss S. is wishing to plant between the two houses, providing *you* have no objection, and on my saying it was your wish also, she said, 'Oh, I am glad of that, then when your Mamma returns we will plant together for, I think it wd. be a great improvement to us both.' ...

I have been wishing, since I have been out so often, for another Necklace, having none but my white one. ... [I] should be very glad if you could buy me one, any sort of colour will please me, not so *the price*, there I must bind you to half a Guinea, at least not much more, and yet I must have bracelets also, and I fear that the sum will not purchase both ... I shall however be perfectly satisfied when you return to hear you say 'Marianne love I did not get you this, or that thing for I thought it would be rather extravagant in your having it' – do not forget this when you read of any fresh wants –

Saturday Morning no Letter! Sunday Morning no Letter! Monday morning still no Letter! What can you be about? – surely *you* are not going to *cut me*. – But I must not complain for you *have been* very very good, and Aunt Ab. says I am an unreasonable Animal to expect another Letter so soon. Pray when am I to expect you *at home?* One body says to me, 'how soon do think your Mama will return Miss Lumb?' and another asks me if Mrs Lumb intends to spend the Winter in London ...

The voices of Marianne, aunt Abigail Holland and friends in Knutsford sound again as one reads the thin and cursive script of this letter.

Copies only survive of her second letter, which must have followed swiftly upon the first.[15] It was dated 'The Heath – Nov. 1 [or 2] 1811' and could hardly have differed more in tone and content:

> My dear Mother, I was greatly shocked to hear from my Aunt Katie's Letter of the death of my poor Aunt Stevenson. You had mentioned her in your last Letter to me as being far from well; but I had no idea her complaints were in the least degree dangerous, and was therefore quite unprepared for the melancholy intelligence, which came to us yesterday. Poor little Elizabeth! what will become of her? She has almost been the constant subject of my thoughts ever since and it is about her I have again taken up my pen, to write to you. Do you not think she could come to us?

Aunt Kitty or Katie, the first to convey the news to Knutsford, has been a shadowy and ignored figure. She was then nearly forty, and had evidently led a more adventurous life in the early years of the century than has ever been realised; she might well have continued to live with Swinton and his young family after their return to England in 1810. She never married and was to die just before she reached the age of fifty in 1822.

What Mrs Stevenson's life had been like after the move from Edinburgh to London and what she died of, we do not know. The almost accidental fragments of news revealed by her sister-in-law Dorothy Landles – her lack of milk after her first child's birth, her fan kept as a curiosity (because it was rare, or finely worked, or a novelty?) – are all that we know of her apart from official records, some of those defective. She had five sisters, one married but separated from a husband of questionable sanity and four who did not marry at all. She herself was not young when she married, twenty-six, and if she had been living with her parents, she was taken from their wonderfully cosy family home at Sandlebridge in the placid countryside of Cheshire and transported to the austerities of a windy Scottish farm – to a venture plagued with money problems that came to an ignominious end.

During her married life of only fourteen years she was shuttled from place to place as William sought to find permanent employment, and quite possibly lost child after child as she did so. Unless there were special circumstances, multiple pregnancies were a married woman's lot at all levels of society and infant deaths only too common.[16] Mrs Dorothy Landles of Berwick, who had looked after Mrs Stevenson when John was born at Saughton, died herself at the age of thirty-one with an infant child, at the time when her brother William was teaching in various parts of Edinburgh. Not long after this there were two more deaths, William's mother at Berwick and his brother Joseph in the Napoleonic war. In 1806 the apparently solid prospect of a fine position for William in the train of the new Governor General of India, Lord Lauderdale, had been denied.

Mrs Elizabeth Stevenson must have been overwhelmed with joy when after all these cruel setbacks a Treasury post with a decent salary was offered to her husband, following a career that had lurched from one disappointment to another. At last she would have the opportunity to display 'the qualities which a man of sense will most regard in the choice of a wife' – those her relation William Turner of Newcastle would recommend to his daughter Mary, who was to marry the Reverend John Gooch Robberds, 'elected' co-pastor of Cross Street chapel, Manchester, in 1810. 'You will not be disposed to exclaim with Mrs W.', Turner joked, 'Is a wife to be an upper-servant, to provide her husband's meals, and take care of his linen?' He advised his daughter, displaying all the serene confidence of an Enlightment liberal who had carefully considered Mrs Wollstonecraft's writings rather than dismissing them out-of-hand, to be 'a companion and helper, to make his home comfortable and his meals pleasant, when he returns from acting the part of a fellow servant in the discharge of those public or more private duties by which he is to make the necessary provision for the common maintenance.'[17]

As Mrs Stevenson was looking forward to settling down and making a home in Chelsea, an enviable place in which to live after Saughton's farm and Edinburgh's decaying old town, there came her sister Ann's death in Knutsford. Elizabeth would have received her bequest of ten pounds and an account of her decease some time in 1809. This relatively minor sadness was followed by a great joy: the birth of Elizabeth in the following year – a daughter who survived infancy and even reached the stage of walking. But Mrs Stevenson's delight in the child who bore her own name and that of her friend's daughter lasted for little more than twelve months, from one winter to the next.

She died just a few months after the move to Beaufort Row. The burial register of Chelsea St Luke, which is very basic in its information at this time (addresses were not given), has an 'Elizabeth Stevens aged 40' under 30 October 1811, with no other possible entry for several years after her daughter's birth.[18] The variation in name, like that found in the Chelsea rate books, is not unusual: by sheer coincidence, an Elizabeth Ann Stevenson who died aged six months is recorded in St Luke's burial register, whereas she appears as Elizabeth Stevens in a burial ground register under 19 October 1813. (By 1813 addresses – Lombard Street in this instance – were being given.) For some reason there is no matching entry of this kind for Mrs Stevenson in St Luke's register of the burial ground on the King's Road, but we can assume that she lies there. Chelsea's old church by the river has a very restricted site and the second graveyard on the King's Road, presented to the parish by Sir Hans Sloane, had been opened as early as 1736. It was closed in 1812, except for relations, and we find that William Stevenson was buried there many years later, presumably in the same grave as his wife.[19]

William Stevenson was left with a son of almost thirteen and a baby girl to care for. His wife, parents, a brother and a sister were dead; his youngest brother was in the navy and the other brother, who had married in 1803, had a growing family of his own to care for in Berwick. William had his work at the Treasury – an assistant keeper's post had been allowed to lapse in 1810 – and was at this time preparing his *General View of the Agriculture of Dorset* for publication. He must have felt able to cope with his son of twelve but not a baby, and presumably neither aunt Katie Holland nor any other female relation wished to keep house for him in Chelsea, common though this was in those circles. Mrs Lumb's younger sister Mary was 'an invalid' in Knutsford at this time, as we have seen; she was to die in the following year. And Marianne's desire to look after her baby cousin was urgent: 'Do, my dear Mama, give *at least* your consent to my proposal – Should Mr. Stevenson have any fears, tell him I will perform the part of a mother to Elizabeth to the very best of my power.' There is a mysterious postscript: 'Pray keep this letter to yourself'. Could she have feared that the Swinton Hollands would take the child?[20]

Flora Masson thought that Mrs Stevenson died soon after the birth of her daughter. Also, 'Mrs Stevenson died within a month of Mrs G's birth – she was put in charge of a shopkeeper's wife – Mrs Withington a friend brought the baby down to Knutsford (see *Mary Barton*) to her aunt Miss Holland (Mrs S's sister) who had just married Mr Lumb' was the somewhat garbled version Ward derived from Meta and Julia Gaskell. He repeated 'within a month' in print, and also gave the name of the friend as 'Whittington'. This last is a mere detail, and Elizabeth Gaskell herself usually knew that she was over a year old when aunt Lumb took her in: 'Though a Londoner by birth, I was early motherless, and was taken when only a year old to my dear *adopted native* town, Knutsford ... '. She had found at the very least a refuge from William Stevenson's troubles in the metropolis.[21]

Her father's association with Lauderdale remained close. Henry Holland, just beginning to make his irresistible way as a doctor in London, found this useful. In February 1812 he was able to attend the House of Lords to hear debates on the Catholic question with a ticket obtained from Lauderdale by Mr Stevenson (spelt 'Stephenson'). Even more helpfully, when in the following month Henry was hoping to go to Lisbon in a vessel of war, 'Ld Lauderdale, Mr Stevenson tells me, will serve me in this point if he can', as well as providing letters of introduction.

In this same letter to his father Henry gave other, more personal details. After retailing Lady Stanley's gossip that when she and Sir John dined with Humphry Davy and Mrs Apreece the occasion was '*monstrously stupid*' – the aristocratic tones ring out – 'for they attended only to each other', Henry continued,

> On Monday I walked out with Mr Stevenson to his house at Battersea [*sic*]. Mr Thomson the surgeon dined with us, a very intelligent, pleasing man, getting on very rapidly in practice. He published a few months ago the London Dispensatory, on as large a scale as Duncan's Edr Dispy; & still more valuable, as respects its matter & arrangement. The botanical part (*I understand*) is particularly valuable.

Stevenson had not yet made his second marriage, to Dr A. T. Thomson's sister, which might account for Henry's further comment that 'Mr Stevenson is troubled with Mr Clennell, as a domestic associate. It is an intolerable grievance, & one which I hope Mr S. will have sufficient spirit to remedy if it continues long.' This letter of Henry Holland to his father again emphasises the level of the social connections maintained by the Knutsford Hollands. He chats about Sir John and Lady Stanley and a sermon by the Knutsford vicar Harry Grey, and retails some gossip he has heard from a visitor: 'Mrs Egerton amused me by the account of a dinner at Tabley, where Sir Peter & Lady Warburton, & Miss Grahame [who had been at Miss Stanley's masquerade] were the sole guests. Sir P, it appears, complains bitterly that he could get only *two glasses* of wine.' Patrician displeasure is again unmistakeable.[22]

Knutsford in the early nineteenth century was not large, little more than two long streets roughly parallel to each other – King Street somewhat lower than Princess Street on a hill sloping down to the town moor, with a number of alleys and outlying groups of houses at Cross Town and Over Knutsford. Princess Street was part of the busy road to London from Manchester, some fifteen miles to the north. But as a town Knutsford seemed pretty and village-like to Maria Edgeworth, 'interspersed with railed-in nice gardens, little *nooky* green spots, and here and there in the fields picturesque paths and cottages', when she first came there in 1813, returning a visit to Ireland made by Henry Holland a few years before.[23]

The Heath or Heathside, at a slight angle to the road running west towards Tabley and Northwich, was later called Northwich Street; it stretched from an inn called the White Bear on the corner of Princess Street for about two hundred yards along to Heath House and one or two neighbours. At the town end were a number of small properties, but where it continued into the country some substantial houses had been built between about 1760 and 1820. They faced a small triangular green across the road and looked out over the wilder heathland beyond on which horse races were held, 'scarcely inferior to any in England for the display of fashionable company'. There was 'a tolerably good plot of ground' on the race-course, where occasional visitors used to play local enthusiasts and 'some of the Young Gentlemen of a large School in this Town' at cricket. Elizabeth Gaskell's friend, the Reverend Henry Green, who came to Knutsford in 1827 to be Unitarian minister of its old dissenting chapel, described the little town as raised 'on a kind of table-land' slightly above the surrounding vale of Cheshire, and spoke poetically of sauntering 'around the race-course, where there is ever a balmy, pure, and refreshing air, and where in their season may be found the dwarf yellow gorse, or the sundew, or the little golden potentilla, or the tiny purple bells of the heather, and others of Flora's wild favourites'.[24]

'The life of a hamlet, a village, a parish, a market town and its hinterland, a whole county, might revolve around the big house and its park', declares a modern historian. The houses of the gentry at this period were hierarchically arranged, their occupants socialising easily with each other, jostling to get invitations from the level above and gracefully patronising the more prominent citizens of nearby towns and villages to keep 'the strings of dependency and influence' in sweet accord. In 1816, for instance, Sir John Leicester asked Lord Cholmondeley's permission to recruit amongst his tenants for his troop of Cheshire yeomanry. It was granted, but there was a reciprocal request for horses, which were supplied, and a local notable was granted the rank of cornet. The links between upper and lower ranks depended upon an endless succession of mutual favours. In the 1826 election at Chester of Robert Grosvenor, 'debtors for upwards of £200' were released from gaol and 'a Freeman's pig' was purchased for £22.

Early commercial directories refer to Knutsford's handicraft trades, largely supported by the 'opulent gentry residing in the neighbourhood, who are numerous'. In 1810 D. and S. Lysons were able to name Sir John Stanley (Alderley), Thomas Langford Brooke (Mere), Thomas Brooke's mother (Over Tabley), Wilbraham Egerton (Tatton), Willoughby Legh (Norbury Booths), Sir Henry Mainwaring Mainwaring (Higher Peover) and George Leycester (Toft). This is very different from, say, a town like Stamford, caught in the single, all-embracing web spun by the great Cecil family of Burghley House.[25]

The nearest mansion to Nether Knutsford was Tatton. William Egerton's seventeenth-century house in red brick was being replaced in 1791 by a severely classical building designed by Samuel Wyatt when the great landscape gardener Humphry Repton appeared on the scene. He had recently suggested to the Legh family of High Legh Hall on the other side of Knutsford that they should divert a turnpike road to improve their privacy and create a picturesque new hamlet at the entrance to their grounds. His associate John Nash encouraged George Legh to ensure that the blacksmith's shop looked up along the road so that its fire might light and cheer the entire village at night, a favour for future generations if not for those cleared out of the way. Repton drew plans for Tatton park in one of his famous Red Books: sketches of 'before' and, beneath a flap, the transformation scene, 'after'. His sketch of an approach to Tatton from Nether Knutsford demonstrated how 'a few miserable cottages' might be rebuilt as tenements in a more uniform style and a 'simple, handsome arch' of a classical kind erected at the end of the town's main street, which would give a more grand entrance to the parkland. In *Mansfield Park* it is Jane Austen's rich, stupid characters who desire radical improvements of this kind and suggest the employment of Repton. The objections of Fanny Price and Edmund Bertram rest on more than aesthetic grounds: they see the disregard of cultural continuity and the disruption of a settled community.[26]

Both William Egerton and Samuel Wyatt died before work was completed at Tatton. Their plans were only partly carried through by Wilbraham Egerton and Samuel's nephew, Lewis Wyatt. The great park with its gardens, lakes and curving, undulating drive is today joined by a leafy lane to the head of the town; the arch is offset to one side. Some cottages were removed, and by the early nineteenth century the premises of a nearby cotton spinning mill had been divided amongst the labourers. Trade of this sort did not really prosper, Henry Green noted, for the town had no canal nearby and was not connected to the railway system until 1862.[27]

In 1811 the population of Nether and Over Knutsford was about 2500 according to the census. Every year in July the races brought great crowds on foot and on horseback to the heath across the way from Mrs Lumb's; the 'dashing equipages with six fine spirited horses' of the aristocracy made a particular impression. As a town it was not large, but it had considerable local importance. By 1821 the population had increased to some 3000, partly accounted for by the recent building of a sessions house in which courts could be held and a 'house of correction', charmingly described by the directories in estate agents' language as 'an elegant and commodious edifice; behind which, is a large and convenient prison', built on a continuation of Princess Street in the London direction. Opposite the sessions house was a decent parish church of brick and stone with square tower, consecrated in 1744 on a site between Princess Street and King Street below.

On the churchyard's southern boundary, with double the amount of land, was the substantial Georgian house, garden and field that came into the possession of Peter Holland Esq. Although his name did not appear as one of those who bound themselves to eat no wheaten bread and moderate their consumption in other ways back in 1800 during a period of wartime distress – unlike Egerton, Legh, Cholmondeley, Leycester, Leicester, Thomas Wright, Strethill Wright and others – he must have soon become a significant point of contact with the gentry whose halls were in the vicinity and who themselves owned many of the properties in Knutsford. His niece Marianne's letter is a clear indication of the Hollands' social status when his other niece Elizabeth was brought to the town as a baby.[28]

The older brother of Elizabeth Stevenson's dead mother and Hannah Lumb was then in his mid-forties. A silver point engraving of him from this time shows a lean figure, high, bony forehead and strong, humorous features. Four out of seven children by his first wife, who had died in 1803, were still living – Henry, Mary, Elizabeth and Lucy. In 1811 Henry was twenty-three, Mary nineteen, 'Bessy' about seventeen and Lucy, the youngest, eleven years of age. The sisters, though they might pay quite lengthy visits to friends and relations, were essentially Knutsford residents.

Peter Holland did not wish to remain a widower after the death of his wife. As he wrote to Lucy Aikin in 1805,

> What I wish to add is all in the way of inquiry. – I want you, Lucy, to give me some account of this 'lovely interesting friend' of yours. Pray tell me why it is that you have never thought of her as a friend for *me*. ... I should have thought we might have been suited to each other. – You say she is 'pretty well'. – Has she bad

health? I have accidentally heard that she had. – Write to me *very soon & tell me every thing about her.*

I have been spending part of the last eight or ten days in the company of a neighbour of yours, Miss Rogers. ... It takes more time than I can bestow, and better opportunities than I possess to get acquainted with any new character. I have liked what I have seen of Miss R., though *now & then* I have had doubts about the goodness of her temper. As you are an excellent painter of characters, pray give me hers – ... You need not fear saying any thing of her. – I am not *too much* smitten to be *excessively* hurt with any remarks you may make.

His own brusque, confident, perhaps ironic character comes over very clearly.[29]

On 21 January 1809, the family Bible records, he made a second marriage, to Mary, the forty-year-old daughter of Esther and Daniel Whittaker.[30] According to Henry Holland she loved the daughters of Peter's first marriage, and was loved by them. Henry reported with sly amusement that his father did not have his usual winter accident that year. Another family arrived in quick succession. First came Charles Aikin in November 1809 ('the little one there seems by all accounts to be quite a *miracle of merriment*', Henry told Lucy Aikin), who was baptised in July 1810 by William Turner of Newcastle at Knutsford. Charles Aikin was followed by Susan in April 1811 and Arthur in March 1813. They were roughly the same age as their cousin Elizabeth Stevenson. Biographers, misled by *Cranford* and her statement that she had been 'brought up by old uncles & aunts, who had all old books, and very few new ones', tended till recently to concentrate on these and her older cousins, almost ignoring the existence of Peter's young second family.[31]

A great deal can be learnt about Knutsford society during the second decade of the nineteenth century, and even more inferred, from a voluminous series of letters written by various members of the Whittaker family. They were connected with the Hollands from at least early 1804, when the young Henry Holland paid a visit to a ladies' school at Bath run by unmarried daughters of 'this agreeable family', great favourites of his aunts at Knutsford. Martha Whittaker, sister of Peter Holland's second wife, married a prosperous music master in Knutsford, Francis Sharpe, in 1809. Their widowed mother and spinster sister, Catherine, were also settled in Knutsford by the end of that year. In the following year they moved to the older part of the town, King Street, taking a house with a garden big enough for peas, beans, cabbages and early potatoes – and perhaps a pig as well. The spring of 1812 saw a move by the Sharpe family, who came to live at Heathside as neighbours of Mrs Lumb, where Mrs Sharpe found it easy to join Mrs Lumb and the two Whittaker ladies for a game of pool. Before long, however, Mrs Whittaker died and Catherine went to live with the Sharpes.

The principal recipient and preserver of these letters was a nephew of Mary Holland and Martha Sharpe, John William Whittaker. His father, mother (née Sarah Buck), and sister (also called Sarah) made frequent visits to Knutsford from their house and farm at Bradford. The letters they all exchanged, although they rarely bear directly upon Mrs Lumb and her affairs, are remark-able for the detail they provide about the concerns, conditions and way of life shared by Hollands, Sharpes and Whittakers. With the exception of William Whittaker, who died on 19 July 1816 at the age of fifty-six, they were intelli-gent, energetic and prosperous.[32]

They all lived on a far better scale than most inhabitants of Knutsford. What Ward later gathered about this period of Elizabeth Stevenson's life from her daughters was characteristically sketchy, suggestive and dubious: 'Cramped but refined poverty – always the same house – a house on the Heath Knutsford nr Mrs Merriman's'. *Slater's Directory for 1869* gives Heath House, Heathside, as the address of Charles Anthony Merriman, a surgeon. One has merely to look at this row of houses today to become aware of the superior quality of their life by provincial standards, an impression reinforced by the letters of Henry Holland that are now available.[33]

Marianne Lumb, who was about the same age as Peter Holland's daughter Mary, was both practical and diplomatic: 'I have measured between the Bed on my side and the Door', she wrote to her mother,

> and I find there is ample room for a pretty *large Crib* (which *I* will pay for) but should you think it will crowd the room too much, or having the child in the room in the night, will disturb you *in the least*, I will most joyfully take my little charge up in to the Garret and sleep there. ...
>
> My allowance is so handsome that it has enabled me to procure for myself many things which I have not the least occasion for, and which for the future I intend to be without, as I shall have double pleasure, when I shall have little Elizabeth to share a part with me.[34]

Mrs Gaskell's daughters were far too inclined to emphasise the indigence of Mrs Lumb. 'They lived in gt poverty at Knutsford', they told Ward; 'the daughter Marianne had resolved to settle all her property on her mother but she died a day or two before coming of age.' Testators did not have to be of age to make a will until after 1837 – a girl of twelve and a boy of fourteen could do so. Chadwick, who saw and described the house at Heathside early in this century, called it 'substantial'. She also found out that Mrs Lumb was consid-ered to have been 'comparatively wealthy', and by the time of her revised edition she was able to add, 'It is said that Marion Lumb, the cripple cousin, who inherited a large fortune from her father, made her will in favour of Elizabeth Stevenson, but she died suddenly without having signed the will, otherwise Mrs. Gaskell would have had considerable means in her own right.'[35]

A discovery by J. G. Sharps, who brought the Whittaker letters to our atten-tion, appears to give some support to the daughters' version. On 8 April 1812 Mrs Sarah Whittaker wrote to her son,

> Mr and Mrs Sharpe have entered upon their Farm and House at Heathside – your Father was commissioned to purchase them some cows. ... he thinks Mr Sharpe a very fine man – who shewed him all over his land, & they had a *vast* of talk. ...

She [Martha] sent me melancholly tidings from Knutsford of the sudden Death of poor Mary Anne Lumb who went to Halifax with her Mother – & died there of a Days illness (Spasms) it is feard before the object of her Journey (making her will) was accomplishd! Poor Mrs Lumb – how this affectin[g] stroke must shock & distress her by depriving her of her sole companion & chief object of affection & perhaps greatly abridging the means of rendering her future life comfortable! She has also a Sister very far gone in a decline – who she was obliged to leave on this necessary but most unfortunate Journey.[36]

This is partly true but also misleading. Marianne did not inherit under the will her father had drawn in 1804. She was not even mentioned in it. But it is very noticeable how often unmarried women in this level of society were provided for by spinster aunts and childless relations. In fact, Marianne received at least one such inheritance (and there may well have been others) under a will that her father's aunt, another Hannah Lumb, had made on 24 November 1797, after the formal separation of 1795. Marianne was left the income from one hundred pounds in trust until she was twenty-one, when she would be paid the capital sum. If she were to die before this age, the money was to go to her mother. The will of this Hannah Lumb, 'gentlewoman', was made only two days before she herself died.[37]

It is certainly correct, as Sarah Whittaker claimed, that Marianne died in Halifax, but it was on 31 March 1812 and several months after her twenty-first birthday, so there is no doubt that she would have been entitled to her great-aunt's £100. Marianne was the very first burial recorded a few days later by the newly settled minister, Richard Astley, at the Northgate-end chapel, known as 'T'cellar hole chapel' because it was entered at gallery level – the most expensive pews were opposite and at the same height as the preacher whilst those in the free seats kept a lowly, wormlike profile below. Her age is given as twenty-one and her address as Knutsford in Cheshire with her widowed mother. She could have looked after Elizabeth for no more than a few months.[38]

Why exactly Marianne went to Halifax in Yorkshire is puzzling. It is not the obvious way to travel to Wakefield from Knutsford, though if she had been on a visit to cousin John Holland of Bolton, it might have been worth taking that route. Had she come into some other inheritance, one that would demand a journey across the Pennines into Yorkshire? Knutsford had lawyers capable of giving advice, though a solicitor, James Stansfield, was a trustee of the chapel at Halifax, which had been firmly Unitarian in its doctrines from the 1760s. Perhaps her journey had something to do with the fact that her uncle by marriage, Samuel Lumb's brother-in-law William Kershaw, lived there, and as an executor looked after the affairs of the family following Richard Lumb's death in 1807. The Lumbs supported Samuel's illegitimate family; they might have wished to do something special for Marianne when she was twenty-one.[39]

If there is anything in these speculations, Marianne would have had in any case to revise a will already drawn – on 17 October 1811, revoking all other wills and leaving everything to her 'dear mother, Hannah Lumb'. It was proved at under eight hundred pounds and referred to 'bona notabilia' (goods worth mentioning, valued at £5 or more) in the diocese of York as well as that of Chester. Swinton Colthurst Holland of Hackney and William Rigby (of Oldfield Hall, near Altrincham), were to act on her behalf; Hannah Lumb and Peter Holland were executors. On the face of it, her mother's material comforts could only have been 'greatly' abridged in some very relative sense.[40]

Mrs Lumb's 'Sister very far gone in a decline', we know, was aunt Mary Holland, who died unmarried not long after on 10 November 1812 at the age of forty-two. Of Peter Holland's sisters, the aunts of Marianne Lumb and Elizabeth Stevenson, only Hannah Lumb, Catharine and Abigail Holland now remained alive, but they were not living with Hannah at this time, if we may judge from Sarah Whittaker's comment that she had lost her 'sole companion & chief object of affection'. Elizabeth Stevenson, we cannot help remarking, is completely ignored. Presumably a toddler could not be regarded as a companion and a niece was not the equivalent of a daughter. In later years, Elizabeth was undoubtedly an object of Mrs Lumb's love.

When she was growing up, was she ever curious enough, and secure enough, to question her aunt about her marriage to the man whose name she bore, Samuel Lumb? Had it been a kind of dynastic marriage, a cool union between two upwardly mobile families? Just why did Hannah Lumb not find it possible to stay with Samuel until he recovered? Did Marianne Lumb ever meet her father after the separation? Whatever the answers to these questions it was a complicated, unsettling tale; and Hannah in the robust pre-Victorian manner might even have gone into detail about the deaths of Mrs Scrimsher and her son, and the fate of his sisters, Elizabeth's illegitimate female cousins. But though a sad tale, best for winter, it was well in the past. Mrs Hannah Lumb could hardly have been in a more favourable social and economic position, thanks to a circle of friends and relations, the protection afforded by her dynamic father and brothers, and various legacies, not to mention her formal separation contract and its legal enforceability.

NOTES

1 Hall, pp. 18, 71; Pigot & Co., *Directories for 1828-9* and *1834*; Samuel Lewis, *A Topographical Dictionary of England*, 3rd edn, London, 1835, 'Knutsford'. See early illustrs in Margaret Howitt, 'Stray Notes from Mrs. Gaskell', *Good Words*, XXXVI, 1895, pp. 604-12; early photos in Payne, Chadwick, 1910, and *The Graphic* (London), 1 October 1910, Supplement. R. H. Watt's drawing (Knutsford Edn, V, *My Lady Ludlow*) purports to be of the house in 1832; his other drawing of Knutsford in 1846 (II, *Cranford*) is clearly stated to be from a Lucy Holland painting, *c.* 1846.

2 JGS: frag. MS, right ⅔ of F leaf; machine-made paper, no wmk; lacking address and date. A longer TS, ML to HL, with address at end, is headed 'Mary Anne [*sic*, despite internal MS spelling] Lumb, 1811'; it has two gaps, said to be of 17 and 15 lines.

3 Irvine, pp. 79-80; Hall, p. 55; SCH to John Watson, HM consul at Venice, Trieste, 3 July 1804 (BL: Add. MS 48413, f. 171); Peter Holland to Josiah Wedgwood, Knutsford, 20

May 1808 (KUL: Wedgwood 2-277); SCH to George Lyall, The Priory, Roehampton, 17 December 1826 (BL: Add. MS 38748, ff. 217-28).

4 *DNB*; Hicks, *Quest of Ladies*, p. 2; George Pegler, 'The Meeting House at Newcastle-under-Lyme', *TUHS*, V, 1931-34, pp. 399-403; Lilian Beard, 'Unitarianism in the Potteries from 1812', *TUHS*, VI, 1935-38, pp. 14-16. See also William Turner II's notice of WW in Joshua Toulmin, *Memoirs of the Revd Samuel Bourn [with] Biographical Notices*, Birmingham, 1808, pp. 258-63.

5 For all such details see JS&PH, LUBL: Swinton's MS, Diary of Expenses and Journal of a Voyage: Liverpool to Trieste, 1805; Malta to Falmouth and Sandlebridge, 1810; also, TS extract from SCH letter, Trieste, 30 July 1806. The 'Diary' qu. by Irvine, p. 80, has not been seen.

6 KUL: Wedgwood 2-264, PH to JW, Knutsford, 22 July 1805.

7 KUL: Wedgwood 2-267, PH to JW, Knutsford, 29 June [1808]; 'Robert Wilson's journal', in *Five Naval Journals 1789-1817*, ed. H. G. Thursfield, Navy Records Society, 1951, p. 168.

8 *Memoirs of Joseph Priestley*, p. 30; KUL: Wedgwood 2-272, Peter Holland to JW, Knutsford, 30 October 1807; DCLH: Anne Marsh Caldwell, TS, *Reminiscences* [wr. Boulogne, c. 1839-40]. DCLH: Anne's MS diary, September 1812–December 1814, has not been read. WT II, *Discourses on the Duty and Reward of Looking to Ourselves Addressed to Young Persons*, Newcastle, 1818, is dedic. to James Caldwell, visited in 1801. For AMC, b. Newcastle-under-Lyme 9 January 1791, see John Sutherland, *The Longman Companion to Victorian Fiction*, London, 1988, and *Letters*, p. 65.

9 Irvine, p. 73; Mineka, *Dissidence of Dissent*, pp. 108-9; Turner, *Warrington Academy*, intro. Carter, p. 69n.; R. K. Webb, 'The Unitarian background', in Smith, pp. 14-15; Alan Ruston, 'Radical Nonconformity in Hackney 1805-1845', *TUHS*, XIV, 1967-70, pp. 1-9. See also KUL: Wedgwood 29-21675, Mrs A. Holland to JW and Peter Holland, Russell Square, 12 December 1816: house in London Field just leased to a Mr Barker.

10 Quotations are supplemented from TS when necessary.

11 CRO: indenture, 17 February 1810 (infm from Mrs Joan Leach); Hall, p. 18; Ormerod, *History of Chester*, p. 493; Kath Goodchild, 'Mr Egerton's pickage, stallage, and shambles', *JKHAA*, Autumn 1981, p. 19.

12 *Memoirs of Edward and Catherine Stanley*, ed. Arthur Penrhyn Stanley, London, 1879; R. E. Prothero and G. G. Bradley, *The Life and Career of Arthur Penrhyn Stanley, D.D.*, 3rd edn, London, 1894, I, pp. 2-4; *Before and After Waterloo: Letters From Edward Stanley*, ed. Jane H. Adeane and Maud Grenfell, London, 1907, pp. 15, 80.

13 SW to JWW, Townhill Farm, Friday 1 November 1811 (WAL: EHC 205c/14; Hall, p. 27); McLachlan, *Warrington Academy*, pp. 38, 88; *Mansfield Park*, ch. 39; Green, p. 113; *Memoirs of Lucy Aikin*, ed. Le Breton, p. 162.

14 DCLH: HH to LA, Knutsford, 21 March 1809; TS, HH to ME, Edinburgh, 2 August 1811, and 22 May 1814. His lifelong correspondence with the two authors is more revealing about the origins and progress of his own distinguished career. See also p. 113 below.

15 The original is not known; Sharps, p. 302n., lists slightly variant copies. The first full text was pr. in Hopkins, pp. 22-4; her source was a copy by Meta Gaskell in HUL: bMS Am 1088 (4490).

16 The Shaen family of Essex, friends of ECG, provides relevant evidence for Davidoff and Hall, *Family Fortunes*, pp. 328-9, 335-40.

17 WT to Mary Robberds, Newcastle, 29 January 1812; Baker, *Dissenting Chapel*, p. 52; M. Wollstonecraft, *A Vindication of the Rights of Woman* (1792), ed. Carol H. Poston, New York, 1975, ch. 3, p. 40. See Chapple, 'Unofficial lives', in Parish, pp. 108-10.

18 GLROL: MF X26/16, St Luke's burials 1778-1812; Chadwick, 'The mother of the author of *Cranford*', *Bookman*, January 1912, pp. 197-8, and Chadwick, 1913, p. 12 (where, however, 29 October 1811 is given as the date of her burial).

19 GLROL: St Luke's burials 1827-38, no. 1309, 27 March 1829 [aged] 57 (MF X26/18); King's Road burial ground book 1789-1863 (MF X26/22a); Bryan, *Chelsea*, p. 152; LCC, *Survey*, IV, p. 87.

20 Sainty, *Treasury Officials*, p. 39; Hopkins, p. 24.

21 Masson, *Encyclopaedia Britannica*, X, 1879; Ward Notebook, f. 4; *DNB*, XXI, 1890 (1st issue); Knutsford Edn, I, p. xviii; *Letters*, p. 28. Cp. Hope, *George Hope of Fenton Barns*, p. 177, and p. 154 below.

22 DCLH: HH to PH, London, 3 February [1812]; London, 20 March [1812].

23 Aikin, *Description of the Country*, pp. 421-5; Lysons, *Magna Britannia: Chester*, pp. 670-3; 1847 tithe map (CRO); *Edgeworth Letters*, pp. 19-20; Butler, *Maria Edgeworth*, p. 211.

24 Hall, p. 77; *VCH Cheshire*; Pigot and Co., *Directories for 1828-9* and *1834*; E. W. Brayley and John Britton, *The Beauties of England and Wales*, VI, 1805, p. 287; Green, pp. 6-7.

25 Harold Perkin, *The Origins of Modern English Society 1780-1880*, London and Henley, 1969, p. 42; Scard, *Squire and Tenant*, pp. 23-8; Mark Girouard, *Town and Country*, New Haven and London, 1992, pp. 35-44.

26 National Trust, *Tatton Park*, rev. 1963; Dorothy Stroud, *Humphry Repton*, London, 1962, pp. 78-9 (with illustr.); N. Temple, 'Pages from an architect's notebook: John Nash and the Reptons at High Legh Hall', *THSLC*, CXXXVIII, 1989, pp. 114-18, 131; Duckworth, *Improvement of the Estate*, pp. 39-55.

27 Green, pp. 16, 70; Hanshall, *History of Chester*, pp. 389-90. (Cp. C. Stella Davies, ed. *A History of Macclesfield*, Manchester, 1961, repr. 1978, pp. 140-3, 162).

28 Green, p. 71 (also WCL: William Beamont's copy, with cutting dated 20 December 1800); CRO: tithe map, 1847 and apportionment, 1848; Scard, *Squire and Tenant*, p. 16; King, *Portrait of Knutsford* (illustr.); Raymond Richards, *Old Cheshire Churches*, pp. 195-7.

29 DCLH: HH to LA, Knutsford, 27 September 1805. PH added his part a few days later (in careless, mostly crossed writing).

30 Cp. Irvine, p. 71: PH married a daughter of Jeremiah (or Daniel) Whittaker of Manchester at Walcot Church, Bath, in December 1808.

31 DCLH: family bible; HH to LA, Knutsford, 21 March 1809, and Edinburgh, 28 January [1810]; *Letters*, p. 562. PH illustr. Irvine, opp. p. 70, and Robert Murray, 'Peter Holland: A pioneer of occupational medicine', *BJIM*, XLIX, 1992, p. 378.

32 Bibliographical appendix, 10; DCLH: HH to Lucy Aikin, Belvidere, Bath, January 1804, and St Michael's Hill, Bristol, April 1804; Hall, pp. 2, 18, 27, 29, 36, 50; WYA: 34D76 (inscription on WW's tomb). Belvidere, HH thought, was 'built originally for a ladies' school'. For Bradford see especially Rae, *Turtle at Mr Humble's*, p. 183 et seq.

33 Ward Notebook, f. 6 (cf. Ward in *DNB*: 'The aunt was poor, and lived in a modest house with an old-fashioned garden on the heath'). ME's 1st letter lists at the end the names of those present at the masquerade; it is a roll-call of the local gentry and their friends.

34 Hopkins, pp. 23-4.

35 Ward Notebook, ff. 5-6; FitzHugh, *Dictionary of Genealogy*, p. 301; Chadwick, 1910, pp. 21, 144, and 1913, p. 98.

36 Sharps, pp. 302-3n.; Gérin, p. 9; SW to JWW, Townhill farm, 8 April [1812] (WAL: EHC 205d/44; Hall, pp. 29-31). Meta later emphasised that her father and mother each inherited money shortly after their marriage and that two servants were increased to three when the 'first (living) baby came' (JGS: MG to Clement Shorter, 10 September 1910, NYPL copy by Mildred Christian).

37 BIHRY: 141, f. 500, HL's will proved at York, December 1797; Westgate chapel registers and inscriptions, outside vault 5 (JGLCW copy).

38 CAH: RG4/3348 (MF); Seed, 'The role of Unitarianism', p. 271. See also Robert Gittings and Jo Manton, *Dorothy Wordsworth*, Oxford, 1985, p. 6.

39 See Millson, *Northgate-end Chapel*, pp. 14, 17, 37, and Eileen Spring, chapter 1, 'The Heiress-at-Law', *Law, Land, & Family: Aristocratic Inheritance in England, 1300 to 1800*, Chapel Hill and London, 1993. The third William Turner did not arrive as the chapel's minister until 1829; other names in the early registers are unfamiliar in a Knutsford Unitarian context.

40 BIHRY: 156B, f. 427, ML's will proved at York, 24 April 1812. Signed in the presence of Sarah William(?s), George Witten and James Partington (see *Letters* index). PH's daughters were staying at Rigby's in 1808 (KUL: Wedgwood 2-276). He was a Manchester merchant who had studied at Warrington Academy c. 1780 and, like Samuel Greg, was a Trustee of Manchester College in 1810.

7

Upper and Lower Knutsford

HANNAH LUMB never left the large and comfortable house she lived in at Heathside, though some of her neighbours seem to have moved fairly frequently – not a difficult matter when houses were often rented rather than bought. 'We have had many changes in this little town amongst the inhabitants since you were here', Catherine Whittaker wrote to her nephew in 1814:

> Mrs Johnson & her family live in the large house near Mr Wrights, where Mrs Grey liv'd; she has Colonel Handfield's house, next to Mrs Lumb's on this side – poor Mrs Streithill-Wright has been dead a few months, after suffering most severely for the last year of her life. Mrs Johnson is the widow of the late Rector of Wilmslow – she has ten Children.

The house and farm to which the Sharpes had moved was owned by the Leicester family, we learn when it was eventually given up: 'Sir J. Leicester has accepted the resignation of that & the farm in Spring – which is thought handsome, the time of regular notice having expired'. The Sharpes probably lived a little further out than Mrs Lumb, more in the country, on the Tabley side of Heath House.[1]

Mrs Lumb's is the largest in a group of four houses, irregular in size and shape, shown in rough outline on the tithe map of 1847. The smaller three on the town side are semi-detached, providing a pleasing variety of roof-lines and chimney-stacks. Gardens and a meadow behind stretched for some distance, as far as the 'house of correction', the mechanical shape of which looks like an alien intrusion on early maps. Mrs Lumb had land enough to be self-sufficient; she could have supplied all the fruit and vegetables her small household would have needed. The man who rented it before her, Samuel Wright, a Knutsford attorney, had planted a Newington peach tree, a nectarine, dwarf greengages and a Morello cherry. At the town end of Heathside sites were more restricted; there were a number of smaller houses in which flourished, according to the 1828-29 directory, a small colony of carpenters, milliners and dressmakers, a plasterer, a nail-maker, an umbrella-maker, shop-keepers and dealers in sundries, smiths and a stonemason, and five taverns.[2]

Hannah Lumb probably lived very quietly. Her Georgian house, built as the first of its group, has been subject to continuous alteration – two bay windows on either side of the central front door were added, one perhaps as late as 1860, and a small extension even later – but Anne Thackeray Ritchie discovered 'a pretty carved staircase and many light windows both back and front' when she came to 'The Heath' towards the end of the last century. Mrs Chadwick, who saw it early in this century, reported 'cosy ingle nooks, and many comfortable window seats', old oak stairs (painted white), panelled rooms and two kitchens, the larger of which had four ovens. Mrs Gaskell retained concrete souvenirs of the house in later life:

> The quaint copper coal-scuttle, with its capacious mouth, and the silver snuffers and tray raise at once a mental picture of that peaceful, old-fashioned home where her powers began to bud and bloom, a home for which to her dying day she retained a romantic attachment, and all the little household gods which came to her from there were cherished with peculiar care. Very precious to her daughters are the pair of blue and white china candlesticks which were used in their mother's nursery at Knutsford.

The garden behind the house still has a well grown and beautiful deodar with drooping branches and fragrant wood. There would have been at least grass to be mown for hay, flowers, bushes, fruit trees – perhaps chickens and a cow. Martha Sharpe on her nearby farm at Heathside was a keen gardener; she had flower beds with dahlias and 'what we here call the polyanthus Narcissus', pretty and sweet-smelling, with 'seven or eight flowers upon one stem.'[3]

Whenever Mrs Lumb took Elizabeth by the hand and led her out of the front door, a few steps would take them onto the road and the little triangular space called 'Market Green' on the six-inch ordnance survey map of 1872. The going underfoot was poor, for all the roads around Knutsford were 'ancle deep with mud in winter, & with dust in summer', farm tracks along which graziers drove their beasts to market. When Elizabeth Gaskell used to 'read' make-believe letters to her own little daughter, introducing the names of all the things Marianne knew, the one supposed to be from Aunt Lumb mentioned 'flowers, geese &c'. Flowers are the sort of thing adults draw attention to, perhaps adding a Wordsworthian gloss that every flower enjoys the air it breathes. But for a small child tall white geese surging uncontrollably by in a compact flock, wild-eyed and stridently honking, are unforgettable.

Knutsford never had a settled market. Beasts and pens were likely to be found in any convenient place, but early photographs show livestock and farm produce being traded where the road widened outside the White Bear, close by the end of Market Green. This inn probably dates from the seventeenth century, but it was not the gabled, half-timbered and smartly thatched structure we see today. It resembled a long, plain-fronted labourer's cottage, with the simplest of thatched roofs meeting the line of three small upper windows – like the old Stag's Head, no longer in use but surviving as an outbuilding of the new Stag's Head, about four hundred yards from where the Sandlebridge home of the Hollands used to stand. When the daily coach to London or to Liverpool, the 'Aurora', pulled in beside the White Bear, the market scene must have been chaotic.

Once round the corner in Princess Street, however, they would have been on a curving 'top street', firmly cobbled or sett-paved, where substantial houses had been or were still being built for prosperous tradesfolk and professional men. Solid shop window frames in Knutsford's main streets gave promise of the 'pretty doorways, arched corners, carved landings and mahogany doors' within. Those fortunate enough to live in the higher part of the town, literally and socially, lived in great domestic comfort. 'The staircases and chimney-pieces are their own original selves, the cupboards were made to dwell in their own particular niches, and it is the passing generations who turn and unturn the keys as they go by', wrote Anne Thackeray Ritchie after her visit. Keys are needed by those with possessions to guard, who live in houses behind heavy doors and garden walls.[4]

A large Georgian building of three storeys with imposing wings projecting onto the west side of Princess Street was to be the home of Peter Holland's young partner, Richard T. Deane. His is a very sad but typical story, even for a prosperous family living in a little country town. Between 1833 and 1840 five children were born to Dr Deane and his wife Mary Anne. By March 1842 Mary Anne and two of the little ones were dead. Two years later Dr Deane married Peter Holland's daughter Susan, on 10 April 1844. A bequest of £300 came to them in 1848 from aunt Abigail Holland's will, but not long afterwards came a dreadful blow. A letter Mrs Gaskell wrote on 12 January 1850 almost certainly refers to their tragedy: 'My head & eyes ache so, with crying over the loss of three dear little cousins, who have died of S. Fever since I last wrote, leaving a childless mother, that I hardly know what I write... '. Two more children were born, but by 1853 they too were dead. Richard Deane himself died in January 1851, aged 46, so that Susan was eventually left a widow with three children of the first marriage. Property, possessions and medical skill did not allow this family to escape the fate of so many in those days, rich and poor alike.[5]

On the other side of Princess Street was a complication of alleys, courts and steps all leading down to King Street. Had Mrs Lumb and Elizabeth as they went by looked left along the short lane to the George and Dragon on the lower level, they would have seen the decent assembly room and card room built by subscription in the eighteenth century for the exclusive benefit of county families and local gentry. Fifty yards further along Princess Street the houses ended and the prospect opened remarkably. Before them stood only the imposing session house with prison governor's house beside it on their right, and on their left the parish church and Peter Holland's Church House, alone in its large garden and field.[6]

A great-grandson of Peter, born in 1855, recalled being carried in a sedan-chair as a child here together with his twin brother and sister:

I mean in the ordinary way of life and not as an artificial 'experience'. One sedan-chair survived in Knutsford long after the others had disappeared off the face of the land, and as the streets of the town were then Cheshire cobbles, and the distances from house to house very short, it was a convenient means of transport. I recall very well all three of us being packed into the chair and the sensation of being lifted off the ground and of the swaying motion as we went along from Church House to the house in High-Street, where my step-aunt, Mrs. Deane, lived.

A sedan-chair had several advantages for those who could afford it. To keep a horse and carriage might cost between £200 and £300 a year. A chair cost about 25 guineas, and could be taken down steps and through alleys a carriage would stick in – obviously useful in Knutsford's many narrow ways, as Lady Jane Stanley and other ladies had found. De Quincey stressed that passsengers did not have to wear pattens and mufflers to walk in dirty streets during bad weather; they could be delivered to the doortep or even taken right into a house, the roof and door of the chair being kept closed until the hall door had been shut.[7]

A little past the prison governor's house a short descent called Adam's Hill went off left to join the end of King Street. There were a number of humble cottages here, both brick and timber-framed (some of them owned by Peter Holland as early as 1797), and on the corner of King Street and Adam's Hill, a very roughly built farm. Across from this, on a steep slope and raised many feet above the level of the road bending south towards Over Knutsford, was the end of many a journey for Mrs Lumb and her niece – the old dissenting chapel now known as Brook Street Unitarian chapel, built towards the end of the seventeenth century on a 'certaine parcell of land the Inheritance of the said Isaac Antrobus called the nearer feild and adjoining to his dwelling house in Nether Knottsford afforesaid'. Isaac was a Knutsford mercer and skinner, who joined with 'Peter Coulthurst of Sandlow Bridge in Little Warford' (from whom the Hollands inherited Sandlebridge) and others in a thousand-year lease of the land and building, a later minister, the Reverend George Payne, tells us in *An Ancient Chapel*.[8]

The chapel is set back from the road. It was next to the much larger Brook House, built by the Antrobus family and later rented to Lady Jane Stanley, a sister of the Earl of Derby and a very grand figure indeed in the town between 1780 and 1803. She was followed in turn by a Miss Legh, a Miss Wright and a Mrs Wyatt. It is difficult now to visualise this corner where Adam's Hill, King Street and Brook Street met as it used to be in the early nineteenth century. The old farm and quaint cottages at the end of King Street are seen in a water-colour of about 1846 by Lucy Holland that was discovered by R. H. Watt and redrawn for the *Cranford* volume of the Knutsford Edition. They remained until the railway was driven through this part of Knutsford in the early 1860s. Eleven cottages by the chapel had been taken down by 1829, when their bricks were used to build a parochial school just below, opposite the farm. A small piece of land directly in front of the chapel was its only burial-ground until another plot was added to one side in 1833, where Elizabeth Gaskell now lies amongst her relations. Otherwise there were only trees, fields and a brook in the valley of the town moor, until the eye was caught by the buildings of Cross Town on the rising land beyond.[9]

The chapel is not a grand building. It resembles chapels at Dean Row (near Wilmslow) and Macclesfield built at about the same time, in the late seventeenth century. Its weathered red brick and small, diamond-paned windows make it look like a small manor house, though it has two external staircases in front, one at each end. Steps lead to doors that open into a three-sided gallery, running around the two small side walls and the longer wall at the back. In the front of the chapel used to be an old three-decker pulpit; in the wall behind this, high windows looked out over the graveyard and through the branches of a large sycamore. Further on there were three magnificent elms, which survived until the arrival of the railway – 'like a buonaparte', John Clare would have said. The services were simple, though the singing was accompanied by musicians – playing a wooden pitch pipe and a flute in the 1820s and 1830s, according to Samuel Leicester, who died at the age of ninety in 1900. To sit in the high-backed pews it used to contain in Elizabeth Stevenson's youth must have given a sense of utter security. The inner walls of this small and homely chapel have always been whitewashed.

The chapel's congregation had become Unitarian as early as 1740, losing members to the Congregationalists and the Methodists during the second half of the century.. An Independent chapel was established in 1803, a Reverend James Turner being its minister for many years. Mrs Lumb and the little Elizabeth would have sat first under a young man, John Smethurst, about whom nothing is said in the history of the old dissenting chapel but that he was the younger brother of the Reverend Robert Smethurst of Stand near Manchester, and was thought to have emigrated to America. He had been educated at Manchester College during its York days, but left in September 1805 before completing his course. He accepted an invitation from the 'small but respectable society' at Knutsford in 1810, continuing until 1819, after which he emigrated. He died in America in 1826. He was succeeded by Joseph Ashton, minister from from 1820 to 1826, years when Elizabeth was mostly away at boarding school, where she would have learnt to compare him and his services with those of the established church. He too had been educated at Manchester New College during its York days, and went on to be successively minister at Halifax, Whitby and Preston. It is not likely that either of these men would have had anything like the impact on Elizabeth of her friend Henry Green, learned, antiquarian and vital, minister from 1827 right through to 1872. When he first came the congregation consisted of about forty adults.[10]

The chapel still possesses a little library, clear evidence of its congregation's special concerns, as much political as religious in Hannah Lumb's case.[11] *An Abstract of the Evidence for the Abolition of the Slave Trade* and Thomas

Clarkson's *The History of the Rise, Progress, and Accomplishment of the Abolition of the Slave Trade*, 1808, an exceptionally popular work, both bear Hannah's name and were presumably presented by her. The famous jasperware anti-slavery medallion of 1787 ('Am I not a man and a brother?'), created by her father's friend, Josiah Wedgwood I, must have been very familiar. Manchester, too, was prominent in the early abolitionist movement. Its local committee contained Unitarians from Cross Street chapel, and their wives and daughters ensured that the number of female subscribers to the Abolition Society was above the national average towards the end of the eighteenth century. For a time Dr Thomas Percival had been a key figure, in contact with abolitionists like Priestley and the Bishop of Llandaff. Thomas Barnes and Ralph Harrison preached against slavery to receptive congregations. Well known Liverpool Unitarians like William Roscoe, James Currie and the Reverend John Yates were supporters; so too was the Reverend William Turner of Newcastle.[12]

Hannah's name is also found in *Sermons* published in 1817 by Ralph Eddowes, a Chester and Liverpool merchant who had emigrated to become a founder-member of an early Unitarian society in America. Roman numerals III in Clarkson and VI in Eddowes perhaps show that she gave at least six books. An 1800 edition of Thomas Percival's *A Father's Instructions to His Children*, bearing Abigail Holland's name, indicates yet another link with Manchester, reinforced by her name on the autobiography of a Unitarian worthy, *Review of the Missionary Life and Labour of Richard Wright*, published in 1824. The subscription list of this shows that the Reverend J. G. Robberds of Cross Street chapel, who had married William Turner's daughter Mary and who was to welcome William Gaskell as a colleague a few years later, subscribed for no less than six copies.[13]

Robberds had come forward himself in 1825 with a tract entitled *An Answer to the Lord Chancellor's Question, 'What is a Unitarian?'*[14] James Losh of Newcastle told Henry Brougham that the classicist Dr Samuel Parr used to speak of Robberds as a 'profound scholar and the best preacher he had ever heard'. His congregation about this time increased his salary and presented him with no less than £1000 in token of their appreciation. Other Holland names are found on chapel library copies of *Six Tracts in Vindication of One God* (1791), the Warrington Academy tutor John Seddon's *Discourses on the Person of Christ, the Holy Spirit, and on Self-Deception* (Warrington, 1793), Newcome Cappe's *Discourses on the Providence and Government of God* (3rd edn, York, 1818), and an 1828 volume of Robert Aspland's theologically conservative periodical, *The Christian Reformer*. William Newcombe's *Observations on Our Lord's Conduct as a Divine Instructor* (2nd edn, 1795), reminds us that in 1808 the Unitarian Society published an 'improved version' of the New Testament, based upon Archbishop Newcome's translation, with introduction and notes by Thomas Belsham.[15]

A more varied walk back to Heathside was through the oldest part of

Knutsford, the narrow and irregular King Street – shops and inns and houses of all shapes and sizes, steps and fronts poking haphazardly into the street. Henry Green took obvious delight in recording that the noble and eccentric Lady Jane Stanley 'disliked to see men and women linked together, i.e. walking arm in arm', so she gave money for pavements of no more than 'a single flag in breadth'. And though she neglected to specify the exact width of the flag, 'in many places the streets and consequently the raised pavements are too narrow to allow of more than a very slender footpath.' Passengers must still be agile enough to hop sideways into the street or stump along awkwardly with one foot on the pavement and the other in the road. Nor can Green resist mentioning another local character: old Molly Coppock, who used to live in one of Peter Holland's cottages, and was so famous for savoury black puddings that George, Prince Regent from 1811 to 1820, ordered some to be sent to London. It inspired Green to adapt Milton's *L'Allegro*: 'How proud good old Molly would be! – nay, how proud the Knutsford puddings, "in their linked sweetness, long drawn out," as they reposed on the royal plate of gold ... '. Her near neighbour was Sally Felton, who sometimes gave more for her apricots than she would charge 'ten or a dozen generations of schoolboys' for the excellent tarts she made from them.[16]

Once fairly into King Street there would have been a number of ways to get back to the upper part of the town. Mrs Lumb and her niece could have gone up Church Hill past the parish church and its graveyard. (A slightly macabre joke was told of Peter: his former patients were always under his eye.) Or they could have continued along King Street, passing by the old court house in a little market square on the town moor side. During the Napoleonic wars it had been the armoury ('ranged muskets, and bayonets and swords') of the Knutsford loyal volunteers infantry; later it housed the books of the working man's library where Henry Green gave the first of his lectures on Knutsford in 1858. There were a number of inns here as well as the centrally placed George and Dragon, which became the Royal George after Princess Victoria's visit in 1832. With coaches calling daily and its elegant assembly rooms, it was a great social centre in the nineteenth century – though back in 1781 the maid had bragged to John Byng that its genteel assemblies included '*on no account*, any tradesmen'. (Nowadays it is happy to welcome members of the Gaskell Society at their annual meetings in Knutsford.) To turn left and go though its arch past the rooms and stables is yet another way up to Princess Street or, as it was sometimes called, 'top street'.

Some dwellings on King Street were, perhaps surprisingly, given Knutsford's genteel reputation, semi-industrial. One old farm, illustrated in *Looking Back at Knutsford* and not long since demolished, had a handloom weaver's gallery in its upper storey. In 1810, Lysons states, there was 'no cotton factory, but a great deal of cotton-spinning and weaving' was done in private houses. The 1821 census records that Nether Knutsford had 227 families 'chiefly employed' in trade, manufacture or handicraft, 132 in agriculture and 140 'not comprized' in either; by 1831, the corresponding figures were 452, 21 and 61. This was characteristic of the whole area. The newly appointed Unitarian Minister to the Poor in Manchester made several thousand visits between January and November 1833 and reported that more than a half of the houses he visited regularly were inhabited by hand-loom weavers. Though power-looms were taking over, domestic weaving could still be profitable in some places until the middle of the century. It was not the only form of work available, as the census recognised, and large families might earn in a variety of ways at different stages of their lives – very erratically, however.

Some weaving work at Knutsford was brought from the silk town of Macclesfield to the east, where the thread was cleaned and spun, 'and given out to the people, who sometimes had to carry the finished product back a distance of twelve miles'. Only the coarsest silk was woven by power. A brilliant journalist, Angus Bethune Reach, described domestic silk-weaving in 1849: living rooms on the ground floor, bedrooms on the first and then up a ladder to the loom-shop in a lofty garret. Middlemen gave out prepared silk, stipulating times and rates for completion. The lowest sort were greys for bandanna handkerchiefs; the rest were fancy articles subject to changing fashion – 'Soom'mut new was always coming up'.

Cotton was brought from Manchester, which, a clever French observer wrote, 'like a diligent spider, is placed in the centre of the web, and sends forth roads and railways towards its auxiliaries, formerly villages, but now towns, which serve as outposts to the grand centre of industry.' Reach describes several of these satellites. It is to be hoped that one of his more depressing accounts, of the 'fast-expiring trade' of hand-weaving cotton on a treadle-loom at Oldham, was not typical of Knutsford. Peter Holland's fellow trustees of Brook Street chapel were a threadmaker, a cotton manufacturer, three tanners and a mercer. Its baptismal register suggests that silk weaving possibly continued until 1850.[17]

If Mrs Lumb and Elizabeth went through Silk Mill Street to reach the higher town, they would have been in a part of Knutsford that bore a considerable resemblance to industrial areas of Cheshire and Lancashire. Its very name comes from a large silk mill factory established in the middle of the eighteenth century, which proved to be unsuccessful in comparison with Macclesfield. Cotton spinning was then carried on, but the mill became bankrupt and the Egertons of Tatton bought it to convert into small cottages built of coarse brick, with thin slate roofs, sash windows having twelve small panes, stone lintels and sills. Semi-circular heads of brick make the doorways a little more decorative.[18] The Egertons' concern went further: just outside the entrance to Tatton Park was a school organised by Mrs Egerton in 1816 to teach reading, cooking and sewing to one hundred girls. Beatrix Tollemache's grandmother used to arrive to take a class, riding in a small carriage with a postilion clad in the Egerton livery of buff and red. A parochial school to teach reading, writing and arithmetic to boys was also established.[19]

Cosy nooks there may have been in Knutsford, but there were also homes and lodging houses without adequate sanitation and water supply, with leaking roofs, unflagged floors, overcrowded and sordid living conditions. The records and accounts of the overseers of the poor are contained in two leather-bound books, each district being a separate entity responsible for its own poor, even if they had moved away. The flyleaf of the first, for Over Knutsford, is dated 10 July 1823; it lists expenses and payments 1822-36. The second relates to the meetings of 'The Select Vestry' for Nether Knutsford, 1826-36, but its records are not as detailed. In the main town substantial men like Wilbraham Egerton, Peter Legh, John Hollins, James Roscoe and Joshua Siddeley were in charge, deliberating over such matters as providing a loom at the workhouse for women and children. Over Knutsford bought a new loom for £3, which was lent on hire-purchase to an individual, Strethill Kinsey, for eighteen pence a week. When Kinsey fell into arrears a later entry reads, 'The Overseer to find him work on the Common where his younger children may be of use to him and where men are earning 2/- a day'. Money was advanced to widows to purchase meat and sell it at a profit – '£2 weekly for that purpose providing she repays it every Monday morning paying 6d a week Interest.' Weekly payments were made to the elderly, widows, orphans, the sick and illegitimate children – fathers especially being strenuously pursued: 'May 2nd. Journey to Stockport, Risdale, Fairfield, Hide and Gorton trying to take Jas Clayton. 3 Days expenses £1. 5. 0'. The landlord of the White Lion asked that a recruit fallen sick of typhus fever be removed; he was sent to the workhouse. A deaf and dumb woman was allowed into the workhouse 'from a consideration of the readiness of Peter Legh Esq., and others of that township to assist the parish generally'.[20]

Elizabeth Stevenson could not long have remained in ignorance. The poor led their often squalid and pitiable lives well within walking distance of aunt Lumb's house and the better parts of the town. Sounds and smells would have been inescapable. The sight of men and boys picking stones on the common or breaking stones 'in a proper manner under the direction of the Surveyor of Roads' would be commonplace. Individuals were known, and the chapel's congregation would undoubtedly have been charitable to those surviving in what has been called 'an economy of makeshifts', especially in times of partic-ular distress. We find that Mrs Holland had with other ladies founded a Female Benefit Society for the poor in 1806; in 1822 Mrs Sharpe joined Lady Maria Stanley, Mrs Egerton, Mrs R. Leycester, Miss Ross and Miss Leigh – for Knutsford, a very exalted group indeed – in proposing a committee of ladies to find a matron and employment for female prisoners in the gaol, 'sadly neglected, & *unemploy'd*.' Her Holland cousins were reputed to 'know the ins & outs of every poor family in Knutsford.'[21]

Whatever charitable part Elizabeth Stevenson might have played, there is no indication that she wished to dwell on the subject of destitution. In *Our Village* (serialised in 1819) Mary Russell Mitford openly confessed her unwillingness to dwell upon the unpleasant sides of rural life, hurrying past the parish workhouse as if it were a prison; 'restraint, sickness, age, extreme poverty, misery which I have no power to remove or alleviate, – these are the ideas, the feelings, which the sight of those walls excites'. Mitford does not ignore darker realities altogether, but she was not a tough commentator like Cobbett, who recognised the propaganda value of a notice he found in Kent: 'PARADISE PLACE. *Spring guns and steel traps are set here*'. There is at Tabley House a framed hand-bill warning of such traps in Cheshire, which Sir John Leicester felt himself 'reluctantly compelled' to set in order to prevent poaching. Despite a series of night-poaching acts, in 1773, 1800, 1816 and 1819, there had been a remarkable increase in offences against the game laws after Waterloo. Not until 1827 were spring guns forbidden.[22]

In the middle of the century Elizabeth Gaskell's fiction achieved national impact by giving a voice to the poor of Manchester, but there is hardly anything she wrote that does the same for the Knutsford of her youth. In an autobiographical essay, 'The last generation in England', which appeared in the American periodical *Sartain's Union Magazine* for July 1849 and which incidentally mentions a lady who did not approve of 'linking', there is a brief allusion to the lower levels of society. She set her scene by listing the grades in a little country town – from the daughters of large landowners of old family right down to

> the usual respectable and disrespectable poor; and hanging on the outskirts of society were a set of young men, ready for mischief and brutality, and every now and then dropping off the pit's brink into crime. The habits of this class (about forty years ago) were much such as those of the Mohawks a century before. They would stop ladies returning from the card-parties, which were the staple gaiety of the place, and who were only attended by a maidservant bearing a lantern, and whip them; literally whip them as you whip a little child; until administering such chastisement to a good, precise lady of high family, 'my brother, the magistrate,' came forward and put down such proceedings with a high hand.[23]

There is little doubt that the behaviour of the gentry in Cheshire changed radically after the turn of the century, though this particular illustration seems rather glib. The essay was later re-worked and expanded as *Cranford;* a 'few peppery words and angry jerks of the head' by the ladies of Cranford serve the equivalent introductory purpose. Nevertheless, some parts of Knutsford in the early decades of the century must have resembled nearby Manchester, where the minister to the poor reported in 1833 on 'the cruel and barbarous sports of bear-baiting, dog-fighting, and other inhuman sports'. 'Pitched battles between man and man' with hundreds and thousands of spectators, and gambling by boys and young men in 'the wide open fields at the out-skirts of the town' were commonplace on a Sunday, he claimed. Henry Green maintained that cockfighting in a pit by the side of the race-course at Knutsford (subsequently converted into cottages and called 'Reform Buildings') continued until about 1820, and had even been patronised by 'an Earl of Derby among the foremost ... principals and spectators.'

A little can be gleaned from Mrs Gaskell's account of certain harsh Knutsford customs in her letter to Mary Howitt of 18 August 1838 (the full text of which has not yet turned up), but it is relatively incidental. A female scold, she wrote, was 'made to ride stang' after work hours, facing backwards on an old, broken-down horse whilst her cries were drowned by the clattering of pots and saucepans. This is little more than local colour of the kind also deployed by her friend Henry Green in his *Knutsford*. It hardly bears comparison with the ominous structural use Hardy made of the comparable 'skimmity ride' in *The Mayor of Casterbridge*.

One of Mrs Gaskell's servants in Manchester told her that the first-of-May custom of hanging a symbolic branch on the front door could ruin the reputation of the 'principal female of the house'. Gorse, nettles, sycamore and sawdust were the Knutsford equivalents of the scarlet letter. Men digging in roadside marl pits for the clay used as fertiliser (before bones took over about 1830) are also mentioned in the letter to Mary Howitt. Servant maids wearing love powders called 'dragons blood' and other rituals of village life are briefly sketched, but on the whole Elizabeth Gaškell seems to have retained her early memories untarnished by savagery or degradation. 'We, of the genteeler sort', she wrote to Walter Landor in 1854,

> rather chose to ignore some of the meanings which I am sorry for now ... I know that a bunch of nettles was an insult; but not equal to a little heap of sawdust, which was the worst affront of all. But of the exact nature of the insult I have not a notion.[24]

Several quainter customs are gently (and anonymously) poured into the flowing volubilities of the second edition of William Howitt's *The Rural Life of England*, published in 1840 with illustrations by Bewick ('the very Burns of wood-engraving') and S. Williams.[25] Howitt's unpublished letter of acknowledgement seems to show that the full text of Gaskell's missing letter contained rather more than we know. It was probably innocuous:

> Mrs Howitt and myself were much interested in your account of the customs and superstitions of Cheshire, which, with your permission, I shall transfer to another edit: of 'Rural Life'. We were a little surprised to find that the English in your neighbourhood were beginning to adopt the German Christmas Tree. It is a beautiful custom, but what I must doubt is that the English have the simple faith necessary to give unction to such a custom. Still it is a very interesting fact.

In the second edition of *Rural Life* we also discover that Howitt had been 'informed by a lady friend that German families in Manchester have introduced this custom of the Christmas tree, and that it is spreading fast among the English there, – pine-tops being bought to market for the purpose, which are generally illuminated with a taper for every day in the year.'

Elizabeth Gaskell was not alone in reporting to Howitt. Maria Jane Jewsbury of Manchester was another of his correspondents. She had, 'half in joke and half in earnest', collected and had bound 'all the half-penny carols and songs' she could find for Mary Howitt in Manchester and its neighbourhood, including the old ballad of Dives and Lazarus. However, Maria Jewsbury died five years before the first edition of *Rural Life* in 1838 and the Christmas tree is not mentioned there. His informant was almost certainly Elizabeth Gaskell. The tone of all such passages is consistent both with the easy-paced literary idealisations of the Howitts and the general tenor of Elizabeth Gaskell's inoffensive accounts of her early life. The poor in Knutsford, 'respectable and disrespectable', did not seem to have pressed upon her conscience in her youth.[26]

NOTES

1 CW to JWW, Knutsford, 18 September 1811, from Hall, pp. 60-1 ('Hector' of Wilmslow, sc. Rev. Croxton Johnson); see also pp. 29, 168.

2 Goodchild *et al.*, *Looking Back at Knutsford;* Girouard, *The English Town*, pp. 92-4, 98.

3 Ritchie, pref. *Cranford*, p. xii; Chadwick, 1913, pp. 33-4; Leslie, 'Mrs Gaskell's house and its memories', pp. 764-5; Hall, pp. 141, 157.

4 RTD, LUBL: ECG, MS diary, p. 37; Hall, pp. 69, 72; Pigot & Co., *Directory for 1828-9*; Ritchie, pref. *Cranford*, pp. xiv-xv. See illustrs in Goodchild *et al.*, *Looking back at Knutsford*, and King, *Portrait of Knutsford*.

5 ECG, MS diary, p. 69; PRO: PROB 11/2086, AH's will; DCLH: family bible; *Letters*, pp. 4, 100, 102, 166, 170, 843. The first Mrs Deane died aged thirty on 30 March 1842. ECG's children were much of an age with hers and used to stay with them in the 1830s (ECG, MS diary, pp. 46, 52). Mrs Joan Leach drew my attention to the 'desolate nursery swept bare', and provided identifying evidence from Knutsford p. c. grave records (c. 1973) and later censuses.

6 For photographs of Church House see Payne, opp. p. 36 (showing graveyard), and Chadwick, 1910, opp. p. 58 (showing garden, visited by Ritchie, p. xxiii). King, *Portrait of Knutsford*, illustr. sessions house and governor's house.

7 Sydney Holland, Viscount Knutsford, *In Black & White*, London (1926), 1928, pp. 7-8; De Quincey, *Works*, XIV, p. 45; Green, pp. 143-4.

8 The next section draws upon Payne's annot. copy in KPL of *An Ancient Chapel*, pp. 2, 16-20, 32, 46; Richards, *Old Cheshire Churches*, pp. 376-8, and *Historical Sketches of Nonconformity*, ed. [Urwick], pp. 447-8.

9 Joan Leach, 'Lady Jane Stanley of Knutsford', *JKHAA;* Knutsford Edn, II, p. viii. For old photos of Brook House, the farm and cottages see Goodchild *et al.*, *Looking Back at Knutsford*.

10 Payne, *An Ancient Chapel*, pp. 26-7, 60; Broadhurst, *Memoir of Smethurst*, p. 19. John Smethurst (1789-1820 [*sic*]) is briefly mentioned under another John Smethurst (1793-1859) in the *DNB*.

11 I am grateful to Mary Thwaite for introducing me to the library and to Joan Leach for greatly improving my knowledge of it.

12 Earl Leslie Griggs, *Thomas Clarkson: The Friend of Slaves*, London, 1936, pp. 64, 95; Clare Midgley, *Women Against Slavery: The British Campaigns, 1780-1870*, London and New York, 1992, pp. 18-23; Ditchfield, 'Manchester College and anti-slavery', in Smith,

pp. 197-8, 210; Raymond V. Holt, *The Unitarian Contribution to Social Progress in England*, London, 1938, p. 135; David Turley, *The Culture of English Antislavery, 1780-1860*, London and New York, 1991, pp. 118-20, 166-7.

13 Elizabeth M. Geffen, *Philadelphia Unitarianism 1796-1861*, Philadelphia, 1981, pp. 37-8, 73-4; Seed, 'The role of Unitarianism', pp. 186-8 (Wright). Percival was 'somewhat mortified' that his eldest son took orders in the Church of England (Turner, *Warrington Academy*, intro. Carter, p. 78).

14 DWL copy in Pamphlets 1813-30, 5. 61. 10, inscribed 'Fanny Holland from her affece Aunt <?>'. This volume also contains pamphlets by Thomas Thrush presented to Miss A[bigail?] Holland, 1825-35 (see p. 230 below), and W. Turner II's *The Day of the Lord: A Sermon ... Repeated* (Halifax, 1830), presented to a Mrs Holland.

15 H. McLachlan, *The Unitarian Movement in the Religious Life of England: I. Its Contribution to Thought and Learning*, London, 1934, pp. 40-1, 185-6; *Losh Diaries*, II, p. 178; Davis, *Dissent in Politics*, p. 204; Mackenzie, *Newcastle upon Tyne*, I, p. 377.

16 Green, pp. 144-7. The following section is based on Green, p. 150; Beatrix L. Tollemache, *Cranford Souvenirs and Other Sketches*, London, 1900, p. 4; Lysons, *Magna Britannia: Chester*, p. 671; *Report of the Ministry to the Poor Commenced in Manchester Jan. 1, 1833*, p. 7; Walton, *Lancashire*, p. 110; Byng, *Torrington Diaries*, II, p. 175. I gratefully acknowledge the assistance of the Reverend R. Cooke of Cross Street chapel (see also Fryckstedt, p. 90).

17 Payne, pp. 5-6 (based on his 'Knutsford in fiction', *GM*, CCLXXIX, 1895); Leon Faucher, *Manchester in 1844: Its Present Condition and Future Prospects*, tr. 1844, repr. London, 1969, p. 15; Angus Bethune Reach, *Manchester and the Textile Districts in 1849*, ed. C. Aspin, Helmshore, 1972; Davies ed., *History of Macclesfield*, pp. 128-35.

18 Cp. illustr. in Goodchild *et al.*, *Looking Back at Knutsford*, and Heather Coutie, 'How they lived on Hillgate: a survey of industrial housing in the Hillgate area of Stockport', *TLCAS*, LXXXVIII, 1994, p. 45.

19 Payne, *An Ancient Chapel*, p. 5; Lewis, *Topographical Dictionary of England*, 'Knutsford'; Hanshall, *Itinerary of Cheshire*, p. 390; Tollemache, *Cranford Souvenirs*, p. 6.

20 Joan Leach, 'Knutsford's poor in the 1800's', *JKHAA*, Autumn 1981, pp. 20-6. Cp. Coutie, 'How they lived on Hillgate', pp. 49-56, and Barry Reay, *The Last Rising of the Agricultural Labourers: Rural Life and Protest in Nineteenth-Century England*, Oxford, 1990, pp. 78-9.

21 Reay, *The Last Rising of the Agricultural Labourers*, p. 54; Payne, p. 41; Hall, p. 147; *Letters*, p. 12 (c. 1837). Payne identifies Mrs Holland as the mother of Mary and Lucy, but she was dead by 1806.

22 W. J. Keith, *The Rural Tradition: William Cobbett, Gilbert White, and Other Non-Fiction Prose Writers of the English Countryside*, Hassocks, near Brighton, 1975, pp. 77, 93-8; Alan Armstrong, *Farmworkers*, London, 1988, p. 72.

23 *Cranford*, ed. Elizabeth Porges Watson, Oxford (1972), 1990, pp. 162-3. Cp. Robert Knipe's 1827 description of rough drunken pranks of the past, qu. Quinlan, *Victorian Prelude*, p. 262.

24 Green, p. 57; M. Howitt, 'Stray notes', repr. *Letters*, pp. 28-31 (see also pp. 292-3); Scard, *Squire and Tenant*, pp. 84-5 (marling); E. P. Thompson, *Customs in Common*, London, 1991, pp. 472-5, 499 (ECG 'a reliable obsserver').

25 Mrs Gaskell's text is quoted closely but not verbatim in *Rural Life*, 1840, pp. 589-90. See Carol A. Martin, 'Elizabeth Gaskell's contributions to the Works of William Howitt', *NCF*, XL, 1985-86, pp. 94-100.

26 WH to ECG, Esher, 30 January 1839 (HUL: fMS Am 1943.1 (120), p. 3); *Rural Life*, 1838, II, p. 213; *Rural Life*, 1840, p. 461 (cp. p. 464, the dreamlike carols); *Mary Howitt; An Autobiography*, ed. Margaret Howitt, London, 1889, I, p. 281; Sheila M. Smith, *The Other Nation: The Poor in English Novels of the 1840s and 1850s*, Oxford, 1980, pp. 15, 102-4.

8

Friends and relations

THE EXTERNAL FACTS of aunt Lumb's life are now fairly clear, but curiosity about the character of this most important figure of all during the obscure years of Elizabeth's childhood is endless. John Stevenson's letters to his sister in the collection of J. G. Sharps provide a couple of trivial clues: she had a dog called Rover and a sense of humour. It is very unlikely that she brought up Elizabeth or her own daughter on the Spartan principles employed by a disciple of Rousseau and Thomas Day. A girl this devotee adopted as a child used to be either taken out in a carriage for pleasure or tossed in a blanket to harden her nerves, alternating with a favourite dog – or so Mrs Gaskell tells us about one of her aunts in chapter 3 of *The Life of Charlotte Brontë*.

In the period to which she appears to refer, the 1790s, most of her aunts would no longer have been children, but it is just possible that Hannah Lumb, or her sister Abigail, was toughened in this way. When Henry Green arrived in Knutsford in 1827 an old lady in his congregation told him that as a child she had been placed in the care of the Reverend John Palmer of Macclesfield, Unitarian minister there until 1779, 'an exceedingly gifted, but ludicrously eccentric man', who thought young people should be 'trained to bear disappointment'. One fine Saturday afternoon she was allowed to ride pillion behind a serving man to see her parents 'at some five miles distance', but as she caught sight of their house, the servant followed orders, turned the horse's head round and went back. Of Elizabeth's maternal aunts, only Hannah, the third child, born in 1767, and Abigail, the eighth, born in 1773, were living when Green arrived. Sandlebridge was six or seven miles from Macclesfield, and it was not at all unusual to send a spare girl to live elsewhere. It certainly happened with Kate Holland of Liverpool and Mary Turner of Newcastle-upon-Tyne in the next generation.[1]

Day's theories would have been well known to the Hollands. He had selected two young girls from the Shrewsbury and London foundling hospitals to raise by his own 'natural' methods and create a model wife for himself – two for safety's sake, of course. 'Simplicity, perfect innocence, and attachment to himself, were at that time the only qualifications which he desired in a wife', wrote his friend Richard Edgeworth, whose own experiment in bringing up his oldest son 'naturally' proved disastrous. He must have had his tongue in his cheek. By 1770 only the girl Day had given the superb name of Sabrina Sidney remained with him. They settled in Lichfield, where her education was continued with ordeals to test her fortitude: pistols were fired by her ears and melted sealing wax was dropped on her arms. In the long run he married someone completely different – a Miss Esther Milnes of Wakefield, in 1778. She had to renounce polite accomplishments, banishing her harpsichord and music books especially, for 'human life is not long enough to throw away so much time on the science of making a noise'.[2]

The two surviving letters from Marianne Lumb, especially the first, addressed to 'My very dear Mother', display an easy and affectionate relationship. She was not in the least inhibited when describing her pleasures and running on about things she wants bought for her in London, secure in the knowledge that her mother would if necessary say gently but firmly, as we have seen, 'Marianne love I did not get you this, or that thing for I thought it would be rather extravagant in your having it'. This is very much Mrs Lumb's note as far as we can tell, both here and in the account given in Elizabeth Gaskell's letters and diary when she was older. 'My dearest Aunt Lumb, my more than mother ... my best friend' wrote Elizabeth Gaskell on 9 December 1837, obviously wanting to record for her own daughter how much she missed 'this most dearly loved Aunt', who had died in the preceding May whilst looking after Marianne during her mother's confinement. Could it have been something like her own childhood she was describing?

> The little girl slept in a cot by Aunt Lumb's bed; Aunt Lumb gave her, her break-fast, sitting on her knee, by a window, with many loving little jokes between them. Aunt Lumb walked out with her, when the weather permitted. And it was to Aunt Lumb, that Marianne ran when in any little distress; and to her that she always clung.
>
> The very day Aunt Lumb was seized with her fatal attack, she had been with Marianne in the Deane's poney-carriage to the Infant school, and was so pleased with Marianne's pleasure.[3]

A painting of Mrs Lumb in later years shows her in a widow's white muslin cap edged with lace, surmounted by a large bow and tied under the side of her chin with another bow, the 'mob-cap' that later generations despised. Some kind of small ruched collar is about her neck. She is wearing a dark silk dress with puffed sleeves, the top hidden by a large, white and lace-edged Vandyke collar together with cuffs made of a fine material like organdie. She sits composedly upright in a high-backed, elaborately carved chair, hands folded and resting on an open book with her spectacles beside it. Her large eyes gaze directly out at us, her Holland nose (a descendant was known in the navy as 'Hooky') is prominent, her lips seem firm but not unkind. It is, or certainly appears to be, a portrait of a mature woman at ease with herself.

It meant a great deal more to Elizabeth Gaskell. She used to show a portrait of Aunt Lumb to Marianne 'to keep alive the recollection of her love and tenderness', obviously wanting to provide a model of female affection and in the stated belief that Aunt Lumb's bodily appearance was 'a fit shrine for so chastened and pure a spirit'. 'Both nuns and mothers worship images', wrote Yeats, 'Presences / That passion, piety or affection knows / And that all heavenly glory symbolize.'[4]

In a more earthly mode Marianne Lumb and her mother used to give family parties like those of their other Holland relations – 'where all are unconstrained & merry', much better than 'formal tea & Card parties, which are in general very *Stupide*', wrote that categorical young lady Sarah Whittaker in 1809. Formal parties apparently met at half-past five and parted at nine, and even if people could not come, 'the compliment was paid, you know, by their being ask'd.' In the winter of 1810-11 Marianne Lumb had a concert and a dance for ten or twelve couples, 'and the Evening finished with a little spouting from some Young *Ladies*. A kind of Ball and supper at the Dutchman's [Peter Holland's] followed'. Marianne Lumb's first letter to her mother mentions that she and Miss Stanley 'fiddled away while the company danced', which proves that even if she was disabled, she was very much part of the merry-making. Martha Sharpe was talented enough to sum up her 'Knutsford Kinsfolk' at this time in a manner that anticipated Dickensian cosiness: 'Believe only that we are as hearty, as fat, & as agreeable, & as snug, as most people, & judge for yourself when you come amongst us.'[5]

There is another source of information about the days of Elizabeth's childhood, small in itself but illuminating in its context. Knutsford Library has preserved a stout little volume of over two hundred pages entitled *The Monitor; or, A Collection of Precepts, Observations, &c.*, printed at Liverpool in 1804 by J. M'Creery [*sic*]. It contains precepts grouped by an anonymous editor in sections entitled Principle, Virtue, Truth, Fortitude, Social Affections, Manners, Time and Industry, Happiness and the like. On its flyleaf is the inscription, 'Elizabeth Cleghorn Stevenson -/ from her affectionate Aunt / H Lumb/ Sepr the 29th, 1821.' Beneath this, just legible, is 'from her affectionate faithful friend/ H. Greg'. Mrs Lumb had given her niece a birthday gift of a book she herself had been given perhaps as many as sixteen years before.[6]

Hannah Greg was, Henry Holland told Lucy Aikin, 'a woman whom I greatly esteem & admire'.[7] Born into a prosperous Unitarian circle in Liverpool, she had joined her husband Samuel Greg, one of Lancashire's greatest mill owners, as an active member of Cross Street Chapel in Manchester. That she was the editor of *The Monitor* is indicated by a junior literary and philosophical society she began in 1812, affectionately called the 'Duodecimo' because there were '12 small people, of small promise, bound up in a small literary form'. It sprang from her own experience in Liverpool of a 'literary box' in which children could put anything they were inclined to write. In her first address as 'Mama-President' she spoke of her 'more accustomed title of Monitor – my nom de guerre on a former occasion of literary inter-course with my dear pupils.'

Many of the pages of *The Monitor* are marked – so many that it is impos-sible to make any precise use of it. But the fond seriousness with which families of this kind regarded the upbringing of their children is evident. A similar work, *The Poetical Monitor ... for the Improvement of the Young* by Elizabeth Hill, went through eleven editions between 1796 and 1831 according to its title-pages. We know that Abigail Holland presented to Knutsford Unitarian chapel the 1800 edition of Thomas Percival's *A Father's Instructions to His Children*. Mrs Greg's motives were like Percival's a generation before: she was so dissatisfied with the children's books available that she produced her own. The first edition of *The Monitor* appeared in 1799, along with another book entitled *Virtue Made Easy ... Being a Collection of Maxims, etc.* gathered from Dr Thomas Townson's *The Poor Man's Moralist* (Liverpool, 1798). Hannah announced in her preface that she had selected the sentiments she wished to impress on her own children's hearts and minds, sensitively adding that the book was compiled by one 'in whom the maternal relation has been almost sunk in a rational and equal friendship'. Margaret Bryan made the same claim – 'I rejoice in the titles of Parent and Preceptress' – in the preface to her *Lectures on Natural Philosophy* (1806). Women of that period have been seen as fighting against Jacobinism on the home front, retaining femininity but extending the bounds of their expertise and influence.[8]

The Gregs had moved about 1797 to a new house they had built near the village of Styal, alongside their great watermill on the river Bollin at Quarry Bank, about six miles from Knutsford in the Manchester direction. She educated her own children, with occasional help from a governess. When they grew older, she ensured that daughters as well as sons were sent away to a boarding school run by the Reverend James Tayler at Nottingham, and later to the famous school kept by the Reverend Lant Carpenter at Exeter and Bristol, where his own daughter Mary maintained with gentle firmness 'an astonishing degree of order' as a monitor amongst the boys. Ultimately, of course, the Greg daughters could not follow their brothers to Edinburgh University. Hannah used to disagree with her husband (who had been flogged by Dr Samuel Parr the Grecian at Harrow even before school began) about the upbringing of their sons: John Greg had to attend the counting house of the Rathbones in Liverpool during his holidays rather than go to John Dalton in Manchester for chemistry as she had wished, though at least one of the daugh-ters was able to attend lectures in Manchester on chemistry and electricity when she was seventeen.

Samuel wrote to a son in 1814, 'Read only what will give you the best use of your faculties and strengthen the mind – what will give knowledge and information – avoid all novels – prating books and books for prating upon.' Mrs Greg tempered this by asserting that 'a good education does not spoil the Man of Business, and a taste for literature, judiciously infused, contributes to form the intelligent merchant as well as the virtuous man.' There is no doubt about the values of the mother of sons as well as daughters in this particular family.[9]

She lived at Styal until her death in 1828. If ever Elizabeth Stevenson went when she was a girl of ten with Dr Peter Holland on his rounds, which included visits to Greg's apprentices at the Styal mill, she would have been able to join in the activities of the Duodecimo society.[10] A 'sort of open house' used to be kept at Quarry Bank, where the 'absence of display and even of knick-knacks, the pale blue walls, the unadorned furniture, the well-filled bookcases, the portrait of George Washington over the chimney-piece' were all admired by visitors. Mrs Eliza Fletcher, who had known William Stevenson in Edinburgh, came to stay with the Gregs in the summer of 1808. She was struck by 'the cultivation of mind, and refinement of manners which Mrs. Greg preserved in the midst of money-making and somewhat unpolished community of merchants and manufacturers.' 'Snow' Wedgwood's praise of the Gaskell household in later years is strikingly anticipated – 'never any bustle & never any dawdling, which makes the beau ideal of domestic occupation'.[11]

Elizabeth would have come within the orbit of a lively, educated woman with a large family, a woman whose advice to one of her own daughters in 1807 was lucid and direct:

> There must be no bustle over your work even when it is the hardest, but you must appear after it when called to meals or company, composed, chearful, neat, remembering that manner, temper, self-denial are the great virtues you are called to exercise – that to be agreeable must be your accomplishment 'par excellence', your forte, to spread an atmosphere of comfort and domestic affections around you – and that to do this it is not brilliant attainments that are necessary – much of female worth and usefulness consists in negatives, never to be inconsiderate, giddy, unneat, awkward, impatient or fretful – never to betray confidence, never to be imprudent, extravagant or foolish, careless or inattentive, unkind, harsh or intemperate ... To perform the detail of such a sketch you will have to study the characters of those you serve (for the Mistress of a family is in effect its Servant).

'Much of female worth and usefulness consists in negatives' might seem almost indefensible as a generalisation, especially in an age when advanced thinkers were giving more emphasis to rights than to duties. But it was a perfect crystallisation of Mrs Greg's experience, which followed Mary Wollstonecraft's belief that 'the rearing of children, that is, the laying a foundation of sound health both of body and mind in the rising generation, has justly been insisted on as the peculiar destination of women', and she followed as far as she could Wollstonecraft's recommendation that girls and boys should be educated together.

She anticipates the Brontë sisters in several ways. She was tough enough to tell William Rathbone that her early reverence for men had declined when she saw how easily they could be 'influenced or governed by violent, or artful women'. 'Were I to educate my Daughters as many Mothers are accused of doing, merely with a view to their relation to your sex, my advice and instruction would be far other than what it will be I hope, in the notion of their being individual and rational and immortal Beings.' She wished 'particularly for an extension of female pursuits that might render single life more eligible, convenient and honourable, and marriage less obligatory.' The daughters of the Holland family embodied both her fears and her aspirations.[12]

Amongst Hannah Greg's friends were several Elizabeth knew in later life or who maintained friendships through the generations with her family.[13] There was the Reverend Edward Stanley of Alderley, keen-eyed, black-haired and lithe, galloping through the lanes with sugar-plums in his pocket for children. It was his wife Catherine who had been so gracious to Marianne Lumb. The engagingly open-minded Stanley had come in 1805 to a neglected parish on the great Cheshire estate of his brother. He and his wife were acutely sensitive to the increasing 'non-intercourse of rich and poor' that caused their friend Thomas Arnold to write to them in 1831 of the nation becoming 'two such distinct classes'. The Gregs were not aristocrats by birth and did not belong to the established church, but they were obviously soul-mates. 'Have you ever been to Quarry Bank? It is such a picture of rational, happy life', wrote Catherine Stanley. 'They actually do not know what it is to be formal or dull: each with their separate pursuits and tastes, intelligent, and well informed.'

When Edward Stanley attended its third meeting of the newly formed British Association for the Advancement of Science at Cambridge in 1833, he fell in with William Turner. Hearing that he was not a clergyman of the established church but a dissenting minister of Newcastle-upon-Tyne, he grasped his hand and cried, 'I know you now, Mr Turner; I have known you long; for I am intimate with your friends in Cheshire, and have heard all about you.' In its early days the Association was led by liberal, Broad Church Anglicans, but Unitarians like John Taylor, James Yates, Lant and W. B. Carpenter, Charles Wellbeloved, William Henry, William Greg and Benjamin Heywood were particularly active in its affairs. Mrs Stanley presented their son Arthur's *Memorials of Canterbury* (1837) to Mrs Gaskell, which makes his initial reserve amongst the Unitarians of Newcastle at the meeting of the British Association in the following year seem a little odd. However, his biographer speculates that his experiences there might have affected his whole life thereafter. (Could Unitarians really be eternally damned?) His mother later wrote a letter full of admiration of *Ruth* to Mrs Gaskell. Delighted with its general truth and beauty, she was also irresistibly reminded of a shared past – the old chapel on Adam's Hill at Knutsford with its 'diamond-paned windows, overshadowing tree, and outside steps.'[14]

Another of Mrs Greg's circle was William Roscoe of Liverpool, M.P., poet, banker and bibliophile, author of the *Life of Lorenzo de' Medici, Called the*

Magnificent (1795), one of John McCreery's finest publications. Roscoe's remarkable collection of old masters, books and prints was designed to illustrate the history of art, thus serving 'some object of public utility' in his Florence on the Mersey. Utility was the universal pick-lock for a new renaissance. He used to belong to a small literary society in Liverpool that had flourished for some ten years until the proclamation against seditious writings of 1792 and the suspension of habeas corpus in 1794 had made it inexpedient to continue. Its members were regarded by the Tory establishment as 'Liverpool Jacobins'. William Rathbone, John Yates, William Shepherd, James Currie, William Smyth (an Anglican) and others supported municipal reform, freedom of worship, relief for Ireland, peace with France and, in a city where handcuffs and shackles were on sale in the shops and where Mrs Fletcher saw one of the last ships under conversion for the slave trade, the cause of abolition – which recalls Mrs Lumb's strong interest and the books bearing her name in Knutsford chapel library.[15]

Reformers had to be careful in private as well as in public. When Smyth wrote to Currie in 1792 conveying the good news that the question for gradual abolition had been carried in the House of Commons, he added 'I shall be satisfied with begging you to be more tender of Planters & Slave Merchants when you speak than when you write. ... You will make no Converts, but many Enemies.' Smyth was the son of a Liverpool banker who had failed in the early 1790s. Though a lively and sociable bachelor, full of songs and anecdotes, he could make no impression as tutor of Richard Brinsley Sheridan's unteachable son Tom, but in 1807 he profited from a great act of patronage: 'Lord Henry Petty gave me the Professorship of Modern History' at Cambridge. (He was actually preferred to Thomas Clarkson the abolitionist for this part-time post.) Petty, M.P. for Cambridge and later Marquis of Lansdowne, was a young but brilliant member of the 'Ministry of All the Talents' in 1806-7, a colleague of Fox and Lauderdale, a patron of Thomas Macaulay and the man who brought Henry Brougham into the Holland House circle. Smyth's inaugural of 1809 made it clear that he did not share the current enthusiasm for political economy and would not lecture on it, though he noted that one of his colleagues had 'been, for some time, soliciting your attention to these most important, but grave and somewhat repulsive subjects.'[16]

There is a letter of 1840 from William Smyth to 'Mrs Gaskell' in the Harry Ransom Humanities research centre at Austin, Texas. It is almost illegible, the handwriting is so appalling, but internal references suggest it was addressed to Mrs Mary Gaskell (née Brandreth), wife of Benjamin Gaskell of Thornes House. Though she herself was a churchwoman, and when she died in 1845 was buried in Thornes churchyard, her son, James Milnes Gaskell, was baptised in the Unitarian chapel at Wakefield and her husband lies in its catacombs. The clever and satirical lady who in 1853 wished people would not look at her as if *she* were the author of a book about an unmarried mother, *Ruth*, was probably Mary Williams-Wynne, who married James Milnes Gaskell in 1832.[17]

Yet another friend of Mrs Greg, the Liverpool doctor James Currie, a tall, heavy ('inclining to robust'), dignified and formal man, both 'grave and energetic', became known as the amateur editor and biographer of Robert Burns. He found himself with a 'huge and shapeless mass' of Burns's papers, unsorted, unannotated, uncensored – 'the complete sweepings of his drawers and of his desk (as it appeared to me)', he had protested in 1797, 'even to the copy-book on which his little boy had been practising writing.' He had to shut himself in his study for several nights on end before he could come to terms with them. He corresponded with Walter Scott in 1800 about ballads they contained and, though immensely busy, he took the trouble to advise Hannah Greg about her first composition, sending the manuscript to the press of one of his and Roscoe's protégés, 'a fellow of genius and fire', John McCreery, on her behalf. This was *A Collection of Proverbs, etc.*, the second edition of which in 1800 was entitled *The Moralist.*[18]

We do not yet know how often Mrs Lumb visited Hannah Greg during the early years of the century and to what extent she knew her associates, many of them Unitarian, but the gift of *The Monitor* shows that she was in contact not only with the local gentry around Knutsford, but with liberal and literate circles in Liverpool especially. They were not perfect. The verses Roscoe and his friends used to read aloud to each other did not impress one bright young man (who already knew the poetry of Wordsworth) in the summer of 1801, Thomas De Quincey. Another clever young man, Macaulay, thought William Smyth a 'finical old bachelor', who read a lot but was 'under the tyranny of printed nonsense'. Currie's biography of Burns, too, is open to criticism. As a doctor he had strong views upon alcohol abuse and sexual adventures; he could not avoid discussing Burns as a self-destructive genius. His reverent, pained and professional diagnosis of the causes of Burns's early death was to persist throughout the nineteenth century. 'Can Currie really not have known the damage he was doing?' Ian Hamilton asks.

But the publication of the four-volume *Works of Robert Burns; with An Account of His Life, and A Criticism on His Writings* in 1800 would have won praise from the open-hearted Robert Cleghorn; it earned well over a thousand pounds for Burns' widow and children. Its list of subscribers shows that Mrs Greg, Miss Greg and Miss Jean Greg ordered two copies each. Currie might have been misguided as a biographer but he was humane and liberal in his private life, advising Hannah Greg about the upbringing of children in partic-ular. Their 'dispositions ought to be studied, *and all interference considered as a necessary evil*', he advised. There is no doubt that Hannah Greg found and improved immeasurably upon the 'little *mental* medicine' she had craved when her own children were raining down upon her in the 1790s. Her culture of mind and spirit must have been transmitted to her own young people and to any others who came within her sphere of influence. The education of children was a primary and inescapable duty. She believed it should be intelligent, sensi-tive and tolerant.[19]

Early directories do not record Mrs Lumb's brother, Peter Holland, as one of the gentry in Knutsford, perhaps because he is listed as a surgeon. In provincial terms he was highly successful when Elizabeth Stevenson was growing up in this little Cheshire town. A pupil at Warrington of John Aikin, M.D., for two years in the early 1780s, he had been 'treated in all respects like a member of the family'. An old acquaintance told Henry Holland that Peter had 'the best head for argument' when he was young that he had ever met. Between 1783 and 1786 he was apprenticed to Aikin's own teacher, the leading surgeon in the North of England, Charles White, F.R.S., a founder member of both the Royal Infirmary and the Literary and Philosophical Society in Manchester. Peter seems to have been established as a surgeon in Knutsford by 1787, to judge from an order for jars in cream-coloured ware sent to Peter Swift, at Wedgwood's Etruria pottery.

By 1800 Holland was attending on one of the greatest of local families, the Stanleys of Alderley. Lady Stanley described how he had inoculated her 'poor little baby', and when it did not take he did the other arm, with the result that five leeches had to be applied to reduce the swelling and inflammation. A lawyer's letter of 1809 reveals that he had also been attending the Earl of Stamford's wife at Dunham Hall near Altrincham; illegally, however, because a condition of his deed of apprenticeship was not to practise within ten miles of Manchester and Salford. The penalty for non-compliance was £1000. Henry Holland, undoubtedly with a parti pris, wrote to Lucy Aikin about the 'conspicuous instance of malevolent feeling' expressed by White, and the 'policy' involved when he returned the bond of apprenticeship. He feared the dispute would reach print, but somehow the business was settled by the noble earl, 'on terms not stated'.[20]

More unexpectedly perhaps, Holland was involved in exploiting the deep rock salt deposits of Cheshire as a partner in a new company near Northwich, for his son Henry looked forward to riding over to see the works in 1800. When in 1803 Henry, who had been sent to school with William Turner in Newcastle, descended Bigge's Main pit on Tyneside he did not fail to send his father a graphic comparison between the ways in which men used to descend – in buckets at the salt mine and by a noose or just twisting their legs about a rope to plumb the much deeper coal mine. On another occasion he mentioned that Turner would like specimens from Cheshire, so that he could describe the strata and methods of salt abstraction in a paper for the Newcastle Literary and Philosophical Society. Peter Holland himself sent a paper on the comparative purity of Cheshire salt to the *Monthly Magazine* in 1804.

These Northwich mines became impressively large. In 1837 some eighty members of the British Association for the Advancement of Science meeting in Liverpool were taken to them by special train, lowered over three hundred feet below ground and provided with an elegant *déjeuner* in the light of thousands of candles. Toasts were drunk, fireworks let off, the national anthem and a psalm sung – 'and, duly enlightened, the whole party ascended to be returned to Liverpool in time for tea.' Northern towns could not hope to rival Oxford or Cambridge, but, Morell and Thackray stress, they could mount remarkable displays to demonstrate the symbiotic relationship between science, technology and material progress.

It is obvious from Henry's schoolboy letters that he knew his father was a typical man of his time – that he would wish to hear about a great ox, the iron works at Lemington, an inclined plane at Benwell colliery, supper with a botanical traveller and David Stephenson, who had widened the Tyne bridge, a lecture on the properties of matter, and, above all, William Turner's first lecture on the history of philosophy (science) to an audience of two hundred people at the Newcastle Literary and Philosophical Society, using the scientific apparatus it had recently purchased. Henry and Turner's own son William had the pleasure of helping to unpack and test it for four or five days beforehand. Peter was evidently more than an unsophisticated country doctor in a Cheshire town, and his son was already showing promise of yet greater things.[21]

But Peter's medical practice was at the centre of his life. In 1813 he told Maria Edgeworth that her old schoolfriend Caroline, wife of Charles Cholmondeley, and her sister Laetitia had both 'injured their health irreparably by the means they have taken to preserve their complexion and beauty – starving – and *taking medicines* perpetually.' And, Maria continues, 'Mrs. H. Leicester (Laetitia Smythe) he thinks actually killed herself by it'. Holland, she wrote, 'knew it professionally.' During the exceptionally hard winter of 1813-14 when there were many deaths, especially amongst the very old and young, he attended Mr Ralph Leycester of Toft's baby son and heir, staying at the hall for ten nights till the poor child died. An easy and familiar letter about medical treatment to Sir J. F. Leicester, who became Baron de Tabley in 1826, has survived. On one occasion Peter Holland stayed with him at his London house. He seems to have treated Sir John's household with julep, draughts and pills every other day or so, judging by the bills that survive, earning about £50 in 1825.[22]

Peter Holland's flourishing practice among the gentry was complemented by the part he played in the earliest recorded occupational health service: for many years he looked after the young pauper apprentices at Quarry Bank mill, Styal for an annual fee of twelve guineas, paying visits at roughly weekly intervals during the winter and monthly ones in the summer. He was professionally discreet in this instance, writing his clinical notes in shorthand but instructions to Mrs Greg for treatment in longhand. In days when one leech under each ear was prescribed for headaches, and eight or ten on the back of the neck for a cold, we may well wonder if he treated his little niece Elizabeth in the usual Draconian way. Senna, calomel, rhubarb and ginger, horehound, ipecacuanha wine, buttermilk, red wine, broth and milk were poured down little throats; clysters, blisters, flannel waistcoats and bread and milk poultices were applied to tender, flinching bodies. Sulphur was prescribed, internally and externally, for 'itch'. The Styal apprentices, aged from about nine to nineteen, were not all local; they were sometimes sent in wagons by their distant city parishes, coming from Chelsea, for instance, where William Stevenson lived, and Hackney, for a time the parish of Swinton Holland.[23]

The Manchester novelist Geraldine Jewsbury, whose father was a cotton merchant and insurance agent, portrayed in her novel *Marian Withers* (1851) a pauper child of the 1790s who became a wealthy millowner. John Withers was a dedicated inventor, who for all his riches refused to forget his humble origins, sending his daughter to good schools but not allowing her to go to Bath, because 'it did girls no good to visit out of their station in life'.[24] But both she and Elizabeth Gaskell must have met more men who resembled Samuel Greg; almost inevitably there was an appropriation of aristocratic values and practices. Factory owners changed into typical gentry, caring for but also controlling their workpeople with the greater strictness demanded by industrial conditions. Habits of paternal authority and deference did not necessarily lapse when mills were built in country valleys. More often than not they continued in all essential respects. Mrs Greg, it is clear, took on the role of the squire's lady after her husband had established his famous cotton-spinning mill, apprentice house, Unitarian chapel, model village and community at Styal. She began an infants school, a sick club, a savings scheme and a woman's club.

The Styal fee of twelve guineas a year was probably quite insignificant to Peter Holland. His brother-in-law, Francis Sharpe, who taught music in Knutsford and in the surrounding district, was earning at least £800 a year ('clear gains') before his death in November 1823, according to his widow, whose long and fascinating letter about his career tells how he was accustomed to dine and stay overnight at his pupils' homes if he wished, his range being as far as Macclesfield to the east, Runcorn on the Mersey and Altrincham near Manchester. Like Peter Holland, whose son Henry was apprehensive about his long rides in the winter on bad roads – Peter had broken his arm when he was thrown out of his gig in 1807 – Francis Sharpe would have spent much of his day outdoors on horseback or in a carriage. When indoors he sat at table next to Lady Warburton, or Mrs Leycester, or Mrs Grey, his wife proudly reported. He exacted proper respect from servants, having his horse or gig brought to the door when 'Mr Hollins & Mr Wright, our most leading Law-men', had to go to the stable for theirs after dining in the steward's room of the local great houses. This is perhaps exaggerated, hardly consistent with Mark Girouard's demonstration of the power and fortunes achieved by attorneys in country towns. Just as striking is Mrs Sharpe's comment that her husband 'considered the Organ [of the parish church] as merely retained, to keep away any other professional Man – & so never gave it up; the emolument was nothing – only 30 guineas (annually).'[25]

Perhaps some things are improved in the telling, made as glossy as possible, but the real prosperity and social standing of the Sharpes and Hollands in

Knutsford do not seem to be in any doubt. It is clear that as a young child Elizabeth Stevenson was enmeshed in a prosperous, comfortable and intricate network of related families, rising in the world. Maria Edgeworth's sensitive antennae waved delicately when she visited the Hollands in April 1813:

> Mrs Holland [neé Mary Whittaker] is a young second wife, with a pleasing appearance and gentlewomanlike manners ... She is *composed* and sensible and amiable and appears to be an excellent wife and mother. Mrs E [Frances Edgeworth] and she *coalesced* immediately. One of the daughters – Bess – is a sweet creature and would adorn either court or cottage. The other sister [Mary?] has a forbidding countenance and a manner reserved till it is *gruff*; but upon knowing her better the 2d. day I found her good and sensible. There is in the whole family a true simplicity of character and a mutual affection which touches and attaches.
>
> I admired their not pretending to be above their circumstances – giving us the style of dinners and going on just the same way that I am sure they always do when by themselves. Mr Holland is doatingly passionately fond of his son and they are all so fond and so proud of him that it is quite delightful to see so much nature and such good nature. Their post comes in at night about ten o'clock and constantly the father watched about that time in hopes of a letter from his son. '*No I don't think there's a letter from him. The man stays to bar the door. He'd come up directly if there was a letter* – Ah no no! there's none!'[26]

It is not known exactly when Peter moved to Church House, home for many years to his servants and large family. Henry Holland had been born in King Street, but one Whittaker letter seems to imply that as early as 1809 Peter was in Church House; most of the letters refer to his living on Church Hill or, more facetiously, in 'Holland House'. As he grew older he found his practice an increasing strain. Gossip held that he talked of giving up medicine and might move away from Knutsford in 1823. His son Henry wrote to Maria Edgeworth in the summer of 1826 that he had at last been persuaded to take a pupil of fifteen years since as a partner ('a sort of worldly marriage'); he was a Mr Ankers, who wished to move away from London for health reasons. For some reason there were 'doubts which hung over' the connection in Knutsford, but by December Henry could tell William Turner that his father was satisfied with 'the general prospects it gives to his future professional life'. The 1828-29 Pigot's directory records William Ankers as a surgeon in Brook House and Peter Holland in 'Higher town', presumably the nearby Over Knutsford. The 1834 directory lists Holland and Dean, Princess Street, under Surgeons. These might have been Peter's professional addresses.[27]

Henry Holland, by the time of Maria Edgeworth's 1813 visit a successful young author with his *General View of Cheshire* and his part in George Mackenzie's *Travels in the Island of Iceland During the Summer of 1810* (Edinburgh, 1811 and 1812), was on the threshold of a glittering career. He had been sent first to a private school in Knutsford, and at the age of eleven in January 1799 he transferred to William Turner's boarding school at Newcastle for four years. A letter home in 1800 contains a nostalgic recollection of riding in Tatton Park with his father, who had told him amongst the spreading beech trees that the opening of Virgil's first eclogue was 'Tityre tu bacco box recumbans sub tegmine fat-chops'. Though Henry later spoke rather dismissively of the lack of 'that exact scholarship which is reached (with disputed advantage) in our public schools', he paid tribute to the appetite for learning that his schooling at Newcastle in Latin, Greek ('Xenophon's account of the Persian laws') and French ('Anarcharsis') had given him.

It was an enviably rounded education that Turner provided in his Percy Street school – little gardens for the boys in which they sowed 'sallad, parsley, & a few flowers', books from a public library in the town, tickets for 'Mr Kinlock's balls', visits to members of the congregation like the Rankins, courses in chemistry and electricity from an itinerant lecturer and frequent walks in the Tyne valley in order to see 'the vast and varied machinery' of the collieries and descend their shafts, to bathe in the river, to view its 'crowded navigation' and visit the great iron bridge at Sunderland.[28]

Henry Holland was a great favourite with the Turners, as were his sisters. Mary stayed for a year when she was a girl in 1802, at which time she had lessons in drawing every Thursday from a Newcastle artist. She 'was then as now, very amusing', Mary Robberds writes in her memoirs. One night during a storm all the bricks of a built-up window were blown into their bedroom. When Turner's daughter said, 'Don't be frightened Mary it is nothing', came the reply: 'Bother, but it is though … for I feel them'. Though she was unhurt, 'the bricks had fallen actually upon her, as she lay in bed'. The family connections were never allowed to lapse. A letter of December 1821 from Mrs Sharpe, for instance, indicates that Mary Holland was again at Newcastle, presumably with William Turner; her sisters Bessy and Lucy were going to spend the Christmas week with his daughter Mary, by now wife of the Reverend John Gooch Robberds, in Manchester.[29]

At the age of thirteen Henry Holland was able to write an 'Account of an Excursion into North Wales. Made in the Summer of 1802', which was presented to his sister Lucy, who might have been responsible for the pencil sketch of the author used as a frontispiece. The title is deceptive. This was no childish tale of a holiday jaunt but over a hundred neatly written pages describing the topography, trades and people he encountered, containing maps, and pen, ink and wash sketches of towns like Conway. He was a precocious and observant boy. There followed a year at Dr Estlin's school near Bristol and two sessions at Glasgow University preparing for a mercantile career, during which period he completed his *General View of the Agriculture of Cheshire*. Manchester College at York does not seem to have been considered, even though the lack of college discipline at Glasgow made it undesirable for the young.

He then very firmly changed his mind, went to Edinburgh at the end of 1806 to take a medical degree, spending two winters in London hospital

schools. There is no indication that he crossed the trail of William Stevenson
in Edinburgh, but he seems to have moved in similar circles. Though only a
student he claims in letters written at the time to have been 'more or less
intimate' with distinguished men like Walter Scott, Playfair, Jeffrey, Henry
Erskine ('Nearly 60 years of age, he still possesses all the sprightliness, &
vivacity of a boy') and, especially, Dugald Stewart. The salon of Mrs Fletcher,
he thought, had 'an exclusively political aspect'. The salon of the wealthy and
captivating widow Mrs Apreece, 'acquainted with Madame de Staël, and
vaguely reported to be the original of Corinne, then fresh in fame', was stimu-
latingly different. He became her friend for life. He went to Iceland with Sir
George Mackenzie, but he did not receive anything like the recognition he
deserved; a modern scholar considers *Travels in the Island of Iceland*
'massively, though clumsily, dependent on Holland's scrupulously prepared
and long neglected text.'[30]

His *Travels in the Ionian Isles, Albania, Thessaly, Macedonia, &c. During the
Years 1812 and 1813* was published in 1815, a fat quarto volume illustrated by
engravings from his own drawings and energetically detailing the scenery,
geology, botany, hospitals, history, demography, politics and languages of the
countries he had travelled through. Like the book on Iceland, it had two
editions. His letters to Maria Edgeworth, several a year during the 1820s,
showed that not only had he determined to allow himself 1200 miles of travel
a year (he rejoiced when steam began to allow even more) but that he was
fascinated by current books of voyages and travel. The names of explorers like
Parry, Frankland and Lyon occur in his letters as often as Davy, Faraday,
Wollaston and Mrs Somerville, or Scott, Southey, Moore and Wordsworth.
'Coleridge is come into society again,' he told her on 25 June 1825, 'as
copious in conversation, as metaphysical, & as much imbued with self-compla-
cency as ever.' He continued ironically, 'He has just published a strange
compound of theology, metaphysics & morals, in a dense [demi?] octavo,
under the title of *Aids to Reflection*. It will be read only by the elect, & understood but by few of these.' But there appear to be no further references in
these dozens of closely written quarto leaves to William Stevenson and his
brother-in-law, Anthony Todd Thomson, even in contexts where they might
have occurred.

Henry moved at the highest levels of London society, becoming a fashionable doctor in Mayfair. He went abroad as travelling physician to the Princess
of Wales for a time – a ticklish assignment in the circumstances – and after his
return produced even more thick volumes; his *Medical Notes and Reflections*
of 1839, based on twenty years' practice in London, went through three
editions. One of his review essays in the *Quarterly* for 1850, entitled 'Natural
history of Man', has been characterised by a major scientific historian as one of
the very few publications before the appearance of Darwin's ultra-cautious
Origin of Species in 1859 that 'closely integrates the question of evolution with
the question of the natural history of man'. His grandson remembered him 'as

a short man with a very clever face, a large choker and a swallow-tail coat'. Eventually he became one of Queen Victoria's physicians-in-ordinary and ended his days as a baronet, one of the four physicians present at the death of Prince Albert in 1861, to be seen with his medical colleagues in the painting and lithograph of 'The Last Moments of H R H the Prince Consort'. His son flew even higher, joining the opulent gentry as the first Lord Knutsford.[31]

Henry Holland's social success has disguised his intellectual achievements, but he certainly surpassed that other bright young man, John William Whittaker, a learned candidate for the professorship of Arabic at Cambridge, a fellow of St John's and domestic chaplain to the Archbishop of Canterbury for a short while. In 1822 he sank back into provincial life for thirty years as vicar of St Peter's, at Blackburn in Lancashire, which was described as a large manufacturing town, 'ill-built, and with a feeble and squalid looking population'. When poor Whittaker wished to marry, his future mother-in-law was devastated to find out that his aunts, including Henry Holland's stepmother, had all been schoolmistresses in their youth – even though as vicar he had an income of £1500 a year. One aunt had even sunk to the level of a private governess, and Mrs Sharpe was of course married to a music master. The Feildens of Feniscowles near Blackburn were 'desirous of being considered & ranked rather among the Squiralty, than the trading population of the County'.[32]

Mrs Lumb, however, was by 1834 listed as one of the Knutsford gentry in Pigot's directory, together with other residents of Heathside at this later date – Charles Cholmondeley Esq. of Heath House (long remembered as provider of pennies, mince pies and hot cross buns to the Sunday scholars), George Reade Esq. and an assortment of Amazons – Mrs Hankers, Mrs W. Hollins, Mrs Moores, Mrs Quale and Mrs Ravenscroft.[33] Hannah Lumb, however, is not so much as mentioned in Henry Holland's letters to his father, Maria Edgeworth and Lucy Aikin, let alone in his *Recollections of Past Life* (1872), which contains only the most cursory reference to Mrs Gaskell herself. Nor does Mrs Lumb make much of a figure in the more gossipy Whittaker correspondence. There are passing references to a card game, a dinner party at her house, an evening at Church House with the Hollands and one or two other meetings with some Turner relations in Knutsford on a short visit.

Perhaps the Whittakers and Sharpes found her tedious. In 1819 Mrs Whittaker wrote about various invitations, including one to Heathside, '*I* have no wish to go *there*.' If this is a reference to Mrs Lumb's, either she was a pleasant cypher or, more likely, she had no special claim upon anybody's attention. Something like this could be said of all Peter's spinster sisters, who were as unimportant as motherless girls to busy wives like Mary Holland and Martha Sharpe. The letter describing Marianne Lumb's death in 1812 only casually mentions Mrs Lumb's sister Mary, 'very far gone in a decline'. Catharine, who died aged almost fifty in 1822, was briefly mentioned as losing

ground in the previous year, but nothing has yet been found in the great mass
of this correspondence about Abigail, who lived on until 1848. It is known
that Abigail lived in Liverpool for several years with the Samuel Hollands in
the early years of the century, but she was back in Knutsford by 1819 and
possibly living with Mrs Lumb, to judge by John Stevenson's letters to
Knutsford in the 1820s, though this is no more than an inference.[34]

Strangely, neither Mrs Lumb nor Peter's family nor the Whittakers seem to
have been close to other Hollands living in the district since the seventeenth
century, some of them descended from Samuel Holland of Sandlebridge's
older brother Peter. He had been an attorney in Knutsford, dying in 1761; his
son John of Dam Head House, just two miles away in Mobberley, lived on till
he died at the age of eighty-three in 1835. John's wife Susannah died in the
following year and his sister Margaret survived until 1842. They are all buried
in the little graveyard of the old dissenting chapel at Knutsford.[35] Gaskell
biographers never mention them, and the only contact so far discovered
between John of Dam Head House and Peter of Church House is a financial
partnership in the Herculaneum pottery of Liverpool.[36] 'But the iniquity of
oblivion blindly scattereth her poppy', wrote Sir Thomas Browne in the great
fifth chapter of *Urn-Burial*, 'and deals with the memory of men without
distinction to merit of perpetuity.'

The Whittaker letters bring to life the occasional pains and frequent pleasures
of the related families wonderfully well. Their proliferating minutiae lead us to
hope that Elizabeth Stevenson's name would appear a few times. After all, her
aunt's house at Heathside, centrally placed in its row, could not have been
more than a few score yards from the house and farm of the Sharpes. Yet only
one probable reference has been found, and that incidental, in a letter of 19
March 1815 written by Catharine Whittaker, aunt of the four Sharpe children
– Edmund, Marianne, Emily and Frances:

> We are all quite well here at both houses. Dear little Edmund has had an unfor-
> tunate accident by which he broke his arm about a fortnight ago but it is now so
> far recoverd that his Uncle Holland yesterday took off the Pastboard & stiff
> bandages which were at first applied in setting it – but he will for some days keep
> it in a Sling – he went one day to spend the day with his cousin Charles [Holland]
> – & in the afternoon Edmund & a little niece of Mrs Lumbs who was there also
> were drawn about by a servant girl of Mr Hollands in a very nice little Carriage
> with four wheels, which we thought it impossible coud be turnd over & which
> all the Children by turns have been drawn in hundreds of times – it was in Mr
> Hollands garden & we conclude that as she was running very fast, she turnd the
> corner so very quick, as to get the fore wheel under the Carriage & so overset it
> – he was taken into the house immediately, & almost before they coud get his
> jacket off to examine his Arm, Mr H. came home from his daily ride – he lookd
> at & felt it, & directly pronounced its being broken – so that it was immediately
> set, & he was carried home by one of Mr H's women servants – preceded by his
> Aunt Holland who broke the matter comfortably to his dear Mother ... [37]

Hannah Lumb's niece Susan, daughter of Peter and Mary Holland, would have been described as the sister of Charles. Caroline, Charlotte and Louisa Holland, children of Swinton and Anne, were nieces of Mrs Lumb, but less likely to have been in Knutsford. The matter seems all the more curious as one notices how often Elizabeth might have been mentioned if anyone had taken a positive interest in her, for instance in April 1816, when the four Sharpe children and the three younger Holland children of roughly the same age-span were mentioned as an attraction to John Whittaker. There was no reference to Mrs Lumb's little ward.

In July 1816 a large family party went to Sandlebridge, which came to Peter Holland after the death of his father Samuel at the age of eighty-two in May:

> The Bartons & Dr. Heathcote are now Mr Holland's Guests – we spent a pleasant day at Sandle Bridge yesterday, in *Fishing*, Walking &c. Part went in a *Cart*, & a Chaise; & Horses accommodated the remainder. Mr & Mrs Sharpe desire me to say how sorry they are you could not join us here – their 4 fine Children are most tractable little Creatures, & we have had abundance of charming Music – Beethoven, Mozart, & Italian music are all the go, except when they compliment my old Fashioned Ear & taste with Handel. Bessy Barton sings 'Comfort Ye &c' in a most superior Style, & I think it worth all the rest – we shall finish this month at Knutsford, & go to the Hollands in a week or ten days.

In December 1817, Henry Holland mentioned measles at Knutsford, but gave no names. (Sarah Whittaker mentions 'the little Sharpes and Hollands, with Bessy Holland', but not Elizabeth Stevenson.) Henry himself was now more than ever convinced of 'the barrenness of Knutsford society' – lost in a whirl of professional business in London, people flitting rapidly before him, unmarried and, as he put it rather idyllically, with 'no time for quiet *house-in-the-country attachments*'.[38]

Perhaps Elizabeth often went to stay with her father in London. Long visits were usual. Women and children had to be escorted, and the general difficulties of travel to distant places – on foot, or by carriage, or when two people had one horse between them, in the tie and ride style – should not be underestimated. On the other hand, Mrs Gaskell states quite clearly in a letter to the Howitts of May 1838 that she was brought up in a 'little, clean, kindly country town' near Old Tabley, that is, Knutsford in Cheshire.

However well she was loved by her mother's sister, she was almost an orphan. Like the heroines of conventional romance, she had no fixed, assured position in an ordinary family. She was in close, probably daily, contact with two sets of cousins of roughly her own age who were living as happily as most children do with their own parents, brothers and sisters. Even the ten children of Mrs Johnston had their widowed mother. Elizabeth must have felt the contrast, especially when she was a little child. There would undoubtedly have been occasions when the difference was brought home to her, when a careless or unkind word reminded her that she had no mother and had never known her either.

In later life she expressed a great sense of loss. George Hope of Fenton Barns, who called on her in 1849, was told that she was 'not twelve months old [*sic*] when her mother died, and that she had no relic of hers'. He was able to send her the letters that had been written to his own mother, one of them within a week of Mrs Stevenson's death in 1811. 'I will not let an hour pass, my dear sir', wrote Mrs Gaskell at once,

> without acknowledging your kindness in sending me my dear mother's letters, the only relics of her that I have, and of more value to me than I can express, for I have so often longed for some little thing that had once been hers or been touched by her. I think no one so unfortunate to be early motherless can enter into the craving one has after the lost mother. ... I have been brought up away from all those who knew my parents, and therefore those who come to me with a remembrance of them as an introduction seem to have a holy claim upon my regard.[39]

The immensely popular, sweetly 'mothering' poetry of Felicia Hemans half-created the very nature of woman in the middle decades of the century. It was learnt by heart by young ladies in every schoolroom and set to music for performance in drawing rooms by Mrs Hemans's sister, Harriett Browne (Mrs Hughes). In Elizabeth's second music book a carefully inserted leaf gives the text of 'The Captive Knight' by Mrs Hemans and is dated 'Aug 29 1828 ECS'.[40] Love between mother and daughter was 'more dominant and vivid in Mrs. Hemans than conjugal love', William Michael Rossetti claimed, probably with his sister in mind. But Elizabeth Gaskell's reply to George Hope is touching, whatever allowances we make for the plangent tones called forth by a born writer's inevitable tendency to mythologise herself and for the larger harmonies of the Victorian convention in which she was composing.[41]

'To be a female and an orphan as well, was to be doubly disadvantaged in an age that valued family and empowered men' is a pattern that undoubtedly shaped both lives and literary strategies in Victorian times. It had an undoubted basis in real life, and for Elizabeth Gaskell an almost superstitious set of associations; her rational 'seem' just manages to save the medieval resonance of 'relic'. Yet it is truly extraordinary that she should have nothing whatsoever that had once been her mother's, such as the fan kept as a curiosity in Saughton; that no keepsake had been left to her, no small object preserved by her father or sent down to Mrs Lumb for the little girl to have when she grew past babyhood. This is precisely what she asked should be done with the diary she began in 1834: 'To my dear little Marianne I shall "dedicate" this book, which, if I should not live to give it her myself, will I trust be reserved for her as a token of her mother's love, and extreme anxiety in the formation of her little daughter's character.'

'Formation' should be understood in a relatively liberal sense. The language of the diary, in which Elizabeth Gaskell can praise the 'beginning of self restraint in the little creature' and commit to the Lord 'this darling precious treasure', indicates careful moral training within a strong religious context. She even believed that it was wrong to show anger in Marianne's presence 'without considering how holy that little creature made the place.' This is balanced by more human phrases like 'we are scrupulous in respecting her little rights', even when Marianne was a tiny girl of ten months. And as her children grew, Patsy Stoneman concludes, Elizabeth Gaskell's attitude 'can be seen clearly in her treatment of her four daughters', brought up with full respect for their individuality, carefully shown the 'arts of housewifery and motherhood' but supported if they wished to take up a career or remain single. Mrs Gaskell sounds here rather like Mrs Lumb's friend Mrs Hannah Greg.[42]

NOTES

1 The story is told in *Historical Sketches of Nonconformity*, ed. [Urwick], p. 415 n., qu. H. Lismer Short, 'Macclesfield's first Unitarian minister', *JUHS*, X, 1951-54, p. 147. Palmer, whose own health was delicate, died aged forty-four on 26 December 1786. See also pp. 53 above and 173 below.

2 *Memoirs of Richard Lovell Edgeworth*, I, pp. 214-17; Roger Lonsdale, 'Dr. Burney, "Joel Collier", and Sabrina', *Evidence in Literary Scholarship: Essays in Memory of James Marshall Osborn*, ed. R. Wellek and A. Ribeiro, Oxford, 1979, pp. 294-301 (quoting *Sandford and Merton*); Lupton, *Wakefield Worthies*, p. 190.

3 RTD, LUBL: ECG, MS diary, pp. 52-3, 56. ECS is said to have attended a school in Chester kept by a Miss Hervey (see Sharps, p. 42n.), but no other evidence has been found.

4 Yeats, 'Among School Children'. See the portrait opp. p. 18 in Chadwick, 1913, sharper than the one usually reproduced.

5 Hall, pp. 4, 16-17, 20, 22.

6 Payne Biog., p. 30; Hopkins, pp. 29-30, 343 (name misread as 'Gieg'). BL copy: 'B H Bright / from his true & faithful fd / H. Greg' (cat. as by [Mrs H. Gregg]; ditto *NSTC*). Mrs Mary Thwaite drew my attention to Hannah Greg's authorship.

7 DCLH: HH to Lucy Aikin, Knutsford, 29 September 1809. For much of what follows see the well-chosen material and qu. from MSS in Spencer, *Hannah Greg*, pp. 6, 11-12, 17, 20-4 (probably James Tayler, rather than his son John James), 28.

8 Marina Benjamin, 'Elbow room: women writers on science, 1790-1840', *Science and Sensibility: Gender and Scientific Enquiry 1780-1945*, ed. Benjamin, Oxford, 1991, p. 40. The Greg(g), Hill and Townson books were all anon., but see *BL Cat.*

9 Spencer, *Samuel Greg*, p. 5. For the life and powerfully liberal ethos of the Bristol school see J. Estlin Carpenter, *James Martineau, Theologian and Teacher: A Study of his Life and Thought*, London, 1905, pp. 16-21, and cp. Davidoff and Hall, *Family Fortunes*, p. 294. When Lant Carpenter collapsed with depression in 1829, however, Mary and her mother were not able to carry on the boys' school.

10 See p. 147 below, and Payne Biog., p. 25; but cp. 'long country drives with an old friend, a doctor [*sic*], going his rounds, twenty and thirty miles at a time' (Ritchie, pref. *Cranford*, p. xxii). See also Murray, 'Peter Holland', pp. 382-6.

11 Spencer, *Samuel Greg*, p. 21; *Autobiography of Mrs. Fletcher*, p. 97; J. A. V. Chapple, 'An author's life: Elizabeth Gaskell and the Wedgwood family', *BST*, XVII, 1979, p. 288. Cp. *Portrait*, pp. 58-61.

12 Spencer, *Hannah Greg*, p. 17; Wollstonecraft, *A Vindication*, chapters 12 and 13, esp. p. 189 [which pr. 'destination]; Marion Shaw, 'Anne Brontë: a quiet feminist', *BST*, XXI, pp. 125-35.

13 For what follows see *Memoirs of Edward and Catherine Stanley*, ed. Stanley, pp. 277-8, 291-2; Prothero and Bradley, *Arthur Penrhyn Stanley*, I, pp. 2-3, 202-9; *Before and After Waterloo*, ed. Adeane and Grenfell, p. 80; Morell and Thackray, *Gentlemen of Science: Early Years*, pp. 25, 228, 242 (but cp. p. 199); Knutsford Edn, III, pp. xv-xvi (*Ruth* letter qu. in extenso); GCL: *The Gateshead Observer*, 30 April 1859.

14 *Memorials of Canterbury* is item 560 in Larmuth & Sons, *Catalogue of Valuable Books ... To be Sold by Auction*, 16 February 1914. Larmuth's title-page of 84 Plymouth Grove mentions 4000 other volumes; this catalogue is therefore incomplete. See also *MG*, 17 and 18 February 1914; Michael D. Wheeler, 'Mrs. Gaskell's reading, and the Gaskell sale catalogue in Manchester Central Library', *N&Q*, CCXXII, 1977, pp. 25-30.

15 C. P. Darcy, *The Encouragement of the Fine Arts in Lancashire 1760-1860*, Manchester, 1976, pp. 3-4, 58-60, 65; Ian Sellars, 'William Roscoe, the Roscoe circle and radical politics in Liverpool, 1787-1807', *THSLC*, CXX, 1969, *passim*; Edward Morris, 'The formation of the gallery of art in the Liverpool Royal Institution, 1816-1819', *THSLC*, CXLII, 1993, pp. 88-91; *Autobiography of Mrs Fletcher*, p. 98.

16 Thornton, *Currie*, pp. 163-5, 189-90; *DNB*; William Smyth, *English Lyrics*, 5th edn, London and Cambridge, 1850, p. xi (autobiographical sketch); Chester W. New, *The Life of Henry Brougham to 1830*, Oxford, 1961, p. 29; *Letters*, p. 309; John Pollock, *Wilberforce* (1977), Tring, 1982, p. 210; Smyth, *Lectures on Modern History*, London and Cambridge, 1840, II, p. 324. For Smyth see K. T. B. Butler, 'A "Petty" professor of Modern History: William Smyth (1765-1849)', *CHJ*, IX, 1947-49, pp. 217-38.

17 See esp. Walker, *Wakefield*, II, p. 646; *Letters*, p. 309; also, *An Eton Boy, Being the Letters of J. M. Gaskell from Eton and Oxford 1820-30*, ed. C. Milnes Gaskell, London, 1939; infm kindly provided by John Goodchild.

18 Thornton, *Currie*, 170-2 (misn. Harriet), 187, 358; *Memoirs of Currie*, ed. Currie, I, pp. 64-5, 271, 286, 405-6; II, pp. 188-9; J. R. Barker, 'John McCreery: a radical printer, 1768-1832', *BSL*, 5th s., XVI, pp. 83-91.

19 Grevel Lindop, *The Opium-Eater: A Life of Thomas De Quincey*, London, Melbourne, Toronto, 1981, p. 53; *Macaulay Letters*, ed. Pinney, II, p. 46; Ian Hamilton, *Keepers of the Flame: Literary Estates and the Rise of Biography*, London, 1992, pp. 94-100; Spencer, *Samuel Greg*, pp. 12-13; *Memoir of Currie*, ed. Currie, I, p. 295; II, p. 176. A Miss Clementina Cleghorn and William Turner of Newcastle were also subscribers to the *Works*.

20 Lucy Aikin, *Memoir of John Aikin*, I, pp. 11, 55; McLachlan, *Warrington Academy*, pp. 75-7; *DNB*; E. M. Brockbank, *Sketches of the Lives and Work of the Honorary Medical Staff of the Manchester Infirmary, 1752-1830*, Manchester, 1904, pp. 60-1; Pickstone, *Medicine and Industrial Society*, pp. 11-13, 18, 47; KUL: Wedgwood, PH 'Surgeon' to Mr Swift, 18 March 1787; DCLH: HH to PH, 27 Cannon Street, London, [1807], and to LA, Knutsford, 29 September 1809.

21 DCLH: HH to PH, Newcastle-upon-Tyne, 29 May [1800], 29 October 1801, 15 September 1802, 12 April 1803, 16 April 1803; WT, MS 'An Account of the brine springs and mines of salt rock, near Northwich in Cheshire' (NLPS: Papers Read at the Monthly Meetings, No. 73; also Paper no. 74, 2 October 1804); W. H. Chaloner, 'Salt in Cheshire, 1600-1870', *Palatinate Studies*, ed. W. R. Ward, Manchester, 1992, pp. 116-19; Morell and Thackray, *Gentlemen of Science: Early Years*, pp. 158-60.

22 *Edgeworth Letters*, p. 21; Hall, pp. 53, 103; CRO: DLT/c34/111, undated (the balance due on 1 January 1826 was £201 6s 7d).

23 Robert Murray, 'Quarry Bank mill 2. The medical service', *BJIM*, XVI, 1959, pp. 61, 63-6, and 'Peter Holland', pp. 377-86; S. G. Checkland, *The Gladstones*, p. 84; Walton, *Lancashire*, pp. 126-8; Rose, *The Gregs of Quarry Bank Mill*, p. 31, chapter 6.

24 Quoted from the analysis in Ivan Melada, *The Captain of Industry in English Fiction 1821-1871*, Albuquerque, 1970, pp. 40-8. See also Easson, pp. 81-6.

25 Martha Sharpe to JWW, 1828 (Hall, pp. v, 23-5; unfortunately, the original MS cannot be found at Leigh, nor is it at Blackburn); DCLH: HH to PH, London, 30 January [1806]; KUL: Wedgwood 2-274, PH (amanuensis, 'sister') to Josiah Wedgwood, Knutsford, 20 November 1807; Girouard, *The English Town*, pp. 109-12. John Hollins, coroner, of King Street and Henry Wright of Church Hill are found under attorneys in the 1834 directory. For the Wrights see Derek Robson, *Some Aspects of Education in Cheshire in the Eighteenth Century*, Manchester (Chetham Society), 1966, p. 116.

26 *Edgeworth Letters*, p. 20.

27 Hall, pp. 5, 169 and *passim*; DCLH: HH to ME, London, 21 & 22 July [1826]; NLPS: Moor Collection 23. i, HH to WT, L Brook Street, 2 December [1826]. Green, p. 113, states that HH was born in the 'house where Mr. Siddeley resides': i.e., in King Street (*Slater's Directory for 1869*). See p. 126 above for Richard Deane.

28 DCLH: HH to PH, Newcastle-upon-Tyne, 29 May [1800], 28 March [1802], and 3 May 1803; HH, *Recollections*, pp. 6-11. The learned antiquarian J. J. Barthélemy's *Voyage du jeune Anarcharsis en Grèce dans le milieu du quatrième siècle avant l'ère vulgaire* (Paris, 1788) had been pr. in a French abridged version for the young (London, 1798).

29 MR, MS 'Recollections', pp. 5-6; MS to JWW, Heathside, 17 December 1821 (WAL: EHC204/34; Hall, p. 128).

30 DCLH: HH, MS 'Account'; HH, *Recollections*, pp. 11-22, 80-90; HH to PH, Edinburgh [1809], HH to LA, Edinburgh, 29 November [1809] and 28 January [1810], TS, HH to ME, Edinburgh, 19 December [1809] (all DCLH); Baillie, *Newcastle and Its Vicinity*, pp. 285-6; Andrew Wawn, ed. *The Iceland Journal of Henry Holland*, Hakluyt Society, London, 1987, p. xii.

31 DCLH: HH to ME, London, 6 November 1823, 9 April [1824], L Brook Street, 25 June [1825] and *passim* ; Robert M. Young, *Darwin's Metaphor: Nature's Place in Victorian Culture*, Cambridge, 1985, p. 66 (though cp. *Darwin Correspondence*, IV, p. 35); S. Holland, *In Black & White*, p. 12; A. M. Cooke, 'Queen Victoria's medical household', *MH*, XXVI, 1982, pp. 313, 321 and plate.

32 *DNB;* Hall, pp. ii, 132, 177; *Losh Diaries*, I, p. 89. See also Hall's edition of Ellen Weeton, *Miss Weeton: Journal of a Governess, 1807-1811*, London, 1936; New York, 1969.

33 Reader, *Professional Men*, p. 16; Green, p. 72.

34 Hall, pp. 96 (SW to JWW, Meersbrook, 20 May 1819), 126; NLW: 4983C, I, p. 19; RTD, LUBL: ECG, MS diary (for 1837), p. 57 ; see also p. 219 below for JS letters. By the time of the 1841 census (transcript kindly provided by Joan Leach) Abigail (aged sixty-five) was living with two servants in Northwich Street, another name for Heathside, whilst Peter Holland's daughter Lucy was living 'near the church' with two servants. Anne Holland (aged forty) and Kate Holland (aged twenty-five) were staying with Mary when the census was taken.

35 John of Dam Head and Mobberley and a 'Miss Holland' living in Princess Street are found in early directories. The 1841 census has Miss Hannah (thirty-five) and Miss Elizabeth (thirty) Holland (neither from Cheshire) living in a Princess Street house, probably the last one before the sessions house, rented according to tithe records of 1847 by John Holland. See Irvine, pp. 47, 56, 157 and appendix B.

36 See p. 170 below.

37 CW to JWW, Knutsford, 19 March 1815 (WAL: EHC 204/13; Hall, p. 64). Edward Hall seems to have read the whole Whittaker correspondence with an eye to ECS.

38 Hall, pp. 75, 78-9 (SW to JWW, 6 July 1816, unlocated), 88; DCLH: HH to Lucy Aikin, Mount Street (London, p. m. 9 December 1817), and Mount Street (p. m. 14 Ju[ne] 1819).

39 Hope, *George Hope of Fenton Barns*, pp. 177-8; *Letters*, pp. 15, 796-7.

40 MRCL: MS F823. 894. C1, music book inscribed 'Elizabeth Cleghorn Stevenson / Heath – near Knutsford / June 12 – 1827' (cf. ECG, *Wives and Daughters*, ch. 6). This is one of four larger music books, all roughly 9 × 11 inches, the last pr. sheet music with MS index. For contents see Hopkins, pp. 34-5; Easson, pp. 24-5; Uglow, pp. 37, 40, 51. 'Manuscript Music, mostly in the handwriting of Mrs Gaskell, 1827, 4 vols' (Larmuth & Sons, *Catalogue of Valuable Books*, item 364; see also *MG*, 17 February 1914).

41 See, Easson, p. 23, p. 249, below and Norma Clarke, *Ambitious Heights: Writing, Friendship, Love – the Jewsbury Sisters, Felicia Hemans, and Jane Welsh Carlyle*, London and New York, 1990, pp. 12, 32-6; Angela Leighton, *Victorian Women Poets: Writing Against the Heart*, New York, etc., 1992, pp. 13-17 (Rossetti qu. p. 16).

42 John R. Reed, *Victorian Conventions*, Ohio U.P., 1975, p. 254; RTD, LUBL: ECG, MS diary, pp. 1, 27, 30, 45; Stoneman, pp. 24-33.

9

Widening circles

ANNE THACKERAY RITCHIE declared, with practised social ease, that Elizabeth 'was always tenderly attached to her father's memory, and proud and fond of him, and he must have been indeed a most interesting and delightful character'.[1] At about the same time a brief introduction to a Minerva edition of *Mary Barton* contained the bald statement that 'Mr Stevenson had been in succession a teacher, a Unitarian minister, a farmer, a boarding-house keeper, and a writer on commercial subjects, and had finally obtained the post of keeper of the records to the Treasury.' This inspired a letter from an E. V. T. to the *Athenaeum* in 1891, written to correct the impression that William Stevenson, 'a man of distinction and ability', had been a 'rolling-stone kind of person'. The letter merely summarises the *Annual Biography and Obituary* for his career, but E. V. T. – whoever that may be – also claimed to be 'one who knew Mrs. Gaskell very intimately' and insisted that she 'always spoke with the greatest pride and affection' about her father. It suggests a father-daughter relationship charged with strong human if not holy emotion.[2]

It could not have been so simple when she was a girl. A few years after she had been taken to Knutsford as a baby, William Stevenson, widower, was married by licence on 11 April 1814 to Catherine Thomson, spinster, by the curate John Rush at St Luke's parish church, Chelsea.[3] To judge from the codicils to Samuel Holland's will, William was by now not in favour at Sandlebridge. The first codicil, dated 29 August 1813, refers to a number of sums amounting altogether to £400 that had been advanced to Elizabeth Stevenson, and directs that the same amount be paid to each of her siblings (Samuel, Swinton, Hannah, Catharine and Abigail) before the division of the personal estate. These loans had not been mentioned when the original will was drawn up in 1812, though sums of money must have been advanced to Mrs Stevenson before her death in 1811.

Then Samuel's own wife Ann died on 1 July 1814 aged seventy-four. The provisions for her in his will were left quite undisturbed by a second codicil, dated 31 January 1815 – after William Stevenson's second marriage. This codicil must have seemed very pointed, for now Samuel's grandchildren, John and Elizabeth Stevenson, were not to receive their joint sixth share of the personal estate at age twenty-one or upon marriage; the executors were directed to pay it instead to Samuel's daughter Hannah Lumb, who was given total discretion: 'to be by her applied to the joint or several uses of my said grandchildren, or to any other purposes my said daughter may think more desirable'. Elizabeth was a small child in Hannah's care, John about fifteen and probably training in some way for a seafaring career. Samuel Holland thus ensured that after his death (in 1816) his grandchildren's' sixth share in the personal estate could not be utilised in any way by their father and stepmother.[4]

Were relations between Sandlebridge and Chelsea ever warm, even at the time of William's first marriage? To the extent that Elizabeth as she grew up became aware of what seems like a climate of disapproval and coolness between her father and grandfather, and gradually came to know about the financial problems that afflicted Stevenson, she would feel more and more the loss of her mother. Her father's second marriage, though to a suitable partner – quite unlike the lady who had married the Earl of Derby and caused his sister Lady Jane Stanley to direct that she be buried elsewhere, 'lest the dust of an actress should mingle with her own' – would exact from Elizabeth conventional expressions of filial love, under which, rightly or wrongly, she later claimed there had smouldered a sense of desolation.

William Stevenson's second wife, called Catherine, was born in Savannah in 1775, and about thirty-nine years of age when she married for the first time. She was one of two daughters of Alexander Thomson, formerly a member of the Council of the Province of Georgia and its post-master general, and his American wife. Her sister was perhaps called Anna, and there were two boys, William John and Anthony Todd.[5] Anthony had been born in Edinburgh on 7 January 1788 when the family were there on leave at the outset of the American war of independence. His godfather, Anthony Todd, was Secretary to the Post Office in Edinburgh; he later became postmaster-general in England and his daughter Eleanor married the Earl of Lauderdale. At the end of the war, Alexander Thomson had like many loyalists returned to Britain, to live in the immediate neighbourhood of Edinburgh on a small pension with 'honourable economy'. Their mother had died about a year after Anthony's birth, but his father's second wife, a widow called Mrs Rainie who had been a good family friend, brought them up after their father's death in September 1798 in a highly disciplined but fond and kind manner. Given what is usually said about Catherine as Elizabeth Stevenson's stepmother, it is more than interesting to note that Anthony is said to have always paid warm tribute to his stepmother's 'care, her precepts, her example'.

As a student of medicine in Edinburgh and a member of the Speculative Society Anthony Thomson was a friend of Henry Brougham, with whom he remained in touch throughout Brougham's spectacular career. He was an even older friend of Henry Cockburn, on whose father's fields of turf and all the hills about Edinburgh they used to play. 'As for the *burns*, he knew every minnow that was in them', wrote Cockburn to his family. They maintained a great attachment to each other, one that might seem surprisingly emotional if we did not recall the cult of sentiment and the vogue of Henry Mackenzie's famous novel, *The Man of Feeling*. Thomson was not especially brilliant, Cockburn thought, but 'sensible, well-principled, and very affectionate'; when he left Edinburgh for England, 'all the kindred houses were sad.' 'His sensibility', Thomson reciprocated in his journal, 'is great and though he endeavours to veil the keenness of his feelings, I have often seen the tear glistening through the smile and a quivering of his lip bespeaks more than he would wish to be perceptible, even to me.'

Dr Thomson lived from 1800 at 92 Sloane Street (the number was later changed to 91), not all that far from Beaufort Row. He had married a Miss Christina Maxwell of Dumfries in 1801. His two sisters were so confident in his abilities that they had 'lent him their little all' without security to help establish him as a general practitioner. In 'less than three or four years' he repaid their loan, and continued a 'never-ceasing care for their comforts in after-life', a dependency that in the case of Anna continued after his death in the middle of the century. In London he achieved 'a large and lucrative practice', which eventually amounted to almost £3000 a year. He must have seen Elizabeth often when she visited Chelsea. His prosperity and his warm and affectionate nature would have provided a contrast to the dryness of his brother-in-law, always hard pressed for money. They had moved in the same circles in Edinburgh; their family connection never lapsed. Anthony was the doctor present at Elizabeth Stevenson's birth, his brother William the miniaturist who painted Elizabeth in Edinburgh when she was twenty-one.

Thomson is known to have played a national part in the passing of the Apothecaries Act of 1815, which led to the first professional body to work on modern lines for qualification and registration; he was also prominent in the parish of Chelsea, especially when the fine new church was begun on a site north of the King's Road to take the place of the old one by the river. Its foundation stone was laid in 1820. He also persuaded his rich patients to establish a dispensary, where he himself came to specialise in diseases affecting the skin. His brother-in-law's facial disfigurement might have been in the case-notes he assiduously collected for a book on the subject, later finished by a relation, Dr Edmund Parkes. He was a remarkably hard-working man, allowing himself only a limited number of hours' sleep a night, publishing a number of standard and useful books on medical matters, some of which went through edition after edition – on pharmacy, the management of sick rooms and botany. The last, published in 1822, is a thick octavo of nearly seven hundred pages. It begins with ten engraved plates, the first four of which were drawn by his second wife Katharine (née Byerley), whom he married in 1820, after the death of his first wife in 1815. This was to be a very significant connection indeed for the young Elizabeth Stevenson.[6]

In December 1826 Dr Thomson left Chelsea, moving to Hinde Street,

Manchester Square, between Hyde Park and Regent's Park, becoming first a licentiate of the College of Physicians of London – with the College of Surgeons a social pinnacle of the profession – and in 1828 the first professor of materia medica and therapeutics at the newly founded University of London in Bloomsbury. In 1835 he had a breakdown through overwork and, on his recovery, he tended to spend his weekends at Long Ditton in Surrey, where he rented a cottage. Towards the end of his successful life – he died in 1849 – he translated a book from the French, *The Occult Sciences: the Philosophy of Magic*, and brought out in 1847 an annotated edition of *The Seasons* of James Thomson, with whom the Stevenson family claimed connection. He had felt the lack of annotations in his youth and more than compensated for the fact in his edition. Sometimes there is no more than a line or so of the poem on a page otherwise packed with encyclopaedic notes in small type, on matters scientific, historical, biographical, etc. Thoughtfully, it was published as cheaply as possible for students.[7]

Two children were born of Stevenson's second marriage. The first was a boy called William, who was baptised by the Reverend William Turner of Newcastle on 12 June 1815. Turner had been the Unitarian minister of Hanover Square chapel in Newcastle since 1782 and was on a visit to London with his wife about this time; he also records baptising two other children there, omitting his usual practice in Newcastle of recording dates of birth as well as baptism in his Hanover Square register.[8] He was a relation in more than one way. Son of William Turner of Wakefield by his wife Mary, sister of Samuel Holland of Sandlebridge, he himself married a Mary Holland of Manchester in 1784. After her death he married again, in 1799, Jane Willets, the sister of Peter Holland's first wife Mary. The other Willets sister, Ann, married Peter's brother Swinton. These interlocking marriages, not untypical in Unitarian circles, might be termed centripetal.

The Stevensons' next child was a daughter called Catherine, born on 7 December 1816 and christened on 11 June 1817 – not on this occasion by a dissenting minister but in the old parish church of St Luke, Chelsea, where John and Elizabeth Galt's son Thomas had been baptised on 23 December 1815 and Anthony Todd Thomson's son Anthony Francis was to be on 31 January 1821. Mrs Chadwick heard that Elizabeth Stevenson 'sometimes worshipped' there, presumably when she was staying with her father and step-mother, in the company of her younger half-brother and sister. Social pressures were always strongly in favour of the established church. The rector of Chelsea from 1805 to 1832 was the Honourable Gerald Valerian Wellesley, a brother of the great duke of Wellington.[9]

It is noticeable, too, that Stevenson did not contribute to thirty articles in Robert Aspland's *Monthly Repository* written by members of the Non-Con club, founded in 1817 to discuss civil and religious liberty. He was never a member. Indeed, Stevenson's name does not appear anywhere in the appendix to Francis Mineka's *The Dissidence of Dissent*, where scores of contributors to the *Repository* are identified from numerous Unitarian and other sources.[10] It is difficult to believe that William Stevenson was a Unitarian at all after about 1817. The Unitarian torch was handed on to his daughter Elizabeth by the Knutsford Hollands, the Warrington and Liverpool Gaskells and the Newcastle Turners. Turner of Newcastle was, like Lewis Loyd, a deputy-treasury of Manchester College. With the exception of Samuel Holland of Liverpool, the others' names do not appear amongst the early subscribers to the college in, say, its Report of 31 August 1810, but they can be found in the 1830s and 1840s. Holbrook Gaskell senior used to send the customary two guineas of Mrs Edward Dimock, William Gaskell's mother, after her second marriage to the Unitarian minister and proprietor of a boys' boarding school at Warrington.[11]

The very scanty evidence about William Stevenson's second marriage suggests that he and his wife did not provide a home and a set of friends for Elizabeth. Maria Edgeworth's childhood was in some respects similar. Her mother had died in March 1773, only ten days after the birth of a third daughter when Maria was little more than five years old. Four months later her father married again, a beautiful but severe young woman. Thereafter, Maria showed all the signs of being a disturbed child. She had already thrown tea in someone's face. Now she got out of a high garret window, and when the maid who rescued her exclaimed that she might have fallen down and been killed, she wailed pathetically, 'I wish I had – I'm very unhappy'. She trampled deliberately on the glass of hot-bed frames and cut out the squares of an aunt's checked sofa cover. These acts of mischief were thought to be just that. 'No one apparently linked them with the distress she felt at the death of her mother and the coming of a strange stepmother', comments Marilyn Butler, even though Maria's own father alluded to 'a common and well-grounded opinion, associated with the idea of a second wife' – in order to deny its relevance.

His new wife seems to have been strict with Maria, always in a high-principled and theoretical manner. Improving oneself was a phrase often in her mouth. She offered affection as a kind of bargain. After only two years with her the seven-year-old child was sent away to school in England, where she won respect by her ability to tell stories to the other girls at night and by occasional pranks like 'walking on the Rails of the stairs going to the Drawing Room & Miss Ford's popping out upon us and crying *So Ladies!*' But high jinks and popularity with school companions were no substitute for the love she desperately needed.

Even whilst living with her loving aunt Lumb, Elizabeth seems to have lacked true friends and companions. Her daughters spoke to Ward of her 'long childhood at Knutsford learning her lessons and eating her lunch at sandpits on Heath'. She herself must have created for them the image of a solitary child, wandering through the dwarf yellow gorse and purple heather that could be found just across the road; 'highly strung and imaginative', Mrs Chadwick heard. Although there were tales of wild romping with her cousins at Sandlebridge, 'one who knew her' told Mrs Chadwick that 'she looked back upon her childhood's days as having been rather lonely.' Lady Ritchie, if she was not Chadwick's source, seems to have been told something similar of this unsettled childhood:

> I have heard that Mrs. Gaskell was not always quite happy in those days, – imaginative children go through many phases and trials of their own, – in her hours of childish sorrow and trouble she used to run away from her aunt's house across the Heath and hide herself in one of its many green hollows, finding comfort in the silence, and in the company of birds and insects and natural things. But at other times she had delightful games of play with her cousins in the sweet old family house at Sandlebridge, where so many Hollands in turn had lived.[12]

Elizabeth undoubtedly lived whilst at Knutsford in what Henry James called the 'dark, dense British social fabric'. There was every opportunity to talk and play with her many friends and cousins, go skating on frozen ponds or dance with them in the parties held in large family houses whilst older uncles and aunts played whist or quadrille in the warm candle-light. Her later life, too, was extraordinarily varied and social; she sought experience avidly, perhaps not so much for its own sake as to provide material for her writing. 'Experience is never limited, and it is never complete', wrote Henry James in his essay on the art of fiction; 'it is an immense sensibility, a kind of huge spider-web of the finest silken threads suspended in the chamber of consciousness, and catching every air-borne particle in its tissue'. Elizabeth Stevenson was growing into James's 'young lady upon whom nothing is lost', so adept did she prove to be in catching 'the very note and trick, the strange irregular rhythm of life' in her fiction, and even more in her letters.

But she was also subject as an adult to self-doubt, especially when she came to have children of her own and began the diary on the infancy of her daughter Marianne:

> How all a woman's life, at least so it seems to me now, ought to have a reference to the period when she will be fulfilling one of her greatest & highest duties, those of a mother. I feel myself so unknowing, so doubtful about many things in her intellectual & moral treatment already, and what shall I be when she grows older, & asks those puzzling questions that children do?

It is odd that she never refers directly in this diary to her own childhood and upbringing. She writes as if she had not been a child at all, but always an apprehensive, conscientious mother whose all-too-human disquiet had brought her into Doubting Castle – 'Now Giant Despair had a wife, and her name was Diffidence'.

Was she so mistrustful of herself because she had been what she now saw in her daughter, a child of acute sensibilities?

If she sees others laughing when she is grave & serious, or is not aware of the joke; she bursts into tears; I fancy it must [be] a want of sympathy with her (at the time) serious & thoughtful feelings which makes her cry, but it must be a morbid feeling I should think, & one that for her happiness had better be checked, *if I but knew how.* Then unexpected pleasure has occasionally made her cry; seeing her Papa after an absence of a few days; and I thought tears were not a common manifestation of joy in children (so young, not 13 months old yet). I feel very ignorant of the best way of managing these sensibilities, so beautiful where healthy, & so distressing when morbid.[13]

Elizabeth Gaskell was subject throughout her life to periods of complete collapse. How far was this the result of simple fatigue from the number of things she took on? Or was it the full bloom of a temperament given its shape when she was very young? Her life was less stable than that of her Holland and Sharpe cousins. There are enough hints that she was disturbed as a child to underscore Lady Ritchie's Romantic explanation that imaginative children suffer more. Continuous affection is more important to young children than anything else, and even if this was provided by aunt Lumb, Elizabeth's serenity could have been shaken by people and factors over which she had little control. Just which particles of her experience were caught in the fine web of her sensibility is very speculative, but it is at least possible to recreate the intimate life of her extended family during the early decades of the century, especially during those highly impressionable years in Knutsford before she went away to school at the age of eleven.

Of the younger people in Knutsford society when Elizabeth arrived we know most about Mrs Lumb's niece by marriage, Sarah Whittaker, who was both lively and clever. On one of her several visits to Knutsford, in early 1810 when she was probably in her middle teens, she began a letter to her brother with seven stanzas of neoclassical verse: 'Songs of Shepherds in rustical roundelays / Formed in fancy & whistled on reeds / Made to solace young Nymphs on Holydays / Are too unworthy of wonderful deeds ... ' The verses were for aunt Martha Sharpe's birthday; she had joined with Marianne Lumb and the Hollands to write 'some lines on the occasion ... on one large sheet and put into the post' – and after tea they acted in *Old Poz,* a playlet for children by Maria Edgeworth. Sarah should have played the part of the heroine Lucy, persistent enough to discover that a magpie had stolen an old soldier's money at the local inn and sweetly capable of restraining her headstrong father – more interested in a dish of chocolate, his gout, goose pie and summary justice than the truth – from leaping to over-positive conclusions. In fact she played the part of Mrs Bustle, a scolding landlady, 'dressed up with pillows' to make her the right size.

These social as well as dramatic roles belong to an older society. Vagrancy was dangerous at the time, 'that's poz!' Life, liberty and the pursuit of happiness had not yet supplanted John Locke's life, liberty and estate. But in a world of personal, face-to-face relations women's wiles in particular could be relied upon to circumvent or dissolve the severities of the law. Maria Edgeworth's imagination was not at odds with conventional morality, nor was it out of key with Knutsford's expectations: 'in one of my scolding speeches', Sarah wrote, 'all my resolutions went & I burst into a fit of laughter which was however graciously received & encore'd.' She merely anticipated the happy conclusion of the tragicomedy, and that evening the celebration had its dramatically satisfying conclusion: 'Fireworks were afterwards let off in the garden by M<r> Wakefield (Mr. H's apprentice) and at supp<er> we were <rega>led with a barrel of Oysters.' If this was Church House, the great garden and field that sloped down to King Street would have been a splendid place from which to release rockets to illuminate the darkness over the town moor beyond.[14]

Amateur dramatics of various kinds were, and continued to be, popular in these circles. Knutsford was also able to support a French dancing master, a Royalist exile called Charles Rogier, who was said to have taught William Pitt to dance in his youth. The statesman was a relative of Charles Cholmondeley, and Rogier once solemnly told him, 'There was nothing whatsoever in Pitt's dancing to indicate what a great man he would turn out.' Henry Green, who knew him, said he 'was in truth an original of the purest water' and went on to talk of his habit of buttonholing or writing long letters to prominent men full of weird ideas. One, according to Green, was a plan of pouring scalding buttermilk on French and Spanish men of war attacking Gibraltar instead of red-hot cannon balls. Was this an embroidery to amuse his audience, many of whom would have known Rogier perfectly well? The young William Beamont, living in Knutsford at the time, records the joy of these French exiles in 1812 on the news of Napoleon's overthrow. The second edition of Rogier's pamphlet entitled A *Word for My King and Country. A Treatise on the Utility of a Rocket Armament, Assisted by Balloons, When Ships of War Cannot Be Accessible*, published at Macclesfield in 1818, shows a means of delivering boiling water to men attempting to scale the rock. It was an age of experimental weaponry: the Montgolfier brothers and William Congreve had shown what could be achieved with balloons and rockets. Rather improbably, however, Rogier went on to suggest that his plan was only intended as a deterrent; the engineer might 'rehearse, now and then, the engine from the port hole, to deter them from their own destruction.' The vicar, Harry Grey, found him improvident in his later years and raised a small subscription for Rogier and his wife, which was doled out in periodical payments. Eccentrics were cared for in this small and close-knit community.[15]

The women of the Whittaker family prove that Elizabeth Stevenson's vivacious talents were by no means exceptional. 'What do you think I am learning now?' young Sarah asked her brother in 1813. 'Not Latin or Greek, not to play the Violin, French Horn or Double Bass. No! I scorn such *unfeminine* pursuits. The soft, plaintive notes of the Flageolet are more to my taste and I can already play several "favourite" airs such as "Tweed Side", "Shepherds I have lost my love" & "Robin Adair".' Her light irony belies her claim to female artistic orthodoxy. She had a brother who was an academic classicist and an uncle who was a professional musician, but she herself could wear her culture lightly. And her culture is demonstrably that of her family circle, whether she was at home in Bradford or on visits to Knutsford.[16]

Her mother had been well educated at Crofton Old Hall school near Wakefield – by 1818 young ladies were 'boarded and instructed in plain and fancy work for thirty-three guineas per annum', other fees 'ranging from ten shillings and sixpence per quarter to five guineas a year'. She was entertained by the town's ladies, including an earlier Mrs Lumb, who showed her a model of Paris and a mechanical wonder called a chronoscope. Pamela Rae quotes a perfect legal spoof she addressed to her widowed father when she was nineteen, entitled 'The Prayr & Petition of SB to Wear a Gause Apron'. The old trimming of her gown being worn and soiled, she proposed to replace it with a gauze apron for an assembly in Bradford,

> for it was not only a saving scheme but a reputable looking one, as the aforesaid pink, red or reddish Satin would shine with great Brilliance through the above mentioned Gauze to the Great Surprize, amaze or astonishment of the Bradfordians, and as Sarah Buck was preparing to unrip, unpick or take off the said trimming, John Buck in the Nick of Time put a stop to these (as she thought Innocent) proceedings to her utter amaze, for would any man gainsay that a Gause Apron is not Genteeler and Handsomer and prettier than a ragged and Dirty Gause Trimming, and moreover consistent with œconomical schemes ... and yr. Petitioner shall ever pray.[17]

Mrs Whittaker's letters show that her mind remained strong and critical in later life. 'I have read Godwins St Leon', she wrote to her son about a Gothic historical novel, '& was much interested by it – the miseries of wealth wh he dared not use & long Life wh that very wealth renderd a torment are described with a masterly hand.' In this book William Godwin, mixing 'human feelings and passions with incredible situations', portrayed the alienation of an alchemist whose supernatural powers brought disaster upon him and his family. Byron, Shelley and Hazlitt all admired *St Leon*, which reached a third edition by 1816.[18] Mrs Whittaker's other reading was nicely varied, including Scott's *Kenilworth*, 'the travels of Anarcharsis', Saint-Pierre's *Studies of Nature* and Crabbe's *Poems*.[19]

She mentions a proposal that the Library subscribers at Bradford should meet about raising 'the Ticketts & Subscription the 1st to 2 g[uinea]s the latter to 10/6'. Knutsford, too, had its 'little Book Club', where ladies could like Fanny Price in *Mansfield Park* be both renters and choosers of books. The Sharpes used to read aloud to each other to lighten household tasks – a common custom in these middle-class circles. John Gooch Robberds offered to read Channing's essay on Milton to his wife, and it was to be one of William

Gaskell's customs at the little house in Dover Street, Manchester, where Elizabeth Gaskell sentimentally recorded in her diary that she thought it 'quite ridiculous' to see Marianne's 'little face of gravity, and earnestness, as if she understood every word.'[20]

Catherine Whittaker earnestly wished to read William Whewell's 'poem of Boadicea' in 1818. At this time Whewell, later to become Master of Trinity and a pivotal figure in Victorian scientific culture, was no more than a brilliant young man (and 'fluent chatterer') admired by her relations in his home town of Lancaster. He had gone up to Trinity College Cambridge on a scholarship in 1812, where John William Whittaker became a friend. His aunt asked that when he next saw Whewell he would remember her to him and offer to bring in his pocket 'any little *scraps* he may have to spare for a friend'. This social context of very amateurish versifying is underlined when with a touch of pride she continued, 'He is, as well as yourself – a very pretty writer.' The great Whewell (when told that science was his forte Sydney Smith riposted, 'Yes, and his foible is omni-science') had a softer side. In 1851 he sent Elizabeth Gaskell his anonymously published holiday translation of *The Professor's Wife, From the German of Berthold Auerbach*. It ends, 'And if you ask who she is, every one will tell you, with a look of gratitude, that she is the guardian angel of the Village poor. She is called, "*The Professor's Lady*".' She must have been the German academic equivalent of a British mill owner's lady.[21]

Knutsford was a small place, but it attracted the usual itinerant lecturers in 'natural philosophy'. In 1814 William Stevenson's old colleague, John Dalton, who was quite accustomed to speak in cities like Edinburgh (where he undercut those who charged five guineas a lecture by asking for only half a guinea), thought it worthwhile to give a course of nine lectures in Knutsford on mechanics, hydrostatics, hydraulics and optics, though he was fast becoming a famous man for his pioneering work in atomic theory. His delivery did not impress Catherine Whittaker.[22] She admired instead his apparatus and models, necessarily used in lectures to unmathematical audiences, a cultural activity that ran in parallel with the popularisations of science found in books by authors well known to William Stevenson and the Holland family, such as the Edgeworths' *Harry and Lucy* series (1780, 1801-25), Jeremiah Joyce's *Scientific Dialogues* (1806) and *A Chemical Catechism for Use of Young People* (1806) by Samuel Parkes. This last was written for his only daughter, who became a friend and protégée of Mrs Gaskell in later years.[23]

A young man like William Beamont, apprenticed at the age of fourteen to a local solicitor, Strethill Wright, in about 1811, was able to go and see a glass, metal and rubber apparatus produce electricity by friction 'at Mr Holland's' and, on a lighter level, sally out to bathe in the Mere Heath brick-kiln pits just to the north of Knutsford. Friends like Dr Heathcote and Charles Barton came to play cricket for two days on Knutsford's heath in the summer of 1814 with the music master Francis Sharpe, Peter Holland's two medical apprentices and local schoolboys, continuing into September with sons of 'our old & much valued friend & favourite, Mr Oswald Leycester', Catherine Whittaker's gracious description of the former vicar of Knutsford. She herself received a notable tribute from Martha Sharpe:

> She is the happiest person I know – having no Cares, & *Making* none – pleased with attentions, but never offended if they be inadvertently omitted – never Speaking, nor even *thinking* ill of any – & warmly attach'd to all her relatives. Not one trait of what is often unjustly implied in the term, *Old Maid*.[24]

As Elizabeth Stevenson's consciousness expanded during her early childhood at Knutsford, the Whittaker and Sharpe families flourished, discovering an even larger circle of friends and widening their own horizons. When John Whittaker's mother and sister moved from Bradford to Liverpool in 1817 after the death of his father, they soon made contact with Peter Holland's brother Samuel, his wife Catherine and their children. Samuel was, like William Roscoe, a supporter of Renshaw Street Unitarian chapel, proprietor of three seats in 1825 and a member of the Liverpool Unitarian Fellowship Fund Society, the president of which was the Reverend John Yates; Richard Vaughan Yates was its treasurer. Their religious dissent did not inhibit the intelligent Mrs Whittaker's unqualified enthusiasm: 'I never saw Mrs S. Holland before,' she cried, '& I think never was so taken with any body on a first acquaintance'. She expressed whole-hearted approval of a branch of the family that became immensely important to Elizabeth Stevenson in her youth and early married years.[25]

They lived in what the younger Samuel called his father's 'Country House' in Wellington road, Toxteth Park. It was not as isolated as John Gladstone's Seaforth House and great estate, several miles down the Mersey from the newly built Liverpool Exchange and exposed to all the gales that came blowing in from the sea. Toxteth Park was still very much on the edge of the town, on land leased on favourable terms from the Earl of Sefton for good quality building along well laid-out streets, some miles from the docks and the old, crowded commercial centre where Maria Edgeworth had found the streets full of 'money making faces, every creature full drive after their own interest, elbowing, jostling headlong after money! money! money!', and the smell of a ship pursued one even to one's bedchamber. The old, stable world with its resident gentry and time-worn customs was giving way to commerce, frenzied speculation and technological change. Only one of Samuel Holland of Sandlebridge's three sons stayed in rural Cheshire. The other two, Samuel and Swinton, were new men, reinventing themselves as they rode, or attempted to ride, the accelerating energies and powers changing the western world almost beyond recognition.[26]

Samuel of Liverpool had an adventurous career. In the 1790s he was a Liverpool ship-owner, in partnership with merchants like Michael Humble of Liverpool, a fellow Unitarian, the mariner Flower Humble, and Dawson Humble, merchant of Bradford. One of their ships, the *Hodge*, purchased in

1794, was taken by the French in the following year. Another, the *Abbey*, bought in 1798, had been an American prize taken in 1779. In the next century the firm of Humble and Holland sent the potters Wedgwood and Byerley a neat little advertisement for their 'unexceptionable good vessel, copper-bottomed and armed', the fast-sailing *Lucy*, which they intended should join the next convoy for the Mediterranean. Samuel himself engaged in privateering, on one of the many Liverpool ships authorised to attack enemy vessels and make them lawful, profitable captures. A story was told that he was on board one of his own vessels in the Mediterranean when it attacked either a British man-of-war or another privateer, '(each vessel having hoisted a wrong colour to deceive an enemy), before the mistake was found out.' This might be a sailor's yarn; it is, as so often, antithetical in shape.[27]

In 1800 the firm of Worthington, Humble and Holland took over the extensive Herculaneum pottery on the shore of the Mersey near Liverpool. Its showroom was in Duke Street, in the centre of the town. A deed of November 1806 includes the names of Samuel Holland of Sandlebridge, gentleman, his son Peter, surgeon, and (for once) John Holland of Nether Knutsford, gentleman – presumably the sleeping partners – and Samuel of Liverpool, merchant. A few years later John Gladstone invested money in the venture, successfully, for his sisters. Besides this, Samuel Holland used to prospect for copper, lead and slate in North Wales, and early in the century he cleverly arranged with Lord Penrhyn for the firm of Humble and Holland to sell all the slates from his great quarries in Caernarvonshire, which were usually brought by sea to Liverpool in any case. (Lady Penrhyn was a relation of the vicar of Knutsford, Oswald Leycester, Peter Holland told Wedgwood.) Samuel's business ventures have been justly characterised as 'highly speculative, fluid and multifaceted'.[28]

Michael Humble was a connection of the Whittakers. Young Sarah had been at school with his daughter Susan and the families were on visiting terms. Once they ate 'Turtle at Mr Humble's – one of 200 lb weight ... ready dressed from Liverpool' – brought there live in tanks like Berwick salmon in the old days and regularly kept in turtle tubs at the entrance to taverns, ready for a feast. Humble became rich enough to purchase Shooter's Hill, a splendid country estate near Doncaster. In Liverpool Sarah Whittaker used to meet every week with another of his daughters, Harriet Humble, to study music, painting and Italian. This was rather awkward, given what turned out to be an unfortunate business connection. For many years Michael Humble and Samuel Holland had been American merchants, but in 1810 Swinton Holland, just returned from Malta, told Josiah Wedgwood of Samuel's unexpected financial losses. Early in the following year Michael Humble was forced to 'return to Trade & Liverpool' because of this failure, the ripples of which spread widely. 'I hear the Young women behave charmingly on this trying occasion', wrote Mrs Whittaker. It was not only the children of the shiftless house of Durbeyfield who sailed captive under hatches into unknown disasters.[29]

The typical Liverpool merchant was 'a mercantilist, a materialist, and an empiricist', operating in highly speculative trade ventures that brought both immense gains and disastrous losses. Henry Holland once wrote to his father Peter that he did not like his 'controversy with my uncle Swinton about advances to my uncle Sam', but Sam became a byword in the family for unwise speculations and financial ups and downs. Swinton had lent him £7000, but had little expectation of seeing it returned. Samuel just does not understand the management of money, he told Josiah Wedgwood.[30] In fact, the partnership between Humble and Holland was abandoned in 1814, when several other houses in Liverpool's important American trade had to declare bankruptcy following the War of 1812. Private lives could not remain unaffected. As Sarah Whittaker's mother wrote in 1817, 'We shall have been here a forthnight next Monday – we traveld in a Chaise with Mary Holland & little Charles, who were coming to visit their uncle Sam Holland, but as his Family & the Humbles are like unto the Houses of "Capulet & Montague" we cannot have much intercourse.'[31]

Her daughter was none too pleased with Harriet Humble's abilities, either. She felt the 'great loss' of Anne and Frances Holland, who were later at Knutsford in the summer of 1818 doing what they could to fit themselves to become governesses after their father's bankruptcy. There were schools for the purpose, but fees could be high and in any case they could profit from the school-teaching experience of their aunts by marriage, Mary Holland and Martha Sharpe. Mary Holland was able to help with Italian. Could they have used young Elizabeth Stevenson and the Sharpe girls as guinea pigs? Mrs Gaskell once wrote to her American friend Charles Norton that he did not understand 'aristocratical feelings' when he made 'a sort of apology to Marianne' about the fact that James Lowell had married a governess. 'My dearest friends, all through my life, have been governesses, either past, present or future', she insisted. At this time, late in 1857, the Brontës might have been in the forefront of her mind, but first-hand experience in her own family was just as relevant.[32]

Samuel Holland had married Catherine, the daughter of John Menzies, a Liverpool accountant, in 1796. Between 1797 and 1804 six children were born, Anne, Charles, Frances (Fanny), Menzies, Samuel and Catherine (Kate) – first cousins of Elizabeth. With the exception of Menzies, who died in his teens, these were all to remain in close contact with her. Charles actually married the younger sister of William Gaskell. The children received their early education from aunt Abigail Holland, Samuel's sister, who lived with the family for several years, but soon the boys were sent much further afield for an education that would not only fit them for a life in business but ensure that they became exceptionally self-reliant.

Charles first went to school in Nottingham, perhaps to the High Pavement school under John Taylor, noted for turning out 'good scholars who were keenly sought after by local business houses'.[33] When he was about thirteen he was placed with Baring Brothers in Malta, presumably through Swinton Holland's contacts. A few years later, 'when educated as my Father thought sufficiently', he was sent off in a totally different direction, to Buenos Aires, where he soon became manager of Messrs Fair & Co, a large business house. A draft of the younger Samuel's memoirs, omitted from the published version, tells of the adventurous existence Charles went on to lead all around the coasts of South America in a trading vessel, an enterprising purchase of his own. The whole continent was ripe for commercial exploitation. Admiralty mapping of islands and coastlines had begun in the later 1820s; Darwin's famous voyage on the *Beagle* (1831-36) was a second stage of these operations, plotting wind forces and surveying 'the desolate maze of channels at the continent's southern tip'.[34]

At other times Charles Holland acted as a commercial agent for Messrs Robertson & Co. in Valparaiso and Lima. In Peru he was caught up in one of Simon Bolivar's wars of liberation and, attempting to trade back country with a Spanish army, was robbed of all his goods. His men and mules simply ran away. The Spaniards played a cat-and-mouse game with him, telling him to confess he was a spy and blindfolding him as if for a firing squad. The British consul eventually obtained his release and, ultimately, redress for the stolen property. In 1833, after a trek across South America with goods from Peru to Buenos Aires, he returned to Liverpool a rich man, leaving business partners established in several cities.

His younger brother Samuel went when he was about nine to a large Moravian school at Fairfield, about four miles from Manchester, just off the Ashton turnpike road. It had been established in the 1770s and with its chapel, college quadrangle and houses was like a little town. Several of the masters were German. A serious outbreak of typhus fever after little more than a year caused him to be taken away. When he had recovered, he was sent with his slightly older brother Menzies to a Anglican school kept by the Reverend William Lamport at Lancaster for two years. There they saw several men hanged 'for misdemeanours' and the return of the survivors of a Lancashire regiment that had been at Waterloo. In 1816 he and Menzies, aged about thirteen and fourteen, were 'shipp'd off in a Brig' (like cargo) from Liverpool to Antwerp, where they were met by one of their father's partners. They travelled by diligence though Belgium along roads 'cut up by the Artillery' as far as Cologne and up the Rhine by horse-drawn boat, ending their journey at a large school kept by a Mr Ziph and a Mr Ruth at Hanau near Frankfurt, where they stayed for two more years. This was not unusual for boys destined to be merchants.

After this Menzies was 'shipped off' – the term is inescapable – to become a clerk in a commercial house in Leghorn for a short while. After about a year, Samuel tells us, he 'fell down in a fit & died'. Samuel, however, was taken into his father's office in York Street as the office boy, first there in the morning to unlock the doors, make the fires, help clean the office and run about the town with letters, till he was promoted to attend to shipping matters at the custom and excise houses. But he still had to hoist and lower goods at their warehouse, walking in from Toxteth Park, running the two miles there and back at one o'clock dinner time, and then walking home in the evening. 'Occasionally', he records stoically, 'when we were very busy I got a 4d Veal Pie in Town for my Dinner.' He seems to have retained the enviable leanness characteristic of Holland men well into later life, as did his brother Charles.[35]

There is hardly anything known about their three sisters when they were young, though Samuel's draft memoirs (not fully utilised in the fair copy that lies behind the printed text) tell us something. Anne, the eldest, was very clever, prudent and fond of books; a great favourite with all who knew her. After aunt Abigail had begun their education, she and her sister Fanny were sent to a school at 'Gettercar' (Gateacre?) near Liverpool. The most striking piece of information, however, relates to the youngest child, Kate, who was born in November 1804. She was attending a school in Liverpool when her mother's brother John Menzies, who lived at Putney, came down in his gig to see their father, who died about August 1813. He asked if Kate, then about nine years old, could return with him. It was agreed, so off she went with him to London, a little girl strapped to the seat of a high, old-fashioned gig in case she should fall out, bouncing and joggling all the way to Putney. Her little figure, diminishing as she left home, almost attains symbolic status. Samuel and Catherine Holland were apparently utterly content that she should stay with her uncle and his wife Mary Anne to be brought up with their own daughters, Anne, Caroline and Lucy. There did not even seem to be any special need or plan: he had merely taken 'a great fancy to her'. Kate was not exactly 'early motherless' like Elizabeth Stevenson, but such apparent looseness in family ties makes her 'craving after the lost mother' seem more emotional than was customary before Victoria's reign.[36]

The great commercial town of Liverpool seemed 'quite a second London' to Mrs Whittaker. It was by this time immensely rich, second only to London, with a town hall containing 'a suite of reception rooms of a splendour, elegance and sophistication that would have satisfied a duke.' It had musical concerts, and visits to the Theatre Royal from actors like Macready – 'a very first rate actor', she and her friends the Heathcotes and Bartons thought. It is evident that they did not share religious objections to the stage, common amongst Evangelicals of various denominations. Mrs Whittaker found there 'a pleasant, Select & rational Society' – the choice of adjectives is perfectly typical – which included Mrs Holland and several other congenial matrons, so she decided to rent a house at Toxteth Park between the Hollands and the Humbles. The rent with taxes was over £80; 'terribly high', she thought, but for this she could obtain dining, drawing and breakfast rooms, a parlour, five or six bedrooms and a garden. Something would be saved, in that she would 'want neither Man, Horse or Carriage – except a Merlin Chair!'

Mrs Whittaker suffered from knee trouble and found it difficult to walk. Joseph Merlin's many ingenious inventions had brought technology to the aid of select society, such as a piano with six octaves that Dr Charles Burney had commissioned. Duets could be played easily, even by ladies in hooped skirts. Merlin also created a mechanical tea-table, which the hostess could rotate by a pedal and bring each cup before her to be filled. A touch on another pedal would open and close the cock of the tea-urn. For locomotion, there was a mechanical chariot with a whip operated by a cord and spring, and a 'way-wise', a kind of mileometer. His Merlin or 'gouty' chair might have been an invalid's chair convertible into a bed, or an invalid's wheelchair with table and an adjustable cradle for the patient's legs. Even the Prince Regent had one.[37]

Young Sarah Whittaker was equally well suited. She got seriously involved in Liverpool charity work, according to her mother, and became secretary of a ladies' society 'for receiving the savings of the poor'. As an inevitable social corollary, she both gave and went to dances. The son of William Roscoe, Henry, 'one of our Figurantes on Wednesday night', met with instant approval from Mrs Whittaker – 'one of the most Engaging Young men I ever saw. Genius, Spirit & Frankness are marked in his Handsome physiognomy'. His brother Robert was a college friend of John William Whittaker's. Sarah was to remain unmarried, however.[38]

Mrs Sarah Whittaker's physical handicaps did not prevent her from travelling about the country and visiting. The freezing Christmas of 1818 saw her staying with her kinfolk in Knutsford, where social life – by her standards if not Henry Holland's – could hardly have been bettered: 'I think I never remember so Severe a Season. ... last night, or rather this Morning between 1 & 2 o'Clock, Mrs Sharpe & I walkd home from Miss Bartons *new* lodgings near the Hollands, after a very gay party – Quadrilles, Country Dances, & some of Bessy's sweetest Songs.' Anne and Bessy Barton were evidently special friends of the Hollands and frequent visitors at Church House. They had even come to Knutsford and taken lodgings in the town. Their father's death in about 1817 had left them scantily provided for, Mrs Whittaker believed, dependent at first on their uncle, a Dr Heathcote, who apparently lived at or near Liverpool. A day or two after the Bartons' party the young Elizabeth, if she herself had not gone away for Christmas, would have been involved in the continuous round of entertainment, because Mrs Sharpe's set all went to dine at Mrs Lumb's. The new year was celebrated with the Hollands. Festive Knutsford evidently suited the Barton sisters, who soon became 'as gay as Larks, with Quadrilles, Concerts and Beaux'.[39]

Late in the following year Bessie Holland was preparing for a visit to her uncle Swinton at Russell Square in London, where yet another relation, Mary Ann Broadhurst, had been spending her holidays. Mary was connected by marriage. She was the daughter of Frances Whittaker (sister of Mary, Esther, Martha and Catharine), who had married the Reverend Thomas Broadhurst of Bath, the utterly unpuritanical dissenting minister of Trim Street chapel.

Sandlebridge Farm, the home of Elizabeth's grandparents, inherited in 1816 by her uncle Peter Holland. See pp. 53-5

Old kitchen fireplace in Sandlebridge Farm. See p. 199

Old Lindsey Row, Chelsea (ECG's birthplace) and Beaufort Row
(her parents' home). See pp. 86-8

Uncle Peter Holland of Church House,
Knutsford. See pp. 116-17

Dr Henry Holland, Elizabeth's cousin, from
a portrait of about 1840. See pp. 148-51

Mrs Lumb's house on The Heath, Knutsford, in 1832, drawn by R. H. Watt,
perhaps from a watercolour by Lucy Holland. See pp. 124-5

The Byerleys' School for Young Ladies, Avonbank, Stratford-upon-Avon,
watercolour painting. See p. 241

above & right] Facing pages from Elizabeth's first music book. See pp. 244-6

Avonbank from the river, sketched in pencil by Elizabeth's schoolfriend,
Jessie Scott, with the help of Katharine Thomson. See p. 241

Inside front cover inscribed 'E. C. Stevenson Avonbank – June 15 1825 Thursday'

Cousin Samuel Holland of Plas yn Penrhyn.
See pp. 289-90

The Slate Mine, aquatint by J. C. Stadler after P. J. de Loutherbourg, 1800.
See pp. 298-9

Reverend William Gaskell,
from *Illustrations of Cross Street Chapel*
(Manchester, 1917). See p. 408

Bust of Elizabeth Stevenson
by David Dunbar, probably Newcastle, 1829.
See pp. 382-3

Though a good preacher, Henry Holland had reported earlier, he was also a fine singer, musician and attender of fashionable parties – 'in short, a gay gentleman'. Henry very much doubted if 'a puritan dissenter who preached 40 or 50 years ago' would acknowledge him as a brother. Broadhurst resigned his pulpit in 1809, to concentrate upon teaching in an academy for young ladies the Whittaker sisters had established in an excellent building originally designed to be a school, as Henry Holland had thought – Belvedere House, Bath. It had been started in the previous century by the dramatist and novelist Sophia Lee and her sisters Harriet and Anne, friends of Mrs Piozzi and Sarah Siddons, whose youngest daughter was a pupil there. They gave up the school, presumably to the Whittaker sisters, in 1803.[40]

In 1808 Broadhurst published *Advice to Young Ladies, On the Improvement of the Mind, and Conduct of Life*, in which he proclaims that girls were 'by no means inferior' to boys and even excelled them in 'liveliness of imagination, quickness of apprehension, and docility'. Broadhurst's book is based upon practice. Young ladies were advised to keep a commonplace book, such as 'Locke's improved, ruled'. He outlined a wide-ranging curriculum that included science as well as religion and humanities, though very few novels from what he contemptuously termed 'the teeming press' were thought suitable for them to read. They would probably do better to practise for the grand ball that the dancing mistress, Miss Le Mercier, was accustomed to hold for the young ladies of Belvedere house just before the Christmas holidays. Sydney Smith used Broadhurst's book as a peg on which to hang his 'Female Education' in the *Edinburgh Review* for January 1810. He approved of his reformist aims, thought him, offhandedly, 'a very good sort of man, who has not written a very bad book upon an important subject', but went on to treat the subject in his own inimitable style – humour (would a mother desert a baby for a quadratic equation?) mixed with more serious grandiloquence ('as the matter stands at present, half the talent in the universe runs to waste').

Mrs Lumb must have given some thought to this school as a possible place for her bright niece. Certainly the oldest Sharpe girl, Marianne, was sent there from 1824 to 1826. The school, however, was not as successful as the Broadhursts would have liked – it was down to twenty pupils by 1818. Frances became depressed. '*He* will be willing to attribute this to the "Want of Reform in Parliament", rather than his own unconciliatory manners with his pupils, to which I fear their failure is attributable' was the hard judgment of his sister-in-law Mrs Sharpe in 1822. Either for this reason, or because William Stevenson's opinion swayed in another direction, Elizabeth was not sent to school at the Broadhursts, where what Sarah Whittaker once called the 'rival cousins' could be found. She strikes a competitive pedal note.[41]

NOTES

1 Ritchie, pref. *Cranford*, p. x; Uglow, p. 613. See Flora Masson to the same effect, *Manchester Guardian* of 29 September 1910 ('used often to talk of him'), and A. Cobden Smith, 'Mrs. Gaskell and Lower Mosley Street', *SSQ,* January 1911, p. 157.

2 G. T. Bettany, ed. *Mary Barton*, London, New York and Melbourne, 1891, p. v; E. V. T., 'Mrs. Gaskell's father', *Athenaeum*, 12 September 1891, p. 352. Anne Ritchie could not identify E. V. T.

3 GLROL: MF, St Luke's marriage register, 1803-18, no. 182. Witnessed by Anthony Todd Thomson and John Swan.

4 CRO: WS 1816: will and codicils, probate (p. 100 above).

5 *DNB.*; infm from a descendant of ATT, Dr Ian Gregg; *Complete Peerage;* Green, p. 144. See also [Katharine Thomson], *Memoir of Anthony Todd Thomson, M.D., F.L.S.*, pr. pr. London, 1850, *passim*, based in part on details supplied by the 2nd Mrs Stevenson. Dr Gregg generously supplied a photocopy of this and other rare items that I have used.

6 Reader, *Professional Men*, p. 41. For Katharine see especially pp. 251-7 below. For Parkes, who was in the Crimea with Florence Nightingale, see W. R. Merrington, *University College and Its Medical School: A History*, London, 1976, pp. 40, 232, 250.

7 ATT, TS of Journal (Dr I. Gregg Collection); [H. Hale Bellot?], 'Memoir of Dr. A. T. Thomson', *Medical Times*, 14 July 1849; *Lancet*, 1849, II, pp. 45-7; New, *Brougham*, p. 356 and n.; *The Seasons of James Thomson*, ed. ATT, preface.

8 On 21 May, Frederick, son of Swinton Colthurst Holland of Hackney and his wife Ann ; on 30 May, Samuel, son of Samuel Clegg of Westminster and his wife Ursula (TWA: 1787/9, Turner's MS Register). SCH expected the Turners in May (KUL: Wedgwood 29-21674, SCH to JW, London, 22 February 1815). Clegg had been an honorary member of Newcastle's Literary and Philosophical Society from 1809.

9 GLROL: MF, St Luke's baptisms, 1813-29 (addresses given as Beaufort Row, Lindsay Row and Sloane Street respectively); Chadwick, 1910, p. 196; 1913, p. 133 (neither indexed). List of rectors in Randall Davies, *Chelsea Old Church*, London, 1904.

10 Alan Ruston, 'The Non-Con club and some other Unitarian clubs 1783-1914', *TUHS*, XIV, 1967-70, pp. 157-8; Mineka, *Dissidence of Dissent*, pp. 136, 394-428. ECG's friend Eliza Fox probably provided one key to contributors, a MS list compiled from her father's notes (p. 400).

11 MCO: MSS Wood 26, f. 117 and 28, f. 46 (HG, 1833, 1835); Wood 35, f. 47 and 37, f. 48 (PH, 1842, 1844); printed annual reports of the Trustees; Pigot and Co., *Directory for 1834.*

12 Butler, *Edgeworth*, pp. 37, 45-57; Ward Notebook, f. 6 verso; Chadwick, 1910, pp. 28-9; Ritchie, pref. *Cranford*, p. xii.

13 Henry James, 'Art of Fiction', *Longman's Magazine*, IV, 1884; RTD, LUBL: ECG, MS diary, pp. 14, 24.

14 SW junior to JWW, n. d. (WAL: EHC 205c/9; Hall, pp. 6-7). Hall dates 'probably January 1810'; cp. DCLH: HH to LA, Knutsford, 21 March 1809, 'Henry Wakefield came to us yesterday from Stockport, to make his trial of the profession'. *Old Poz* appeared in *The Parent's Assistant* (1796), designed for children in their early teens (Butler, *Edgeworth*, pp. 159-65).

15 Green, *Knutsford*, pp. 134-6 (also WCL: WB's annotated copy); Joan Leach, 'The French master', *GSN*, XII, August 1991, pp. 12-16; Black, *European Warfare*, pp. 45-6, 53.

16 SW junior to JWW, 8 August 1813 (WAL: EHC 205/20; Hall, p. 47).

17 WYA: 34D76/47: Sarah Buck to her father, Crofton, 9 October 1773; prayer and petition, November 1779. Qu. from Rae, *Turtle at Mr Humble's*, pp. 20, 27, 42-3. See also Juliet Barker, *The Brontës*, London, 1994, p. 117.

18 See the critique in *Collected Novels and Memoirs of William Godwin*, ed. Mark Philip, London 1992, I, pp. 30-3; George Woodcock, 'Things as they might be: things as they

are', *DR*, LIV, 1974-75, pp. 690-2.

19 SW to JWW, Townhill, Saturday 16 February 1811 (WAL: EHC 205d/29; not in Hall); Hall, p. 111. J. J. Barthélemy, *Travels of Anarcharsis*, tr. William Beaumont, 2nd edn, 1794; J. H. B. de Saint-Pierre, *Studies of Nature*, tr. Henry Hunter, London, 1796, 1799; William Crabbe, *Poems*, 1807, or perhaps *The Borough*, 1810.

20 Hall, p. 54; MCO: Robberds 1, JGR to MR, Nottingham, 13 September 1826; ECG, MS diary, p. 4. For Channing's 'Remarks on the Character and Writings of JM' (1826) see Howe, *Unitarian Conscience*, pp. 182, 359, n. 67.

21 Hall, pp. 54, 58, 75-6, 92 (CW to JWW, Heathside, 19 June 1818), 178. See also unpublished Whewell correspondence at TCC, especially Add MSS c. 88[91-3]; and for Auerbach, Peter Skrine, 'Mrs Gaskell and Germany', *GSJ*, VII, 1993, p. 43.

22 Musson and Robinson, *Science and Technology*, pp. 101-11; Jacob, *Cultural Meaning*, pp. 142; DCLH: HH to PH, Edinburgh, 8 February 1807; Hall, pp. 58-9 (CW to JWW, 18 September 1814).

23 The death of Mrs Hodgett's husband in a chemical experiment in 1851 shocked Mrs Gaskell. Wife and daughter were left very badly off and, although Anne Holland came to live with them for a few months, the possibility of a school or daily governessing was discussed. See *Letters*, pp. 145, 148, 156, 159, 180, 833. (Re-date letter 116: [March 1851]). For Joyce see p. 217 below.

24 WCL: MS 284, diary of WB, 10 and 17 June 1816; WCL: G. A. Carter, 'William Beamont (1797-1889) and the town of Warrington in the 19th century', Liverpool University diploma in local history, 1983, p. 3; Hall, p. 168 (MS to JWW, February 1828, specially noted by Hall).

25 G. E. Evans, *A History of Renshaw Street Chapel and Its Institutions*, Liverpool, 1887, pp. 119, 140 (a valuation for each pew); SW to JWW, Liverpool, 9 August [1817] (WAL: EHC 205d/129; Hall, p. 86).

26 Davies, *Memoirs of Samuel Holland*, p. 2; Checkland, *The Gladstones*, pp. 82-3; Aikin, *Description of the Country*, pp. 375-6; *Edgeworth Letters*, p. 10.

27 Williams, *Liverpool Privateers*, p. 240n.; R. Craig and R. Jarvis, *Liverpool, Registry of Merchant Ships*, CSR, XV, 3rd s., Manchester, 1967, pp. 8, 59; C. Northcote Parkinson, *The Rise of the Port of Liverpool*, Liverpool, 1952, pp. 129-37; KUL: Wedgwood 87-15751, H & H to W & B, Liverpool, 21 June 1808. Flower Humble of Bradford (later of Walker and Durham) was elected an honorary member of the Newcastle Literary and Philosophical Society in 1796.

28 Aikin, *Description of the Country*, p. 371; Mayer, 'On Liverpool pottery', pp. 202-7; Brooke, *Liverpool As It Was*, pp. 417, 477-8; Checkland, *The Gladstones*, p. 81; KUL: Wedgwood 2-267, PH to JW, Knutsford, 8 April 1808; Malchow, *Gentleman Capitalists*, p. 19.

29 Rae, *Turtle at Mr Humble's*, pp. 76, 152; Hall, pp. 15-16, 92; KUL: Wedgwood 29-21665, SCH to JW, Knutsford, 13 September 1810.

30 S. G. Checkland, 'Economic attitudes in Liverpool 1793-1807', *EconHR*, 2S, V, 1952-53, pp. 58-9; DCLH: HH to PH, 3[?] Lisle Street, L. Square, 29 January [1812]; KUL: Wedgwood 57-31901, SCH to JW, London, 4 September 1819.

31 Tolley, 'The Liverpool campaign against the orders in council and the American war of 1812', pp. 121-4; SW to JWW, Liverpool, Saturday 9 August [1817] (WAL: EHC 205d/129; Hall. pp. 85-6).

32 Hall, pp. 92-3, 108; Kathryn Hughes, *The Victorian Governess*, London and Rio Grande, 1993, pp. 17-20; *Letters*, p. 488. An 'Anna Stevenson' was probably a governess. See JGS: TS, John Stevenson to ECS, Ship Recovery, Gravesend, 13 June [1827], p. 285 below.

33 David Wardle, *Education and Society in Nineteenth-Century Nottingham*, Cambridge, 1971, pp. 121-3. I must thank Mrs Caroline Kelly (Hallward Library, University of Nottingham), who tells me that his name does not appear in the admission registers of the period.

34 Adrian Desmond and James Moore, *Darwin*, London, 1991, pp. 105-6. See Irvine, ch. 6, 'Holland of Liverpool', and appendix D for a partial transcript of SH's draft.

35 SH, *Memoirs of Samuel Holland*, ed. Davies, pp. 1-4 (with portrait); Aikin, *Description of the Country*, pp. 232-3, with plate of Fairfield. Cf. *Losh Diaries*, I, pp. 130, 135, II, p. 12 (sons to go to Rouen for two years and Germany for one in 1821). CH's likeness in later life is reproduced in *Portrait*, no. 8.

36 See appendix D; Irvine, pp. 158-62 (paper about Menzies family in possession of Fanny Holland, 1870). It is possible that Samuel Holland's business problems were a factor.

37 Girouard, *The English Town*, p. 29; Quinlan, *Victorian Prelude*, p. 113; SW to JWW, Liverpool, 9 August 1817 (WAL: EHC 205d/129; Hall, pp. 85-6, also 104); Richard D. Altick, *The Shows of London*, Cambridge, Mass., 1978, pp. 72-4 (with illustrs).

38 Hall, pp. 88-9. Sir Henry Roscoe later became a famous man and a friend of Mrs Gaskell's.

39 Hall, pp. 95-6: SW to JWW, 3 January 1819 (unlocatable letter). See also Hall, pp. 88, 99, 116-17.

40 Jerom Murch, *A History of the Presbyterian and General Baptist Churches in the West of England; With Memoirs of Some of Their Pastors*, London, 1835, pp. 148-9, 199; DCLH: HH to Lucy Aikin, Belvidere [*sic*], Bath, January 1804; *The Memoirs of Susan Sibbald (1783-1812)*, ed. Francis Paget Hett, London, 1926 (not seen; infm and ref. courtesy of Mrs Elizabeth Bevan, BaCL).

41 *Advice to Young Ladies*, Bath, [1808], pp. vii-viiii, 56, 76-7, with Preface dated Camden-Place, Bath, 9 September 1808 (BL: 8415. ccc. 50, presentation copy to wife); 2nd edn, lightly rev., London, 1810, Belvedere House, Bath, 26 March 1810. See also Hall, pp. 1, 35, 40, 52, 64, 94, 99, 133; endnotes, pp. viii, xi.

10

Happy families

ELIZABETH STEVENSON WAS brought up in the Knutsford area amongst lively, intelligent and enterprising people, but an investigation of her extended family shows how the provincial was raised to or brought into association with a national level of importance, whilst retaining strong roots in the English counties. Swinton Holland, for example, went from strength to strength. He became a very rich man indeed. After his travels to America, Italy and Malta, he had finally settled down as a partner in Baring Brothers and company, in December 1814. From 30 June he was to have a one-sixth share of the whole concern; two years later, on the retirement of Henry Baring, he held a quarter share. He became the trusted, rather pedantic controller of the Bishopsgate Street counting house of this once princely firm, 'an honest right-spirited man, but somewhat brusque and unpolished', rather lacking in boldness and leadership. By the time Mary Ann Broadhurst arrived he had moved from London Fields to Russell Square, and had six children living – Edward and Caroline, born in Trieste in 1806 and 1807; Charlotte and Louisa, born in Malta in 1808 and 1810; Frederick and George Henry, born in London in 1814 and 1816.[1]

Life, of course, was not all roses. A daughter, Jessie, had not survived infancy, and Caroline was epileptic. Dr Henry Holland told his father in 1812 that she was irritable and fretful, having had four fits on the day before. He did not have, he wrote, 'the slightest faith in the efficacy of Dr Darwin's prescription for her'. She was looked after in country lodgings for a time; in 1818 Swinton was seeking somewhere suitable for her along the Harrow road. Eventually she was sent to Knutsford, and Peter and Abigail Holland were appointed amongst her several guardians in the will her father made in November 1827. An annuity of £500 a year was assigned to her care. A copy of a Bible, annotated 'Caroline Holland / from her affectionate mother / A Holland' and dated 17 December 1824, was given to Abigail Holland in 1829. It eventually came to Mrs Gaskell.[2]

In June 1831 a new situation was being sought for the Holland daughters' former nursery governess, who had become Caroline's companion and housekeeper. We surely hear the living tones of aunt Swinton, as she was called, when Elizabeth Stevenson wrote to her friend that Miss Swinerhath was 'of discreet age, and a more kind-hearted, faithful creature never was.' Apart from this, poor Caroline is never mentioned, though she must have been living in Knutsford at the very time her cousin became engaged and married. She did not die until 9 October 1833 at the age of twenty-six. She was buried a few days later in the graveyard of the old dissenting chapel, and lies under the stone of John Colthurst of Sandlebridge, gent.[3]

In 1819 Swinton was able to settle £28,000 in 3 per cent Consols and three life policies for £1000, £2000 and £5000 on his wife and children, and also to purchase a splendid estate, 'The Priory' at Roehampton, in an exclusive area where 'the beauties of the surrounding scenery, and the contiguity to Richmond-park' had induced many rich people to build villas. Finance had made him wealthy and famous enough to be the subject of a Dighton carica-ture ('A View of Holland') and for 'The Priory' to be included in a published set of engravings. His brother Peter Holland and nephew Henry were both accustomed to 'trifling dabbling in French funds' as they rose and fell, doubt-less with Swinton's expert but cautious advice. 'No one, who cannot bear these jolts & ruts', wrote Henry with great sangfroid to Maria Edgeworth, 'ought to tie himself, even by the slightest thread, to the great stock-jobbing machine of modern Europe.' It was nevertheless his Whiggish opinion that 'this modern supremacy of the Barings and Rothchilds [*sic*]' was better than 'the necessitous and plundering armies of the Wallensteins and Tilley's' during the religious conflicts of the seventeenth century.[4]

In Swinton's home one could meet men from all the countries the house of Baring traded with, in effect from 'nearly all the civilised world', Lucy Aikin claimed. At one dinner party she met a harmless-looking old abbé and a sharp-looking little Corsican surgeon who were going out to be with Napoleon on St Helena; 'the longest, leanest, brownest, most ungainly mortal' she had ever set eyes upon, a senator from Carolina, who was so astounded at the tales of borough jobbing that he longed to 'witness the humours of an English election'; and a Mr Haldimand, 'one of the ablest and most enlightened mercantile men in London', who talked learnedly of usury laws and the like, 'observing that ladies now studied political economy'. As the proud brother of Jane Marcet, he was probably engaged in a little advertising; Mrs Marcet had already added *Conversations on Political Economy*, 'standard for later Benthamites', to her even more famous best-seller, *Conversations on Chemistry, Intended More Especially for the Female Sex* (1806). Dr Holland was there, 'but he was so seized upon by the Italians that one had nothing of him.' Swinton Holland could put his relations in touch with an intellectual world as well as geographical, financial and trading ones.[5]

He seems at some time to have taken a town house in Park Lane, which in the 1820s was becoming very fashionable and rapidly more expensive, its views stretching over Decimus Burton's improved Hyde Park to the distant hills of

Surrey. The house was not part of the magnificent Grosvenor estate, though his nephew Henry lived for half a century after 1822 in one of its houses in Brook Street – left, according to him, 'villainously out of repair' and on an expensive sixty-year lease exacted by the agents of the 'noble extortioner'.[6] We happen to know that Elizabeth Stevenson used to visit Swinton's family in London, for in later years she told Frances ('Snow') Wedgwood that at about age twelve she used to enjoy one of her Wedgwood uncle's jokes when he and other undergraduates visited them from Cambridge. She was probably a little younger, perhaps going there on a visit before she went to school when she was ten or eleven.[7] It was in Park Lane, Meta and Julia Gaskell told Ward, that their mother used to stay sometimes with her uncle Swinton – 'a partner of Barings', they did not fail to point out, and, with one of their characteristic antitheses, 'she was very beautiful in shabby dress – cousins vice versa'. Swinton himself not long before had told Josiah Wedgwood that his daughter would find his own regular habits and hours 'an antidote to the London gaiety, which all young Ladies expect when visiting the Metropolis'.[8]

In 1822 Earl Sommers put his manor, advowson and estate of Dumbleton, some nineteen hundred acres of freehold land 'of a very superior quality', on the market. The quiet little village of Dumbleton is well away from the main road between Evesham and Cheltenham, below Bredon Hill, where the bells in summer time sounded clear and the coloured counties of Gloucestershire and Worcestershire lay below. Its church is Norman and Early English – still a perfect village church. The rectory was enlarged in about 1700. The manor was co-extensive with the parish, with the exception of a farm that belonged to Jesus College, Oxford, the rectory itself and glebe lands (the incumbent being 'upwards of 60 years of age'), together with a small property belonging to T. P. Staight. It was advertised as 'only 95 miles distant from London, very convenient for occupation.'[9] In June 1823 Swinton bought it, for eighty thousand pounds – 'full value' in his opinion. He paid for it out of his own resources, but also sold trust stock in English Funds to reinvest in New York State canal stock, he told Josiah Wedgwood, in a correspondence that is stuffed with information about money, investments, possible taxes on earthenware in the next budget and the like.

On 27 December 1827, however, Swinton took up his pen to sign a cheque in Mr Baring's counting house, fell back and died within a few minutes, Henry Holland recorded in his manuscript journal. He was only fifty years old, 'in perfect health, & abounding in all manner of worldly prosperity'. Swinton's autobiographical memoir at Barings effusively praises the 'Omnipotent Ruler of the Universe for having elevated his situation in life.' A modern historian finds this document 'rich in sanctimonious prosing', but his nephew Henry is more charitable, finding 'a simplicity and single-mindedness in his character' amidst the 'utmost activity of worldly concerns'. However unexpected his death, he had made a lengthy will only a month before, in which he asked for his funeral 'to be as plain as is consistent with propriety and that all needless parade may be avoided'. In it Abigail Holland received £100, his brothers Peter and Samuel and Hannah Lumb £50 each, 'as a small token of my affection for them'. Henry, who was an executor with Josiah Wedgwood, reported to Maria Edgeworth that he had judiciously disposed by his will of a large property of about £400,000. He provided another, almost inconceivable standard of prosperity against which William Stevenson could be measured by a girl in her teens, even if the shabbiness of her dress is unlikely.[10]

As the old hall at Dumbleton near the church was ruinous, Swinton's son and heir, Edward, decided to create a model village and build for himself, his wife and family a large new mansion of honey-coloured Cotswold stone, designed by Humphry Repton's architecturally versatile son George in a kind of Tudor Gothic style. The elaborate contract for erecting this mansion house, dated 9 January 1833 and annotated with a series of payments of £19,800 in total up to 9 September 1837, has survived. 'It will be a nice large house', Catherine Darwin wrote rather acidly in 1832 after an extended visit to Swinton's widow, Mrs Anne Holland, and her daughters Charlotte and Louisa, 'but Edward will be awfully pompous when he is master of it, for he can hardly contain his importance now'. The interior is full of first-rate panelling and moulded plaster ceilings, with an especially fine hall and staircase, to judge from old Victorian photographs, which show even more elaborate carving than exists today. The stairs are lit by a beautiful lantern in the roof above. The large drawing room looks out over formal gardens, which now contain magnificent Lebanese and Atlantic cedars, presumably planted by the Hollands. The typical triangular shapes of young cedars are visible in old photographs. An ornamental lake can be seen beyond, and to one side are picturesquely steep little hills in parkland on which animals peacefully used to graze. Edward ordered new carriage drives to be made though his property, which was entered by pattern-book lodges and gates. In 1832 the Holland ladies were staying a few miles away at Overbury, another great house, rented from Merton College and crowded with pictures 'not always of the most delicate description', Elizabeth Gaskell joked with her friend Harriet Carr. The impression of rapidly increasing wealth and position is very strong. Meta and Julia Gaskell might well contend that Hannah Lumb was poor in comparison.[11]

Swinton might not have been very sophisticated, but his was a branch of the family rising greatly in the world and, perhaps, not over-burdened by its dissenting conscience on the way. His son Edward Holland, who went up to Trinity College, Cambridge in September 1823, would have had to attend college chapel and make the Church of England subscription required before taking his degree. His brother Frederick became vicar of Evesham. Edward went on to become a leading figure in his county, helping to found a famous agricultural college at Cirencester, becoming its first Chairman of Council in 1845 and, soon afterwards, advancing thousands of pounds of his own money to ensure its continuance. His role in the Royal Agricultural Society became just as influential.[12]

When at Cambridge Edward associated with families that were already famous in national life and provided one figure of international significance. Edward was a contemporary of Hensleigh and Robert Wedgwood, and knew Charles Darwin's older brother Erasmus well. Dr Henry Holland, too, though not a Cambridge man, was a great friend of Erasmus Darwin, whose sister Catherine complained with mock-annoyance that Bessie Holland knew more about Charles Darwin and his voyage on the *Beagle* than she did. Edward Holland had once lent Charles (a young Cambridge undergraduate strangely fascinated by beetles, who had not yet been inspired by reading Alexander Humboldt's *Personal Narrative* and John Herschel's *Preliminary Discourse on the Study of Natural Philosophy*) 'a horse to ride in the park with' when he was in London in 1829.[13]

Domestic life, even in these privileged circles, was precarious. Hensleigh's sister Fanny, only twenty-six, pious, humble and unselfish, was suddenly taken ill at Maer Hall with vomitings and fever during the 1832 cholera epidemic. She seemed to recover, but then died quite unexpectedly, to the great distress of her family. Her sister Elizabeth sent Mary Holland in Knutsford the sad news, which Henry Holland heard when he arrived there after a short tour of Skye, Mull and other Western Isles. His own children were at that time being cared for at Knutsford after the death of their mother in early 1830. His letter of condolence to Hensleigh Wedgwood is dated 1 September, and speaks of arriving 'yesterday', which means that he must have missed a happier event, the wedding of his cousin Elizabeth Stevenson to William Gaskell on 30 August.[14]

These families were connected by marriage in more than one way, interrelated in what Peacock's Mr Flosky might have called 'a compound ratio of ramification', especially through the daughters of the Reverend William Willets, the kind and bookish Unitarian minister who had married Catherine, sister of the first Josiah Wedgwood.

Back in the 1770s the first Josiah Wedgwood, who was a Unitarian, had sent one of his young daughters with two little Willets cousins to the school kept by Philip Holland and his wife at Bolton. When Mrs Holland was not about, the minister used to give the boys seed cake, raisins and a glass of sweet wine in his room. She was inclined to be strict, believing that good conduct should count when 'making out the bills of merit as well as Greek and Latin' – she too must have had reservations about the utility of classical learning. A little later Wedgwood sent his son John there accompanied by his cousin John Willets; they were soon joined by the two younger Wedgwood boys, Jos and Tom. 'Philosophical apparatus' – air-pumps, electrical machines and the like – was to be ordered from London for their experiments. Wedgwood's own largely self-education in scientific subjects had already been initiated by his brother-in-law William Willets, Joseph Priestley and the Birmingham Lunar Society.[15]

By 1779 the Wedgwood daughters were back at Etruria with a governess, Everina Wollstonecraft, Mary's sister, and soon a home school had been set up for the boys to add a more commercial type of practical education to their grounding in classics. Various cousins and one of Dr Robert Darwin's boys, Robert Waring, also studied with them. The connection was a close one through several generations. Dr Robert married Josiah's daughter Susannah. His famous son, Charles Darwin, married Emma, daughter of the second Josiah Wedgwood. Charles's sister Caroline married Josiah Wedgwood the third. Names recur. Keeping the generations apart in one's mind is not easy. Several family homes were in the same part of England, in the north midlands near Newcastle-under-Lyme and the Welsh border, not very far from Knutsford.[16]

George Stubbs's painting in 1780 of the Wedgwood family in the grounds of Etruria House in Staffordshire shows Josiah and his wife at their ease on a seat beneath a great tree whilst their seven children, four of them on horses by Stubbs's insistence, are rather more carefully placed (statically at play) before the verdant landscape of the park. The painting is emblematic rather than expressive; calm, uncrowded and stiffly harmonious, displaying a domestic group conscious of the facts of possession and the decent conditions of landowning life in a flourishing provincial economy. Typically, for an age when the fine arts were intertwined with industry, Stubbs was rewarded for his professional work with large, specially made ceramic tablets suitable for enamel painting, a technological triumph from Wedgwood's kilns. The somewhat earlier commissioning of young John Flaxman's neoclassical designs for Wedgwood's newly perfected 'Jasper' body, dense, white and silky to the touch, is the most famous association of this kind. Their Greek motifs and perspective, figures in bas-relief, strong lines and a variety of colours, including blue, black, green, yellow and lilac, proved incredibly successful.

Around the turn of the century the sight of Dr Robert Darwin (well over six feet and twenty stone) travelling around and about Shrewsbury in a tiny chaise painted bright yellow, which fitted him with only an inch or so to spare on either side and was drawn by smart black horses, must have provided the greatest contrast in the world to the lean doctor Peter Holland riding in a dogcart on his rounds in Knutsford and its surrounding lanes. No coachman would have had to go before Peter into the houses of poorer patients to see if the floors would bear his weight.

In 1802 Samuel Holland of Sandlebridge had been able to capitalise on a valuation he had made some years before. He conducted complicated, delicate negotiations on Josiah Wedgwood's behalf for the purchase of the Maer estate in Staffordshire, charging sixteen guineas for his services – which, in a gentlemanly manner, he invited Wedgwood to tax if he thought the bill excessive. In the event, with a Mr Lloyd of Manchester in the offing, Josiah paid out nearly £30,000.[17]

It was worth it – an old Elizabethan house right off the main road, set in extensive gardens stretching down to a lake, surrounded by woods and the little hills of Staffordshire, with its own neat church standing high across the way. Maer Hall, about nine miles away from Etruria and the smoking chimneys of the nearby pottery, became a favourite with the family. There the Wedgwoods used to entertain their neighbours – the Tolletts of Betley, the Sneyds of Keele and the Caldwells of Linley Wood. In the next generation Robert Darwin's son Charles was to experience its Stubbsian felicity. He was enraptured:

> Life there was perfectly free; the country was very pleasant for walking or riding; and in the evening there was much very agreeable conversation, not so personal as it generally is in large family parties, together with music. In the summer the whole family used often to sit on the steps of the old portico, with the flower-garden in front, and with the steep wooded bank, opposite to the house, reflected in the lake, with here and there a fish rising or a water-bird paddling about. Nothing has left a more vivid picture on my mind than those evenings at Maer. I was also attached to and greatly revered my uncle Jos: he was silent and reserved so as to be a rather awful man; but he sometimes talked openly with me.

Fortunately Charles Darwin had the good sense to marry a Wedgwood daughter, Emma, who sustained him through a life in which frequent bouts of ill-health ran their course along with thoughts that changed western views of human origins and destiny. Dr Henry Holland was consulted about his mysterious illnesses, but even he could not be expected to cure the *blue devils*. Peacock's Mr Flosky held the view that tea had shattered everybody's nerves, late dinners made them slaves of indigestion and the French revolution caused them to shrink away from true philosophy, destroying in the more refined part of the community all enthusiasm for political liberty. They were, so to speak, the low spirits of the age. But no doctor could cure the most famous of all the Darwins, whose illnesses are now regarded as psychosomatic. 'The way to produce fine fruit is to blight the flower', opined the darkly oracular Mr Flosky.[18]

Between the eternities of evolutionary time members of these clever, affluent families continued to thrive in human history. Business, finance, science, technology and medicine were the source of their wealth. They were fascinated by their interrelationships, and ready to admit any intellectuals who could contribute to what they devoutly believed was the progress of the human species. In the eighteenth century Richard Edgeworth's encounter in 1766 with the scientist and poet, Erasmus Darwin, and the midlands Lunar group had marked an epoch in his life. They used to meet at the manufacturer Matthew Boulton's house near Birmingham – on the Monday nearest the full moon for a simple, practical reason, to make travelling easier. Josiah Wedgwood the potter, the engineer James Watt, the industrial chemist James Keir and others composed an informal 'pioneer research establishment', in touch with leading figures in Europe and America. Benjamin Franklin, who had visited William Turner of Wakefield, was a notable correspondent.[19]

Fifty or more years later Edgeworth's daughter Maria met leading figures of another age on her visits to England – Jane Marcet; 'little slight-made' Mary Somerville, one of the finest scientific authors of the age; Henry Holland's friend, Sir Humphry Davy, famous for his electrochemical discoveries and for being 'the martyr of matrimony' (he had wed the vivacious Mrs Apreece, widow of a Leicestershire baronet); Mrs Siddons, telling entertaining anecdotes of the stage; John Herschel the astronomer, whose extraordinarily influential *Preliminary Discourse* was for Maria 'price 6*sh. worth any money*'; and, on one occasion in Sir Henry Holland's house, the poet Robert Southey, who 'looked like a worn out Italian actor with very black eyebrows and a very grey-mop-head', accompanied by a tediously voluble and successful lawyer, Sir Edward Alderson.

Maria's eyes were elsewhere:

> Dr. Hollands children are very fine happy looking children and he does seem so to enjoy them. His little boy in reply to the common place *aggravating* question/observation put to children of 'Who loves you – nobody loves you in this world Im sure' replied 'Yes there is somebody – Papa loves me I know -Im sure'. And throwing himself back on his on *his aunt Mary's* lap he looked up at his father with such a sweet confident smile! The father was standing between Alderson and Southey – The one sure he had him by the ear and the other by the imagination but the child had him by the heart and looking over the lawyer's gesticulating arm the father smiled and nodded at his boy and with an emphasis in which the whole soul spoke low but strong 'Yes I *do* love you'. Neither the lawyer nor the poet heard it – to the best of my opinion.

It is a stylistic set-piece; nevertheless, one based upon a tiny incident in an intellectual community that contained men, and a few women, with international reputations. Though Elizabeth Stevenson's name has not been found in any of the various correspondences, by this point she was twenty years of age, intellectually alert and sparklingly competent. The world was open to her – up to a point.[20]

Aikin, Edgeworth, Somerville and Marcet were exceptional beings. On the whole middle-class women and children in the early decades of the century tended to lead separate lives, as John Stuart Mill noted, often in a complicated and continuous interchange of visits with each other, their male relations deigning to appear when affairs permitted. 'The first 6 weeks of Mary Holland's visit', wrote Mrs Whittaker to her son in 1820,

> I was very dull & Stupid in my nervous quiescent State, & just began to revive before she left us – & by the time she had paid her visit to Aunt Sam [Holland], was so anxious to have her back again that I woud take no denial, & bro't her here almost nolens volens. If you *knew* our Mary, you coud not help being charmd with her – she is in ev'ry point so truly excellent, with so much sincerity temper, wit & information as to be almost unique, but few know how to appreciate her character – for it can only be known to those who are most intimate with her, & she does not like what is calld visiting –

She & Sarah made me almost a mad cap with their sportive vagaries – Mary was desirous Sarah shoud return with her to Knutsford, where I know the Christmas will be passd so cheerfully that I promoted the plan with all my might & having at length persuaded your Sister that I can do extremely well without her – she will go next week for 3 weeks or a month.

Clerical families were perhaps not as patriarchal:

Henry Turner & his Wife are also expected at Mr Hollands part of the time – Lucy & Bessy both at Home – besides the 2 Bartons & the Sharpites & Mr Holland, between whom & Sarah there is always an amusing war of quizzing & teasing, so I shall quite enjoy her being there, & perhaps fetch her home, if I can screw up my courage (for a winter Journey) to the sticking place.[21]

Henry Turner was yet another relation, son of William Turner of Newcastle, grandson of William Turner of Wakefield and 'the young and pure-souled minister' of the High Pavement chapel in Nottingham. He was first educated by the Reverend Edward Moises in Newcastle Grammar School, went to the University of Glasgow for a year at age sixteen but soon transferred to Manchester College York. In 1817 he accepted the important Nottingham post and in June 1819 married Catharine, the only child of John Cole Rankin and his wife Catharine (née Holland), who belonged to the Hanover Square congregation; she was also the only descendant of her grandfather, the Reverend Philip Holland of Bolton. Henry died soon after, in 1822, and his widow then opened an excellent school, which offered girls an education to match that provided for boys. It was in their house that James Martineau, who was to lead nineteenth-century Unitarians in their quest for a more mystical, intuitive and emotional religion than could be found in the rationalist Priestley tradition, had been inspired to turn away from engineering to the ministry – to the dismay of his parents, though they finally accepted his decision.[22]

Sarah Whittaker duly met the Henry Turners at Knutsford in early 1821 whilst she was staying with the Sharpes:

I drank tea yesterday at Mr Hollands to have some chat with our old friend Henry Turner – he and his wife are spending a week here. She is a pleasing nice-looking woman, and appears a very suitable spokeswoman for her husband who is not more talkative than formerly; he appears to me not at all altered since he left Bradford; we are going to meet them this evening at Mrs Lumb's ...

On this occasion Elizabeth Stevenson would have met an accomplished young woman who could take the lead in conversation. Her Holland cousins of the same generation seem to have been more complicated beings. Sarah's clear, trenchantly expressed opinions about the daughters of Peter Holland's first marriage, Mary, Elizabeth and Lucy, carry conviction. She wrote that it was three years since she had seen Bessy Holland. 'She is a very amiable, pleasing girl, much less clever than Mary, but more calculated to be generally pleasing, from having tried more to be so, but I do not relinquish my former favourite.' Their sister Lucy seemed to her 'rather a curiosity; a jumble of untrained ideas, of cleverness in some things, & stupidity in others'. Lucy was quite tactless, blurting out whatever came into her mind, though fortunately 'her perfect good temper makes her take well the laughter which it is impossible to restrain at her odd speeches without wishing to make her ridiculous.' 'Miss Mary Holland gains very much upon acquaintance. Lucy is a good-natured goose': Maria Edgeworth's decisive judgment whilst on a visit in the following May smartly endorses the characterisation of these cousins of Elizabeth Stevenson, who was then ten years of age. Lucy, the youngest of the trio, was double that.[23]

However, women of the Holland family do not appear to have been repressed by their menfolk. In 1821, on one of Henry Holland's dashing annual journeys, he swept his sister Mary off to the Lakes, where he introduced her to Wordsworth, dragged 'from his poetical den' for her benefit. To amuse Mary, moreover', Henry wrote, 'I got him into a discussion on the elementary principles of Poetry, when he threw himself out upon his peculiar doctrines, with much emphasis, & a good deal of eloquence.' (There is a bare reference to this visit in the Wordsworths' correspondence. Mary is not mentioned at all, and Henry is described as 'the Albanian Traveller, and otherwise less agreeably distinguished' – a reference to his part in the trial of Queen Caroline.) After a visit to Southey, they travelled over the moors to Newcastle, where Henry left his sister as he went north to see the third of his Tory poets, his favourite Sir Walter Scott at Abbotsford.[24]

In the following year, scarlet fever ran through the Sharpes's house at Heathside, 'after poor little Fanny took it – but we are all now quite well,' Mrs Sharpe wrote, '& the House has been so Smok'd, and *coal'd*, & *heat'd*, that I hope we may receive our Bath friends in safety ...' In July we learn from Henry Holland that because of a 'feverish attack' Bessy had gone to uncle Swinton's 'country house at Roehampton' to recover. She had been overfatigued by an expedition 'under [James] Mackintosh's protection, to the Ventilator of the H of Commons', the special gallery where ladies could hear debates. In late 1823, Mary was in London at her brother's house for the season, reading Latin, Greek and German with Henry and deep in a French history of Venice with his wife, whilst Bessy was with the Caldwells at Linley Wood. Mary's health might have been delicate for a time in the mid-1820s, for Henry once wrote that he had news from Knutsford of his poor sister, 'who is too much of a permanent invalid'.[25]

Mary, Bessy and Lucy went together to the Lakes about this time, taking their cousin Anne Holland of Liverpool.[26] One of the journals that the sisters jointly kept on this occasion proves that they were confident enough to establish their own personalities and strike sparks off each other. (What else could provincial young women do, if they did not possess the strong intelligence and individuality of a Mrs Somerville?) Harriet Martineau described, in a chapter of *How to Observe*, only too appropriately entitled 'mechanical methods', the way one should keep a journal, beginning with the preparation of 'a set of queries, so prepared as to include every great class of facts connected with the condition of a people, and so divided and arranged as that he can turn to the right set at the fitting moment.' But the sisters were not impelled to join such a male and Benthamite tradition. Their journal is swift, allusive and informal, distinctly literary in nature. The earliest booklet is missing, so the main text begins abruptly, after a leaf bearing pencilled drafts of verses about one of Elizabeth Gaskell's favourites, 'sainted' George Herbert, and, on the verso, a pencil sketch of their landlady at Grange.[27]

There is a good deal of description of country, weather, distances and terrain – fairly conventional but lit with quotations from minor poets. We first meet Bessy 'in the rockiest part of Borrowdale', sketching Grange and its beauties and pitying her sisters, who had stuck to the dull road whilst she was 'in the midst of Nature's wildest works, in the heart of her untrained woods, & her careless handiwork of rocky beds'. Prompted perhaps by Wordsworth's lyrical ballads, she wrote sympathetically of a poor girl who opened the gate for travellers; born with only one hand, she demonstrated how she could still knit stockings. On an expedition to Wast Water all three sisters were struck by the affecting tale of a near-illiterate inhabitant called Winifred Strickland, who lived at Wasdale Head and had never been over the hill to Rosthwaite. She had brought up her motherless niece, but lost her when she went to live in Wales with her father, called Casson, a prosperous slate proprietor. He must have been either William or Thomas Casson, two brothers from Seathwaite who took control of Diffwys, the mother quarry of Ffestiniog, in 1800 and made profits large enough to achieve the status of gentry. They thought Anne Holland's father Samuel would be able to help the desolate Winifred keep in touch with her relations in future.

On leaving Winifred's clean and decent house, Lucy took a different way back. Her impetuous bounds inspired Bessy to pen a comic fantasy, seeing Lucy as a mountain goat:

> She stands on the edge of a steep precipice, then darts down the wildest part, and before you can distinguish her, bounds up a mountain on the other side – leaps a brook, and is suddenly on another crag – I don't know whether she browzes yet, but if she does, the wild fern does not suffice, as she continues to browze on our eggs & bacon and bread & butter with a tolerable twist.

A little later, Mary took over the writing (and characterisation): 'Then we turned our eyes downwards & saw Lucy below, crawling like a great black spider among the rocks. However the spider proved a 'Lucy-long-legs' and got to the top as soon as we did.'[28]

By the black lead mine of a Mr Bank's they saw 'fine old yew trees' mentioned to them by the Wordsworths, but Mary did not so much admire them as wonder if their landlady, Sally Yewdale, had not been cradled in one of them. Her dirty and untidy ways were unpleasant, but the sharp-tongued Mary managed to keep her temper by writing sarcastic remarks and an uncomplimentary 'Song – written at Rosthwaite', six 10 line stanzas in which she pretended Sally was really a witch:

> They heard her go muttering down the dark stairs,
> And supposed she was backwards repeating her prayers:
> A strange looking fish was hung up on the hall,
> Which they never went near, lest it on them should fall,
>   For they thought 'twas a spell
>   As they could not well tell,
> For what other use she could keep it so long ...

A good 'country pudding' improved the atmosphere a little, but gave rise to a parody of her dialect: 'Well, I'se sure I'se sae glad you like the pudding – I did na knaw whether ye'd like it or na; or I could hae made mair o' it; but I thought, what, its nae matter o' making mair nor they'll eat.' However, Winifred Strickland's husband Miles appeared unexpectedly, and cheered them up with his stories of ladies who had needed his help and two young men on Scawfell, one completely 'crag-fast'. He said he had a feeble-minded lodger from London between sixty and seventy, called Gaskell, whose rich brothers had boarded him at Wast Head – a hard drinker if he could get it, only just manageable sometimes. His own cousins in Wales, the Cassons, were 'terrible rich', he said.

Eventually, the sisters made their departure in a jolting cart, after what was called a 'witch-like squeeze from the hand of our elegant Hostess, & something which we hoped was a *blessing*'. They passed the time with bad puns and badinage, Lucy becoming unnecessarily serious about the subject of growing older – 'as usual', wrote Bessy, for they were sensitive about their age and, no doubt, unmarried state. They reached Buttermere Inn, from which the landlady's husband took them on an expedition to see Scale Force, which, Bessy exulted, 'dashed in one single foaming stream 156 feet! when it rests awhile among the rocks, & again foams forward in a much broader stream, but not so very high'. She viewed the scene with an artist's eye: 'a tree blown from the rocks lies prostrated near the bottom of the first high fall, and covered with moss, forms a good foreground.'

The sisters were keeping much more than what Dorothy Wordsworth once modestly called 'a neatly penned Memorial' of a few interesting months for her niece. They set themselves to write entertainingly, almost certainly for the family audience at Knutsford in the first place. Lucy in particular was portrayed as young, gauche and precipitate. The older two seem to have more control over their own personas – Bessy appearing sensitive and artistic, Mary self-confident, critical, direct. Because Samuel Holland's daughter Anne evidently thought it her family duty 'to poke' about slate quarries and enquire about quality, quantity and price, Mary was derisive: 'On the same principle *we* ought to go into all the apothecaries shops we meet with & ask the price of magnesia, rhubarb, &c how much they give for a dose, & at what price per ounce they sell it.' She also maintained that Bessy's picture of Sally Yewdale showed her looking too clean and tidy; it needed to be '*grimed*'. These were Elizabeth Stevenson's older Knutsford cousins – well-educated, hardworking, artistic and lively at best, forceful and sarcastic at worst.[29]

Louise Swanton Belloc's 'Elisabeth Gaskell et ses ouvrages', published as early as 1867, has been largely overlooked. Ward quoted several passages from it in his notebook and yet, at the end of his *DNB* article, dismissed it, biographically speaking, as a 'slight notice ... partly founded' on the obituary in the *Unitarian Herald* for 17 November 1865.[30] This is somewhat misleading. For one statement in particular Louise Belloc had evidence that was definitely not taken from the obituary. Elizabeth, she wrote, was affectionately cared for by 'une femme distinguée' (Mrs Lumb), 'dont la tendresse lui inspirait une reconnaissance passionnée, mais lui attirait en même temps la jalousie de ses cousines. Leurs railleries, en comprimant l'essor de ses épanchements, la forcèrent à se replier sur elle-même.' Lucy was something of a special case, but that the sisters might once have been so jealous of Elizabeth and her unique relationship with aunt Lumb as to inhibit the natural effusiveness for which she was so well known in later life, and, indeed, cause her to turn in upon herself, is thought-provoking to say the least.

Louise Belloc, a very experienced author who used to spend three hours every day except Sunday writing herself, considered this an advantage for a future author:

> Elle y gagna; ses facultés se développèrent par l'étude; le blâme la mit en garde contre les illusions de la vanité, et s'il lui en resta une défiance d'elle-même qui a pu quelquefois la faire souffrir, son tact en devint plus sûr et plus délicat. A cette époque, elle observait beaucoup et ne dissipait pas: elle amassait pour l'avenir.

The comment is sensitive, anticipating Henry James's 'young lady upon whom nothing is lost', but what biographical authority did Louise Belloc possess?

In the 'Notice' we find her quoting from a letter that her 'digne et vénérable amie', Maria Edgeworth, had written to her on 2 February 1849, to accompany a copy of *Mary Barton*, 'l'œuvre d'une très-respectable dame, animée, j'en suis sûre, des meilleures intentions.' This sounds rather distant, and from what Edgeworth wrote to both Mary Holland and Honora Beaufort it appears that she did not really know the author of *Mary Barton* – 'It is written by Mrs. Gaskell a friend & I believe a relation of the Hollands'. A far more personal connection is represented by a copy of Louise Belloc's *Pierre et Pierrette* (Paris, 4th edition, 1849, published in a series for the young, for whom she had written and translated a good deal) in Manchester Central Library. Perhaps intended for Florence and Julia, born in 1842 and 1846 respectively, it is inscribed 'humble hommage à Madame Gaskell, ou plutôt à ses enfants. Louise Sw. Belloc'.[31]

In addition, the Library contains an unsigned copy of her 1856 translation of *Cranford*, which Louise Belloc's old friend Mary Clarke Mohl is thought to have arranged. Mrs Gaskell was herself staying in Paris with Madame Mohl in February and March 1855, meeting innumerable people, including Louis Hachette, who published this translation in his 'Bibliothèque des chemins de fer' series. No less than six of her seven novels were published by Hachette, in translations generally superior to the 'nombre prodigieux de romans anglais' that appeared in France during the middle of the century.[32] If Louise Belloc, Irish by birth, had not actually met Elizabeth Gaskell on this occasion, as did her young German translators, Ida and Anna Mohl, there were many other visits to France. In any case, the outspoken Madame Mohl, always ready to fight for her friends and not given to understatement, might well have told Louise Belloc how Elizabeth had been repressed by her older cousins. There is yet another possibility. In 1867 the son of Louise and her husband, the academic painter Hilaire Belloc, wooed and married in England a friend of Mrs Gaskell's, Bessie Rayner Parkes. Bessie is said by Robert Speaight to have accompanied Mrs Gaskell to Yorkshire when the *Life of Charlotte Brontë* was being prepared, and in Manchester Central Library there is a copy of her *Ballads and Songs*, London, 1863, inscribed to 'Mrs. Gaskell with the writer's affectionate respects, May 18th 1863'.[33]

But how true is the story itself? When a young friend of Elizabeth in Manchester, Edward Herford, heard that William Gaskell was going with her to Knutsford as an acknowledged fiancé in March 1832, he supposed that they would have to call on the Miss Hollands. 'Oh! I should not much like to be they', he wrote in his diary. 'If I were one of them I would tell the Miss H's that they only plagued me because they were envious, tho' I dare say they would not care for that; perhaps they are *above* such things: they are certainly *beyond* them – dear old maids'. Not too much reliance can be placed upon the flippancy of a youth of seventeen, who might not have known the older Holland sisters at all well. Mrs Gaskell's second daughter Meta Gaskell, who obtained a copy of Madame Belloc's memoir for an unknown correspondent in 1881, was dismissive, though she thought it 'quite authentic' on the whole: 'The *jealousy* of the cousins was a mistake. They were rather older than my Mother, and dictatorial as elder girls sometimes are to younger ones.' More than mere seniority is at issue, however. The three cousins had learning, spirit and energy, and more significantly still, literary knowledge and ability. Did they have aspirations that went beyond the family circle?[34]

When he later came to write a preface to *Cranford* for the Knutsford Edition, Ward took some pains to establish 'Mrs Gaskell's strong affection for those high-minded and benevolent ladies', Mary and Lucy Holland, always thought to be the models for Miss Deborah and Miss Matty. (By this time Bessy had married the Reverend Franklin Howorth and moved away from Knutsford.) He quotes from some brilliantly written letters by Mary Sibylla Holland describing life in Church House when they were very old: 'Aunt Lucy said to me this morning, "Don't take ginger wine to-night, Sybil love, there's not much left, and Mary will not like another bottle opened, as there is no company but you".' She also reported, 'The old ladies, though dissenters, and even on bad terms with the parson, keep a rigid hold on the house-pew ... It was re-lined with baize in 1801. Date in brass nails on the door. The corners are wide and the hassocks large, and I am ashamed to confess that the seclusion was not uncomfortable.' Like Henry Green, Mary Sibylla Holland seems to have succumbed to the comfortable pleasure of creating 'characters' out of individuals who were undoubtedly somewhat eccentric and memorable in real life, especially in their old age.

Ward takes advantage of this amiable eccentricity to soften any harsh impressions readers might receive from *Cranford*, wisely suggesting too that Mrs Gaskell had written 'with a freedom of treatment not out of harmony with affectionate personal attachment'. This could well be valid. All relationships have their ups and downs. Perhaps more to the point, disturbed children invite, receive and resent teasing. Stir in with this the envy of others that even successful authors cherish. It produces a volatile mixture – especially in happy families that do not always tell their wrath.[35]

NOTES

1 Irvine, p. 80; Hidy, *House of Baring*, pp. 38-9, 78 (cp. p. 43: Swinton was in Malta until 1810 and died in 1827); Ziegler, *Barings*, pp. 93-6. Sir Thomas Lawrence's fine portrait of the partners in 1806 is repro. in *London – World City*, ed. Fox, opp. p. 278.

2 DCLH: HH to PH, 3[?] Lisle Street, L. Square, 29 January [1812]; JS&PH, LUBL: SCH, 'Diary of a Voyage', etc., unpaged, 26 July 1818 ; PRO: PROB 11/1736/6485, SCH's will, dated 17 November 1827, proved London, 28 February 1828; RTD: *The Holy Bible*, Clarendon Press, 1823, inscribed 'Mrs Gaskell's Bible bequeathed to her by her aunt Mrs Abigail Holland'.

3 Chapple, 'Five early letters', p. 5; CRO: MF 1/4. 190, ODC burial register, as daughter of the late Swinton Holland. The index entry for Caroline Holland in *Letters* (pp. 200, 386) is wrong; this Caroline was Henry Holland's daughter.

4 KUL: Wedgwood 29-21680, copy settlement, 11 September 1819; Lysons, *Environs of London*, I, p. 317; NPG: Dighton portfolio 1810-20; R. Ackerman, *Repository of Arts*, etc., no. 50, 1 February 1827; DCLH: HH to ME, London, 22 March 1821. HH had just read and admired J. C. F. Schiller's history of the Thirty Years' War.

5 LA to E. Aikin, Adelphi, 1 May 1819, in *Memoirs of Lucy Aikin*, ed. Le Breton, pp. 117-19; Greg Myers, 'Science for women and children: the dialogue of popular science in the nineteenth century', in *Nature Transfigured: Science and Literature, 1700-1900*, ed. John Christie and Sally Shuttleworth, Manchester and New York, 1989, pp. 172-3, 199.

6 LCC, *Survey of London*, ed. F. H. W. Sheppard, XL (The Grosvenor Estate in Mayfair, part 2), London, 1980, pp. 15, 264-5; DCLH: HH to ME, Mount Street, London, 15 October [1821].

7 Irvine, p. 80-1; J. A. V. Chapple, 'An author's life: Elizabeth Gaskell and the Wedgwood family', *BST*, XVII, 1979, p. 288. FW thought Henry Allen Wedgwood was meant, but if Elizabeth was twelve, he was at Cambridge rather earlier, 1817-21.

8 Ward Notebook, f. 8; KUL: Wedgwood 57-31900, SCH to JW, London, 20 March 1819. Mrs Anne Swinton, a widow since December 1827, seems to have been living in the Park-Lane area. See KUL: Wedgwood, A. Holland to Mr Howarth, 32 Norfolk Street, 5 July [1829], and Chapple, 'Five early letters', pp. 3, 5 ('3 L', in crossed writing, should read '32').

9 JS&PH, LUBL: Annotated *Particulars 1822*, Worcester; A. E. Housman, 'Bredon Hill'. See also J. C. L. Ellis-Mitchell, *Lands called Dumbleton*, n. d.; Susan Oldacre, *The Blackmith's Daughter: The Strange Story of Ann Staight*, Gloucester, 1895. I am grateful for help given by HWRO staff.

10 KUL: Wedgwood 29-21670, JW (copy) to SCH, Etruria, 5 December 1811, and 29-21686, SCH to JW, London, 12 December 1822; DCLH: H. Holland, MS Journals I, and HH to ME, L Brook St, 28 January [1828]; Ziegler, *Barings*, pp. 93-4. In September 1875 Dumbleton was sold for £180,000, with just over £8,000 for the timber (Day & Yewdall, Coverdale & Son, Leeds, 20 August 1979, reciting part of Conveyance).

11 Joseph Stratford, *Gloucestershire Biographical Notes*, Gloucester, 1887, p. 337; Colvin, *Dictionary of English Architects*, pp. 678-9; Chapple, 'Five early letters', p. 19; JS&PH, LUBL: contract and photograph album; *Darwin Correspondence*, I, pp. 270, 275. The Hall was enlarged in 1879 and now belongs to the Post Office Fellowship.

12 Roger Sayce, *The History of the Royal Agricultural College at Cirencester*, Stroud, 1992, pp. 8, 13, 34-9, 63. After his death a gold medal was struck in his honour and is awarded annually to the best student for the diploma in estate management.

13 Venn, *Alumni Cantabrigienses; Darwin Correspondence*, I, pp. 17-18, 76, 118, 270, 357, 365; *Darwin, Huxley: Autobiographies*, ed. de Beer, pp. 30, 38.

14 *Darwin Correspondence*, I, p. 269; KUL: Wedgwood 57-31775, HH to HW, Knutsford, 1 September [1832]. See also p. 425 below. I am grateful to Ian H. C. Fraser for valuable assistance.

15 H. A. Ormerod, 'Extracts from the private ledger of Athur Heywood of Liverpool Merchant and Banker', *THSLC*, CIII, 1952, pp. 105-7; KUL: PH to JW, Bolton, 11 August 1776 (W/M 7); Philip Holland jr to [JW], Bolton, 24 September 1780 (29-21655); Robert E. Schofield, *The Lunar Society of Birmingham: A Social History of Provincial Science and Industry in Eighteenth-Century England*, Oxford, 1963, pp. 42-5. The Wedgwood Accumulation contains many letters between JW and the Hollands about money, e.g. 29-21661 (wet-press copy – a James Watt patent), JW to PH, 25 July 1811: £1700 in estate of 'late aunt Willet'.

16 See appendix B for Willets; also Robin Reilly, *Wedgwood: A New Illustrated Dictionary*, Woodbridge, 1995, and the biographical register in *Darwin Correspondence*; Barbara and Hensleigh Wedgwood, *The Wedgwood Circle: 1730-1897 Four Generations of a Family and Their Friends*, London, 1980, pp. 11, 61-75, 89, 106-8, 132, 136, 219; Schofield, *Lunar Society*, pp. 131-2.

17 Chadwick, 1910, pp. 23, 71; KUL: Wedgwood 21-3711-3718: eight letters of 1802 from SH to JW. See esp. SH to JW, Sandle Bridge, 22 November 1802, and Newcastle [-under-Lyme], 18 December 1802.

18 Wedgwood, *The Wedgwood Circle*, p. 175; *Darwin Correspondence*, II, pp. xix-xx; *Darwin, Huxley: Autobiographies*, ed. de Beer, pp. 30, 38, 56; Thomas Love Peacock, *Nightmare Abbey*, London, 1818, chs 5-6. Flosky is based on Coleridge.

19 Schofield, *Lunar Society*, pp. 45-8; Inkster, *Science and Technology in History*, pp. 35, 77; Butler, *Edgeworth*, pp. 33-4; Bonwick, *English Radicals and the American Revolution*, p. 29.

20 ME to Sophy Ruxton, 8 December 1830. See *Edgeworth Letters*, pp. xviii, 321, 382, 443 (qu. ME to Sophy Ruxton, Welbeck Street, 8 December 1830), 471; J. A. V. Chapple, *Science and Literature in the Nineteenth Century*, London, 1986, pp. 5-7, 22-6.

21 SW to JWW, [Toxteth] Park, 10 December 1820 (WAL: EHC 207/107; Hall, p. 107).

22 Laws, *Scola Novocastrensis*, II, p. 131; Wardle, *Education in Nottingham*, p. 162; Hunter, I, pp. 176-7; Short, 'Presbyterians under a new name', in Bolam *et al.*, *English Presbyterians*, pp. 256-7; Carpenter, *Martineau*, p. 24; *Martineau*, ed. Drummond and Upton, I, p. 24; William Turner to Jane Turner, Manchester, 6 July 1822 (NLPS: Moor Collection 50); HM to JM, 15 July 1822 (MCO: MS Martineau 2, shorthand abstracts transcr. W. S. Coe). There is a valuable High Pavement collection in Nottingham University library.

23 SW junior to JWW, Heathside, 14 January 1821 (WAL: EHC 204/24; Hall, pp. 108-9); *Edgeworth Letters*, p. 212.

24 DCLH: HH to LA, Mount Street, 5 October [1821]; HH to ME, Mount Street, 15 October, [1821]; *Wordsworth Letters*, 2nd edn, III, Part 1, p. 83. Dorothy Wordsworth 'spoke highly of Mary Holland', J. G. Robberds wrote to his wife from Keswick, 15 September 1830 (MCO).

25 MS to JWW, Heathside, 22 June 1822 (Hall, p. 141); DCLH: L Brook Street, 24 July 1822, London, 6 November 1823, and L Brook Street, 25 June [1825].

26 DCLH: 'Lakes 2' [?1824]; wmk dated 1821. The same wmk occurs in one journal of their Welsh tour (see p. 467 below). A new chapel was opened at Seathwaite when they were there (p. 27).

27 Harriet Martineau, *How to Observe. Morals and Manners*, London, 1838, p. 232. Another, more finished pencil sketch of Sarah Yewdale by Bessy is glued to the back cover of the journal. Herbert at Bemerton and Nicholas Farrar seem to be the subject of the poetic drafts.

28 Lakes journal, pp. 2, 9-14. See *The Memories of Sir Llewelyn Turner*, ed. J. E. Vincent, London, 1903, p. 17; Lewis and Williams, *Pioneers of Ffestiniog Slate*, pp. 10-11.

29 *Wordsworth Letters*, 2nd edn, III, Part 1, p. 271. Quotations from Lakes journal, pp. 14-19, 23-4, 30-6, 40-8; 25, 29.

30 E.- D. Forgues, tr. *Cousine Phillis [etc.]* ... *Nouvelles Précédés d'une Notice sur Mrs Gaskell, par Mme Louise Sw. Belloc*, Paris, 1867, repr. 1869. See Ward Notebook, ff. 1 recto, 5, 16, 19, 26, 32 (all verso), 33. Ward used the sixth impression, 1879, of the reprint (*Cat. Bibliothèque Nationale, Auteurs*), but the 1st edn text quoted above is identical. I am grateful to Christine Lingard of MCL, Caroline Arnaud and Frances Twinn for help in my research.

31 A. N. Wilson, *Hilaire Belloc*, London, 1984, p. 21; Forgues, *Cousine Phillis*, pp. 2-3, 9 (see also pp. 27-9: Marianne Gaskell to Mme Mohl qu.); Waller, p. 11; ME copy extract, courtesy of J. L. Bolton (cf. Butler, *Maria Edgeworth*, p. 455n.); *CH Gaskell*, pp. 88-91; M. Prévost and R. D'Amat, *Dictionnaire de Biographie Française*, V, Paris, 1951. *Pierre and Pierrette* is not in the Plymouth Grove sale catalogue (see p. 156, n. 14 above).

32 M. C. M. Simpson, *Letters and Recollections of Julius and Mary Mohl*, London, 1887, pp. 17-19, 61, 149, 165, 217, 126; Margaret Lesser, *Clarkey: A Portrait in Letters of Mary Clarke Mohl (1793-1883)*, Oxford, 1984, pp. 25-7; *Letters*, pp. 326, 333, 925 (amend index); A. B. Hopkins, 'Mrs Gaskell in France 1849-1890', *PMLA*, LIII, 1938, pp. 545-66.

33 *Portrait*, p. 99; *Letters*, pp. 902; Marion Elmina Smith, *Une Anglaise Intellectuelle en France sous la Restauration: Miss Mary Clarke*, Paris, 1927, p. 127; Uglow, p. 311-12; Robert Speaight, *The Life of Hilaire Belloc*, London, 1957, pp. 2-7. Only three ECG letters, nos 229, 230 (incomplete) and 231, have survived from the 1855 Paris visit, but see E. G. Franz, 'Heidelberg und Heppenheim in Erzählungen und Briefen der englishen Schriftstellerin Elizabeth Gaskell', *Archiv für hessische Geschichte und Altertumskunde*, n. s. 32, Darmstadt, 1974, p. 495.

34 MCL: Herford, MS diary, I, p. 45 (see p. 398 below); MEG to 'Sir' [J. W. Cross?], Plymouth Grove, n. d., associated with a letter dated 24 November 1881 (PUL: AM 18163). See in particular the Holland sisters' Barmouth notebooks, ch. 16 below.

35 Knutsford Edn, II, pp. xix-xxii; Ward Notebook, f. 38, citing the ref. to Mme Belloc in Simpson, *Julius and Mary Mohl*, p. 126; Blake, 'A Poison Tree'.

11

Et in Arcadia ego

IN THE SECOND and third decades of the century the four cousins who were about the same age as Elizabeth and living at Heathside, near neighbours of Mrs Lumb, naturally received a good training in music. Edmund Sharpe had to learn pretty little pieces of poetry by heart and sing songs to his father at the pianoforte; he had a good ear and at age four could bear his part in duets and trios. His music-making was never abandoned, even when he became a successful architect and author. As a child he used to say two little hymns by Dr Watt (the 'busy bee' and 'let dogs delight') along with his sister Marianne. Isaac Watt's *Divine and Moral Songs for the Use of Children* (1715) are regarded as 'the beginning of a new more positive vision of childhood', their exceptional popularity confirmed by literally hundreds of editions. Marianne Gaskell was taught the 'busy bee' when she was about three, 'but I do not know if she attaches much meaning to the words', wrote her mother realistically.[1]

It was not long before Edmund's education was given the priority usually afforded to boys. He was sent first to the Knutsford grammar school under the Reverend Peter Vannet. Vannet had about fifty pupils, most of them boarders, and charged thirty-five guineas a year for all except six foundation scholars. When Nicholas Carlisle published *A Concise Description of the Endowed Grammar Schools* in 1818, he recorded that 'the Eton Grammars' were used and 'the system of Education' was like that of Eton. (The inscription on the tombstone of Vannet's wife is in Latin and quotes a Greek text.) However, Edmund soon went on to another school at Runcorn and then to Dr Charles Parr Burney's school in Greenwich, where by a curious chance Thomas Day's Sabrina, rejected by him as a wife but helped by his friends after his death, had become the respected and popular housekeeper.[2] Edmund finished his education at St John's College, Cambridge and took orders. Very likely he was the composer of some pretty 'manuscript duett quadrilles' that Elizabeth Stevenson later secretly copied for a friend. 'They are written by a half-cousin of mine,' she wrote slyly, 'a young Cantab, whose *sole* talent lies in music.' His sisters were left to study at home, reading Thomson's *Seasons* and continuing with their singing lessons, not to mention going to the dentist in Manchester and, in 1823, riding upon the pony they had been given by John William Whittaker.[3]

By the time Marianne Sharpe was eleven, she could read Scott's *Guy Mannering* to herself and an English history to her mother, who had promised to read some of Shakespeare's historical plays with her 'as a great Treat'. The next sister, Emily, was reading *Pilgrim's Progress* and, according to her mother, 'enters into it very fully'. The following year the two girls were to read Spenser's *Faerie Queene*. Unless aunt Lumb was extremely possessive, Elizabeth Stevenson might well have shared at least some of these lessons in her early years and would have been at least as advanced in her reading.[4] There is no firm evidence, however. Her mind was later full of classic fairy tales by Charles Perrault and others, as her story 'Curious if True', which appeared in the *Cornhill Magazine* for 1860, cleverly demonstrates, but it is not at all certain just when she might have first encountered the children's works pouring from the presses since the 1780s, especially Mrs Anna Letitia Barbauld's *Lessons for Children from Two to Three Years Old* (1780) and the constantly reprinted *Fabulous Histories* (1786) by Mrs Sarah Trimmer, later entitled *The History of the Robins*. She could have revived them for her own children, or read them then for the first time. She later asked a friend if her baby's trotting about did not remind her of a hymn by Mrs Barbauld, 'If you fall, little lamb, you will not be hurt. God has spread under you a carpet of soft grass', continuing, 'Perhaps these Prose hymns are rather a *dissenting* book, and may never have fallen in your way; and I don't like all of them, but my eldest girl used to quote that hymn to her second sister when she could just walk, so I think the pleasant remembrance of those days has fixed it in my mind.'[5]

Other, less famous works were almost certainly read when she was young. Mrs Lumb's friend and cousin, the Reverend John Holland, who had written a sympathetic review of Mary Wollstonecraft's *Vindication of the Rights of Woman* in 1792, was 'devotedly attached' to teaching the young of both sexes. He produced for them a number of books on religion, history and geography. 'The labour which he devoted to the preparation of catechisms, series of questions, and lectures, was incredible', wrote a successor. With his school-master brother Thomas he published a 'pretty little volume' entitled *Exercises for the Memory and Understanding, with a Copious Appendix of Questions, Without Answers, on Mrs. Barbauld's Lessons and Hymns, on the Calendar of Nature, and the Evenings at Home* in 1798. 'We are "here today, & gone tomorrow", as the fat scullion maid said in some extract in Holland's Exercise book', remembered Mrs Gaskell in later years.[6]

The brothers had some claim to be the originators of the interrogative system of teaching. In 1812, John Holland published *A Series of Questions on the Holy Scriptures, with References to the Bible for Answers*, which was used at William Turner's church for children of fourteen to seventeen and could be obtained for two shillings in the vestry. Miss Richmal Mangnall, a relation of the Hollands who took over as headmistress of Mrs Sarah Whittaker's old school, Crofton, became a celebrity in 1798 when she published the most famous textbook of this kind, *Historical and Miscellaneous Questions, for the Use of Young People*. Pupils had to learn answers by heart for 'repetitions'. They were 'the pride and terror of several generations of school-girls', including Charlotte Brontë, who came to Cowan Bridge with a personal copy; a work reprinted, revised and adapted throughout the nineteenth century in both England and America. According to Miss Margaret Holland of Mobberley, she also gained more by her school than any female she ever knew.[7] In 1820, however, John Holland suffered some kind of breakdown ('a nervous irritability of a constitutional character'), resigned his post and was unlikely to have been particularly involved with Elizabeth's education after this date. He died in 1826 aged 59. His brother Thomas died three years later.

Given the long-standing Edgeworth connection with the Hollands, and the fact that many of the *Harry and Lucy* series had appeared before 1820, it is not surprising that Maria Edgeworth's books for children were known at Knutsford. Henry Holland wrote that in 1821 Maria Edgeworth had sent his little sister Susan 'delightful books'.[8] Elizabeth Stevenson presumably saw these, and was thoroughly familiar with many standard works of literature. As a girl, she says, she loved one of Dorothy Wordsworth's favourite novels, *The Fool of Quality; or the History of the Earl of Moreland*, written by Henry Brooke and first published in five volumes between 1764 and 1770. Thomas Day claimed that he could find nothing worthwhile written in English for young children, and. little that would appeal to them, except for part of *Robinson Crusoe* and 'a few passages in the first volume' of *The Fool of Quality*. As for Day himself, Elizabeth's brother later mentioned that when she was nine she had read his celebrated Rousseauistic *Sandford and Merton*.[9]

Brooke's novel is not often read today, even by specialists, but this tale of a gay, heroic but not perfect boy, neglected by his family and thought a fool for his virtues, could not fail to appeal. The dozens of interpolated stories and amusing dialogues between the author and his friend, which lay bare the fictiveness of the whole, answer instincts both primitive and sophisticated:

> *Friend.* But how long, I say, do you propose to make your story?
> *Author.* My good friend, the reader may make it as short as he pleases.

Perhaps her 'old uncles & aunts' possessed the authorised two-volume condensation of 1781 by John Wesley, who was more interested in the book's morality than its entertainment value. He deleted a third, suppressed Brooke's name and retitled it *The History of Henry Moreland*. He must have thought that the story with his 'improvements' would inculcate intelligence, sensibility, virtue and happiness – synonyms for educators of that era.[10]

As far as the younger children of Peter Holland – Charles, Susan and Arthur – are concerned, only random, tantalising details of their upbringing can be found. Susan, 'a very fine noble Child though perhaps she will not grow up pretty', and rather comically said to be 'a *beautiful* Child but no *Holland*', was very much Elizabeth Stevenson's age – only a few months younger.[11] When in February 1814 Henry Holland decided to begin his career as a fashionable doctor in London, he was accompanied by his step-mother Mary, who was going to stay in and about the capital for two or three months. Lucy Holland, then thirteen, had been for some months with William Turner in Newcastle and was to continue to live there for the time being, so her older sisters Mary and Bessy on this occasion cared for the three little ones.

Mrs Mary Holland, whose few letters in the Whittaker collection are not very interesting, was often ill during these years – 'she has for some time past been subject to bilious attacks, which are accompanied by a very gouty affection ... they are very painful & often last a long while & leave her very languid & exhausted'. We can assume that the older half-sisters were probably responsible for much of the education of the three young ones. ('What will she blame me for now?' Charles Darwin used to think as he entered a room where his sister Caroline, 'too zealous in trying to improve' him, waited to guide his first steps in learning.) Though details are few, Mrs Sharpe can be relied upon for a brisk summary of the household's tone and nature. She told her nephew in 1821 that Sarah Whittaker on a visit to the Hollands found 'the regular pursuits of the young ones' were 'like her own, *rational*'. She 'drew, & read, & work'd, & walk'd, & play'd jokes on Uncle Peter to admiration', which suggests a distinct lack of stuffiness in Church House.[12]

Nevertheless, there appears from the Whittaker letters to have been a strange bias in the upbringing of Susan Holland. In summer 1820 Mrs Sharpe announced that her daughter Marianne was off 'with her friend Susan to Sandlebridge for a week', taking a packet of new books presented by Marianne's godmother, M. A. Yates, and planning 'many little Schemes of enjoyment'. The farming was now in the hands of a manager, but the old and substantial farmhouse in Little Warford was probably very much what it had been in the grandparents' days, with its comfortable sitting parlour and stone floor (only the half near the 'nice large oldfashioned stone Chimney piece' carpeted), 'a monstrous grate always well heaped up with Coal & a "goody Cupboard", always well stocked with mince pies buns & tarts'. Fires in the bedrooms were kept up night and day during the winter. Its peace and rural seclusion – through Over Knutsford, some miles along the rolling road towards Chelford and then into deeper countryside, with little more than an old smithy, mill and pond nearby – made it a children's paradise.[13]

There is no mention whatsoever of any part Elizabeth Stevenson had in this rural idyll, though she was probably in Knutsford early in the summer. Perhaps Mrs Sharpe had eyes for her own child alone:

> She was much admired, I assure you – not for her beauty, but her *prattle*. C. Heathcote took a wonderful fancy to her, & says she has more *Mind* than any Child of her Age he ever met with – Bessy Holland (who is anxious to have her with Susan as much as possible) says she is a very Sensible engaging little thing.

If maternal affection has not distorted the record, we are again forced to consider the attitude to Elizabeth of her older cousins. Why was Bessy Holland anxious to have Marianne Sharpe with Susan as much as possible, rather than Mrs Lumb's little ward? It is hard to believe that Elizabeth at age ten lacked *mind*: her brother even hoped that she could 'get money enough to buy Hume's History' before he returned from his next voyage. Perhaps she was neither sensible nor engaging at that time – in a difficult phase, common enough in the best regulated families.[14]

When Charles Aikin Holland was nearly twelve, in 1821, he was in hot water at his Manchester school:

> I have a great Idea that Mary & her Brother will prevail upon Mr. Turner to take Charles at Christmas & so he will not return home at all for the Vacation but go from Manchester to Newcastle – & it would on many accounts be best – for I am sorry to find that his Conduct is known here, & Mr. Harris was under the neces-sity of telling the Boys who was the Culprit, so that secresy is out of the question.

Perhaps only someone with the charity of a relation, the Reverend William Turner, could be prevailed upon to take a delinquent boy. He seems to have agreed, for Charles's mother travelled to Manchester in December to see Charles before he went 'to spend his Holidays with Mary at Newcastle'. By the following June Charles and Arthur Holland were back in Knutsford, 'both grown and improved in appearance'. William Turner was educating the two boys as he had once educated their older brother Henry for four years from 1799.[15]

Charles Aikin Holland makes an occasional, favourable appearance in Mrs Gaskell's letters, but Arthur, born in March 1813 and therefore just two or three years younger than Elizabeth, is a bit of a mystery. He is ignored altogether in Gaskell studies. It is recorded in Irvine's *History of the Family of Holland* that he died young and Joseph Hunter, who could even supply the names of three siblings who had died in infancy, does no more than mention him. But Maria Edgeworth, whose own father's four marriages produced twenty-two children (the oldest forty-five when the youngest was one), caught sight of him in October 1830 just before he was due to go to Dublin for some months – to spend them, she thought, with a surgeon called Hutton. He would be able to take over 'a sort of pyramidical tin flower pot' full of dahlias, mignonette and honeysuckle that she had admired at Mrs Holland's; Lucy would arrange to have one specially made for her by a Knutsford specialist.[16] Yet this young man, with whom Elizabeth Stevenson grew up at Knutsford, is not mentioned in her surviving letters, which date from 1831.[17] When families were so large and mobile, perhaps it was not too difficult to mislay one, but he survived until he was twenty, dying on 25 August 1833; he was interred a few days later at the old dissenting chapel in Knutsford, a month and a half before his cousin Caroline Holland.[18]

Elizabeth Stevenson was closely related to the Hollands of Knutsford and remained in constant contact with them for the rest of her life, something that could not be said about the family of her father's second marriage or his brother Robert Stevenson's. It would be particularly useful to have more information about Susan Holland, the cousin closest in age to Elizabeth, who by 1830 had grown from 'the least of things' to 'five feet seven well measured and really a very fine girl', Maria Edgeworth thought. Her friendship in the years after Elizabeth's marriage to William Gaskell seems curiously overwrought. About Christmas 1833 Elizabeth exulted, 'Sue has refused every invitation but to me! there's a compliment – and she has had 5 to my certain knowledge. ... Susan brings her guitar which is very charming the darling [-] how I do love that girl.' But in August 1838 she was mortified: 'After all, and my dear Lizzy I have struggled with my touchy temper about this', Elizabeth wrote to her sister-in-law, '*Susan* & Lucy are going (for 10 days or a fortnight to Scotland), tomorrow – we offered Sue her choice of time or place almost – to go with us!' Lucy, perhaps still able to bound like a giddy goat about the hills, would be able to offer Susan untrammelled freedom, whilst Elizabeth had two little children to entertain. Meta was little past the crawling stage. As for Marianne, 'I try to employ her in making candlelighters, pricking pictures, counting out articles &c, but she is soon tired of any *one* employment', sighed her conscientious mother, who would obviously have welcomed the distraction provided by a cousin with a guitar.[19]

Understandably, if disappointingly, we know much more about the Sharpes and Whittakers, whose letters are so far the best source that has been discovered for the Hollands at Knutsford in the early decades of the nineteenth century. It is easy to assume that all their children were brought up in very similar ways. However, the strong likenesses between these families can prove subtly deceptive, if the tensions that lurk in religious and political differences are ignored, particularly where Unitarians are concerned.[20]

The name of 'Peter Holland of Nether Knutsford, Surgeon' is found in a deed of 1792 as a trustee of the old dissenting chapel and his formal allegiance at least did not lapse. In 1828 he wrote a letter to John Long enclosing the chapel deeds and promising to be accountable for money. Like Hannah Lumb he presented books to the chapel library, which was formally established in 1833 (the date on the bookplates). In the interval, according to an early Unitarian monthly typically 'devoted to religious, moral, and social progress', *The Christian Freeman*, Elizabeth Stevenson was encouraged to teach in the chapel's Sunday school: 'Many a one now grown up to womanhood dates her first religious impressions from her kind, earnest and intelligent instruction'. Peter, his first wife, five of his sisters and two of his daughters were eventually buried in the chapel's little graveyard.[21]

The Sharpes, on the other hand, were faithful members of the Church of England, ever wary of dissent. Rivalry between church and chapel in the Manchester area was increasing rapidly during the early decades of the nineteenth century. When Charles Aikin Holland was born in the house right next to the parish church, Mrs Sharpe rather acidly wrote to her clerical nephew that 'her *very large* fellow has none of the marks *you fear* – in short I suspect that so far from having "a Church on his *Back*" he will have nothing to do with it *in any way* – but this is between ourselves – You are right dear Willy in believing that it will be our wish to inculcate the principles of religion early into our dear little Babe,' – and then follows a more human proviso, 'if he live to lisp his prayers'.[22]

Other people stirred the pot. Mrs Frances Broadhurst proclaimed that Margaret Heathcote, who saw a good deal of Mrs Mary Holland at Swinton's house in Hackney, was 'quite disturbed at her being so *Hollandized*'. A Whittaker aunt remembered Peter 's '*odious sneering* at one who had neither the will nor the power of retort', Catherine Whittaker. 'You probably know he is a Deist,' she went on portentously, '& sorry I was for his children; I had it from his own mouth.' It was an old accusation. In 1819, W. J. Fox in 'The duties of Christians towards Deists' painstakingly reasserted the differences between Deists, who rejected divine revelation, and Unitarians, who accepted the authority of the Bible and the Christian revelation as they understood it. The aunt continued, 'Dr Holland I fancy from what I saw of him has profitted from his pupillage; the only thing I saw to admire in him was his great attention to Mrs Holland – *there* he *shone!*' These religious differences remained unresolved. When she died in 1840 Mrs Mary Holland was not buried in the graveyard of the old dissenting chapel, but in that of the parish church, just across from Church House. The same grave holds her sister Catherine Whittaker and their mother Esther.[23]

Elizabeth Stevenson would have been too young to appreciate Knutsford's celebration of Wellington's victories in September 1812, when church bells were rung and loyal emblems made with white sand on the street. An effigy of Napoleon with chaplain and executioner was followed by a great procession to the prison, and many of the gentry and 'all the respectable male inhabitants of this Loyal little town' held a grand dinner at the Angel Inn in King Street. Some time after seven that evening 'Old Bony' was borne to the racecourse and thrown upon a great bonfire 'amidst universal shouts of approbation & Huzzas'. Was she held up at aunt Lumb's front window to gaze wide-eyed at the flames and tumult across the way?[24]

This effervescent display of national unity soon collapsed. With peace came economic distress and the beginnings of class strife, nationally organised. Led at first by gentlemen like 'Orator' Hunt and Sir Francis Burdett, a radical who represented the city of Westminster and who had been committed to the Tower for breach of parliamentary privilege in 1810, vast meetings called for household and then universal suffrage. Many of the middle-class reformers in Manchester were Unitarians, opposed to the pretensions of Tories and the established church (no longer able to depend upon church-and-king mobs as it had in the 1790s) if out of sympathy with the drilling and marching and huge meetings of popular radicalism. Three of the most famous were members of Cross Street chapel and well known to Elizabeth Gaskell in later years: John Edward Taylor, who became editor of the newly established *Manchester Guardian* in 1821, Richard Potter, known as 'Radical Dick' and later M.P. for Wigan, and John Shuttleworth, a voluble cotton and twist manufacturer.[25]

Revolution was feared. The pressures of economic distress were visible in strikes, marches and assemblies. Six troops of Cheshire yeomanry cavalry had been raised by Sir John Leicester in the summer of 1803, Peter Holland becoming surgeon to the regiment and Francis Sharpe ('gent.') a cornet in the Knutsford troop. In March 1817 five of these Cheshire troops were called out and marched to Manchester. Two troops of Manchester and Salford yeomanry cavalry were specially embodied from merchants, manufacturers, publicans and shopkeepers. Riot acts were read, and magistrates ordered out the cavalry with 'judicious promptitude', to use a phrase in the history of the Cheshire regiment. On 28 June 1819 a great radical meeting at Stockport (about fourteen miles from Knutsford) was addressed by Sir Charles Wolseley. 'I was at Paris during the taking of the Bastile', he declared, 'and I can assure you that I was not idle on that glorious occasion'.[26]

The climax came on 16 August 1819 in Manchester on an area near St Peter's church. Several hundred special constables had been enrolled; the Manchester and Salford yeomanry, regular infantry and cavalry, together with a troop of the Royal Horse artillery, were stationed nearby; the Cheshire yeomanry (some four hundred men under Lieutenant-Colonel Townshend) were waiting in St John's Street. Processions with bands poured into the town. Hunt's carriage was followed by a female committee dressed in white. For the first time, special reporters came from distant towns. The lowest estimate of numbers was fifty thousand, the highest more than three times that. The magistrates sent messengers for the troops, but the Manchester and Salford yeomanry, easily first on the scene, were soon in difficulties. Regular hussars arrived and were ordered into action by a magistrate. The Cheshire yeomanry, which appeared 'in excellent order', and the infantry soldiers in waiting took no part in the dispersal. Sixty-seven soldiers and twenty horses were struck by sticks and stones, but amongst the crowd, altogether eleven people died and about four hundred were injured.[27]

Elizabeth, young as she was, could not have escaped some knowledge of these dire events. A principal witness at Peterloo was the Reverend Edward Stanley of Alderley, who printed a critical account of the dispersal and gave evidence at a subsequent trial. Thomas Belsham was outraged, and always added 'never to be forgotten, and never to be forgiven' whenever he referred to it in later years. Swinton Holland, rich as he was, thought the 'misdeeds' of the magistrates should be punished, but feared association with 'Hunt & his rabble'. In Knutsford, Mrs Whittaker held similar views: she was passionately convinced that Manchester magistrates were 'abettors of the Ferocious Yeomanry in their brutal attack upon a quiet & orderly assembly', but distressed to think that 'Honest rational Whigs' like Lord Fitzwilliam who wished to investigate the affair would become associated with the mob and 'such reformers as Hunt & Sir C. Wolseley.'[28] Wolseley was a man of means who helped provide bail for those arrested after Peterloo and was himself imprisoned for eighteen months for the violent speech he had made at Stockport. Earl Fitzwilliam was in fact dismissed from the Lord-Lieutenancy of the West Riding for attending a meeting at York on 14 October 1819.[29]

There is no doubt that Peter Holland was squarely on the side of the authorities. He sent a letter to Sir John Leicester, then in London, about the end of October 1819, in which (despite his age) he speaks of having ridden more than forty miles, and then scrawls recent 'intelligence' of increases in troop size, change of command and subscriptions of money. By November his son was able to tell Maria Edgeworth that 'a Church & King Club, – 2 companies of foot & two field pieces, & the convenience of daily rumours from Manchester, keep alive the high note of alarm; which as far as I can see, is rapidly dying away in London. Here financial terrors are predominant.' A second letter from Peter to Sir John in December says that travellers at Altrincham, where he had been at headquarters, 'reported that all was quiet & that they saw no appearance of any assemblage of radicals.' Four troops had been deployed, including the *Mere troop* at Bowdon and Dunham and 'the *Knutsford & Tabley*' at Cheadle. He did not expect trouble; as he commented, 'the radicals are too well aware of the amount of military force in the neighbourhood.'[30]

Knutsford families then fell out with each other over another contentious national issue. When George the Prince Regent came to the throne he attempted to prevent his wife Caroline from becoming Queen, and, almost unbelievably, considering his own behaviour, his pliant government agreed to proceed against her in parliament for immoral conduct. Henry Holland had been her doctor for part of the time whilst she was travelling on the Continent – against political advice and with a handsome Italian courier. Henry's father, spending a week in London as Sir John Leicester's guest, 'almost with the freshness & vigour of a boy's enjoyment', was there to see the triumphant return of what he called the 'good Queen', and came back to Knutsford with 'a variety of anecdotes' about the behaviour of the mobs that supported her. Even his son complained that 'the distresses of the country, poor laws, corn laws, bullion laws, & reform in Parliament' were all forgotten in the excitement.[31]

The case was discussed everywhere, for months on end. Everybody had a view. Though he wished to remain silent, Henry eventually gave evidence in the Queen's favour and, after the case against her had been dropped, was a pained witness on the day of the coronation when she was forbidden to enter the Abbey and Westminster Hall. In Knutsford, Mrs Sharpe complained that she and the Hollands had to avoid '*the* Subject, by tacit agreement – for the Doctor's evidence has completely decided their opinion in favour of her Queenship – & they are violent, so to avoid useless Squabbles, nothing is said.' In the following year, professionally, he stood over the death bed of 'the unfortunate Princess'. *The* subject must have come to the ears of a bright girl nearly ten years of age.[32]

Relations were better in April 1821, when Mrs Mary Holland and young Susan visited Mrs Whittaker at Liverpool whilst the boys Charles and Arthur visited with the Samuel Hollands. Their favourites the Bartons were staying nearby with the Heathcotes, who gave an evening party with music and dancing. There was also a ball and supper at Mr Richard Yates' in Duke Street. Mrs Whittaker believed this 'Gay Scene' did her good; it was 'the most stylish thing' she had seen for a long time, and she thought it also pleased Mrs Holland. Peter Holland, however, caused problems. In September Mrs Sharpe felt impelled to write at length on the subject to her nephew, saying that her sister Mary and her daughters had managed to persuade Henry Holland 'to give his Father the advice he often stands in [need] of in matters of *civility* & *temper* &c.' Henry had even come through the rain to see the Sharpes,

> & was so affectionate & kind that there was no refusing his *very* earnest desire that we would go to them *that Eveng* or *the next*. He said Mary was to go with him to Newcastle & *she* too made it her particular request that we would go to see them …
>
> So we went – & they were all most pointedly kind as if to acknowledge that we had done *some violence to our feelings* in going – & when *he* enter'd the drawing room he came up to each separately & altho' with a very confused manner very *kindly* greeted us.

Peter's wife and daughters worked hard to re-establish good relations with Martha Sharpe. They even brought up reinforcements in the shape of Hannah Lumb and the Unitarian minister:

> Mrs Lumb & Mr Ashton were there afterwards – & we had a very pleasant Eveng – Mr H. was pointedly civil – desired Mr S. to go with him to look at a new Horse &c … Bessy yesterday came to borrow some Books for Eveng reading as the Doctor strongly recommends his Father to read to them aloud & to keep up that & other pursuits (in preference to politics &c *as they infer'd*), that might serve to divert the mind from more perplexing matters.[33]

Though Mrs Mary Holland was her sister, Martha Sharpe was growing away from the family. Henry unexpectedly became engaged to Margaret Emma, youngest daughter of James Caldwell, in 1822. The Caldwell family were old friends, and the daughters very attached to Peter Holland, Henry told Maria Edgeworth. On the visit of the bride-to-be, Mrs Sharpe at Heathside was quite overlooked. Her sarcasm was muted: 'I took it all in good part & said very quietly that it was better of the two, to have been quite forgotten than to have been thought unworthy of being consider'd a member of the Family.' We can sense her feelings of affront and exclusion when she calls them 'The Clan Holland' – all gathered together at Linley Wood '& tomorrow the grand Event will take place!' One can read hurt between the lines: 'all hands have been at work to prepare the wedding Garments & poor Lucy has been all fidgets about new Gowns & *mis*fitting black Satn Shoes.' Henry gave a summary of his marriage settlement to Josiah Wedgwood, who was a trustee. Amongst other arrangements, Henry was to be paid £1000 on the day of his marriage, £2000 was to be placed in trust and £5000 was to come to him on the death of James Caldwell. His wife was to receive certain interest on these monies, and any property she inherited was to be settled on her.[34]

The ways began to part after the death of Francis Sharpe in November 1823. 'Knutsford I am persuaded', wrote Mrs Whittaker, 'will never do as a residence for his family, altho' the Hollands have paid every attention, both in the medical & Sisterly way, & Mary & Martha woud I daresay be again the affectionate pair they always were in their youth' – which implies a degree of estrangement. Mrs Martha Sharpe had no desire whatsoever to stay in Knutsford, removing as soon as she could to Lancaster, where Mrs Whittaker had already established herself, and yet another sister, called Esther, had married a successful wine merchant, Benjamin Satterthwaite. The two younger Sharpe girls were placed in an academy there, whilst Marianne was sent to be finished at her aunt Frances Broadhurst's school in Bath. Life in Knutsford, in the three or four decent families that Jane Austen thought sufficient, could be very snug. It wasn't always so. 'Et in Arcadia ego' is an ambiguous phrase.[35]

Many things remained the same. Wills that had been made at the time of Peterloo lay quietly to one side whilst the Cheshire Regiment of Yeomanry Cavalry mustered for a week's exercise in Liverpool or presented a sabre to Lieutenant-Colonel Townshend at a sumptuous dinner in the Angel, Knutsford. Perhaps they were read over again when troops were sent to Manchester during rioting over the introduction of power-looms in 1826. On a domestic level, distance improved relations between Hollands and Whittakers. Mrs Mary Holland wrote to the vicarage at Blackburn in April 1829 to congratulate the J. W. Whittakers on the safe birth of a second son and to give various items of news, such as a forthcoming visit from Henry Holland, '& his nice wife, with their four darling children', and another visit promised by 'the two dear Ems', Emily Sharpe and Emily Broadhurst. Susan will be pleased, she wrote, that Emily Broadhurst would be staying in Knutsford, for she

> is very impatient for this fresh importation from Bath, & dearly loves all her cousins, indeed it would be strange if she did not. I think you would scarcely know my tall girl, she has outgrown all her sisters, but the best of it is, that with her rapid growth she enjoys the most uninterrupted health, & is blest with the happiest temper & flow of spirits I ever saw. Her sisters think there never was so nice a girl, which you see will spare *me* a world of trouble, as *my* account of her might be suspected. I think your good Aunt Sharpe is tolerably happy in her children, & I know you will agree with me in this opinion.

Mrs Holland then goes on to mention the loss of an only son in the Yates family, but has nothing to say about William Stevenson's death in the previous March. Mary Holland, she reported at some length, was taking an interest in a little deaf and dumb girl's candidacy for the special school in Manchester. Charles Aikin Holland had chosen to be a lawyer and was starting modestly in a Liverpool solicitors' office, Lowndes and Robinson. Lucy and Arthur are not mentioned, so perhaps it is not significant that Susan's friend now appears to be Emily Broadhurst.

In October 1829 Mrs Sharpe had very sad news. Henry Holland's wife was mortally ill and they had already lost one small girl of three. Mary and Lucy Holland were helping with her nursing, but back in Knutsford, she had been told by Bessy, Mrs Mary Holland had a growing tumour above the thigh. It was more uncomfortable than painful and might last for many years, she thought. Susan Holland, nice-looking, 'a very sweet girl, most amiable in disposition, & very gentle in temper', was staying in Lancaster, but of course in 'painful suspence' and unable to 'feel in spirits to enter even into a limited party'.[36]

Emma Holland died early in the following year. Peter's wife Mary, and Peter himself, lived on for many years, and there is scattered evidence that a certain amount of connection was maintained. In July 1836 J. G. Robberds met two Miss Sharpes and their mother in Lancaster; they were glad to hear that they would probably see Mrs Lumb & Mr and Mrs Gaskell, together with little Marianne, in a few days' time. In a letter of 1838 Mrs Gaskell briefly mentioned that 'the Sharpes' had been singing duets a year or two before. In 1851 William Whewell told her that her relation Mr B. Satterthwaite had recently died, 'very rich; as was likely to be the case with one who of late appeared to live mainly for that end'. He had been one of Whewell's oldest friends.[37]

The early decades of the nineteenth century saw changes more profound than the merely personal. The old order of rank, wealth and property of the previous century was beginning to mutate and realign itself quite remarkably. In a lengthy will written in her own hand between December 1800 and February 1803 Lady Jane Stanley of Brook House, Knutsford had bequeathed considerable sums of money: £600 each to her two upper female servants and an extra year's wages to every servant that had been with her three years, £500 to the aged and infirm of three parishes, amounts between £50 and £500 to twenty-one ladies (mostly spinsters, but to others 'for her sole and separate use independent of, and free from the debts, power or control of her husband, or future husband, and for her to apply and dispose of as she shall think proper'), £6000 to members of her family, and sums between £500 and £1250 to infirmaries at Liverpool, Manchester, Chester and Bath, lunatic hospitals at Liverpool and Manchester, an asylum for the indigent blind (one was established at Liverpool in 1790), Manchester hospital for the relief and assistance of lying-in women, and the Philanthropic Society of St George for the promotion of industry and reform of the criminal poor.

A powerful campaign against the poor laws reached its zenith in the years after 1815 – 'the most flagrant breach of the principle of dependency on which the old society rested', according to Harold Perkin. In 1817 a select committee of the Lords proclaimed that

> abuses have undoubtedly been introduced into the general administration of the Poor Laws of England; but the Committee are nevertheless decidedly of opinion, that the general system of those laws, interwoven as it is with the habits of the people, ought, in consideration of any measures to be adopted for their melioration and improvement, to be essentially maintained.

This was an attempt to have the best of both worlds, to palliate rather than abolish, in order to maintain a link between past and future, and resist a radical movement of mind that had united Whigs and Tories of all shades, Malthus as well as Coleridge, and persuaded a select committee of the Commons that poor relief 'not infrequently engenders dispositions and habits calculated to separate rather than unite the interests of the higher and lower orders of the community.'[38]

The Knutsford community in Elizabeth Stevenson's youth was so mixed that it was more like shot silk than a tapestry – sometimes dull, sometimes spectacularly black, at other times iridescent with changing colours. What she wrote about her early life is mostly bright, as far as we know. There is little about the poor, nothing about the many servants her family employed. But who can tell what she glimpsed, saw, felt, mulled over, forgot and later recalled, not perhaps as a concrete fact but as a quality or half-recollection? One thing is certain: she and her family were rising in society and always in danger of acquiring the attitudes of the arriviste. The values of their simpler presbyterian inheritance were always being tested, as the young Henry Holland had stressed and a disillusioned Anne Marsh Caldwell was to discover.

Marianne Lumb, we know, used to meet Mrs Edward Stanley, wife of the vicar of Alderley, at Miss Isabella Stanley's. In 1851 Mrs Gaskell encountered her as a widow at Mrs Davenport's of Capesthorne, that splendid house just a few miles from Knutsford, with its private chapel and great conservatory designed by Joseph Paxton, full of camellias and sweet-scented geraniums, where 'clean, wholesome country-looking children' were taught.[39] Elizabeth was friendly with their son, who became a famous establishment figure, Arthur Stanley, Professor of Ecclesiastical History at Oxford and Dean of Westminster, as well as his wife, Lady Augusta Bruce. Sir Henry Holland knew him too. Such connections, and there must have been many more, argue a continuity of knowledge and interest. Elizabeth would have heard tales about the autocratically charitable Lady Stanley of Brook House. She would certainly have read Henry Green's account of her, because she helped him when he was preparing his lectures on Knutsford. He quotes a long letter from the German philologist Jacob Grimm about the place-name Knutsford, which indicates that Mrs Gaskell had previously written on Green's behalf.

But what did she think when she was young of the story that Lady Jane used to walk out 'with a gold-headed cane, or rather staff in her hand; and she was very tenacious of the right which her noble birth gave her of keeping the wall from whomsoever she met', so much so that she once gave a vigorous blow on the shoulder to a surprised countryman who did not give way? Green, a Victorian of 1858, turned this into a complaint about the contemporary decay of good manners towards ladies; he also called Lady Stanley a 'lofty dame' and said that the countryman 'did not know her peculiarity'. This seems close to nonsense. If the story is true, her patrician manner and assumptions were unmistakable.[40]

Precise details may be irretrievable, but the more complex pattern of Elizabeth Stevenson's later responses to aristocracy and the old social order must have begun in her youth. By the time of the little group of early letters written to her friend Harriet Carr, she was ironically aware of ambivalence:

> I have been at so very many races, and reviews in my long life, that I think they have quite lost their charm for me, but I should like to see the King, Queen & all the Royal family, proper and improper. In spite of my 'political principles', I can not help admiring high blood, and aristocracy. And what do you think of Paganini, is he so very wonderful, as people say, and did you go into hysterics with the violence of your emotions, as I have heard of people's doing.

Moral and political principles war against fascination. She had a feeling for the mystique of royalty: she also knew about William IV's belated and childless marriage to the unfortunate Adelaide of Saxe-Meiningen ('doomed, *poor, dear, innocent young* creature to be *my* wife') and his ten illegitimate FitzClarence offspring by the actress Mrs Dorothy Jordan. Nor is the apparent change of subject to Paganini and his violin a diversion from her theme. She recognised the kinship between myths of aristocracy and of virtuoso genius, and was humorously able to resist complete surrender to them.[41]

Elizabeth's letters to Mary Howitt about her childhood, so often used for lack of better evidence, are selective. They transform her early experiences. Shades of 'professional' authorship settle upon her prose. She obviously fell in with the Howitts' perception of the wishes of the literary public, writing, for instance, with determined charm of 'Old Tabley', an ancient house on an island site no more than two miles through the Cheshire countryside from her home at Heathside:

> Here on summer mornings did we often come, a merry young party, on donkey, pony, or even in a cart with sacks swung across – each with our favourite books, some with sketch-books, and one or two baskets filled with eatables. Here we rambled, lounged and meditated: some stretched on the grass in indolent repose, half reading, half musing, with a posy of musk-roses from the old-fashioned trim garden behind the house, lulled by the ripple of the waters against the grassy lawn; some in the old crazy boats, that would do nothing but float on the glassy water, singing, for one or two were of a most musical family and warbled like birds: 'Through the greenwood, through the greenwood,' or 'A boat, a boat unto the ferry,' or some such old catch or glee.[42]

This attractive passage describes more than one arcadian visit in her youth. A similar record can be found in the Hall letters when Mrs Sharpe took her children back to Knutsford in 1828, to help make up a 'family party of fourteen at Mr Holland's dinner Table every day – & those chiefly young ones'. They had gigs and ponies, and there were two joyous sailing parties on Tabley mere, '& all our Old Friends rich & poor welcomed us most heartily and made much of us'. Mrs Sharpe renewed acquaintance with the poor she had once helped, but apart from this daily life seems almost legendary in quality. For many middle-class women and children hard work was optional, true leisure always available. Cushioned by money and servants and friendly owners of great estates, they could afford to indulge in the fashionable cult of informality. 'Men and women began to lounge and recline rather than sit up straight', writes Mark Girouard; 'increasing value was put on the spontaneous expression of emotion, on sensibility rather than sense, on love matches rather than arranged matches, and on life in the country rather than in the town.'[43]

Lower Tabley Old Hall, begun in the late fourteenth century, was enlarged right up to the seventeenth, when it was the seat of Sir Peter Leicester, author of the *Historical Antiquities of Cheshire* in 1673. Sir Peter had a chapel built alongside his hall, to which a tower was added in 1724. Everything was carefully maintained, with its furnishings, when in the 1760s John Carr of York built for Sir Peter's descendant a beautiful Palladian house on higher ground above the mere known as the Moat. The old hall still slept below, a visible symbol of continuity. In Elizabeth Stevenson's time, the new house was inhabited by the fifth baronet, Sir John Fleming Leicester. He was a considerable patron of artists, Turner in particular, who in 1808 painted two atttractive canvases, 'Tabley ... Windy Day', showing the Moat lashed into a miniature fury, and its matching piece, 'Tabley ... Calm Morning'. The former is still at Tabley, together with a large and impressive John Martin, 'The Destruction of Herculaneum and Pompeii' – Sir John's last major purchase, commissioned shortly after 1821 – and two orgulous pictures of himself on horseback, with unsheathed sword, depicted as a Colonel exercising the King's Cheshire Yeomanry Cavalry on the sands at Liverpool in 1824. (No need to take the cult of informality too far.)[44]

Elizabeth Gaskell, if she had seen these paintings, was not seeking to achieve anything like their sublime, grandiose effects in her descriptions. A lost commonplace book she compiled when she was twenty-one contained 'gracious and smoothly flowing' descriptions of 'landscape with the hush of serenity upon it', rather than 'the splendid or the terrible aspects of nature'.[45] Her letter bears this out:

> And when the meal was spread beneath a beech tree of no ordinary size (did you ever notice the peculiar turf under beech shade?) one of us would mount up a ladder to the belfry of the old chapel and toll the bell to call the wanderers home. Then if it rained, what merry-making in the old hall. It was galleried, with oak settles and old armour hung up, and a painted window from ceiling to floor.

Fortunately, two fine Victorian photographs show the exterior and interior of the old hall, which no longer exists. Times change, and we change with them.

> The strange sound our voices had in that unfrequented stone hall! The last time I was there during the fall of rain from one of those heavy clouds which add to a summer day's beauty, when every drop of rain is sun-tinged and falls merrily amongst the leaves, one or two of Shakespeare's ballads: 'Blow, blow thou winter wind,' and 'Hark, hark the lark at Heaven's gate sings,' &c. were sung by the musical sisters in the gallery above, and by two other musical sisters (Mary and Ellen Needham from Lenton near Nottingham) standing in the hall below.[46]

Mary Sibylla Holland a generation later wrote of the woods near Old Tabley as 'a miracle of beauty' and of the harmony of 'the old, old crumbling hall and Church, and the quiet mere and the old boathouse, and the lovely budding beeches and limes, and the carpet of wild flowers below'. Elizabeth Gaskell's responses are deepened by the pastoral tradition she invokes, mediated and intensified by musical settings of Shakespeare songs from *As You Like It* and *Cymbeline* by Dr Arne and Schubert. There is no hint that human beings ever encounter a Vale of Despond or a Doubting Castle. After all, Bunyan's allegory was condemned by one Unitarian minister as 'needless discouragement ... not warranted by divine revelation'.[47]

Looking back with charged emotion, discovering a perfect past not truly lost, is a general Romantic inheritance: 'I listened motionless and still; / And, as I mounted up the hill, / The music in my heart I bore, / Long after it was heard no more.' Elizabeth betrays a special sensibility for 'old solitary manor-houses, surrounded with trees, grey with lichens, and with their painted windows, from which one may in fancy catch a glimpse of the inhabitants of former days walking through long dark avenues'. The cult of an imaginative childhood here finds one of its most beguiling forms. In another century and another country Augustin Meaulnes would find himself in an avenue by a wood, where he suddenly felt inexplicably happy and the sound of children's voices heralded their actual appearance. He had come upon the lost home and joyous life of his childhood, *le domaine mystérieux* and *la fête étrange*.

But Alain-Fournier transformed the picnics of his youth at Loroy and other 'châteaux de Sologne presque tous merveilleux de goût, d'élégance, de poésie dans ces paysages sauvages' into a mythopoeic work of art, *Le Grand Meaulnes*, 'the most delicate rendering so far achieved of the romantic adolescent consciousness', wrote Robert Gibson in 1968. Elizabeth Gaskell's art at its best, as in *Cousin Phillis*, could recreate summer joys and tender human growth, but reaches beyond them to what she felt was a necessary maturity. In her early letter to Mary Howitt she could only lapse into shallow, winsome enthusiasm, 'Oh! I am particularly glad you are thinking of describing some of these solemnly poetical places.'[48]

Perhaps this is too severe. Her brother John once reminded her of the time when she used to stroll in a Cheshire park 'where the old abbey (am I right –) is – or in that where we had once upon a time a sail in a punt together when

Elisabeth was a little girl of ten years old & liked brother John to kiss her'. It is a striking reminder of her life as a girl, of which we know so little and which she almost always re-visited within the safe confines of fiction. As George Eliot wrote at the end of the fifth chapter of *The Mill on the Floss*, 'such things as these are the mother tongue of our imagination, the language that is laden with all the subtle inextricable associations the fleeting hours of our childhood left behind them'.[49]

NOTES

1 Hall, p. 55; Robert Jolley, *Edmund Sharpe 1809-1877*, University of Lancaster Visual Arts Centre, [1977]; Thomas Walter Laqueur, *Religion and Respectability: Sunday Schools and Working Class Culture 1780-1650*, New Haven, 1976, p. 11; RTD, LUBL: ECG, MS diary, pp. 66-7. I am grateful to T. Mannix (see 'Edmund Sharpe 1809-1877', *GNL*, XIX, 1995, pp. 13-15).

2 Hall, pp. 91, 104-6, 110, 128; *VCH Cheshire*, III, p. 234; Robson, *Education in Cheshire*, p. 54. Maria Edgeworth wrote a fictionalised version of Sabrina's story in *Belinda* (1801). See Lonsdale, 'Dr Burney, "Joel Collier", and Sabrina', pp. 304-7.

3 Hall, pp. 77, 109, 115, 157, 159; ECS to Harriet Carr, The Heath, Knutsford, 8 August [1831] (Chapple, 'Five early letters', p. 19). 'The Lancashire Witches. Duett Quadrilles', dated 'ES Oct 1831', occurs on a disjunct leaf in her last MS music book. See p. 154 above, and also p. 244 below.

4 MS to JWW, Heathside, 10 November 1822 (WAL: EHC 204/42); Hall, pp. 149, 154.

5 See Philip Yarrow, 'Mrs Gaskell and France', *GSJ*, VII, 1993, p. 30; Butler, *Edgeworth*, pp. 61, 156-7; Easson, pp. 20-1; Uglow, pp. 27-8; PUL: ECG to Mrs Maria James, Plymouth Grove, 1 September [1851]; Iona and Peter Opie, *The Classic Fairy Tales*, Oxford, 1974.

6 Ruth Watts, 'Knowledge is power – Unitarians, gender and education in the eighteenth and early nineteenth centuries', *GE*, I, 1989, p. 38; Archibald Sparke, *Bibliographia Boltoniensis*, 1913 (annotated copy at Bolton); Baker, *Nonconformity in Bolton*, pp. 66, 70; *Letters*, p. 17. *DNB*, 'John Holland', Obits: John, *MR*, XXI, 1826, pp. 430, 495-6; Thomas, *MR*, n. s. III, 1829, pp. 721-2. I must thank Barry Mills, BLAA local studies librarian, for his help.

7 *DNB*, 'Mangnall'; Turner, *A Short Sketch*, pp. 33n., 43; Rae, *Turtle at Mr Humble's*, p. 22 (describes 1818 prospectus); Lupton, *Wakefield Worthies*, p. 218; Barker, *The Brontës*, p. 174; *Brontë Letters*, I, p. 145; Irvine, pp. 61-2 (MH to Abigail Holland, 10 February 1838, mentioning a recent visit by 'Mrs. Gaskell and Miss Lucy Holland').

8 See Gaskell, *Wives and Daughters*, chapter 14; Butler, *Edgeworth*, pp. 455n., 505; DCLH: HH to ME, London, 22 March 1821. Waller, 'Letters addressed to Mrs Gaskell', pp. 9-12, prints a long critique of *Mary Barton* that Maria Edgeworth sent to Mary Holland from Edgeworthstown, 27 December 1848.

9 *Letters*, p. 562; TD, *The History of Sandford and Merton, A Work Intended for the Use of Children* (1783-89), London, 1791, I, p. iv. See p. 219 below.

10 HB, *Fool of Quality*, chapter 2; Quinlan, *Victorian Prelude*, p. 30.

11 SW junior to JWW, Knutsford, 1 December 1811 (WAL: EHC 205c/15; Hall, p. 28).

12 Hall, pp. 55, 63, 68, 110 (MS to JWW, Heathside, 6 February 1821); *Darwin, Huxley: Autobiographies*, ed. de Beer, p. 9. HH began his professional career in January 1816 at Mount Street and went to Lower Brook Street in 1820 (*Recollections*, p. 151).

13 For Sandlebridge see p. 53 above, and SW junior to JWW, Knutsford, 15 January 1810 (WAL: EHC 205c/10; Hall, pp. 8-9). See also Hall, pp. 79, 105; *GSN*, VII, March 1989, pp. 2-4.

14 M. Sharpe to JWW (MS not seen; n. d. given, Hall, p. 106). See JGS: TS, John Stevenson to ECS, London, 7 May [1820], p. 228 below. David Hume's histories appeared in many editions from 1754; they were continued by Tobias Smollet and others after 1793.

15 MS to JWW, Heathside, 19 September 1821 (WAL: EHC 204/31). Hall, p. 125, reads 'Sedburg' (JWW's school) instead of 'secresy'. See also Hall, pp. 128, 141; HH, *Recollections*, p. 7.

16 *Memoirs of Richard Lovell Edgeworth*, II, p. 382; *Edgeworth Letters*, pp. 421-2; *Letters*, pp. 166, 241.

17 BPMH: ECS to Anne [Burnett], 'Thursday Eveng' [Summer 1831]; qu. in full, *Portrait*, pp. 11-12; since the discovery of the Carr letters, re-dated c. June 1831. See also P. J. Yarrow, 'Mrs. Gaskell and Newcastle', *Archaeologia Aeliana*, 5th s., XX, p. 141.

18 CRO: MF 1/4. 190, ODC burial register; Strachan, TS, 'Record of graves and inscriptions', no. 118 [no year date].

19 See *Edgeworth Letters*, p. 421; *Letters*, pp. 4-5, 8, 20, 23, 26 (indexing defective: add [letters] 3, 4, 10, 11), and ECG, MS diary, p. 74. For Susan and Richard Deane see p. 126 above.

20 Unitarians are omitted from K. D. Brown, *A Social History of the Nonconformist Ministry in England and Wales 1800-1930*, London, Oxford, Toronto, 1988, as 'well outside' Evangelical orthodoxy with always fewer than four hundred ministers (p. 17).

21 CRO: EUC 9/4408/18, PH to Mr Long, 13 [Nov?] 1828; *CF*, XIII, 1869, p. 59. Chadwick states she taught before she was fifteen (1910, p. 28) and fourteen (1913, p. 17) – to allow for what she came to think was three years rather than two away at school.

22 Read, *Peterloo*, p. 26; SW to JWW, Knutsford, 30 November 1809 (WAL: EHC 204/1; Hall, p. 5). A straw in the wind: 'our' is crossed out before 'religion'.

23 See Hall, p. 55; endnotes, pp. vii, ix (two unlocatable letters, selected by Hall); Carpenter, *Martineau*, pp. 104-5; Knutsford parish church record (c. 1973), grave 125. Peter Holland died in 1855 and Catherine Whittaker in 1844.

24 Hall, p, 34. Some in Knutsford sanded *against* Catholic emancipation in 1829.

25 Rudé, *Hanoverian London*, pp. 247, 249; Slugg, *Manchester*, pp. 173-4; Read, *Peterloo*, pp. 58-9, 71; Seed, 'Liberal culture in Manchester', p. 5; H. McLachlan, 'The Taylors and Scotts of the *Manchester Guardian*', *TUHS*, IV, 1927-30, p. 32.

26 *The Earl of Chester's Regiment of Yeomanry Cavalry: Its Formation and Services 1797-1897*, pr. pr. Edinburgh, 1898, pp. 8-10, 52-7; Hall, pp. 88-9; DCLH: Henry Holland to Lucy Aikin, St Michael's Hill, Bristol, April 1804; Read, *Peterloo*, pp. 81, 108-10; Walmsley, *Peterloo*, p. 122.

27 *Earl of Chester's Regiment*, pp. 74-80; Read, *Peterloo*, pp. 127-40; Walmsley, *Peterloo*, p. 149.

28 [Fox], 'Belsham', *MR*, n. s. IV, 1830, p. 252; KUL: Wedgwood 59-31901, SCH to JW, London, 4 September 1819; Hall, p. 97; Walmsley, *Peterloo*, pp. 162, 191-2, 222-5.

29 See Read, *Peterloo*, p. 39, 192-3; Walmsley, *Peterloo*, pp. 187, 316-17; J. R. Dinwiddy, *Radicalism and Reform in Britain, 1780-1850*, London and Rio Grande, 1992, pp. 117, 122.

30 CRO: DLT/c34/109, 110: PH to JFL, Knutsford, Sunday evening, [postm. 28 October 1819] and Knutsford, 13 December 1819 ; DCLH: HH to ME, 10 November [1819]. I must thank Mrs Joan Leach for drawing the CRO letters to my attention.

31 HH to ME, Mount Street, 27 June [1820]; Hall, p. 103. See Perkin, *Origins*, pp. 208-17, and Walton, *Lancashire*, pp. 155-7.

32 HH to ME, London, 23 August [1821]; HH, *Recollections*, pp. 114-46; Hall, pp. 106-7. See also Edgeworth correspondence of 1814 and 1815 (NLI: MSS 10, 166; analysis courtesy of C. Fahy), and for a truly partisan account, Brougham's 'George IV' in his *Historical Sketches of Statesmen*, *Works*, IV, London and Glasgow, 1860, pp. 5-49.

33 Hall, p. 116-17, and MS to JWW, Heathside, 19 September 1821 (WAL: EHC 204/31;

Hall, pp. 124-5). PH had been in a 'bothered state' at Edgeworthstown (*Edgeworth Letters*, p. 421).

34 MS to JWW, Heathside, 7 October 1822 (WAL: EHC 204/41; Hall, p. 146); DCLH: HH to ME, L Brook St, 24 July 1822 and 21 November 1822; KUL: Wedgwood 29-21633, HH to [JW], London, 26 June 1828.

35 *Earl of Chester's Regiment*, pp. 103-7, 112; Hall, pp. v, 104, 163-9 (quotation, p. 167; MS unlocated); endnotes p. vii. See also E. Panofsky, *Meaning in the Visual Arts*, New York, 1955.

36 MH to JWW, Knutsford, April [1829]; MS to JWW, Lancaster, 22 October 1829 (WAL: EHC204/63, 64; neither in Hall).

37 JGR to MR, Lancaster, 28 July 1836 (MCO); *Letters*, p. 17; TCC: WW to ECG, 12 January 1851; Mrs Stairs Douglas, *The Life of William Whewell, D.D.*, 1881, p. 376 [annotated copy, CUL].

38 Leach, 'Lady Jane Stanley', pp. 5-9; Aikin, *Description of the Country*, pp. 348-50; Perkin, *Origins*, pp. 189-91 (incl. his quotations).

39 See ECG's 1852 description in 'An unpublished Gaskell letter', *GSN*, X, August 1990, pp. 4-9, and P. de Figueiredo and Julian Treuherz, *Cheshire Country Houses*, 1988, and p. 109 above. Mrs Davenport's journals, 'sent every Saturday to her sisters' (copied extracts of which, 1841-43, are in JRULM: Kay-Shuttleworth MSS 221) have not been found.

40 *Letters*, pp. 165, 402, 491; *Letters and Verses of Arthur Penrhyn Stanley*, ed. Rowland E. Prothero, London, 1895, pp. 380-1; Green, *Knutsford*, pp. 27-9, 145. See also Uglow, p. 534.

41 ECS to HC, Brandon Street, 18 June 1831 (Chapple, 'Five early letters', p. 3); Stanley Weintraub, *Victoria: Biography of a Queen*, London and Sydney, 1987, pp. 26, 30, 54, 67; Claire Tomalin, *Mrs Jordan's Profession: The Story of a Great Actress and a Future King*, 1995, chapter 21, esp. p. 309. See also Appendix G.

42 See M. Howitt, 'Stray notes', pp. 605-6 (with engravings), repr. *Letters*, pp. 15-16 (comma omitted after 'musing').

43 Hall, endnote, p. i (a brief quotation: original MS not found); Mark Girouard, *Life in the English Country House: A Social and Architectural History*, 1978, repr. London, 1979, pp. 214-15.

44 John Young, *A Catalogue of Pictures by British Artists in the Possession of Sir John Fleming Leicester*, London, 1825; Christopher Hussey, 'Tabley Old Hall' and 'Tabley House', *Country Life*, 14-28 July 1923; Peter Cannon-Brookes, *Tabley House near Knutsford Cheshire*, 1991 (both profusely illustr.). The old hall collapsed in 1927. As much as possible was rescued and incorporated in an 'Old Hall Room'; the damaged chapel and tower were moved to a new site beside Tabley House.

45 J. R. Coolidge, 'Life and letters of Mrs. E. C. Gaskell', unpublished TS, J. G. Sharps collection (copy in LUBL). See appendix E below.

46 Moss, *Pilgrimages in Cheshire*, pp. 63-7 (photos). Lenton suggests the sisters were connected in some way with the Reverend Henry Turner. A letter from his widow to William Turner is dated from Lenton, 21 February 1822 (TWA: MF).

47 MSH to Lucy Holland, Knutsford, May [1874] (*Letters of Mary Sibylla Holland*, ed. Bernard Holland, London, 1898, p. 23); Mineka, *Dissidence of Dissent*, p. 127.

48 *Letters*, p. 14; Alain-Fournier, *Le Grand Meaulnes*, intro. Robert Gibson, London, [1968], 1980, pp. xix-xx, lxxxi-ii, cxxxii, I, chapter 11; Wordsworth, 'The Solitary Reaper'.

49 See JGS: MS, JS to ECS, Blackwall, 8 and 10 June [1827], p. 284 below.

12

Father and brother

IT IS NOT KNOWN exactly how much time Elizabeth spent at Knutsford before she went to school, but all the indications are that this quiet little country town in Cheshire was her real home for her first ten or so years. Her father and brother could hardly have led a more different kind of life. They were not successful new men of the age like most of the Hollands, able to ride the whirlwind of change. Caught in more traditional spheres, they found themselves battling against unprecedented economic and social forces in the post-war years. It was a time of exceptional instability. Victory had turned sour. Businesses and banks were failing, agricultural labourers setting fire to barns, the unemployed marching and workers calling strikes. William Stevenson in London, with a wife and two young children to support, was in very respectable employment, but for some reason he needed more than his Treasury salary of several hundred a year. Perhaps investments upon which he and his wife relied had failed. His son John was in his late teens, unmarried, still casting about for an assured profession, which would inevitably involve some sort of premium and initial expenses.

William did find sources of extra income, though they demanded unremitting, detailed work. A letter in 1814 from Swinton Holland to Josiah Wedgwood begs for details of manufacturing in the Potteries and encloses a copy of a series of questions from Stevenson, who was contributing to David Brewster's *Edinburgh Encyclopaedia* rather more than the single article on Chivalry that is mentioned in his obituary. He was about to write an article on England – a 'bold subject to undertake', Swinton thought – which would include details of pottery manufacture, from raw materials to value added and markets, the conditions and wages of the workers, the number of women and children employed, their usual food, education and industrial diseases, labour-saving improvements and so on. Stevenson hoped to see Swinton at London Fields when the winter roads were better; 'I shall probably trouble you further respecting the imports & exports of England to & from the Mediterranean', he ended.

Brewster was a busy scientist, well known for his invention of the kaleidoscope, which did not however prove very profitable. But he was also the author of over 300 scientific papers and a great populariser of science, becoming eventually the first lay principal of Edinburgh University. The first two numbers of the *Encyclopaedia* had come out in May 1808, printed in double columns on large quarto pages, but Brewster endured numerous problems and delays. Half-volumes at a guinea apiece were issued over many years, and the full eighteen volumes with a supplement were not complete until 1830 – by which time it had been beaten to the post by James Millar's *Encyclopaedia Edinensis* (6 volumes, 1827).[1]

Other unpublished letters show that Stevenson had attracted the attention of a Mr Stewart, probably the famous Professor Dugald Stewart, whose lectures on political economy about the turn of the century 'unfolded the elements and the ends of that noble science, and so recommended it by the graces of his eloquence that even his idler hearers retained a permanent taste for it', wrote Henry Cockburn. Stewart has been called 'perhaps the most effective teacher and disseminator of ideas of his time' by a modern scholar. At his hospitable house in the Canongate of the old town Maria Edgeworth had met a catholic mixture of scientists and men of letters in 1803, about the time when Stevenson lived in and about the Scottish capital; later Stewart helped her edit her father's memoirs for the press.[2]

He was good enough to recommend Stevenson to Macvey Napier, the editor appointed by Constable for a supplement to the fourth, fifth and sixth editions of the *Encyclopaedia Britannica*. In May 1814 Napier sent Stevenson one of the earliest invitations to contribute to this expensive and precarious enterprise.[3] In the preliminaries James Cleghorn's signature is given as A and Stevenson's as C. They were in distinguished company. Contributors included Stewart himself, William Hazlitt, James Mill, Francis Jeffrey, Walter Scott, Sir William Hamilton the mathematician, William Playfair the architect, Thomas Malthus, Dominique Arago the astronomer and William Turner of Newcastle – a mixture of intellectual brilliance and scholarly worthiness. By April in the following year Stevenson had an article on Abyssinia and two on Academies (learned and army/navy) almost ready.

A letter of July 1815 to Napier, however, is full of distress: 'I most readily acknowledge that a charge of negligence or misrepresentation might have been justly brought, if you had not altered [part of it]. ... I cannot, in any degree accuse myself, of inattention arising from the cause you mention & plead guilty – In fact I was at the time I wrote that part oppressed with business.' The fault does not appear to have been completely disastrous, because Napier took articles on Albania and the Aleutian Isles off his hands. Stevenson also wrote that Lauderdale would be away from town and the Treasury in recess till the middle of October, which would enable him to prepare America – a reminder of more spacious days for men of letters who were public servants, like Thomas Peacock and Charles Lamb. In the event America was provided by David Buchanan. On 6 February 1816 Stevenson explained that Antrim and Armagh would have been finished had it not been for the illness of his Treasury assistant and asked to see the B list of articles wanted. But Napier seems to have had enough. The articles are not very striking, and no contribution by Stevenson is found beyond the first volume, which appeared in two parts in December 1815 and June 1816. Where he might have been expected to appear in later parts as the author of topographical or agricultural articles, the usual signature is James Cleghorn's A.

There was, however, a very special friend willing to look out for his interests in Grub Street journalism, no less a man than William Blackwood. By 1816 the Edinburgh bookseller had left South Bridge Street by the University and moved into the new town, to fine and spacious premises in Princes Street, and was developing the career as a publisher that was to make his a household name. In April 1817 he issued the first number of the *Edinburgh Monthly Magazine*, with Thomas Pringle and James Cleghorn as editors ('the one beast was like unto a lamb, and the other like unto a bear'), though the dullness of the result ensured that they were smartly dismissed after six numbers. Two bright young men, John Gibson Lockhart and John Wilson, took over, and the monthly eventually came to be known as *Blackwood's Magazine*.[4]

Stevenson's many letters to Blackwood can be read through in the National Library of Scotland, along with office copies of the firm's answers. They run from 3 February 1817 to 28 December 1827; sparsely at first, most thickly from 1821 to 1824.[5] They overlap chronologically with a dozen letters in the Sharps Collection written by John Stevenson to his young sister, which begin in late 1819. These correspondences are very characteristic, and lay bare what was in effect the last act of two private tragedies.

The first letter from William Stevenson to Blackwood was written on 3 February 1817 from the Treasury, which provided him with postal franks if he could not send material by the publisher's usual monthly parcel from London.[6] It begins with the apologies that are to be a leit-motiv:

> I am afraid you will conclude that I have been principally occupied with the 'Voyages'; – this however has not been the case. The annexation of the Commissariat to the Treasury, & the arrangements necessary for the annexation of the Irish to the British Treasury, have required much closer, & longer official attendance than I formerly gave. ... Beside my encrease of official duty, the sudden death of Mr. Joyce threw entirely upon me, the execution of a literary work, in which he & I were jointly engaged; & this work required immediate & close attention.

Jeremiah Joyce had been one of those arrested for treason in 1794 with Horne Tooke. He never managed to throw off the stigma, though he became one of Robert Aspland's circle and secretary of the Unitarian Society. From his pen came numerous scientific and other works, some of which the publishers insisted should be printed under another name, and others which appeared in new editions after his death in 1816. An 1817 edition of *Systematic Education*, which Joyce wrote with William Shepherd and Lant Carpenter, is one possibility or, more likely, the second edition in 1821 of Joyce's *A Complete Analysis or Abridgement of Dr. Adam Smith's ... Wealth of Nations*, a work that will be seen to harmonise with Stevenson's interests, not to mention those of his daughter.[7]

The 'Voyages' was Stevenson's major work, a *Historical Sketch of the Progress of Discovery, Navigation, and Commerce from the Earliest Records to the Beginning of the Nineteenth Century*, which he at first promised could go to press in the middle of April 1818. It was the last volume of *A Collection of Voyages and Travels* begun by R. H. Kerr in 1811; eighteen volumes in all were published by 1824.[8]

Defects in quality and presentation of the *Historical Sketch* sprang at least in part from the conditions under which Stevenson wrote. On 25 July 1817 he confessed that he had taken on too much work; when he had finished some pieces for Dr David Brewster (India and Ireland) he was going into the country for a few weeks, because he absolutely needed 'some relaxation'. (He does not, unfortunately, say where.) About April 1818 he wrote that he had been very unwell and was waiting for his assistant at the Treasury to return, 'after which for 6 or 8 weeks' he could devote his time entirely to the 'Voyages'. More letters bring more excuses. In November 1821 he promised two sheets a week and a conclusion in two months time. By the following June he had only finished the historical part ('30 or 31 sheets – leaving 9 or 10 for the Catalogue'), and was beginning to prepare a selective catalogue of texts. Nevertheless, he urged Blackwood to go to press – probably to spur himself on. Crucially, no terms had been agreed between the two men, old friends now locked in a highly unsatisfactory professional relationship.[9]

In February 1817 he had asked Blackwood, as publisher, to tell Brewster that he could not finish India before the middle of March 1818. Fifty or more entries, several lengthy and scholarly, are attributed to Stevenson in the final list of contributors – Chivalry, Complexion, Captain Cooke, Cornwall, Cromwell ... The list is very miscellaneous – Dreams, Druids, Druses ... Jamaica, Jews, India, Ireland, Kent and so on, though the majority are geographical in a broad sense. The popular economist J. R. McCulloch, first professor of political economy at London University, praised Stevenson's 'statistical articles' in the encyclopaedia. The article on England was a history, followed by a statistics, that is, a lengthy dissertation on geography, natural history, agriculture and many other matters, prepared by Stevenson. He was responsible for both the history and the statistics of France. In Dreams he cites Locke, Hartley, Dugald Stewart and P. J. G. Cabanis. India, which gave him a good deal of trouble, runs to nearly one hundred pages. He wrote a good deal for Brewster, but the list of his contributions ends unexpectedly with 'Netherlands, and articles signed (W. S.)'.

In 1820 the young Thomas Carlyle, striving to keep body and soul together in Edinburgh by teaching and hack-writing as Stevenson had done some fifteen years before, already suffering from his famous combination of despondency and digestive problems, began to contribute. In effect he took Stevenson's place: in volumes 14 to 16, published between 1820 and 1825, he dominated just the areas of biography, history and geography that the older man, struggling with the 'Voyages', might otherwise have been expected to provide. Carlyle was on the spot, and hungrier, his table 'covered with manuscripts and first copies and proof-sheets and pens and snuffers and tumblers of water and pipes of tobacco'. 'I *must* compile that trash for their Cyclopaedia,' he cried to Thomas Murray, 'tho' it were ten times stupider and I ten times sicker'. He ran into difficulties with The Netherlands in July 1821, for which he was unable to find materials, and therefore the article is attributed to both Carlyle and Stevenson in the final list. Stevenson perhaps had better access to sources in London. In 1821 he mentions that he has examined 'all the American Reviews, Magazines & other likely Books, in the Royal Institution, & in the Library' and says he is writing to the London Institution for information.[10]

Informally, Stevenson acted as a London reporter for Blackwood, though this gradually declined as his own concerns became more pressing. Some of the great political movements during the later 1820s – anti-slavery, Catholic emancipation and so on – go unmentioned. In February 1817, however, he wrote about two of Scott's novels recently published together, *The Black Dwarf* and *Old Mortality*, giving a fair account of their reception. The first, he wrote, was not much liked: the story is not very interesting or probable; the catastrophe is badly managed; & the character of the Black Dwarf partakes too much of malignity & insanity'. The other, however, was 'a very high & firm favourite, & tho' there are passages in Waverley, Guy Mannering, & even the Antiquary, of a higher order than perhaps any passage in this Tale, – yet it is more equable, & in point of delineation of character fully equal to those works'. He was also a sounding board for *Blackwood's Edinburgh Magazine*, which Blackwood had handed over to its flamboyant new editors in October 1817. Lockhart and Wilson at once began to attack everybody, bringing about complaints, objections, law-suits, challenges and, of course, rising sales. 'I was much amused with the last No. of your Magazine', wrote Stevenson rather primly in 1820, 'but I think you want variety – you want more solid food with your piquant sauces'. It proved to be a most unwise suggestion.[11]

Elizabeth's brother John had like his grandfather and uncles adopted a seafaring life, but when ashore mostly stayed with his father and stepmother at 3 Beaufort Row. He seems to have written quite adult letters to his little sister as soon as she was old enough to understand. One of December 1819 refers to an earlier letter to which he had not received an answer and goes on to hope that she had enjoyed her Christmas with so many young friends. He writes comically to her about his awkwardness whilst dancing at a party. 'But you have read Sandford and Merton', he went on, 'and fancy to yourself you see the gouty gentleman standing on the hot iron plates, first lifting up one leg then the other, and you will have some idea of the figure your brother cut'. She must then have been at Knutsford, because he ends with love to relations there, 'aunts Lumb, Kate, Abb and [Mary] Holland' and cousins Bessy and Lucy.[12] He expected to join a ship called the Lady Nugent, which had arrived from Madras in early December and was due to sail again at the end of January. It was a private vessel of 514 tons, Captain Robert Swanston, belonging to Calcutta and nearly double the size of an ordinary trading ship. In 1820 it was licensed as an extra ship by the East India Company, which needed vessels at least of this size, but in the event John did not sail in her.[13]

There was no chance that John could join the royal navy like his grand-father. Its rapid expansion during the Napoleonic wars had been followed by a severe contraction. By 1817 the great majority of its officers were beached, the remaining naval hierarchy 'clogged, aged, incompetent in many respects'. In 1839 the youngest admiral was sixty-five, the oldest ninety, and it was even difficult to find a senior officer fit enough to take a command at sea. William Gladstone's brother, born in 1807 and the son of a very rich man, was excep-tional. He managed to find a captain to take him as a midshipman in 1820, and after the combined influences of the politician William Huskisson, Sir George Cockburn, Lord Melville and the Duke of Clarence had been brought to bear, he obtained a lieutenant's commission in 1826. Like William Price in Jane Austen's *Mansfield Park* (1814), he owed his success to patronage. But it was a short career. By June 1835 he was on half-pay, for the rest of his life.[14]

On 1 March 1820 the Court of Directors of the East India Company resolved that 'Mr John Stevenson be granted Free Mariners Indentures on the usual conditions', to sail in trading vessels to the East. His father had to put up a bond of £500.[15] The Company itself, established in 1600, was in a declining condition, losing its exclusive trading privileges and increasingly influenced by Robert Clive's 'legacy of territorial conquest and acquisition' in the eighteenth century, when he had been granted sweeping civil and military powers as Commander-in-Chief. Control at such a distance, when ships took a year for the round trip from London, was impossible. Private traders as well as the Company operated from the Red Sea in the west to Canton in the far east, often using ships built in the region; their cotton, indigo and opium trading patterns were largely independent, and at the Company's charter renewal in 1813, it was stripped of all except its monopoly of the tea trade to China.[16]

For the time, there was a pause. John's next letter to Elizabeth, written in March 1820, shows that he had gone to Berwick rather than Bombay:

> I will attempt to give you some idea of the business that took me down there –
> First then, you must understand that to be a burgess of Berwick it is necessary to
> be either the Son of a freeman or to serve 7 years' apprenticeship in the town. In
> either case you have a vote when you have attained the age of 21 – The advan-
> tages of being one are that when you reside in the town you have your children
> well educated free of expence and that you have likewise a few pounds per annum
> according to your seniority.[17]

Berwick was one of fourteen freeman boroughs where the right of election was vested in the burgesses of the town, numbering about one thousand, by no means all of whom lived there. At election times it was venal and expensive, 'almost as famous for its elections, as for its smacks and salmon'. It cost candidates thousands of pounds in bribes to get elected, at ten guineas a vote. The many 'Treasury appointees employed in the customs, garrison, army, navy, excise and tax collectors' of Berwick could swing elections to candidates nominated by the Treasury. In 1754, not many years after John's grandfather became a freeman, John Wilkes had stood as a candidate, spending some £3000 in bribes to electors. The story that he managed to arrange for some of his opponent's supporters sailing from London to be shipped to Norway 'by accident' is more symbolic than true, however.[18]

The merry-go-round began again in the general election of 1820. 'As this election gave me a good opportunity of taking up my freedom without expence and at the same time afforded me a chance of seeing my Berwick friends before my departure', John continued, 'I thought it a pity to lose so many advantages – The member I went down to vote for was Admiral Milne, who had set up in opposition to Col. H St Paul the old representative.' Colonel Henry Heneage St Paul had been elected for Berwick in 1812 and 1818. In March 1820 he was again a candidate, together with Lord Ossulston (who became Earl of Tankerville in 1822) and Admiral Sir David Milne. The *Berwick Advertiser* for Saturday 11 March 1820 gave the state of the poll on Friday as Lord Ossulston 448, Colonel St Paul 332, with Sir David Milne trailing at 313. The windows of the town, 'particularly those near the town hall', it fulsomely reported in the manner of Dickens's *Eatanswill Gazette*, 'were filled with all the beauty and fashion of the neighbourhood'.[19]

John had sailed from London on Sunday for an election beginning on Wednesday, but contrary winds prevented them arriving before Friday. 'We had sixty votes in two smacks for the Admiral', his long account continued, 'who as he depended entirely upon us put off the election as much as possible by polling one every quarter of an hour'. If no voters appeared after a quarter of an hour, a proclamation was read three times; if a voter then came before the third, the whole process began again and could not conclude until an hour had elapsed. John was one of eighteen who were not yet freemen, but the guild of burgesses required forty-eight hours' notice. Sir David Milne just managed to squeeze out his remaining votes and last until the poll closed on Saturday night. 'The Sunday intervening enabling us to make up the 48 hours', John explained, 'we were made free on Monday Morning, voted directly after & carried the election by 17 – 18 being made free'.

John wrote in youthful high spirits that 'one great advantage we had was having all the ladies on our side. It certainly was animating to see all the Berwick Belles wearing our favours and so warmly joining in the cause.' He was a young buffer, if we compare him with Mary Clarke, who as Madame Mohl was to become one of his sister's greatest friends in the years to come.

She went to an election at the London Guildhall in the 1820s and 'was half-killed, but did not care a fig', she wrote forthrightly. More than ever it made her wish to be a man, living in the public eye, working for the public good and having 'a busy life instead of sitting by the fireside imagining'. The last thing she wanted was to be an election belle. She was soon rejoicing in Elizabeth Fry's governmental mission to report on the prisons of Ireland: '*There's* the beginning of women's rise to power and government – not through love and men's ridiculous passions, but by sheer moral force and intelligence.'[20]

John's name appears in the Guild minute book under 13 March 1820 as the eldest son of William Stevenson, 'Clerk of the Papers in the Treasury and one of the Burgesses of this Corporation', and it is followed by that of John Sinclair, eldest son of Sir John Sinclair, 'of the City of Edinburgh, Baronet'. Stevenson's name is accordingly found as a voter in the MS poll book for 8-13 March 1820. The *Berwick Advertiser* of 18 March gives the final state of the poll (Ossulston 470, Milne 373, St Paul 356) and records that the two victors were carried up the High Street in chairs to the sound of martial music.[21]

John continues his long letter with an account of a visit to his Berwick relations in this spring of 1820, to see aunt Elizabeth, widow of Robert Stevenson, and his cousins – particularly Isabella, who was his sister's correspondent and like her, nearly ten years old:

> She is a remarkably fine girl, lively, intelligent, and good tempered – The whole of the family are indeed uncommonly well behaved and are very forward in their studies – The only advantage however that Isabella has over you is in musick. She often gave me a tune, and I think plays very well for her age – I should have liked very much if you could have learned likewise but I am almost afraid from what I have heard that wishes are vain –

It sounds, almost unbelievably, as if Elizabeth had reaped no advantage from living with aunt Lumb so near the musical Sharpe family at Heathside. He then writes with a flourish:

> My aunt made me a present of my grandfather's sword and dagger and my uncle Roberts pistols with which I am practising firing at a mark – I am going I believe likewise to learn the cutlass exercise – I have been told by several people that 9 out of 10 that go to the E. Indies die there but I must comfort myself in the same manner the officers of the army and navy stationed off the W. Indies did when they drunk as their first toast after dinner, 'A sickly season and plenty of new rum'. I hope at least we shall have the chance of a skirmish with the Malays.

At this stage John aspired to be the complete man of action in his generation of cousins, although there were three Stevenson boys in Berwick. Joseph Stevenson, born in 1806, was the most successful. He became a well known historian and archivist, whose entry in the *Dictionary of National Biography* records a long, weirdly diverse and highly productive scholarly career. He was a protean version of his uncle William. He became in succession a minister in the Presbyterian Church of Scotland, a sub-commissioner of the public records, a married clergyman in the Church of England, an editor of the Rolls Series, a Roman Catholic priest and, at the end of his long life, a Jesuit.[22] One of his brothers, William Berry, went to Bengal as assistant surgeon and the other, John, became an attorney. Their sister Isabella was born in 1810. A disentailing deed of 1842 shows that she was still living, but she does not appear to have married. The letter of early 1854 in which Elizabeth Gaskell started to put her daughter Marianne 'a little au fait as to the family', her only relations on her father's side, is tantalisingly incomplete at this point. Meta Gaskell's 'exact copy of some pencil notes' Mrs Gaskell made on an envelope postmarked 1853, later found in William Gaskell's desk, has a brief comment about her: 'unmar: crooked'.[23]

Three other daughters – Elizabeth Wilson, Marianne and Robina Dorothy – were born between 1812 and 1818, all of whom later married. Mrs Gaskell suggested that her eldest daughter call upon Marianne, now Mrs Manisty, wife of a Queen's counsel on the Northern circuit. 'She is sister to Mrs [Elizabeth] Church, the wife of the clergyman who died within 2 months at Torquay, & of Joseph Stevenson the clergyman at Leighton-Buzzard.' A visit to Leighton Buzzard in 1854 was not a success: 'Mr Stevenson good & conscientious but I don't like Mrs Stevenson, she is fussy and under-bred. Nice girls.' The daughter of George and Dorothy Landles, Margaret, who married a William Paulin and lived until at least the 1880s, is not mentioned in the portion of the letter to Marianne that has survived. She seems to have had little contact with her Berwick relations in later life.

However, John's letter tells us that the Chelsea and Knutsford connection with Berwick was still fresh in the early 1820s, fostered by her brother and with the second Mrs Stevenson's support:

> I have a small gold seal with your name on which we wish to send you if we can get a conveyance – I do not know if you have got Paul & Virginia and the Exiles of Siberia, if you have not, tell me and I will send them at the same time. My mother has been proposing that if you can manage to come up this Summer, she will ask your cousin Isabella to come up to meet you, and my father will take you down in the autumn. ...
>
> Enclosed you will find a letter from Isabella who I think writes better than you, tho' she is not as forward as you in french and arithmetic – I do not mean this as a reproach my dear sister, but only to spur you on, particularly as both your writing and your cousin's is far superior to that of many girls of your age.

Some of the earliest Gaskell letters known were sealed with a small oval design in which appeared a script 'Elizabeth'.[24]

Elizabeth, or The Exiles of Siberia [and] Paul and Virginia appeared in a single volume in 1820, translated from French originals by Helen Williams.[25] It went through a number of editions. The first tale, one of tears and sensibility – check not the kindly gush! – had appeared in English as early as 1809 and become very popular. Elizabeth's brother probably sent it in the first place because of the name of the heroine, who undergoes protracted dangers in a long journey from Siberia to beg pardon from the czar for her exiled father. But John, who called his stepmother mother, we notice, just might have had more in mind when he sent his sister this affecting little tale. The heroine derives her 'character compounded of boldness and sensibility' from both parents: 'her father disclosed to her the grand and sublime features of virtue; her mother, those qualities which were consolatory and amiable: the first, taught her how virtue was to be revered; the second, how it was to be cherished.' In the utmost perils and when secret terrors stole upon her heart, she would repeat, 'Father! mother!' And over all brooded the spirit of a father who inspired but was also owed love and duty.[26]

John's letters to his young sister are not very adroit, but who knows what lessons she learnt from his brotherly exhortations? The story of *Elizabeth* is a continuous display of the heroine's self-sufficiency. She has male companionship in the shape of an old missionary as she crosses steppes, forests and rivers, but he gradually fails and dies. Nature is no Romantic nurse or guardian in this tale. It is either simply beautiful, as in the description of a premature Siberian spring, or dumb and indifferent like nature in a Hardy novel – icy lakes, snowstorms, forests, 'immense heaths covered with a great number of tombs: many of them had been violated, and the bones of the dead bodies (remnants of an aboriginal people which might have remained eternally in oblivion if the golden ornaments buried with them had not revealed their existence to the eyes of avarice,) were scattered about in various directions.' After many trials the heroine at length exchanged a father for a husband, and was thereby eventually restored to a patriarchal order – but only superficially. Her quest had been very definitely her own.[27]

In his letter of March 1820 John wrote that 'Mr Roe who lived next door is dead and we have got Mr. Galt there, whose children being about the age of William form nice play fellows for him'.[28] Galt was at this time in his life a successful version of William Stevenson, writing whatever he could to raise money – although he had an even larger basic income, of £600 a year. In early 1819 he had found employment as a parliamentary lobbyist for a Scottish canal company and come to live in London for a while.[29]

Jenny Uglow very plausibly suggests that an account of Galt by Katharine Thomson also contains a pen-portrait of Stevenson.[30] Katharine had first met Galt, an 'ungainly man: of height above the common, with a common-place, though somewhat handsome cast of features', when she was in her early twenties and he was living in Lindsey Row. They met, however, 'in one of the small tenements in Beaufort Row' belonging an intimate friend, 'a specimen of the pure literary man of the olden time' who worked as a clerk in the Record Office; 'added to which, he had the onerous office of eking out the powers of a certain nobleman's brains to do their work. He was, in short, a private secretary.'

Galt was, Thomson declares, 'a male Scherazaide', to whose long stories told in a strong Scottish accent evening after evening his friend listened 'with a philosophic incredulity, never expressed, but pictured in a face to which nature had lent no charm' – the skin disease attributed to salmon out of season, no doubt. Galt would stride into his little drawing room full of life and intellectual vigour and propound endless schemes to his silently sceptical friend – 'the last wearer of the willow hat; a blessed, but not a becoming invention', remarks Katharine Thomson mischievously, adding that 'on the same principle a gambroon coat was assumed in summer'.

> He neither smoked, nor talked, nor played at cards, so that the copious talk of Galt seemed to be designed by his good angel on purpose for his amusement. ... Galt was just discovering the *saleability* of his own powers; he was penning 'The Ayrshire Legatees.' 'I can write a sheet a night,' said he, addressing his friend. I remember the cold 'humph!' which sounded to me very much like 'the more's the pity.' Our secretary did not approve of rapid composition.

It seems unkind but hits the mark.

According to his obituary Stevenson wrote for the *Retrospective Review*, though no contributions have been identified. Back in 1816 Coleridge had advised John Murray the publisher that he had 'often thought that there might be set on foot a review of old books, *i.e.*, of all works important or remarkable, the authors of which are deceased, with the probability of a tolerable sale.' Henry Southern, a young graduate of Trinity College, Cambridge, took up the idea in 1820. Articles for this short-lived review could be particular or general and were, as usual, anonymous. It is known that William J. Fox contributed. A polemic against the inadequate commissioners appointed to arrange for the publication of documents in the state papers office would have been well within Stevenson's competence, and could hardly be thought of as catchpenny work.

Dibdin was later to assert that a slashing assault on his *Library Companion* in the *Westminster* (almost certainly by William Stevenson) was by 'the reputed editor' of the *Retrospective Review*. Nicholas Harris Nicholas joined Southern 'in editing a revival' of the *Retrospective* in 1827. Its first two numbers contained 'violent attacks on the Antiquarian Society, from the Council of which Mr Nicolas was a few months since rather unceremoniously ejected for certain radical Notions which he was pleased to start', T. Crofton Croker wrote maliciously to Blackwood. These articles 'created a great stir amongst a certain dirty Set,' he went on, 'and in consequence sold the Retrospective Review far beyond what it otherwise would have done.' Stevenson could have been an assistant editor, scraping a few more guineas together in the great publishing machine of modern Britain – to compensate for losses in the stock-jobbing machine, maybe.[31]

His neighbour John Galt continued to write at length and without effort, often under pseudonyms – elementary school textbooks (some three thousand pages) and articles as well as several fine short novels. It was these that brought him into close contact with Blackwood, who responded at once to Galt's initial proposal and went on to publish what Galt himself regarded as 'a kind of local theoretical history, by examples' of west Scotland, rather than novels as such.[32] The first was *The Ayrshire Legatees*, the instalments of which ran in the magazine with great success from June 1820. In a letter to Blackwood of 22 June Galt writes that he has consulted 'our friend Stevenson', who agreed with him that 'the price of novels is so variable it is not easy fixing any thing regular but he conceives something from 5 to 7 Gns per sheet should be the price besides the printers bill'.

Barry W. Proctor wrote about this time to Blackwood, 'What do you think Colburn has given Lady Morgan for her "Italy" which will be shortly printed in one vol. 4°? – I am told (as a secret) 2500!!! I'll marry an authoress if possible.' Galt does not seem to have achieved anything like this amount, only some hundreds of pounds for several publications, often paid in bills not due for twelve months or more. Almost miraculously in these circumstances, his full creative powers were suddenly released. The series of short novels he now composed, based squarely upon memories of his Scottish childhood (*The Ayrshire Legatees, Annals of the Parish, The Provost* and *The Entail*), have been described by Ian Gordon as the first *roman fleuve*.[33]

With them he achieved a kind of popularity that totally eluded Stevenson, whose imagination remained in chains. Even more painful must have been his knowledge of the speed and energy Galt was displaying next door at number 2 Beaufort Row, where, Ian Gordon tells us, he was 'sometimes working on so many things simultaneously that only a flow-diagram would chart his activity'. Reading through the letters Galt sent to Blackwood about this time gives a strong impression of an energetic author forging ahead, producing with ease just what would sell in the literary market-place. There does not seem to be more in his correspondence with Blackwood than the one passing reference to 'our friend Stevenson', though in the parallel correspondence Galt is mentioned on a number of occasions. On 13 June 1821, for instance, Blackwood took pleasure in sending Stevenson a copy of the *Ayrshire Legatees*, announcing that the *Annals of the Parish* had been popular and that 'this species of writing is really our friends forté [*sic*].' The *Annals*, published in the spring of 1821, had been at once recognised as Galt's first masterpiece.

On 19 October Stevenson mentions dining with Mrs Galt and the children but goes on to say that he had not seen Galt before he had gone off to Edinburgh to stay with Blackwood; otherwise, he could have transmitted an explanation of when he expected to finish his own 'Voyages' book. He apologises for 'latterly so much delay', and proposes to Blackwood another prosaic brainchild – 'a useful, interesting, & saleable Book', a comparative work on 'The British Empire & its Inhabitants at the Beginning of the reigns of George III & George IV'.[34]

His financial troubles to some degree were bound up with the entangled affairs of his wife. Ward was told one version that Mrs Gaskell's daughters, Meta and Julia, had heard from some source and come to believe many years after the fact: 'Sometimes she went to visit her father in Chelsea he had married again – a bad step mother who [went?] into debt (bailiff &c) These were very sad visits for EG'. The bailiff sounds a melodramatic touch, but was not unlikely. Just a few years before Richard Brinsley Sheridan had written in desperation to Samuel Rogers that bailiffs were 'going to put the carpets out of the window, and break into Mrs. S.'s room and *take me*'.[35] Stevenson could have been in similar straits. As he wrote to William Blackwood on 7 March, probably in 1822, apologising for not sending copy and for a silence of some months,

> You are of course aware that Mrs Stevenson, before her marriage, was in partnership with her Sister: on her marriage [1814] a settlement of their concerns took place, which was considered final. Towards the close of last year however, circumstances occurred, which rendered it absolutely necessary that all their joint concerns should be again gone into: & as on many accounts, it was desirable that they should not be submitted to a stranger, I was compelled to undertake the task.

The money Catherine Stevenson and her sister had lent their brother Dr Thomson had presumably been repaid by this point. The allusion to new circumstances remains unexplained. Stevenson continues,

> It has occupied all my leisure time for two months. that is, ever since I last sent you MS. & this you will not be surprized at, when the nature of the task, & my comparative inexperience are considered.
> When I got your letter, I was just on the point of closing this troublesome & unpleasant business: & till I had actually closed it, I did not like to write to you.

This letter heralds a series of appeals for money to his old friend William Blackwood in the 1820s. He must have been earning about £300 a year on his progressive scale at the Treasury by this time, but from what he kept on writing to Blackwood about debts falling due, he was in a state of near-desperation for several years before his death in early 1829. There is no hint of this whatsoever in his obituary. Yet as Elizabeth came into her early teens, she must have become more and more aware of the infinitely depressing state of her father and the little household in Chelsea. Nor was there any sign that her brother John was going to revive the family fortunes in the land of opportunity.[36]

For the sons of poor men, and especially those who desired to make obscenely large fortunes, India beckoned as it had since the seventeenth century. Some were avaricious rogues, like Sir Matthew Mite in Samuel Foote's play of 1773, *The Nabob*, a term that became standard. Others were more scrupulous. Maria Edgeworth tells how the Princeps family had six sons prospering there – two were merchants, two underwriters; the others an engineer and an essayer at the mint. Four of the boys had been through a regular course of education at the East India college at Haileybury near Hertford:

Mrs. Marcet assures me that there are no young better informed better princi-
pled or better conducted than those who now go out as Writers to India. With
the danger to their morals much of the danger for their health has decreased.
They are all in good health and speak without any horror of the climate.

Maria gave a description of the intake derived from, amongst others, the
Reverend Thomas Malthus, the Professor of history and political economy.
They preferred to take boys at sixteen years of age.[37]

John Stevenson was by 1820 in his early twenties, and seems to have
attended some sort of institution in London. His next two letters to Elizabeth,
the first addressed to Miss Stevenson, Mrs. Lumbs, Heath, Knutsford, continue
the pedagogic theme (this is the letter that refers to Hume's History), but also
talk of his drill from seven till eight in the morning, the need to be 'in the city'
for navigation at ten, fencing from four till five and dancing from six till seven.
'Ask my aunt if she ever read Moliere's Cit turned Gentleman', he quipped in
the first letter; 'this account will put her in mind of it'. He also sent Mrs Lumb
a comically ornate hairdressser's advertisement from the papers in return for
some verses she had sent him, and told his sister that he had sent her seal and
a small work box, 'which I hope you will keep in remembrance of me ... A
good long letter will be as acceptable a present as you can send me', ending
with a reminder to her to answer a letter from Isabella as soon as she had time.
It is possible that Elizabeth Stevenson came up from Knutsford on this
occasion to see her brother off on his first long voyage as a free mariner. Her
daughter Marianne said her mother told her that 'she could only just
remember her brother when he went to sea', and came up from Knutsford to
London to wish him goodbye; but if so, John's letters give no indication.[38]

His second letter was written from Portsmouth on 12 June, where his ship
was detained by contrary winds, which prevented them from setting course for
Madeira in the usual way after leaving the Channel.[39] Though this letter could
belong to either 1820 or 1826, *The Calcutta Kalendar and Post Office
Directory, For 1821* (under November 1820 arrivals) shows that John sailed as
a free mariner on a ship called the *Lady Ráffles*, an extra ship hired for the
season, along with colonels, a major of light dragoons, a captain of native
infantry, medical men and cadets. Captain James Coxwell's log lists the names
of half-a-dozen young ladies amongst the twenty-four passengers: two Miss
Angelos, Miss Matthews, Miss Neate, Miss Wyatt and Miss Hawkins, together
with another free mariner, Simpson Catt. 'The Weather looking so very wild',
as Captain Coxwell noted in his log, and prevailing winds from the south-west
in the channel did not prevent the initiation of shipboard pleasures designed
to while away a long voyage. 'We are very gay', wrote John, 'having a band
who play tunes a great part of the day in fine weather and we have dances in
the Evening'. They eventually sailed from Portsmouth on 14 June 1820.[40]

Such entertainment should not disguise the dangers so easily dismissed in
Maria Edgeworth's letter. The captain's log records a ship's boy, James

Whitney, falling overboard in July and drowning despite the lowering of a boat and every effort made to save him. An able seaman was also drowned on the way out. Even when the ship reached India safely, Coxwell had to record a number of deaths amongst his crew as well as several 'Run at Calcutta'. They ran from one set of perils into another. In 1823 Bishop Reginald Heber, a connection of the Leycesters of Toft and the Stanleys of Alderley, left England to become Bishop of Calcutta. In 1824 his chaplain died of fever in Dacca, then his physician died suddenly, and he himself, often ill and overworked, died in Trichinopoly two years later. More than spicy breezes blew soft o'er Ceylon's isle.[41]

Whilst John was at sea, his father gave Blackwood an account of the Queen Caroline pains-and-penalties bill that was introduced before the House of Lords in July 1820. He displayed the expected loyalty to his patron as the long process dragged its slow length through the summer and autumn:

> Lord Lauderdales speech is regarded as the best against the Queen & Lord Greys for her. The former I believe made many Converts: & his way of considering the case as made out by her own witnesses was certainly the least objectionable.
>
> After all, it is, & is likely to be a dreadful business, & has gone far to loosen the ties between nearly all classes of people & the Governmt: in the City, those who were the staunch Ministerialists exclaim loudly against it.

The Clerk to the Privy Council was not so impressed: 'Lord Lauderdale made a violent speech the other day', he wrote on 15 October, 'and paid himself in it a great many compliments.' Sir Henry Holland used to tell a story against Lauderdale, who at one stage suggested that one of the Queen's associates must have been a vulgar person, for she spoke in a provincial dialect. An opposition member immediately asked if the lady spoke Italian with as broad an accent as the noble Earl spoke his native tongue.

Galt based some of *The Ayrshire Legatees* upon the trial. A supporter of Queen Caroline, Dr Pringle, is made to say:

> I was in the House of Lords when her majesty came down for the last time, and saw her handed up the stairs by the usher of the black-rod, a little stumpy man, wonderful particular about the rules of the House, inasmuch that he was almost angry with me for stopping at the stair-head. The afflicted woman was then in great spirits, and I saw no symptoms of the swelled legs that Lord Lauderdale, that jooking man, spoke about, for she skippit up the stairs like a lassie. But my heart was wae for her when it was all over ...

Stevenson was as close as Galt to these events, and though we do not know what he thought of the way in which Galt exploited them in *The Ayrshire Legatees*, he could be generous about *The Entail*: 'I have read & am much pleased with Mr Galt's Book; tho' the Annals are still my favourite ...'[42]

Caroline's legal advisers, Brougham and Denman, and radicals like Matthew Wood and Burnett were for the Queen; older Whigs like Lords

Hutchinson and Lauderdale were against her and on friendly terms with George IV. Some, like Grey, James Mackintosh and Lord John Russell, possibly a majority, were undecided and formed a 'judging group'. Stevenson does not mention the evidence given on her behalf by Sir Henry Holland, and we might guess that the remains of his connection with the Knutsford Hollands were weakened by his position in the train of Lauderdale. The whole country followed the trial. Mobs gathered daily outside Parliament, the Queen's counsel, Brougham, was devastating in cross-examination, government majorities were declining all the time. Eventually the bill was dropped. Professionally, for Stevenson at the Treasury, it was taking valuable time – it was on this occasion that he promised Blackwood to write at the rate of two sheets a week at least – 'when this Queens business is at an end'.[43]

By November 1820 John had at length reached Calcutta, 'after a most tedious passage of five months and a half', about which he has little to say, apart from a mention of the two drownings and the capture of two immense sharks, so large that he could insert his head and shoulders between their jaws.[44] The young ladies aboard cannot have been too diverting, or interested in him. His journal letter of 29 November to his young sister, almost all about India, is long and highly coloured – he writes of 'tigers, alligators, and snakes of the largest size', dead bodies of men, women and children floating down the Ganges and funeral pyres. He was impressed with the 'most magnificent country houses or rather Palaces' and botanical gardens, a river twice the breadth of the Thames and as crowded with shipping, the leisurely life of the rich Europeans with dozens of servants ('if you have no servant you will most probably dine with Duke Humphrey, as none of the other servants will wait upon you'), caste differentiations amongst the Hindus, carriages, palanquins, mosquitoes and, of course, the weather. He seems there to have joined a ship called the *Earl Kellie*, a ship of 530 tons built in Calcutta in 1815 and belonging to that port. It was preparing to sail to Bombay and after to Canton, then the only port in China open to European trade – 'as difficult to enter as Heaven and as difficult to get out of as Chancery', Charles Reade had joked.[45]

John Stevenson does not mention John Holland's *A System of Geography, With a Series of Geographical Examinations* (1798, etc.), but it would have been useful.[46] He asks for news of Rover, and how her lessons agree with her, and what progress she is making in music. Perhaps the Sharpes had relented. He begs his sister to send him long letters, though she was only ten years old: 'You will have plenty of time and take long paper ... and tell my aunt Ab that as I am at such a distance politicks will be very acceptable in her letters after all domestic news has been related'. Abigail Holland, as is shown by her presentation copies to the chapel at Knutsford of pamphlets by Thomas Thrush, a naval captain who resigned his commission on becoming convinced of the unlawfulness of war and who was, as a Unitarian, in controversy with Archdeacon Wrangham, had a lively interest in current affairs. In response to this plea, she would undoubtedly have written about the second Berwick election and his father's part in it.

William Stevenson had to answer a call that in his son's absence he could not deny. On 15 July 1820 the *Berwick Advertiser* had carried the news that Sir David Milne had been unseated for bribery. St Paul took his place, but died after a brief illness on 1 November. The ensuing parliamentary vacancy was contested in December between Sir Francis Blake and James Balfour of Whittingham House, Dunbar. Balfour, who had accumulated a fortune of £300,000 in less than ten years as supplier of provisions to the British Navy whilst in Indian waters, furnished 'several very excellent letters of Introduction' when John Stevenson went to the East Indies, Stevenson told Blackwood. 'The Nabob', as Balfour came to be called, returned to Britain, married a daughter of Lauderdale in 1815 and purchased the Whittinghame estate in East Lothian. The obligations of the patronage system could not be evaded. Although Stevenson was hard pressed in London and had not intended to go down to Berwick, the election would be a close one, 'as the adverse party had sent, & was sending a great many London Votes'. Stevenson also confessed that he had not visited his home town for six years. He did not think he would be able to get back in less than a fortnight.[47]

The *Berwick Advertiser* reported a buoyant speech Sir David Milne made for Balfour at the new election, in the course of which he unblushingly proposed that all his friends had done wrong 'was paying those Burgesses who came from a distance a little too liberally'. The poll book for 7 December 1820 shows that William duly voted for Balfour. So too did his brother-in-law, George Landles, cooper of Berwick. In vain. Sir Francis Blake won by eleven votes. Berwick was, as John Gladstone discovered a few years later in 1826, 'a dear and slippery representation'. Gladstone won his election by three votes, but was soon unseated for bribery, treating and the like. He never forgave the town. It was, like so many others, providing copy for satirists like Dickens. In his ancient, loyal and patriotic borough of Eatanswill everything was conducted on the most liberal and delightful scale, and Mr Pickwick's servant Sam Weller was paid a shilling a head for 'pumping over independent voters' who had supped too well through the 'mistaken kindness of the gentry' the evening before.

Balfour was far from being cast down by his failure at Berwick. He went on to purchase estates in the Highlands, including Strathconan, and became a deputy-lieutenant and Member of Parliament, leaving a fortune well over a million pounds when he died in 1845. After wholesale evictions had cleared the Strathconan estate in the 1840s, his grandson, Arthur Balfour, was able to invite John Gladstone's famous son to enjoy its excellent sporting facilities.[48]

In January 1821 John Stevenson was still waiting aboard the *Earl Kellie* at Calcutta.[49] It was a 'country ship', he told Elizabeth, meaning that it was a vessel built in India, distinguished by its 'golden-hued' sails. The Calcutta vessels carried rice to the west from Bengal to Madras, or opium and other goods to the east, finishing at Canton. John reported that his ship was entirely manned by lascars who did not speak English, were given less time for their meals and had to work for much longer hours as well as on Sundays. (The captain of the *Lady Raffles* made a point of recording in his log every Sunday that no work had been done.) Designed for speed these vessels were often heavily armed. Though reasonable seamen, lascars were not inclined to fight and sepoys were often carried for this purpose. An English captain and a few other officers were regarded as essential, if expensive. John had to work hard, but 'taking it all together' he believed he would like the service very much when he was better acquainted with Bengali, he claimed.[50]

This is not entirely credible. His narrative displays a degree of sturdy, insular distaste for native mores and customs: 'They never use spoons and it is certainly rather disgusting to see seven or eight of them sitting round a small earthen pot filled with rice and curry and by turns putting their hand in, taking out a handful and pushing it into their mouths with their thumbs'. The lively memoirs of a soldier who was carried in one of the country vessels ('a fine class of ships, and of considerable tonnage') a few years later provide a rather more acceptable reason for revulsion: the type of cargoes carried enticed cockroaches, scorpions, tarantulas and enormous centipedes.[51]

John had bought a piece of muslin for Elizabeth, but added that he had been too busy to go ashore to purchase it himself. He claimed to be 'very much disappointed and even alarmed' at not hearing from Elizabeth or any of his friends since his arrival, begged for good long letters from his aunts at Knutsford – 'Remember how delighted I shall be to receive them and let yours be long likewise' – and again asked after Rover. The life he had adopted could not have been more active and open-air, but these letters home intimate something unexpected. He was not really a man of action at all. During the long sea voyages of weeks or months on end, he was finding that much of his emotional existence was either inward and literary or centred upon his family in England. The young man who cut an awkward figure on a dance-floor did not take after the dashing and legendary Clive of India, whose mother was a Gaskell and who as a boy is said to have appalled the Hollands by leaping from one ball of a gatepost at Sandlebridge to its fellow. Nor are there any signs that John discovered in his eastern career the secret of Warren Hastings's love of Indians and affection for their country.[52]

NOTES

1 KUL: Wedgwood 57-31896, SCH to JW, London, 26 January 1814; Mrs Gordon, *The Home Life of Sir David Brewster*, 3rd edn, Edinburgh, 1881, pp. 37, 43, 53-4; Morell and Thackray, *Gentlemen of Science: Early Years*, p. 534. LUBL's copy of Brewster's *Encyclopaedia*, once owned by the Leeds Philosophical and Literary Society, is in the original parts.

2 Cockburn, *Memorials,* ed. Miller, pp. 20-4, 169-70; Butler, *Edgeworth,* p. 198; *Edgeworth Letters,* p. 147.

3 See BL: Add. MSS 34, 611, ff. 69, 198, 219, 242, 337, WS to MN, [recd]28 May 1814, 12 April [1815], 20 May [1815], 21 July 1815, 6 February 1816.

4 Tredrey, *House of Blackwood*, pp. 22-4, 245. See also David Finkelstein, 'Early nineteenth-century Scottish publishing', *GSJ*, VIII, 1994, pp. 82-4.

5 References below are by date only; all but one of the Stevenson letters used have been indexed in a single NLS volume. See also Alan Bell, 'Some recent acquisitions of publishing archives by the National Library of Scotland', *PH*, III, 1978, pp. 39-40.

6 NLS: WS to WB, Treasury, 3 February [18]17; for franks see 8 November [1820].

7 John Seed, 'Joyce and radical intelligentsia', pp. 104-5; *BL Cat.;* McLachlan, pp. 253-4; *Letters*, pp. 148, 902.

8 See *NSTC* I. i: S3816, K447. K448 is Kerr's *General View of the Agriculture of Berwick*, 1809, part of Sir John Sinclair's series.

9 NLS: WS to WB, all from Treasury, 25 July [1817], [c. April 1818], 22 November [1821], 11 June [1822] and 23 December [1822].

10 Roger L. Tarr, *Thomas Carlyle: A Descriptive Bibliography*, Oxford, 1989, pp. 404-5; J. R. McCulloch, *The Literature of Political Economy* (1845), repr. LSE no. 5, London, 1938, p. 148; *Carlyle Letters*, I, pp. 229, 373, 377, 379, 384, 396; NLS: WS to WB, Treasury, 22 November [1821]. G. B. Tennyson, in 'Unnoted Encyclopaedia articles by Carlyle', *ELN*, I, 1963-64, p. 111, calls attention to the dual authorship.

11 NLS: WS to WB, Treasury, 3 February [18]17; 8 November [1820]; John O. Hayden, ed. *Scott: The Critical Heritage*, London, 1970, p. 9; Sutherland, *Scott*, pp. 194-200; Tredrey, *House of Blackwood*, pp. 24-39.

12 JGS: two identical TSS, JS to ECS, Beaufort row, 27 and 28 December [1819]; address at end: 'Miss Stevenson' (Copy of the earliest letter to her to have been preserved).

13 IOLR: L/MAR/B, ships' logs 1702-1856; *East-India Register and Directory, For 1820*, London, 2nd edn, private ship licences; Parkinson, *Trade in the Eastern Seas*, pp. 142-5, 170. I am most grateful to Tim Thomas of IOLR for his expert assistance.

14 Dandeker, 'Naval officer in English society', *BJS*, XXIX, 1978, pp. 311-12; Checkland, *The Gladstones*, pp. 135-6, 168, 284. See a similar case in *The Journal of Sir Walter Scott*, ed. W. E. K. Anderson, Oxford, 1932, pp. 209, 251.

15 IOLR: B/170, Court of Directors, p. 1200; Gérin, p. 33, (but JS is not in the Bonds vols 1819-20). On 18 October 1820 Bombay was notified (E/4/1040, p. 85) and on 1 November 1820 Madras (I/4/924, p. 579).

16 Philip Lawson, *The East India Company: A History*, London and New York, 1993, pp. 103-5, 127, 141-3; John Keay, *The Honourable Company: A History of the English East India Company*, London (1991), 1993, p. 451.

17 JGS: three TSS, JS to ECS, Beaufort Row, Sunday [19 March 1820], annotated 'MISS STEVENSON. 1820'. Two copies lack everything after the signature; otherwise very minor variants.

18 R. G. Thorne, *The House of Commons 1790-1820*, 5 vols, London, 1986, I, pp. 43, 80; II, pp. 307-10; J. Holladay Philbin, *Parliamentary Representation, 1832: England and Wales*, New Haven, Conn., 1965, pp. 142-3; Gilmour, *Riot, Risings and Revolution*, p. 301.

19 *Col. St. Paul of Ewart*, ed. G. Butler, 1911, I, p. clxxi. For Milne see Clowes, *Royal Navy: A History*, VI (with engraved portrait).

20 MC to C. Fauriel, Cold Overton, 23 June 1826 and 1 July 1827 (Lesser, *Mary Clarke Mohl*, pp. 71-3).

21 BRO: B1/25. John is still listed in the 1842 printed *Freemen's Roll of the Burgesses or Freemen* as 'Mariner EICS'. His death or disappearance could not have been reported.

22 ECG wrote to him in 1853 when he was vicar of Leighton Buzzard. See CUL: Add 7348/10/19, ECG to J. M. F. Ludlow, Plymouth Grove, 25 June [1853].

23 *The East-India Register and Directory, For 1825*, London, 1st edn, Bengal, p. 131 (rank dating from 18 February 1823); *Letters*, p. 272 (perhaps the natural son of Joseph was no longer living); Ward Notebook, f. 7 verso (in Meta's hand; it was noted that John and William were dead). See also A. W. Ward, *Collected Papers*, Cambridge, 1921, IV, p. 416n.

24 *Letters*, pp. 272, 863; Chapple, 'Five early letters', pp. 6, 15. See also p. 13 above (Mrs Robina Robertson).

25 By S. Cottin and J. H. B. de Saint-Pierre respectively.

26 The second edition of W. R. Bowles' translation, London 1815, cites in its preliminaries approval from the *Edinburgh Review*. See also pp. 9, 11, 78, 143.

27 Cf. Angela Leighton, *Victorian Women Poets: Writing Against the Heart*, New York, etc., 1992, pp. 24-31, on Felicia Hemans' poetry and Madame de Staël's *Corinne* (1807).

28 Galt's name is pencilled into the Chelsea rate book for Lady day 1820 (CPL). He had married on 20 April 1813 and three boys were born by 6 September 1817 (Jennie W. Aberdein, *John Galt*, Oxford and London, 1936, pp. 79, 90).

29 I have drawn extensively upon Gordon, *John Galt*, p. 20 et seq.

30 Uglow, pp. 21-2; [Thomson], *Recollections of Literary Characters and Celebrated Places*, London, 1854, II, pp. 100-5.

31 Richard and Edward Garnett, *The Life of W. J. Fox*, London, 1910, p. 52; Thomas Dibdin, *Reminiscences of a Literary Life*, London, 1836, II, pp. 737-8 (see p. 275 below); *Wellesley Index*, III, p. 562; IV, p. 802; Samuel Smiles, *A Publisher and His Friends: Memoir and Correspondence of John Murray*, ed. Thomas Mackay, London, 1911, p. 122; TCC to WB, 52 Charlotte Street, Portland Place, 15 January 1828 (NLS: MS 4021, pp. 106-9 verso).

32 See John Galt, *Annals of the Parish*, ed. James Kinsley, [1967], Oxford, New York, 1986, pp. vii-ix.

33 NLS: MS 4005, f. 27, JG to WB, London 22 June 1820; MS 4007, f. 228, BWP to WB, [?1821]; Gordon, *Galt*, pp. 41-64.

34 NLS: copy letter books (chronological order); WS to WB, Treasury, 19 October 1821.

35 Ward Notebook, f. 7; *The Letters of Richard Brinsley Sheridan*, ed. Cecil Price, Oxford, 1966, III, p. 246.

36 NLS: WS to WB, Treasury, 7 March [1822]; Sainty, *Treasury Officials*, p. 39.

37 Peter Mudford, *Birds of a Different Plumage: A Study of British-Indian Relations From Akbar to Curzon*, London, 1974, pp. 92, 109; ME to FE, 7 January 1822 and 23 January 1822 (*Edgeworth Letters*, pp. 312-13, 328-9).

38 JGS: three TSS (light violet one has a superior text), JS to ECS, [London], 7 May [1820]. See also Rubenius, p. 254, who cites a copy of MA's letter in LUBL.

39 JGS: three almost identical TSS, JS to ECS, Portsmouth, Monday 12 June [1820], address at end: 'Miss Stevenson'. The 12 June fell on a Monday in 1820 and 1826.

40 IOLR: L/MAR/B/106A, log 28 April 1820-30 August 1821 (incl. return voyage); Parkinson, *Trade in the Eastern Seas*, p. 99; *Calcutta Kalendar*, Appx, p. 106; *East-India Register and Directory for 1820*, 2nd edn, London, n. d., pull-out list.

41 Derrick Hughes, *Bishop Sahib: A Life of Reginald Heber*, Worthing, 1986, pp. 72, 83, 88, 113, 177-80; Malcolm Barnes, *Augustus Hare*, London, Boston, Sydney, 1984, pp. 13-15. See also Uglow, pp. 227, 244.

42 NLS: WS to WB, 8 November [1820], Treasury, 23 December [1822]; *Greville Journal*, I, p. 39 and n.; Galt qu. John MacQueen, *The Rise of the Historical Novel*, The Enlightenment and Scottish Literature, II, Edinburgh, 1989, p. 153.

43 Christopher Hibbert, *George IV: Regent and King, 1811-1830*, London, 1973, chapters 11-12; New, *Brougham*, chapter 13, 'The Queen's Trial'; Ford, *Henry Brougham*, pp. 319-44; Austin Mitchell, *The Whigs in Opposition 1815-1830*, Oxford, 1967, p. 145.

44 JGS: three TSS (superior text dated '1821'), JS to ECS, Calcutta, 29 November [?1820];

address at end: 'Miss E. Stevenson / 29 Nov. 1821 / No. 2 -' The next letter (see p. 231 below) dated Calcutta, 15 January 1821.

45 See Parkinson, *Trade in the Eastern Seas*, pp. 31-5, 57-8, 331-2, 343-6; Mudford, *British-Indian Relations*, pp. 68-73 (good illustrs); *Bengal Almanac, and Annual Directory, For 1822*, Calcutta, n. d., list of shipping: *EK* owned by Cruttenden, Mackillop & Co; Captain I. Edwards in *1823*, R. Edwards in *1824*.

46 MCL has *A General Atlas* (1799), owned by 'C[atherine?] & A[bigail?] Holland', passed on to the Gaskell family in their Dover Street home by 1842. I am grateful to the MCL Language and Literature Librarian, Christine Lingard, for a great deal of help with my research.

47 Davis, *Manchester College*, pp. 81-2; *Col. St. Paul*, ed. Butler, p. clxxi; Thorne, *House of Commons*, V, p. 92; NLS: WS to WB, 2 December [1820]. This election is not listed in Lamont-Brown, *Berwick*.

48 Checkland, *The Gladstones*, pp. 156-7, 343; Dickens, *Pickwick Papers*, 1836-37, chapter 13; Richards, *Highland Clearances*, I, pp. 394.

49 JGS: three TSS (light violet one with better text), JS to ECS, Ship Earl Kellie, Calcutta, 15 January 1821, address at end: 'Miss Stevenson, Cheshire'.

50 See Parkinson, *Trade in the Eastern Seas*, chapter 11, 'The Country Trade'. William Carey had produced a Bengali grammar and three-volume dictionary (Mudford, *British-Indian Relations*, p. 108).

51 Doveton, *Reminiscences of the Burmese War*, p. 11.

52 *Letters*, pp. 75-6 ('when I was a child his exploits were traditional in the neighbourhood'); Mudford, *British-Indian Relations*, pp. 74-6, 82-8.

13

The education of an author

THERE ARE MANY indications in William Stevenson's letters to Blackwood that he was under continuous strain. Sensibly, he took inexpensive holidays that were probably very necessary for his health, physical and mental. A letter of 1824 shows that he had kept up a habit of his student days: 'In my rambles – for my annual journeys are generally rambles & on foot – I visited the Isle of Wight – particularly that singular & beautiful tract called the Undercliff – the New Forest, & the Isles of Jersey & Guernsey.' Victorian intellectuals like Leslie Stephen defined Muscular Christianity as the duty to 'fear God and walk a thousand miles in a thousand hours' – not with any particular object, unless 'statistical walking' could be regarded as a way of transcending lesser theological differences. However, one journey William took, probably in 1821, seems to have had a special purpose.

In a letter of 31 July he revealed to Blackwood that he intended to go into Cheshire about the 8 or 10 of September and would return in the beginning of October. As far as we can tell, Elizabeth's education was about to be continued away from Knutsford. There is no doubt that Elizabeth's father would be the guiding spirit, as R. L. Edgeworth had been for his daughter. 'I had not for some years the happiness to be at home with him', Maria Edgeworth wrote. 'But even during the years that I was absent from him his influence was the predominating power in my early education.' Whatever family connections there were with schools at Bath and at Liverpool, William Stevenson's choice of a boarding school elsewhere must have been decisive.[1]

Elizabeth's eleventh birthday was evidently significant. A copy of the second edition in two volumes of a work called *The Female Mentor; or, Select Conversations*, published by T. Cadell, jr and W. Davies in 1798, has recently come to light. On the flyleaf of the first volume is a date and inscription: 'E. C. Stevenson / from her Father / on her birth day / Sep 29 – 1821'.[2] It was evidently one of several rather old-fashioned gifts. Besides Hannah Greg's *Monitor*, we know that William Cowper's *Poems* was presented 'by her father and mother' in 1823, and they inscribed the 1821 edition of Thomas Gray's *Works* for her on 2 August 1825.[3] The editor of *The Female Mentor* was

'Honoria' ('Mrs Philips' is pencilled below) and the original dedication was to a Mrs M. Hartley, Belvedere, Bath, dated London 10 January 1793. Belvedere then housed the school run by Sophia Lee, before Frances Whittaker appeared on the scene. The second volume has a dedication dated 30 June 1796 to Elizabeth, Baroness Amherst, 'as a testimony of esteem and gratitude'. What connection William Stevenson had, if any, with these circles in Bath is unknown, but his general educational intention is patent.[4]

In *The Female Mentor* Honoria is supposed to be the daughter of Amanda, 'the mother of a numerous offspring', who was accustomed to teach both her own children and those of her friends.[5] As they grew older, they 'gradually swelled into an improving and rational society' that met every fortnight, many of them being 'young ladies just entering the world'. This may all be a convenient fiction, though it resembles at a slightly more exalted social level the Duodecimo society Hannah Greg began a decade or so later. The conversations of this Bath coterie, embellished with numerous quotations in prose and verse, form the substance of the work.

Conversation 8, 'On Novels', is typical. Young men might profit from the reading of novels by having 'feelings of virtuous love' awakened, Amanda declared. Young women should of course avoid them. But, she concluded 'with a smile', she might allow them to read 'the Female Quixote, in which a rich, amiable, and beautiful young woman had so filled her head with romances, that she fancied every man who approached her a lover in disguise'. The theme of youth entering the world was commonplace in the eighteenth century, as was satire of female susceptibility born of delicacy and a desire to please. Charlotte Lennox's *The Female Quixote*, published in 1752, made fun of naive earlier fictions of this type. Jane Austen's *Northanger Abbey*, written about the turn of the century, is a more classic instance.[6]

In Conversation 10, 'On Learned Ladies', Amanda proposes a model of disguised knowledge to intelligent young women. Their minds should be formed by the noble and pathetic; they should enrich their imaginations with the fine arts and at least understand modern languages. Men are said to be inclined to set undesirable limits to female acquirements – which ideally could extend to reading Homer and Virgil in the original and writing verses. A lady would therefore 'carefully keep out of view all pedantry of learning, and let her expressions run though the easy vein of unpremeditated language.' She should know the 'technical terms of art' – and gracefully ask gentlemen to explain them. Family duties should in any case always come first. Jenny Uglow has rightly stressed the conflicts to which this kind of dual allegiance gave rise in the 1790s, when even Mary Wollstonecraft made motherhood primary.[7]

The roots of some of these views go back at least into the late seventeenth century. In Conversation 11 on the subject of female education the author cites *Sur l'Education des Filles* by François Fénelon, whose *Télémaque*, translated into English by Smollett and others, had given currency to the word 'mentor' in both languages. *L'Education des Filles* is raided for maxims about the raising of children: 'Be as indulgent to them as possible; be not irritated by their faults, but pity their weaknesses. Suffer them to be gay and familiar before you, that you may know their real dispositions', and so on. This book by a Catholic bishop, 'living, too, during the reign of that tyrant bigot Lewis 14th', found new admirers in liberal Unitarian circles. The diary Elizabeth Gaskell kept when Marianne and Meta were children in effect provides many illustrations of its precepts put into practice.[8]

Elizabeth Stevenson was then just eleven years old, but this conventional birthday gift from her father, like Mrs Lumb's on the same occasion, was in all probability intended to be taken with her when she left Knutsford for a boarding school in Warwickshire run by connections of the second Mrs Stevenson. There, suitably primed, she was fortunate enough to receive one of the best educations available to girls – for life, as it were.

Ward was told that 'from 14-16 or 15-17 She went to school to Miss Byerley at Stratford on Avon where she used to be left in the holidays – was taught Latin there, was a good Latin scholar'. Mrs Chadwick at first gave similar information, though she made it clear that Maria Byerley was not alone but assisted by her younger sisters. By the time of her second edition Chadwick had heard from former pupils. She altered her text to read 'about fourteen years of age' and a period of three years. Aina Rubenius was the first to produce evidence that Elizabeth was at school with the Byerley sisters for no less than five years. (Her early study entitled *The Woman Question in Mrs. Gaskell's Life and Works* is a mine of, for once, accurately documented information.) It is worth noting that when the works of Anna Barbauld were published in 1825, Lucy Aikin's memoir quoted letters in which Mrs Barbauld had insisted that the years between nine to thirteen or fourteen were the best time for a girl to go away to school. Thereafter, the kind of *savoir-faire* she would need until 'she is married or likely to be so' should be learned 'partly at home, and partly by visits to genteel families'.[9]

If Elizabeth was at the Byerleys' school from 1821, she went first when it was at Barford. The father of the Byerley sisters, a relation and partner of Josiah Wedgwood, had died in 1810. The partnership was dissolved, but one son remained as a salaried employee and some provision was made for Byerley's large family, for his debts turned out to be larger than expected. With a loan from Josiah and an allowance from his sisters, the daughters established a school for young ladies, at first in Warwick itself. Frances and Maria were assisted by Ann, Elizabeth, Jane Margaret and Katharine in this courageous enterprise. Frances and Elizabeth did not teach for long, and Katharine also gave up teaching when she married, at the age of twenty-two, William Stevenson's friend and new brother-in-law, Anthony Todd Thomson, at Barford church on 1 February 1820. Dr Thomson's first wife had died in 1815; he was then forty-two years of age, a widower with a son and two daughters. Within a year of the second marriage a son was born to the Thomsons, followed by the two more sons and five daughters who survived him.[10]

Unfortunately, no records of the school have been preserved for the year 1821 (after the move to Barford in 1817), but if Elizabeth had been sent there in that year on Katharine's recommendation, it was not altogether wise. Josiah Wedgwood, we notice, sent his own two youngest daughters, Fanny and Emma (called 'the Dovelies'), to Mrs Mayer's finishing school at Paddington Green, London, in January 1822. On 12 October he wrote to Maria at Barford that circumstances would force him to bring to an end the allowance he had till then made to her mother. Maria wrote courteously in stoic acceptance of his decision four days later, but on 5 November 1822 Katharine sent from 91 Sloane Street a letter written in her neat, small, fluent hand that even now, as one peers at its sadly faded writing, startles by its uncompromising pungency of statement.[11] Her brothers could not assist: they were themselves in need of help. One might survive on few hundred pounds capital borrowed from her husband, another was merely a clerk in a mercantile house. As for her brothers-in-law, William Parkes (husband of Frances) was 'reduced to poverty' with six children to care for and the other, William Lowndes (husband of Elizabeth), was earning very little at the bar. She continues,

> Mr. Thomson will, I am *sure* do something for my Mother, whose ill-health he has witnessed, as she was very ill last year at our house; & I need not say, that I would sooner starve myself, than see her in want. But he *cannot* support her entirely; for although he has, by industry, &, I may say, by talent, raised himself in his profession, & has an excellent practice, yet he has five children, & a Sister whom he supports entirely.

Could this be the sister whose affairs were entangled with Elizabeth Stevenson's stepmother, causing her father such stress in the previous March? It looks like it. After a passionate appeal to Wedgwood to continue the support – which drew a remarkably speedy but very dusty response: 'You were too young at the period of the dissolution of the partnership to form any just opinion upon the case, and you are probably not better informed upon that matter now' – Katherine's letter ended rather weakly with 'It gave me sincere pleasure to hear a few days since, from Dr. & Mrs Holland, of Mrs Wedgwood's convalescence.' This is a reminder that Henry Holland's very recently married wife was a Caldwell of Linley Wood, not far from the Wedgwoods' Maer Hall. Though the connection with Katharine Thomson seems more significant in this context, Wedgwoods and Byerleys were also relations of the Hollands in Sandlebridge and Knutsford.[12]

Fortunately, Katherine's trust in her sisters soon proved to be justified – and her rhetoric a little hollow. By early 1823 the school was flourishing again, as successful as the contemporary school in Edgbaston run by Sarah Bache and Phoebe Penn, where they too united 'Mental and Moral Culture' with 'a greater Attention to elegant Accomplishments'. Moreover, the Byerley family were in a position to rally round their mother and the invalid daughter who lived with her. With noteworthy sensitivity Maria suggested to Josiah on

9 August 1823 that various separate contributions should still be paid through him:

> I believe the motive that influences us is not a romantic or useless feeling or I would not trouble you with it. It appears to us very important that my mother as she advances in life should have no cause for lessening the few comforts she at present enjoys, & I feel that if she felt herself in a state of dependence upon her children or friends that her mind would never be at rest.

This certainly dates from the period when Elizabeth was at the school, and it shines with a quality of mind and spirit that could hardly be missed in a small establishment of some thirty or forty girls.[13]

The school had begun to falter in its Warwick period, but the sisters had resolved never to separate – 'as our plan is to teach every thing without masters', Maria wrote to Wedgwood, with either female independence or feminine delicacy. She also told him about the offer of the much more convenient house at Barford, a pleasant Greek-Revival mansion, its two-storey frontage made imposing by unfluted, attached Ionic columns, four round flanked by two square. Its lawns and gardens were let, but the school retained an exclusive right of walking in them. Inside there was a large mirror over the fireplace to lighten the principal room and its ornate ceiling. A long room facing the garden to the east might have been the schoolroom and above were bedrooms and attics shared by the girls. It was a usefully compact house, she noted, large enough to take twenty-five boarders but allowing them to employ no more than three indoor servants and a laundry woman.[14]

Barford was a village with grassy meadows tucked into a curve of the river Avon where a stone bridge crossed it, about three miles south of Warwick. It had an old ('dilapidated') parish church of St Peter, which the girls attended on Sundays, and an unpretentious parsonage. Opposite the church was the little cottage in which the farm workers' leader Joseph Arch was born, in 1826. He is eloquent on his mother's refusal to pay deference to or receive charity soup from 'a most despotic parson's wife, a kind of would-be lady pope'. Long afterwards he claimed in his autobiography to have become disaffected at the age of seven, when he saw his father with all the other 'poor agricultural labourers in their smock frocks' go up last to communion. Were they preceded in the 1820s by the Byerley sisters and their girls filing out of their rented pews? A major landowner in the district was the Byerleys' banker, Edward Greaves of Avon Side house, Barford, who was for a time Arch's employer. Edward's brother John was to become connected with the Hollands by marriage.[15]

Maria, Ann and Jane Byerley still needed all their strength of mind, for 1824 brought a severe dispute with the landlord of Barford House, which involved notice to quit with many expensive repairs to be done upon removal. A financial compromise was eventually reached, but the remaining three sisters removed their school altogether, renting an eighteenth-century mansion called Avonbank next to the church in Stratford-upon-Avon, a few miles from Barford. The building was a fine one, with a covered passage to its main entrance in the fashionable street known as Old Town. A watercolour shows two projecting wings and a steep-pitched roof with elegant dormers, the whole surrounded by trees above which rises the spire of the church. Ten demure young ladies in pairs are about to follow their mistress into the house. Behind it were lawns and an underground boathouse with brick arches though which boats could emerge onto the river.[16]

A sketch book of Jessie Scott, who was at school with Elizabeth, contains a copy of Dr Johnson's letter to Lord Chesterfield, and several pleasing pencil sketches of Avonbank's garden. One, captioned 'Avonbank Green House', depicts a large building with what looks like a statue of an eagle on its pediment. In others, school and church, almost lost in trees, are seen from a river viewpoint, very like that of the engraving in Smith's *Warwickshire* of 1830, reproduced as a frontispiece to *A Quest of Ladies*. This has the legend, 'Late the Seat of Lord Middleton, now of Miss Byerleys'. Most interesting of all is Jessie Scott's view of the river and the church in which Shakespeare was buried, annotated, 'Done with Mrs A. T. Thomson'. The use of her married name suggests that Katharine's connection with the school did not lapse after her marriage, even though she was living in London. She helped keep unwanted male teachers at bay, presumably on occasional visits to Stratford and her sisters.[17]

The three sisters took possession of their imposing new residence in May 1824. By August 1827 Sarah Byerley, the invalid sister, could tell Wedgwood that they were beginning 'this half year's *toils* in good spirits as their house is quite filled'. The 1831 census records fifty-seven females in residence there. It was even rumoured that Avonbank had been considered grand enough for Princess Victoria. Florence Nightingale, too, was taken there on a visit at the age of ten in 1830, though it is notorious that her father considered that he was the only person capable of instructing his clever daughter in Greek, Latin, Italian, mathematics and 'the philosophy of the human mind' (text by Professor Dugald Stewart). A large oval room with high, almost conical ceiling probably served as the schoolroom, whilst the pupils slept above in rooms on the first and second floors.

It was very far from being a Yorkshire school at twenty guineas a year and doctor's fees. An itemised bill of 1832 for a Miss Radford of Leeds charges £26 5s 0d for half a year's board and instruction, but includes separate amounts for dancing, drawing, drilling, Italian, French, English and Composition, Writing and Arithmetic, together with a string of extras like linen, hair-dressing, mantua-making, medicine, dental work, travel and seven guineas board for the Christmas holidays. The total came to just over £74. Drilling might have been in declensions, but a comical letter from Lucy Aikin claims that just as French ladies had cast off their stays and *petits talons* after the French revolution, English ladies had learned to march from the drill sergeant and now *stepped out*.[18]

Avonbank's fees were high. When there happened to be employment, Joseph Arch's father earned about ten shillings a week. Joseph himself claims that he received a good basic education in an endowed village school at Barford, but at nine he had to begin work as a bird scarer at fourpence for a twelve-hour day; a year later he became a plough-boy at three shillings a week, the rate still current in Barford thirty years afterwards. All that, however, was on a different plane of existence – Jude the Obscure's. The Reverend Lant Carpenter's school for boys in Bristol charged fees of 100 guineas a year in 1819-21; the Reverend John Relly Beard of Salford charged from 50 to 70 guineas per annum in the 1830s, with extra fees for languages, music, dancing and the use of the library.[19] Similarly, the education of Elizabeth Brand Scott at Avonbank cost altogether about £130 for a year in the 1820s. This sum covered Dancing and Italian at four guineas each, French and Drawing at three, 'Writing and Arithmetic' at a guinea and a half. 'English and Composition' cost one guinea – not as much as wine and carriage hire combined at twenty-five shillings. Pupils like these could only come from the most affluent section of the middle class.[20]

Who paid these considerable fees for Elizabeth over several years? Her father was struggling, desperate for money. There is no indication that he paid anything at all. Perhaps the Byerley sisters were prepared to charge less for a relation by marriage, Anthony Thomson being the brother of the second Mrs Stevenson. And Mrs Lumb, of course, had been left in complete charge of the money that her father had left in her sole control, obviously in informal trust for John and Elizabeth. She could surely, if necessary, make up any shortfall from her own resources.

Latin is not specified in Miss Radford's bill, though Katharine, younger and more brilliant than her sisters, had learnt it from her brother in exchange for teaching him Italian. Chadwick quotes from a letter about Ann by a relative: 'One of the sisters, Ann Byerley, who married a Mr Coltman, was very clever and a good Italian scholar, but deaf as a post'. In Knutsford public library is an old book, entitled *Le Maître Italien dans sa Dernière Perfection ... Par le Sieur De Veneroni*, Nouvelle Edition, Amsterdam, Chez Pierre Brunel, 1713. Once possessed by Francis Willoughby, it is signed by Elizabeth Cleghorn Stevenson. It also seems that Ann Byerley acted as the housekeeper when Elizabeth was at this flourishing school.[21] 'All my life', wrote Sarah Martineau of a similar establishment, 'I have been so thankful to have been to a really first rate and high toned school, and I must always try to persuade parents to send their daughters to school for some period of their life.' On the other hand, Mrs Mayer's finishing school at Paddington Green was regarded by Charles Darwin's younger sister, rightly or wrongly, as a place of 'Incantations & Whippings', and French history never got beyond Charlemagne, for the arrival of each new girl caused them to begin again with Clovis.[22]

Mrs Gaskell once made a cheerfully improbable statement to her eldest daughter Marianne, whose teacher in Hampstead thought she was 'too fond of gaiety', that she herself was 'five years at Miss Byerley's & never drank tea out of the house *once* let alone going to plays etc. etc. etc. etc.' There is one indication that Elizabeth was not confined to the house and grounds of Avonbank in term time. Her first piece of prose to see print, sent to William Howitt in 1838, was a short account of Clopton Hall, based on a visit made one autumn day in the past to the home of one of the narrator's old school-fellows, 'the daughter of a Mr. W –, who then lived at Clopton.' William Howitt told her that the house had been sold to a 'Mr Want of Welcome', who, quite uninterested in Clopton and its traditions, was modernising it. He included the little piece by Elizabeth ('to Howitts disgust said by critics to be the best thing in the book', Ward was told) in his *Visits to Remarkable Places* in 1840.[23]

Miss Wyatt was probably a day pupil, for Clopton Hall was very near Stratford. The Thomsons, too, used to take the pupils abroad for holidays, though we do not know if Elizabeth ever went with them. The only specific date known for such a trip is 1835. There is a letter in which Mrs Gaskell wrote of 'a very happy month with 17 aunts, cousins, and such like' in Aber, North Wales, which might have taken place whilst she was a schoolgirl in the 1820s. It might even have been about the time when Wordsworth walked up the vale of Aber as far as the waterfall and saw 'an odd sight – fifteen milkmaids together, laden with their brimming pails. How cheerful and happy they appeared! and not a little inclined to joke after the manner of the pastoral persons in Theocritus.'[24]

In her second edition Mrs Chadwick quotes from a letter by a near-contemporary of Elizabeth:

> [It] tells of the happy Christmas parties to which the young ladies of Avonbank were invited. One of the houses to which the merry schoolgirls went, is the one in which Miss Marie Corelli now lives – Masoncroft. Many of the pupils spent their holidays at school like Elizabeth Stevenson, on account of the expense of the long journey by stage coach. The Christmas holidays finished on the last day of January.

Marie Corelli used to live, much later of course, in Church Street, Stratford. It is also clear from the context that Chadwick had seen both Miss Radford's bill and a letter by her:

> One of the pupils, writing from Avonbank to her parents at Leeds, says: 'We have been to several parties; one was at Mrs Parkes; we had a very pleasant evening. The next night we went to Mrs. Shirley's. It was "twelfth night," we had a large twelfth cake, and we all drew characters. We had a blind Irish harper to play to us while we danced. He also told us tales which were very amusing, particularly as they were told in Irish. The party broke up about twelve.'

The Parkes reference shows that not all the school's connections were with the established church. The oldest sister, Fanny Byerley, had married William Parkes of a prominent Unitarian family of Warwick in 1811. They were married by Dr Samuel Parr, who was curate of nearby Hatton but also notorious for being a Whig and a staunch friend of dissenters. He attended the Unitarian ordination of William Field at Warwick in 1790, when Belsham gave the charge to the new minister, formerly a fellow student at Daventry of William Stevenson. Priestley preached the sermon.[25] Forced by business failure in 1818 to sell their house in Warwick ('combining the advantages of a Town Residence with the beauties of a country retirement'), William and Fanny Parkes moved first to Bloxham and then to Solihull near Birmingham in 1820. They were now, a son reports, 'very poor, and had a limited supply of servants'. Priestley's granddaughter Elizabeth, 'a woman of great charm, with genial and kindly manners and a gift of vivacious narrative', was to marry the Birmingham politician Joseph Parkes, nephew of William Parkes and son of his brother John, in 1824.[26]

Phyllis Hicks quotes extensively from an elaborate book Fanny Parkes, the first of the sisters into print, published in 1825, *Domestic Duties; or, Instructions to Young Married Ladies, on the Management of Their Households and the Regulation of Their Conduct*. Plain, moral, humane and wise advice was given in two contending voices, as Jenny Uglow notes, one advising young women to suffer and be still, the other stressing their rights as well as duties. Fanny is exactly like Amanda of *The Female Mentor* when she recommends young women to avoid any 'appearance of pedantry'. 'Much of female worth and usefulness consists in negatives', Mrs Greg had written too. 'Light Reading, Drawing, Music, Light and Ornamental Needlework' – diversified by dancing to the harp and amusing Irish tales – are what they should visibly enjoy in the drawing room whatever they studied in private. And always they should remember a simple truth, that though 'the sphere of duty, assigned to women, considered singly, is limited to one family and to one circle in society', their collective influence is incalculable and extended even to 'unborn generations'.[27]

The school had a harp and a grand piano, the latter obtained as early as 1810. Thousands of pianos, at high but not impossible prices, were being manufactured by firms like Broadwood. Young ladies could take advantage of the flood of songs, ballads and simplified transcriptions provided by specialist publishers. Both Jane Byerley and Katharine had been carefully taught to play before they took up teaching and when Jane was about to join the school, Maria told Wedgwood that they would 'venture to undertake the instruction of dancing', though a little later two of the sisters wanted to go to London in the vacation for further instruction.[28]

A small oblong book of about nine by five and a half inches, with forty-six pages ruled for music, is a unique piece of evidence. On the inside cover is written 'E. C. Stevenson – / Avonbank June 15 1825 / Thursday', and all but a few pages are filled with manuscript songs and piano pieces, mostly written in an early hand – the sloping cursive of letters to Harriet Carr in May and August 1832 – but sometimes in imitation print. Here and there are written various names, the majority of these in pencil, some illegible, others too near the edge of the page to be clear. They include Clare Phillips ('Symphony Macbeth'), 'The Cypress Wreath – Copied from Miss Lond', Sophia Smith ('Swiss Valtz'), Louisa Kennett ('Le Garçon Volage'), Louisa Holland, almost certainly the daughter of Swinton and Anne Holland ('Auld Robin Gray'), Mary Anne Eyr<e> ('Blue Bells of Scotland'), Sara Priestley ('Celui qui sut toucher mon coeur') and an Emily, perhaps Hamilton ('Partant pour la Syrie').[29]

The pupils' own musical arrangements are only moderately competent, like the incidental music perhaps composed to open a domestic performance of *Macbeth*,[30] and sometimes crude or plain wrong, such as the monotonic 'Rang [Ranz] des Vaches', which has no name pencilled against it and might therefore be Elizabeth's own. This piece, unlike the others, has a description: 'A song or rather National Air of the Swiss – It was forbidden to be played by the French as it caused the desertion of the Swiss Guards'. According to the *New Grove Dictionary of Music and Musicians*, Swiss *Küher- und Sennenlieder* songs had political implications from early in the century, following a festival near Interlaken in 1805 and the appearance of the first genuine collection of Swiss folksongs, *Acht Schweizer-Kühreihen mit Musik und Text*. By the fourth edition of 1826 it contained seventy-six songs. Sophia Smith's very amateurish 'Swiss Valtz' testifies to the general vogue at the time for such music. The source of Elizabeth's annotation is unknown, but she could have found a model in publications like *The Harmonicon, A Journal of Music*, where in the 1824 issue Charles Dibdin's moving and justly famous 'Tom Bowling' is headed 'Song, The Sailor's Epitaph ... on the death of his brother, Captain Thomas Dibdin'.[31]

Fast, triple-metre peasant dances and songs imitating Alpine folkmusic were internationally popular. Sara Priestley's 'Celui qui sut toucher mon coeur' is annotated 'Tyrolienne'. The setting is on the whole professionally competent. Its few errors might be Sarah's, misreading commercial publications, though Ignaz Moscheles did not bring out the first volume of his *Tyrolese Melodies* until 1827, the year in which the famous Rainer family made their first visit to England. On the other hand, *The Harmonicon* of 1824 contains J. N. Hummel's 'Air, à la Styrienne', which evokes yodelling in the Austrian Alps, and a piece in Elizabeth's music book entitled 'Mozart's Waltz' contains bars in yodelling style – perhaps a kind of uninhibited homage to genius.

Musical compositions of this standard were beyond the capacities of Avonbank's pupils. Similarly, the several Scottish pieces in the book ('Locheil March', 'My lodging is on the cold ground', 'Cease your funning', and 'I'm wearing awa' Jean') were probably taken from commercial sources. A contemporary of her father in Edinburgh, George Thomson, began publishing his collections of national airs in 1793. Burns was one of those who provided words; composers as great as Haydn and Beethoven were called upon to provide settings. Louisa Holland's version of 'Auld Robin Gray', however, is annotated 'Burrowes', presumably John F. Burrowes, the composer and organist of St James, Piccadilly for some forty years. A contemporary list of music gives 'Cease your funning' to Fiorillo, possibly Federigo Fiorillo, violinist, prolific composer and arranger of popular songs.[32]

A name pencilled in several times, mostly with Scottish airs, might read 'E C Eidle', though no two versions are identical. Pronounced in a German manner it could be a joke against herself, for the book, which begins well with titles, words, etc. ends with many pages of musical notation alone, often very roughly done. Some pieces are not very difficult, the kind that slender-fingered girls can rattle off with amazing facility at twice the proper speed, though the ornamental turns and Scotch snaps of a spirited version of the 'Bluebells of Scotland' demand some dexterity in the performer.

All in all the book evokes the visits of the Byerley sisters to London, surely for up-to-date music as well as dance-steps, and the collaborative musical culture they encouraged in their pupils. We can tell from the riotous typography, engraved curlicues and lithographic illustrations of title-pages for publications like '*O! Say Not Woman's Heart is Bought*', *A Favourite Ballad Sung with the Most Rapturous Applause by Miss Stephens at the Theatre Royal, Covent Garden* that publishers were successfully tempting innumerable private performers in schools and drawing rooms. In 1825 Charles Darwin and his brother Erasmus used to go to the Theatre-Royal, Edinburgh, to hear Catherine Stephens, a popular soprano of the time, 'encored to such a degree that she could hardly get on with the play.' Their sisters at home were full of envy.[33]

The next important piece of evidence is an incomplete letter from Jane Byerley to her ex-pupil Elizabeth, dated from Avonbank, 14 June 1826. Elizabeth was probably back in Knutsford with her family; the Swinton Hollands and Lucy Holland had travelled there in May.[34] Jane mentions a Miss Master, and a 'dear trio' that had returned on a visit – Emma, whose husband was at the Warwick Assizes, Jane Pickard and Sophy, the daughter of a Colonel Banow. Ideals of womanhood come over strongly. Of Sophy, who had stayed at Avonbank for many weeks, Jane writes,

> I am proud to say she gives promise of being an honor to our sex; she is a noble-minded intelligent ingenuous creature, and in fact she is everything I wish her to be and all that I fondly hoped she would be, when I used to study her youthful mind, and narrowly watch her opening dispositions: at seventeen the character is *nearly formed*, and I am thankful to say that Sophia's principles and religious feelings are such that I could almost depend on her acting conscientiously in any situation or assailed by any temptations; she has been introduced in the gay world of Cheltenham and she has left the place sick of its miscalled pleasures, and with as simple a taste as when she entered it; and we found that in this quiet place she

was never dull and enjoyed truly a rural walk and more even that [than] the gaiest ball or rout: such is your friend Sophy ... [35]

Jane Byerley seem to have little conception of the heightened, liberating forms of social life experienced in spas and resort towns. One wonders if she had felt the swiftly spreading influence of the Evangelical revival, so alien to cool and rational Unitarian culture.[36]

In 1824 one of Charles Simeon's most earnest students, the Reverend Francis Close, became at first curate and two years later incumbent of St Mary's church, Cheltenham. He fought high churchmanship in education with as much energy as he attacked racing and gambling and profligacy under the wing of Colonel William Fitzhardinge Berkeley, representative of a powerful Gloucestershire family – Liberals in politics where Close was a Conservative. From 1810 to 1826 this little town of a few thousand souls had been wonderfully developed into a Regency spa and social resort of great architectural merit with a population of twenty thousand, swelled by retired officers from the navy and the army, or by nabobs from India with great wealth and ambitions to build. It was visited by many a notable figure – the Duke of Wellington, Byron, Jane Austen and, in 1823, by four Dukes, three Duchesses, six Marquises, five Marchionesses, four Bishops, ten Earls, eight Countesses, fifty-three Lords, seventy Ladies 'besides a host of Honourables, Baronets and foreigners of title and other persons of distinction', which had included the Tennysons from the year before when the drinking of Alfred's father, the Reverend George Tennyson, sent him there for a cure. The poet's uncle complained there were so many mahogany faces about in church that he fancied himself in India.

Harriet Martineau's father came in a vain attempt to recover health during 1826, and in the following year appeared the future Queen Adelaide, accompanied by Miss Fitzclarence, one of William's daughters by the vivacious comedy actress Dorothy Jordan. The town, not far from Stratford and even nearer to Dumbleton, had a reputation for being ostentatious and full of fortune hunters. Balls, card assemblies, plays, auctions, lounge libraries, promenades to the sound of music, the cavalcade of the hunt 'four-in-hand upon stage coaches in the appropriate costume – the Berkeley scarlet mounted with a black velvet collar and a fox thereon worked in silver, the lining yellow' – all declared that cakes and ale would not be forsworn because some were virtuous. As the Evangelical William Wilberforce had said of the gay families of Hull in his youth, 'No pious parent laboured more to improve a beloved child with sentiments of piety, than they did to give me a taste of the world and its diversions.'[37]

Jane's letter continued in flowing prose:

Poor Sophy has lately had a severe trial in hearing of the death of her favourite brother Henry in India; this sad news she received shortly after she had left us and her letters were most melancholy, her attachment to this brother was so warm and her feelings so violent that had she not been influenced by religious resignation I fear she would have been inconsolable for a very long time.

The thoughts of Elizabeth Stevenson, nearly sixteen at the time, must have gone flying to her brother John, whose colourful letters from the east were far from silent about the dangers of his naval career. Jane Byerley's stress upon religious resignation, and yet obvious preference for the girl she calls the 'warm hearted and enthusiastic Sophy' in comparison with her lovely, inter-esting-looking and decorous friend Jane Pickard (both 'fondly attached'), manifest a desire both to lift her pupils' feminine spirits and to recognise the real hazards of existence, multiplied for women. She neither idealised nor advocated renunciation of emotional life.

'I believe you were at school with the Priestleys', she continues, 'but I am not quite sure; you will be sorry to hear how melancholy are the circumstances of both sisters at this moment'. Sarah (whose name appears in the music book) was consumptive, taken rather hopelessly to Devon by her friends. As for her sister Marianne,

> if you did not know her you will remember hearing me speak of her for she was a pupil I dearly loved and ever considered she possessed uncommon strength of mind and for her years a most unusual portion of devotional feeling; I never knew any girl of her age whose actions were so entirely regulated by religious principle, and mark the consequence of this beautiful regulation of mind: she had been engaged to Mr. Charles Skey many years in fact I believe ever since they were either of them old enough to form any attachment: when they were thinking of soon being united Mr. Skey's father failed and his son was ruined: Marianne was much urged to give up her engagement for there seemed no hope of his being ever able to maintain her – but no one could prevail upon her to think of such a thing for an instant and she declared herself more attached and bound to him than ...

Here the copy breaks off. In the *Morning Post* for 29 September 1910, B. R. B. (Bessie Rayner Belloc, née Parkes), who says she remembered Mrs Gaskell vividly and 'was privileged on one occasion to enter deeply on a subject very near to Mrs. Gaskell's heart and conscience', affirms that two grand-daughters of Joseph Priestley, brought in infancy from America after his death, were schoolfellows of Elizabeth Stevenson. All three women, she continued, played strenuous parts in later life (one surviving to a great age) and 'bore emphatic witness to the lasting impressions of an ideal sincerity in word and deed communicated by the teachers of their youth.' There is always an element of *post hoc, ergo propter hoc* about such assertions. In this instance we are fortu-nate in having the evidence of Jane Byerley's contemporary letter.[38]

It shows just such an emphasis, based explicitly upon her religious beliefs. The Byerley sisters and many of their pupils had strong dissenting connections and were often Unitarian in background like the Wedgwoods. Yet Emma and Jessie Wedgwood were confirmed in Maer church on 17 September 1824, and in the following year Allen Wedgwood, Evangelical but undemanding, was given the living of Maer by his cousin Josiah. Similarly, in Barford the pupils seem to have attended the parish church with its humble labourers, and later the church at Stratford, where the vicar once sent a message asking that the young ladies should not wear large hats that obscured their faces. But certain broadly religious values cut across sectarian divisions. Elizabeth's insertion on 29 August 1828 of a poem by the popular Mrs Felicia Hemans in her second music book reminds us that Mrs Hemans' best-known poem, published in an annual in 1826, is entitled 'Evening Prayer at a Girls' School'. One stanza reads:

> Her lot is on you – to be found untired,
> Watching the stars out by the bed of pain,
> With a pale cheek, and yet a brow inspired,
> And a true heart of hope, though hope be vain;
> Meekly to bear with wrong, to cheer decay,
> And, oh! to love through all things – therefore pray!

This is as almost as far from being a clarion call for female independence as it could be; nevertheless, as Leighton comments, 'the tone of exhortatory melancholy captures a potent combination of resilience and weariness, heroism and victimisation, importance and hopelessness in its female audience.' More and more, independent women like the Byerleys were educating middle-class girls, striving to inspire them but also to prepare them realistically for the 'lot' of women in the nineteenth century, a fate that might include marriage but also living with dignity and security as single women, like the sisters themselves and two of Mrs Gaskell's four daughters.[39]

In 1836 'Jane the Just', as she was called, wrote to Josiah Wedgwood in her fast, open hand that her brother-in-law William Lowndes had succeeded in becoming Commissioner in the Court of Requests at Liverpool. In the same year Ann Byerley, 'forty-seven, stout and deaf as a post' – the phrase seems inescapable – married Samuel Coltman, a retired widower living near Bakewell, who was generous enough to allow Maria and Jane when they retired in 1840 to divide their time between his house and that of Dr A. T. Thomson, who had a country house at Ditton on Thames. Maria died in 1843, leaving her property to her sisters, in a form we have met so often, 'for their separate use & benefit independently & exclusively of any present or future husband & without being in any wise subject to his debts, control or management'. Economic freedom for the unmarried Byerley sisters was important, a condition of the moral independence they had so evidently achieved.[40]

In about 1846 ('It is 20 years since I have been at dear Avonbank') Mrs Gaskell wrote to a Mrs Montagu to ask if she ever saw 'dear Miss Jane', from whom she had received a letter when ill with measles the previous spring, Kate Thomson (probably Mrs Thomson's step-daughter) or any of their old schoolfellows. An even later reference comes in an unpublished letter Elizabeth Gaskell sent in 1853 to Jane's sister, Mrs Ann Coltman: 'I often want to hear something of Miss Jane. I have called once or twice at Dr

[Edmund] Parkes', but never when she has been in London.' The approval
Ann Coltman had evidently expressed of *Ruth* – coming as it did from 'one,
whom I knew of old', wrote Elizabeth, 'to dislike any thing forward or
immodest or unwomanly' – was especially welcome. She ends with 'believe me
to remain my dear "Miss Anne", yours truly & affectionately E. C. Gaskell'. If
this is affection rather than affectation, there survived a bond with her schooldays that might lapse but was not broken.[41]

In the years that followed Jane evidently kept up with her many friends and
relations. In the August of 1854 she was to visit Mark Philips and his sisters,
'where Mrs Thomson & daughter are now staying'. There is no other mention
of either Katharine Thomson or Jane Byerley in the Gaskell letters, but Mrs
Gaskell definitely knew, and in 1852 visited, Mark Philips, first M.P. for
Manchester after the 1832 reform act, and his brother Robert, M.P. for Bury,
finding them as hosts 'very kind & good natured not very gentlemanly'.
Robert Philips used to allow the public into his grounds at The Park, 'with the
understanding that there shall be no trowels carried'. Both men were members
of her husband's congregation at Cross Street.[42]

Phyllis Hicks prints two letters of December 1854 from Jane Byerley to
Sam Coltman in extenso. Written from Brighton, they display a polished
concern for the health of Mr Coltman and unobtrusively modulate into excellent advice – for him to look on the brighter side of things and not talk
gloomily to his wife in the night. She goes on to speak sentimentally of the
young children in her circle, and even more emotionally of 'the dear little
Queen', who met the messenger coming with dispatches from the Crimea on
the stairs: she 'burst open the paquet & sat down on the stairs to read them
through, weeping all the time at the accounts of the killed & wounded! is not
that nice?' The question pulls one up short for a moment. The context is that
of a fragile Victorian woman's lot as well as that appropriate to the queen of a
fighting nation.

The second letter from Jane speaks of 'a juvenile party to please the little
darlings here' and a treasure of a servant who will 'do all the nursing & waiting
&c & Eliza can cook & do all the scouring.' Servants in their station of life
were expected to be as disciplined and as warm-hearted as her best pupils had
been. 'You remember what a delightful nurse Mary was', she writes, 'what a
sweet temper, what a clean creature, & she has raised herself in the opinion of
every one by her devotion to her Mother'. Jane's bust, executed by 'Pepper of
Brighton' in 1858 – a photograph of which Mrs Chadwick managed to obtain
for her second edition to place alongside David Dunbar's bust of one of the
splendid young women she had helped to form – makes her look classically
keen and stern, a modern sybil like George Eliot, but we can now imagine the
thin lips melting into a fond or touching smile. Did she, like her sister Ann,
preserve relics of Barford and Avonbank, the most affecting of which was 'a
bracelet of hair of old pupils with turquoise clasp'?[43]

There remains Katharine Thomson, a mother of eight and a prolific author. John Aikin had shown the way with his *Annals of the Reign of King George III* in 1816; his daughter Lucy, strongly encouraged by Henry Holland, provided another model with her *Memoirs of the Court of Queen Elizabeth* in 1818. Katharine, concluding that 'the most readable biographical works of the day' were written by women like Miss Aikin, brought out the first of her own historical works, *Memoirs of the Court of Henry VIII*. The *Memoirs* appeared in 1826 when she was in her late twenties. Her husband became a professor at the University of London a little later, and the indefatigable Brougham, a moving spirit in its foundation as a secular university without Anglican tests, soon recruited them both as contributors to the publications of one of his parallel enterprises, the Society for the Diffusion of Useful Knowledge. Henry Cockburn and the young Gladstone seem to have read Katharine's 'Wolsey' as early as 1828. She was something of a pioneer, for there were only two women amongst Brougham's thirteen biographers of eminent persons, Sarah Austin ('Niebuhr') being the other.[44]

By no means all men disapproved of women using their intellectual powers. The successful barrister James Losh of Newcastle, a member of William Turner's congregation, made a point of informing Brougham that Quaker women were 'generally better forward in Literary matters than the men, as they have the same kind of education and more leisure' in which to write for the Society. And about this time the young Macaulay wrote in his defence of the new University of London, 'A man who thinks the knowledge of Latin essential to the purity of English diction, either has never conversed with an accomplished woman, or does not deserve to have conversed with her.' There was in some circles a general tone of approval and encouragement.[45]

Katharine's *Henry VIII* drew a volubly enthusiastic letter of praise from a young neighbour in Sloane Street whom she had known for some years, 'L. E. L.' (Letitia Elizabeth Landon), something of a publishing prodigy. Her volume of poetry entitled *The Improvisatrice* went through six editions in 1824. The money she received for her books, enhanced by payments from the remunerative and decorative literary annuals so popular at the time, enabled her to support her penniless family in some style after the death of her father in 1825, though she lived alone, either for practical reasons (a room of her own) or, Katharine Thomson suggested in *The Queens of Society* (1861), to exist as an *esprit fort*, like Corinne. Elizabeth Browning noted the intimate friendship that existed between three London-based authoresses – Mrs S. C. Hall, 'poor L E L.' and Mrs Thomson, whose work was 'sown abundantly' in the periodicals of the time.

There was sometimes a psychological cost. As a famous professional author L. E. L.'s life was frantic, 'wildly gay in public and sick with anxiety in private'. She became involved in scandal. Katharine, friend and sober matron, gave her welcome advice. Laetitia wrote gratefully, 'I wished to be able to tell you I had taken some steps towards change; and I also wished, if possible, to subdue the bitterness and irritation of feelings not to be expressed to one so kind as yourself. I have succeeded better in the first than the last.' But she seems to have been both guileless and a victim of uncharitable envy. Plunging into an unwise marriage she went out to West Africa as the wife of the governor. Shortly afterwards, in 1838, she died in mysterious circumstances, perhaps by her own hand. Dr Thomson, her friend and physician for fifteen years, gave evidence at the inquest.[46]

'Take the life of girls in general', L. E. L. had written in one of her last essays, on Scott's heroines, 'they know nothing of real difficulties, or of real cares; and there is an old saying, that a woman's education begins after she is married'. Katharine was the very antitype of poor Letitia Landon. She succeeded in marriage, society and authorship, which extended, notably, to works of fiction.

Constance, A Novel, which Katharine brought out anonymously in three volumes in 1833, is very readable. She begins with the rather facile argument that fact combined with fiction, both probable and natural, must provide a useful moral lesson. One of her minor characters, a physician who had made his own way in the world 'by pure and honourable means', loving both the science and the practice of his profession, a man of real sensibility who knew how to console without deluding, sounds very like her husband Anthony Thomson. A long descriptive passage at the end of book three in *Constance* is designed to evoke and embody the 'deep interest of cultivated minds' in 'sacred ruins', ancient castles and the Norman town of Câudebec, 'lying as it were in the compass of a nut-shell' formed by the surrounding hills, full of the bustle of trade, with vines and villas and vistas, the 'jabber of French, in every variety of cadence' and 'slight, but admirably cooked dinner' taken there of *éperlins*, stewed eels, flummery, fruit and Gruyère cheese – 'somewhat *au maigre*, for it was Friday'. What we would now regard as the travel-supplement sensibility of the Howitts was far from unique in those days and could swing easily from the antiquarian to the epicurean. A daughter added to a reprint of Thomson's memoir in *The Medical Times* for 1849 that this hard-working man knew how to take 'the necessary autumn holiday' and relax by visits at home and abroad.[47]

The hedonistic touring in *Constance* is incongruously succeeded by a highly moral and sentimental resolution of the main plot, in a novel that for once continues after the marriage of the hero and heroine. Constance (an orphan of course) possessed 'a depth of feeling, impassioned yet pure', a need to love and be loved that had been denied her in her youth but which she finally discovered in the trials of life. She and her clergyman husband were at long last reconciled with Sir Charles Marchmont, the man who had once loved her and with whom she continually found herself unsuitably linked, brought together at the sickbed of his own motherless child.

This sentimental story takes place in genteel society, amidst card parties, race meetings and balls. There are scenes in Bath crescents and its pump room, a Malvern hotel, London streets and various thinly disguised places in Warwickshire, where the 'amazons of the neighbourhood' chase assiduously after partners for the dance and for life. The moral optimism of the novel's core is associated with satire of 'contracted society' and petty amusements. Type names and characters appear – Mr Puzzleby the lawyer or Dr Creamly, a pleasing young physician at Bath who was fortunate enough to realise that his profession might be better practised amongst the frequenters of municipal dinners with good old-fashioned ailments like gout and heart attacks than amongst those whom prayer and fasting kept inconveniently healthy.

The five Miss Tribes, who lived in 'a large, rickety, banging and slamming sort of house, famous for breezes' and full of screams for doors to be shut, have been identified by Hicks with the 'large, disorderly family' of Katharine's own youth, though Susan Ferrier in *Marriage* (1816) had shown what good fun could be had with 'five awkward purple girls', Bella, Becky, Betty, Baby and Beeny. A feeble literary man in *Constance* 'died of an elegy which he had stayed too long in a damp church-yard to write'. A young lady 'was one of those unhappy victims whom the desire of gentility immolates on the altar of constraint'. As for her father, 'confined chiefly within the precincts of a retired village, his self-estimation, like a fungus in the shade, had grown out to a prodigious extent'. It is very amusing, but there is something very smart and sharp about Katharine Thomson in this vein.[48]

The identifiable satiric portraits in *Constance* caused a public complaint in the *Gentleman's Magazine* for March 1834. In March 1825 had died a good friend of the Byerleys, the eccentric Dr Samuel Parr, Johnsonian perpetual curate of Hatton for the last forty years of his life but invited, like Sydney Smith, to all the grand Whig houses. He kept a private academy for boys, several of whom were brothers of the Byerley girls. The most famous had been Tom, the son of R. B. Sheridan, a merry lad who had stayed with Parr for six years, mixing gunpowder with his tobacco, sprinkling pepper on his wig and playing other pranks. Parr himself had a very convivial side. His May Day celebrations at Hatton were famous – invitations went out to high and low for concerts, races, theatrical shows, fairs and dancing. Chapters 13 and 14 in Book one of *Constance* are devoted to descriptions of these class-free jollifica-tions and Parr's household. He might have been just too old for Elizabeth Stevenson to meet while she was at Stratford, as he flew over the land 'at full gallop' and scoured 'town and country with four clerical-looking long-tailed horses', but she could have learnt a lot about him in his later years from Katharine's novel.[49]

Mrs Thomson, quite unimpressed by his reputation, describes him with the kind of caustic control that Jane Austen employed to hit off Mrs Musgrove in *Persuasion*. She writes of 'a bulky man, of about sixty years of age, but in the full vigour of a constitution which neither his habits of profound thought, nor of immoderate eating, had as yet, in any great degree, impaired.' The passage abounds in such 'unbecoming conjunctions'. Sydney Smith, a connoisseur of wigs who had already published a comic excursus on Dr Parr's wig, had in effect anticipated her description of the 'standing-out, well-powdered wig, containing hair enough to stuff a moderate sized pillow' that made him look 'in the eyes of his simple parishioners, of far more importance than any bishop they had ever seen.' It soon became proverbial. John Gooch Robberds once wrote to his wife from Dunkeld on 12 July 1835, 'Take a number of old wigs, such as Dr Parr's, and a number of scrubbing brushes rather the worse for wear, touch them with an enchanter's wand, and let them swell into hills and woods', and she would know what Scottish scenery was like.[50]

Life causes many to appear ridiculous as they age, but Katharine indulges in a kind of burlesque that is more like Jane Austen in a pet or Thackeray with a villain than Elizabeth Gaskell. In fact, although a short, friendly reminiscence of Parr had appeared in *Blackwood's Magazine* for November 1825, by the time Katharine wrote she might have read De Quincey's comprehensive and biased demolition of the 'Birmingham Doctor'. It had appeared in four issues of *Blackwood's* in 1831. She is following established conventions. There are softer touches in her portrait, however, especially at the very end of *Constance*, and it then corresponds pretty well with her own non-fictional account of Parr in her *Recollections of Literary Characters and Literary Places* in 1854. Here she stresses the way in which he was an old-fashioned 'parish priest' (rather than parson) and the sense of community he encouraged in the teeth of disapproval and ridicule from the local gentry in Warwickshire.[51]

Katharine Thomson was one of those ambitious women of the early nineteenth century who as professional authors had to face what Norma Clarke terms 'a complex mixture of permission and prohibition, deriving from their sex'. Felicia Hemans is a clear case in point. Some, like the Manchester sisters Maria Jane and Geraldine Jewsbury, at first had considerable success, though Maria's eventual decision to marry brought moods of self-doubt, depression and uncertainty about her future role in life. After her wedding in August 1832 she was taken to India as a chaplain's wife, and died from cholera little more than a year later. The unconventional Geraldine is said to have published work of lesser quality after a marriage proposal *she* had made, in 1859, was turned down. Katharine's Thomson's marriage, however, seems to have been no bar; she flourished as an author, without any obvious domestic problems, using her talents as an artist to help her husband with the drawings of his book on botany as well as keeping up her own stream of publications even whilst travelling abroad, and caring, presumably, for the ten surviving children of his two marriages.[52]

To her memoirs of Raleigh in 1830 were added in the next two decades memoirs of eighteenth-century historical figures and scenes – the duchess of Marlborough, the Courts of Queen Anne and Queen Caroline, and the Jacobites. 'I never saw any person so full of life, animation & enjoyment as Mrs. Thomson – the people are all in love with her', wrote Samuel Coltman in

September 1844. 'She is writing the history of the Jacobites for which she is to have 300£ from her bookseller, she writes faster than I can read.' Alongside the memoirs flowed a stream of three-volume novels. *Constance* was followed by *Rosabel, A Novel, in Three Volumes* in 1835 and *The Lady Anabetta* in 1837, still published anonymously. They were not as successful, but this did not inhibit her from producing yet more fiction in the 1840s, especially historical romances.[53]

In 1842 came another novel with an intriguing title, *Widows and Widowers: A Romance of Real Life*. She was again profiting from her experience; her preface announces that it was based upon an actual case of poisoning some fifty years before, the 'first detected instance of poisoning by prussic acid, or rather by laurel-water, which is the basis of prussic'. Her husband had published on toxicology, but what had brought this case to the front of her mind? L. E. L's sad death in Africa, presumably. In 1847, the year before Elizabeth Gaskell's *Mary Barton*, she published two three-volume novels and another book of *Memoirs* in two volumes.

Katharine Thomson had strong journalistic talents. L. E. L's guileless and imprudent life furnishes a section in her *Recollections of Literary Characters and Celebrated Places* in 1854, along with light and fluent accounts of Coleridge, Charles Mills (a chivalrous and 'laborious gentleman writer') and John Galt, with its probable portrait of William Stevenson. There are atmospheric descriptions of Hatton Rectory and Holland House, the statue of Charles James Fox in its entrance hall, its gilt chamber, great drawing room and library of 15,000 volumes. She had known Cockburn, Jeffrey, Bulwer Lytton, Thackeray and Sir James Mackintosh, a colleague with Brougham in the founding of London University, a philosopher and historian whose conversation was the most delightful Maria Edgeworth had ever heard, who impressed Charles Darwin in exactly the same way, but whose great promise was never fulfilled. Mackintosh, the husband of Kitty Wedgwood, was in London for a time after 1823, when Thomson attended his youngest daughter in her last illness; by 1827 he had become 'resident genius' for a time at Maer Hall. He was a great reader of novels and a fan of Jane Austen, maintaining that 'the test of a true Austenian was *Emma*', not the highly praised *Mansfield Park*. How far did such opinions circulate amongst his relations?[54]

Katharine wrote prolifically and easily for several different publishers. Towards the end of her life she was able to deploy a striking and very appropriate quotation for a woman like herself if not L. E. L.: 'the literary career, always to good men, honourable, has become one of the most remunerative professions to the gifted of our time.' She was a model of literary production for Elizabeth Gaskell – as John Galt had been for William Stevenson – rather than a pattern of attitude and style, but there is one special, affectionate portrait in *Constance* that is possibly based upon her older sister Maria Byerley – a woman whose 'buoyant, satirical mirth of girlhood, which usually made free with the weaknesses and peculiarities of others', had matured into 'that keen, and yet good-natured, perception of character without which a person may have a respectable share of sense, but must always prove a dull companion.' The author of *Cranford* seems not unlike.[55]

There is, however, a more obvious parallel between Elizabeth Gaskell as an author and Katharine Thomson. Early in the second volume of *Constance* a visit was made to an old and haunted house, where Constance was told the story of the young, gay and fair Margaret of Marchmont, whose picture was in the house ('a laughing landscape in the background and a lamb at her feet') and whose tomb was 'in yon church'. She had caught the plague and, in a trance, was buried alive. 'She was the lady, miss', whispered the old house-keeper with Gothic relish, 'who walked out of her grave, and eat part of her own arm.' The resemblance to an anecdote of Charlotte Clopton in Elizabeth Gaskell's first prose publication, the short account of a visit to 'Clopton House', is not in the least accidental. Katharine wrote in a footnote that a tradition of this kind was attached to a portrait in Clopton Hall, Warwickshire. Both must have visited the house at some time from Barford or Avonbank, and both thought the gruesome story worth publication. Katherine had done so, in a larger context, some five years before Elizabeth sent her letter to William Howitt in 1838, though it is always possible that the latter was re-writing a piece composed during her schooldays.[56]

It is hard to believe that they did not keep in constant touch with each other, though this cannot be demonstrated. There was a considerable difference in age and temperament, and in life-style for many years. Katharine had begun to publish extensively at a much younger age than her relation by marriage, who was soon embedded in the kind of provincial life satirised in *Constance*, nowhere near the booming literary machine of the metropolis and its sophisticated intellectual society. Elizabeth's father had died at a time when he might have begun to introduce her; there is little sign that she was able to make visits and take part in London literary life before 1848. Her cousin Dr Henry Holland was far more in touch than she was in her early married years. There is one piece of evidence of considerable importance, however, to show that the connection with Katharine Thomson was not broken. Elizabeth Browning once told Miss Mitford something she had heard from a friend of Mrs A. T. Thomson: that *Mary Barton* 'was shown in M. S. to Mrs. Thomson & failed to please her; and in deference to her judgment certain alterations were made.'[57]

Nothing more is known than this. When exactly Katharine might have seen the manuscript is difficult to determine. It is likely that she was consulted some time in 1846, perhaps about the first volume only. William and Mary Howitt were also involved, but Katharine was as much of a professional in the literary market-place as they were – and also a writer of novels, which they were not. She was able to give artistic advice on fiction at a critical stage in Elizabeth Gaskell's development – though the most interesting point of all, what revisions she might have suggested, is quite unknown. A great deal is known about those who gave Elizabeth literary advice after *Mary Barton*. Katharine Thomson's name is never mentioned, perhaps because she lived mostly abroad. In July 1849 Dr Thomson died, attended by his nephew and former pupil, Dr Edmund Parkes; his widow took her numerous children to France not long afterwards – 'I never before saw such vigour & self command', wrote Samuel Coltman. She was still there in the November following when Jane Byerley and her companion Miss Bright were staying with her. In the July of 1852 Katharine was expecting Jane to visit her near Lake Constance. In fact, she gave up continuous residence in London altogether. Yet she never failed to produce her novels and historical works. She eventually died at Dover of typhoid fever in 1862.[58]

There is little doubt that of all the Byerley sisters Elizabeth Stevenson knew – Frances, Maria, Anne, Elizabeth, Jane, and Katharine – the last was the closest to her as a future novelist, far more sharp, sophisticated and cosmopolitan when she was young, but not unlike the Elizabeth Gaskell of the 1850s and 1860s. There is nothing to match the hundreds of pages of Fanny Parkes's *Domestic Duties* except Elizabeth's comical little list of 'Precepts for the guidance of a Daughter' – '8: Talk German so fast that no one can ascertain whether you speak grammatically or no./9: Don't gobble; it turns maidens and turkey-cocks purple ... ' Maria and Jane Byerley delighted to the same extent in society and travel, but it was their sister Katharine who circulated in good London society, travelled abroad, published memoirs and novels and combined it all with marriage and motherhood. Though Elizabeth Gaskell never managed to complete her long-projected 'Life of Madame de Sévigné' – incidentally, one of Katharine's Queens of Society – her *Life of Charlotte Brontë* and *Sylvia's Lovers* make the historical direction of her interests very clear.

The Byerley sisters would all have influenced her moral being. Katharine was closest to her as an author. Not perhaps as a friend. Her characterisation of William Stevenson was hardly flattering, and in 1862 she published an easy skim through the literary and social history of two or three centuries, entitled *The Literature of Society*. As she came into the nineteenth century, she had an obvious opportunity to notice *Mary Barton*, *Ruth* or *North and South*. Instead, we find *Jane Eyre* and *Adam Bede* singled out for special praise, which might show good taste but is certainly lacking in family feeling.

NOTES

1 NLS: WS to WB, Treasury, 31 July [?1821] and 31 August 1824; G. Himmelfarb, *Victorian Minds*, London, 1968, pp. 206-9; Butler, *Edgeworth*, p. 57.

2 See *GNL*, XVI, August 1993, pp. 13-15. I must thank Jenny Uglow for the reference and its owner, Mr C. C. Waghorn, for generously providing photocopies.

3 MCL: Larmuth & Sons, *Catalogue of Valuable Books*, items 425, 430, 504. Gray, 'Presented by Rev. W. Gaskell to E. C. Stevenson' – either the date or the presenter is improbable. William did not begin to study for the ministry until 1825, and this copy, 'given to her by her father' (*MG*, 18 February 1914) fetched £5 15s.

4 An aunt of Lady Stanley of Alderley knew a Mrs Hartley at Bath in 1796 (J. H. Adeane, ed., *The Girlhood of Maria Josepha Holroyd 1776-1796*, London, New York, Bombay, 1896, p. 360). Baron Amhurst of Montreal, Kent, died on 3 August 1797; Elizabeth, his second wife, died on 22 May 1830 (*Burke*).

5 A plate of 'Amanda' dated 25 June 1798 is from a picture by Coates, engraved by I. Neagle.

6 See Kenneth L, Moler, *Jane Austen's Art of Allusion*, Lincoln, Nebraska, 1968, pp. 17-28, 162-4.

7 Uglow, pp. 31-2, and summary note 10, p. 626.

8 *OED; Losh Diaries*, I, p. 29 (for 1813); Anita C. Wilson, 'Mother and writer: A study of Elizabeth Gaskell's diary', *GSJ*, VII, 1993, pp. 67-79.

9 Masson, 'Gaskell', p. 104; *DNB* (cp. Knutsford Edn, I, p. xix: 'the Miss Byerleys'); Ward Notebook, f. 7; Chadwick, 1910, p. 90; 1913, p. 65; Rubenius, p. 19n.; *The Works of Anna Laetitia Barbauld with a Memoir by Lucy Aikin*, London, 1825, I, pp. xix-xxi. See also *Letters*, pp. 292, 837; Whitfield, p. 8; Hopkins, p. 343; Henry James, *Washington Square*, end.

10 Wedgwood, *The Wedgwood Circle*, pp. 138, 144-7, 157, 183-8, 190; Hicks, *Quest of Ladies*, pp. 28, 61-2; 'Memoir' of ATT, *Lancet*, 1849, pp. 46-7; [Thomson], *Memoir of ATT*, p. 24. For what follows I have relied heavily on Hicks, *Quest of Ladies*, pp. 56-7, 66-71, 87, having been unable to locate or consult her MS sources apart from the Wedgwood correspondence. See also Reilly, *Wedgwood Dictionary*.

11 KUL: Wedgwood 13-12261(draft), JW to MB, 12 October 1822; 13-12262, MB to JW, Barford, 16 October 1822; 13-12313, KT to JW, 91 Sloane Street, London, 5 November 1822.

12 KUL: Wedgwood 13-12314, JW to KT, Etruria, 7 November 1822. This is again a draft, but many of JW's letters, such as the long series to Mrs Frances Byerley, mostly about money (13-12362 to 12425), are wet-press copies.

13 KUL: Wedgwood 13-12263 & 66, MB to JW, Barford, 12 February 1823 and 9 August 1823; Davidoff and Hall, *Family Fortunes*, pp. 297-8.

14 KUL: Wedgwood 13-12242 & 44, MB to JW, Warwick, 10 January 1816 and Barford, 10 February 1817. See especially Edward Chitham, 'Elizabeth Stevenson's schooldays', *GSJ*, V, 1991, pp. 1-15.

15 *VCH Warwickshire*, IV (with 1820 picture of the church, now fully restored); Lewis, *Topographical Dictionary of England*, 'Barford'; *Joseph Arch*, ed. Warwick, pp. 7, 15-20; Horn, *Joseph Arch*, pp. 2-5, 13; *VCH Warwickshire*, VIII, pp. 516. In some villages few labourers received communion (Reay, *The Last Rising of the Agricultural Labourers*, p. 64).

16 Hicks, *Quest of Ladies*, pp. 76-79; illustr. 'from a drawing by C. W. Ratcliffe', Chadwick, 1913, opp. p. 70. Avonbank was pulled down long ago, like the house that succeeded it.

17 SSBT: Jessie Cuthbertson Scott, sketchbook, marbled board covers, $10^{3}/4 \times 7^{1}/4$", presented by A. Francis Steuart in 1930. Covering letters identify Jessie as the sister of Mrs James Steuart, née Elizabeth Brand Scott (1806-36). I am most grateful to Mairi Macdonald and the helpful staff of SSBT for assistance.

18 Hicks, *Quest of Ladies*, pp. 1, 80-7; Sir Edward Cook, *The Life of Florence Nightingale*, London, 1913, I, pp. 12-13 (1830 visit not mentioned); *Memoirs of Lucy Aikin*, ed. Le Breton, p. 416.

19 Horn, *Joseph Arch*, pp. 4-6; G. E. Mingay, *A Social History of the English Countryside*, London and New York, 1990, p. 103; *Martineau*, ed. Drummond and Upton, I, p. 18;

John Seed, 'Unitarian ministers as schoolmasters, 1780-1850', *TUHS*, XVII, 1979-82, pp. 174-5.

20 NLS: MS 3109, ff. 233-43, TS, Maria I. Steuart [grand-daughter of Mrs James Steuart], 'A lengthening chain', 1942, p. 2 (see Appendix G and Sharps, pp. 501-3). Elizabeth Scott and her sister Jessy were at the Byerleys' school 1820-25. I am grateful to Professor K. J. Fielding for his help.

21 P. B. H[icks], 'Mrs. Gaskell and Warwickshire', *Birmingham Post*, 25 July 1930 (SSBT cutting); Hicks, *Quest of Ladies*, pp. 12, 23, 34, 65 (illustr. from *Warwickshire*). A 'Mrs Mortimer – or "Morty" as she was usually called … a very faithful dependent, and quite a character' (according to 'one of the former pupils' cited in Chadwick's 2nd edn), perhaps succeeded her as housekeeper when Ann married in 1836.

22 Chadwick, 1913, p. 66 (cp. 1910, p. 91); Hicks, *Quest of Ladies*, pp. 102, 127; Sarah Flower, *Great Aunt Sarah's Diary 1846-1892, Prefaced by the Early Reminscences of Charles Edward Flower*, pr. pr., n. p., 1964, p. 9 (see also p. 47: 'Avonbank purchased'); *Darwin Correspondence*, I, p. 9 and n.

23 *Letters*, pp. 16, 836-7; *Mary Howitt: An Autobiography*, I, pp. 126-30, 259; II, p. 28 (*Visits*); HUL: fMS Am 1943.1, 120: WH to ECG, Esher, 30 January 1839; Ward Notebook, f. 13 verso. Sharps, p. 29, suggests that the original sketch might have been written as early as 1825.

24 Hicks, *Quest of Ladies*, pp. 65, 81; [Thomson], *Memoir of ATT*, p. 17; *Letters*, p. 16; WW to Sir George Beaumont, Hindwell, Radnor, 20 September [1824], *Wordsworth Letters*, 2nd edn, III, part 1, p. 278. See p. 288 below.

25 Chadwick, 1913, pp. 74-5; Hicks, *Quest of Ladies*, pp. 18, 25, 59-60, 65; Field, *Memoirs of Parr*, I, pp. 216-7, 289-90; II, pp. 278-82; Derry, *Parr*, pp. 69-71; McLachlan, *Unitarian Movement*, p. 124, Hole, *Pulpits, Politics and Social Order*, p. 26n.

26 *DNB*; Jessie K. Buckley, *Joseph Parkes of Birmingham*, London, 1926, pp. 2, 6, 17-18. See also p. 239 above.

27 Qu. from Hicks, *Quest of Ladies*, pp. 65, 72-5; Uglow, pp. 38-9.

28 KUL: Wedgwood 13-12334, FB to JW, Warwick, 4 January 1810; Mary Burgan, 'Heroines at the piano: women and music in ninteenth-century fiction', *VS*, XXX, 1986-87, pp. 54-7; KUL: Wedgwood 13-12229 & 31, MB to JW, Warwick, 3 December 1811, and 25 April 1812.

29 MCL: MS F823. 894. C1. See Appendix G for other schoolfellows, and p. 241 above; 15 January 1825 was in fact a Wednesday.

30 Cp. John Addison, arr. *The Introductory Symphony … Macbeth*, in *A Shakespeare Music Catalogue*, ed. Bryan N. S. Gooch and David Thatcher, Oxford, 1991, II, no. 6972.

31 Copy of Julian Savory: London, II. ii, 'A Collection of Vocal and Instrumental Music', pp. 242-3. I am grateful to him for his performance of the music in Elizabeth's book and for valuable commentary on its qualities.

32 Leslie Orrey, 'Solo song', *The Age of Beethoven*, ed. Gerald Abrahams, London, etc., 1982, pp. 555-6, 591-2; *The Harmonicon*, II. ii, pp. 140-1. ECS writes in 1831 of copying a Tyrolese song from her cousin's book (Chapple, 'Five early letters', p. 4). 'Partant pour la Syrie' is attributed to Vollrath, at present unidentified.

33 Charles Humphries and William C. Smith, *Music Publishing in the British Isles, From the Earliest Times to the Middle of the Nineteenth Century*, London, 1954, pp. 35, 309-10; *Darwin Correspondence*, I, pp. 19, 22.

34 JGS: incomplete TS, JMB to 'Elizabeth', Avonbank, 14 June 1826; also qu. *Portrait*, p. 8; MCO: Robberds 1, JGR to MR, Nottingham, 11 May 1826. MCL has Edward F. Rimbault's *A Little Book of Christmas Carols with the Ancient Melodies to Which They Are Sung* (Cramer, Beale, & Co., n.d.), inscribed on the flyleaf 'Elizabeth Cleghorn Gaskell'.

35 Perhaps the Sophia Barrow of the presentation copy of Beattie's *Minstrel* (see Appendix G), or even a Sophy Basson (see p. 337 below). In a second music book of 1826-28

(MCL) appears what looks like Charlotte E. Banno< >, a Spanish Serenade copied on 7 March 1827. See p. 284 below.

36 Lucy Aikin thought that the Evangelical party had become powerful enough to 'give the tone to society at large' (LA to W. E. Channing, qu. Quinlan, *Victorian Prelude*, p. 116).

37 Gwen Hart, *A History of Cheltenham*, Leicester, 1965, pp. 175-6, 187-91, 199-204; Robert Bernard Martin, *Tennyson: The Unquiet Heart*, Oxford, 1983, p. 38; MCO: MS Martineau 2, Coe transcripts, HM to JM, 1826; Platts and Hainton, *Education in Gloucestershire*, pp. 61-3; Girouard, *The English Town*, pp. 77, 108 (WW qu.)

38 See *Letters*, p. 902; *Langham Place Group*, ed. Lacey, p. 139. See also p. 192 above.

39 Hicks, *Quest of Ladies*, pp. 81-2; *Wedgwood Circle*, pp. 194-8; Leighton, *Victorian Women Poets*, pp. 11-14; Stoneman, pp. 32-3. See pp. 154, 240 above.

40 KUL: Wedgwood 13-12359, JMB to JW, Stratford-on-Avon, 13 November 1836; Hicks, *Quest of Ladies*, pp. 102-3, 113, 116, 119ff.

41 Chadwick, 1910, p. 118; *Letters*, p. 52; PML: MA 4500 (Gordon Ray Collection), ECG to AC, Plymouth Grove, Manchester, 2 May [1853]. Mrs Montagu is unidentified, but Dr Parkes was with Florence Nightingale in the Crimea (Hicks, *Quest of Ladies*, p. 122).

42 *Letters*, pp. 45-6 (misindexed), 182, 848; *GSN*, II, August 1986, p. 11. The name of Clare Phillips is pencilled in Elizabeth's Avonbank music book; a Caroline Phillips is mentioned in a letter from Jane Byerley. See p. 336 below.

43 Hicks, *Quest of Ladies*, pp. 124-8 ; Chadwick, 1913 (not 1910), opp. p. 122. Jane died in 1868.

44 DCLH: HH to LA, Mount Street, [early 1818] and [pre-10 July 1818]; 'Grace and Philip Wharton' [K. and John Cockburn Thomson], *The Queens of Society*, rev. ed., [1861], p. 509; New, *Brougham*, pp. 348, 361-89; [Thomson], *Memoir of ATT*, p. 23; *Memoirs of Lucy Aikin*, ed. Le Breton, p. 98; ATT journal, and HC to ATT, Edinburgh, 16 June 1828 (Dr Ian Gregg); *The Gladstone Diaries*, ed. M. R. D. Foot, I, Oxford, 1968, p. 177.

45 JL to HB, Newcastle-upon-Tyne, 11 October 1828 (*Losh Diaries*, II, p. 184); T. B. Macaulay, 'The London University', *ER*, XLIII, 1826, p. 331.

46 Hicks, *Quest of Ladies*, pp. 90-1; Leighton, *Victorian Women Poets*, pp. 47-56, 67; 'Wharton', *Queens of Society*, pp. 193, 199, and *Recollections of Literary Characters*, II, pp. 71-98; EBB to R. H. Horne, [London, 5 February 1844] (*The Brownings' Correspondence*, VIII, ed. Philip Kelley & Ronald Hudson, Winfield, 1990, p. 187).

47 *Constance*, I, p. iv; II, pp. 235-7; III, p. 306; E. A. R. [Elizabeth A. Rodd, née Thomson], 'Notes', 1912 (Gregg Collection).

48 *Constance*, I, pp. 141, 147, 198, 201-2; III, pp. 166, 207, 324.

49 *GM*, n. s. XIV, 1863, pp. 245-6 (KT obit.); Field, *Memoirs of Parr*, II, pp. 321-4, 427-37; Derry, *Parr*, pp. 62, 105n. Charles Parr Burney was his godson.

50 Hicks, *Quest of Ladies*, pp. 83-5, 99-101; MCO: MSS: Robberds 1, f. 5 (from notebook, 'Granny's "Recollections" and some letters JGR', 4to, unpaged, marbled boards, which Miss B. Hartas Jackson kindly allowed me to consult).

51 De Quincey, 'Dr Samuel Parr or Whiggism in its relations to Literature and other writings', rev. for *Works*, V, repr. Edinburgh, 1880, p. 61; 'Wharton', *Recollections*, II, pp. 192-3.

52 Clarke, *Ambitious Heights*, pp. 6, 155-61, 217-23. See also R. C. Alston, *A Checklist of Women Writers 1801-1900, Fiction Verse Drama*, London, 1990.

53 *Anne Boleyn* (1842), *Ragland Castle: A Tale of the Great Rebellion* (1843), *The Chevalier: A Romance of the Rebellion in 1845* (1844), *The White Mask* (1844), *Carew Ralegh: A Historical Romance* (1847), *Tracey; or the Apparition: A Tale of the Last Century* (1847).

54 *Edgeworth Letters*, p. 332 (in 1822); [Thomson], *Memoir of ATT*, p. 18; *Greville Journal*, I, p. 247; *Darwin, Huxley: Autobiographies*, ed. de Beer, pp. 30, 39; *Macaulay Letters*, II, p. 72. After the death of his wife in 1830 Mackintosh continued to live at Clapham with

their children until his own freakish death in 1832 (Wedgwood, *Wedgwood Circle*, pp. 200, 207, 218).

55 *DNB*; *BM Catalogue*; 'Wharton', *Literature of Society*, II, p. 315; Hicks, *Quest of Ladies*, pp. 100-1.

56 [Thomson], *Constance*, II, pp. 59-60; Knutsford Edn, I, p. 506; Uglow, pp. 37-8, 118-21; p. 243 above.

57 EBB to MRM, Florence, 13 December [1850], *The Letters of Elizabeth Barrett Browning to Mary Russel Mitford 1836-1854*, ed. M. B. Raymond and M. R. Sullivan, Winfield, 1983, III, p. 317; Uglow, p. 182.

58 *Mary Howitt: An Autobiography*, II, p. 28; Hicks, *Quest of Ladies*, pp. 120-2; E. A. R., 'Notes', 1912.

14

Home and abroad

THE NEXT LETTER from John Stevenson to Elizabeth that has survived in the Sharps collection is an incomplete manuscript of a journal letter written in a thin and sloping hand.[1] John apparently sailed round India to Bombay in the *Earl Kellie* in January or early February 1821. He did not then go on to China – the price of cotton was thought to be too low – but to Rangoon for timber instead. Rangoon, on a main branch of the Irrawaddy in Burma about twenty-eight miles from the sea, had a lucrative trade in teak, 'the finest wood imaginable for shipbuilding because it resisted sea water and did not splinter under gunfire'. Burmese teak was not the best, but it was cheap and plentiful. Over one hundred ships of European type had been constructed there since the late eighteenth century, and many Calcutta ships were built of teak also. The *Earl Kellie* was stout enough to survive two severe gales on the way.[2]

The port of Rangoon, John thought, was 'but a miserable looking place', having 'nothing but mud huts, there being no European Inhabitants'. This is a little exaggerated, but corresponds pretty well with the impressions of an artistic young officer, T. A. Trant, who termed it 'exremely dismal' a few years later. One would never guess it from the heroic and picturesque prints that were published at the time. The country had a native ruler, Bagyidaw, who had become King of Burma on his grandfather's death in 1819; he had then deliberately moved his capital away from Rangoon – to Ava, even higher up the river, deep in the hinterland. Bagidaw himself was weak and moody, his court of Ava arrogant and exacting. It was a recipe for trouble. There were continuous Burmese incursions into Assam on the borders of India, and at other times an influx of fugitives from Burmese rule, all creating frontier problems for the East India Company. A kind of cold war was being waged.[3]

Bagidaw had placed many restrictions upon trade at Rangoon. According to John Stevenson,

All the guns, powder, firearms &c are obliged to [be] sent on shore where they remain until the ship sails again – the inhabitants are extremely saucy & very little justice is to be obtained by a European if he is illtreated – One [of] the men employed working on board, being extremely saucy, I kicked him, when he immediately went on shore & lodged an information against me & next morning a guard of soldiers was sent off to take me out of the ship. When I got ashore I was taken before the Magistrate, (I forget the Rangoon name) & had not our Captain been a very good friend of the government I should not have got off without a couple [of] days confinement in the Stocks, which was the case with the chief mate of a ship here a little while ago.

A naval officer, Lieutenant H. L. Maw, confirms the assertion about arms, which were customarily retained until port dues had been paid, and also proves that John's imperialist attitude was not untypical. Maw was prepared to use the point of his cutlass on 'wretched Bengalees in the row-boats', though this was a few years later, in battle conditions. Native workers generally were thought to present 'a mass of obstinate inertness', and the Burmese, in a phrase of Henry Havelock recalling William Stevenson, considered 'nearly as superstitious as the Highlanders of Scotland'. Other westerners complained about legal injustices and the venality of the magistrates at Rangoon.[4]

A little later John seems to have gone on a second voyage there, followed by a stormy return passage of twenty-five days to Calcutta in September. After spending some months in the city, he joined another vessel, the *Marianne Sophia*. This was probably a barque of 293 tons, built in America and owned by Palmer & Co. in 1824.[5] He sailed on the short voyage from Calcutta to Madras, perhaps in the February of 1822, by which time Elizabeth would have left Knutsford and been away at school in Warwickshire. There are unfortunate gaps in John's surviving correspondence; little more is known of his movements in these years. A letter from his father to Blackwood dated 16 June 1823 happens to note in passing, 'My Son John too is doing uncommonly well: he is chief mate of a vessel of 500 tons belonging to Calcutta, & sailed in January for the Red Sea'. He gave no name for this country ship.[6]

In January 1823 William Stevenson reported to Blackwood that Galt was 'ill with the lumbago, & a kind of nervous complaint'. He believed that Galt's latest book, part of which had been read to him, would be good, though he believed that he was running a 'considerable risque' by appearing to compete with Scott. Neither Blackwood nor Stevenson suspected that Galt was at this very time secretly treating with a rival publishing firm for his new novel, *Ringan Gilhaize*, designed to give a more sympathetic view of the Scottish covenanters of the seventeenth century than Scott had in *Old Mortality*. Blackwood was angry to lose Galt's most serious and impressive book to Oliver and Boyd, and William Stevenson lost his friendly neighbour, for in the late summer of 1823 Galt moved his family back to Scotland. Boyd advanced him £100 for the new novel, plus £50 for a third edition of his *Life and Administration of Cardinal Wolsey* (1812) and £100 for *The Spaewife* not long afterwards.[7]

Stevenson crawled on through the *Historical Sketch of the Progress of Discovery, Navigation, and Commerce*, originally promised for April 1818. In early 1823 he was disappointed that Blackwood had not ordered printing-off to begin. As he struggled on, Messrs Spottiswoode's compositors managing to perform wonders 'considering the crabbedess' of his writing, he changed his mind about shorter pieces. He proposed a series of papers 'of solid & permanent value' on political economy, about which he claimed to have very definite ideas. It was becoming a controversial subject. David Ricardo's *Principles of Political Economy* appeared in 1817, though the ebullient John Wilson was antagonistic.[8] Carlyle, too, translated the Swiss economist J. L. Sismondi's long, critical article on the subject for Brewster's *Edinburgh Encyclopaedia* in 1823-24, a piece of hack-work kept very dark and even now not well known. 'Classical' economists were accused of ignoring the dire human consequences of *laissez-faire* doctrines. The broad critique, which Stevenson shared, was summed up by John Stuart Mill: 'Utility was denounced as cold calculation; political economy as hard-hearted; anti-population doctrines as repulsive to the natural feelings of mankind'.[9]

Blackwood was enthusiastic. Stevenson's proposed papers were just right, worth ten guineas a printed sheet in the first instance; the fee might be increased if they went well, he wrote.[10] But Stevenson's next two letters were oddly cautious. He had to meditate deeply, 'examine what I have to advance, & the proofs of it, in every possible point of view'. Then on 16 June 1823 he wrote of 'an unexpected & sudden demand' for money. Could Blackwood advance him £40? 'This with the £10 you advanced to my nephew William', he added, 'will make £50'. He went on, 'By the bye, you will be glad to learn that William is placed in the Bengal Establishment as assistant surgeon; he is at present at Bencoolen', and added the reference to John Stevenson's voyage as a mate to the Red Sea.[11] The personal touches show that Stevenson was appealing to Blackwood, whose own son William went to Calcutta in 1826 to join an East India company regiment, as a friend. 'Direct to me under cover to the Earl of Lauderdale London', he ends. Lauderdale was then staying in Warren's Hotel, Waterloo Place, a few hundred yards from the Treasury – very convenient if Stevenson wished to keep his request secret for any reason.

Blackwood sent the money, but the pace of work on the *Historical Sketch* did not pick up. On 5 August 1823 the excuse was that he had been obliged to take his daughter, presumably Catherine, to Ramsgate. She had been 'ordered to the sea side by her Uncle Thomson'. (Later in the century Janey Morris wrote of the homely therapy available there: 'One is made in a kind of pie with the sea-weed'.) In September Stevenson confessed that he had stayed on longer than intended, because the sea air cured 'violent headaches' he had been suffering from. And on his return to Chelsea he said that he had been 'till very lately – very much occupied with a new assessment & valuation of the Parish, which as a Member of the Parish Committee, under the local act, I was obliged to attend to'. Now, at last, he told Blackwood, he was free.[12]

The beautifully kept minutes of the committee set up for Chelsea under an Act 'for the better assessing and collecting the parish rates' show that Anthony

Todd Thomson was present at its first meeting on 6 January 1823. The committee met frequently, with varying numbers present. On 27 February there was an especially large turn-out, with the Honourable and Reverend Dr Wellesley in the chair. Stevenson's name does not appear in the minute books until 29 August 1823, when he was present as a member of a new committee appointed 'to equalize the Rates of the parish, and to examine and confirm the new assessment preparatory to the making of the next poor rates'. Thomas Hobbyn was in the chair, and it was agreed there should be a fine of five shillings for non-attendance, though this seems to have been a mere gesture. Stevenson was present at the next meeting but one on 4 September, in which the examination of the books was completed, but he did not appear at any of the weekly meetings that followed. The committee generally was reduced to its core members.[13]

Something was going very wrong in these months. In early October 1823 Stevenson again asked for ready money – £20, 'either in Cash, or in such a shape that I can immediately convert it into Cash' before the eleventh of the month. In November he reminded Blackwood that nothing had been agreed about terms for the *Historical Sketch*. He begged for liberality in payment, appealing explicitly to their 'long friendship' and promising 'greater punctuality in any future transactions'. He wanted as much in money and 'the rest in as short Bills' as possible. 'Indeed I must trust to you being able to let me have £30 *now*', he wrote emphatically, and added, despondently,

> The second point in which I need & request your assistance is this: the procuring as much literary employment as I can, that will pay me well. My reading, especially latterly, has been very general; – but the bent of my inclination & I think the predominant power of my mind, is to subjects that require & admit methodical & close reasoning – such as Political Economy – the general principles of Politics – the Philosophy of the human mind &c.

Desperation did not jolt his mind out of old, familiar tracks, but the more solemn intellectual style of the Scottish enlightenment was quite alien to the light and popular writing Blackwood wanted for *Blackwood's*. Stevenson was even prepared to sell himself to the booksellers to be boiled dry, to borrow a vivid phrase from Mary Clarke Mohl. He wrote that he was 'not fond of looking over MSS and preparing them for the Press', but if Blackwood could help him to form 'a connection of this kind with a London Bookseller', he would 'esteem it a particular favor.'[14]

Blackwood's reply of 5 December 1823 was canny. He sent an order on Mr Cadell for £30, making £100 in all. He praised the finished *Catalogue*. He spoke of the pleasure it would give him to be liberal. But with inconvenient candour he confessed that he found it so difficult to fix a total price for the *Voyages* that he must ask Stevenson for his own suggestion, mentioning that had he finished as expected, two years before, upwards of £2000 worth of stock would not have been lying entirely dead in the interval. 'Take all this into account and write me what your ideas are.' This was a real poser. Blackwood then reminded him of the proposed articles at ten guineas a sheet on political economy, not yet begun, and hoped that he would be able to do something for Stevenson when in London next. 'Alex Chalmers is at present the Man of all Work for the Trade', he noted, but he was 'getting old and failing'. In his opinion Stevenson was for his 'general information as well as letters much better-fitted to be useful to the Trade than ever Chalmers was.' 'You may rest assured', he promised, 'that I will leave no stone unturned to get you brought fairly in contact with the Gentlemen of the Chapter Coffee House.'

The Chapter coffee house was a famous inn near St Paul's with strong literary associations, from Johnson to the Brontës. Alexander Chalmers was an Aberdonian who had settled in London and formed a connection with the firm of George Robinson of Paternoster Row. The editing of multi-volume works was his forte: a biographical dictionary in thirty-two volumes, a 'British Essayists' in forty-five volumes, an 'English Poets from Chaucer to Cowper' in twenty-one volumes and so on. The complete list is awe-inspiring. He was a convivial man and a popular conversationalist, whose 'intimacy with the principal London publishers' always secured him a seat at the regular dinners of the Stationers' company. His prodigious output was perhaps slowing down, but he outlived Stevenson, dying at the age of seventy-five on 10 December 1834.[15]

The *Historical Sketch* was finished early in the new year, but Stevenson took a while before he could bring himself to request £150 more – through no disposition to make 'a keen bargain', he claimed, but his 'present difficulties in respect to money' – nearly £200 was wanted to free him – were mixed up with the consideration of what he deserved. He would like £50 on account, as much in money as Blackwood could spare and the rest in as short bills as possible. 'I shall only add that if you can accomodate me, you will give me the strongest additional motive to regular work in any thing I may write for you in future', he pledged. This awkward and difficult letter was written (at top speed, like the rest) on 31 January 1824. By the 11 February he had not heard anything from Edinburgh, and was reduced to writing urgently for £34 needed to meet a debt due on the 20th. 'I have not been under such pecuniary difficulties since I came to London', he cried; 'they have arisen from a combination of circumstances such as I trust will not occur again'.

William Blackwood, publisher and friend, answered this despairing plea. On 17 February we find Stevenson acknowledging a draft of £75 in full payment – most dispiritedly. At the price of 8 shillings, he could see, even the sale of all the copies would gain little for Blackwood. 'I think that £175 – which you say is more than you had laid your account with paying me, – even if I had finished the work in as many months as I have taken years, – is little for such a work – less than £5 a sheet', adding in dejected humility, 'I cannot however complain, reflecting on the loss you have sustained from my delay, however much I may suffer & be embarrassed'.[16]

He did not even have the consolation of bringing out a masterpiece that won him instant fame. The *Historical Sketch*, a substantial tome of over 500 pages together with a *Catalogue* of about 100 pages, finally appeared in May 1824, at 14 shillings. The preface, dated 30 March 1824, stated that it was 'strictly and entirely an independent and separate work'. Stevenson had analysed printed evidence about the ancient world through to the discovery of America in four long, detail-packed chapters, assembling quantities of information about slavery ('an infamous trade'), improvements in navigation, measurement of the arc of the meridian, progress in trade, the principal exports of Norway and many other subjects. His last chapter covers voyages from the middle of the fifteenth century to the beginning of the nineteenth, stressing 'commercial character and relations' rather than war. Commerce, he believed, acted like gravity; and, with Whiggish optimism, he asserted that it directly or indirectly spread 'the civilization, knowledge, freedom and happiness of Europe' all over the globe. One wonders if his son John would agree.

The *Catalogue* is selective and evaluative. Stevenson's obituarist wrote in a footnote that 'he gave considerable offence in the arrangement of this list to an eminent literary character and an intimate friend of his own, by omitting the mention of a book of travels which that gentleman had written, and which Mr. Stevenson deemed unworthy of insertion.' He must have meant Galt, whose *Voyages and Travels* (1812), which did not meet Henry Holland's expectations either, is ignored, nor does Galt's *Letters from the Levant* (1813) appear.

The public already enjoyed a rich diet of exotic voyages and travels, as the reviewing journals prove. *Blackwood's* printed a simple announcement of the work, and the supplement to the *Gentleman's Magazine* of December 1824 was briefly complimentary: 'the whole is ably performed'. J. R. McCulloch praised its *Catalogue*, but damned the *Sketch* as lacking in 'the elaboration and research necessary to give real and permanent value', adding that it appeared to be a hasty piece of work – ironically in the circumstances.[17]

Whilst his father in London was struggling to cope with duns and mounting debts, John's maritime career was reaching an exciting climax. He would have reached the Red Sea some time in 1824, but we know nothing about his movements until his next surviving letter, this time addressed to Mrs Lumb at Knutsford. The top portion – it is another manuscript – has been torn irregularly away, so the name of his ship is unknown, but its conclusion (a flourishing 'Your very affe Nephew Jno Stephenson') is legible.[18] The contents show that he was caught up in dramatic events. A fragile peace had broken. The first Anglo-Burmese war had begun on 17 January 1824 with a skirmish in a satellite state on the eastern frontier of India. Minor battles were fought in islands off the north-western coast of Burma, and on 5 March Lord Amherst, the governor-general, made the formal declaration of war.

The future novelist Captain Frederick Marryat was involved in its early stages.[19] He had commanded HMS *Beaver* at St Helena from March 1821 until just after the death of Napoleon in May. Later that year he escorted the mortal remains of Queen Caroline to Cuxhaven in another vessel, the *Rosario*, and afterwards captured a number of smugglers in the Channel. He published a pamphlet entitled *Suggestions for the Abolition of the Present System of Impressment in the Naval Service*, much to the Admiralty's displeasure, but there were times during the Napoleonic wars, his French biographer points out, when towns like Portsmouth and Plymouth were in effect besieged by the press-gangs. In April 1823 Marryat took command of the *Larne* (a 6th rate, 20 guns) and in July sailed for the East Indies. Once there, he left his wife and baby with an English family in Ceylon, taking their ten-year old son for a three-week cruise to Madras. The *Larne* was then caught up in an expedition to attack Burma, so the young lad (the future General W. T. Layard) joined Marryat's ship as a volunteer first class and his three-week holiday cruise was extended to three years.

Marryat sailed on to Calcutta, from which Sir Archibald Campbell and his staff embarked for the Andaman islands in the Bay of Bengal, commanding a combined naval and military force of over ten thousand infantry and artillery, naval gunboats, armed brigs, schooners and row-boats. Wilson lists the names of the transports for the Bengal Force that sailed in April 1824. The *Earl Kellie* (but not *Marianne Sophia*) is named in this group, which carried mostly European troops. So too is the *Diana*, the first steam vessel that had ever appeared in the East. Built as a private speculation and purchased for £10,000, it was said to be imperially terrifying to the natives – when in operation, for in untidy reality it was subject to mechanical and navigational problems in the complicated river system of Burma. The first division of the Madras Force, mostly native troops, also sailed in April; the second division left on 22 May, but the names of the transports are not to be found in any of John's letters.

A naval aide-de-camp at this time, Lieutenant Maw, conveys a vivid impression of the organised chaos inevitably produced when ill-combined forces swing into action, beginning in the Andamans but continuing through the multiple actions to come. On 11 May 1824 Campbell's forces attacked Rangoon – their river pilot a merchant captain who had been engaged in the eastern trade, Captain Marryat in command of the royal naval flotilla that sailed up the Irrawaddy. The city, however, was deserted. Monsoon rains poured down. Heavy fighting lasted for months on end in the surrounding countryside. Marryat and his men were in the thick of combined naval and military operations, repelling fireships, boarding Burmese vessels, breaching stockades and constructing bridges. A contemporary wrote of 'a body of jolly blue-jackets brushing past us helterskelter with Captain M. [Marryat] at their head'. Documents show that sometimes the transports were involved in operations – *Satellite*, *Good Hope* and *Moira*, for example – and their personnel praised in dispatches, but naval ships, gun-boats, mortar-vessels and *Diana* bore the brunt of the action along with Campbell's military forces. The dense jungle was full of Burmese soldiers and concealed stockades, constructed either of teak logs or green bamboos that were even better at resisting cannon-ades than more solid defences.[20]

The exceptional loss of men through battle and sickness forced the *Larne* to withdraw in September, so Marryat missed the great battles of December 1824 alluded to in the journal letter of early 1825 by John Stevenson. In its torn opening can be read the words 'Rangoon', 'I mentioned in my' – presum-ably something like 'earlier letter a fierce attack which the' –

> Burmese had made on the town in which th<ey were re>pulsed with great loss – Not discouraged with this they have since our departure made a third & were again repulsed, with a loss, says the papers [*sic*] of 10, 000 men – It is now confi-dently affirmed that we have nothing further to do than march up to Ava the Capital & shall meet with no further resistance – This however I much doubt. I think it improbable that the Burmese will give over so easily, both from what I have seen & read of their character & from the small number of men they have as yet brought into the field – not above 40, 000 & in a Kingdom like that of Ava where every man is a soldier they ought to be able to raise 400, 000 at least.

The Burmese, under a brave and brilliant general, Maha Bandula, had made a series of major assaults at the beginning of December, their fire rafts on the river illuminating the golden pagoda at Rangoon as if it had been noonday. They were heavily defeated, though it proved as difficult to fight up-country as John Stevenson believed and the war went on for more than a year. His reference to the 'papers' suggests that he had not been as fully involved in the fighting as Captain Marryat and his jolly blue-jackets, though his missing letters might have been full of exciting action and lent to others for that very reason. Nor was he severely wounded like Lieutenant Maw, who was invalided home via St Helena, where he 'of course visited the tomb of Napoleon', taking away pieces of willow and geranium sprigs to strike in England as souvenirs.[21]

Though Snodgrass had made it clear on his title page that he was 'detailing the operations of Major-General Sir Archibald Campbell's Army', a review in the *Quarterly* by the formidable John Barrow of the Admiralty ended with a stinging series of reproaches for the book's neglect of the part played by naval forces as a whole. John's journal letter mentions problems with sepoys carried in civilian vessels by sea and the difficulties caused by caste requirements – 'more particularly the case with the Bengal army which consists in a great measure of Rajapoots. The Madras regiments from having a greater number of Pariahs amongst them have behaved much better'. John's vessel would have been hired to transport East India Company's troops – some Muslim, others Hindu of high and low castes, 'with whom the higher will no more associate than with Europeans', Barrow alleged. John might also have mentioned 'the usual followers of an Indian army, equal in number to the army itself, crowding the ships, and always in the way'. Captain Doveton maintained that 200 soldiers on one ship of 450 tons were accompanied by 400 camp-followers during a voyage of several weeks.

Barrow's sardonic review gives a more global view of the naval operations, their jealousies, friction and disorder. Europeans were plagued with their own kind of 'caste' problems, placed as he maintained they were under army rather than royal navy command:

> The regular India ships taken up for the conveyance of troops are manned chiefly with Lascars; and their masters – captains, as they style themselves, are high and important personages; the company's cruisers [Bombay Marine] are manned with English, Hindoos and Mussulmen -
> The governor-general and council ... placed the whole under the command of the quartermaster-general, who was probably sea-sick during the whole passage. The consequence was, as might have been expected, that all were commanding and none obeying. The gentlemen of the company's cruisers, who have long been aspiring to take rank with the officers of the navy, and to wear the naval uniform, were not sorry not to obey the officers of the navy; the masters or captains of the Indiamen did not deign to obey the gentlemen of the company's cruisers.

When Rangoon fell, Barrow continued with his case for the prosecution, 'provisions, stores, and ammunition were indiscriminately lying on the beach' and – a nice touch – boats laden with gunpowder were run over by men 'with lighted segars in their mouths'. John was lucky to return to Calcutta alive and whole. The army was almost totally dependent on Bengal and Madras for supplies, a ship taking four months to make the return journey. However, a more relaxed view of the gossip and hospitality of what became known as 'King's or Scandal wharf' at Rangoon is not hard to find. It became part of the war's romanticised iconography. 'Rangoon from the Anchorage, / Drawn on the spot by Capt. Kershaw, 13th Light Infantry' was published by William Daniell a few years later.[22]

Calcutta had become John's shore base. By 31 October 1824 he was listed as 'Free-mariner, 1820' amongst the British and foreign inhabitants.[23] At the close of his 1825 journal letter to aunt Lumb John made some revealing complaints. He had gone ashore, 'not to dance, for I never do', and found nothing but people dancing, 'no <con>versa<tion> – not even small talk – not even cards'. Some paper at this point was torn away when the seal was opened, but it seems that where he had hoped for 'manners, ideas, & intellect' he found only 'figures, silence or stupidity':

> You may think this severe but remember it is only spoken of India Shopkeepers, or their wives & daughters. The former of whom, have their intellects concentrated on the sole idea of making money, & the latter on dancing for really nothing else seems to have attraction for them & if I were asked where their heart laid should certainly say in their heels –

But drinking and gaming were declining, according to an anonymous 'Letter from Calcutta' in a work called *The East-India Sketch-Book*. 'We read,

– we think, – and we publish', it proclaimed; women's interests now extended well beyond turbans, novels and *liaisons*. It makes John's sharpness sound rather priggish. His sarcastic words must disguise a deeper dissatisfaction, and he sounds thoroughly discontented as well as envious:

> Of the more respectable classes I can say but little for there country officers are never admitted, but I could shrewdly guess that even in those priviledged circles, the principle care of the gentleman is, how he may make a fortune, & of the lady, how she may spend it – if married – or to get a husband if not.

The less idealistic Henry Solly accepted as a matter of course that his sister on her marriage in 1835 would go to India with her husband to join his brothers in a vastly profitable business. 'My sister', he wrote, 'would have to accompany him to Calcutta, where they were to reside for three years, when in all probability they would be able to return home with a considerable fortune'. They did.[24]

Disappointment as well as the homesickness so common amongst those long away probably dictated the manner in which John ended this particular letter:

> I hope you & every one else continue to be satisfied with Elisabeths progress. If she writes to India again, persuade her to be more liberal in the length of her letters – If she only gets into the habit of keeping a journal the difficulty of filling up her paper would soon cease – And now my dear Aunt, once more farewell – Give my best love to Bessy Holland & all *enquiring* friends & believe me to be
>
> Your very affe Nephew
Jno Stevenson.

In 1824 his father's promised articles on political economy began in the May issue of *Blackwood's*. They were hard going. 'One must read very doggedly and attentively as your Essays are not childs play' was Blackwood's restrained comment on 25 May. In his fourth article Stevenson was still promising yet more preliminaries on 'the general investigation of the mode in which we arrive at truth, in the principal departments of human knowledge', before he could even start upon political economy.

On 30 July he acknowledged the receipt of 12 guineas and put another proposal to Blackwood: a series of papers reviewing the reviews – not exactly an original idea. The very first number in January 1824 of a new quarterly, the *Westminster Review*, contained a famous article in which James Mill initiated 'a regular and systematic course of criticism' of periodical literature. On 31 August Stevenson floated yet another idea: a book done in 'a plain, practical & popular manner, not bibliographical in what related to the choice of Books – nor too scientific or recondite in what related to the directions for studying them'. He had been outraged at Thomas Dibdin's bibliomaniacal *The Library Companion; or, the Young Man's Guide, and the Old Man's Comfort, in the Choice of a Library*. He was recovering his energy.[25]

But again there came a pause. In October the *Westminster* published a review of James Mill's *Elements of Political Economy*. Stevenson was clearly falling behind. A curt note from Blackwood on 20 October 1824 asked if he was ill, and also enquired whether Galt was in London and what his movements were. This crossed a letter from Stevenson, saying that the delay had been occasioned by his desire to treat the subject of his fifth paper on political economy really well. He also promised a preliminary paper on periodical publications, 'pointing out the object & the path to be pursued' – Blackwood's heart must have sunk – and asked about his earlier proposal of a library companion. Galt, he said, was going to Canada. Blackwood sent a very mild reply, even accepting the proposal of a library companion, but Stevenson was no substitute for the irrepressible Galt, who had recently proposed a selection of elegant extracts from books of travel, a 'Views of Scottish Life and Manners' from his own tales and a modern novel to be entitled *The Housekeeper* – to the rival firm. But he was beginning to send in 'tentative peace-offerings' to Blackwood, a publisher who was what he needed to produce his best work, one who would fight back. A recalcitrant De Quincey a few years before, in 1821, had been too much for Blackwood to bear. 'I can only excuse your letter which I rec'd today', he riposted with heavy sarcasm, 'by supposing that you were hardly awake when you wrote it.' One can only admire Blackwood's patience and constant encouragement of the dilatory William Stevenson.[26]

The November issue of *Blackwood's* contained Stevenson's 'On the reciprocal influence of periodical publications and the intellectual progress of this country', an introductory piece almost devoid of solid content. Blackwood was forced to tell his friend, on 24 November 1824, about complaints that the political economy articles were 'so long of coming to the point.' People thought 'pages of metaphysical discussion' were both wearisome and unwanted. Those capable of sustained attention might be satisfied with the clearance of intellectual rubbish, but Stevenson should remember 'the Babes predominant among our readers and that they cannot digest strong food', he wrote sardonically. His colloquial vigour of mind contrasts greatly with Stevenson's long-winded competency: 'The great matter is to come directly to the Scratch as the Bruisers say, and not to talk about it.'

Yet Blackwood was still kind, giving his old friend good advice in a letter of 21 December 1824. His style would suit 'a large separate work', but

> in a monthly Miscellany I fear so much metaphysical discussion, and dry reasoning upon preliminary matters, will prevent your valuable papers being read at all. If, with all my partiality for what you write, I feel this, what are ordinary readers to feel? ...
>
> I also send you back your Paper on the Reviews as I would be very anxious if it were possible to have your article on Charitable Institutions in the same Nr and you perhaps could shorten this a little. Do not think me unreasonable in asking you to abridge, for I assure you that this is one of the greatest difficulties I have

with Maga, the getting papers kept within proper bounds. You are so fond of having every thing clearly made out and are so given to logical deduction, and well founded reasoning, that you are always apt to think that others require as much to satisfy them as you do yourself. Nowadays the good folks will not always digest such strong food, and the short hand method may be occasionally indulged in.

Some modern historians find matter to admire in his economics papers, which take their place in *Blackwood's* sustained attack on the kind of hard-edged political economy reckoned to be 'revolting to the best feelings of our nature'. Stevenson likened classical political economists to Milton's Chaos, who 'umpire sits, / And his decision more embroils the fray' – a quotation he, or Jeffrey, had once applied to the dubious *Mysteries of the Cabiri*. He also objected to the use of algebra or calculus as an equivalent for reasoning in political economy – models of this type imply that economics could be a science as certain as mathematics – anticipating in this respect Carlyle's more wide-ranging critique in 'Signs of the times', where he proclaimed that human beings had become 'mechanical in head and in heart, as well as in hand', and Peacock's satire of a John McCulloch persona (Mr MacQuedy, the son of a demonstration) in *Crotchet Castle* (1831). The days when Erasmus Darwin the poet had happily taken 'the Infection of Steam-enginry' were far behind, and so too were Stevenson's rational calculations to improve the Highlands of Scotland.[27]

Stevenson agreed to compress his papers and humbly confessed that his 'style of thinking & writing' was 'more adapted to longer works than a Magazine'. Then with improbable optimism he proposed 'a set of works in the more common & popular types of education, adapted not to children – but to youth of from 12 – to 16 –' He must have envied Galt's success in this field – and was just possibly thinking of his own daughter's education at Avonbank. In the event only one more paper on political economy appeared, in February 1825. His article on periodical publications had come out in the previous November; it was headed 'No. I' and promised more at its close. But it was the first and last.

In effect Blackwood had abandoned these items, awkward and shaming though it must have been. Nothing more appeared in the magazine, despite another humble letter from Stevenson of 31 January 1825. 'I was much disappointed at receiving such a short letter from you', he began, and again asked for advice. He expressed a keen sense of intellectual failure: 'I feel that I have not done what I might & ought to have done: I am also sensible of a tendency to plan many things'. Blackwood finally wrote on 19 February 1825 that he approved the idea of an educational series and reminded him of the suggested library companion, but, strangely, Stevenson did not respond.[28]

At the end of that year many country banks failed, and the government reacted by proposing to restrict their note issues and those of Scottish banks as well. After a time Blackwood wrote again, perhaps having seen an analysis of the crisis in the *Edinburgh Review* for February 1826 which argued against the superior merits of the Scottish system of banking. He told Stevenson on 21 February 1826 that he had not been able to see him when in London the October before, but he had been impressed by a speech of Lord Lauderdale's, 'by far the most able that has been delivered on the Small note Bill'. If Stevenson's views were similar, he could surely obtain all the papers and information he might need from Lauderdale and compose a paper on the 'Scotch system of Banking'. A plain, forcible and spirited one, he urged, not too long and with as little preliminary matter as possible; it would go well in an issue devoted to the present state of the country.[29]

Again, there seems to have been no response from William Stevenson, who, even if he had seen the very favourable reference in the *Edinburgh* article to his predecessor at Manchester, Lewis Loyd, by now an experienced partner in 'one of the first banking houses in the kingdom, (Jones, Lloyd, and Co.)', might not have cared too greatly. Stevenson had found a new outlet for his talents and a new lease of life. The House of Blackwood could go on without him. He no longer cared to seek ill-paid hack-work from the gentlemen of the Chapter coffee house. There was no need to snatch at ideas in the *Westminster Review* any more. He had become a contributor.

The *Westminster Review* came into being when a number of young Unitarians, perhaps introduced to each other by W. J. Fox, joined forces with James Mill and Benthamite radicals. The literary or 'flowery' half of the review (chronically short of copy) was at first edited by the young Henry Southern, whilst the traveller and linguist John Bowring looked after the political side.[30] The articles are anonymous and difficult to assign. Hardly any of Southern's papers survive. Bowring, who seems to have at one time been in a worse state than Stevenson – bankrupt with 'half a dozen little ones' to support – names many of the early contributors in his later *Autobiographical Recollections*: his patron Jeremy Bentham, T. Perronet Thomson (M.P. for Hull, said to be the first writer on economics to employ calculus), J. A. Roebuck, the lawyers John and Charles Austin, the Unitarian preacher turned physician Southwood Smith and the radical Albany Fonblanque, but not William Stevenson.[31]

The first issue of January 1824 opened with W. J. Fox's survey of the state of the nation and included the assault on contemporary periodical writers by James Mill. Mill demonstrated with considerable trenchancy how the journals, Whig as well as Tory, were inevitably subservient to 'the aristocratical classes', by which he meant great landowners and their hangers-on, the clerics and lawyers who shared power and the profits of misrule. He then went on to dissect the *Edinburgh*, with extensive quotations. The amount of space allowed to Mill and to other contributors was enviable. This new and clearly important quarterly was attractively printed in single-column format, fat and expensive at six shillings a number. It very soon paid well, at the rate of £20 for a sheet of sixteen pages.[32]

In January 1825 appeared a learned, elaborate and indignant review of the 'bibliomaniacal trifling' in Thomas Dibdin's *Library Companion* that briefly but closely echoes some of the adverse remarks on it in a letter Stevenson sent to Blackwood in November 1824. It is almost certainly his, though the sobriety of the letter in no way anticipates the parody and liveliness of parts of the review, especially its first page or so: 'Our worst fears are realized, poor Mr. Dibdin is mad from title-page to colophon.' Had another editor been improving Stevenson's copy?[33]

In July came a lengthy, favourable account of Alexander Henderson's *History of Ancient and Modern Wines*, with no acerbities. It contains many learned additions and corrections – classical especially. Several of the obscure sources of Stevenson's *Historical Sketch* are again displayed. His obituarist's assertion that he changed his mind about classical learning and 'became more favourable to its general diffusion' in later life is consistent with one of this reviewer's urbane comments: 'we miss those classical allusions, and that familiarity with the ancients in their domestic circle, which throws a powerful charm over the first part of the work.' It sits oddly with a buoyant, utilitarian attack upon classical education by an unidentified reviewer in the same number: 'Must we conclude that education is a useless labour, that nature does all, that man, at twenty-four, having been denominated a master of arts, springs up a lawyer, a statesman, or a physician, to act and govern by intuition; and, well imbued with syntax and port, to transfer his hand from the reins of four greys to those of the state.'[34]

In October 1825 appeared a detailed review, again attributed to Stevenson, of Lord Braybrooke's edition of Pepys' *Diary*. There is an obscure reference to a French traveller called Denon also found in the *Historical Sketch*, but if Stevenson is the author, he has changed his tactics. His material is almost entirely derived from the text under review and there is no ballast of lengthy footnotes and scholarly references. This review, described as important by a modern scholar, is an exposé of king and government in the Restoration period, a historical equivalent of James Mill's critique of contemporary 'aristocratical' politics. It is a biased, well-written, fluent and readable piece. The style is remarkable: full of confident authority, spiritedly sarcastic – even insolent. The original diary, it states condescendingly, was deciphered by one of Magdalen college's 'more laborious children', and 'the head of a noble family, or, more properly speaking, the possessor of a splendid mansion, by virtue of which he enjoys authority in the College in question, took upon himself the more honourable, but less irksome, duty of editor.'[35]

If it really is by William Stevenson, he was responding to the spirit of the *Westminster* in a way that he never had with *Blackwood's*. Benthamites were nothing if not against aristocracy. The carelessly abusive tones of a man like young Henry Southern ('Dear Fox, – We have had a kick-up with our publisher … ') seem audible. The editors did not hesitate to alter and radically recast articles submitted, and might have done so in this case. It is not easy otherwise to reconcile the comments on the 'interest' and 'good job' that made Pepys secretary of the Admiralty (though he is said to have exerted himself 'with a degree of diligence, not often exhibited by the administration to which he belonged') with Stevenson's own position at the Treasury and continuing connection with the Earl of Lauderdale.[36]

The January 1826 issue of the *Westminster* saw Stevenson's review of Charles Mills's *History of Chivalry, or Knighthood, and Its Times*. Like Kenelm Henry Digby's *The Broad Stone of Honour*, it was one of the many books on chivalry published between 1815 and 1830 that preceded the charismatic Young England movement in the politics of the next decade. ('I had rather be Lord John Manners than any young man who has passed through the University', sighed the great Master of Trinity, William Whewell.)[37] This review resembles both Stevenson's 'Chivalry' article and the *Historical Sketch*, though it lacks a flock of learned footnotes. Moreover, a few scientific idioms of his early reviewing again appear; he is aware of deceptive affinities and apparent analogies. Mere antiquarians, he contended, are superseded in an age when botanists have become vegetable physiologists, 'the laws of organization and of animal life have, in many instances, been illustrated by the entomologist; and contributions to the same interesting and mysterious topics have been supplied by the conchologist raising his studies from the inner shell to the animal which inhabited it.' This is for him 'the real utility of science' in a modern age.[38]

About this time Henry Holland wrote to his old teacher William Turner that apart from astronomy and geology, more progress in the natural sciences was being made in France and Germany – a view strenuously urged by David Brewster and that 'irascible genius' Charles Babbage. British scientists thought about establishing a European Academy, but eventually, in September 1831, the first meeting of the British Association for the Advancement of Science was held at York – 'the most centrical city for the three Kingdoms', as Brewster put it in a letter to John Phillips of the Yorkshire Philosophical Society.[39] Holland went on to report that the older Brunel had driven his tunnel about 300 feet under the Thames, the first royal medal of the Royal Society had been awarded to John Dalton (after too much neglect and cavilling), whilst South had been given the other medal for his discovery of the revolution of double and triple stars. The younger Herschel was gaining a reputation that his talents fully deserved. Back in 1809 Henry had written enthusiastically about Humphry Davy's discovery of new metals – he 'seems to think *archium* the most proper termination, *barytarchium, strontarchium, sodarchium* &c'. Not long afterwards he noted that Davy had given his first lecture at the Royal Institution to seven or eight hundred people, with a good deal of action, 'elegant language, & a superabundance of tropes & similes', all adapted to the taste of a fashionable audience. But by the mid 1820s Davy had in his opinion failed to carry on his career as an experimentalist, in favour of 'a few excursions to Country Seats' and becoming a figure in society.[40]

In the welter of information that is characteristic of Holland's letters he makes frequent references to travel books, but unfortunately there is a chronological gap about the time when he might have mentioned Stevenson's magnum opus, the *Historical Sketch*. In any case, the initial connection between the two men in London had never blossomed and his name does not occur again in Henry Holland's known correspondence. Stevenson had been one of Brewster's authors, but he was not interested in the progress of the physical and experimental sciences, only in those that could be assimilated to his historical and classical knowledge.

As a typically 'philosophical' historian looking for patterns and meaning, he condemned Charles Mills for his failure to analyse 'the causes which, during the middle ages, attained, or retarded, or kept stationary, the mind and condition of the human race', and for feebly slurring over the baneful influences of chivalry on contemporary society. Selfless bravery, loyalty, and gallantry were misguided in their day and unwanted in this. However, 'Attention and respect to women, of a more soft and guarded character than that which would mark our conduct to our own sex, are quite compatible with a proper treatment of them as our companions and co-operators in intellectual pursuits'. Theory collapses at the end of Stevenson's article when he cannot resist a dig at Letitia Landon, who had been praised by Charles Mills for singing the glories of chivalry. He expressed an unchivalrous 'wish that all who admire L. E. L.'s poetry may admire his prose, and the more substantial wish, that all who purchase the Troubadour and the Improvisatrice, may purchase his History of Knighthood.' Did he not know that L. E. L. was a woman? Is the disapproval more than scholarly? Many were envious of her success in the literary marketplace.[41]

It must have been even harder for Stevenson not to feel pangs when the youthful prodigy John Stuart Mill, son of James, gave an early display of his powers in the July 1826 number of the *Westminster*. His virtuoso analysis of Sismondi's *Histoire des Français* recreates the barbarisms of the middle ages and, driven by passionate disapproval of chivalric myths, often focuses in its negative way on the same topics as Stevenson: 'If it could be proved that women, in the middle ages, were well treated, it would be so decisive a proof of an advanced stage of civilization, as it would require much evidence to rebut.' William Stevenson was not without passion: his review of Charles Mills contains an emotional defence of Herbert of Cherbury's freethinking Deism and, in this context, strong praise for the Reverend Robert Hall's famously eloquent and often reprinted sermon of 1800 on 'Modern Infidelity', from which he quotes a specimen:

> Lord Herbert, the first and purest of our English freethinkers ... did not so much impugn the doctrine or morality of the Scriptures, as attempt to supersede their necessity, by endeavouring to show that the great principles of the unity of God, a moral government, and a future world, are taught with sufficient clearness by the light of nature.

This passage might have enshrined Stevenson's own beliefs at this stage in his life. But whatever the state of his religious opinions, the minute philological and antiquarian details of the review prove him to be still the scholar, as he had been since the time when he used to associate with classicists at Daventry Academy. In contrast, J. S. Mill's writing was forceful, cogent and uncluttered; the assured scope of his learning manifest in his fine control of both the French language and historical sources.[42]

Stevenson was a footsoldier in 'the march of mind', a cant phrase of the day picked up by Peacock in chapter 2 of *Crotchet Castle*:

> 'God bless my soul, sir!' exclaimed the Reverend Doctor Folliott, bursting, one fine May morning, into the breakfast room at Crotchet castle, 'I am out of all patience with this march of mind. Here has my house been nearly burned down, by my cook taking it into her head to study hydrostatics, in a sixpenny tract, published by the Steam Intellect Society, and written by a learned friend who is for doing all the world's business as well as his own, and is equally well qualified to handle every branch of human knowledge.'

Henry Brougham's Society for the Diffusion of Useful Knowledge, begun in November 1826 as a major enterprise in the field of mass, secular education, initiated a Niagara of treatises, usually containing thirty-two octavo pages of packed information in double columns of small type for sixpence. Brougham himself began the 'Library of Useful Knowledge' by publishing *A Discourse on the Objects, Advantages, and Pleasures of Science* in March 1827. Amongst the many subjects planned was one by Stevenson, but when written it went astray:

> Sir, Having been informed by my relation Dr A. T. Thomson – that I am to be paid for the loss of my MS. on Agriculture, which I sent to the Committee of the Society for the diffusion of useful knowledge about 18 months since – I shall be obliged to you to inform me, at your earliest convenience, when & how I am to receive payment.

The date of this reproachful letter, 26 June 1828, shows that he was one of the earliest contributors.

A follow-up letter of 1 August shows that he had not received any reply. When it did come, it annoyed a harassed and perhaps dying man:

> Sir In reply to your Note respecting my MS. on agriculture, I beg to state that I have no copy of it: nothing indeed but references & a very few short Notes. I mentioned this to Mr Brougham when he told me the expense of re-copying would be defrayed: & in reply he says in a note now lying before me 'I am not without hopes: but if you have to write it again, of course the loser is bound to pay for *that*'. ...
>
> I should also wish to know, whether there is such ground for hope of the recovery of the MS. as to render my setting about writing it again unnecessary. Mr Brougham's note is without date, but I think it was written at least 4 months ago, so that I am afraid the chance of recovery is now very small.

In 1827 Harriet Martineau had sent in a 'Life of Howard the Philanthropist'. She was told it was in type, but when she humbly asked to be paid some part of the £30 promised, it could not be found. Years afterwards, she says, it turned up, 'not only dirty, but marked and snipped' – obviously made use of by others – at the bottom of a chest. There is no more Stevenson correspondence with the Diffusion Society, but when he was overtaken by his final illness, his obituarist tells us, he 'was occupied in preparing for the press a series of treatises intended for the edification of the agricultural classes, projected by that eminent friend to intellectual improvement, Mr. Brougham'. This may be the 'Farmers' Library', which Brougham thought would be more practically useful to 'your Wiltshire yeoman' than propaganda for scientific agriculture. A wheel had turned full circle. Stevenson's financial reverses began at a farm. Twenty-five years of work and drudgery had taken him no further forward.[43]

NOTES

1 JGS: incomplete MS, two conj. 4to leaves (crowned posthorn wmk), 'No 3-' [JS to ECS]; TS version adds nothing. 'To my sister – /- No. 3' is written across the last page; this portion of a letter contains what appear to be inconsistent details – headed 'Jany', 'Marianne Sophia / At sea', and 'Feby 1st'; 'Calcutta May 5th' in the body of the letter.

2 See Morse, *Chronicles of the East India Company*, IV, pp. 1-6; Bayly, *Indian Society*, p. 117; Harvey, *History of Burma*, pp. 284, 353; Crawfurd, *Journal of an Embassy*, pp. 349, 446-7; Parkinson, *Trade in the Eastern Seas*, pp. 324, 331.

3 Aung, *History of Burma*, p. 210-11; Harvey, *History of Burma*, pp. 297-304; Woodman, *Making of Burma*, pp. 57-9; [Trant], *Two Years in Ava*, p. 23. Cp. Cooler, *British Romantic Views of the Anglo-Burmese War*, pp. 1-3. Trant's breadth of interests and powers of description are excellent: see, e. g., pp. 208-26, on Burmese character, dress and customs, and the passages on landscapes and architecture quoted by Cooler.

4 Maw, *Memoir of the Burmese War*, pp. 23, 88; Havelock, *Memoir of the Three Campaigns*, pp. 19, 112; [Trant], *Two Years in Ava*, pp. 274-5.

5 *Bengal Almanac, etc., For 1824*, 3rd edn, Calcutta, 1824. Captain Robert Cornfoot.

6 See p. 264 below; Parkinson, *Trade in the Eastern Seas*, pp. 48, 110.

7 NLS: WS to WB, Treasury, 11 January [1823]. When paralysis eventually gripped Galt, his doctor A. T. Thomson made an application on his behalf to the Royal Literary Fund in June 1838; he was awarded a grant of £50 (Gordon, *Galt*, pp. 14, 61-8, 140).

8 NLS: WS to WB, Treasury, 18 February [1823]; Treasury, 21 March 1823; Hilton, *Age of Atonement*, pp. 37-42. A 2nd edn of the abridgement of Adam Smith's *Wealth of Nations* was published in 1821.

9 *Carlyle Letters*, I, p. 259n.; F. W. Fetter, 'The economic articles in *Blackwood's Edinburgh Magazine*, and their authors, 1817-1853', *SJPE*, VII, 1960, pp. 89, 103, 217; *The Early Drafts of John Stuart Mill's Autobiography*, ed. Jack Stillinger, Urbana, Illinois, 1961, p. 102.

10 Payments to Stevenson can be found in NLS: MSS 30657-8.

11 NLS: WS to WB, Treasury, 29 March 1823, 26 April [1823] and 16 June 1823. His namesake first appears in the *East-India Register and Directory for 1823*, 2nd edn, without date or precedence; cp. p. 223 above.

12 NLS: WS to WB, Treasury, 5 August [1823] and 20 September [1823]; Tredrey, *House*

of Blackwood, pp. 70-2; Smiles, *John Murray*, p. 217; Jack Lindsay, *William Morris: His Life and Work*, London, 1975, p. 232.

13 GLROL: P74/LUK/27, MS, minutes under dates cited.

14 NLS: WS to WB, Treasury, 2 October [1823]; Treasury, 28 November 1823. See D. Hume, *Treatise of Human Nature* (1739-40), ed. Ernest G. Mossner, Harmondsworth, 1969, p. 42; J. A. V. Chapple, 'William Stevenson and Elizabeth Gaskell', *GSJ*, I, 1987, p. 3; Young, *Edinburgh*, p. 63.

15 Rees, *Literary London*, pp. 39-40; *DNB*.

16 NLS: WS to WB, 8 January 1824; Treasury, 31 January 1824, 11 February 1824 and 17 February 1824.

17 *Historical Sketch*, preface, pp. 398, 497, 502, 513, 527; *ABO*, p. 213; DCLH: HH to PH, 3[?] Lisle Street, L. Square, 29 January [1812]; McCulloch, *Literature of Political Economy*, p. 148.

18 JGS: frag. MS, two conj. 4to leaves (wmk 'KINGSFORD 1822'), JS to HL, [?Calcutta, ?early 1825], endorsed '1825 not wanted'. There is no TS; see Sharps, p. 17.

19 I rely here on Gautier, *Marryat*, pp. 50-65. More generally, see Graham, *Great Britain in the Indian Ocean*, pp. 346-62.

20 Pearn, *Rangoon*, chapter 6 ('The War of 1824'); Intelligence Branch, *Frontier and Overseas Expeditions*, pp. 16-25; Snodgrass, *Burmese War*, pp. 51, 91, 105; Wilson, *Documents of the Burmese War*, pp. 25, 46-7, 91-3; [Trant], *Two Years in Ava*, pp. 14, 285; Maw, *Memoir of the Burmese War*, pp. 11-16; Doveton, *Reminiscences of the Burmese War*, cited by Gautier, p. 63n. Snodgrass and Wilson provide large-scale folding maps.

21 Woodman, *Making of Burma*, chapter 4; Aung, *History of Burma*, pp. 210-16; Maw, *Memoir of the Burmese War*, p. 88.

22 Barrow, 'The Burmese war', *QR*, XXXV, 1827, pp. 512-14; Parkinson, *Trade in the Eastern Seas*, pp. 45-50, 285; Doveton, *Reminiscences of the Burmese War*, pp. 126, 288, 373; Cooler, *Romantic Views of the Anglo-Burmese War*, plate III. Wilson, *Documents of the Burmese War*, p. 94n. denies that the army QMG was in command.

23 *Bengal Almanac, and Annual Directory, For 1824*, 3rd edn. This listing continues, by inertia probably, until the early 1840s. Cp. Berwick's list of freemen.

24 *The East-India Sketch-Book: Comprising an Account of the Present State of Society in Calcutta, Bombay, &c.*, London, 1832, I, pp. 204-12; Solly, 'These *Eighty Years*', I, pp. 241, 303.

25 NLS: WS to WB, 30 July 1824; WS to WB, Treasury, 31 August 1824. For further details see Chapple, 'William Stevenson and Elizabeth Gaskell', pp. 4-5.

26 NLS: WS to WB, Treasury, 20 October 1824; Gordon, *Galt*, pp. 69-72; Lindop, *De Quincey*, p. 244.

27 Milton qu. *Blackwoods*, XVI, 1824, p. 210n. See Fetter, 'Economic articles', p. 96; Perkin, *Origins*, pp. 244-51; [TC], 'Signs', *Edinburgh Review*, XLIX, 1829; Marilyn Butler, *Peacock Displayed: A Satirist in his Context*, London, Boston, Henley, 1979, p. 190.

28 NLS; WS to WB, Treasury, 31 December 1824 and 31 January 1825.

29 NLS: MS 30309, ff. 121 verso – 122, WB to WS, Ed[inburgh], 21 February 1826 (wrongly indexed; almost illegible wet-press copy); 'Banking System of England', *ER*, XLIII, 1826, pp. 272, 281-6, 297-8.

30 Nesbitt, *Benthamite Reviewing*, pp. 31-3, 135. Nesbitt did not know that Stevenson was a contributor, but see *Wellesley Index*, III, pp. 529-31, et seq. (rev. IV, p. 802) for references and attributions.

31 Stephen Conway, 'Bowring in Government Service', *Bowring*, ed. Youing, p. 30; *Autobiographical Recollections*, ed. Bowring, pp. 65-77.

32 *WR*, I, pp. 1-18, 206-68; *Draft of Mill's Autobiography*, ed. Stillinger, pp. 89-99; Nesbitt, *Benthamite Reviewing*, pp. 36-7.

33 *WR*, III, 1825, p. 189; NLS: WS to WB, Treasury 3 November 1824; Chapple, 'William Stevenson and Elizabeth Gaskell', p. 5.

34 *ABO*, p. 210; *WR*, IV, 1825, pp. 93, 136, 152.

35 *WR*, IV, 1825, p. 408; Nesbitt, *Benthamite Reviewing*, p. 50.

36 Garnett, *W. J. Fox*, pp. 51-3; Nesbitt, *Benthamite Reviewing*, pp. 130-5; *WR*, IV, 1825, p. 413.

37 See Mark Girouard, *The Return to Camelot: Chivalry and the English Gentleman*, New Haven and London, 1981, pp. 42-3, 56ff.; Kevin L. Morris, *The Image of the Middle Ages in Romantic and Victorian Literature*, London, etc., 1984, pp. 103-4; Blake, *Disraeli*, p. 170.

38 *WR*, V, 1826, pp. 60-2, 65, 68-9. Cp. Chapple, 'William Stevenson and Elizabeth Gaskell', p. 2; Knight, *Scientific World-View*, pp. 90-5.

39 NLPS: Moor Collection 23. i, HH to WT, L Brook Street, 2 December [1826]; Morell and Thackray, *Gentlemen of Science: Early Years*, pp. 44-59, 88, and ed. *Gentlemen of Science: Early Correspondence, of the British Association for the Advancement of Science*, London, 1984, pp. 22-3.

40 DCLH: HH to PH, Cannon Street, 24 November [1809], and 3[?] Lisle Street, L. Square, 29 January [1812]; HH to ME, L Brook Street, 25 June [1825], 12 December [1825] and 16 November [1826].

41 *WR*, V, 1826, pp. 80-1, 101; Nesbitt, *Benthamite Reviewing*, pp. 88-91.

42 Mill, 'Age of Chivalry', *WR*, VI, 1826, pp. 62-103; *WR*, V, pp. 95-8 (Herbert). Hall was a long-standing friend of Sir James Mackintosh, and his sermon had been in substance given at J. S. Estlin's Lewin's Mead chapel, Bristol (*DNB*).

43 WS to Thomas Coates, Paper Office, Treasury, 26 June 1828; Treasury, 1 August 1828; Treasury, 11 August 1828 (UCL: MSS, correspondence and papers of SDUK); Smith, *Useful Knowledge Society*, pp. 9, 59; New, *Brougham*, p. 348, 353; *Harriet Martineau's Autobiography with Memorial by Maria Weston Chapman*, 3rd edn, London, 1877, I, pp. 140-1.

15

Advice to a young lady

THE TIME HAD come for Elizabeth Stevenson to enter upon the world. Jane Byerley's letter of June 1826 indicates that she had left school altogether, been on a visit – perhaps to see her cousins in Dumbleton – but returned to Knutsford without calling in at Stratford on her way back. What was in store for her after the summer holidays? It is unlikely that she had to prepare herself to become a superior kind of teacher like the Byerley sisters, or a professional writer like Harriet Martineau. Dr James Currie's treatment of his daughter Jean gives a clue. Of aunt Lumb's generation, he shared the educational values of Scotland and liberal circles in Wakefield, Knutsford, Liverpool and Manchester.

Jean Currie had, typically, been sent away from home to a school in Newcastle-upon-Tyne run by a Mrs Wilson, perhaps the 'talented and intellectual lady' who kept a large school in Ellison Place. When Jean was about to leave in 1803, her father advised her to be very selective in her choice of future correspondents. 'Nothing in nature is more frivolous than the intercourse by letter between two giddy or romantic misses, to say the best of it', he wrote with ponderous solemnity. On her return to Liverpool, he made it clear, he wanted her to continue her studies 'in the line of improvement'; also, to be useful at home, reading to him and, if she had time, copying – for, he wrote rather movingly, he felt 'the hand of age'. He was pleased with the plans she sent him: 'I shall be proud to find that my daughter is not a mere every-day woman, courting amusement, and weary of thought; but one who has resources in her own mind, and who aspires to the friendship of those of both sexes who are truly estimable.' Daughters fortunately make allowances for their fathers. Jean sounds too good to be true, and it is utterly impossible to imagine Elizabeth Stevenson taking Dr Currie's advice about letter-writing.[1]

But William Stevenson would have agreed with him. For men of this generation personal 'improvement' was no less important than social 'utility'. In the diary of the Whig and Unitarian James Losh, we can see that he intended to give his daughters 'all the advantages of education' and, something that Stevenson could not achieve, leave them 'enough to maintain them as gentlewomen, should they remain single'. And so Losh's daughter Celia was sent in 1817 to stay with her uncle's family in Rouen for six months – conventionally, to 'improve in drawing, dancing and speaking the French language', but also to make up for an education till then wholly domestic, 'to habituate her a little to act for herself and to acquire self possession and ease by mixing and conversing with strangers.'

Some of the consequences of the relative freedom bestowed on young women in these circles are amusingly displayed in Katharine Thomson's second novel, *Rosabel*, published in 1835. Its heroine – motherless of course – reacts against the 'state and form, and economy, and improvement' in her home. 'I hate economy,' she cries, 'and I never will give in to improvement – sermons by the hour, and backboards a yard long'. *Rosabel* is a historical novel, set in the late eighteenth century, but its relaxed authorial stance belongs to the 1830s. This is explicit when the author speaks: where once 'a parental fiat' was all in all, 'ours are times of independence'; or, political economists now say that 'tedious, old-fashioned sort of charity' must be abjured. There is nothing surprising about the assured and dashing tone of Elizabeth Stevenson's letters to Harriet Carr.[2]

In the winter of 1826 she seems to have been in London with her father, a man able to give great quantities of theoretical aid and advice 'in the line of improvement', to the extent that she was prepared to listen. She is said to have continued her studies in Latin, French and Italian with him, and to have regarded Goldsmith, Cowper, Pope and Scott as her favourite authors – not exactly a showy set, but soon to be greatly expanded. Her presence at 3 Beaufort Row in Chelsea is suggested by a letter from John Stevenson, dated 5 December, which belongs as far as one can tell to 1826.[3]

His ship *Catharine*, 535 tons, had been built in London in 1819 and sometimes sailed to and from Madras and Bengal for the East India Company.[4] It was in the river below Woolwich, prevented by a strong adverse wind from making progress but hoping to reach the company's docks on the north side of the river at Blackwall within a few days. Transformed in 1806, they were the largest and best equipped docks in the world; the mast-house was 117 feet high and a 'dominant landmark for homeward-bound sailors' as they sailed up the Thames. 'The Weather is abominably cold', John complained, 'for we have no stoves on board; we have very hard work beating up the river and I have [a] four hour watch to keep every night.' He expected to see his sixteen-year-old sister in Chelsea on the following Saturday, once the ship had gone into dock.[5]

She might have stayed in London for some months, but exactly where she was is not known until the early summer, when a letter from her father dated 2 July 1827 refers to her having been at Knutsford for above a month. In that month Henry Holland thanked Maria Edgeworth for the volume of *Little Plays for Children* she had sent. His wife and children passed the entire summer at Linley Wood and Knutsford until October. In December Knutsford and Tatton celebrated a major occasion: the coming of age of William Egerton,

Captain of the Knutsford troop of Cheshire cavalry.[6] Elizabeth could have been at Knutsford for the celebrations, but equally, off on a round of visits. Her second music book, dated 12 June 1827, is full of popular songs like 'On the banks of Allan water', together with Italian, French and German pieces, and contains headings like 'Copied from L. A. D. H. February 1826', 'from Louisa K's' and 'Copied from Charlotte E. Banno< >', with the date 7 March 1827. She might have had her friends' books with her in Knutsford, but it is more likely that she did her copying at their houses.[7]

If Charlotte E. Bannow was a sister of the beautiful, warm-hearted and enthusiastic 'Sophy Banow' Jane Byerley mentioned to Elizabeth, she was the daughter of the Colonel Banow who in June 1826 had left meretricious Cheltenham for Bath. 'They are looking for a house in Devonshire', commented Jane with mild asperity, 'but I do not expect they will ever be settled but will grow tired of every place after a year's residence.' A visit to Bath, or to soft and relaxing Devonshire, sounds more social than anything else, not a serious preparation for teaching or authorship. A good marriage was another matter. Young spinsters were very mobile in those days.[8]

In the middle of 1827 John wrote three letters to Elizabeth at Knutsford. It was clear in the first letter[9] that he was no longer staying at Beaufort Row, as he mentions lodgings, which seem to have been in Chelsea. He had joined a ship called *Recovery* – 443 tons, Captain H. C. Chapman, according to *Lloyd's Register of Shipping, For 1828*. The Captain stated that he would be 'seriously displeased if he heard any officer making use of an oath', John told her in his third letter. He was expecting to sail for Bombay on 15 June 1827, calling at Portsmouth on the way for passengers and sailing from there on the 24th. It was not an East India Company charter in that year. A letter from William Stevenson to Elizabeth refers to 'another of Mr C. Forbes ships' sailing a little later in the summer.'[10]

He was very definitely in correspondence with his sister now. 'I was much amused with your account of your loadstone hill – indeed with your whole narration of your travels', he wrote in answer to a lost letter, and was pleased to hear that she had begun a journal; he hoped for long extracts from it. At this point in his letter of 8 and 10 June he quotes what must be the earliest phrase from her correspondence that has been accidentally preserved, trite though it is:

> Sophia, last Sunday, shewed me the caricature you drew – I think the [?danger *deleted*] idea very good. They were all well – I have not yet seen Capt Roberdean –
> 'I must now conclude, my dear John, with desiring' but where is the conclusion – and dear – not dearest – oh fie! I hope you will not be so hurried next time you write –
> I hope Aunts Lumb [as well a *deleted*] and Abb intend writing soon, as I shall be disappointed if I go away without a letter from them – I received one from my Aunt at Berwick the day before yesterday inclosing one from Isabella – they had

not till then concluded moving but they are now finally settled in their new house – I have written to Isabella, & asked her for a lock of her hair – what sort of answer do you think I shall get-? Her last letter to me was in a very friendly style, as also my aunts –

The whole family was in constant correspondence, Elizabeth included. John even suggested that she should write to him twice before his ship left England, since packages could be forwarded from Portsmouth. He gives a description of a grand farewell party – 'twenty five ladies, mostly young, but hardly one pretty', dancing for hours after a dinner 'in the first style' on the newly holystoned quarter deck, hung with awnings and decorated with gay flags. He expresses his usual distaste: 'I wished fifty times their toes had *stuck* to the deck', betraying what modern theoreticians regard as an all-too-typical 'masculine' formation of the age.[11] He nevertheless engaged in a detached but sentimental dance with his young relations, Elizabeth as well as Isabella:

> Have you commenced your plan of early rising & walking yet? How I should [like] these fine mornings to have a stroll with you in that park where the old abbey (am I right -) is – or in that where we had once upon a time a sail in a punt together when Elisabeth was a little girl of ten years old & liked brother John to kiss her – You see how saucy I am grew [*sic*] now you are away –
>
> I have seen Logan, but only for a short time – the packet with all the letters is sent to the Treasury so I have not yet seen it -
>
> June 10th
>
> I have seen it – I mean, I received it yesterday & did you think I was going to throw away your hair as closed in the little packet – So I have deposited both safe in my writing [desk?] I hope next time you will give me leave to look.

A letter of 13 June from Gravesend[12] thanks his sister for writing so often and so well: 'I think you have a talent at letter writing for truly your epistles are remarkably good.' His flirtatiousness, so odd in a man of nearly thirty, continues – 'we expect to leave here tomorrow for Portsmouth when our passengers join us – about twenty-three in number and thirteen ladies – most of them young', or, 'I had a long conversation with Sophia L- on Saturday evening – She is very pleasant and spirited certainly, but what a pity she is so ugly – Were she only plain I could bear it, but her mouth – it is enough to frighten one, and her beetle eyebrows – her lover ought to be blind.' More sensibly, he expressed his pleasure with two letters Elizabeth had sent her father, 'particularly the one containing a criticism on Lord Byron's poetry', but then went on to describe his third mate, 'Wm [or Mr]Greig' – 'he seems pleasant and agreeable but I believe in a ladies eyes personal description goes first – Well then – he is very dark with long black whiskers, thin faced, not very tall and rather good looking – are you satisfied? aetat 23 but by your reckoning 28.'

The third letter in this group,[13] probably written on 29 June 1827, announces that his ship was detained at Portsmouth by adverse winds.

Passengers had come on board. As second officer he had been placed at the head of a table where ladies and gentlemen sat alternately, 'contrary to the usual custom'. All the ladies except one were plain, he remarked wryly, and she – even more wryly – 'seemed much inclined to enter into a flirtation with a young cadet' who sat between them. Every evening, he reported, there was dancing and music, as unpleasant for him, presumably, as his duty to carve at table, but he liked the passengers and was 'getting very intimate with the Doctor', who was 'going to propose establishing a newspaper' for the long voyage to India.

They could have done with someone like Thomas Moore, who in 'almost continuous calms' when on a voyage to America fascinated all on board with his brilliantly dramatic wit and melodious singing.[14] John's letters give the opposite impression: he was far more withdrawn, in the company of ladies in particular. 'I should so like so much to have heard from you once more before leaving England', he cried at last,

> Give my best love to my aunts Lumb and Abb and remember me to aunt Holland and cousins Bessy and Lucy.
>
> > Ever my dearest Sister,
> > Your very affecte. Brother
> > Jno. Stevenson.

Adverse winds continued to prevent John's ship from leaving Portsmouth, we learn from the most valuable letter of all in the Sharps collection. It is from Elizabeth's father, the only one to her that has ever turned up.[15] His comments on reviews of Scott's *Life of Napoleon* and Thomas Moore's *The Epicurean* in the *Literary Gazette* fix the year as 1827:

> > 3, Beaufort Row,
> > [Monday] July 2d.
>
> My dear Elisabeth,
> I enclose a letter from John dated from Portsmouth on Friday where he was detained by strong West Winds. I should not be surprised if he were still there; as the wind, tho' more moderate is still adverse to his getting out of the Channell. I suppose he will tell you the news: He seems very comfortable and likes the Captain and Doctor, as well as the passengers. His sitting at the head of the table and being obliged to carve will be of service to him; but I should imagine his being left handed will be against this operation. He seems to have expected a letter from you whilst he was at Portsmouth; but he should have reflected that you had no idea he was still there: but imagined he was beyond the reach of letters. As he expects however, a packet of letters to be sent by another of Mr C. Forbes ships, which sails the 13 of this month, you must have a long letter here by the 10 or 11, and request one or both of your aunts to write please.

Family correspondence was a duty. The aunts were expected to write to John and, though Elizabeth had left Avonbank, she was expected both to compose epistles and continue her studies. Whether this was to prepare herself to be a wife who was a model of hidden erudition is unclear. At least he treated his sixteen-year-old daughter as a literate adult, even if she needed to be kept at her books:

> I am glad to learn by your letter to your Mother that you are busy working for yourself: you must however, work a large portion of the day, if you have little or no time to read – as you have now been at Knutsford above a month. I hope you [are] again applying to your Latin and Italian; Let me know, when you write, in what manner you spend your day – I mean, so far as work or study is concerned.
> I send the last No. of the Literary Gazette, which contains a review of Scott's Life of Napoleon, or rather long extracts from it. It was to have been published on February [Friday?] but I believe is not actually out yet. The Literary Gazette also contains a review of Moore's Epicurean – but I can hardly judge from what they say, what sort of work it is. I dare say, very gaudy. I suspect from the style, the review is written by Miss Langden [Landon?].

The review of Scott's *Life of Napoleon* was indeed a long collection of extracts. It was advertised as published on the back page of the *Literary Gazette*, along with Moore's *Epicurean*. Moore was already well known for his *Irish Melodies*. His reputation was made as soon as the first set was issued in 1808. They are sung, with feeling, to this day. Other *Melodies* followed, and from 1818 he began publishing a series of *National Airs*. The first number of these contained the popular 'Oft in the stilly night', which duly appeared in Elizabeth Stevenson's second music book.

The *Literary Gazette* reviewer effusively declared that *The Epicurean* would 'ever rank as one as one of the most exquisite productions in English literature, alike valued for its lustre and purity' – the complete opposite of the sour opinion De Quincey published in the *Westminster Review*. Stevenson evidently suspected something of the same kind. Mackintosh and Emerson were using 'gaudy' of dreams and fables about this time, according to the Oxford English Dictionary. It was not even necessary to invoke 'utility'. Moore's only novel, a philosophical prose romance set in third-century Egypt, is a tissue of visionary mysteries and marvels. It echoes mythopoeic works like Shelley's *Alastor* and Keats's *Hyperion*, and as a novel is lacking in substance. One of Stevenson's favourite words was 'luminous', but by this he meant intellectual rather than mystical clarity.[16]

He did not condescend to notice L. E. L's poem 'The White Ship' in the same issue, but continued with some items of news:

> I believe it is since you went that – after I had written 3 Letters to him – Mr Loundes himself called at the Treasury, with my little book he had kept so many years: Since that he called again – when I was not there – but whether to re-borrow the Book a third time I cannot tell.
> Mr Lojan [Logan?] is arrived, John saw him once: he brought back the parcel and letter Mr Bilz had sent by him to poor Margaret. I delivered them to Edward – Mr Lojan's cousin, who called at the Treasury with these things – told me he had a cousin in the Martin: and that she was last seen in a dreadful tempest not

far from Madagascar – in which she is supposed to have foundered – Mr Lojan says the report in India was that – she had been wrecked on the Coast of that Island and the crew murdered by the natives.

She must have felt the incongruity: a young man who ran the same professional risks in the eastern seas was the loving brother who encouraged her interest in playful uses of language – 'I should not have known her at all', he had written about an acquaintance. 'She is grown very course, & her manners are very much *vulgarified* – is there such a word'? On another occasion he asked, 'By the bye what is the meaning of this phrase? – are apple pies in better order than other pies?'[17] Her father, too, was pleased that she had begun to keep what John had once called her log:

> If you should go into Wales, I expect you will keep a regular journal of what you see and remember.
> Your Mother will write by this opportunity and she will tell you all other news respecting Catherine &c. She and I wrote to her yesterday – and enclosed your letter, – one from John and one from William – so that, today when she gets to Billericay she will be much gratified by receiving 4 letters at once. I shall hope to have a long letter from you before the 10 – and the letters for John by that day.
> Your affectionate Father,
> W. Stevenson.

Miss Stevenson.

Her half-sister Catherine, then in her early teens, was off to a village in Essex a little way east of London, situated on high ground with scenic views over fertile countryside. It was noted for the number of Dissenters living there, but these seem to have attended Baptist, Quaker and Independent meeting houses. Why exactly Catherine went is unknown. Nor is it certain that Elizabeth travelled into Wales in this summer of 1827. The reference in a later letter to 'a very happy month' at Aber, a small village in North Wales about five miles from Bangor on the coast road, 'with 17 aunts, cousins and such like', has been firmly tied to William Stevenson's conditional clause, and the holiday extended to six weeks by reference to a later sentence in Elizabeth's letter: 'I remember when I first came from spending a very happy fortnight at Plâs Brereton (near Caernarvon, you know) to Liverpool I used to get on a sort of knoll from which I could see the Welsh hills, and think of the places beyond again.' This is not impossible, but Elizabeth might have been alluding to two quite distinct visits, at uncertain dates. The importance of Wales to Elizabeth Stevenson, both in her youth and in the years to come, was considerable.[18]

A local poll book shows that Plas Brereton was a small gentleman's residence about a mile north of the old town of Caernarfon and its great castle. The house was inhabited in 1831 by a Henry Turner. His father William Turner lived nearby from 1809, in a house called Parkia that he had enlarged; it looked down on a beautiful part of the Menai Straits. This William Turner had begun life as a quarryman in the Lake District, worked for minerals in

Ireland till 1798 and in 1800 purchased the Diffwys quarry near Ffestiniog on the other side of Snowdon, just about the time when the Liverpool firm of Holland and Humble began to sell slates from the quarries belonging to Lord Penrhyn. A decade or so later both William Turner and Samuel Holland senior were working quarries near Llanberis, just a few miles from Caernarfon.[19]

Samuel Holland junior's memoirs contain no more than a passing reference to William Turner, but the unbelievably anecdotal autobiography of his eleventh child, Llewelyn Turner, states that Samuel Holland senior rented Plas Brereton 'in the early part' of the century. Elizabeth might have stayed at Plas Brereton when she was very young. Rather later, Samuel junior and Llewelyn, who was born in 1823, would tramp the hills together and exchange visits when the Hollands had moved to Merionethshire, to live near a quarry they had opened near Ffestiniog. The friendship did not lapse. Llewelyn was Samuel's best man when in 1850 he married Annie Robins of Alesly Park in Warwickshire.

In the early decades of the nineteenth century a social circle of enterprising new men must have been forming in North Wales, to the dismay of the Welsh inhabitants, who 'complained that a *tramp*, who walked over the country and got what ought to have been theirs, was unbearable.' A visit to Plas Brereton would have removed Elizabeth from the placid, near-pastoral life of aunt Lumb's house in Cheshire by Knutsford heath, her father's scholarly home at Chelsea, the elegant school for ladies at Stratford-upon-Avon and the more sophisticated 'vortex of London Society' her rich cousins moved in. She would have stepped into almost another world, socially, culturally and topographically. Llewelyn claims that in his boyhood it was common 'to see men stripped naked to the waist and covered with blood fighting in the streets of Caernarfon', which were full of old guns, relics of the French and American wars. His father always kept great house-dogs, to scare the tramps going from place to place in gangs. Was Elizabeth taken by her cousin Samuel, as Llewelyn was, to see the house where a woman had been brutally murdered with a sickle by a gigantic Welshman? Would the sparkling gooseberry wine as good as champagne and ginger wine made in the half barrel at Parkia, the 'glorious thick cream and fruit' generously given to neighbours, the hams and bacon cured on the premises and the turkeys, ducks and hens have reminded her of her grandparents' old home at Sandlebridge Farm?[20]

'My father was engaged in speculations in Wales ... ' is the beginning of a section of Samuel Holland's somewhat disorganised memoirs. The word 'speculations' is charged with ambiguity: a gamut of meanings ranging from distant, high-risk investment in the expectation of high profits to much closer, utterly pragmatic investigation of many relatively small possibilities – Samuel Holland the younger's end of the scale. His father had in 1818 begun to quarry for the excellent Ordovician slates, fine-grained and blue-grey in colour, found in the Snowdon range, far to the west of Liverpool and the lowlands of Cheshire. His first quarry was at Rhiwbryfdir in North Wales, about a mile away from Turner and Casson's quarry at Diffwys, a thousand or so feet up in the mountains at the head of Dyffryn Maentwrog, also known as the Vale of Ffestiniog. Slates were carried by mule or carted some miles down steep tracks from the high quarries to quays along the river Dwyryd, which was here not much above sea-level and navigable at high tides as far as the village of Maentwrog. The valley flattened out and the Dwyryd wound westwards between steep slopes of smaller hills through the 'most romantic portion of the fertile and highly picturesque vale'. The slates were loaded into shallow-draught boats and sailed or rowed down to the broad and sandy estuary of Traeth Bach, rich in shellfish gathered when the tide fell, for transference to sea-going ships.

A little downstream from Maentwrog was the property of W. G. Oakeley of Plas Tan y Bwlch, from whom Holland rented his quarry. His substantial hall (now a study centre) and its grounds were situated high on a hill across from the village and its bridge, well shown in an engraving after an 1836 sketch by David Cox the elder.[21] In earlier days the learned Thomas Love Peacock had stayed like a hermit in a cottage at Tan y Bwlch, 'associating with no one, & hiding his head like a murderer', a suspicious local told his friend Shelley in 1812, but his highly original novel *Headlong Hall* in 1816 was soon to prove how strongly, if conventionally, he responded to the scenery of this beautiful north-western corner of Wales.[22]

After very few years Samuel Holland became dissatisfied with the man who ran his quarry (he lived in the Grapes Hotel at Maentwrog and got drunk every evening), so in March 1821 he sent for his eighteen-year-old son Samuel in a hurry to take over. He caught the steam packet that sailed from Liverpool across to Bagillt on the Dee estuary, and then had to make the greater part of his journey west on foot with his carpet-bag. Like his spare and healthy cousin Dr Henry Holland, he was a heroic walker, but in places there were no regular roads, only footpaths and cart-tracks over the mountains. In 1826 a Lancashire commercial traveller on horseback died in Snowdonia on his way to remote Ffestiniog. When Samuel finally reached his father on the third day after setting out – he did not sleep on the second night as rats were running about in his room at an inn – he was told how he might learn 'the art of Quarrying' and advised to stay in lodgings in a decent house rather than in a hotel.[23]

From 1821 onwards Samuel Holland was one of the pioneers of the north Wales slate industry, a small capitalist finding and working slate and ironstone quarries and copper mines, running sheep on local hills, taking trips to Ireland, the Isle of Man and Putney (where he stayed with John Menzies) in the course of business, immersed in road improvement, purchases, agreements, legal quarrels with the distant speculators of the Welsh Slate and Copper Mining Company, political agitation to alter the duties paid on Welsh but not English slates and complicated arrangements for their transport. His efforts follow on and merge with those of that great speculator William Madocks, owner of the

Tan yr Allt estate a few miles to the north and west of Maentwrog, who had in the early years of the century diverted the Glaslyn river as it ran into the sand and marsh of the next estuary to the north, Traeth Mawr, in order to reclaim a thousand acres of land near Penmorfa, on some of which was built the 'toy' town of Tremadog. It is still a famous example of town planning, T-shaped, with public buildings that included a classical town hall and, in happier days, a gothic privy and a woollen mill 'in a style that was the very opposite of satanic'. Following his initial success, Madocks had in the course of several years and with major setbacks managed to throw a great embankment across the whole estuary of Traeth Mawr, to reclaim even more land and establish the larger town of Porthmadog, leaving little Tremadog in a time-warp.[24]

The contrast between old and new landscapes is made emphatic in chapter 7 of *Headlong Hall*, the seat of Harry Headlong Esquire in the vale of Llanberis. Three visiting philosophers walk from the hall to Tremadog 'through the sublimely romantic pass of Aberglaslynn' and along 'the edge of Traeth Mawr, a vast arm of the sea, which they then beheld in all the magnificence of the flowing tide', and out along one arm of the embankment, not yet completed. They marvel at the scene but simultaneously mourn for what has vanished – 'whatever consolation may be derived from the probable utility of the works which have excluded the waters from their ancient receptacle', Peacock commented. 'The mountain-frame remains unchanged, unchangeable; but the liquid mirror it enclosed is gone.' Tremadog, 'a city, as it were, in its cradle', sparks off a typically Peacockian debate on the return walk, in which 'the multiplied comforts and conveniences of life diffused over the whole community' are set against the children of the poor slaving amidst the 'dizzy and complicated motions of diabolical mechanism' in cotton-mills, 'death-doomed from their cradles'. As they approach Headlong Hall on their way back, the stately verbal ritual of their arguments is broken by a tremendous explosion. A fellow guest, the landscape-gardener Mr Marmaduke Milestone, Esquire, was improving 'the capabilities of the scenery' about the hall with gunpowder. He takes his name from Humphry Repton, who, coincidentally, had proposed engraving the Egerton family arms on an obelisk or milestone to show the grandeur and extent of Tatton Park.[25]

Financially, Madocks was almost ruined by his latest enterprise. One of those who attempted to come to his rescue was Shelley, who leased his rebuilt cottage of Tan yr Allt high on the mountain above Tremadog and publicly pledged his own fortune to this 'work of national benefit'. His assistance, one can only say, was Shelleyan; 'the friend of the unfriended poor' infuriated the local gentry. He did not stay long at Tremadog. After a mysterious night attack on their house, he and his wife left the district altogether.[26]

Madocks added a harbour to Porthmadog at a cost of over a thousand pounds in 1825 – 'a very speculative year', Samuel junior rightly claimed. The first of its new quays was made for his slates. This gave a far better outlet to the quarries above Ffestiniog, in years when mining speculation was at its highest, now able to compete with Lord Penrhyn's quarries on the other side of Snowdonia. Poor Madocks, however, was forced to leave Wales soon afterwards and died in France in 1828. Samuel Holland's father eventually ended his chequered career by sometimes taking his meals alone at his son's house – 'a sign that he & Sam had had a tiff, ten to one about their mining speculations', wrote Mrs Gaskell. 'Edward Holland allows Uncle S. 200£ a year as long as he does not speculate, and Sam is to mention if he does. Now Sam's notion of speculations and Uncle Sam's differ widely – so you may fancy the uncomfortable work that sometimes ensues.'[27]

But the Hollands were always a close-knit family. Whilst the men looked out for each other's financial and business interests, their wives and daughters took full advantage of the houses and estates they managed to acquire. Elizabeth's first visit to North Wales was one of many taken by herself and by her cousins, dating at least from Henry Holland's in 1802. Her father's firm expectation that she would keep 'a regular journal' of what she saw and remembered, shows that such visits, however pleasurable in themselves, had to have some kind of educational purpose. Similarly, when Martha Sharpe wrote in 1823 that the Hollands were all well '& the Junrs very much delighted with their Mountain Tour', she takes an over-simple view of a visit to Samuel and a stay in Barmouth made by Mary, Bessy and Lucy Holland of Knutsford. It is possible to deduce more complex aims from the journals they wrote. The kind of freedom that Katharine Thomson's Rosabel enjoyed is evident enough, but their serious characters are revealed and 'improvement' lurks underneath.[28]

Of three journals relating to this tour, only the first and third have been found. The first, entitled 'Journal of an (intended) expedition to Barmouth in the year 1823', was almost certainly the longest and, like the surviving Lakes journal, was intended to be more than a mere record. Nine lines of blank verse by 'Millman' (Henry Hart Milman) on Welsh mountain scenery were first quoted as an decorative epigraph. The main text, in Mary's hand, begins when the party set out from Knutsford in a carriage on Wednesday, 6 August, Mary and Lucy 'spouting scraps of poetry to each other'. Uncle Samuel Holland's house at Toxteth Park was reached that evening, but they found it more difficult than expected to get a passage on a steam-packet from Liverpool.

Mary's irony at this point is subtle, amusing and significant:

> Our hearts and spirits began to flag a little: particularly when we reflected it was not the *habit* of the Holland family to make expeditions solely with a view to pleasure, and *therefore* it was never likely to answer. The Hollands are a useful, working, money-trying-to-get family, and not intended for an ornamental or pleasure-taking race.

All three sisters wrote to be read – by their aunt Lumb amongst others, if we may judge from the fact that at Barmouth they received letters from her, and also from Peter Holland, Henry Holland, his wife, cousin Anne and so on. 'The idea of breakfasting without letters! almost an unheard of thing' is an exclamation by Lucy near the end of the first journal worth pondering. Journals, like commonplace books and letters, were passed around families as a matter of course. The fact that the second notebook of this tour is missing is in itself suggestive. But how did their male relations react to Mary's bantering truth-in-jest? Indulgently, in all probability. They knew that they were 'useful, working, money-trying-to-get' men. What else should they be? It was what allowed their womenfolk to play and to indulge in the more superficial delights of fine writing.[29]

Passages like the following, in the handwriting of Lucy but not untypical of her older sisters, are bookish in more than one sense:

> I read Beattie's Minstrel & thought the epithet 'silent mountains' very correct. They give one the idea of *silence* & *stillness* so completely. – *I* cannot account for this, but Mary will have it that there is nothing more simple, 'as we know if we think about it that there is a very thin population in those high regions, & there can be no great towns.' So we know if we come to reason calmly upon it that where there is less talking, there is more silence.

The punctuation is a little defective here, but we can easily gather that if ever the schoolgirl Elizabeth Stevenson asked her older cousins about poetic style, she might receive a dry and literal reply from Mary and a more ambiguous response from Lucy. Yet Mary was perfectly capable of exaggeration and literary pastiche. Once when Lucy did not return in time for a meal she wailed, 'Our affectionate hearts took fright, and so loud & vehement were their throbbings, that we could hear each others beating: Bessy's sounded like the golden string of a lute, and mine like the silver chord of a guitar.'

Mary had just written that Lucy had been

> rather grumpy tonight because she is not 'either pretty, or witty, or handy, or clever, or' a long list of et ceteras, which I cannot remember. 'She cannot draw, or *cast a sum*, or dance, or make poetry, or in short do anything; and she should so like to be something. Its fine talking, but she is good for nothing: she must be very *spiritual* for she has neither head, nor body.' – We endeavoured to administer a little comfort to her, but in vain; 'She has no quickness, nor attention, nor observation: she should so like to be sharp & quick.' So we were obliged to leave her deeply impressed with a sense of her own cyphership, and consoling herself with uttering loud yawns just like Sally Felton.

In fact, Lucy's writing in the journal is keen, lively and literate. As the youngest, still ambitious but able to see her own future in her older, unmarried and blue-stocking sisters, she was letting off steam. She displays the kind of yearning that might have been felt by her younger cousin Elizabeth in the ambience of Knutsford, though as far as is known, Lucy did not profit from the wider perspectives of a boarding-school education. A few lines later she found release in a petty riposte: 'Mary was rather grumpy this morning because it was a wet day – & every time she looked out of the window, she said "Oh dear", & at last got a silly novel to read, instead of employing herself rationally.' There is no reason to assume that the sisters were fundamentally quarrelsome. All three probably played familiar roles – with each other, and for the benefit of the wider family circle.[30]

NOTES

1 *Memoir of Currie*, ed. Currie, II, pp. 262-7 (JC to JC, Liverpool, 17 June 1803, qu.); Bruce, *Handbook to Newcastle*, p. 94.

2 *Losh Diaries*, I, pp. 67-8, 188; K. Thomson, *Rosabel*, I, pp. 7-8, 304; II, p. 11. For Losh see *DNB (Missing Persons)*.

3 JGS: TS, JS to ECS, Ship Catherine Below Woolwich, 5 December; annotated in pencil, 'Dated 6 December 1826'. Cp. Chadwick, 1910, p. 138: wrong about the date of John's disappearance, but possibly right about the authors his sister read.

4 *Lloyd's Register of Shipping, For 1827;* Hardy, *Supplement*, pp. 60, 80, 355: 22 April 1819 – 16 February 1820; 24 June 1829 – 22 May 1830; 10 August 1833 – 8 June 1834. *Catharine* was a popular name; I assume that it was not the ship that belonged to Palmer & Co. (like the barque *Marianne Sophia*) in the port of Calcutta, 490 tons, built in Rangoon in 1813 (*Bengal Almanac, and Annual Directory, For 1823*).

5 *London – World City*, ed. Fox, pp. 229, 230 (illustr.); Sheppard, *Infernal Wen*, p. 111.

6 WS's letter dated 1827 by internal references (p. 286 below). See also DCLH: HH to ME, L Brook Street, 29 July 1827; *Portrait*, p. 5; Butler, *Edgeworth*, p. 165; *Earl of Chester's Regiment*, pp. 111-12.

7 MCL: MS F823. 894. C1, unpaged, pp. [27, 42, 45]. Other dates: 23 August 1828 and 14 May 1828. See p. 154 above.

8 JGS: TS, JB to ECS, Avonbank, 14 June 1826. Transcriptions of proper names are often doubtful.

9 JGS: incomplete MS, two conj. 4to leaves (wmk 'I RUMP 1816'), JS to ECS, Blackwall, 8 [altered figure] June, with internal date of 10 June [1827].

10 See p. 286 below for WS letter, and Hardy, *Supplement*, pp. 49-50, 64, 74. JS's letters suggest that the first mate was called White; the third mate was William Greig. The ship's logs for 7 June 1830 to 13 May 1831 and 9 July 1832 to 30 May 1833 (IOLR: L/MAR/B/106C) have been seen. JS's name is not found amongst the officers in the 1830 voyage; the fourth officer, H. T. Brown, died at Calcutta on 28 October.

11 See Herbert Sussman, *Victorian Masculinities: Manhood and Masculine Poetics in Early Victorian Literature and Art*, Cambridge, 1995, pp. 5, 13, 46-8.

12 JGS: three TS copies, JS to ECS, Ship Recovery, Gravesend, 13 /17 June [1827]; address at end: 'Miss Stevenson, Mrs. Lumbs, Heath, Knutsford.' One TS is dated 13 June and two 17 June. These agree in manifest errors – 'Blackwell', 'Eecovery', etc., but have 'about 23' for 'eatat 23' [sc. aetat] in the first, which is headed 'Copy'.

13 JGS: two TS copies, almost identical, JS to ECS, Recovery, Portsmouth, 20 [29] June [1827]; address at end as above. WS's letter of 2 July below would date this 29 June 1827.

14 Howard Mumford Jones, *The Harp That Once – A Chronicle of the Life of Thomas Moore* [1937], New York, 1970, pp. 59, 68.

15 JGS: three TSS, with typing errors but no truly substantive variants, WS to 'Elisabeth', 3 Beaufort Row, 2 July [1827]. The whole text of this letter is given.

16 H. M. Jones, *Thomas Moore*, pp. 104, 202, 262-3; *The London Literary Gazette; and Journal of Belles Lettres, Arts, Sciences, &c.*, Saturday, 30 June 1827, pp. 401-5, 417-29. Miss 'Langden' is not mentioned in the *Wellesley Index;* cp. p. 251 above.

17 JGS: incomplete MS, JS to ECS, Blackwall, 8 and 10 June, and TS, 13 June [1827].

18 T. Wright, *The History and Topography of the County of Essex*, II, London, 1835, p. 544; ECG to Eliza Gaskell, 17 July 1838 (*Letters*, p. 16); Gérin, pp. 29-30. See p. 243 above.

19 SH, *Memoirs*, ed. Davies, pp. 1, 4. I am indebted to Dr David Gwyn for information about Plas Brereton and the Turner family. In this section I rely greatly upon SH junior's memoirs (NLW), Malchow's *Gentleman Capitalists* and M. J. T. Lewis, *Sails on the Dwyryd* (including all quotations from SH's diary in NLW). I am most grateful to Dr Michael Lewis for expert advice and assistance.

20 *Memories of Sir Llewelyn Turner*, ed. Vincent, pp. 12, 16, 48-50, 58, 66, 71-3, 215-18.

21 Lewis, *Topographical Dictionary of Wales*, 'Maentwrog'; Knutsford Edn, III, opp. p. xxiv (W. Radcliffe's engraving, from T. Roscoe, *Wanderings and Excursions in North Wales*, London, 1838). See Lewis, *Sails on the Dwyryd*, pp. 21, 83.

22 *Letters of Percy Bysshe Shelley*, ed. F. L. Jones, Oxford, 1964, I, p. 334.

23 SH, *Memoirs*, ed. Davies, pp. 4-6; Dodd, *Industrial Revolution*, pp. 129, 326. The steam packet *Cambria*'s regular service began after her launch on 17 May 1821 (F. Neal, 'Liverpool shipping in the early nineteenth century', *Liverpool and Merseyside*, ed. Harris, p. 177).

24 SH, *Memoirs*, ed. Davies, pp. 10-14; Paul Coones and John Patten, *The Penguin Guide to the Landscape of England and Wales*, Harmondsworth, 1986, pp. 264-6.

25 Butler, *Peacock Displayed*, pp. 31-2, 47-8; Stroud, *Repton*, pp. 79, 83.

26 See Richard Holmes, *Shelley the Pursuit*, London, 1964, chapters 7 and 9.

27 SH, *Memoirs*, ed. Davies, pp. 11-12; Millward and Robinson, *Landscapes of North Wales*, pp. 95-9; Dodd, *Industrial Revolution*, pp. 42-4, 125, 214-16; ECG to Eliza Gaskell, 14 Dover Street [17 July 1838] (*Letters*, p. 17).

28 MS to JWW, Heathside, 15 October 1823 (WAL: EHC 204/51; Hall, p. 165).

29 DCLH: M, B and LH, Barmouth journal 1, pp. 1-2, 66, 68, 79.

30 DCLH: M, B and LH, Barmouth journal 1, pp. 51, 61, 64. For Sally Felton see p. 130 above.

16

Social life in Wales

SOMETHING VERY LIKE the nature, and, occasionally, the exact details of Elizabeth Stevenson's experiences on her early visits to Wales can be found in these journals kept by her cousins on their visit to Barmouth. On 9 August 1823 Mary, Bessy and Lucy left the house of the Samuel Hollands and went down to the quayside at Liverpool. There they 'were hauled into a wet boat', Mary's hand '*tenderly clasped* by a rough looking sailor', to be rowed to the *Druid*. Two fellow passengers appeared, ladies 'who looked as if they might be come on purpose to be sick.' Bessy asked for help from a man she thought was the Captain, but he turned out to be a West Indian planter or overseer from Jamaica. He was kind to them, but also warmly defended slavery. Wind and tide proved so adverse that eventually the *Druid* returned to Liverpool. (Lucy rather scattily wondered what town it was when churches and houses came in sight.) These set-backs made Mary advise the Hollands never to go on a tour of amusement with a party of their own relatives, 'unless they have some usefully-dull scheme in view, which may in some degree take from the pleasure of their plan.'

Bessy then took over the comic description of their travels, revealing that Lucy's gown had been cobbled up for the excursion 'out of an old stout silk, which had lain by some 19 years'. It soon 'began to split, & shew symptoms of rapid decay in every direction; like the envelopements of an old Egyptian mummy, on being again exposed to the air.' Lucy and Anne went to buy 'a cheap cottage stuff' in Liverpool. All three had to 'cut out the skirt & raddle it up that night', as uncle Sam told them that the *Llewellyn* was due to sail at 7 a. m. At 5 o'clock on Tuesday 12th, he roused them with 'All hands ahoy'.

Their light amusement at their own behaviour sharpened in tone when it was directed at other passengers on this larger steam-packet – smart young ladies and their attendant beau, who lisped and began his sentences with ''Pon my soul'. An uncouth man 'with the face of a hog – dignified by the title of Mayor of Pwllhely' was caricatured, and they found odd characters fit for a farce promenading up and down: 'an immense John Bull figure, with a segar puffing out in the centre of a red round face trying to sing at the same time to the music' of the ship's band, and another John Bull, 'most likely a Yorkshire clothier'. However, the Welsh coast from Conway to Bangor, and the beauty of Bangor and the Menai strait, delighted them – their raptures only modified by the 'packet's giddiness' and 'black soot falling in a shower' upon their clothes. It was a cheap voyage, costing five shillings each for fifty miles.[1]

At Bangor they stayed at an inn, where Mary, 'knowing in Welch small cattle', carefully examined their beds. Lucy was now the one 'in the dumps' because her gown needed to be sewn. Her sisters revealed that she was pretending they were '3 dress makers settled in a little room in a narrow street, to get a pinching livelihood by dint of stitching! and the idea afflicted her picturesque spirit'. They then took a 'car', a vehicle for two or three on either side with luggage stowed in the middle, and galloped along the picturesque road to Caernarfon. As it was the Assizes, 'Bessy and Lucy took each separate walks into the town, in the hope of meeting with a young counsellor, or some young sprig of an attorney', wrote Mary. 'No success however attended their attempts. *I* as the matron of the party staid quietly at home.' She was thirty years of age.

On they went to the 'beautiful and romantic vale' of Beddgelert, enraptured with the scenery, the practical costume of Welsh women and the playing of a blind harper – 'jangling and discordant notes', but a national custom that was new to them. Lucy rambled off across meadows looking for a waterfall, found one that 'fell into a translucent pool, quiet & cool', where she 'sat some time in profound meditation, trying to quote & to sing'.

> Longing to taste the pure stream I scrambled down a stone wall, (shewed my legs a little, but the Genius of the stream was asleep) and found there a picturesque pail, 'made as it were by more than mortal hands' (hem! Miss Lucy) which I lifted to the water, and actually quaffed a waterfall! I was intoxicated with delight!

At last they reached their cousin Sam Holland's cottage at Pen Trwyn y Garnedd, by the wharf where the slates were transferred to boats on the Dwyryd. The vale of Maentwrog, Lucy wrote, '*seems* the abode of innocence & peace, but Sam says the inhabitants are *rogues*, or *topers*, or *cheats*, or swindlers, *or* sportsmen, or runaways, or debtors &c &c.' Perhaps business was poor at this time. Certainly Tan y Bwlch was disappointing: the 'beautiful grounds' were at that time 'in rack & ruin – & every thing going to waste'. Sam's little house, fortunately, was comfortable and much cleaner than the inns they had been staying in.[2]

In the narrow valley of the Dwyryd between its low hills the slate boats with their square or fore-and-aft sails glided through the water – a pretty sight that once inspired a Mrs Skrimshire to paint a charming watercolour, inspired no doubt by the Genius of the stream. But voyages began after the hard task of unloading the heavy slates from carts and 'handing' them on board. The boats were so dependent upon spring tides that Sundays were not sacrosanct. Night work was often unavoidable. In early days Samuel himself lent a hand: 'Was up till one o'clock, got flour from Boats, and counting slates' is a typical entry in his diary. Sometimes sailing was impossible; the men had to row, standing up and facing forward with a pair of long sweeps. Whenever the boats ran aground on the shifting sandbanks in the winding channel, the men had to plunge into the water to free them, remaining in sodden clothes till their work was done. In 1832 a man was drowned when one of Holland's loaded slate boats went aground.[3]

There is no sign that the Holland sisters noticed or sympathised with workers in such conditions. Their cousin Sam, though a slate proprietor, was prepared to endure them himself if necessary as well as spouting easy generalisations about the inhabitants of the vale for the sisters' benefit. They adopted his views, took pleasure trips in his '7 shilling boat', rode his horse Kitty and a 'skeleton which he had bought for 7 & 20 shillings', walked, sketched and admired the vale by moonlight, and continued to quote poetry. Rain kept interrupting plans for Lucy to ride side-saddle on the skeleton, which turned out to be very frisky when Sam tested it. 'Hurra! die todten [*sic*] reiten schnell!' reads a footnote. Mary studied German at intervals, unless the day was wet and dull, in which case a novel would do.

Bessy, it was first thought, could ride behind Sam on Kitty, sitting on a piece of carpet and wearing her brown stuff bathing dress for a riding habit. Then, Lucy writes, 'Sam who is very spirited in all his plans as the reader will have perceived in the above Carpet concern, & Skeleton scheme, proposes to cover the cart, not with a carpet, but with the sail of a ship' for an excursion to the quarry in the hills above. The road they took went through Ffestiniog, where they met and praised the generous landlady of the inn, Miss Martha Owen, who promised them food on the way back. They jolted and jogged 'over the most horrid road possible', which sometimes was so steep and narrow that the wheels scraped against the rocks on either side.

There follow passages that their male relations would regard as useful and improving. They even interest, because of the rarity of such descriptions at this early date, modern historians, and might have satisfied William Stevenson if he ever saw anything comparable in a journal kept by his daughter Elizabeth:

> At length we reached the quarry proceeded to a place where the men were just going to blast, so had to hasten back for a few minutes out of the way: after the explosion had taken place we returned to the spot, & saw the men at work beneath us, preparing holes for the insertion of gunpowder: some slung by a rope half-way down one side of the chasm, working away with as much care as we 'sit on a sofa and sew up a seam'. After leaving this spot we went to another of the same kind, only on a lower level, going under an archway in the rock to get to it.
>
> Then we went to see the men who were splitting the slate & cutting it into the different sizes, which are called Queens, Duchesses, Countesses, Ladies, &c &c. The splitting the large thick pieces is the most curious thing: by merely inserting a chisel between the layers, they are divided as easily & smoothly as possible.

After looking over the quarry, (during which time we were once or twice obliged to run & take shelter under a little shed, when by three loud shouts the men gave notice that they were going to let off a blast) we went to the farm house, and there lunched on oat-cakes & butter, with some buttermilk to drink: the women in the cottage could neither of them speak English: one was a countrified likeness of Charlotte Wedgwood.

Martha Owen refused payment for her food and drink on their return to Ffestiniog. Though the journal abounds with instances of Holland frugality, in this instance the sisters showed a proper concern for her finances: they 'had recourse to stratagem' and left a payment with Sam.[4]

On Wednesday 20th they set off walking to meet the Tremadog chaise that was to take them to Barmouth. The tide delayed them at the Traeth Bach crossing, so, Mary recorded, 'Lucy very quietly got out her work bag and took the opportunity of mending her gloves, while Bessy and I betook ourselves to reading'. A horse at length appeared in the distance, looking as if the wind and the waves had been its grooms, ridden bareback by a Welsh maid 'who looked as though she had just sprung from the sea; (though not exactly resembling Venus)'. Their ancient courier took over and led them across the broad sands, though the horses were sometimes up to their bellies in water. Eventually they reached drier land, and the guide asked for 1/6d, which they paid quietly, as they had 'no means of knowing whether this was the regular charge or not'. Previously, they had refused to be charged 1/3d a mile by the driver of a carriage to Caernarfon; they had found the rate was 1 shilling before they started.

On they went, along a terrible road to the dramatic site of Harlech castle, where they imagined themselves in the time of Edward I, with troops marching out of the gate, 'banners flying and harps playing the martial air which still goes by their name.' The road to Barmouth was vile, sometimes over sand, at other times in the beds of streams, but eventually they reached the most comfortable inn so far, the Conygeddol Arms. The Miss Gregs had just left the day before. At the post office there was a letter from Agnes Greg and another from Fanny Edgeworth; both were young women like Bessy, in their mid-twenties. Cheerful and clean lodgings (three rooms) were found in the lower town, at £1 4s 0d a week, with an extra 5 shillings for the landlady's cooking and the use of her fire. When they mentioned the lack of a sofa, the she brought down a flock mattress and spread a quilt on it. Their sitting room had an indirect view of the sea, and, they quoted Keatsian verses,

> we can hear
> At silent noon, & eve, and early morn
> The sea's faint murmur.

Bessy preferred this part of the town to the high row of houses on the Dolgellau side (all taken), as she liked 'the gapesay' and traditional Welsh women looking 'very picturesque in their neat hats'.

The Hollands were forced by local custom to cater for themselves, but they were 'very near the cake shop, and just opposite the shop where you may purchase grocery, drapery, hosiery, stationary, literature &c &c &c.' The same shop had a circulating library, 'and really contains better books than one shd have expected: many of Scott's works, & Byron's: Tours in N. and S. Wales: the Pioneers: Pamela (which we got out: but I don't like at all: it is very dull, and Pamela herself is a great goose)', wrote Mary. Fenimore Cooper's American frontier novel of that same year, 1823, was more of a novelty than Samuel Richardson's tale of a servant girl whose soul was as valuable as that of a princess, so affecting to a female audience of the previous century.

The sands were not very firm but full of shells, which they thought little Susan Holland would like to gather. Lucy went down to the sea to bathe, whilst Mary went with her 'to amuse herself with watching the other sea nymphs – Comfortable machines – 10d a dip – The same woman watches over bodies & clothes', Bessy noted. Mary's comment was that there were 'many curious figures ready for bathing' and, with a touch of cultural envy, 'some Welsh nymphs ducking away at a little distance, to whom it seemed matter of small importance *where they* dressed or undressed themselves.' Bessy, she thought, 'looked very elegant in the water in her *riding habit*.' This joking must have been a family trait, for Sam sent them a parcel at Barmouth, addressed to 'Cousins Mary, Bessy, & Lucy *bâch*', dated from 'Bachelor Hall – Plas Pen Trwyny garnedd Amsterdam'.[5]

When three young ladies and a gentleman came to stay in the same lodgings, Lucy let her imagination run loose:

> However we 'comfort' ourself with thinking that the *Journal* which was growing rather flat, & spiritless (in spite of 'the high heathy Hills' in the last page) will now become full of entertaining matter. – These people *must* be *made out*, & then they most likely will be very odd, & mysterious. – The Lovers of Romance may expect much interest, in the details which we *may now* be able to give them, of 'the melancholy expression' constantly residing in the countenance of the female in black. – Of the beautiful singing we hear from their apartment every evening accompanied by the gentleman's flute. – Of our hearing 'Edward' pronounced in a soft voice, when the door is ajar. – ...
>
> Let them be *perfect* strangers I beg. – Fortune is propitious to my wishes the new comers are perfect strangers, & likely to be so always. We did not get a sight of them that night – but suspect they had mackerel for their supper – & the supposition we found upon this circumstance is that they are a family addicted to a good many meals a day – we will say 5 – & make a point of a hot supper before going to bed –

On Sunday 24th, because the parish church was at some distance, Mary stayed at home but Bessy and Lucy went in heavy rain to three interconnecting rooms where an Irish gentleman read the Church of England service and preached to a congregation which included most of the English bathers, all sitting on planks of wood laid across chairs. He was eloquent, but 'too Calvinistic' for their taste, so that evening all three tried the large, handsome Welsh Calvinist chapel, where the singing, their principal motive for going, was excellent. But the extempore Welsh of the preacher astonished them 'with the odd sounds he made & the recitative into which he finally worked himself'. All the while, 'the people answered him with their groans.' Men then came to collect money, which the Hollands, 'not knowing what for, & not being very full in the pocket', at first refused, but were told it was for the poor.

They were even more amazed when a second preacher got up. They even 'wished the man would but choak himself, as he was so near it sometimes – He distorted his face, & made it look very horrid & then asked for candles to be put about it that it might be seen better.' The difference from the decorum of Unitarian services must have been extreme. However, the matrons in the congregation were thought to look very respectable, dressed as they were in 'Sunday Hats, long gloves, & small handsome silk shawls'. Bessy added that there was 'always a pretty girl' in every group of Welsh people, 'for there is abundance of picturesque *female* beauty'; and then, engagingly, above a caret mark, 'N. B. The men are frights.'

The first Barmouth journal displays a keen sensibility for flowers, sky, sea and landscape, but also reveals many of their minor obsessions, including a stress upon the fact that their appearance was neither smart nor fashionable. In the Lakes they were very aware of what gentlefolk wore. Prevented from going to church by floods of rain, Lucy commented, 'Such smart lilac silk pelisses & veils & Bonnets were seen coming back from Church that we [*sic*] should have cut a queer figure in my stained, peaked Bonnet my [tarry?] Keswick Gloves, & Annes Boots.' It was the same in Barmouth. 'Much gaiety abroad today', Mary wrote; 'most of the ladies very smart: we cut a shabby figure: but we flatter ourselves that "gentility will out" even through our old blue cotton gowns.' At one time they had a discussion 'as to the comparative gentility of coming to a place like this in fine things or not – well for us to lean towards the latter opinion', added Bessy tersely. Though their father wrote to give them 'pretty carte blanche' about staying on an extra week or so in Barmouth, inelegant economy was ever on their minds.[6]

It was a recurring topic, even if liberally laced with irony. One wonders if Peter Holland's expenses were such that his daughters really did have to watch the pennies. By 1823 his oldest son, Henry, was a rich man, so Peter was responsible for the education of two boys of ten and thirteen and his youngest daughter Susan. His three older daughters probably looked to him to supplement their own incomes, but prudent expenditure might have been part of the fabric of their beings. Though their brother was to become a baronet and their nephew a viscount, their grandfather had once been 'grazier of Marthall cum Little Warford'. In comparison aunt Lumb was responsible for the expenses of one young lady attending a school run by relations.

A letter from their brother Henry giving news of the coming of two society ladies, the Miss Rumbolds, set them to relining their bonnets – as usual, Lucy was cast down at the sight of a needle – and meditating a letter to be left in the post office, telling the ladies that they should return at once as their house in London had been 'burnt down to the ground, their brother broken his neck in leaping from a high window out of the flames, their sister Lady Temple scorched dreadfully and all the little Temples a good deal singed.' A little later, Mary and Bessy, out for a ride on two great, clumsy hired hacks and wearing shawls for riding habits, 'met an open carriage with 2 ladies in mourning, & servants in black'. It turned out to be the Miss Rumbolds, whose 'servants behind seemd vastly amused by us and our horses, & gear – accustomed perhaps only to seeing the ladies in Hyde Park ride.'

This superior acquaintance had to be kept up, so on Sunday they took Miss Rumbold to the rooms where service was held. (She found it too Calvinistic also.) On this occasion William Wilberforce, sick and old, who not long after a great debate in the House of Commons on the abolition of slavery had retired for a time to Barmouth, joined the congregation with his wife and children. Uneasy that he was given an armchair when many ladies were standing, 'the little man', who had to live encased in a steel and leather girdle for many years at the end of his life, 'fidgetted about a good deal, offering it first to one & then another & nobody would take it'.

Afterwards, Lucy wrote slyly, Miss Rumbold, Miss Bessy Rumbold and the Hollands 'walked about very fashionably for some time – & then returned, as vulgarly hungry – & *knew*, (which made us more so) that Miss Rumbolds were on the point of dining *then*, and we were not to dine till 4'. In the evening, the Hollands slipped into the gallery of the Welsh chapel to hear the singing but slipped out just as a collection for the poor was being taken. 'We were glad to escape this, as we were uncertain whether we should come under the class to *subscribe*, or be *subscribed for*', wrote Mary. Apparently she was the strict guardian of the purse, Lucy often without ready money.

On 1 September it was raining as usual, so Mary stayed at home and wrote letters to aunts Lumb and Turner. In the journal she recorded, 'Miss Bessy Rumbold much struck with Lucy – thinks her a sweet unaffected girl – (*Mem* I heard nothing they said of *me*, but I dare say they *thought* the more).' In fact, they all got on very well together; the Hollands might lack their '*blue ornaments*' when they went to drink tea, but were pleased to find that their friends paid 'more attention to the ornaments of the mind than of the body.'

A return visit demanded, or was said to demand, economy: 'We must sport two pieces of tallow instead of one; and make better tea, and get some cakes (*Mem.* to pinch my sisters for it afterwards – one teaspoon full of tea plenty for us three; and they may go to bed before candle light time for a night or two).' Mary could not resist giving a exaggerated description of their own style when the ladies came to tea. It is a queer but humorous compensation for the reality, the contrast between their own careless, shabby appearance and the smart mourning of their fashionable friends: 'Bessy wore her striped muslin, trimmed at the bottom with three heights of flounces; (we were not near enough to discern whether the flounces were Mechlin or Valenciennes lace, but the effect was very good) ...', Lucy a 'sweet pretty coloured dress: the material well adapted to the rambles which a sea-side life tempts one to take ...', and she herself 'that very elegant coloured muslin' which her aunt Swinton gave her, her 'waist encircled with a ribbon of the same delicate lilac colour: and a muslin handkerchief with a triple row of frilling served as my calyx'.[7]

'3d /Tour in Wales / Barmouth &c', is a small notebook that begins *in medias res*. The first internal date, '*Thursday*. – (2nd day of our gentility)', can be shown to be 11 September.[8] They were then enjoying various meetings with the two Miss Rumbolds, but on the last day of their gentility, Sunday, 14 September, they said farewell. 'Such are the ups and downs of life!' wrote Bessy. 'At Bangor we were 3 mantua-makers, at Barmouth the most intimate friends of a Baronet's daughters & a Lord's & Bishops nieces'. Her humorous snobbery is soon qualified. Just before they left, she displayed disgust with the behaviour of some new arrivals, a lady and gentleman who left their 'poor maidservant ride outside in the drenching rain. – & yet they did not look like a new married couple which would have been the only thing to palliate such conduct.'[9]

The Holland sisters then took a carriage to Dolgellau, where Mary had some fun imitating the speech habits of a guide: 'that indeed as the weather was not so fine – that indeed we should have a good view, but not so good indeed as bright indeed but ladies indeed were very different from gentlemen indeed'. Tiring of his vacillations, they asked his opinion about a chaise. And, 'having obtained it in deed & in truth, we *decided* – got into a chaise, & drove to Bala'. From Bala ('"famous for its Lake" Hem Hollands' Geography') they drove over bleak moors in drizzling rain till they reached 'the great Irish road', now the A5, and came to 'a little Paradise in the Wilderness', Canniogie. The accommodation was excellent, but the charge for it high. Unfortunately, the 'Cash-keeper' had just burnt the proof contained in previous bills, so 'for the first time', Lucy wrote, 'we treated Boots & maid rather shabbily.'

Then they drove north into the beautiful vale of Conway as 'the clouds dispersed, the sun brightened the hills in the distance, the road (the new Irish one) was excellent – and much exceeding in beauty *any* we have yet seen!' Bessie's enthusiasm was unrestrained:

> It is quite unequalled in my opinion – winding its way half way up one hill – you see the old road considerably below – & still lower the Conway's darkly tinted & deep waters gushing over it's rocky bed – wooded down to edge. ... The fall of Conway – where its waters dashing from high, are caught in one rocky basin after another – till they reach the base of a rock – & having caught new spirit, continue foaming & dashing on. But who can describe this romantic spot? Think of this being the mail coach road![10]

Conventional ardour for the picturesque drowned any appreciation of one of the most stupendous engineering achievements of the age, Thomas Telford's improvement of the road through wildest north Wales and on to Holyhead.[11]

There followed an easy journey to St Asaph, where Mary took her sisters into damp grass to clean their shoes and save 6d thereby, then on by Holywell and Hawarden 'through dullish country' to Chester. Just short of the city Lucy records an incident that strongly contrasts with Bessy's feelings for the maid left out in the drenching rain, for 'Mary made a hungry ragged Irishman run after our Car for a few yards to seize upon a Loaf which she held out to him.' The poor man's running, '& his queer legs – & his joy & haste & rags had a droll appearance' looking like this. Here she drew a little sketch. 'We repented that we had not given him the Dolgelle cheese which of course we should have no opportunity of eating now, as we were going into society & civilized life again & to have regular dinners.'

They could not have recalled Wordsworth's early poem, 'The Old Cumberland Beggar':

> So helpless in appearance, that for him
> The sauntering horseman throws not with a slack
> And careless hand his alms upon the ground,
> But stops – that he may safely lodge the coin
> Within the old man's hat ...

Wordsworth's transcendental message of a leech-gatherer beside 'a pool bare to the eye of heaven' belongs to another realm of thought, but Stephen Gill has noted the change in Wordsworth's public reputation from the poet apparently content 'to starve his mind in solitude', as Lucy Aikin had put it in 1808, to the 'poet of humanity' who, William Ellery Channing thought, would 'break down the factitious barriers between human hearts'. God had revealed himself in human hearts as well as in external nature and the scriptures. Channing's view accords with the desire of a chastened Elizabeth Gaskell in 1838 to illustrate a truth enshrined in this same poem: 'That we have all of us one human heart.' Wordsworth himself came to regard this phrase as the key to his poetry of lasting value.[12]

In Chester they found not only aunt Abigail and Mrs Samuel Holland, over from Liverpool, but a friendly group with Mr S. Humble, who was 'like Mrs Burchell, except that he does not say "Fudge".' He might have been the Stephen who was the son of Dawson Humble, wool-stapler of Bradford, a relation of Mrs Sarah Whittaker. He ordered a bottle of cider at the Hop Pole inn for the Welsh contingent. They joined forces with a Sarah and a Kitty and all had a jolly time, visiting the Cathedral, St John's Church (with, they were told, its figure of a Knight Templar 'exactly as you find them described *in scripture*'), relating their adventures and – as one might have expected – reading the Welsh journal. At length, bidding a reluctant farewell to the Liverpool people, they drove in a car through a Cheshire drizzle to Knutsford,

with 'some thoughts of going a Tour of pleasure every year'. There is a final
date: 20 September 1823.[13]

Samuel Holland the younger had lived in various places during the early
1820s. He had lodged first with a clergyman's widow in a village near
Ffestiniog for twelve shillings a week, and then in the old turnpike cottage
across the road from his wharf on the river Dwyrwd, at Pen Trwyn y Garnedd.
As well as his cousins from Knutsford, Samuel's mother and sisters Anne,
Frances and Kate visited him now and again from Liverpool. He paid an active
young housekeeper called Mary Wynne nine guineas a year to look after him.
She remained with him or in his service for nearly fifty years and never asked
for an advance of wages, he reports rather ambiguously.

He and his men improved the wharf and his father caused special sloops
carrying twenty to thirty tons to be specially built in Liverpool, the first being
called the *Experiment*. They could carry wheaten flour and other goods into
the neighbourhood and reload with slates for the voyage back to the estuary
and its sea-going ships. Bathing and lounging in the lazy resort of Barmouth,
with its endless views out over Cardigan bay and sunsets that rival those of the
Bay of Naples, or sightseeing on foot or horseback or in carriages, must have
provided an enormous contrast to unrelentingly arduous work amongst the
more confined vistas of the upper Dwyryd valley.

Elizabeth Stevenson would have come first to this part of Wales at a time
when abominably difficult tracks were being turned into roads, pack-animals
and sledges giving place to wagons. 'Degenerate travellers sought the idle
discomfort of the stage-coach or post-chaise instead of riding their own
horses', writes the historian of the industrial revolution in North Wales, A. H.
Dodd. Transformations like those of Telford and Madocks were wrought by
and for speculators, many of them English rather than Welsh, some of them
supremely practical men like Samuel Holland, forcing change upon some of
the wildest country places left in Britain and supported by national sources of
finance. In 1825, Samuel initiated the sale of his father's leasing rights for his
quarry to the absentee investors of the Welsh Slate Company. Fortunately,
Swinton Holland was able to act extremely successfully for his brother and
nephew when it came to bargaining in London. They made a great profit.
Unemployed then by his standards, Samuel pursued various other minor
ventures, farmed and raised hay for his horses and mules.

In 1828 he was able to set about developing a quarry of his own higher up
the mountain at Rhiwbryfdir, borrowing money from uncle Peter Holland of
Knutsford and Edward Holland, who had just left Cambridge and inherited
the Dumbleton estate when his father died unexpectedly at Christmas 1827.
Then, against the opposition of all the farmers and river boatmen of the
district, who feared for their livelihood and who managed with support from
London speculators to get the first enabling bill in Parliament thrown out,
Samuel after some years succeeded in establishing a tramway from the quarries

above Ffestiniog down to Porthmadog. It is said to have been narrow-gauge to save money on land, but poor mountain land was cheap; narrow-gauge allowed the kind of very sharp curves demanded by the terrain that a broader gauge would not. Wagons and carriages were pulled up the vale by horses but rolled down the incline by themselves, with the horses 'in Boxes made for the purpose, at the tail end of the Train ... feeding all the way while coming down' – such as realises one's ideas of felicity in the equine sphere, dear Miss Jane might have said.[14]

The Vale of Ffestiniog had already suffered from deforestation in the previous century (Maentwrog oak was famous) and now the landscape was being radically altered again, aesthetically in the grounds of the great house overlooking the meadows of the lower vale that belonged to the local landlords of the Oakeley family, but more drastically for the sake of new industry and commerce, the quarries and mines and roads and trackways that horribly disfigure the hills above to this day. Slate quarries normally rise in tiers up the mountain-side; even if the slate is taken from underground shafts, enormous piles of waste are created. The continuous sharp sounds of slates being split and dressed would be sometimes lost in greater explosions with reverberating echoes that could be heard miles away.

The population of the valley grew and changed in nature; nonconformist chapels, market halls and schools were a-building and the older Welsh way of life altered in Dyffryn Maentwrog almost beyond recognition – largely at the behest of men like Samuel Holland, who, however, was not altogether typical: he at least settled in the district, learnt to speak the Welsh that was mostly used in North Wales and had 'plenty of interesting information to give about the state of the people, farms, quarry-men, &c., in that part of the world'. He was 'not a "bookish" man', wrote a clever young lady from Manchester, Catherine Winkworth.[15]

Ever active, cousin Samuel used to walk the twenty-three miles northwards over the pass of Beddgelert to do business in Caernarfon on the Menai Straits and then walk all the way back, his head doubtless seething with schemes. In 1825 when the Welsh Slate Company took over his wharf and cottages, he lived for a while at a farm, but in 1827 he managed to rent on a long lease and get possession of Plas yn Penrhyn, Borthwen Fawr and Beudy Gwyn, all places in or close to the village of Minffordd, on the hill across Traeth Mawr from Porthmadog and above the Dwyryd as it snaked through the sands of Traeth Bach to Tremadog Bay. He immediately started making additions and alter-ations to the Plas yn Penrhyn farmhouse, boasting that he had 'roofed *all* in Sept. 1830'. It never became architecturally noteworthy, but was undoubtedly a comfortable place to live in and popular with visitors.[16] Samuel had put down his roots in Wales and intended to be hospitable. Relations like Henry Holland, Frank Holland and Isabella Rankin visited him, and in July 1832 came Professor Adam Sedgwick of Cambridge University. The previous summer he had been on a geological tour of North Wales with one of Samuel's more distant relations, Charles Darwin, when they had failed to spot glacial evidence in the area of Nant Ffrancon and Lake Idwal.[17]

Elizabeth Stevenson might have visited her cousin's cottage by the wharf on the river Dwyryd when she was young, but Plas yn Penrhyn is where she is known to have stayed many times. 'It is not surprising', comments Dr Merfyn Jones, 'that it was back to this incomparably beautiful and significance-laden borderland between Glaslyn and Dwyryd, Caernarfonshire and Merioneth, that the writer in her returned in the Welsh chapters of her fiction.'[18] Nowadays, Sam's house is up a secluded lane, its hedgerows 'bright with foxgloves and honeysuckle, intertwined with ivy, brambles and ferns', with glorious views over hills and sea. Bertrand Russell used to rejoice that he could see across the valley from it to where Shelley had lived at Tan yr Allt, still visible as a white house on the hill amongst dark trees. Samuel Holland might not have been a 'bookish' man, but he established a book club and acted as its secretary for fourteen years. More organiser than reader, he acted as auctioneer at the annual sale of books – unlike Harry Headlong, who 'by dint of lounging over them after dinner, when he was compelled to take his bottle alone' was 'seized with a violent passion to be thought a philosopher and a man of taste.' Samuel was also involved with the first school opened for Ffestiniog village on 27 May 1829; like the Oakeleys, he was a great patron of education for the dissenting quarrymen of North Wales. He was on his way to becoming high sheriff of Merioneth and representing the county as a Liberal Member of Parliament in later years.

In June 1829 Samuel's mother and sisters came from Liverpool to live with him permanently:

> My sisters lived with me for many years at Plas yn Penrhyn and also my mother for a great part of this time, but my father did not come to reside with me until 1832, bringing an old sailor, Man-of-wars man W. Jones with him, we had always visitors and friends staying with us, after I had completed my alteration at the house, erected stables, cow house, &c, which I had in some measure completed by the year 1829, amongst my visitors was my cousin Miss Eliza Steveson [sic] (afterwards Mrs Gaskell who wrote so many novels) one of which she began to write, while staying with me.[19]

The printed text reads 'began or wrote'. (It is worth remembering that these recollections are printed from miscellaneous, untidy and repetitive manuscripts, dictated and written, and composed in old age, like Henry Holland's memoirs.) Elizabeth liked her cousin's house and family so much that in September 1832 she took her new husband there on their honeymoon trip. She might have thought, too, of the shellfish in Traeth Bach and William's fondness for cockling.[20]

In an essay Mrs Gaskell wrote about company manners in grand French salons, there is a sudden excursus that evokes past social life in 'the heart and depth of Wales'. Dinner-parties at this time often depended upon little sailing-vessels on voyages with cargo to Bristol or Liverpool returning with commissioned private purchases, like a chest of oranges, that would serve for an occasion. Acquaintances lived ten or twelve miles apart over bad and hilly roads, so the state of the moon was an important consideration for guests. Then, 'after the gentlemen had left the dining-room it was cleared for dancing'.

> The fragments of the dinner, prepared by ready cooks, served for supper; tea was ready some time towards one or two, and the dancers went merrily on till a seven or eight o'clock breakfast, after which they rode or drove home by broad daylight. I was never at one of these meetings, although staying in a house from which many went; I was considered too young; but, from what I heard, they were really excessively pleasant, sociable gatherings, though not quite to be classed with Madame de Sablé's salons.

Peacock's spirited description of the Christmas ball for the 'beau monde of the Cambrian mountains' in chapters 11 and 13 of *Headlong Hall* confirms several of these details for a slightly earlier time, starting from the Spenserian moment when 'the ivied towers of Caernarvon, the romantic woods of Tan-y-bwlch, the healthy hills of Kernioggau, the sandy shores of Tremadog, the mountain recesses of Bedd-Gelert, and the lonely lakes of Capel-Cerig, re-echoed to the voices of the delighted ostlers and postilions'.

Elizabeth's stepmother, we shall see, considered her too young to wear a tartan silk about this time, but this is probably the only thing that life in the Chelsea household had in common with her early experiences at Plas yn Penrhyn. At neither place was she in any danger of encountering a mysterious entremets that reminded her of eating a tender white kid glove with Béchamel sauce, 'under the name of Oreilles de Veau à-la-something'. She describes an easy, friendly and informal way of living, based upon money enough to maintain a good standard of comfort if not as grand as that of the Oakeleys of Tan y Bwlch – 'after dinner, slip-slop sleepy talk; a little music; a good deal of lounging on sofas and easy chairs; a great longing for tea, which comes in about 8, lasts till nine' was her account, admittedly much later, in 1848.[21]

But as at Knutsford, there was another life led nearby. In the early decades of the century a Welsh quarryman earned between 9 and 18 shillings a week, an agricultural labourer between 9 and 12 shillings. Her cousin's boatmen, despite their tough, dangerous and sometimes fatal job, did not gain this much and had to earn money in other ways to survive. 'The Boatmen this day stood out for more Wages, but have not yet surrendered', wrote Samuel in his diary on 10 March 1823. On the following day: 'The Boatmen returned to their work again and did not succeed in getting the price up.'[22]

When Elizabeth Stevenson left school, it seems clear, she had real choices. Though her father was in financial straits, aunt Lumb must have cared for her welfare. She did not have to earn her living, perhaps not even prepare to earn her living. She could travel deep into the Welsh valleys to relax with her Holland uncle, aunt, cousins and sociable friends by the coast, return to the Byerleys of Avonbank in Stratford-upon-Avon as a welcome visitor, or grandly reside in the more splendid houses of rich relations in London and Gloucestershire. If these pleasures palled, she could sink back into the familiar comforts of life with aunt Lumb and her kin, as long as she kept up the course of study her father thought proper. Her friends and cousins in Knutsford were clever, literate, humorous and certainly able to write, as their journals so amply demonstrate. Elizabeth must have been aware of models worth imitating, ideally in friendly competition.

But this pleasingly varied stability of her existence was always under threat. Beneath the ripples on the surface were deeper gulfs that threatened to overwhelm her ageing father, notwithstanding his ability to make some extra income by his pen. Quite apart from his increasingly frantic letters to Blackwood in the mid-1820s, his 'will' shows that by July 1827 he had been obliged to make use of his wife's dowry.[23] This fact might have been kept from her, but she knew that her brother, so attached to her and so encouraging to a future author, was in a dangerous profession, facing perils of the sea and land every day of his life abroad. Her father had told her about another ship, the *Martin*, last seen in a 'dreadful tempest not far from Madagascar', and not thought of concealing the belief that her crew had been murdered by natives when she was wrecked on its shores.

NOTES

1 DCLH: Barmouth journal 1, pp. 1-13. The steam service to the Menai Straits was very new at this date: see Neal, 'Liverpool shipping in the early nineteenth century', p. 177.

2 DCLH: Barmouth journal 1, pp. 14, 18, 20, 24-6, 28-9.

3 I rely here on Lewis, *Sails on the Dwyryd*, pp. 22, 37-40, 85-7, 96-9 (incl. useful maps). The watercolour provides an attractive cover illustration, with a matching photograph, p. 38.

4 DCLH: Barmouth journal 1, pp. 29-37, 58. Cf. Lewis and Williams, *Pioneers of Ffestiniog Slate*, pp. 22-6; MCO: MSS Robberds 1, JGR to MR, Ffestiniog, 13 July 1831 (Martha Owen).

5 DCLH: Barmouth journal 1, pp. 19, 39, 41-8, 58.

6 DCLH: Barmouth journal 1, pp. 49, 52-7, 66, 68; Lakes journal, pp. 36-7.

7 DCLH: Barmouth journal 1, pp. 68-9, 71-82; David Newsome, *The Parting of Friends: A Study of the Wilberforces and Henry Manning*, London, 1966, p. 37; Pollock, *Wilberforce*, pp. 234, 286.

8 'Barmouth / August 22d / 1823' inside its cover probably relates to two lines of simple German exercises on the first page. It is perhaps a subsidiary notebook: on p. 21, 'While my Sisters were writing the journal … ' occurs in Mary's hand.

9 *DNB* and *Burke* give Sir George Berriman Rumbold, who became the 2nd Bart in 1791, married in 1783 and had four daughters, including Caroline, Maria and Emily, born in 1786, 1788 and 1790 respectively.

10 DCLH: Barmouth notebook 3, pp. 3-7, 9-15. Assignment of hands is not always certain.

11 See Paul Johnson, *The Birth of the Modern: World Society 1815-1830*, London, [1991], 1992, pp. 181-3.

12 DCLH: Barmouth notebook 3, pp. 21, 25-6; *Letters*, p. 33; Easson, p. 22; Stephen Gill, 'England's Samuel: Wordsworth in the "Hungry Forties"', *SEL*, XXXIII, 1993, pp. 842-4.

13 DCLH: Barmouth notebook 3, pp. 26-33. Stephen Humble and his wife Susan lived at Quarry Cottage, Idle (Rae, *Turtle at Mr Humble's*, p. 219).

14 Dodd, *Industrial Revolution*, p. 97; SH, *Memoirs*, ed. Davies, pp. 11-22; Lewis, *Sails on the Dwyryd*, pp. 38, 40, 74, 100-1. See p. 336 below (JB to ECS).

15 *Letters and Memorials of Catherine Winkworth*, ed. [S. Winkworth and M. J. Shaen], pr. pr. Clifton, 1883-86, I, p. 164. She was a friend of Mrs Gaskell and a fine translator of German hymns. See Peter Skrine, *Susanna and Catherine Winkworth*, Occasional Paper II. ii, The Hymn Society, London, 1992.

16 SH, *Memoirs*, ed. Davies, pp. 9-10, 13-14, 23; MS, ff. 37 verso-38; Irvine, p. 90.

17 Mary Robberds to W. Turner, 18 October 1840 (photocopy: see Chapple, 'Unofficial lives', in Parish, p. 112); SH, *Memoirs*, ed. Davies, p. 24 (MS, f. 125: 72); Millward and Robson, *Landscapes of North Wales*, p. 83; *Darwin Correspondence*, I, p. 136n. Plas yn Penrhyn is plate 2 in Malchow, *Gentlemen Capitalists*.

18 For an analysis of ECG's knowledge and use of Welsh places, people and language in her fiction, see R. Merfyn Jones, '"No barrier against agony": Elizabeth Gaskell's North Wales', *JMHRS*, 1993, pp. 271-83.

19 See Joan Leach, 'Summer outing to North Wales', *GSN*, IV, August 1987, pp. 18-20, 24; SH, *Memoirs*, ed. Davies, pp. 20, 23, 25; MS, f. 125: 72; *Headlong Hall*, chapter 1; Wynne Evans, *Education in Industrial Wales*, pp. 212-17.

20 *Letters*, pp. 2-3, 850. William's part of the joint letter (LUBL) they wrote from Plas yn Penrhyn on their honeymoon is often quoted inaccurately, but see *GSN*, IX, March 1990, pp. 5-7.

21 'Company manners' [*Household Words*, 1854], Knutsford Edn, III, pp. 499-503; *Letters*, p. 61. See also *Letters and Memorials of CW*, I, p. 164 for a ball given in 1848.

22 Malchow, *Gentleman Capitalists*, p. 44; *Letters and Memorials of CW*, I, p. 16; Lewis, *Sails on the Dwyryd*, pp. 92-9. See also p. 298 below.

23 For details see p. 330 below.

17

Authors and would-be authors

A CONSIDERABLE PORTION of a manuscript letter from John to Elizabeth, dated 16 July, written at sea during his 1827 voyage to Bombay, has survived. Though it is neither yellow nor sea-stained nor peculiarly fragrant (like the ocean letters in *North and South*), its scrawl suits the unusual heading: 'Ship Recovery / At Sea Lat. 38-30N / Long. 15-10W.' He was some three hundred miles west of Lisbon, at the beginning of the long sweep out into the Atlantic that sailing ships needed to catch favourable winds for the voyage round the Cape of Good Hope.[1]

John's letter, evidently dashed off at odd moments when professional demands permitted, begins with a stanza of poetry, 'Once more upon the waters! yet once more ... ', which can be identified as from Byron's *Childe Harold's Pilgrimage*, book three. 'Swift be their guidance, whereso'er it lead', he quotes, and then adds with calculated bathos, 'only to Bombay though'. After taking a week to get clear of Portsmouth, his ship met 'nothing but fair winds and fine weather'. The ladies – he does not mention the men – could have their work tables out in the mornings and a promenade or dance in the evenings. The first number of the newspaper, mostly written by John and the doctor, had appeared, and the band used to play John's favourite pieces, like 'There nae luck about the house' and 'Blue bonnets over the border', in the open air daily during his evening watch from four till eight. He was as fond of Scottish airs as his sister. Mrs Monkland's *Life in India; Or, The English at Calcutta*, a mixture of three-volume novel and travelogue, bears out John's account. The ladies' round-house cabin in the after part of the ship contained a pianoforte, music, books and drawing materials; a newspaper was issued and it was chosen as a kind of coffee-room for passengers.[2]

The literary bent William Stevenson was nourishing in his daughter about this time is also displayed by John, in an parody of inflated style:

Last night whilst the meandering moon shed her pellucid rays on our decks, illuminating with her splendour the figures of those our passengers who were amusing themselves with the mazes of the dance & at the time when lovers vows are most softly breathed, when the nightingale, sweet harbinger of the approaching darkness is first heard, ...

He soon dropped parody (as his sister was to do) in favour of a long burlesque description of the traditional ceremonies of crossing the line – 'Mrs Neptune a handsome young sailor, dressed in a sprig muslin gown & a high french bonnet, the Doctor in a black coat & powdered wig, tight pantaloons &c ... ' At the end he asks Elizabeth if she had the patience to read it all and continues, evidently at a different time:

> I give credit to my new adversary for the ingenuity she displays [in defending her cause *deleted*] – & must confess that like Milton's Belial she possesses the power of making the worse appear the better cause
>
> You are staring Elisabeth. What do you think this is – Why I am engaged in a controversy in the newspaper with some of our lady passengers & happening to take up this letter instead of the sheet I had been writing upon, I commenced my intended answer.
>
> It has been just determined we are to go into the Cape so I have no time to write this letter again, as we are within a few days sail of it & have very bad weather.

The bad weather, however, called forth a vivid, mimetic realism that more truly showed his talent as a writer than the easy parodies and set-pieces:

> The motion was so violent that every moment some dish or other was flying away to Leeward & carrying with it plates, glasses & every thing that had the courage to oppose its fury – If any ...

His rapid pen-strokes now crosshatch the lines of writing on the first page –

> one happened to rise from his chair in order to reach any thing, away went the chair & when he offered to sit again, away went he. Sometimes when one felt oneself falling, one would catch at the next chair or the table cloth to save oneself – either expedient produced consequences equally disagreeable – Either away went both of you oversetting your next neighbour, he his next and so on untill the lee side of Cuddy brought you all up, huddled one upon another or the table cloth giving way, down would come dishes & all their paraphernalia, & if you should have a leg of mutton in your lap, perhaps you might have the consolation of having the Caper sauce along with it.
>
> Below in the cabins it was no better – every now & then a trunk or a table breaking adrift & taking such complete possession of your apartment, that you are obliged to keep jumping from one side to another to keep your legs from being broken; even should you succeed in seizing it: presto! away the ship gives a lurch, & holding on, you both go together into the scuppers – At length in despair you resolve rather to face the pelting of the pitiless storm on deck – the moment you show your nose out from the hatchway however a sea breaks over you. At first you think you are overboard & begin to strike out, till a violent shock
> ...

He had reached the end of the page, but did not continue to write across on the second. Duties on board might have demanded his attention at this point; he was, after all, a sea-going officer and not a man of letters.

No more is known of this particular voyage, which would have ended about December 1827. In that same month John's father approached Blackwood after a long silence, to say that a manuscript entitled 'Twelve Years of a Sailors Life written by himself' had been put into his hands; he thought it would do for some articles in *Blackwoods*. It contained 'adventures & observations, while with a Cattle hunter, some hundred miles up the Country from Buenos Aires', and a spell on board the admiral's sloop off St Helena, 'during part of the time Buonaparte was confined there'. In addition there was an account of several voyages in the East Indies' coasting trade, ending

> with many curious particulars respecting the Burmese War – the manners &c of the Burmese, while he was in a Transport employed – during the whole of that war, in carrying Troops &c from Madras to Rangoon. He was often ashore & engaged in an attack on one of their Stockades.
>
> Wherever he was, he seems to have seized every opportunity of becoming acquainted with the natives: & has thus been enabled to mix with his personal narrative much curious information. I know it is genuine & may be depended on.

John Stevenson's cousin of about the same age, Charles Holland of Liverpool, had been sent off to Buenos Aires in about 1817, because there were family trading connections with South America, though there is no evidence that John accompanied him. Napoleon was at St Helena between 1815 and 1821, until his death on 5 May. John was in London or Berwick from December 1819, as we know, and had joined the *Lady Raffles* by June 1820 for a voyage to India. It is possible that like Frederick Marryat he went to sea in his teens and was at St Helena, though this has not been substantiated. The details of the Burmese war certainly fit his career, and it is possible to speculate, given the endorsement '1825 not wanted' on his letter to Hannah Lumb about the war, that his father was cannibalising some of his journal letters for publication.[3]

There was no shortage of such items. A general article about 'The Hindu Chinese Nations' had appeared in the *Edinburgh Magazine* for February 1826, Captain H. Cox's *Journal of a Residence in the Burmhan Empire* being one of the books under review. Blackwood commissioned G. R. Gleig to review Major Snodgrass's *A Narrative of the Burmese War* as the lead article for his February 1827 issue. In the *Edinburgh Magazine* for September 1828 appeared a review of R. Rickards' *India; or Facts Submitted to Illustrate the Character and Condition of the Native Inhabitants*, and in the following December came a long and enthusiastic review of the second edition of Bishop Reginald Heber's *Narrative of a Journey Through the Upper Provinces of India, From Calcutta to Bombay*. Even the *Literary Gazette* for 29 December 1827 printed an exotically descriptive letter from the Burmese capital of Ava. The narrative offered to Blackwood by his former contributor was hardly unique and could not have been accepted for publication.

In the years after Elizabeth left school she stayed at her father's house in Beaufort Row, but is difficult to know exactly when, apart from the implication in her brother's letter of 5 December 1826 that she was in London, and her father's statement in early July 1827 that she had been at Knutsford above a month. We are in no doubt how she viewed her London visits in retrospect:

> Long ago I lived in Chelsea occasionally with my father and stepmother, and *very, very* unhappy I used to be; and if it had not been for the beautiful, grand river, which was an inexplicable comfort to me, and a family of the name of Kennett, I think my child's heart would have broken.

This comes from fragment of a letter to Mary Howitt, itself undated but possibly, from its position in the source, between May and August of 1838. Mrs Gaskell was writing to a comparative stranger, revealing intimate family experiences otherwise hardly known, which might explain her daughters' distress and the editor's apology for publication of unauthorised extracts from their mother's letters. 'Long ago' suggests early childhood, but Elizabeth was a contemporary of Louisa Kennett at Avonbank school in 1825, and an Ann Kennett lived at 13 Beaufort Row from March 1827 according to the rate books.[4]

In 1838 Elizabeth was writing about her youthful unhappiness from a distance in time, after a watershed in her life, when youthful tempests of emotion had at length subsided, leaving their invisible scars. But throughout her teens William Stevenson's financial problems, and those of his wife, were unresolved, as his will and letters to Blackwood prove. Whenever she visited Chelsea, she would have found a hard-pressed man, in debt, buried in work, his health deteriorating as the years went by. As far as we can tell, his second wife and her children were no special comfort to Elizabeth. They too must have been afflicted by her father's problems. Other London experiences for a bright and sensitive girl as she met her relations – all those rich and successful uncles and cousins – must have provoked almost unbearable comparisons.

Dr Thomson and his wife Katharine were particularly enviable. He had made 'a considerable fortune' by the time he left Chelsea in 1826 to live in nearby Kensington. His memoir in the *Medical Times* of 14 July 1849 emphasises the value of his published works, produced when he had 'the largest practice in his part of London'. He also received a professorial appointment in the new University of London. There is no sign that William Stevenson, learned as he was, formerly a classical tutor at Manchester College and a contributor to major reviews since early in the century, had ever been considered for a post when in the 1820s the university opened its gates and let 'the King of Glory in, for I have no doubt that knowledge, in all its majesty, is destined to make that its palace', Henry Cockburn put it grandiosely in a private letter to his friend.

This industrious medical man – his eldest daughter could not remember him without a pen in his hand 'when not in society or professionally engaged'

– was helped in his work by his wife; and Katharine Thomson herself, when not confined to her thriving nursery, was at the outset of her career as a published author, in contact like William Stevenson with the dynamic Henry Brougham, and starting to produce all those histories and novels. (Her husband must have abandoned an early view that women should be given a chemical education: 'It diverts their attention from the perusal of works addressed solely to the imagination, which frequently draw false views of human nature and create an artificial and vitiated sensibility highly prejudicial to domestic happiness.') To cap it all, Katharine was herself a step-mother, much younger than Elizabeth's. The Thomson household, and perhaps that of John Galt, would have fascinated Elizabeth, unless her sea of troubles in Chelsea swamped everything else.[5]

As for Henry Holland, he was almost a being on another planet. Some eighteen years younger than William Stevenson, he had finished his *General View of Agriculture* at an early age and achieved an income of over £1200 a year by about 1820. He moved to one of the best addresses in London, Lower Brook Street in Mayfair, where his young family could enjoy the pleasures of Hyde Park; cows, deer and swans were 'within a quarter of an hour's walk from the door'. In town he mixed with men and women like James Mackintosh, Humphry Davy, Madame de Staël and Mary Augusta, Lady Holland. We do not have to rely on the names he himself celebrated in his memoirs. A Maria Edgeworth letter of 1822 includes Dr Holland in 'all the best scientific and literary society in London' that visited the houses of Mary Somerville and Jane Marcet on a daily basis. For two months in the autumn every year he roamed all over the globe wherever he fancied, limiting his professional income, he tells us, to £5000 a year to ensure that his life and lines remained free. In the late summer of 1827 he had been on a journey of over 1200 miles by land and sea, in Scotland, Ireland and South Wales. He took twelve days for this, he boasted to William Turner, two of which were spent at his wife's old home, Linley Wood, and he then went on to Knutsford for the christening of his daughter. He was to receive royal patronage and a baronetcy.[6]

In comparison, whatever money on top of his salary William Stevenson managed to gain by writing for the *Retrospective Review* and the *Westminster* was insufficient. He was always on the look-out for additional income. In May 1827 R. P. Gillies came to London and, following a suggestion of Sir Walter Scott, set up a quarterly review of foreign literature with William Fraser. Gillies wrote discursively in his memoirs of 'palmy days for authors', when they might make as much as £1000 a year, but also of quarrels with Fraser, rivalry, debts and writs, all of which prevented him from doing more than feed 'the press with hasty scrolls' – just like Stevenson. Fraser left to set up the *Foreign Quarterly Review*, and it has been suggested that Stevenson might have been introduced to this by Dr Thomson, who had connections with the editor. Possible contributions are an article on the 'Rural Economy of Switzerland' in January 1828 and another on the 'Classification of Languages' in the

November following. There are parallels with Stevenson's other reviews in subject matter, mannerisms of style, such as the use of terms in threes, and his methods, especially his habit of learnedly pointing out and correcting errors.[7]

One last contribution by William Stevenson to the *Edinburgh Review* appeared in May 1828, on John Jamieson's *Supplement to the Etymological Dictionary of the Scottish Language*. Stevenson opens with a claim that such a dictionary's cultural value is as great as its philological: 'its true and most important character is that of a vast treasury of facts relating to the history of the northern parts of the empire, or rather of that period in the history of the races by which they are peopled, which is now fading from recollection'. Indeed, Stevenson suggested, Jamieson would do well to produce another, more popular work on Scottish language and culture, which is very like the advice his daughter borrowed from Robert Southey – 'how good & well it would be if every Parish priest would write down what he hears and learns about his own Parish, as traits of customs & manners & character might thus be preserved as Memoires pour servir.'[8]

Stevenson then proposed a more subtle idea. The work should bring out 'the influence of the varying opinions, character, and manners of a people, upon their language; and of the re-action of the language upon their habits and opinions.' He cites here an 'early treatise of Michaelis, by no means equal to his after fame', in which, a modern scholar believes, 'language is seen entirely as a product of usage' by speakers both literate and illiterate, perhaps for the first time. As Michaelis neatly expressed it, 'language is a democracy where use or custom is decided by the majority.'[9] But after a few instances, Stevenson let himself be sidetracked into a long discussion of shall/will usages and settled down to an easy-paced selection of 'curious and interesting' examples.

Some of these have an obsessively personal ring, as when he refers to 'a number of services and petty payments, exceedingly troublesome, vexatious, and degrading, as well as inconvenient, were regularly inserted in the leases, and as regularly enforced, even in the Lothians, and consequently within a short distance of the metropolis of Scotland'. England had its drawbacks too: 'in Chelsea parish, the road before the Hospital is shut up on Landsmark day, in consequence of the parish claiming a right to it; and the Governors of the Hospital denying the justice of the claim'. But he has more pleasant memories, seen when he expands Jamieson's derivation of Fairntosh – 'which, in our recollection, designated a kind of whisky, then unrivalled for its purity and fine flavour.'

He raises our expectations when he mentions 'a volume of Mr Coleridge's earliest poems, published in 1797', containing 'songs of the Pixies' – but then, typically, he refers to the introductory note rather than to the poem. Stevenson was not a man to linger imaginatively in a Spenserian or Miltonic cave by the Devonshire Otter. A poetic sensibility is something his daughter did not inherit from him. Even his historical sense can sometimes let him down. In the course of objecting to Jamieson admitting words from minor contemporaries, he commented that one could 'not always trust to the exactness of Sir Walter Scott in this particular; nor be sure that he does not occasionally coin a well-sounding archaism, when it is too much trouble to recollect one.' While it is true that in Scott's rich and diverse vocabulary of some 30,000 words are a few he made up himself, the great majority of his unfamiliar words are either revivals or drawn from a true knowledge of the old Scots language. In any case scholarly exactitude is not a virtue of what Scott himself only too readily confessed was a 'hurried frankness of composition'.[10]

Stevenson and his daughter did not have the consolation of being able to rejoice in the worldly success of John. The last two of his letters to have survived are from Beaufort Row and dated 30 July and 18 August; they probably belong to 1828.[11] The name of the ship he was joining for an eastern voyage is not yet known. It was not one of the extra ships chartered for a single voyage by the East India Company, for Hardy's *Supplement to a Register of Ships* shows that none of these sailed after 20 July in that year.

The two letters prove that he wanted to give up his naval career altogether and stay in England, but could not afford to do so. In the first he complains that he could not come down to see his sister, who was almost certainly at Knutsford – 'among so many aunts and cousins as you now have around you', he wrote, 'I might not feel so much at ease as I could wish'. Perhaps she was one of the fourteen mostly youthful relations at her uncle's table who had 'two joyous sailing parties on Tabley mere' with Mrs Sharpe in 1828, presumably in the summertime. Elizabeth's second music book, as we have seen, contains an inserted leaf dated 29 August 1828. In this part of the book, too, are the dates of 14 May and 23 August 1828. She might even have been flirting, for at the foot of a page between these two is pencilled – in a hand that resembles that of her early letters (rather than that of a young man) – 'May I go somewhere to have you to myself', and portions of leaves are sometimes cut out for no apparent reason. It seems clear that however much she felt for her brother, she was leading a full life of her own during this summer.[12]

John, with a new appointment to a ship in the offing, had to stay in London; he did not dare be out of the way if needed by his captain. His swiftly written letter of 30 July veers uncontrollably between mere gossip and passionate emotion:

> Do not for an instant think it is because I do not like it: how could such an idea come into your head – I would give worlds to see you – to walk with you – to enjoy your conversation – but (supposing the thing to be possible) seeing you for so short a period – having continually before me the certainty of parting so *very* soon, of perhaps parting with you for ever – I could not really be happy – and besides among so many, I would not as much as I wished have you to myself – I may be selfish – nay I dare say I am selfish in this but I cannot nor ever would wish to help it –

It vexes me more than any thing else that I have by so near a chance missed seeing you[13] – but I will not repine any more – You yourself seem convinced that nothing is to be done in England – thus it seems I must be contented to be a banished man for what use is it returning and having nothing to do – on three pound a month what can I save – what can I do – It is better to make up my mind to remain abroad – to quit even you who are all to me and the more I saw of you, the more I should regret quitting you – so in one way it is perhaps better I should see you no more – it will save me one pang.

To stay in India was not lightly undertaken. When John Losh misconducted himself at college in 1824, his father James offered him the chance of returning to Durham when the term of his punishment was over or a cadet-ship in India. The latter was accepted by letter within a few days – '"joyfully" as he says', added Losh suspiciously. But John Losh remained 'cold and distant in his manner', and the day of his leaving, 'the last in all human probability' that he would spend with him, wrote his ageing father pessimistically, 'was not free from agitation and anxiety … May God preserve him from all evil!' John in fact survived the Burmese wars, becoming one of the few British officers with a grasp of the Burmese language, and by 1833 could be recommended to Lord Brougham as 'a distinguished linguist and a most promising officer', a Lieutenant in the 9th Madras Infantry.[14]

However, dispassionately considered, it was hardly fair of John Stevenson to transform what could have been just another voyage for a sailor into a sentence of banishment, and at least appear to place some of the responsibility for this on the advice given by his seventeen-year-old sister. His extravagant turns of phrase (Dryden would advise an accompaniment of sharp violins), and even the dashes that serve for punctuation, seem to parody the style of the novel of sensibility. But she might have been clever enough to note that immediately after he wrote of his 'pang' foregone, he turned to small talk:

> They are all here except Papa going down to Scotland where they intend to remain till the end of September – They leave on Tuesday the 5th of next month and go by Berwick in order to leave Elisabeth – so Papa will have seven weeks of it to himself –
>
> The Kenetts are hardly yet recovered – they are really terribly boisterous – the colonel who is a very quiet man does not much seem to admire it – he continues to be in high favour with all who have seen him – Captain Roberdean has at length contrived to get clear of his sisters – if he is wise he will snatch the oppor-tunity and marry the first woman that comes in his way – they will take care to keep him single whilst with them –

John was nevertheless in low spirits. Positive remarks are bald and conven-tional, negative ones expanded:

> I am so vexed with the disappointment of all the hopes I entertained when I arrived in England that I have no spirits to write about myself – I have no doubt I shall manage very well in the voyage I am about to undertake – the Captain seems a very pleasant man and the chief mate – Brown by name, appears one likewise –

This is all the *good* I can tell regarding myself. ... I certainly cannot agree with Bessy in thinking Charles handsome, and his manners are very stiff – it would be long before I could be intimate with him and I should always feel inclined to pick my words before I spoke in his company – his own he seems to select with the greatest thought and care be the subject ever so trifling – What would Bessy say if she was to hear this of her lover – but perhaps with her he is warm and animated – She may inspire him perhaps – Remember me to her –

If this is an allusion to their older cousin Bessy Holland, born a few years before John and in her early thirties, it is not too kind. Her writing in the Barmouth journals was full of sensibility, and she was, we recall, thought to be an amiable girl, not anything like as clever as her sister Mary, 'but more calculated to be generally pleasing, from having tried more to be so'. She had refused an offer of marriage, Henry Holland told Maria Edgeworth in January 1830, and remained unmarried until on 24 September 1835 she became the wife of the widowed Franklin Howorth of Bury – a man of 'singularly pure and elevated character', whose 'faithful and searching demands upon the conscience of his first hearers', James Martineau wrote of his fellow-student at York, meant that he 'had to be got rid of with their old chapel'. He sounds a little difficult. Indeed, he was later to abandon Unitarianism and set up a 'Free Christian Church'.[15]

The conclusion of John's letter was a self-conscious plea for total sympathy:

Do you know my spirits have been and are so low that I have not laughed this month and I am getting the name of the silent man – I shall write again before I go, and Mama will write to you on Monday – this day fortnight I shall I dare say be taking my last look of everything *here* – a comfortable idea for one so fond of England as I am – Farewell my dearest Sister – Give my best love to my aunts Lumb and Abb and all enquiring Cousins –

> Your very affecte Brother
> Jno Stevenson

His farewell letter of 15 August 1828 to his sister harps upon accustomed themes. He has not heard from her. He says he is afraid that she is offended with him for not coming to see her. He is likely to sail soon. He will remain in India. 'Repining is of no avail'. Suddenly he blurts out that he had brought her a piece of tartan silk from India – 'but Mama thinks you rather young for it yet – there is enough for a gown and she will give it you next winter'. Elizabeth was then very nearly eighteen. He sent her a copy of a popular Christmas annual, *Friendship's Offering* – a 'delicately printed, lustrously bound, and elaborately illustrated small octavo volume, representing, after its manner, the poetical and artistic inspiration of the age', according to John Ruskin, whose first poems appeared in it a few years later.[16]

John hoped that Elizabeth would keep it for his sake, and he also sent some seeds for her to 'raise an opposition garden to Bessy'. The trivia flow on, always tending to the wryly negative:

There is some talk of Johanna's being married to a Mr Mc Somebody not quite *thrice* as old as she is, but rich and agreeable – They seem here to think it will be the best thing she can do, for it will enable her to sit at her ease all day doing nothing – for my part I should be sorry to see her thrown away for I should call it nothing else – There is some talk too of an attachment between Louisa Kennet and Mr Miller the surgeon – I pity him if he gets her, that is if he is not prepared beforehand to yield up the management of every thing to her and make himself a cypher in his own house.

The Colonel is not yet gone to France; he does not take either of his sisters with him which I am rather surprised at and which they are much disappointed at – perhaps he is afraid of their exposing him by being so noisy – Sophia Slade talks of writing to you – when she will I can hardly say.

Discontents and unsatisfied desires eddy about his sister, now almost a figure of his own creation. If she herself was as heartbroken as she told Mary Howitt she had been, there is no sign whatsoever that John recognised this. The joie de vivre of his earlier writing has gone. His present miseries were laid open to her; her duty was love and sympathy. In an uncanny way this August letter reminds us of letters his sister was to write in adult life, when her light-hearted gossip and scandal-mongering were occasionally queerly mingled with expressions of frustration and yearning.

The end of this 15 August letter from John lays bare the root of his disappointment. East India House in the City was a literary refuge. Charles Lamb kept ledgers there for thirty-three years and at the time of his retirement in 1825 was paid a salary of £750 a year. John, as a mere free mariner, was not so fortunate:

I have just got the final answer from Smith and Elder – they are extremely sorry to decline taking my book &c. &c. but dare say Longman would take – as a sort of douceur for thus disappointing me, they enclosed a friendships offering and a book on the present state of slavery in the West Indies – to end my hopes of being an author.

He might have thought of approaching Smith and Elder because they were known for Indian publications. In 1827 they had published a book by M. J. Horne, entitled *The Adventures of Naufragus; Written by Himself*, which purported to give 'a faithful account of his voyages, shipwreck, and travels, from his first outset as a midshipman in the East India Company's service, till he became a commander in the Indian seas', etc., etc. It reached a second edition in 1828, and no doubt they were looking for something different, which they soon found in Lieutenant Maw's *Memoir*. John's work would not serve. He could do no more than pass on to Elizabeth the gift book he had received from them, *Friendship's Offering*, one of their own publications. Ironically, Smith and Elder were to raise his sister's reputation to its highest point.

The relationship between brother and younger sister was shot through with ironies and ambiguities. His early letters were sententious but encouraging.

He tried to stimulate her rivalry with her cousin Isabella in Berwick, not too wisely but with good intentions. They are good models in many ways – full of fun, jokes and news, of electioneering at Berwick and voyages to the east, exotic accounts of Indian scenes and customs, warfare at Rangoon, storms at sea and social life on board British ships. He seems the typical older brother and jolly sailor. Mrs Gaskell's daughters transmitted the memory of him as 'a pickle – much attached to her', which certainly accords with the style of his early letters. All this must be weighed against his evident lack of social ease, his thwarted literary ambitions and the increasingly jaundiced view of life and human motives that colours his later missives.[17]

Did John realise that ultimately he was trying to will her to succeed in literature where he had so clearly failed? There is a point in his letter of 30 July 1828 where he does for a while forget his own concerns and comment upon the beginnings of his sister's literary career:

> You have really made out a very pretty story of Captain Barton – it would almost make the foundation of a novel [-] it was indeed a narrow escape of Kitty's and must have given her a tremendous fright – though I have heard <and> read many stories of them, I never saw a quicksand a<nd hard>ly believed them to be so dangerous as was generally <spoken?> off.[18]

This rescue probably occurred on the very estuary that Mary, Bessy and Lucy Holland had crossed with an ancient courier on horses up to their bellies in water during their 1823 tour to Barmouth, Traeth Bach. Elizabeth Stevenson was following in their literary footsteps, telling perhaps the very first of her Welsh stories. It has not survived, but cries out for investigation of its context, which turns out to be the life she shared with Holland relations in Wales and an unexpected sequel set in Warwickshire.

In Samuel's Holland's memoirs he referred very incidentally to a neighbour, Captain Barton. Some time between 1825 and 1828 J. J. Barton had bought a house at Cae Canol, the next house to Plas yn Penrhyn, just about the time Samuel Holland was improving it.[19] Barton, who is not recorded as a royal naval officer, built upon the nearby foreshore of the sandy estuary of Traeth Bach at Aber-ia (better known today as the Italianate village of Porthmeirion) a quay at least 600 feet long for the transference of slates from Dwyryd sailboats to sea-going ships. He is described as 'a shadowy figure' who eventually became 'old, fragile, part deaf and part blind', and whose commercial attempt to rival Porthmadog was a miserable failure.[20]

Kitty was almost certainly Samuel's sister Catherine, the one who had been brought up at Putney with her uncle Menzies' family. Then in her mid-twenties, she was presumably staying with her brother Samuel at Plas yn Penrhyn, in all probability at the same time as Elizabeth if the latter had been inspired to make a story out of her rescue from a quicksand. A letter Mrs Gaskell later wrote to William Gaskell's young sister Eliza speaks about the wedding in Wales of this cousin, usually called Kate, to a Richard Greaves in April 1838 – white chip hat, orange flowers, pale lavender satin pelisse trimmed with swansdown. She continues dramatically, 'They ford across the Tratte, a most dangerous place by the way full of quick sands, are married, breakfast at the beautiful little inn near there, & the whole party accompany the happy pair for a stage or two'.

Had they been going to Porthmadog the party could have driven easily across William Madock's embankment, but south of Plas yn Penrhyn was the wide, distinctly unimproved estuary of Traeth Bach with Captain Barton's quay on its northern bank. Travelling in this direction, the party would go by an old route mentioned by Giraldus in 1188 and shown in the early Ordnance Survey map, across the sands from Abergafran below Minfford to Talsarnau and along to Llanfihangel y Traethau, by which, according to the topographical dictionary of 1833, 'the road from Harlech over the sands to Tremadog passes'. No mention is made of quicksands, but tidal estuaries are always tricky. At Llanfihangel was an ancient church dedicated to St Michael.[21]

Greaves is a name that Samuel Holland mentions a number of times in his memoirs. In particular he tells us that John Whitehead Greaves came to the Tan y Bwlch hotel in 1834 to work 'what was called Lord Newborough's quarry', the third of any size to be opened in the neighbourhood after Samuel Holland senior's. (The Old Vein at Diffwys, the foundation of the industry, had been worked for some decades before 1800.) John Whitehead Greaves, expected by his family to emigrate to Canada from the booming slate port of Caernarfon, was instead excited by the industrial potential of North Wales and joined in partnership with another English adventurer, Edwin Shelton. He found a place to live at 'Tanyrallt issa' near Tremadog. In 1835 John joined Samuel Holland in working an iron-stone quarry near Abersoch across the bay on the Lleyn Peninsula (though this was given up after a year's trial), and members of the Greaves family were present on 20 April 1836 for the grand opening of the Ffestiniog tramway. John can be identified as the son of a Quaker, John Greaves of Radford Semele by Warwick, and Mary (née Whitehead) of Barford, who according to a deed of 1834 had another son called Richard living at Shottery, no more than a mile or so away from Avonbank and the Byerley sisters' school. John and Edward Greaves of Barford were in fact his elder brothers.[22] Members of the Greaves family in Warwickshire were as thoroughly involved in stone quarries, lime and cement works and the like as their representative John Whitehead Greaves in North Wales.[23]

Their private life was prosperous and kept separate from business affairs. Both Richard and his father were bankers, described as gentlemen in documents. Elizabeth Gaskell seems to have lost touch with the family after her marriage, but she re-visited the 'land of clover & good food' around Warwick and Stratford-upon-Avon during the spring of 1849. After *Mary Barton* and the whirl of lionising she encountered in London, she sank back into the cushioned existence of the 'very pretty, really old-fashioned cottage' at Shottery, where 'the scents through the open hall door were all of sweet briar and lilac and lilies of the valley: where we slept with our windows open to hear the nightingales' jug-jug, and where the very shadows in the drawing room had a green tinge from the leafy trees which over hung the windows'. This cottage could have been the home of cousin Kate and her husband, Richard Greaves.

Bessy Howorth and Anne Holland – whose 'excellent sense, and a very fair proportion of satirical power, which she is not at all unwilling to exert', were intended to save Elizabeth Gaskell from the mysterious effects of being lionised in London – also stayed at Shottery at this time. They told each other ghost stories, visited a curious old house called Compton Winyates, on the way back from which Mrs Gaskell herself claimed to have seen a ghost – her story is transmitted by Augustus Hare – and went to 'dine at Mr Greaves at Radford, the father of Mr R. Greaves.' Kate's husband, Richard Greaves, seems not long afterwards to have moved to The Cliff, Warwick, becoming a J.P. and a pillar of the community. He died on 29 April 1870, leaving £200 in his will towards the establishment of a public bathing place for the citizens of Warwick on the bank of the Avon. He also expressed the hope that the 'days of persecution for religious opinions will speedily cease' and left £500 to the little Unitarian chapel in the High Street. Its former minister, the Reverend William Field, had been forced into lengthy polemics with his *Letters Addressed to the Calvinistic Christians of Warwick* in 1820. Mrs Gaskell wrote about 1850 that she had been separated from these cousins for nearly eighteen years, but that with them were 'associated some of the happiest recollections' of her childhood.[24]

By this time in mid-century the Byerleys had long since given up teaching in Warwickshire. Avonbank was purchased for 200 guineas by yet another family connection, Charles Edward Flower, whose father had married Richard Greaves's sister Selina in 1827. Charles writes in his early reminiscences of a visit to North Wales with his brothers William and Edgar in 1835 to uncle John Greaves, whose 'sharp, short manner' kept him in great dread. On 13 May 1852 the Unitarian minister Thomas Madge married Charles to Sarah Martineau at Newington Green chapel. Sarah remembered several parties and dances in early 1849. She went through the snow in a dog cart to the Greaveses at Radford, stopping for dinner at a pastry cook's at Leamington on the way, and found a twelfth night party going on. This was followed by a dinner at the Flowers' Brewery House in Stratford on the following day, at which the wife of Dickens's brother Fred 'played very brilliantly in a grand style – the incomparable sonata of Beethoven – I wonder which it is?' The business connections of John Whitehead Greaves in Wales in the 1830s had evidently led to an exceptionally pleasant extension of Elizabeth Gaskell's social round.[25]

A few months after her 1838 letter about the romantic wedding of Kate Holland and Richard Greaves, she lightly reproached her sister-in-law Eliza, then staying at the old walled town of Beaumaris in the isle of Anglesey: 'You never mention Capn Barton. Is he "to the fore" yet? Did you ever see Mr Greaves?'[26] Beaumaris had become a fashionable bathing place. It was on the coast, opposite Mrs Gaskell's favourite village of Aber on the mainland across the Lavan sands, which could also be dangerous in certain states of the tide; in foggy weather the bell of Aber was rung to guide travellers across. Beaumaris was a port with regular steam-packets to Liverpool and Ireland, 'lucrative commands' according to De Quincey at the beginning of the century.[27]

Exact identities are doubtful, and more research needs to be done, but the links between Warwickshire and North Wales compose a kind of delicate web in which people and incidents were caught up from a very early stage in Elizabeth's writing career. The story-telling habits of this particular circle are manifest. Her father, brother and the Byerley sisters had also provided not only a good education but positive examples and encouragement. Aspirations to authorship were by no means hopeless. From a broadly similar provincial and Unitarian background Harriet Martineau succeeded in obtaining literary work in the 1820s, through the *Monthly Repository* in the first instance and with the assistance of William Fox and others. When Harriet's father was ruined in the financial crash of 1825-26, she had no doubt that she would have to rely upon herself. Her deafness ruled out teaching or, as she caustically put it, 'going out into the cold dark sphere of governessing'. The death of her one and only fiancé removed what she perhaps less well characterised as 'the temptation' of love and marriage. Elizabeth Stevenson had financial security, and was not to escape the mixed blessings of wedlock, which she managed to combine with her writing and must be regarded as the source of her 'maternal thinking'.[28]

Unfortunately, the journals Elizabeth was on more than one occasion urged to keep by her father and brother have not been found. The journals kept by her Knutsford cousins give us some idea of their probable nature. Her little story 'The Sexton's Hero' in *Howitt's Journal* for 1849 harks back to the vast stretches of sand at Traeth Bach and Aber, and later, Silverdale on the Lancashire coast. The life and times of her family, which Jenny Uglow found so often in the published fiction, began early. Stories like 'The Well of Pen-Morfa' and 'The Doom of the Griffiths', both set in the Tremadog area, might well be youthful compositions. The former might have been revised, or revived, when she met her Greaves cousins again in mid-century. The latter, she told Charles Norton, was 'an old rubbishy one, – begun when Marianne was a baby, – the only merit wherof is that it is founded on fact'. It is said by a daughter to have been written at Plas yn Penrhyn – though its setting might have inspired the assumption.[29]

The Vale of Ffestiniog, however, provides the most poignant instance of a connection between married life and authorship, for it was to North Wales that the Gaskells took the ten-year-old Marianne and their infant son Willie in the summer of 1845. They were given rooms in the inn at Ffestiniog where there had been scarlet fever, which Marianne caught. They all left and went to Porthmadog, where Marianne recovered but, to her infinite distress, little Willie died on 10 August.[30] 'To turn her thoughts by her husband's advice she began to write' is a sentence Ward underlined in his notes from the Gaskell daughters, continuing, 'She had previously written two poems (one on a still born child of her own,) the other ['romantic' inserted nearby] on a stag), and the beginning of a short story.'[31]

Kate Greaves's sister, Fanny Holland, had a small house in Porthmadog about this time and knew the landlady of the house in which Willie had died. A recently discovered letter of March 1847 to Fanny displays the mercurial volatility of Elizabeth Gaskell's character – not unlike her brother's. She writes with deep emotion of a nurse she felt it was ungrateful to part with, a Miss Fergusson, who had been with them in Wales and 'who was *so tender* to my poor darling boy'. But she strongly disapproved of the way in which Miss Fergusson was managing Marianne and Meta. As she fervently avowed to Fanny, who sympathised with '*both*' her feelings, 'All those awful days are stamped in my heart, and I don't believe Heaven itself can obliterate the memory of that agony, – and I am haunted by the thought of the person who knew him most & loved him most at last, going to leave our house which ought to be her home – and our doing. He died in her arms too.' But there is also a paragraph in this deeply felt letter which demonstrates her inability, as her mind raced on, to resist 'news afloat':

> Do you know if Mrs Hughes ever got a workbox I sent (through Lizzy when she came over to see her mother,) to Jane-Anne Hughes. Give my love to Mrs Hughes. We all mean to write to her oftener than we do. Wm is engaged morning noon & night; what a curious adventure of Mr Rowland Wms! Tell me about Sophy Greave's engagement – I never heard a word of it.

Who was Mr Rowland Williams, and what was his curious adventure? Williamses in North Wales are as common as blackberries. Could he have been a relation of the David Williams, a solicitor from Pwllheli, who took over Cae Canol from his brother, made great alterations, built a tower, which he called Castell Deudraeth (or Bron Eryri), and preceded Samuel Holland as Merioneth's first Liberal M.P.? Unfortunately, there seems to be no Rowland in his family tree.[32]

It is, however, an uncommon name, and there was a Rowland Williams at this time, a surgeon of Tremadog, who probably moved in the same circles as the Hollands. Some years before he had an adventure that was reported in the *Caernarvon and Denbigh Herald* of 24 December 1842. Riding along the edge of the Ffestiniog railway he saw a train of wagons loaded with slates coming down, so he sensibly dismounted and turned his horse into a recess of the wall. But the nervous creature backed into the train as it passed, plunged and reared in fright and fell on Williams. The horse then fell over an edge many feet high without hurt. Rowland Williams suffered a broken collar bone and several ribs. If this is rather too early to be the curious adventure in question, it did involve unusual circumstances in a wild land that was still being tamed.[33]

And who was Sophy Greaves, the engaged lady? She was a sister of Richard, remembered with her children in his will. Charles Edward Flower knew her as one of his five young aunts at Radford, 'a tall girl in white with a long broad sash', who acted in spirited charades at a succession of parties and taught him how to dance the new-fangled polka before she married in 1847. She sounds very like Elizabeth Stevenson in Manchester some fifteen years before, if waltz is substituted for polka. And who did Sophy marry? It has yet to be discovered. The material that presented itself to Elizabeth Gaskell sometimes seems endless, and so does research.[34]

NOTES

1 JGS: ?unfinished MS, two conj. F leaves (wmk 'MUNN & STEPHENS 1824'), JS to ECS, Ship Recovery At Sea, 16 July & 11 August [1827]. See Parkinson, *Trade in the Eastern Seas*, pp. 99-102 (with chart), and p. 284 above. I am grateful to E. B. Gaskin for expert advice.

2 Monkland, *Life*, London, 1828, pp. 19, 30; *QED*.

3 *Letters*, p. 21; *Portrait*, p. 6; NLS: WS to WB, Treasury, 28 December 1827; Gautier, *Marryat*, pp. 27, 50. See p. 172 above.

4 *Letters*, pp. 797-8, from Margaret Howitt, 'Stray notes', [September], p. 606; apology in flyleaf of October issue. See also pp. 3, 245 above.

5 HC to ATT, Edinburgh, 16 June 1823 (Gregg Collection); [K. Thomson], *Memoir of ATT*, p. 15; [R. Radford], 'Portrait Gallery – 14: Anthony Todd Thomson, M.D., F L.S. (1778-1849)', *University College Hospital Magazine*, XXXVIII, 1953, pp. 160-1.

6 NLPS: Moor Collection 23. i, ii: HH to WT, L Brook Street, 2 December [1826] and London, 20 September [1827]; HH, *Recollections*, pp. 7, 165, 228-31; *Edgeworth Letters*, p. 321.

7 R. P. Gillies, *Memoirs*, 1851, III, pp. 143, 165, 196-213; [?Bellot], 'Memoir of Thomson', p. 3; research material kindly sent by Wilma R. Slaight, Archivist, Wellesley College, 17 September 1993. The researcher also noted Stevenson's use of 'luminous'.

8 *Letters*, p. 508. Cp 'Discourse', in Harriet Martineau's *How to Observe. Morals and Manners*, London, 1838.

9 J. D. Michaelis, *Influence of Opinions on Language, and of Language on Opinions* (1760), tr. 1769. S. Parr recommended this to Dugald Stewart c. 1816. See Aarsleff, *Study of Language in England*, pp. 102, 143-7.

10 David Murison, 'Two languages in Scott', *Scott's Mind and Art: Essays*, ed. A. Norman Jeffares, Edinburgh, 1969, pp. 212, 218-20.

11 JGS: MS, two conj. 4to leaves (no wmk), JS to ECS (Address: 'Miss Stevenson'), Beaufort Row, 30 July [1828], with TS and MS copies. Also, two TSS with accidental variants only, JS to ECS ('Miss Stevenson'), Beaufort Row, 15 August [1828]. Dated by perpetual calendar and A. Barclay, *A Practical View of the Present State of Slavery in the West Indies*, London: Smith, Elder, & Co., 3rd edn [1828].

12 P. [70]. See pp. 210, 154 above.

13 This suggests that Elizabeth had been in Chelsea just before 30 July 1828. The second music book would repay closer study and comparison with, e.g., Chapple, 'Five new letters', pp. 4, 12-14. Its 14 May 1828 date (associated with French and German texts) might belong to London.

14 *Losh Diaries*, II, pp. 8-9, 211, 225-6.

15 DCLH: HH to ME, L Brook St, 8 January [1830]; Hunter, p. 179; Knutsford parish church register; *Martineau*, ed. Drummond and Upton, I, pp. 30-3; Carpenter, *Martineau*, p. 38; FH, *A Brief Statement of the Rise and Progress of the Christian Church, Rochdale Road, Bury, and of Its Doctrines and Principles*, London and Bury, [1855], pp. 4, 11. I must thank librarians of BuCL and RL for information about FH and his publications.

16 Ruskin, 'My first editor' [W. H. Harrison], *Works*, XXXIV, p. 94, qu. Derrick Leon, *Ruskin the Great Victorian*, London, 1949, repr. 1969, p. 31.

17 *The Letters of Charles and Mary Lamb*, ed. Edwin W. Marrs, Jr, Ithaca and London, 1975, I, p. xxxiv; HUL: advert bound in Maw, *Memoir of the Burmese War*, 1832; *Portrait*, pp. 4-5; Ward Notebook, f. 9. I am grateful to Mrs Virginia Murray for informing me that there is no record of the submission of John's book in the John Murray archives.

18 First pr. in Sharps, p. 42n. The paper was torn when the seal was ripped open.

19 'I took *Dorlan Goch* for several years – from Mr Davies of Borthwen bach – & eventually sold it for him – to Mr John Williams, in 1840 who bought & lived at *Cae Canol* which he bought from Cap. Barton, who built [it *deleted*] a large House there'; with side entry stating that a Mr Cartwright 'sold it to Barton' (NLW: MS, f. 38; *Memoirs*, ed. Davies, p. 15). Captain John James Barton of Cae Canol is recorded in *Pigot's Directory* for 1835.

20 Lewis, *Sails on the Dwyryd*, pp. 61-3; [Smith and Lewis], *Commissioned Sea-Officers of the Royal Navy*. I am grateful to Steffan ap Owain and the record office staff at Dolgellau for identifying Captain Barton.

21 ECG to Eliza Gaskell, [28 (*sic*) March 1838] (*Letters*, p. 13); Lewis, *Topographical Dictionary of Wales*, 'Llanfihangel'; Lewis, *Sails on the Dwyryd*, p. 58. From July 1837, however, the law no longer demanded that dissenters' marriages be celebrated in the parish church; Quaker marriages had always been exempt.

22 SSBT: DR149/157/65, 28 February 1834; Irvine, p. 84; SH, *Memoirs*, ed. Davies, pp. 19-20, 24-5; Wynne Jones, *Eagles Do Not Catch Flies*, pp. 1-2, 15; Lewis, *Sails on the Dwyryd*, pp. 9-10; Lindsay, *North Wales Slate Industry*, pp. 87, 142. The *IGI* records nine children of John and Ellen Greaves christened 1844-60, and an adult christening of John Whitehead Greaves under 7 April 1858. John Greaves, 'son-in-law', was a trustee under John Whitehead's will, dated 5 July 1821 (SSBT: DR318/5/vii).

23 A letter from John to his brother about railway shares, a mortgage, bills due and common land ends with a reference to loading a barge for him (SSBT: DR469/180: JWG to RG, Tremadoc, 28 October 1839). See also *VCH Warwickshire*, II, pp. 194, 204; III, pp. 35, 243; William West, *The History, Topography and Directory of Warwickshire*, Birmingham, pp. 670-1; numerous SSBT deeds, etc.

24 See *Letters*, pp. 71, 79-81, 134, 792 (n. d., c. 1850?); Augustus J. C. Hare, *The Story of My Life*, London, 1896-1900, II, pp. 224-7; Uglow, pp. 227-8, 239; Sharps, pp. 539-40; WRO1: C1453/Wills/Book 2 (copy), R. G's will proved D. R., Birmingham, under £100,100.

25 Flower, *Great Aunt Sarah's Diary*, pp. 1, 10-12, 47.

26 ECG to Eliza Gaskell, 14 Dover Street, [17 July 1838] (*Letters*, p. 21). See Sharps, p. 42n.

27 Lewis, *Topographical Dictionary of Wales*, 'Beaumaris'; De Quincey, 'Autobiographical sketches 1790-1800', p. 211. *IGI* records Bartons in Beaumaris: Richard and Mary Barton (son Alfred bp 13 October 1824); William and Alice Barton (son Thomas bp 28 August 1819).

28 Webb, *Martineau*, pp. 49-52; *Autobiography of Harriet Martineau*, I, pp. 117, 128-31, 143-9. Cp. *Harriet Martineau Letters*, ed. Sanders, p. 19: 'My sisters are provided with excellent situations as governesses' [in September 1829].

29 Sharps, pp. 41, 97n., 267; *Letters*, p. 488.

30 Ward Notebook, f. 14, *DNB* and Knutsford Edn, I, p. xxvii. Date given as 1844, but cp. Sanders, *Gaskell*, p. 17, and Bulmer, *Unitarian Chapel, Cairo Street*, p. 42 (inscription:

William Gaskell, their son, 9m 18d; but the space above is blank). Willie was born 23 October 1844, baptised at Cross Street chapel on 23 January 1845 and died 10 August 1845. Brief obit. in *CR*, 1845, p. 660: at Port Madoc, N. Wales, only son of Rev. William Gaskell. See also Appendix G.

31 In *DNB* Ward gives the family tradition that it was a wounded stag. But cp. E. C. Gaskell, *The Life of Charlotte Brontë*, London, 1st edn, 1857, I, pp. 97-8, in which a poem of this title was ascribed to CB.

32 *Letters*, p. 844, [17 October 1851]; LUBL: ECG to FH, Upper Rumford Street, [9 March 1847]; SH, *Memoirs*, ed. Davies, p. 15 (MS, f. 38). Fanny was a cousin, not an aunt (error in *Portrait*, p. 34).

33 I am grateful to Dr Michael Lewis for drawing my attention to Dr Rowland Williams and his mishap (MJTL to JAVC, 28 April 1994).

34 Flower, *Great Aunt Sarah's Diary*, pp. 2, 5-6. See also p. 414 below.

18

A chapter of endings

A T SOME TIME in the late 1820s William Stevenson was working on the last of his books to be published. It was, like Katharine Thomson's *Wolsey*, one of the 'Lives of Eminent Persons' for Brougham's Diffusion of Useful Knowledge Society. Cockburn had seen her text by the June of 1828, and the Lives were published together in 1833, anonymously. Stevenson is not named in the Society's original list of fifty-seven authors, but there is no reason to dispute the attribution in his obituary.[1] It begins, typically, with an analysis of different types of biography, in order to determine the kind to which a life of Caxton should belong. Then follows an enumeration of 'the modes and materials used for translating knowledge' before the invention of printing – wood, leather, papyrus, paper, ink and the manuscript book – and, at length, the life of Caxton and notes on other early printers. It is melancholy to see that someone who knew Elizabeth Gaskell very well, James Martineau, was able to record the full names of all the authors of the series in his personal copies, now in Dr Williams's Library, with one exception: 'By – Stephenson', he wrote. This is yet another indication that Elizabeth's father had lost touch with the Unitarian community, and perhaps a sign that Elizabeth had not said much to Martineau about her father.

He was in harness till his death. He seems to have been in good health in the summer of 1828, when the July letter from his son John spoke of his remaining in London from early August till the end of September, whilst Mrs Stevenson and her children went to Scotland, dropping off Elizabeth Stevenson of Berwick on the way. He was probably glad to be free to do what he wanted – but unwise. His obituary speaks of him working 'until repeated attacks of illness obliged him to relinquish all mental exertion.' He was actually thought to have recovered on Friday, 20 March 1829, but suddenly lost his sight whilst sitting at tea with his family that evening. Then he lost the use of his right side, was carried to bed 'and spoke only once afterwards'. By Sunday he was dead.[2]

Amongst the Blackwood papers is a final Stevenson letter written in a neat little hand on the Wednesday following, 25 March 1829. It was from Elizabeth Stevenson's half-brother:

Sir,

Though not personally acquainted, I have often heard my poor Father speak of you, and I am sure you will be very sorry to hear of the death of my Father, on Sunday morning last; he was seized on Friday evening by a Paralytic shock, he was speechless from Friday night, at ten o'clock, till he died. He was senseless from Saturday morning. He was cupped, on Saturday forenoon, and every assistance was given till the last moment. He was opened, on Monday morning, by the surgeon who attended him, and by my cousin; they found that he had an enlargement, of the heart, and that an abscess, had formed in his brain, and that a blood-vessel had burst in the head. He did not seem to have any pain. Mama is better than we could expect. She would be much obliged to you, if you would send your Magazine the same as if Papa had been in life; but if you would direct it to No 3 Beaufort Row Chelsea.

I am Sir
Your obliged Servant
William Stevenson.

William's cousin was Dr Alexander Thomson, Anthony's son by his first marriage to Christina Maxwell. A student at the London University Dispensary in George Street, he was old enough to help his father in editing a book on cutaneous diseases in 1829, but was soon to be expelled for his part in a bitter quarrel at the university. William himself was only about fourteen at the time, which probably accounts for his lack of savoir faire. His step-sister was more adept when she begged a copy of *Adam Bede* from John Blackwood thirty years afterwards – a 'slightly impudent' request she acknowledged as she expressed her great delight in the genius of the unknown writer – adding the comment that 'some Mr Blackwood was for auld acquaintance sake extremely kind in assisting in the education of a half-brother of mine, since dead.' Once again, we can admire the generosity of William Blackwood and see that he transferred to the son, possibly from about this time, the kindness he had always displayed to his father.[3]

His obituarist's claim that the 'literary and scientific world has sustained a great loss' is a conventional assertion. That he was 'a man remarkable for the stores of knowledge which he possessed, and for the modesty and simplicity by which his rare attainments were concealed' is much more credible, but not only his treatises 'for the edification of the agricultural classes' were left unfinished, his personal affairs turned out to be in a state of chaos. In the very month of July 1827 that he had written to Elizabeth showing no signs of distress, he had been 'obliged to make use of part of the money' his wife Catharine had brought as her dowry by selling some of the Bank of England stock belonging to her. He had at that point drawn up a kind of will, but neither signed it before witnesses nor given it a date.

He declared it was 'but just and proper that she and her children should receive ... in the first place the principal and interest of what she brought' him on marriage. If there was not enough 'in the Stocks' at his decease (which shows how pathetic was the fortune he had been able to make in comparison with his Holland relations), the furniture and books at Beaufort Row should be sold to make up the sum of £800 for his second family. Any residue he wished to be divided equally between his wife and children, John and Elizabeth, William and Catherine. He appointed 'Alexander Thomson M D, of 91 Sloane Street my Brother in law', to be his executor.

Mrs Stevenson had to appear personally on 12 June 1829 before the Surrogate to swear that when in July 1827 she had agreed to the sale of her stock, her husband had promised to make a will to provide for re-investment. She then affirmed that in November 1828 he had given her the paper 'purporting to be and contain' his last Will and Testament, 'folded up but not endorsed or enclosed in any envelope', telling her that he had written it when he sold the stock. There is no indication why it was not signed and witnessed on this occasion, well over a year later; she merely states that she had kept it 'in the self same plight and condition' as when she received it and had not after a diligent search been able to find any other will or testamentary paper. She also swore that her brother Anthony Todd Thomson, now living at Hinde Street, Manchester Square, was the intended executor.[4]

John Barnes, gentleman of 19 Seymour Place, Euston Square, and Alexander Thomson esquire of 4 George Street, Euston Square had already made affidavits on 30 May 1929 to the effect that they had known Stevenson for several years before his death and were well acquainted with his handwriting, which was that of the paper before the court. Barnes is a name that occurs in John Stevenson's letter of 30 July 1828: 'Mr Barnes who was with Mr Thomson has returned from Van Diemans land and is going to study in London'. Barnes was, perhaps, a botanist, an assistant to Professor A. T. Thomson by 1831, and also for a long time a close friend of his son Alexander, though the friendship had broken down by this date.[5]

All this suggests that William Stevenson suffered the first of his 'repeated attacks of illness' in November 1828. Was he too ill at this time to sign the document he had drawn up? Or did he perhaps consider that he could repay the money he had borrowed before too long? Wills used to be put off for as long as possible, but Mrs Stevenson might very naturally have wished for some proof of his intentions? She was not exactly in an enviable position, approaching her middle fifties, with a husband, whether she knew it or not, nearly sixty years of age, overworked and in a poor state of health. His grown-up son John had sailed for the East a few months before and had stated his intention of staying there for good. Her own children, William and Catherine, were in their early teens. The family was in continuous financial straits. On the other hand, given the help she and her sister had extended to Dr Anthony Thomson at the beginning of his successful career, she might reasonably rely on the Christian charity for which he was well known. Indeed, Katharine Thomson emphasises his 'never-ceasing care of the comforts' of his two sisters 'in after-life'.[6]

John Stevenson's last letters suggest that Elizabeth was in Knutsford during the summer of 1828, even though her slightly younger cousin and namesake was still visiting at Beaufort Row. A copy of part of a solitary letter from Mrs Stevenson to Mrs Lumb (all that is known)[7] is dated from Chelsea on 15 June 1829, the day that the will was granted probate. 'I often think how fortunate it was her (Elizabeth) being with us when her poor Father died; & it must always be a source of comfort to her to think that she had seen him', she began in graceful conformity to social norms. The last phrase perhaps implies that Elizabeth had not been called to London until a late stage of her father's illness. The letter then continues just as smoothly but more problematically:

> Often did he intend writing to you about Elizabeth and frequently spoke to me about her. Indeed both he & I considered her much improved altogether and although he said little, I could easily see that he felt proud of his daughter. I do not recollect at present that in any one instance he was either hurt or vexed about her.

A. B. Hopkins, who was the first to print in full all that the family had so carefully preserved, thought that although the letter was evidence of earlier problems, it nevertheless reflected credit upon all concerned. Later biographers have been less inclined to take it at face value. Is there an implication that at the age of eighteen Elizabeth had caused trouble at some time in the past, whatever her subsequent improvement? Anne Thackeray Ritchie wrote of unhappiness at Knutsford and a consequent retreat to the lonely safety of the green hollows of the heath, seeking silence and 'the company of birds and insects and natural things'. Elizabeth could have been very young then, chafing at the restraints so often imposed upon children; but when she herself writes that she 'occasionally' lived in Chelsea with her father and stepmother and was '*very, very* unhappy', the reference to the comfort provided by the Kennett family suggests that a severe emotional crisis occurred at some time after March 1827 when Mrs Kennett began to live in Beaufort Row. In any case, Elizabeth seems to have been inclined to remove herself entirely from difficulties, to find refuge elsewhere, by river or heath, or with sympathetic friends.[8]

Even if we ignore (with difficulty) the novel that is so evidently connected with her early experiences, *Wives and Daughters*, the 'common and well-grounded opinion, associated with the idea of a second wife', as Richard Edgeworth had put it, casts the shadow of a fairytale ogre over her life. The only letter that has survived from Elizabeth's father does not breathe a word of the financial disasters that afflicted the household at 3 Beaufort Row. If she was largely shielded from these, they were all too ominously present for the second Mrs Stevenson. Her future and that of her children, born after a marriage relatively late in life, was insecure, dependent upon the charity of others. Did her insecurities cause her to be sharp with an exceptionally lively young lady entering upon a world that was obviously going to like and admire her? Or was she dealing with a difficult and passionate young woman? The Victorian matron always known as 'Mrs Gaskell' until recently was unusually open to a stranger when she told Elizabeth Barrett Browning something that made Mrs Browning reply, 'Imprudent marriages are the most prudent marriages according to my philosophy – and experience – for I too have made an imprudent marriage. ... For my part, I congratulate you, dear Mrs. Gaskell, from the bottom of my heart, on having made an imprudent marriage.'[9]

The last portion of Mrs Stevenson's letter to Mrs Lumb reverts to suave commonplaces:

> Her conduct at the time of her Father's and my distress was certainly very beautiful and more like a person much older. Indeed she was a very great comfort to me, my own girl being young and consequently not so thoughtful. I shall ever love Elizabeth as my own child, and trust that nothing will ever break that friendship which I trust is between us at this time, and also the love that she and her brother and sister have for each other.

The protestations are elegantly turned – and not necessarily false. She does not go so far as to claim that Elizabeth reciprocated her love, only that she trusted there was a friendship between them at that time. But it is inconceivable that aunt Lumb would have written in such terms. Before long the widowed Mrs Stevenson left the sad little house in Beaufort Row altogether.[10]

Swinton Holland's will had provided for The Priory and real estate in Toxteth Park, Over Peover, Barnshaw and other places in Lancashire and Cheshire to be administered in trust for the benefit of his wife and children. An annuity of £2000 a year was arranged for Mrs Holland. After her father's death in March 1829 Elizabeth might have stayed with her widowed aunt Anne, who was at Norfolk Street in the middle of 1831, her cousins, Charlotte and Louisa (who were each left £15,000 in trust) and their brothers Frederick and George. The sort of town pleasures her relations in London could afford may be judged from Elizabeth's gossip. She wrote to her friend Harriet Carr that 'the good people in Park Lane' had been giving 'what sounds like a most delightful dance, only dances always do sound delightful', she continued with swift urbanity, 'but they had an excellent projector, who made capital "flirting places" in the balcony, and Gunter, and Weippert's band, & Colville's flower show'.[11]

New evidence about Elizabeth's movements and those of her relations is contained in a letter Mary Holland wrote to Mrs Mary Robberds at Manchester in September 1829.[12] Mary was very anxious about Emma, Henry Holland's wife, who had been ill with a rheumatic attack whilst her husband was in Ireland. Her health had been poor for some time, and Henry used to send her off with the little ones to Hampstead, 'one of the most beautiful villages near the metropolis' according to William Stevenson in *Brewster's Edinburgh Encyclopaedia*. John Constable the painter made it his refuge about this time. Whenever Henry could snatch a moment to ride there from town, the family used to ramble on the open heath 'without hats, hoods, or waiting maids; caring little what was going on beneath the huge cloud of smoke below'. By August 1829 Emma was in Hampstead again, when her little daughter Elinor died suddenly, Mary Holland being with her at the time. A house was then taken at Broadstairs to try the benefit of the sea air for wife and children. On Henry's return from Ireland, Emma was well enough to take a pleasant steam trip to Margate and back with friends. Then he was off again, on his autumn travels, this time to Brittany and the Vendée.[13]

By September Emma and Mary had left Broadstairs to stay at 'The Priory', Roehampton, together with Emma's children – Henry Thurstan, Francis James and a daughter, Emily-Mary. As Mary Holland confided to Mrs Robberds,

> Emma and I like being here very much, we are perfectly quiet, but we have plenty of books, and the children. More especially my darling Franky. Then in this showery weather it is a great thing to have a nice garden & grounds to turn into when there is a dry, or sunny gleam: to conclude, anything is better, to me at least than being in London. ...
>
> We have one book here which would amuse your husband, if he has never read it: Fuller's British Worthies. It is so quaint, sly, and full of bad puns, & humour. I borrowed Mr Eccles' history from Miss Aikin when I was at Hampstead ... We are reading too Mrs Cappe's life aloud in the evening, as Emma had never read it, and she is much amused by it. We have a great variety of other books, in all styles, of all languages, and on all subjects so we shall not want 'food for the *moind*'.

The connection with Manchester Unitarians still seems strong:

> One sort of food tho' I am rather in want of, & that is of Manchester news. I want to know how Mrs Wood is, for she will *not* write to me herself: whether Mrs Henry is come home & many other particulars – Also whether your [ear] trumpet is of any use to you. ... Then I want to know something about my *literary concerns*. Forrest's bill ought to be paid, & I will give directions to that effect at Knutsford, if you will take the trouble to pay it for me. But then I want to know whether you have received payment for any of the books, that I may tell them what money to send you. So please to send either me, or them, word. I have received much commendation of the Easy lessons from various quarter<s> Catharine, Charlotte Wedgwood, Mrs Coltman, Emma, &c &c. So I do hope it will be useful.[14]

The way in which this long letter emphasises the bookish culture of these intertwined and prosperous families is interesting enough; its indication that Mary Holland had published a textbook is new. Mrs Sarah Trimmer's *Easy Lessons for Young Children* of 1786 went through a number of editions. If Mary was not herself an author, she might have arranged for a reprint. However, Thomas Forrest was a bookseller, printer and stationer in Market

Street, Manchester, and reputed to be the only one who would 'allow the publications of the Unitarian body to lie on his counter'.[15]

On the last page of this letter Mary writes, 'I grew quite fond of old Mrs Aikin. She was so kind & affectionate to me, particularly during the week Henry was away, when I was anxious & unhappy about Emma'; and a few lines later continues, 'I have most comfortable accounts of Bessy in Gloucestershire, and most cheerful letters from her. I do hope she is at last regaining spirits & strength, & ... '. The last page ends at this point, but scrawled across the writing on the first the unexpected continuation of her sentence emerges like an austereogram from the cross-hatching:

> this is such a relief to my mind. My Aunt Lumb and E. Stevenson have joined the party there now and they are planning all sorts of gaiety – trip to a Bath Ball at Cheltenham & I know not what beside. Susan is at Lancaster, so poor Lucy is alone at home, which is rather hard upon her. However my conscience is clear as I have no doubt about my being where I ought to be now.

Before long Emma had to be nursed through her last illness. She was again seriously ill at Roehampton in November, with Mary Holland looking after the children. She seemed to rally – early in the new year she was able to make two of her children shed tears by reading them an abridgement of the *Snow Woman* – but she was dead by February 1830. Black-edged mourning paper again appears in Henry Holland's correspondence. Deeply affected, he took refuge in a desire to make 'some hasty journey without stopping any where', he wrote to Lucy Aikin. Mary seems to have had a visit to Edgeworthstown to recuperate her strength, but by the summer Henry's children were in Knutsford, 'under the admirable care', he wrote, 'of my sister Mary, who is almost a Mother to them' – not quite as impassioned as Elizabeth Gaskell on Hannah Lumb. In September 1831 Mary was looking after the children at Maer with the Wedgwoods. But the fact that his two little boys were going away to school determined Henry to take a second wife. He became engaged to Saba, daughter of his old friend Sydney Smith, and the Archbishop of York married them in early 1834. She now took charge of his children and the house in Lower Brook Street, supplanting Mary.[16]

A second letter from Jane Byerley to Elizabeth in the Sharps collection, dated 4 November 1829, begins in a more relaxed manner, 'Without wasting my paper in apologies, I will candidly confess myself a very bad correspondent, and unworthy of the long and amusing letters you have from time to time sent me but I am not ungrateful ... '.[17] Either Elizabeth was not heart-broken over the death of her father in the previous March, or she had not revealed her feelings to her old teacher in these 'long and amusing letters'. It is unlikely that she had left the gay world of Cheltenham, a dozen or so miles to the south, 'sick of its miscalled pleasures'. She had been enjoying life amongst the new gentry of Gloucestershire with her aunt Lumb and Bessy Holland, presumably staying on or near the estate her cousin Edward had inherited. 'You describe a most happy kind of life, such as realizes ones ideas of felicity in the country', wrote Jane to her with Horatian serenity, adding that she had been within a few miles of Dumbleton that summer when she had stayed at the foot of Bredon Hill with a Mrs William Parker, 'Lucy's old friend and *correspondent* Jane Paget'.

William Parker and his brother Hubert, she explained, were pastors of Great and Little Charleston. Last summer, Jane told Elizabeth, Mrs William Parker was near her confinement and stayed at home, but after a week at Malvern William and Hubert Parker met Jane Byerley at Ross and escorted her with Miss Cockburn and another pupil down 'the enchanting Wye, crossed the channel to Clifton and then travelled to Charleston thro' the fine part of Gloucestershire.' She returned to Stratford 'full of charming recollections of the past three weeks'. It is obvious that the Byerleys and their like were decent gentlefolk taking quiet country holidays rather than racketing in Cheltenham. Jane went on to ask what Lucy was about and which of Elizabeth's cousins were in London – 'I hope Mrs H. Holland is better than when you wrote.' In this midst of all this simple chat was one nugget. Anna Thornton, presumably another Avonbank pupil, had just written a long letter from Scotland, where she had seen Mrs Stevenson and her children. Though they were well, she reported, they were 'not I fear very comfortably settled at present'. And, Jane comments tantalisingly, 'She will have much to contend with in her new mode of life.'

What exactly is meant by this is unknown, but Mrs Catherine Stevenson might have been living near Edinburgh, for Jane immediately continues by saying that Anna had spent two days at Bonaly. This was Henry Cockburn's rural paradise in the Pentland Hills, where he had converted a farmhouse by adding a 'large Norman tower, designed by Playfair'. He created a feudal setting, in which it was his custom to gather his friends, sensibly pitching a tent in the country nearby for the children. The cultured and hospitable place, with its picturesque library and grassy walks, was well known to his boyhood friend Dr Thomson and was still being hymned by Katharine Thomson in 1862.[18]

Cockburn's eldest daughter ('a fine, noble girl', Jane Byerley was happy to proclaim) had just left Avonbank,[19] where 'Mr Jeffrey the Reviewer and his wife' had come to see her:

> We thought him very interesting and as he was, I fancy, in a happy frame of mind away from home, we did not discover much of the tart and disagreeable manner we have heard so much of – we see many Scotsmen here, for we have a new young physician from the North countries – he is a namesake of our brother-in-law in London but no relation, being a son of Mr Thompson of Duddington nr Edinburgh. We like him extremely, for besides being clever in his profession, he is remarkably agreeable in society *and musical*. Come and see this paragon- We have lately had a visit from Caroline Phillips – you remember how sweet a child she was.

Jane then gives some news that might have brought Elizabeth's brother
forcibly to mind and reminded her of religious obligations in a world where
death was commonplace:

> Poor Sophy Basson had lost a brother and a sister since you knew her ... all
> dearest to her are separated by death or distance, but she is a good religious girl
> and I firmly believe does her duties as a daughter conscientiously and resigns
> herself to God's will.

The letter ends with love from Marion [Maria] and Ann Byerley, a request
to be remembered 'particularly and kindly to Mrs Lumb and to Lucy' and
'Believe me, dear Elizabeth, Your ever affectionate friend, Jane C. Byerley.' It
reveals the usual cat's cradle of relationships, but one extending rather notably
to intellectual Scottish families and including, in some strenuous but unspeci-
fied manner, Elizabeth's stepmother. Perhaps Mrs Stevenson had gone to her
other brother, the artist William John Thomson. After living in London for a
time, at 41 Craven Street, Strand, he had gone back to Edinburgh and
prospered; by 1829 he had recently been elected a member of the Scottish
Academy. He would obviously be acquainted with fellow Academy painters
like Sir George Harvey, but a letter of condolence on the death of William
Blackwood in 1834 indicates that he moved in good Edinburgh society more
generally.[20]

Elizabeth's friendship with her stepmother, if it existed at all, was not kept
green for long. From the address and conclusion of this Jane Byerley letter of
late 1829 we can deduce that after Elizabeth's Gloucestershire visit she went
back to her assured home with her aunt Hannah Lumb at Knutsford. A few
years afterwards, in December 1833, we find Mrs Gaskell writing to her
husband's young sister, 'Sam (the wretch) has never been over, & I am longing
to hear all about the Thomsons. My little miss of a ½ sister is to be married this
Christmas – only 17 this 8th of December.' She probably refers here to her
husband's brother Samuel, who in 1833 was a valued house-surgeon at the
Stockport Infirmary near Manchester but who had been up in Edinburgh
gaining prizes for medicine at the university for two years from 1830. He
could easily have remained in touch with fellow students. The casual indiffer-
ence to her half-sister expressed in this letter is obvious, even studied, and very
possibly indicates the strength of an impulse to detach herself psychologically
from the emotional stresses of Beaufort Row and her father's last days.[21]

The length of the coolness or estrangement is underlined even more
strongly by letters she wrote in 1855. They make it clear that she, a seasoned
traveller if not in Henry Holland's class, was seeing her 'unknown half-sister'
and stepmother after a gap of about twenty-five years. Mrs Stevenson might
have been living in Glasgow then, and her daughter had married Archibald
Black of Dunoon. Ward also gathered (via Meta and Mrs Robina Robertson)
that Catherine died childless and her brother William died young of consumption. He was said to have settled as a medical man in Bridlington, sometimes

known as Burlington. This is plausible. The East Riding town, about a mile inland, was a busy resort with a mineral spring, developing its sea front by the little harbour of Bridlington Quay with an esplanade, bathing machines, lodging houses and a new chapel of ease for the influx of visitors. The white cliffs of Flamborough Head to the north subside to the long stretches of a fine sandy beach, safe, strewn with shells and popular with children. Here Charlotte Brontë was moved to tears by her first sight of the sea in August 1839, and correspondingly amused by the absurdly crowded evening parade of gentlefolk upon the little pier. It is tempting to believe that the 'bachelor doctor of Burlington' Charlotte's friend Ellen Nussey was civil to (because she thought he was a safely married man) might have been William Stevenson – a 'pragmatical thing in breeches' inane enough to believe that a woman's animation must mean she wished to dedicate her life to him. Local directories name seven physicians and surgeons of 'that improving town' in 1840 and six in 1851, but William's name does not appear. Perhaps he was no more than an apprentice there.[22]

In the first edition of *Haunts, Homes, and Stories* Chadwick stated that John Stevenson had been lost at sea about 1827 when he was a naval lieutenant on an East Indiaman, and then, intriguingly, altered this to 'mysteriously disappeared from his ship when at port in Calcutta' in her 1913 revision. Thomas Seccombe had a similar story: John, 'who had been a regular visitor at Knutsford, disappeared mysteriously at the close of a voyage in an East Indiaman.' Sandars also makes him disappear on a voyage to India, but was told by a grandson of Mrs Gaskell, Bryan Holland, that 'the family always supposed the ship in which he sailed to have been captured by pirates', which might be a confused recollection of William Stevenson's letter of July 1827 to his daughter. Hopkins, always reasonable, mentioned both Calcutta and pirates, but claimed like Chadwick without hard evidence that William Stevenson heard of John's loss before his own death, an assumption also made by Gérin, who wrote that this brought Elizabeth to Beaufort Row to comfort her father in late 1828 or early 1829. In fact, nobody has discovered what happened to John. A relevant *Calcutta Kalendar*, one that names the ships and passengers that came into Calcutta during the winter after what was probably an August 1828 sailing, has not yet been found.[23]

Elizabeth must have known her brother well, and as she grew older she was surely able to read between the lines of his letters, sensitive to the undertones of chagrin and personal failure as well as to the very real disappointments of a man who wished to change his career entirely. Yet in later life she hardly mentioned the name of the brother who had written so passionately about leaving her – 'the more I saw of you, the more I should regret quitting you – so in one way it is perhaps better I should see you no more – it will save me one pang.' Slight evidence that she did mention him on one occasion comes from nearly a century afterwards. Marianne Gaskell told Clement Shorter that her mother had said she could only just remember her brother: 'I think she said when she was quite a young girl, that she remembered coming up to a visit to her father from Knutsford to wish her brother good bye. I think she must have been about twelve years old when she paid that visit.' Aina Rubenius, who cites this letter, was careful enough to note that John had written to his sister after 1822. Ward was told that John, a lieutenant in the merchant navy, '*absolutely disappeared*' on his third or fourth voyage – She was then abt 17 or 18.' The italicised words are doubly underlined. This is more accurate, but their mother's reticence about both her father and brother provides a psychological mystery to set beside the historical one.[24]

A new piece of information may show that the pirates did not capture John on the voyage out and that he arrived in India safely, though it does nothing to solve the mystery of his disappearance from his sister's life. In a list of 'Europeans not in the Service of His Majesty or the Honourable Company, Residing in Calcutta', etc., in a Calcutta directory for 1831 appears the name of John Stephenson, 'Free Merchant', rather than the usual 'Free-mariner, 1820' of the Bengal directories. The same information is given in a Calcutta directory for 1835, but one always suspects a failure to cancel such information if the compilers were not told specifically to do so. After several years they were still unable to give an address for him, and it is noticeable that Hannah Lumb's will, signed on 31 December 1834, makes no mention of him though money had been left in her hands by his grandfather. And unless he unexpectedly joined the colours (like Coleridge), he is not the private in the 3rd dragoons who died at Cawnpore in June 1838.[25]

The dearth of later references to John by Elizabeth Gaskell (ignoring her fictional figures of young men lost) is almost unbelievable. He was twelve years older, but she had met him and corresponded with him throughout her girlhood. His letters prove how hard he tried to be a figure in the life of his much younger sister, perhaps aware that the second Mrs Stevenson was naturally bound up in her own two little children. Much of Elizabeth's correspondence is missing, but there is no reference to John in the scores of unknown letters that have turned up since the edition of 1966. On present evidence there must have been a kind of deliberate suppression of painful recollections.[26]

Perhaps he died in the East. The mortality rates for Europeans were terrible, beginning with deaths on the voyage out, as ships' logs show, and continuing with the effects of 'the climate', which can sometimes be interpreted as liver disease after a diet of Hodgson's pale ale, claret, sangaree and Madeira. By 1830 cholera was raging through the whole of south and southeast Asia. The young William Gaskell would have heard Dr John Bowring, Foreign Secretary of the British and Foreign Unitarian Association, regret 'the removal of some from Calcutta, and the death of others, – for death has there extended its empire as well as to other places' in a speech at Salford in June 1830. Asiatic or Indian Cholera, as it was called, reached Moscow, St

Petersburg and the Baltic ports as early as 1831. Maria Jane Jewsbury, married just after Elizabeth Gaskell, landed in Bombay – 'alias biscuit-oven, alias brick-kiln, alias burning Babel, alias Pandemonium, alias everything hot, horrid, glaring, barren, dissonant, and detestable' – early in 1833. She died of cholera later that year.[27]

Or perhaps John had sent from abroad some kind of disillusioned rejection of England and English life. Captain Doveton writes of European soldiers deserting for the sake of attractive Burmese women. His own servant was perhaps more commercially minded than susceptible: he disappeared, and was later heard of running a grog-shop at Rangoon. The East India Company lost its monopoly of the tea trade in 1833, laws were passed allowing dissenters to take special oaths for India service and British private shipping and navigation were encouraged. John Stevenson, established as a free merchant of Calcutta, would have been in a favourable position had it not been for an economic downturn in the 1830s and 1840s. But all we know is that he was nothing like as fortunate as a former sailor in the maritime service of the East India Company, Robert Anderson, who in 1834 when the marine was abolished was able to come back to an assured position in the Branch Bank of England at Newcastle.[28]

Elizabeth's early correspondent Harriet was the daughter of a former St Petersburg merchant, George Carr, who had been made an honorary member of the Newcastle Literary and Philosophical Society in 1793. A former Newcastle solicitor, Thomas William Carr of Gray's Inn, a friend of Henry Holland and father of an affectionate family greatly loved by Maria Edgeworth, also became an honorary member in the 1790s. George Carr was still in St Petersburg in 1821, but must have retired from business, for on 3 April 1828 he was appointed Agent of the newly established Branch Bank of England in Newcastle at a very useful salary of £1000 a year, to supervise the supply of gold coin to country banks and the collection of money from the various Receivers of Inland Revenue. The bank had a deliberate policy of finding such agents from outside the banking profession.

Another St Petersburg merchant, Matthew Anderson, had become an honorary member in 1793 and was still there in 1821, just like George Carr. 'Mr. Anderson is our principal Russian agent', wrote James Losh to Brougham in 1825, 'and has a brother in an official situation at Petersburg'. It is obvious from Elizabeth's early letters that Harriet Carr's family maintained connections with St Petersburg, and Harriet later married a Matthew Anderson, who seems to have built himself a house in the township of Jesmond, to the north of the smaller Newcastle of those days. Robert Anderson became Sub-Agent of the Branch Bank of England in Newcastle after the death of George Carr at Cronstadt on 6 December 1836, aged seventy-seven.[29]

NOTES

1 See p. 251 above; Smith, *Useful Knowledge Society*, p. 59.

2 *ABO*, p. 213. See p. 318 above.

3 NLS: WS junior to WB, 25 March 1829 (lightly edited); *Letters*, pp. 531-2; [K. Thomson], *Memoir of ATT*, p. 15; [Radford], 'Anthony Todd Thomson', pp. 162-3: Merrington, *University College Hospital*, pp. 11-12; *Lancet*, 21 August 1830, 23 October 1830, 5 March 1831. George Street became part of Gower Street.

4 PRO: PROB 11/1757/383, proved at London, 15 June 1929. I am grateful to J. Harrison for advice about the original will (PROB/5099). Gérin's account of it, pp. 36-7, is not accurate in some of its details.

5 Dr Ian Gregg cites information in the preliminaries of Alexander Thomson's letter to Brougham, *Reasons Why the Expulsion of Alexander Thomson, M B From the London University Should Be Reconsidered*, pr. pr. Paris 1831. See also p. 337 below.

6 [K. Thomson], *Memoir of ATT*, pp. 8-9; [Radford], 'Anthony Todd Thomson', p. 161.

7 LUBL: TS, Shorter and Symington, 'Transcripts of Letters ... Mrs E. C. Gaskell'. The whole of what survives is quoted above.

8 Ritchie, pref. *Cranford*, p. xii; *Letters*, p. 797-8; Hopkins, pp. 29-30 (cp. Uglow, pp. 54-5).

9 EBB to ECG, 7 October [1853] (pr. in context, Waller, pp. 42-6). ECG seems to have accepted William Gaskell very quickly. Cf. his letter of [29 March 1832] in Appendix F below.

10 A different name is pencilled into the Chelsea rate book for April 1830.

11 *Portrait*, p. 161; Chapple, 'Five early letters, pp. 1-5, 12.

12 MCO: MSS Robberds 1, f. 156, MH to MR, The Priory, 10 September [postmarked 1829].

13 DCLH: HH to ME, London, 21 July [1826], and L Brook Street, 14 August [1829] (mourning paper); *London – World City*, ed. Fox, pp. 463-4, with illustr. of Constable's 'Hampstead Heath with London in the Distance', c. 1827-30. Chadwick's claim (1910, p. 145) that Elizabeth Stevenson paid frequent visits to Lower Brook Street about this time seems unlikely.

14 Francis James, born 20 January 1828, baptised by William Turner in London on 31 January 1829 (Irvine, p. 73; TWA: 1787/9). For Mrs Coltman (Ann Byerley) see p. 242 above.

15 Slugg, *Manchester*, p. 60. MH's *Easy Lessons* has yet to be identified. Thomas Forrest published the *Report* of the British and Foreign Unitarian Association in 1830; Forrest and Fogg were the Manchester publishers of William Gaskell's *Protestant Practices*, 1836.

16 DCLH: HH to Maria Edgeworth, L Brook Street, 10 November [1828], 8 January [1830] and 3 August [1830]; also, HH to LA, L Brook Street, [February 1830], and 19 January [1834]; *Darwin Correspondence*, I, pp. 166, 365, 373, 428.

17 JGS: TS, JMB to ES (Mrs. Lumb, Knutsford), 4 November 1829. See above, pp. 3, 246. No letters from ECS to JMB have so far come to light.

18 ATT, Journal; 'Grace Wharton' [KT], *The Literature of Society*, London, 1862, II, pp. 307-9.

19 Dr Louise A. Yeoman kindly informs me that two letters of 1823 to Mrs Cockburn and Mrs Jeffrey in NLS do not mention schooling.

20 Long, *British Miniaturists*, pp. 436-7; NLS: MS 4039: WJT to Alexander Blackwood, 57 North Street, 22 September 1834. (BL: Royal Literary Fund, Case File 652, not seen).

21 *Letters*, p. 4; JS&PH, LUBL: *Testimonials of Mr. Samuel Gaskell*; WCL: TS, R. G. Guest-Gornall, *Samuel Gaskell*, p. 4.

22 *Letters*, pp. 358 ('25 years and more'), 532 (William dead by 1859), 871 ('24 years'); Ward Notebook, f. 1 verso, 108; Barker, *The Brontës*, p. 315; *Brontë Letters*, I, pp. 197-9,

203, 383-9, 606; W. White, *History, Directory, and Gazetteer of the East and North Ridings of Yorkshire*, 1840 and 1851. Ellen Nussey deleted 'Burlington' from the MS.

23 Charles (Knutsford Edn, I, p. xvi, II, p. xxii): John (Knutsford Edn, IV. p. xxiii); Chadwick, 1910, pp. 2, 138; Chadwick, 1913, pp. 2, 94; Seccombe, ed. *Sylvia's Lovers*, p. xiv (corresp. with Meta Gaskell in 1910); Sandars, p. 7; Hopkins, pp. 14-15, 40; Gérin, p. 36. See p. 228 above.

24 Ward Notebook, f. 9, adding, 'See *Cranford* (Peter) See paper on *Disappearances* in *Household Words*'; repeated with John's correct Christian name in Ward's *DNB* article on ECG; LUBL: MA to CS, 10 December [1914], cited Rubenius, p. 254. Marianne also told Shorter that her sister Meta had ordered her solicitors to burn remaining documents.

25 *The Calcutta Annual Directory and First Quarterly Register ... 1831*, Calcutta, n. d., p. 367, and *1835* (cf. p. 233, n. 21 above); 'Bengal Burials' (IOLR: MF, LII, no. 75; no further search made). Bengal directories list JS as a free-mariner until 1841. See also p. 270 above and p. 377 below.

26 Important new letters are published; a supplement to *Letters* is being prepared.

27 Durey, *Return of the Plague*, p. 8; Parkinson, *Trade in the Eastern Seas*, pp. 70-5; *Report of the Proceedings*, p. 18 (see p. 422 below); MJJ qu, *Victorian Women Poets: An Anthology*, ed. Angela Leighton and Margaret Reynolds, Oxford UK and Cambridge USA, 1995, p. 28.

28 Doveton, *Reminiscences of the Burmese War*, pp. 371-4; Crawfurd, *Embassy to Ava*, Appendix, p. 17; Lawson, *East India Company*, pp. 156-60; Phillips, *History of Banks*, pp. 207-8.

29 *Edgeworth Letters*, pp. xxii, 190-1, 305; DCLH: HH to ME, 7 July 1819; NLPS: Hon. Members' file, *Twenty-Eighth Year's Report*, 1821, and *A List of the Ordinary Members*, Newcastle, 1831; Phillips, *History of Banks*, pp. 204-8; *Losh Diaries*, II, p. 178; Chapple, 'Five early letters', pp. 6, 14, 16, 22, 26, and 'Two unpublished Gaskell letters from Burrow Hall, Lancashire', *GSJ*, VI, 1992, p. 67; information kindly provided by F. Whitehead, M. Norwell and E. M. Kelly.

19

Newcastle and elsewhere

AFTER THE END of her schooldays, the death of her father in the spring of 1829 and the disappearance of her brother came the years in which Elizabeth blossomed into a vital, even dazzling personality, needing, like Isobel Archer in *The Portrait of a Lady*, only to be *placed* in order to discover much of her identity. But, to begin with the most basic matter first, evidence about her movements is scanty and contradictory. Chadwick asserted that she spent two years in Newcastle-upon-Tyne with one of its most famous citizens, William Turner, a relation and Unitarian minister of the Hanover Square congregation there for over fifty years.[1] A. W. Ward in the *DNB* had claimed 'two winters' with Turner and his daughter Ann in Newcastle. His notebook shows him swiftly dashing down in the style of Mr Jingle, 'Spent 2 winters [now?] in *Newcastle* (at Mr Turner's a Unitarian minister founder of institution public character – a bust of him) – another in Edinburgh (18 or 19) where she was much admired (several artists & sculptor [*sic*] asked to [take?] her portrait)'.

In a list of corrections Meta Gaskell sent Thomas Seccombe for his edition of *Sylvia's Lovers* (1910), she was anxious that he should make it clear that Elizabeth had a real home with aunt Lumb at Knutsford after her father's death – 'only diversified by long visits to her uncle in London, a cousin in Essex, and friends in Edinbro', and to a connexion, Mr. Turner at Newcastle'. Any visit to uncle Swinton in London must have been before his death in 1827. The 'cousin in Essex' is a mystery at present, perhaps connected with the visit of her half-sister to Billericay not too long before. It is definitely known from Mary Holland's letter to Mary Robberds that Elizabeth was at Dumbleton with aunt Lumb and Bessy Holland in September 1829, and Jane Byerley addressed a letter to her at Knutsford in the following November. The first letter to Elizabeth Carr of Newcastle proves that she was back with aunt Lumb by 18 June 1831.[2]

Her first stay in Newcastle might therefore have been during the winter of 1829-30. If she went on with Ann Turner to Edinburgh, as is usually claimed, it must have been in or after the summer of 1830, because Ann paid her monthly contributions of one shilling a quarter to Hanover Square chapel from November 1829 to May 1830 without a break. She made no quarterly contributions for August and November 1830, February and May 1831 (paying five shillings in the following August) and was very likely away from Newcastle during this period. The opening of Elizabeth's letter to Harriet Carr suggests that a second visit to Newcastle had begun before Harriet went off to London on 3 December 1830, so she might also have been visiting in Edinburgh with Ann Turner during the first part of 1831 before going south again to rejoin aunt Lumb.[3]

In the summer of 1831 Elizabeth was with aunt Lumb, but at lodgings in Brandon Street, Woodside, a pleasant residential suburb and resort being developed on a small headland across the Mersey from Liverpool. Here she stayed quietly from about June to September, associating with friends in the neighbourhood (William and Mary Worthington and John Gooch Robberds) and some of the Liverpool Hollands, whose house in Wales was then being improved. They took pleasant sails up and down the Mersey and made little trips over the broad river to Liverpool by the regular steam-paddle boat services. James Law's 'Plan of Birkenhead' of 1844 shows Brandon Street near the Woodside ferry pier, leading to Hamilton Square. The ruins of Birkenhead Priory – ancient walls and grotesque stone faces, ivied and nested in by birds, Nathaniel Hawthorne noted later – were being engulfed by the brick and stone houses of a modern town. A handsome church, begun in 1819 and built of the same red free-stone, had been built in part of the Priory's grounds.[4]

Elizabeth then returned from Woodside to 'Knutsford. The Heath' in September or early October 1831. Aunt Swinton Holland and her daughter Charlotte had only just left Mrs Lumb's house, and Elizabeth had also been on a short visit to Sandlebridge with the cousin nearest her in age, Susan Holland. Her life during the previous two years, roughly from her nineteenth birthday to her twenty-first, ill-documented and relatively little studied, demands at least as much attention as the time she spent in Knutsford and Stratford-upon-Avon, for these were small towns and hardly to be compared with the great working towns to which she paid extended visits. They were years of relative freedom after the ordeal of her father's illness and death, years of self-discovery, but within totally new kinds of community and inevitably affected by their shared assumptions. It seems most likely that her father's place as mentor was taken by the Reverend William Turner of Newcastle-upon-Tyne. It would be difficult to find a more forceful and unequivocal character.[5]

The sails of little slate convoys used to catch the light on the pastoral waters of the Dwyryd and its estuary. On the 'black and busy' Tyne in north-east England darker steamships, at first wooden rather than iron vessels, made their appearance as early as 1814. There were still hundreds of sails on the Tyne – Newcastle was a major port for the German or British Ocean, with a population of over 50,000 in 1831 – just as there were a surprising number of windmills on its valley sides, but both ships and machinery for grinding corn were gradually being replaced or converted to steam power. By 1827 the steam-vessel *Hylton Jolliffe* was running regularly to and from London during the summer season. It could be erratic. In June 1831 George Carr wrote from London that he was returning by steamer sailing on a Tuesday evening and would be with them on Friday. When he had not arrived nine days later, he was thought lost. It turned out that the vessel had been detained in Yarmouth Roads and it did not reach Newcastle till a day or two later. The perilous alternative was to travel by stagecoach – laden with baggage above and in chests slung beneath, eight passengers outside and four within, as well as a coachman and a driver perched on top of the lot, bold enough to start at a full gallop. The journey from London inside the Wellington coach cost £4 10s (inside) and took about thirty-three hours.[6]

Travellers north in the first quarter of the nineteenth century on the east coast roads through rural England would have to almost slide down a steep incline called Bottle Bank when they reached the Tyne at Gateshead, viewing if they dared the town of Newcastle rising across the water, built on 150 acres of hilly land cut by burns falling to the river. Newcastle had once been enclosed like Berwick within fortified walls. About twelve feet high and eight feet thick, they were gradually being demolished to make way for the needs of an increasing population but considerable stretches still survived. In 1830, travellers could avoid Bottle Bank by taking a newly formed circular route by St Mary's Church, Gateshead, and more safely admire across the river the sight of Newcastle's ancient castle keep and the beautiful lantern of the medieval St Nicholas' church (its clock only recently lit by gas-light), the new County Court for Northumberland built in 1812, with fluted Grecian columns and massive pediment standing high over the bridgehead, and to the right, a classical church of the late eighteenth century with circular interior and elegant spire dominating the skyline of the town, All Saint's. An engraving of the prospect from the south-west on Thomas Oliver's fine *Plan* of 1830 shows that beyond the centre were more hills and the smoking chimneys of industry.

The ends of cobbled medieval alleys, known locally as chares, running down towards the waterside in the older town appeared as travellers went over the Tyne bridge, but they were lost amongst the tall warehouses of the quayside and obscured in a forest of masts. Newly built ships were even launched with their masts standing. The broad river was exceptionally busy, despite the hazards of its notorious bar at Tynemouth. And as at Hull lower down the east coast, no early nineteenth-century artist would think of drawing the port without a busy little steam-packet and its characteristic plume of smoke in the foreground amidst the billowing sails of keels, barques and sloops of up to three or four hundred tons burthen.

The single bridge over the Tyne, rebuilt after devastating floods of 1771 and widened by David Stephenson in 1801, led into a complication of toilsome, winding and ascending streets reminiscent of Edinburgh. A little to the west of the bridge were stairs leading up to the castle, lined on both sides with shops selling old and new clothes. But Newcastle was rich. In the late eighteenth century its annual income was £25,000; only three other English towns – London, Bristol and York – could afford to provide special residences for their mayors. A grand Mansion House dating from the late seventeenth century stood on the narrow street called the Close. It had its own riverside quay to the rear, from which on Ascension Day the Mayor, as a judge of the Court of Admiralty, would lead a procession of gaily decorated and painted barges with other boats on a survey of the Tyne. Henry Holland describes the 'splendid show' they made in 1800, when as a lad he had the extra delight of seeing the mayor's hat knocked off and torn to pieces by the wadding of a gun discharged from the Quay side. In 1827 it was less lively, but the local artist J. W. Carmichael did his best to add colour and drama to his painting of the event.[7]

Beside the Mansion House stood a chapel of United Secession Presbyterians; just across the street was the beginning of the many flights of stone stairs needed to climb the steep Toothill bank, past a Particular Baptists' Chapel, to Hanover Square. Here a decent chapel had been opened in the first decades of the eighteenth century, its entrance facing towards the river. They had also erected 'several genteel and well-built houses' but had not been able to complete the whole square. At one end of Hanover Square were erected a few houses, called Russell Square; leading out of the other end into the town was Clavering Place, which acquired its own chapel of United Secession Presbyterians early in the nineteenth century. All these buildings were just within the western wall, between White Friar Tower (by then an ice house) and Denton Tower.

Institutional religion flourished and mutated. Before the turn of the century Hanover Square chapel had acquired a vestry with an 'excellent library, of some extent', merged with another congregation in 1797 and been enlarged in 1810 to allow the installation of a new organ. It then had '1670 running feet of seats' and could contain well over a thousand people, according to Thomas Oliver's *New Picture of Newcastle-upon-Tyne*. The Presbyterian chapel in Clavering Place, not fifty yards from Turner's chapel, was established in a building designed by John Green and had opened in 1822 with the Reverend James Pringle as minister.[8]

These two chapels and the fine houses built for a select number of 'opulent' citizens were high above the river with views out over the Tyne valley, still pleasantly rural in its western reaches. Today, Toothill Stairs remain to serve their old purpose, but the Mansion House below and many of its neighbours have gone, the steep bank has been landscaped and of the four chapels only the one in Clavering Place remains, adapted for commercial purposes. The other, Turner's Unitarian chapel, has been thoroughly rebuilt as a warehouse and is almost unrecognisable both within and without, flanked by a great van-park that reaches to a short remaining section of the old town wall on the height above the river.

The Bank of England chose Clavering Place in 1828 for one of its earliest provincial branches, established after the banking crisis of the middle of the decade. Protests from the Newcastle chamber of commerce did not impress the relevant committee, which calmly noted on 20 March 1828 that the branch was ready to open 'with Agent and Sub-Agent, both local men' and that others in the area were supportive.[9] It took over a large dwelling house, now obliterated by the railway. Its fine double-fronted neighbour, owned by Sir Robert Shaftoe Hawkes, a prosperous woollen and linen draper of the Side, in 1831, survives to show the quality of what has now been almost entirely wiped out. Local supporters of the branch bank could not have warned the Bank of England that the superior location chosen in Clavering Place was also on the corner of the undrained and ancient Baileygate. Damp spoiled the notes, dead cats (some skinned) used to be flung over its side wall with other rubbish and an old lady had to be paid a shilling a week to chase away the urchins from the front entrance. George Carr lived there with his family, but after 1838 his successor took the branch to settle in Richard Grainger's masterpiece, Grey Street, where the staff grandly transacted their business behind eleven Corinthian columns surmounted by a double row of balustrades, carefully set in a curving range of buildings designed as a single unit on a rising slope.[10]

Houses down near the water, especially along the Quay to Sand Gate in the eastern wall, were packed like fish in barrels – 'Newcastle, particularly in its lower part, is a veritable slum', d'Eichthal asserted. It was in these narrow streets that the press-gang used to operate, as a piece collected for the 1812 publication, *Rhymes of the Northern Bards*, records: 'They've prest my dear Johnny / Sae sprightly and bonny, – / Alack! I shall ne'er mair d'weel, O', sang Henry Robson for the lass he left behind. 'Had he staid on the Tyne, / Ere now he'd been mine, / But oh! he's far over the sea, O.'[11]

Most of the better houses higher up had gardens and, almost uniquely within a walled town, there survived a sixteenth-century mansion and thirteen acres of formal grounds next to an open space called the Nun's Field. When Sir Walter Blackett died the town council declined to purchase his property. Its new owner in 1782 gave it his own name, Anderson Place, and it was finally developed by Richard Grainger between 1834 and 1840. Harriet Martineau's contemporary articles in the first volume of the *Penny Magazine of the Society for the Diffusion of Useful Knowledge* (1840) on 'The Newcastle improvements' were designed to publicise what Grainger 'saw in vision, as he now declares, the new town as it has arisen under his hands – terraces, squares, long ranges of streets, all fronted with polished stone, instead of the peculiarly ugly brick of which the old town was built.'

This is very unfair to some of the town's pleasing Georgian houses, but the 'hunger for improvement and indeed grandeur' of the men and women of Newcastle is indisputable. A group of merchants 'On 'Change' were recorded in paint by Joseph Crawhall, industrialist and artist, in about 1826. He portrays many recognisable portraits of the industrial elite, wearing a wonderful variety of clothes – some in trousers, some in knee breeches and stockings and others sporting riding breeches and boots, but all with long coats and top hats. It was a time of sartorial transition, but he, and they, were assured of their own worth and expectations. 'How this appetite for grandeur grew and was eventually satisfied' is the theme of *Tyneside Classical*, by Lyall Wilkes and Gordon Dodds.[12]

With Grainger is coupled the name of John Dobson, pupil of John Varley the water-colourist and father-in-law of Sydney Smirke, the final architect of the British Museum, but Newcastle was fortunate in its other architects, such as John Green the younger, who designed a building in the latest Greek Revival style for the museum and library of the Newcastle Literary and Philosophical Society at the bottom of Westgate Street. A Temple of the Arts and Sciences like the contemporary British Museum, it was completed by 1825 at more than three times the cost the Society's Committee had intended; they were empowered to raise £5000 upon a mortgage of the premises at 4 per cent interest. The mortgage was eventually cleared many years later by the great engineer Robert Stephenson, on the understanding that the annual subscription would be lowered from two guineas to one. The original 'new' Assembly Rooms, higher up Westgate Street on the other side and designed in delicate neoclassical style by William Newton in the 1770s, rivalled those at Bath. The central glass chandelier of the seven in its ballroom cost six hundred guineas, Eneas Mackenzie was careful to report – somewhat improbably.[13]

Brilliance was needed, whatever its cost (and source). 'When we neared Newcastle', Gustav d'Eichthal wrote after setting out from 'Durham's mean streets' on 3 September 1828, 'we found the sky darkened by smoke from the steam-engines and the coal-dust burned at the pit head to get rid of it.' The master-works of architects and stone-masons were being shrouded in grime all over Britain. Town halls and churches came to look as if they had been carved out of coal. (Within living memory in larger towns like Manchester, babies put outside in prams to sleep in the open were at the mercy of the sooty air that speckled delicate skin.) Just to the west of Newcastle in 1781 excellent house coal had been discovered at Wallsend; pit after pit had then been sunk to exploit the Main Seam all the way along to South Shields by the sea. By 1826 most of the two million tons imported into London came in ships from these deep collieries along the Tyne, inspiring wonderfully individual vignettes ('*tale -pieces*') by Bewick as well as what his brother called 'coally Tyne Poetry'.[14]

And 'along the steep slopes of the banks of the river', the observant young Frenchman continued,

> is an unbroken succession of glassworks, pottery works, foundries, lime kilns, rope works, shipyards, paper mills, etc. Fifty steamboats are in service on the

river, used either as tugs for the ships or to carry passengers. The journey [to Shields] costs 6d. Since a boat with a 7 or 8 horsepower engine only costs £500, entrepreneurs can still get a good profit. Last year the master of the boat we were on, an ex-seaman, managed to save £100 when all his expenses had been paid. A large number of spouts on staiths are to be seen along the river. These are large balances connected to the mines by railways, which are used to load coal on to the ships. These spouts have made superfluous a large number of the keels or boats which used to carry the coal on to the waiting ships. The keel men therefore did all that they could to prevent the building of the spouts.

The keelmen even went to law to prevent the spread of these mechanical coal-drops, but in vain. John Bell, the scholarly collector and antiquarian who had published *Rhymes of the Northern Bards* in 1812, took down in an unsteady hand, 'almost certainly from a live performance', this parody of the *Keel Row*:

> As I cam through SandGate
> through Sandgate
> As I cam throwgh Sandgate
> I heard a Lassy Whine
> itts ower with the Keels now
> the Keels now. – the Keels now
> its ower with the Keels now
> upon the Coally Tyne.[15]

Elizabeth Stevenson in her youth might have been taken like her cousins to see the major quarries at Ffestiniog, which ultimately supplied about a quarter of the cheap, durable roofing slates of the endless rows of houses in Britain's industrial conurbations, but lower down the vale and at Sam Holland's Plas yn Penrhyn the devastation and worst aspects of industry would have been relatively imperceptible. In Newcastle and the lower Tyne valley they were unavoidable. At William Turner's services his congregation heard charitable sermons on the many accidents in northern coal mines – in a Jarrow colliery explosion of August 1830 forty-two men and boys were killed. There was continuous industrial strife, leading to the importation of lead-miners to take the place of recalcitrant coal-miners. The barrister James Losh, who owned shares in mines but also mistrusted the good sense and faith of his fellow-proprietors, was frequently called upon to act as mediator in bitter industrial disputes.[16]

Even more apparent, below Hanover Square, at the bottom of the steep Toothill bank, were a sugar refinery, a glass-house, a soap works and a foundry. Their rising fumes would have mingled with those of the banquets given by the mayor as he made sure of spending much of his £2000 a year entertainment allowance in the kitchens of the Mansion House, something that Dr Henry Holland, who had been to one of these Ascension Day Feasts as a boy, came to regard as useful but also 'rather a heavy tax on English social existence'.[17] Just over the town wall from Hanover Square, George Stephenson and his son Robert had opened a workshop early in 1824 to make locomotives for the first passenger railway from Stockton to Darlington. They were not far from Robert and William Hawthorn's engineering shed on Forth Banks as it turned north from Close Gate by the river, a works reduced to a mass of ruins by a great fire on 10 March 1832.

In Stephenson's locomotive works, a great deal was still done by hand; wheels were 'driven onto their axles by sledge hammers', lifting accomplished by portable shear-legs and pulley-blocks. The most famous engine of all, *Rocket*, was built there in August 1829 and taken by road and boat via Carlisle for the famous Rainhill trial or 'ordeal' on the Liverpool-Manchester line in the following month. Elizabeth could not have escaped hearing of this event, wherever she was. Stephenson's success was such that an order was placed at the Newcastle works for four more engines, completed in the very months when we might assume she first came to the town. A pottery, lime kilns and 'Mr Potter's large *common Brewery*' were also established nearby, across a small burn. The direction of the wind would have been very significant.[18] Back in the eighteenth century a new Infirmary had been built a little higher up on Forth Banks, as practical an institution as the glassworks the boy Henry Holland visited on the same day in 1802. Its 'Operation room' was placed at the top of the building, so that the screams of a patient would be quite inaudible, he told his father, 'though he should roar (to use Mr Turner's expression) like *a stuck pig*'.

This was canny Newcassel, a town 'comparatively in its intellectual nonage' when Turner came in September 1782, but one that was by the time of Elizabeth's arrival filling in and paving over its burns, tearing down its slums and creating a distinctively classical northern city designed to combine elegance with utility, like Edinburgh – not quite as improbable a place for a young lady's entrance upon the world as it might seem. Sedan chairs were still in use – Knutsford was not the only old-fashioned place – competing from 1824 with the hackney coaches in St Nicholas' Square that took three persons for two shillings anywhere in the town.[19]

The fountains in John Dobson's magnificent Vegetable Market were 'supposed to resemble those of the Borghese Palace in Rome', but sensibly built of Kenton stone from local quarries. As Harriet Martineau did not fail to note, once the town had been improved in convenience and beauty, and habitations for 'an increased population of the most valuable class' provided, Grainger turned his mind to manufacturing and commerce. 'His plan comprehends the junction of several railroads, the formation of extensive quays, the erection of ranges of manufactories, and on the high grounds behind, of villas and terraces', all these to be built on a country estate to the west of the town. This particular plan he could not carry into effect, but Newcastle's railway station shows that a new architecture was growing out of the old: John Dobson's imagination had been successfully captured by a 'new class of structures erected for purposes unknown to the present age'. They would be 'constantly seen by thousands and tens of thousands of persons, and might therefore do much towards improving the taste of the public', he enthused, provided their designer took advantage of both the spacious dignity native to the classical style and technological innovations such as the curved iron ribbing to support the roof, produced by Messrs Hawks and Crawshay of Gateshead for him 'after experimenting with bevelled rollers'.[20]

In the early nineteenth century industrial development was bringing about revolutionary change along what Milton had called the 'coaly Tyne' as long ago as 1628. Tyneside had an extensive system of broad-gauge wooden wagonways for scores of years before the coming of public railways with steam-engines and iron rails, but a few years after d'Eichthal's arrival it fulfilled the proposals Richard Edgeworth had made back in the 1760s for baggage wagons linked together and responded, with a difference, to his advocacy of iron rails and stationary steam engines. The first section of the Newcastle-Carlisle railway – James Losh had been its Chairman of Directors – was opened on 9 March 1835. Stephenson's locomotive *Rapid* and Hawthorn's *Comet* were delayed for a short time to wait for the Mayor of Newcastle and his party from the Mansion House in the state barge, which had been held up by small boats and the state of the tide. Four years later the whole line was completed. Smoke, danger and grime could be forgotten for a while in the novel beauty of the engines with their shining brass-work and the eight-tone organ whistle of *Tyne*, invented by a musical vicar – though Stephenson's *Atlas* had a steam-whistle that sounded, with richer Yeatsian symbolism, like a peacock's scream. It heralded a new age.[21]

William Turner of Newcastle lived on to see all these changes though he had been born as long ago as 1761. After education at Warrington Academy and Glasgow (as an occasional student for one session) Turner came to Hanover Square chapel, his first and only post, in 1782, at a salary of £100 per annum. He married Mary, daughter of Thomas Holland of Manchester, younger brother of the Reverend Philip Holland of Bolton, in the summer of 1784. They had a family of five boys and two girls, but Mary survived no more than three months after the birth of her daughter Ann on 21 October 1796. Two of the boys, Thomas and John, died aged eleven months and twenty-six months respectively in the 1790s. Turner married for a second time in 1799. Jane, then about forty years of age, was the eldest daughter of the Reverend William Willets. There were no children of Turner's second marriage. Philip Holland Turner survived until the age of twenty-one, but died on 22 September 1811; the Reverend Henry Turner died in 1822, leaving only the Reverend William Turner of York and Halifax living out of the five boys.[22]

Turner's eldest child, called Mary after her mother, was born on 24 February 1786. Her upbringing, typical of middle-ranking Unitarian families, parallels Elizabeth Stevenson's in many ways. After school in Newcastle-under-

Lyme and Manchester and happy holidays at Sandlebridge as a small child,
Mary returned to her father's home, where she was taught by her kind, firm
stepmother Jane until she was old enough at about the age of eighteen in 1804
to go on 'several pleasant & improving journies'. Her first visit was to London
as a guest of relations like the John Wedgwoods; not unexpectedly she was
shown 'many curious & beautiful things'. She had lessons in singing and
drawing, and met the Unitarian essayist and poet Mrs Barbauld, whose poem
'Eighteen Hundred and Eleven' so impressed Wordsworth, and her brother
John Aikin, M.D., who had been elected an honorary member of Newcastle's
Literary and Philosophical Society in 1796 and retired to Stoke Newington,
where he wrote book after book. Henry Holland was to spend a month with
him in 1804 and writes of expeditions to the docks, where he saw an East
Indiaman refitting, and visits to the playhouse to see Mrs Siddons as Jane
Shore. Contemporary Unitarians had no objections whatsoever to the theatre.
The Theatre Royal, both the old one and the new, was a major feature of
Newcastle's civilised architecture.[23]

Mary also attended the fashionable lectures of a scientific genius at London's
Royal Institution. Humphry Davy's discoveries of new elements were fast
making his reputation as a leading scientist of the age. His larger theories about
the unified, ethereal and active powers of nature inspired large and fashionable
audiences as well as men like Coleridge, though nothing of this comes through
in Mary's recollections. She was probably too young and at this point unpre-
pared. Davy, however, was affected by the spirit of a transitional age. He
sought Romantic sublimity – combined with Enlightenment utility.

Utility was still the watchword at any level: what might appear to be mere
drawing-room accomplishments for languid young ladies were pressed into
service when Mary returned to Newcastle. Her father was not only one of the
founders of the Newcastle Literary and Philosophical Society in 1793, he was
one of its two secretaries and a lecturer. He gave three pairs of scientific
lectures a week during the winter, in the morning for country members and in
the evening for townsfolk. Not unexpectedly he attended the very first meeting
of the British Association for the Advancement of Science in York as one of
Newcastle's representatives, speaking for his provincial philosophical society at
the great dinner on 27 November 1831. His wife encouraged Mary to act as
her father's assistant in Newcastle by drawing his diagrams on the blackboard
– privately beforehand, of course, to avoid possible objections, Mary reports,
though this literary and philosophical society was perhaps the first of its kind
in the country to admit ladies as members at about the turn of the century. A
printed notice dated 7 April [1831], for a lecture on 'Hebrew Learning' by the
Reverend John Whitridge, preserved in the grangerised NLPS *Reports*, is
annotated, 'N. B. Ladies are particularly requested to attend'.[24]

A course cost two guineas, but ordinary members and young people under
eighteen paid one, and ladies half-a-guinea. Mary ingenuously confessed that
her work helped her to understand the lecture, and she enjoyed it much more

than the duty of writing down the sermon she had heard on a Sunday in Hanover Square chapel to be read aloud after tea: 'We did not much like this, but we were obliged to do it; and my Father & Mother always made the evening pleasant for us by singing & talk.' A few pages of self-examination now in the Newcastle Literary and Philosophical Society's library shows how serious she was as a young woman in 1810:

> I hope the writing down what occurs in reading, or in conversation will tend to correct this defect [inattention], as it will supply a motion to constant attention; and I hereby certify (to myself) that I do this not with any intention whatsoever of display, or with any ostentatious view, but entirely for the improvement of my own dispositions and character. ... I know that much is expected from my Father's daughter ...
>
> Much more is expected from young women in the present age than formerly; many in the higher ranks having set a laudable example of employing their leisure, which a freedom from worldly care affords, in improving their own minds.

There was a second round of visits, firstly to Mrs Catherine Cappe of York, an old lady, author of many pamphlets on education and a warmly interfering supporter of Manchester College, which had by 1803 moved to York. William Turner junior was a tutor in mathematics there with John Kenrick, an exceptionally learned classicist. Here was an opportunity to meet the students at tea parties in her brother's lodgings in the main college building and without embarrassment (except for her increasing deafness) find a husband in the narrow circle of a sect always spoken against. She did in fact marry one who had been a student there, John Gooch Robberds, in 1811, but not until she had been on yet more visits to Holland uncles at Bolton and at Manchester and to the eccentric Dr Peter Crompton at Eton House, Wavertree, near Liverpool. He was a relation of Anne Marsh Caldwell and became a great friend of Dr William Winstanley. Mrs Crompton bore Mary off to meet 'the celebrated Mr Roscoe', whose house 'was adorned with beautiful paintings and statuary', and others like Dr Currie, Dr Shepherd and Mr Yates – the group that Hannah Greg knew and which James Audubon visited. There was nothing unusual in sending daughters on lengthy 'improving' visits to families sharing the same set of values.[25]

If William Stevenson had wished his daughter to prepare herself to be a governess, her time with the Reverend William Turner in Newcastle would have been invaluable. The 1779 Act allowing dissenters to teach, especially modern subjects, had led to a decline of the Newcastle grammar school; Turner's own school was one of some thirty-six or more in and about the town by 1800. Henry Holland's early letters to his father evoke the breadth of its activities and Turner himself reveals his methods when he quotes with evident approval an assessment of Priestley's technique at Warrington Academy, particularly its informality and freedom:

I do not recollect that he ever shewed the least displeasure at the strongest objections that were made to what he delivered; but I distinctly remember the smile of approbation with which he usually received them; nor did he fail to point out in a very encouraging manner, the ingenuity or force of any remarks that were made, when they merited these characters.[26]

Even more pertinently, Turner and his daughter Ann were involved in the upbringing of several of the Norwich Martineau family. Harriet Martineau's father had married Elizabeth Rankin of The Forth, Newcastle, a large house and garden standing amongst fields and a square of trees just outside the Gunner Tower in the west wall. In 1809, when Harriet was seven, her mother and aunt crammed her, two sisters and 'little James, aged four, and in nankeen frocks' into a postchaise for a journey that took several days in order to spend the summer with their grandparents, Robert and Ann Rankin. Their names occur in Turner's 'Register of the Minister and People who regularly assemble in Hanover Square' and his daughter refers to the Rankins as their greatest friends. (Elizabeth Stevenson asked Harriet Carr to remember her to them 'very affectionately'.) The Martineau children of course visited the Turner family. Ann Turner, then about fourteen, was instrumental in relieving Harriet's childish fears and encouraged her 'to confession and morning and nightly prayer'. This put Harriet, she affirms in her autobiography, 'as it were, into my own moral charge'. Ann actually went back to Norwich with the Martineaus on a return visit and took charge for a while of Harriet's religious development, though her influence did not last long.[27]

In her autobiography Harriet speaks of her religious difficulties with the ancient foreknowledge-freewill controversy, and mentions 'a rebuke administered' to one of her family by William Turner, 'who disapproved inquiry into what he took for granted to be an unknowable thing.' This would never stop Harriet. By 1830 she had left Ann Turner far behind and was associated with W. J. Fox's 'free-thinking and free-living clique', to use the words of James Martineau, who at first considered their practice of telling each other their faults and temptations 'unhealthy and repulsive'. He must have changed his mind about Fox at least, perhaps after hearing his great speech at Manchester in July 1830, for he paid a visit to the family in 1832, during a 'black fortnight' when Fox and his wife were outwardly harmonious but quarrelling in private. By 1834 the scandal of Fox's separation from his wife, taking the eleven-year-old Eliza with him, and his association with Eliza Flower, caused Harriet to refuse to see him again. Her brother, however, kept up the connection with a man whose independent writing and preaching were highly regarded by many Unitarians.[28]

When William Turner's son Henry, minister at Nottingham, married Catharine, daughter of John Cole Rankin of Newcastle and his wife Catharine, relationships were strengthened, though after Henry Turner died prematurely in 1822 she was distressed to find that the contact between her aunt Elizabeth's family at The Forth and the Turners had declined for a time. Other connections flourished, however. Harriet Martineau's older and prettier sister Elizabeth ('Lissey') married a surgeon who by 1827 was living in the fashionable and newly built Eldon Square, Thomas M. Greenhow.[29] He was an important doctor in the midwifery of the city and a stalwart of the Literary and Philosophical Society, giving talks on modern British poets, vaccination and, on 5 April 1831, 'a sensible paper upon the advantages of establishing at Newcastle-upon-Tyne an University or Academy upon an extensive liberal plan', especially for the middle classes of the community. J. Green provided a gothic, castellated drawing of the proposed college, which, however, was overtaken by the establishment of the University of Durham in the following year, where Greenhow became professor of Medical Ethics.[30] William Turner was very fond of this family – he recorded the baptisms of four of their children between 1821 and 1831 – and when Harriet came up for the winter of 1824 she spent 'seven or eight delightful days' with Mr Turner as well as with her other relations, returning yet again in 1827 for medical treatment from Dr Greenhow.[31]

After the final collapse of the Norwich Martineaus' manufactory in June 1829, the daughters, like Samuel and Catherine Holland's, had to fend for themselves for a time. Harriet's increasing deafness forced her, she told Fox, 'to depend on my pen alone'. Mary Robberds testified to the difficulty she had experienced when educating her own children because of deafness. One of Harriet's plans, before its time, was to set up a correspondence course for 'the further and happier culture of educated girls after leaving school'; her circular proposed a fee of 25 guineas per annum, 'or less if confined in schools'. Her sister Ellen, whose lessons she had heard as a girl, was asked in August to go as a governess with the older married sister Elizabeth Greenhow, to teach her daughter Frances. The Greenhows were members of Turner's congregation and, Harriet said, Ellen would be able to study with him.[32]

Even if there was no question of Elizabeth Stevenson studying with William Turner for this particular purpose at about the same time – on the assumption that the money left by her grandfather in Hannah Lumb's charge was sufficient to enable her to live independently – her 'improvement' would not have been neglected. The educational ethos and organisation of these families could hardly have been stronger. William Turner might not have asked her to prepare diagrams for his lectures, but he would have attended to the development of her intellectual and moral powers, living as he did amongst the most forward-looking citizens in a town proud of being the most important provincial centre between Leeds and York to the south and the capital of Scotland to the north.

NOTES

1 Chadwick, 1910, pp. 154, 162. See especially P. J. Yarrow (to whom I am grateful for much help), 'Mrs Gaskell and Newcastle upon Tyne', *GSJ*, V, 1991, pp. 62-4, and 'Mrs. Gaskell and Newcastle', pp. 139-40.

2 Ward Notebook, f. 10; JGS: MS corrections, Plymouth Grove, Manchester, n. d., in Meta's hand (see p. 338 above). About Newcastle Meta added, 'She *didn't* spend "two winters" there', though she and Julia were Ward's original source. For Billericay see p. 288 above.

3 Chapple, 'Five new letters', p. 2; TWA: 1787/18, Members' monthly [later quarterly] contribution book, Ann Turner contributions Feb. 1829-Feb. 1832. Her father's subscription was 2s and James Losh's 3.

4 Baines, *Liverpool*, p. 580; McIntyre, 'Docks at Birkenhead', pp. 110-11; MCO: JGR to Mary Robberds (née Turner), Llangollen, 6 July 1831; N. Hawthorne, *English Notebooks*, ed. Randall Stewart, New York, 1962, p. 48 (28 February 1854). A. J. Worthington and D. N. Thompson of BCPLA gave me valuable assistance.

5 Chapple, 'Five new letters', pp. 12-14. See the bibliographical appendix for basic reference works: Bruce's *Handbook*, *Oliver's New Picture*, Middlebrook's *Newcastle* and Oliver's excellent *Plan* and *Key* of 1830.

6 *A French Sociologist Looks at Britain: Gustave d'Eichthal and British Society in 1828*, tr. and ed. B. M. Ratcliffe and W. H. Chaloner, Manchester, 1977, pp. 56, 63; Phillips, *History of Banks*, pp. 206-7; *Sopwith*, ed. Richardson, p. 56.

7 Girouard, *The English Town*, pp. 28-9; Carmichael and Welford, *Tyneside Life and Scenery*, p. xi and illustr.; DCLH: HH to PH, Newcastle-upon-Tyne, 29 May [1800]. A Northern Academy of Arts was established in 1827 by T. M. Richardson, J. W. Carmichael and H. P. Parker.

8 NLPS: grangerised copy, Mackenzie, *Newcastle*, I, pp. 107, 169; II, pp. 370-6, 378-9, 395; *Oliver's New Picture*, pp. 56-61; Harris, *Christian Character*, pp. 14-15; Charlton, *Newcastle Town*, pp. 84-5; Baillie, *Newcastle and Its Vicinity*, p. 273. See also TWA: 1787/159, sixteen scrapbooks relating to the Unitarian chapel's history.

9 Sir John Clapham, *The Bank of England: A History*, Cambridge, 1944, II, p. 112; p. 340 above. Maberly Phillips did not think Carr belonged to a northern family.

10 See Phillips, *History of Banks*, pp. 208-9; Wilkes and Dodds, *Tyneside Classical*, pp. 81-93 (illustr. opp. p. 85); Girouard, *The English Town*, pp. 176-7, 183-8.

11 Henry Robson, 'The Sandgate Lassie's Lament', in *Rhymes of the Northern Bards: Being a Curious Collection of Old and New Songs and Poems, Peculiar to the Counties of Newcastle upon Tyne, Northumberland, and Durham*, ed. John Bell, junior, Newcastle, 1812, pp. 301-2.

12 HM, 'The Newcastle improvements', p. 137; Johnson, *Birth of the Modern*, pp. 45-9; *Tyneside Classical*, pp. 19, 30-1. The painting, now in the librarian's room of NLPS, is repr. in Watson's *History*, opp. p. 10. I must thank the Librarian, Margaret Norwell, for much information about NLPS paintings and sculpture.

13 Welford, *Men of Mark*, p. 60; Watson, *History of the NLPS*, p. 92; Wilkes and Dodds, *Tyneside Classical*, pp. 14-15, 38; Andrew Greg, 'The Society's building and its architect', in *Bicentenary Lectures*, pp. 27-47; Girouard, *The English Town*, p. 130 (illustr.); Mackenzie, II, p. 231.

14 *A French Sociologist*, ed. Ratcliffe and Chaloner, p. 66; *Memoir of Thomas Bewick*, ed. Bain, pp. 69, 77, 236.

15 *Songs From the Manuscript Collection of John Bell*, ed. D. I. Harker and F. Rutherford, Surtees Society CXCVI, Leamington Spa, 1985, pp. 95-6. An old spout is illustr. in Carmichael and Welford, *Tyneside Life and Scenery*, opp. p. 31.

16 Lewis and Williams, *Pioneers of Ffestiniog Slate*, p. 30; Sykes, *Historical Register*, II, p. 274; *Losh Diaries*, I, p. xv, II, pp. 112, 134, 140-2.

17 Watson, *History of the NLPS*, p. 5; HH, *Recollections*, p. 10.

18 Middlebrook, *Newcastle*, pp. 140-1, 192; Sykes, *Historical Register*, II, p. 346; Oliver, *Plan*, nos: St Nicholas' 43, St John's 216; *Reference*, pp. 2, 10; *Oliver's New Picture*, pp. 56-7; L. T. C. Rolt, *George and Robert Stephenson: The Railway Revolution*, London, 1960, pp. 80, 146-7, 160-76, 180.

19 DCLH: HH to PH, Newcastle-upon-Tyne, 28 March [1802]; Harris, *Christian Character*, p. 11; *Oliver's New Picture*, pp. 15-16.

20 HM, 'The Newcastle improvements', p. 178; Wilkes and Dodds, *Tyneside Classical*, pp. 76-7, 104, 122-4.

21 M. J. T. Lewis, *Early Wooden Railways*, London, 1970 (illustr.), pp. 110-231, 292-9 (incl. Edgeworth quotation); Maclean, *Newcastle and Carlisle Railway*, pp. 37, 41, 79.

22 TWA: 1787/9, WT's MS register, and 1787/117, MS copy of gravestones, St Andrew's, opp. p. 16 of Harris, *The Christian Character;* Hunter, I, pp. 175, 177; *DNB;* Jane Turner obit., *MR*, n.s. I, 1827, p. 126; NLPS: Moor Collection 18 (20 October 1784, congratulations to WT on his marriage).

23 MR, MS 'Recollections', pp. 1-5 (see Chapple, 'Unofficial lives', in Parish, pp. 110-11); DCLH: TS, HH to Peter Holland, Stoke Newington, 17 January 1804; Girouard, *The English Town*, pp. 177, 186.

24 Lawrence, 'Humphry Davy and Romanticism', pp. 217-21; Watson, *History of the NLPS*, pp. 213-17; Morell and Thackray, *Gentlemen of Science: Early Years*, pp. 68, 90 (also p. 137: WT a northern 'leading light'); Davidoff and Hall, *Family Fortunes*, p. 443.

25 TWA: 1787/9, WT's MS register; MR, MS 'Recollections', *passim;* Davis, *Manchester College*, p. 79; *CR*, n. s. VIII, 1852, p. 639 (Winstanley). The few MS pages in NLPS are anonymous, but the hand is probably that of Mary Robberds (née Turner).

26 Laws, *Scola Novocastrensis*, II, pp. 109-14; Yarrow, 'Mrs. Gaskell and Newcastle', pp. 139-40; Turner, *Warrington Academy*, intro. Carter, p. 26.

27 See *Autobiography of HM*, I, pp. 18, 28-34, 43; Oliver, *Plan*, St John's 293, and *Reference*, p. 11; Mary Robberds, MS 'Recollections', p. 6; Chapple, 'Five early letters', p. 10. In 1828 Ann Rankin asked Turner to accept the gift of a chair from his friends (NLPS: Moor Collection 40, AR to WT, The Forth, 31 December 1828).

28 *Autobiography of HM*, I, p. 108; MCO: MS Martineau 2, Coe transcripts, 5 May 1830; 27 Feb. 1832; Webb, *Martineau*, pp. 95-9; Carpenter, *James Martineau*, pp. 147, 161; Brenda Colloms, '"Tottie" Fox: her life and background', *GSJ*, V, 1991, pp. 16-18. See p. 422 below.

29 MCO: MS Martineau 2, Coe transcripts, 14 November 1824; NLPS: Moor Collection 31, J. Martineau to WT, York, 10 May 1827.

30 Prothero and Bradley, *Arthur Penrhyn Stanley*, I, p. 203; grangerised *Report 1832* (Green's drawing); Seed, 'The role of Unitarianism', p. 239-40; *Losh Diaries*, I, pp. 99, II, pp. 18-19, 109; Gordon Dale, 'Newcastle's medical Schools, *Medicine in Northumbria*, p. 211; Derek Tacchi, *Childbirth in Newcastle upon Tyne (1760-1990)*, Whitley Bay, 1994, pp. 10-11.

31 MCO: MS Martineau 2, Coe transcripts, 7 October and 14 November 1824; TWA: 1787/9, WT's MS register (information kindly supplied by Stephen Harbottle).

32 MCO: MS Martineau 2, Coe transcripts, 17 July and 18 August 1829; *Harriet Martineau Letters*, ed. Sanders, pp. 16, 19; *Autobiography of HM*, I, pp. 128, 139-43; MR, MS 'Recollections', p. 8.

20

Northern values

TURNER REMAINED a joint secretary of the Literary and Philosophical Society for over forty years. In his first address to the members he followed 'an excellent writer' (Priestley) in proposing that a provincial philosophical society should be 'regulated, in some degree, by local circumstances' rather than by the general interests of science, such as extensive experiments, voyages of discovery and, before the days of agents, 'the reward of literary adventurers, and the like'. The arts were not ignored; they were, however, subordinate to the investigation of what was 'improvable'. Derek Orange notes how very characteristic the word was of the man and the period.[1]

The early papers of the Society were recorded in manuscript if they did not find their way into print fairly swiftly. A paper he read on 8 August 1797 might appear from its title to be no more than desultory notes – 'Observations on a tour through parts of York and Lancashire' – but much of it is precisely focused on just the kind of information that would stimulate both thought and practical results. He called Wakefield 'a handsome town, beautifully situated' and stressed its artistic treasures, but he did not fail to describe in detail an industrial process of 'fulling' by hammers, formerly the work of women treading cloth in a tub. An eighteenth-century man, one of his favourite words was 'particulars'.

At Halifax, he came across ironworks, canals and cotton manufacture – processes, he says, scarcely mentioned in Dr Aikin's *Description of the Country Round Manchester*. Turner filled the gap for the benefit of his Tyneside audience. His lengthy technical account also led him into a serious moral consideration of manufacturing. The introduction of machines can undoubtedly bring 'riot and disorder', but unlike Ruskin, he praised them as 'most wonderful productions of human genius', turning out cheaper and more uniform articles, competitive with foreign goods. On the other hand, to make children from the age of six work in close rooms for ten hours a day was horrifying; childhood is a time when mind and body should be encouraged to 'unfold themselves'. The custom of hiring 'by wholesale, for a term of years, the children of a distant parish', thereby breaking 'all the ties of parental love and filial affection', was in his eyes particularly detestable. They were, he quotes a friend as saying, '*white negros*', brought down from St Giles in covered wagons, 'slave vessels on wheels'.

Turner ended with natural history (an' ingenious friend at Knutsford' had told him about the Earl of Stamford's goldfish being attacked by the larvae of a large water beetle) and mineralogy, which he characterised as 'the discovery of things which may be turned to use, and meliorate the condition of society.' It was 'highly presumptuous', he contended, to misapply the science of mineralogy for 'dressing out theories of the earth', and he quoted a friend's analogy of a fly on the surface of an orange. It could drive its proboscis 'through bitter oil contained in those cells, or even ... into the insipid fungous substance beneath them'. It had no chance of discovering the orange's 'real formation and structure'. This is a parallel to his dislike of the foreknowledge-freewill controversy. His mind was clear, keen, practical and efficient, but utterly unmetaphysical.[2]

His lectures for the Newcastle Literary and Philosophical Society were pragmatic. After a decade or so the growth of the Society's library to some 8000 volumes had in Turner's eyes almost defeated the original conception. He was not against libraries. His very successful vestry library for his congregation in Hanover Square had begun way back in 1787, but he did not wish the Literary and Philosophical Society to be turned into a mere reading club. In 1802 it was proposed that a special science lectureship should be set up, a Baconian New Institution for 'such natural philosophy as shall not vanish in the fumes of subtile, sublime, or delectable speculation, but such as shall be *operative in the endowment and benefit of man's life.*' There was strong local support for this: the Duke of Northumberland made a donation of £200 towards the purchase of apparatus from the estate of Dr Garnett of the Royal Institution, the Bishop of Durham £100. It was kept in a special room and in constant use thereafter. Natural, experimental sciences were clearly regarded as fundamental for the prosperity of the region, though the appointment of William Turner as official lecturer, however appropriate, ran into powerful opposition, resignations and ill feeling. Enlightenment can never expel nature; it will always spring back.[3]

He was paid two hundred guineas for each course at the beginning, and worked hard for his money until he finally gave up in 1833. There are some very clear examples of the part he played. The wood engraver Thomas Bewick praised his great talents as a lecturer on various scientific subjects and obviously thought him a friend. When in 1797 Bewick quarrelled with his partner (and former master) Ralph Beilby about whose name should adorn the title-page of the *History of British Birds*, he agreed to accept the decision of Turner and three members of the Literary and Philosophical Society – William Charnley, one of the town's largest booksellers, Robert Doubleday, manufacturer and author, and Solomon Hodgson the printer.[4]

In 1812 Turner gave an account to the Society of 'the moveable Steam

Engine lately introduced in the colliery at Middleton, near Leeds'. Robert Stephenson paid tribute to Turner for his readiness to assist him with instruments and books, such as a volume of the *Repository of the Arts and Sciences*, 'and with counsel, gratuitously and cheerfully' given – at a crucial time when he was a boy in his teens sharing his Newcastle school knowledge with his untutored mechanical genius of a father out at Killingworth. Years later he told Samuel Smiles of Turner's help, inspiring a typically Smilesian moral in a footnote to volume 3 of his *Lives of the Engineers*. In 1815 a friend described George Stephenson's safety lamp to a meeting of the Newcastle Literary and Philosophical Society; it was George, however, who dealt with the questions in his strong Northumbrian accent. Turner would have been at the public dinner on 1 November 1817 in the Newcastle Assembly Rooms with Charles Brandling of Gosforth House in the Chair at which Stephenson was presented with an inscribed silver tankard and a large sum of money, and he would undoubtedly have been privy to the caustic letter James Losh sent to Sir Humphry Davy, who was unwise enough to object in writing to the public honouring of a rival inventor of a safety lamp for use in the mines. In the following year Henry Holland told Maria Edgeworth that Davy had been 'a good deal teazed of late by this Northumbrian controversy as to the real discoverer of the Safety Lamp', not yet settled; 'the papers, anonymous & otherwise, already published on the subject, make a tolerably sized volume.'[5]

The archives of a local philosophical society like that of Newcastle, still flourishing and always welcoming to strangers, contain fascinating material. In 1821 its officers were exercised in mind about 'indiscriminate admission' to see a recently acquired mummy and appointed a sub-committee to consider how to take it out of its coffin. Henry Holland was consulted and his reply neatly copied into the Society's records. His letter ends with ensuring that his old master, and Newcastle, were made aware of

> Mrs Somerville our great female Mathematician and Philosopher here, to whom La Place sends all his works … I know not whether ever you heard of this extraordinary woman, whom Dr Wollaston and Young were to consult about their mathematical writings; – artists, about their philosophical instruments; mineralogists, about their rare minerals; – scholars, about Greek. La Place had heard that only three women in England had read and would understand his *Mechanique Celeste* …

Two of these, a Scotch woman and an English women, both turned out to be Mary Somerville. Holland's conclusion is more equivocal: 'I may add to these various eminent qualities, that she paints as a first-rate artist; plays and sings well, is extremely simple and modest, pretty, & engaging in her manners.' She knew, however, where her own priorities lay. She missed the meeting of the British Association for the Advancement of Science at Cambridge: 'The improvement of my girls being the object of our stay in Paris', she wrote to Whewell, 'I wish to give them time to profit by their opportunities.' Perhaps such a well balanced personality should have been consulted about the purchase of Byron's *Don Juan*. It raised a tempest of opposition in Newcastle. Parodies, squibs and letters filled the pages of the *Newcastle Courant* and the *Tyne Mercury*, and occupied the time of meetings. It must have been hugely enjoyable for all concerned.[6]

By the time Elizabeth Stevenson arrived at Newcastle late in 1829, these were triumphs and battles of the past, but Turner's lectures, in special accommodation, were still being regularly given for the benefit of 'the merchant, the manufacturer, the miner, the engineer, the shipwright, and the navigator'. His energies were inexhaustible. He had campaigned for the removal of civil disabilities from dissenters, the emancipation of Roman Catholics and Jews and the abolition of the slave trade, supported Sunday schools and charity schools, taken collections for Manchester College and become its official Visitor, established a Unitarian Tract Society in Newcastle, written numerous articles and the history of his old academy at Warrington. During the Napoleonic wars Newcastle had raised an armed association of nearly 1200 men for home defence. Turner was Chairman of the Police Association in 1803, being 'willing on an emergency to exchange his usual weapon, the pen, for the constable's staff', his obituarist quipped. He had evidently become a local legend in the course of his long career, but hagiographers had abundant material and anecdotes to draw upon.[7]

In the town he had played a major part with the vicar of St Nicholas, the Reverend John Smith, in establishing the Royal Jubilee School in 1810 for poor boys, in 'a noble, chaste and substantial building' planned by John Dobson near the Keelmen's Hospital. It was non-denominational, Turner becoming one of its two secretaries; which caused several gentlemen to withdraw their patronage because of what they saw as the 'rapid and alarming increase of the Dissenting interest'. Soon afterwards, the wife of a French traveller, M. Simond, on a visit to the boys' school told Turner that the boys would need wives and that he had better start a school for them. So one was begun, but in 'a plain brick building'. Losh attended an anniversary meeting in 1814:

> It was indeed a most interesting sight – 180 girls in the most perfect order, neat, clean and well behaved and very many of them receiving rewards for their good conduct or acquirements. All of them belonging to poor, many to profligate parents, and none of them in a condition to have obtained the advantages they are now enjoying without the aid of the admirable institution under the care of which they are now placed.[8]

Turner also joined with a very select group of Newcastle men to set up a Literary Club for the discussion of wide-ranging papers, on geology as well as literature, education in addition to mining. He was prominent in beginning Newcastle's Society of Antiquaries and a Natural History Society. He gave lectures in chemistry free to 'a very numerous class' in the Mechanics' Institution. Lord Brougham paid tribute to his efforts and was careful to quote Turner's opening address when the Institution was established in 1824; it recommended the study of any subjects except '*controversial* divinity and *party* politics' – a kind of London University for the working classes, established in far-off days when value-free study of science and literature was thought to be an attainable ideal. Not surprisingly Turner was an active member of the local committee for Newcastle of the Library of Useful Knowledge. So was his friend and Hanover chapel stalwart, the Whig barrister James Losh. Like the Earl of Lauderdale, Losh could express his political allegiance in the language of salmon: 'The moment I received your letter', he once wrote to Lord Brougham, 'I sent my clerk to Mr. Hopper, the great master of the art of parboiling' – but goes on to say that the river in December 1830 was too full of ice to allow a salmon to be caught.[9]

In early 1830 Turner's lectures were on mineralogy and geology, ringing the changes on the lectures on zoology and botany he had given in the last two seasons. In May his son and namesake, formerly a tutor at Manchester College in York but recently appointed minister of 'T'cellar hole chapel' at Halifax, gave six lectures on 'The Origin and Progress of Civil Society'. If Elizabeth did not meet him on this occasion, she would undoubtedly have done so at some time, for he was named as an executor of Hannah Lumb's will along with Edward Holland of Dumbleton. The following winter William Turner senior gave a series of lectures on optics and astronomy. It is not known if Elizabeth actually attended any of these lectures, but it is quite possible that she did.[10]

It is inconceivable that Elizabeth Stevenson would not have gone regularly with Ann to services in Turner's chapel. The Hanover Square congregation was open and liberal by nature, a characteristic of many southern congregations also. Henry Solly's grandparents in Leyton, though friendly with Priestley, 'would not have tolerated for a moment the "Old Meeting" in Marsh Street being called a Unitarian Chapel.'[11] The 'securities and papers' of Turner's chapel were copied into a book which, like its annual reports, was open for inspection by all. According to Turner's statement of the congregation's objects in 1811, it was 'a Voluntary Association', belonging to no one sect and holding no special set of doctrines – a common enough stress, though one notices that Richard Wright's *An Essay on the Unity and Supremacy of God, and the Subordination of Jesus Christ* is advertised at the end for 6d and Turner himself was Priestleyan in background. But Turner added that the pastor, whilst reserving his right to give a personal exposition of the Scriptures, should not offend any kind of Christian.

The order of service was not prescribed. It usually began with a psalm and a short prayer, followed by reading of passages from the Old Testament, a more general prayer and a lesson from the New Testament; these might be accompanied by exposition. Then two more psalms and a sermon were concluded by 'a short intercessory prayer'. The preface to his *Offices of Public Worship, For the Use of Unitarian Christians; Selected and Partly Composed by William Turner* (Newcastle, 1824) is revealing. Long extemporary prayers, he thought, allowed the minds of young people to wander, and he confesses that an early habit of hesitation caused him to 'precompose'. According to a Daventry student in 1787 Turner had been successful enough in extemporary prayer but had been asked to read his prayers by the congregation. Turner did not wish to inhibit 'free prayer'. There was full liberty to diverge from his suggested texts, but they did not include responses, which were not in his view useful for dissenting congregations. They could, if they wished, help compose a 'Symphony' by joining in the parts he had italicised. A fourteen-page pamphlet has survived, giving anthems the choir actually sang in 1828; they include several from Handel's *Messiah* and works by Kent, Eddow, Sparrow, Arnold and Mason.[12]

Differing views were held amongst the congregation on the subject of baptism, Turner carefully noted. The celebration of the Lord's Supper on the first Sunday of every month was, he regretted to say, thinly attended. James Losh, who took this complaint very seriously indeed, recorded in his diary that he always administered the sacrament in 'a simple and rational manner'. Turner seems to have used the occasion of an invitation to be minister at Nottingham after the death of his son Henry in 1822 by making known his intention to refuse but also pointing out certain things that disappointed him in Newcastle. This was a successful tactic: a solemn meeting was held and Losh was able to record the numbers of communicants increasing to forty or fifty.

A later sermon on the Lord's Supper, printed at Newcastle in 1828, reminds us of a larger context, however. Turner preached it on 17 February, 'Previous to a Meeting of the Congregation for Petitioning Parliament for the repeal of the Corporation and Test Acts'. Once again the long struggle of Unitarians to achieve political freedom had been renewed. This time it was successful. James Losh attributed it to 'the *march of the intellect*' (with no Peacockian overtones) rather than the wisdom of politicians. His joy is almost palpable. Like the 'cleanliness, good order, and, above all, employment and kind treatment' in the lunatic asylum he went to visit soon afterwards, it was for him yet another proof of the glorious progress of the decade. Elizabeth Stevenson came to Newcastle on a swelling tide of optimism and good feeling amongst dissenters. It was soon to meet Evangelical cross-currents, however.[13]

Religious instruction at Hanover Square was highly organised, and it seems likely that if the pattern Turner had so diligently established continued, Elizabeth might have been expected to teach 'the plain catechism' to the younger children or exercise the older ones by using works like John Holland's *Questions*. Turner's own little volume, *An Abstract of the History of the Bible, For the Use of Children and Young Persons, With Questions for Examination*, an improved version of which had been published at Newcastle in 1807, had achieved a much better printed sixth edition by 1816. It was intended to be a family-companion for Sunday evenings. Prayers, readings, recitals from the Scriptures and 'our best English poets', together with exercises in sacred harmony, were the staple fare. Or perhaps she would have been asked to help educate the children of the poor in the Sunday school for girls – 'regularly visited and well managed by the young ladies' and examined every quarter by the ladies as a whole, with prizes on the last Sunday in the year, Turner noted in his *Present State of the Congregation*. Unfortunately, the Sunday school minutes were not kept between November 1827 and 4 March 1832, the very period when Elizabeth was there.

Several of Turner's congregation were involved in printing, publishing and bookselling, responsible for the town's liberal newspapers, the *Newcastle Chronicle* and the *Tyne Mercury* (Hodgsons and Mitchells), as well as books, magazines and tracts. W. A. Mitchell was a prolific author himself. The radical John Marshall and Emerson Charnley, whom Dibdin called 'the veteran emperor of Northumbrian booksellers', were also prominent. Turner's Newcastle Unitarian Tract Society, founded in 1813, flourished in this fertile soil. Elizabeth Stevenson could hardly have avoided reading some of its publications, several of which were by Turner himself, such as numbers 15 and 16, the titles of which plainly indicate the nature of his religion: *The Excellence and Advantage of Public Social Worship* and *A Serious Address to Heads of Families, on the Subject of Family Religion*. Look after the interests, morals and religion of servants, he exhorts, but without imposing upon them; family prayers should be without ostentation, after guests had gone, or even omitted on occasion.[14]

Two Sermons given in the area by his son-in-law J. G. Robberds, stressing the duty of Christians to work for the improvement of their fellow-men, were printed in 1829. A longish anti-Calvinist piece by Hannah Lumb's friend, William Turner of Halifax, entitled *Remarks on the Commonly Received Doctrine of Atonement & Sacrifice*, appeared in the following year. This was a trenchant piece. Turner insisted that 'vindictive justice' was a contradiction in terms; God was 'slow to wrath and plenteous in mercy'. He speculated about the motives of strict Calvinists and the psychological consequences of a doctrine that condemned so many to everlasting damnation. Fortunately, he thought, the number of moderate Calvinists was increasing – a tendency which affected Elizabeth Gaskell in later years, who on meeting Charles Bosanquet wrote to Charles Eliot Norton, 'I told him what *I* did believe – (more I suppose what would be called Arian than Humanitarian,) – and among other things said I had only one antipathy – and that was to the Calvinistic or Low Church creed' – tactlessly in the circumstances.[15]

A good deal of American material was re-published by the Newcastle Society. Tract number 31 reprints a sermon by the Reverend William Ellery Channing that had created a sensation in New York. To Trinitarians in all denominations its very title was paradoxical: *The Superior Tendency of Unitarianism to Form an Elevated Religious Character ... Dec. 7, 1826* (Newcastle, 1827).[16] Number 44 is entitled *One Hundred Scriptural*

Arguments for the Unitarian Faith. Recently Put in Boston. Numbers 45 and 46 are similar, and if we are now well aware that Elizabeth Gaskell was basically uninterested in the doctrinal and controversial aspects of Unitarianism, we can be sure that Turner would have drawn her attention to number 48, Caleb Stetson's *On Piety at Home*, reprinted at Newcastle in 1832. It praises unhistoric acts in an organic way that George Eliot would find sympathetic:

> As human life is made up of a succession of moments, unimportant when considered singly, so character is formed by a long series of acts, insignificant perhaps in themselves, but, as units in the sum of moral existence, and germs of deep-rooted habit, they will influence our whole future destiny.

From home, Stetson argues, our God-given sympathies must be extended to social life; 'both happiness and virtue are promoted by a large and free communion of mind with mind, and of heart with heart'. But home is the centre and its duties must come first, especially the education 'which nothing but parental affection can impart'. How Elizabeth would have regarded one exhortation (quoted from Channing) after her experiences in Chelsea is impossible to determine: 'God never places beings in a relation to each other,' he had written, 'without giving them strength to perform the duties arising from it'. Stetson was reassuring: affliction might for a time overshadow domestic happiness but never wholly destroy it, and home's affections and virtues were as available to the poor as to the rich and distinguished. The values of this tract, however effusively propounded, are central in the Unitarian tradition and identical with those that run through her later life.[17]

She would have been hard put to escape the lectures on the 'Evidences and Doctrines of Natural and Revealed Religion, and on the Corruption, Reformation, and Present State of Christianity', delivered in the Hanover Square vestry to men and women alternately on free Sunday mornings. Turner prided himself on being up-to-date with the relevant literature; the vestry library contained hundreds of works, issued and received by a young member of the congregation for half an hour before the morning and evening services. Heads of families were encouraged to use Sundays with their children, 'encouraging the younger ones to exercise their privilege (*task* let it not be called) of repeating Mrs. Barbauld's or Dr. Watts' hymns ... '. Was Elizabeth involved in the selection of books for the 'juvenile library' to be housed in a special bookcase in the girls' school, which Turner presented to the congregation in 1832? On Sunday and Wednesday evenings 'persons' would meet to read sermons and similar treatises, 'certainly a very agreeable and profitable way of spending a part of the Lord's day evening for young men, and persons of any age who have no families', he declared. Priestley, too, had set up an evening discussion group for young men and women at the New Meeting in Birmingham. Was this the way in which the sexes met, an opportunity to find a suitable marriage partner?

The question was not a casual one for Unitarians. When James Losh took his daughters to dinner and an evening at the Mansion House in December 1831, they met a large party of officers, which sounds promising. But the soldiers were not, he wrote in his diary, 'very suitable company to *meet us.* ... The officers, with few exceptions, appeared to me to be what are called *scamps.*' Any set of jolly young fellows might strike a serious-minded old father, acutely aware of morals and money, in this way, but his daughters had not only to suffer from the attentions of light-hearted fortune-hunters but from a pointed lack of attention in what should have been more acceptable quarters.[18]

Turner himself had been a secretary of the Newcastle Bible Society together with the vicar of St Nicholas for some twenty years. Meetings could attract three thousand people. In August 1831, Losh found himself asked as a vice-president to take the chair at the annual meeting. It was expected to be difficult:

> The intolerant or evangelical (as it is called) party had determined (in imitation of their Brethren in London) to propose the expulsion of *Unitarians* from the Soc'y upon the ground that they are not Christians. They had issued circular exhortations to *all Christians* to bestir themselves for the destruction of a '*Soul-destroying Heresy*', and they had actually put up placards, all over the town, to the same effect.

In the acrimony between churchmen and dissenters about the time of the reform act of 1832, it was claimed that any collaboration in bible, school and tract societies was discreditable and hypocritical. Dissenters were said to be privately unrestrained in their insults and lies. 'Such conduct may be quite in character with a dissenting teacher, and a factious liberal, but a disgrace to any Clergyman', wrote one hot-tempered controversialist.[19]

Losh was able to report that the Newcastle attempt to expel Unitarians failed completely, but it shows the growing strength of intolerance, which led William Gaskell a few years later to protest about their treatment by fellow Protestants:

> We have been refused the Christian name; we have been stigmatized as blasphe-mers, enemies of the cross of Christ, and deniers of the Lord who bought us; we have been made the objects of a kind of holy horror; and the place usually assigned to us is with Infidels and Atheists in this world, and with dread spirits of evil in that which is to come.

The distinguished preacher and Master of the Temple, Christopher Benson, who had in earlier Newcastle days as curate of St John's church been a friend of Turner, renounced acquaintance with him 'on account of his Unitarianism', Lucy Aikin wrote to Channing in America, 'and has publicly preached that this faith was contrary to morals!' (He later preached against the Oxford Tractarians.) In December 1831 Losh quite naturally showed hurt disapproval of a charge by the Bishop of Durham, well written but not a '*candid* defence of the church establishment', he thought. The way in which the bishop had lumped '*Socinians*', '*Popery*', 'Infidelity and Atheism' and 'Fanaticism' together without distinction he thought neither fair or liberal, lacking in the Christian mildness 'nearly allied to true good manners' – ungentlemanly, then. In fact, a would-be emollient newspaper article (right of private judgement on both sides, much to admire, etc.) of January 1832 reveals that Turner had felt bound in conscience to resign from the Bible Society.[20]

The boot could be on the other foot. In 1832 William Turner of Halifax brought out his *Lectures on Protestant Nonconformity*, with the aim of strengthening dissenters in their principles and providing them with historical justification. His teachings of mathematics, physics and the science of mind at York belonged to the older Unitarian tradition of Locke and Priestley. In Lecture 5 he began on objections to the Church of England. Though he refrained from attacking individuals, he clearly thought he had full licence to be as rude as he wished about its doctrines, constitution and liturgy. He condemned addresses to Christ that contained phrases like 'by thy holy nativity and circumcision' and 'by thine agony and bloody sweat' unequivocally: 'language which is shocking, monstrous and horrible ... '. In comparison his father's writings seem much less polemical. Turner of Newcastle writes simply of doing the will of God in joy and mutual love, of acting as a disciple of Jesus and always in his name, looking forward with hope and trust.[21]

Sectarian differences could ruin marriage chances. Henry Solly was the son of a rich Unitarian merchant in the City of London. The main family house was out in the country at Leyton, but his father had another house in the city and even used to take a house for the winter in the West End. Here the family gave parties at which literary lions like L. E. L., Winthrop Praed, 'Barry Cornwall' and his daughter Adelaide Procter would appear – 'dazzling lights, many guests, beautiful music; brilliant talk ... '. In 1829 Solly's father rented a house in Portland Place and the family attended the chapel in York Street, St James's Square – Unitarian since 1824 and presided over by a man Charles Dickens admired 'for his labours in the cause of that religion which has sympathy for men of every creed and ventures to pass judgment on none', the Reverend Edward Tagart. Tagart had begun in poverty, but his marriage to the widow of Harriet Martineau's older brother, much against the wish of the Martineaus, had brought him a useful fortune. A young man, Edward Herford, found him friendly but totally possessed by the values of the rich, 'certainly ... most abominably aristocratic for a dissenting minister', keeping a splendid (Dickensian) table with fish, turkey, saddle of mutton, plum pudding, Stilton cheese, ale and wine, and urging the old arguments for 'the legitimate influence of property', which included voting as the landlord wished if houses had been taken on that understanding.[22]

All this respectability, wealth and position in society notwithstanding, Unitarianism 'had been the fatal obstacle on my brother's part to marriage with a most charming and loveable young lady', Henry Solly maintained; and 'a similarly serious objection, from precisely the opposite point of the theological compass' was maintained by a Cheshire county family to their eldest son marrying his sister Charlotte. Elizabeth Gaskell later suspected the same kind of objections to her own unmarried daughters. Religious and social prejudices are not always easily separated, for Solly somewhat ingenuously admits that whilst his parents, who had been 'on terms of intimate friendship with Dr. Priestley and Mr. Belsham', had never uttered a disrespectful word about the London Unitarian ministers, they 'were looked down upon by some of the wealthy laymen of the connection' and spoken of by his own brothers 'in jesting and disparaging language'. And when James Losh heard W. J. Fox preach in London his praise was mixed: 'Mr. Fox has not a good voice, has a provincial accent, and by no means a graceful or even pleasing manner; still, however, he gives one the idea of a strong minded and well informed man.' Losh had the previous day been in very superior company, talking intimately with the Prime Minister, Lord Grey, about prospects for the great Reform Bill; on the other hand, his diary makes his general social values plain. Some of the young men who came from Manchester College to preach in Hanover Square might not have measured up, notwithstanding their religion.[23]

John Seed has shown by cross-referencing chapel registers with directories and other sources that Turner's congregation included one gentleman, thirteen professional men, eighteen merchants and manufacturers, four schoolmasters and nine small dealers and retailers. Solicitors and physicians, printers and booksellers, editors and sugar-refiners, corn-factors and coal-fitters were typical of those who paid quarterly pew-rents ranging from one shilling to one and a half guineas in 1807. The chapel sittings show that there were box pews for strangers and the charity scholars; the boys' and girls' Sunday schools seem to have sat on benches at the back of the gallery. In the main body of the chapel were pews rented by the families we meet in Elizabeth Gaskell's earliest letters, all prosperous members of the congregation: Robert and Ann Rankin (next to William Turner's family pew; their servants sat nearby with his), George Carr, George Burnett senior and junior, James Losh, George Waldie, John Cole Rankin, Jane Welbank, Joseph and Ann Ward Morton, whose son Andrew has 'a Portrait Painter' pencilled in after his name. (His friends ensured that in December 1828 he was given the Literary and Philosophical Society's commission for Turner's portrait rather than an artist with an established reputation.) Nor was the chapel without music; organist's and choristers' receipts about 1830 still survive.[24]

The congregation Turner led so firmly did not ignore the poor. It celebrated George III's jubilee in October 1809 by providing beef, bread, porter, tea and lump sugar, which they were permitted to consume at home. By 1829 the quarterly collection for the poor regularly raised three or four pounds, which meant that about twenty individuals each received sums of around four shillings each quarter. At the chapel's annual meeting a committee used to be appointed, James Losh the almost inevitable chairman. The grasp of Whigs and radicals not only on the chapel's affairs but also, after the repeal of the Test and Corporation acts, their energies freed, on many other aspects of Newcastle life must have been a source of pride and satisfaction. Losh's political reward was to be chosen Recorder of Newcastle in 1832 – 'somewhat singular', he wrote with proud objectivity, for a reformer and a conscientious Unitarian. Elizabeth had to tread cautiously when she was with her Liverpool relations, who were strong Tories: 'Oh! how tired I am of the Reform Bill', she had cried to Harriet Carr on 1 September 1831, 'and my Aunt and most of my cousins, are quite anti-reformers, and abuse Lord Brougham and think him superficial.'[25]

A public dinner for nearly one hundred people in the Assembly Rooms was officially given to celebrate William Turner's service of fifty years to the city on 21 December 1831. James Losh was in the Chair and the thirty-one Stewards included the great town clerk, John Clayton, George Carr, Dr T. E. Headlam, the Reverend Anthony Headley, John Hodgson M.P., Dr J. Ramsay, Sir M. W. Ridley, M.P., William Ord M.P. and Sir John Swinburne. Other men of wealth and influence, like the Mayor of Newcastle, Archibald Reed, were present. This occasion might have been something of a riposte to the Newcastle Bible Society members who had attempted to eject him. George Carr's gentlemanly letter to the secretary, expressing his pride in 'being considered as great an admirer and as affectionate a friend as any of the valuable friends of Mr Turner can possibly be', has survived as an example of his supporters' tone. A long and learned letter from another friend, the Reverend John Collinson, vicar of Gateshead, regrets his inability to attend. Turner's own Hanover Square congregation made him a presentation of an inscribed silver salver in January 1832, £320 was subscribed for him from within the congregation – the management committee minutes show the sum increasing from £200 in October 1831 – and his likeness was engraved. Turner was 'deeply affected on the occasion', it was reported.[26]

But there is one great omission in Elizabeth's earliest letters to Harriet Carr: religion. Her aunt Hannah Lumb, uncles Peter and Sam Holland were still Unitarian; she had been staying in the household of the Reverend William Turner, where practice was faithfully maintained. Was she less serious in this respect than her companion Ann Turner, whose commitment seems to have been strong? Would her correspondent, a gay young lady like Harriet Carr, have found the subject rebarbative? The total absence of religion in her known early letters (many have yet to be discovered) stands in strange contrast to the occasionally effusive piety of the diary Elizabeth Gaskell began to keep a very few years later, in March 1835. The emotional experiences of marriage to a young clergyman, the still-birth of their first daughter and the blessed survival of the second, Marianne, must have deepened her religious sensibility immeasurably.[27]

One point about her life at this period, however, can be regarded as certain. Socially speaking, the families she associated with would have been more likely to produce a marriage partner for a Unitarian than the little society at Knutsford, pleasant though it was – 'all inland thoughts and views'. With his extensive circle of acquaintance amongst the best people in Newcastle, Turner was able to provide more than a pious home and a sound education, and the Hollands of Liverpool moved in an equally wide sphere – 'all full of rail ways and canals and the great bustle of a commercial seaport town', wrote Miss Edgeworth.

These were years remarkably full of weddings amongst friends and relations like the Hollands and Wedgwoods – with the exception of Bessy Holland. In his confidential letter of early 1830 to Maria Edgeworth her brother insisted that whilst her menfolk approved of her decision, no pressure had been brought to bear on her:

> I may swiftly mention further, that in addition to the great risk to a health not robust from the bad climate of B. [Burton?] Agnes, there were other very unfavourable circumstances attending the engagement (I make no allusion here to mere money matters, which I little regard in a question of this kind) which have more than once before been on the point of setting it aside.

Burton Agnes is a small place, in the wolds a few miles behind Bridlington on the east coast. One of the most beautiful houses in Yorkshire was owned by the Boynton family; otherwise there were 6 or 700 inhabitants in the village and neighbouring hamlets, mostly farmers and labourers with a few land-owners – W. D. T. Duesbury, John Ward and William St Quintin in 1840. Had Bessy come to live there she would have found the climate bracing, winds sweeping inland from the north and east, though Burton Agnes itself is not low-lying. For a time in the latter part of 1838 Henry Nussey was the curate of the Reverend C. H. Lutwidge, vicar of the rich living of Burton Agnes with Harpham, but he did not propose to Charlotte Brontë until early in the following year, also unsuccessfully.[28]

It is in a marriage context that we could view any visit or visits Elizabeth made to Edinburgh with Ann Turner. In the summer they would have been able to climb the steep slopes about the Castle or Carlton Hill, wander about the irregular streets of the old town and pay the customary thrilling visit to Holyrood House to see where Mary Queen of Scot's Riccio had been murdered. They could have joined the Edinburgh promenade along Princes Street so vividly described by Carlyle:

> The crowd was lively enough, brilliant, many-coloured, many-voiced, clever-looking (beautiful and graceful young womankind a conspicuous element): crowd altogether elegant, polite and at its ease tho' on parade; something as if of unconsciously rhythmic in the movements of it, as if of harmonious in the sound of its cheerful voices, bass and treble, fringed with the light laughters; a quite pretty kind of natural concert and rhythmus of march; into which, if at leisure, and carefully enough dressed (as some of us seldom were) you might introduce yourself, and flow for a turn or two with the general flood.[29]

Elizabeth and Ann would probably have experienced the kind of visits, breakfasts and tea-drinkings, suppers, assemblies and parties described by Lucy Aikin during a visit she made in 1811-12, where she encountered a 'charming mixture of people of fashion and people of literature' at Lady Apreece's and was told a scandalous story by Mrs Fletcher. Even the 'very shabby and very Scotchy' parts of the old town could put on fresh garments during the winter-time. In February 1831 there was, Henry Cockburn wrote,

> Deep and universal snow here; silent streets – save when the house top avalanche comes plump on some startled wight, waiting in delicate raiment till the bell be answered; sparrows sitting chittering round the cans, but ever and anon descending, like Tories on a sinecure, round a ball of well laid horse dung, reeking through the clear air; ... the long white of the pavement interspersed with streaks of glorious black slides – along which, to the delight of the boys and the scandal of the decorous, a Solicitor General is seen running and skimming.[30]

They might have been less censorious at the sight of a gypsy-bachelor kind of young woman rejoicing in the snow. The city had doubled in size since the beginning of the century, and Ann and Elizabeth had several useful connections to turn to account, though one of the most likely was a doubtful proposition. A Unitarian congregation existed in the new town. No evidence has survived to show that they joined it. In 1826, the Reverend W. J. Bakewell wrote to William Turner from 17 Young Street, Charlotte Square, to say that he had a good house nearly opposite the chapel but that he needed more than his stipend of £130 a year to survive decently in the Scottish capital. His address in Edinburgh's new town was a good one; the chapel had been newly opened in 1823, quite close to Charlotte Square and well away from the old town with its sordid tenements. But the congregation was then in a parlous state. Bakewell stayed about a year, his successor was asked to resign in the autumn of 1829, a young Irishman, Thomas May, temporarily supplied the pulpit in 1830, and only in August of the following year did the chapel revive with the appointment of Bartholomew Stannus. R. K. Webb considers his lectures characterised by 'an aggressive Unitarian tone'.[31]

Mrs Gaskell's daughters said that she and Ann Turner stayed with friends of her parents in Edinburgh. The brother of the second Mrs Stevenson and Anthony Todd Thomson, William John Thomson, did not live far from the chapel. He lived at several addresses, all in the new town, and by 1826 was living at 47 Northumberland Street, where we might assume the widowed Mrs Stevenson and her family visited him. He was a versatile painter, especially of miniatures, landscapes and genre subjects – paintings with titles like 'The Duke and Duchess of Roxburgh, Lady Matilda Bruce' and 'The Blind Beggar of Bethnal Green'. In 1830, having moved to 57 Northumberland Street, he exhibited 'John Wood Esquire' and 'William Thomas Trotter, EIC Civil Service'; in 1834 'Musical Boy', 'Lady at her Study' and 'Mrs Gaskill'. If this last is the well-known miniature of Elizabeth now in the John Rylands

University Library of Manchester, it belongs to a later visit, for he wrote 'Painted by W. J. Thomson June 1832 Edin~' on its back. William Thomson could have introduced her to her father's old friend, William Blackwood, and his commissions obviously brought him into good Scottish society. He married first Helen, daughter of Captain James Colhoun, and after her death in about 1812, Anne McCulloch, by whom he had two or three children.[32]

Other acquaintances might have been met through Henry Cockburn. Not only was he the boyhood friend of Anthony Todd Thomson but his eldest daughter was the 'fine, noble girl' who had been on a tour of the Wye valley with Jane Byerley during the summer of 1829. There was Anna Thornton, who had given Jane news of Mrs Stevenson and her children in Scotland, and gone on to mention a two-day visit to Bonaly, Cockburn's retreat in the Pentland Hills. These were recent occurrences. Then there were Elizabeth and Jessie Scott, old schoolfellows who had been presented with a fine copy of Beattie's *Minstrel* bound in crimson and gold a few years before. Anna Thornton, we recall, had only recently left Avonbank, where 'Mr Jeffrey the Reviewer and his wife' had come to see her. Jeffrey had given up the *Edinburgh Review* in 1829, but still advised its new editor, Macvey Napier, who seemed hard and proud in manner but was a man 'with a warm, true heart, and a taste for kindness'.

Jeffrey's house in Moray Place, Edinburgh, was magnificent, greatly superior to equivalent London mansions and with fine views over the Forth. When Macaulay told him that dancing could not be allowed on the upper floor of the new houses in London's Russell Square, 'he laughed and said that if the Elephant who danced at Covent-Garden Theatre could be got up to caper in his drawing room he should have no objection.' Jeffrey was immensely fond of his wife and daughter. He wrote reviews and law-papers in the drawing room or his wife's boudoir rather than his study, he did not let more than a few minutes pass without some loving look or caress, he took them with him in his carriage when called away on business. Macaulay

> was surprised to see a man so keen and sarcastic, so much of a scoffer, pouring himself out with such simplicity and tenderness in all sorts of affectionate nonsense. Through our whole journey to Perth he kept up a sort of mock quarrel, like mine with Hannah and Margaret; attacked his daughter about novel-reading, laughed her into a pet, kissed her out of it, and laughed her into it again. She and her mother absolutely idolise him: and I do not wonder at it.

His mimicry was superlative. He was greatly given to flirting with pretty and clever women in the late 1820s, according to Carlyle in his brilliant reminiscences, 'all in a weakish, mostly dramatic, and wholly theoretic way (his age now fifty gone)'. If Elizabeth Stevenson did manage to meet this improbably aged man in the intervals of his political career, which began to take off when he was appointed Lord Advocate in December 1830, it would again contrast greatly with her own father in his last years, and not only in worldly prosperity.

The Edinburgh society Jeffrey knew was splendidly informal. He maintained that he could go into a number of houses at any time and talk at his ease with his female favourites whenever he had leisure. On the eastern slope of Costorphine Hill stood his own summertime retreat, Craigcrook, where like Cockburn at Bonaly he delighted to entertain his friends. In the event, Elizabeth did not find her life's partner in Edinburgh, but a more favourable milieu would have been hard to find – providing theology did not interpose.[33]

NOTES

1 Orange, 'Rational dissent and provincial science', pp. 210-19; Watson, *History of the NLPS*, p. 224.

2 NLPS: WT, No. 59, MS 'Observations on a tour', unpaged (pr. *Monthly Magazine*, September and October 1797). Turner's MS 'Some observations on the custom of lifting in Lancashire' was not copied out; it appeared in the *Monthly Magazine* (cf. *Letters*, p. 30).

3 Joan Knott, 'The vestry library of the Hanover Square Unitarian Chapel, Newcastle-upon-Tyne', *LH*, I, 1969, p. 154 (Appendix I, MA thesis, University of Newcastle, 1975); Watson, *History of the NLPS*, pp. 81, 212-18; Orange, 'Rational dissent and provincial science', pp. 215.

4 *Memoir of Thomas Bewick*, ed. Bain, pp. xix-xxi, 113, 123, 241-2. Bewick's silhouette of Turner is on p. 114.

5 S. Smiles, *Lives of the Engineers. The Locomotive. George and Robert Stephenson*, London, 1861-62, III, pp. 63, 114 (para and note cut from the 1879 edition); *Losh Diaries*, I, pp. 73-4; Rolt, *George and Robert Stephenson*, pp. 24-33; Watson, *History*, pp. 144-7, 212-24; DCLH: HH to ME, London, January [1818]. The full text of Losh's letter can be found in Lonsdale, *The Worthies of Cumberland*, IV.

6 NLPS: grangerised *Reports*, 1820-21, copy of HH to WT, Mount Street, London, 3 November 1821; NLPS: *Miscellaneous Papers*, 1812-31, minutes, cuttings, printed ephemera; TCC: Add MS a. 212^{126}, MS to WW, Paris, 19 April 1833.

7 Obit: *CR*, n. s. XV, 1959, p. 364. See especially Harris, *The Christian Charecter*, and Orange, 'Rational dissent and provincial science', *passim*.

8 *Unitarian Chronicle, and Companion to the MR*, No. 1, February, 1832, p. 6 (WT's speech; girls' school); Middlebrook, *Newcastle*, pp. 156, 165; Kenrick, 'Memoir', p. 364; WT, *A Short Sketch*, p. 26; *Losh Diaries*, I, pp. 4, 11, 29, 39 (qu.), II, pp. 177; Mackenzie, *Newcastle*, III, pp. 452-5;

9 *Introductory Address at the First Meeting of the Literary, Scientific and Mechanical Institution, May 11, 1824*, Newcastle, 1824; H. Brougham, *Practical Observations on the Education of the People*, 13th edn, 1825, p. 34 (repr. Shannon); *Losh Diaries*, II, p. 186.

10 Yarrow, 'Mrs. Gaskell and Newcastle', pp. 140-1; CRO: PROB 11/1883, HL's will, signed 31 December 1834, proved at Chester on 17 August 1837. Elizabeth was to receive £80 a year during Abigail Holland's life and half the remainder after her death, the rest being divided amongst the eight nieces – Mary, Bessy, Lucy, Susan; Anne, Catherine, Frances; and Elizabeth herself. Five letters written in shorthand (unread) from WT of Halifax to his father, November 1837–June 1839, are in NLPS: Moor Collection 52.

11 A main source below is WT's *A Short Sketch of the History of Protestant Nonconformity [and] Present State of the Congregation Assembling in Hanover-Square*, Newcastle, 1811, p. 29 et seq; cp. Solly, *'These Eighty Years'*, I, p. 55.

12 Mackenzie, *Newcastle*, II, p. 380; DWL: MS 69/10, 'An address ... forms of prayer'. The music pamphlet is with other printed material and ephemera in TWA: 1787/113, an

exceptionally valuable resource for WT. *New Grove Dictionary* gives John Arnold (c. 1715-92), James Kent (1700-76) and William Mason (1725-97); Eddow and Sparrow remain unidentified.

13 *Losh Diaries*, I, pp. 121, 147-8, 169, 172, II, pp. 7, 59-60, 65-6, 80.

14 TWA: 1787/78/1, Minutes, order and admin. book, Sunday School 1789-1847; Seed, 'The role of Unitarianism', p. 242; *Rules of the Unitarian Tract Society ... With An Address on the Objects and Plan of the Society*, Newcastle, 1813; *A List of the Members of the Newcastle Unitarian Tract Society, November, 1830* (kindly supplied by E. A. Rees, Chief Archivist, Tyne and Wear). Turner's own pamphlets have imprints that include S. Hodgson, T. & J. Hodgson and J. Marshall.

15 W. Turner III, *Remarks*, Newcastle, 1830, pp. 11, 13, 17, 48; *Letters*, p. 648; Uglow, p. 451.

16 Earl Morse Wilbur, *Our Unitarian Heritage: An Introduction to the History of the Unitarian Movement*, Boston, 1925, p. 423; Howe, *Unitarian Conscience*, pp. 99-104; Andrew M. Hill, 'Channing and British Unitarianism: sowing the seeds', *TUHS*, XIX, 1987-90, pp. 71-7. Alan Seaburg, Curator of manuscripts at Andover-Harvard Theological Library, kindly searched the records of the American Unitarian Association on my behalf, but there are no letters to Turner.

17 Stetson, *On Piety at Home*, pp. 5-10. Stetson is not in *DAB*, but he published several works 1830-44 (*BL Cat.*)

18 WT, *A Short Sketch*, pp. 34-6; TWA: 1787/1/1: Management committee minutes 1829-45, 9 September 1832; Davidoff and Hall, *Family Fortunes*, p. 145; *Losh Diaries*, II, p. 129.

19 Harris, *Christian Character*, p. 23; *Losh Diaries*, I, pp. 83, II, pp. 70, 77, 80-1, 86, 117, 128; Seed, 'The role of Unitarianism', p. 355; Quinlan, *Victorian Prelude*, pp. 126-33; M. A. Gathercole, *A Letter to Charles Lushington, Esquire, M.P.*, London, 1835, p. 58.

20 William Gaskell, *Protestant Practices Inconsistent with Protestant Principles: A Discourse Delivered in Renshaw Street Chapel, Liverpool, June 16th, 1836, at the Provincial Meeting of the Presbyterian and Unitarian Ministers of Lancashire and Cheshire*, London and Manchester, 1836, p. 13; LA to WEC, Hampstead, 1 June 1830, *Memoirs of Lucy Aikin*, ed. Le Breton, p. 208; O. Chadwick, *Victorian Church*, pp. 62-4; TWA: 1787/113, 'Friendly remarks', cutting (Harris, p. 23, does not mention this).

21 Turner III, *Lectures*, pp. 61, 111; Carpenter, *Martineau*, p. 34; Turner II, *Two Sermons ... in the Unitarian Chapel, Alnwick*, Alnwick 1829, pp. 12-13, 20.

22 MCL: Herford, MS diary, I, n. p., Feb. 1835 (cf. Seed, 'The role of Unitarianism', pp. 204, 223); A. J. Cross, 'Charles Dickens, Edward Tagart and Unitarianism', *FF*, XLII, 1989, pp. 59-66; Webb, *Martineau*, p. 49; Peter Ackroyd, *Dickens*, London, 1990, pp. 504-7, 1116. Turner baptised Helen, dau. of Edward and Helen Tagart, on 6 February 1829 (WT, MS register).

23 Solly, *These Eighty Years*, I, pp. 132, 136, 300; *Losh Diaries*, II, p. 137 (18 March 1832).

24 Seed, 'The role of Unitarianism', p. 240; Yarrow, 'Mrs. Gaskell and Newcastle', pp. 141-2; TWA: 1787/12, Minister's book of members, c. 1810-1834, which contains a plan of the chapel (60 x 48 feet) and its library (18 feet square); *Losh Diaries*, II, p. 74; TWA: 1787/159/11.

25 Mackenzie, *Newcastle*, I, p. 77; TWA: 1787/1/1, Management committee minutes, 9 August 1829; TWA: 1787/29, Poor names and distribution book; *Losh Diaries*, II, p. 144; Chapple, 'Five early letters', p. 11.

26 Sykes, *Local Records*, II, pp. 334-6; TWA: 1787/115, GC to W. Hutton, Clavering Place, 5 December 1831; J. Collinson to WT, Gateshead, 6 December 1831; TWA: 1787/1/1, Management committee minutes. TWA: 1787/115 is a scrapbook about the dinner, incl. *Report of the Proceedings*, Newcastle, 1832, the *Unitarian Chronicle and Companion to the MR*, No. 1, February, 1832, and many related letters.

27 The most informed studies of her religion are by R. K. Webb, 'The Gaskells as Unitarians',

Dickens and Other Victorians: Essays in Honour of Philip Collins, ed. Joanne Shattock, London, 1988, pp. 144-7, and Michael Wheeler, 'Elizabeth Gaskell and Unitarianism', *GSJ*, VI, pp. 25-41.

28 *Edgeworth Letters*, pp. 421-2; Chapple, 'Five early letters', p. 16; DCLH: HH to ME, L Brook St, 8 January [1830]; Edward Baines and W, Parsons, *History, Directory, and Gazetteer of York*, II, East and North Ridings, 1823; W. White, *History, Directory, etc.*, 1840; *Brontë Letters*, I, pp. 132n., 185-8, 205n.

29 See Carlyle, *Reminiscences*, ed. Campbell, p. 367. Carlyle also wrote, rather implausibly, that the promenade had gone by 1832.

30 *Memoirs of Lucy Aikin*, ed. Le Breton, pp. 82-92; FC to Sir Thomas Dick Lauder, February 1831, qu. Bell, ed. *Lord Cockburn*, pp. 20-1. The Solicitor General was Cockburn himself.

31 Youngson, *Classical Edinburgh*, p. 270; NLPS: Moor Collection 3, WJB to WT, 17 June 1826; Hill, 'St. Mark's Unitarian church, Edinburgh', pp. 151-4; memoir of George Harris, *CR*, n. s. XVI, 1860, p. 720; Webb, 'The Gaskells as Unitarians', p. 158. The Reverend Andrew M. Hill, whose help I gratefully acknowledge, found no reference to Ann and Elizabeth in the records of the congregation (AMH to JAVC, 24 September 1979).

32 Uglow, pp. 63-4; infm from Dr Ian Gregg; Long, *British Miniaturists*, London, 1929, pp. 436-7; Foskett, *Collecting Miniatures*, Woodbridge, 1979, pp. 216-17; McKay, *Royal Scottish Academy*, pp. xxxix-xlii, 'Catalogue'. See p. 337 above.

33 TBM to S. M. Macaulay, Court House Pomfret, 15 April 1828 (*Macaulay Letters*, I, pp. 237-40); Carlyle, *Reminiscences*, ed. Campbell, pp. 59n., 319, 327, 330.

21

Grave and gay

BY THE THIRD decade of the century only one of William Turner's five sons, William, was still living and had long since left home. The father, then in his early sixties, was almost preternaturally hale and hearty. He joked that he did not even know that he had a stomach when a parishioner complained of internal problems, and he was still reading without glasses at the age of ninety-five. But his second wife Jane had died on Christmas Day 1826 after a 'long & distressing illness'. His funeral sermon, which like her obituary mentions 'her own, perhaps extreme, dislike of publicity', is deliberately impersonal in its nature, but the tone of a letter he wrote to her in 1822 from Mary's married home in Manchester shows a truly affectionate relationship between them. All the indications are that Mary and Ann Turner had lost a loving stepmother a few years before Elizabeth Stevenson is known to have come to Newcastle, not long after she had taken leave of her own stepmother.[1]

Mrs Chadwick, probably using an 1827 *History, Directory, and Gazetteer of Newcastle*, stated that Turner's home was in 13 Cumberland Row. The road running out to Hexham and across the Pennines to Carlisle began by Newcastle's demolished West Gate, between a hospital built in 1814 to testify public joy at the peace of Amiens and the House Carpenters' Hall of similar date (in which a congregation of Antinomian Baptists used to meet). Thomas Oliver's map shows the beginnings of ribbon development at this point, beyond the massive remains of walls that had once encircled the whole town. A terrace of 'very neat and commodious houses' called Cumberland Row had been built on the north side of the road where the hill out of town became markedly steeper. They were relatively modest in size, each with a very small garden in front and a larger one behind. Immediately opposite number 13 where Turner once lived were the long back gardens of some finer, late Georgian houses; these faced south and looked out over the river valley. The engineer Robert Stephenson lived in one of these from 1829. A little higher up the hill a new cemetery had been opened in the same year to relieve the crowded churchyards in the town; it was 'tastefully laid out with serpentine walks' and lit by lamps at night, answering 'very well as a speculation in a pecuniary point of view' even if its non-utilitarian flowers and shrubs did not flourish in the early years.[2]

Turner's house was well above the worst parts of the town and in a 'healthy and airy' situation for private dwellings, but it was far from grand. It is now 248 Westgate Road, one of three houses where the street levels have been converted into a motor cycle shop, but to judge from number 252 a long flight of steps once led up to its front door on the first floor – where rock bands now practise. There was a cellar below, a second floor and attic rooms above with small dormers and sloping ceilings. Turner lived in it with his unmarried daughter Ann and perhaps a servant or two. The house must have felt lonely, though visitors would have brought it to life – and no doubt caused problems with sleeping arrangements in such a small place.[3]

But there is no certainty that Elizabeth Stevenson actually stayed in Cumberland Row, unless she did so on an unknown early visit. Local directories are unhelpful for the years 1829-32, but the Reverend William Turner's address is given as Clavering Place in the subscription list of Oliver's *A Plan of the Town and County of Newcastle* (preface dated 22 January 1831) and two letters of December 1831 are addressed to him there. The 1832 list of those entitled to vote in St John's Ward, which includes householders as well as freemen and must therefore have been issued after the Reform Act of June, also gives the Clavering Place address for our William Turner. (Other men of the same name in Newcastle can be eliminated.) This address makes sense of a retrospective passage in Elizabeth's letter to Harriet Carr, who lived in the Branch Bank of England premises on the corner: 'here [in Woodside] I cannot go to the window, and make signs to a nice kind little friend of mine to put on her bonnet, and dash and fly over to me … '. Cumberland Row is much too far away for signs to be seen.[4]

The best evidence, however, is the contribution book of the chapel, where Ann Turner's address is shown as Clavering Place between February 1829 and February 1832. In his *Reference to A Plan*, Oliver identified those who owned or leased property on the west side of Clavering Place, that is, in St John's Chapelry, as Sir Robert Shaftoe Hawks, Isaac Cookson senior, Miss Cath. Mary Longstaff, Mrs Margaret Pollock and the Trustees of the United Secesssion chapel. Across the roadway, but in St Nicholas' parish, were properties of Sir Robert Hawks again, Robert Hopper Williamson and, of all names, John Steavenson. This John, however, was a member of the Newcastle Literary and Philosophical Society from 1823-24 to about 1844. Williamson, Recorder of Newcastle till 1829, 'a Whig of the old school' who died in 1835, had long before given up his membership of the Society, because he 'dreaded (and not without reason) the levelling and disturbing influence of scientific discussion and observation'. The other men were all members in 1831. Presumably, any one of the houses on the west side of Clavering Place might have been Turner's temporary rental. He moved to Albion Street in October 1832, and by December of that year William Turner, Dissenting Minister of Albion

Street, is recorded as having voted for Sir Matthew Ridley and J. Hodgson, the Whig candidates.[5]

His temporary Clavering Place address, however, was one of the best within the city walls. It had been prosperous enough to display large, patriotic and tasteful illuminations on occasions like the coronation of George IV. Later in the nineteenth century the houses sank to the condition of warehouses, with rows of ham and sides of bacon displayed in their drawing rooms. Almost every building has nowadays been obliterated or rebuilt in the carefree English way, but the two great houses of Sir Robert and the Recorder on the east side have been restored. No houses remain of the west side, where William Turner seems to have lived with his daughter in the years when Elizabeth visited Newcastle after her father's death.[6]

Ann Turner has hardly done more than peep above the printed surface of history till recently. She had a cough – 'the most troublesome one I ever heard', wrote Elizabeth to Harriet Carr, 'and I used to fancy it must make Mr Turner feel very uncomfortable'. But apart from such trivia her character is revealed in two of her own letters that have survived.

The first, dated 10 October 1835, was written to her sister Mary Robberds in a flowing, almost calligraphic hand. At first it is full of family gossip – the tooth-ache of her nephew Charles, for instance, that affected his good looks and prevented him from being in Newcastle to hear a series of lectures on phrenology and animal physiology by George Combe. At this time Edinburgh was the centre of the new movement; Combe and other enthusiasts were striving to become a part of the British Association for the Advancement of Science. But more than the vogue for phrenology and physiognomy made appearances so important to Ann, who called Mrs Combe 'very ladylike', possessing 'quite the manner of one who has been accustomed to good society.' There follows a page of sympathy for her sister-in-law in Nottingham, Catharine Turner, whose mother was gravely ill but who would soon have to begin again with the 'bustle of the girls' in the school she kept; then news of the dissolution of a very short-lived partnership of solicitors, Henry Rankin and a Mr C., to the great surprise of the former, who had, according to Mr C., 'behaved in the most honourable and gentlemanly way'. One of Catharine's pupils was back in Newcastle under the care of Dr Headlam, Ann went on; he was optimistic about her 'remaining tendency to complaint in the spine' but she was unlikely to return to school till summer. Ann was also sorry to hear that William Holland was not well, 'a sad prospect for his poor wife.' And so it continues, with more news of people's health and sensible remarks on the problem of an audience for Combe's morning lectures. The subjects are various, but related in a composed and even manner, nothing like a 'heterogeneous mass of nonsense', as Henry Holland described one of Elizabeth Gaskell's letters.

One final piece of crossed writing in this missive to Mary Robberds is noteworthy:

Did you say anything to my [Bank?] about my money. I quite forgot to ask Mr Robberds what he thought of James Turner's proposal. I think William [her brother] rather preferred the idea of buying into the funds though the interest would be less because when once done any small sum might be added without any additional expence.[7]

A firm grip upon the money that would enable a single woman to live in a ladylike manner is even more evident in a letter Ann wrote to her father, known – even notorious towards the end of his career – for his generosity. His obituarist acknowledged that it had become a real weakness. 'Have you a penny upon you?' he is said to have asked a friend when approached by a beggar, 'I *owe* this poor man one.' Once Turner's nephew sent him a bank-note for £50, with the admonition, 'I fear from the account you give me that it will only assist in enriching some Knave, who has imposed upon your good-nature ... Do, pray, then learn to say – *No* – when you are asked to lend money or to become security for money'. James Aspinall Turner, a rich and convivial man who used to sing Lancashire comic songs at parties, was also a practical philanthropist. He persuaded Harriet Martineau to write her *Devotional Exercises for the Use of Young Persons* in 1823, supported Manchester's Ministry to the Poor and visited Irish families in 'the hollow low part of Oxford Road' on the left hand going from All Saints Church to town for the District Provident Society. It was a district 'almost exclusively inhabited by the lowest Irish', he claimed, 'one of the most unpromising sections' allotted by it. After initial failures in the sixteen houses assigned to him, he managed to persuade ten feckless inhabitants to lay aside part of their earnings. He believed he was entitled to preach to his uncle upon 'worldly wisdom, and business-like prudence' if upon nothing else.[8]

The opening of Ann's letter to her father defies summary, if its complexity is to be appreciated:

Saturday Morning May 21st [?1836]

My dear Father,

    I am afraid I am going to do, and to own that I have done, what you may consider very impertinent, but I hope you will forgive me if you *do* think me so. I went yesterday (as you once gave me leave to do at any time) to look for the date of some engagement in your pocket book; and there I saw an account of some transactions with regard to the New York Stock, which, together with a letter which was on your table (and which I acknowledge I ought not to have looked at as I saw you put it into your pocket without saying what it was about) leads me to fear that you have been obliged to sell this Stock, and, from your having transacted the business not through Mr Rankin or Mr Carwell, but through a person of the name of Bell, whom I do not know, I fear that it is sold to enable you to answer some obligation which he or some other needy person has prevailed upon your kindness to take upon yourself. If this be so, there will then only be the money in the Society' s hands remaining of what you had, and

I cannot help looking forward with some anxiety; not, my dear Father, on my own account, but on yours.

Should your life be prolonged as we *earnestly pray* that it may for *many* years to come; and you should feel your duties in the chapel too much for you, how grieved would your children be to see you compelled to continue them because you cannot do without the income arising from them: yet if you suffer unworthy or at best improvident persons to find that they can prevail upon you to pay their debts out of your own property, it will all dwindle away: and then what is to make your latter years comfortable.[9]

She is on mental and emotional tiptoes, but her syntactical control is complete, a fitting vehicle for her assurance and diplomatic skill. She confesses that she is not as good a manager as her dear mother had been, though she had followed her example in the only way that she 'ought not to have done so, in not keeping regular accounts'. She begs pardon for her presumption, reminding her father that letters about money were the only ones he never showed her and that he had thought her 'impertinent' when two years before, at the desire of her widowed sister-in-law Catharine, she had tried to discover how the £300 his congregation had invested in securities for him had gone. She makes a positive request (in the emollient form of 'Will you therefore excuse me for suggesting?') that he should transfer to his son William 'the shares in the Society and the remainder (if there be any) of this Stock'; he could then claim with perfect truth that he could not 'undertake to be answerable for *any* debts or bonds of any sort.' A good argument. An incontestable one follows:

I know indeed that in her ever kind thoughts for me as unmarried: my Mother once said something of considering this Stock as mine, but *that* I would never have considered it: but should insist upon an equal division between my brother, my *two* sisters and myself, of anything that should remain of your property: and should there not be enough to supply my wants I can by some means add to it. But I *cannot* bear the thought of *your* wanting the comforts whi<ch your> advancing years will require, or being dependent for them <on the> kindness of your friends ...

I have taken this way of addressing you because I feel that I can do it better than by speaking. I have only again to entreat your forgiveness and subscribe myself your affectionate and grateful daughter

Ann Turner

Direct evidence of Ann's influence on Elizabeth Stevenson is lacking, but she must have been one of the last people able to influence Harriet Martineau and was a mature woman of nearly forty when she became Elizabeth's companion. There are times when this letter reminds us of Mrs Catherine Stevenson's protestations, but there is more evidence on which to judge. The letters from daughter and nephew also demonstrate the truth of William Turner's reputation in Newcastle for impulsive acts of charity – indeed, they were probably preserved for this very reason. The Minute Book of his congregation shows that he attempted to give up his retirement pension in 1844 and in 1847. When he was about ninety years of age, in 1851, the death of his daughter Ann brought a suggestion that he should give up 'half of its former Amount, viz 30 Pounds per Annum'. The congregation, to its credit, refused on all three occasions.

There is a complication. This last offer actually came in a letter from William Turner of Halifax, announcing with respectable common sense that his father's 'present severe bereavement of course reduces in some measure his expenditure'. The merely human and the somewhat saintly are intertwined with considerable ingenuity by all concerned. A fine example is the long missive, neatly written in a small, elegant hand on a large folio sheet and signed 'Your affectionate Father Willm Turner', that he had sent to his daughter Mary on 29 January 1812. He had carefully waited till she had settled in as the wife of the Reverend John Gooch Robberds of Cross Street chapel in Manchester, he told her, but his heart had 'often of late engaged the head to meditate upon' her future. There was much stress upon the usual duties expected of a minister's wife (which Elizabeth Gaskell was to resist in her day), but he also adds that it was 'only fair and reasonable' for her to lay out the ministerial stipend as far as possible among the congregation that paid it: 'You will thus, as well as by a mutual interchange of good offices in other respects, strengthen your husband's interest with his people.' She inscribed this letter with affectionate irony, 'My Father's Pastoral Epistle'.[10]

When James Aspinall Turner had a '"mad scheme" (as some people term it)' of building an extensive cotton factory in Liverpool, he told his uncle he was ambitious for it to be as much of 'a *charitable Institution* in every true sense of the word, as any planners of an Infirmary'. At the same time he insisted that it must not affect his family and home life: 'I mean that if the tide were to wash it all away it would not be needful to give up a single comfort or convenience, or even luxury, which I now can provide for my family.' To regard luxuries as necessities is truly remarkable.[11]

Uncle Samuel Holland was a by-word in the family for his speculations. Catherine Winkworth was told that he had once been 'enormously rich, but had lost all his money at once'; his later enterprises always needed watching closely and were in fact being monitored. Swinton Colthurst Holland was quite unlike his brother. A prudent and exceptionally successful financier, his will shows the care he had taken to provide for his wife and daughters. His son Edward was on his way to becoming a great man in Gloucestershire, as we see from his splendid obituary in the *Gloucester Journal* for 9 January 1875. Samuel Holland junior, too, was a good provider. His mother and sisters were able to come to live with him at Plas yn Penrhyn in the late 1820s, followed by his father in 1832. About the time Elizabeth Stevenson visited Newcastle dispositions were being made for the support of wives and unmarried daughters right across the family, and even if Aunt Hannah Lumb protected her from worries on that account, the stay with Ann Turner could not have failed to bring home to her the position of single women. Ann and her sister-in-law Catharine were being forced to take such matters out of the open hands of William Turner, as far as they were able, and in this they had the support of their younger male relations. Nobody could have known that he was going to live to be nearly a hundred. He was in his last decade as a minister. Sensible arrangements had to be made.[12]

Until now, whatever degree of support the Hollands of Knutsford might have given the old dissenting chapel over the generations, Elizabeth had not lived in a minister's family. Nor, perhaps, had she met a character so firm in his own principles and central to the moral and intellectual life of a major town. Turner was known as well-informed, ready with information, with 'a quick eye for things as well as words'; not visibly studious, having an intellect 'more characteristically receptive and retentive than original and creative', a man 'the bent of whose mind was altogether to the practical and tangible, rather than to the speculative or mysterious'. Combing through the sale catalogue of his library produces little of what was then called polite literature: 'Thomsons Poems', 'Browne's Religio Medici', 'Butler's Hudibras', 'Rambler, 4 vols', 'Rogers' Human Life, a Poem', 1819, 'Shakespeare's Plays' and 'Aikin's Poems'. Samuel Butler's satire of scholastic arcana – 'Where Entity and Quiddity, / The ghosts of defunct bodies, fly' – was surely more to Turner's taste than Thomas Browne's suprarationality – 'I love to lose myself in a mystery, to pursue my reason to an *O altitudo!*'[13]

Did the young Elizabeth read Turner's copy of 'Thomas a Kempis in French'? Did she, like George Eliot, respond to its gospel of selfless renunciation? It seems unlikely, but at least she was not in the position of George Eliot's Maggie Tulliver, who had no sensible authority and guide in her youth. Turner was very far from being the sort of superior clergyman 'to be met in the best houses'. He would have ensured that a schoolgirl's 'soul untrained for inevitable struggles' became aware of the life led by others 'condensed in unfragrant deafening factories, cramping itself in mines, sweating at furnaces, grinding, hammering, weaving under more or less oppression of carbonic acid ...'.[14]

In *The Mill on the Floss* Mrs Tulliver's remaining 'bit o' pleasure' was to have her daughter's hair 'plaited into a coronet on the summit of her head', which George Eliot scorned as the 'pitiable fashion of those antiquated times'. In the wonderfully clear photograph of Elizabeth Stevenson, 'from the bust by D. Dunbar', which Ward used to illustrate volume 6 of the Knutsford Edition and dated 1829, a coronet of this kind can be seen.[15] David Dunbar the younger lived for some years in Newcastle and had worked with one of England's greatest and by then most expensive sculptors, Sir Francis Chantrey, known for his ability to train his assistants. The bust of Elizabeth Stevenson possesses the clarity and definition that Chantrey taught. Classical drapery on the shoulders is thrown back to reveal the slim column of the neck, head turned to one side as if to display the controlled looping of the hair about the ear and its gathering to a coronet. The pose also shows the smooth roundness yet strength of Elizabeth's features, like those of a young Roman matron.[16]

She had lighted upon a time and place where Northern Whigs and Radicals, celebrating the decade of political successes that culminated in the Reform Bill of 1832, were ensuring that their leaders were fittingly commemorated. Dunbar's practice in the north grew commensurately. Besides carving ornamental works in marble for Lord Durham, he modelled 'an admirable bust' of James Losh to be cut in marble for the Literary and Philosophical Society, according to a cutting from the *Tyne Mercury* of 31 May 1831 (repeated from the *Dumfries Courier*). Another cutting from the *Newcastle Courant* of 7 February 1832 refers to him as 'Mr D. Dunbar of this town'. His bust of Losh (incised 'Dunbar Sc.') now stands in the Society's main library. A cast of the bust of Lord Brougham, presented by G. Burnett on behalf of its sculptor, E. H. Baily, at an anniversary meeting in 1832, is now lost.[17]

Turner himself was memorialised. His strongly modelled bust, again by Baily, in 1829, stands today at the head of the entrance stairs to the comfortable library. Head and neck are bare, a loose cloth thrown about the shoulders in the Chantrey manner. It stands opposite a full-length portrait of him by his friend Andrew Morton; both works were commissioned by the Society as 'a lasting Memorial' of his 'eminent and gratuitous services'. In the portrait Turner, in dark gown and white bands, gazes calmly out at us as he points to an open book by his side. The anniversary meeting of 5 February 1833 also took note of a letter from David Dunbar about the present of a bust of Earl Grey, which in its *Report* keeps queer company with 'a cast taken from the skull of King Robert the Bruce, discovered at Dunfermline in the year 1819'. In the same year a 'large picture by Mr. Train, representing Highland Scenery, with the introduction of Macbeth and the Witches', was accepted for the committee room. Members of the Society were conscious not only of a decade of reform but also of forty years of personal achievement. They were in a sense claiming their own special place in the weirdly diverse ascent of the British nation.

In this context it is not surprising that Elizabeth was modelled in the first place and that Dunbar's bust made her appear to be a typical product of the enlightened society to which she belonged, proclaiming her in stone (or plaster) to be that 'noble-minded intelligent ingenuous creature' the Byerley sisters had striven to form. Underneath she was a more lively being. She took the opportunity of telling Harriet Carr (on 31 August 1831) that Mr Losh told her 'cousins in town that he thought [her] bust so very like Napoleon': the combination of her strong Holland nose and hair plaited like a laurel wreath gave real point to the joke.[18]

Science, history, classics and divinity (Belsham, Priestley, Aikin *et al.*) bulk very large amongst the hundreds of lots in the sale of Turner's books when he finally left Newcastle. Henry Holland's *Cheshire* and Stevenson's *Historical*

Sketch were there; so too are 'Greenhow on Vaccination' (1825) and Turner's own addresses and sermons on subjects ranging from inoculation against the regular scourge of smallpox in 1792 to *A Short Abstract of the Late Controversy in Calcutta, On the Doctrine of One God, the Father, and One Mediator, the Man Christ Jesus, As Professed by Native East Indians* (Newcastle, 1825), the first part of an account of a dispute with Baptist Missionaries by the first Indian to write at any length in English on important matters, Ram Mohun Roy. He was a remarkably independent Hindu thinker who became convinced that both Hinduism and Christianity had once been strictly monotheistic. His ideas were introduced to British Unitarians by Thomas Belsham. There was hardly any prose fiction in the sale, apart from 'Galt's Annals of the Parish, and seven other vols'. Notoriously, at the anniversary meeting of the Newcastle Literary and Philosophical Society on 1 March 1831, a proposal to purchase the Waverley Novels with author's introduction and notes was defeated, and in the following year a more wide-ranging amendment was carried: 'that it is not the plan of this Society to admit novels into the Library.'[19]

The title of a book by a Newcastle author of the previous century catches the eye in Turner's sale catalogue: 'Astell's (Mary) Essay in Defence of the Female Sex, 1697'. Unitarians were well aware of women's rights and potential. Turner began his 1812 'pastoral epistle' to Mary Robberds by noting that she had read several relevant books – John Aikin's 'judicious remarks', Thomas Gisborne's advice on 'the general duties of a wife' and Mary Wollstonecraft – and would therefore be aware of the mutual obligations in a marriage.

An independent-minded woman like Mary Wollstonecraft was greatly admired. She had been influenced by Richard Price and Hannah Burgh of the Newington Green community; there was a copy of her *Thoughts on the Education of Daughters, With Reflections on Female Conduct in the More Important Duties of Life* in the vestry library at Hanover Square, and Turner actually quoted from the famous *A Vindication of the Rights of Women* (1792) in his letter. Nevertheless, there is a powerful stress in the rest of his 'pastoral epistle' upon the particular duties of a *minister's* wife. She must know the congregation, avoid gossip, mediate, teach both her own family and the 'lower classes of the congregation, either in charity and Sunday schools, or otherwise', care especially for them as a woman ('See Mrs Cappe's excellent Paper on Female Visitors in Hospitals') and encourage her husband in his ministerial duties 'by cultivating a prevailing cheerfulness, both of the countenance and heart.' Elizabeth Stevenson, who was to become the 'dear colleague' of Mary Robberds, was being fostered by a man who was demanding and inflexible in certain crucial respects. However, he had a sense of humour and his wife's amusing scribble around the edge shows that life in his home was not always ruined by theory and ideology: 'I shall have plenty to say for Miss Aikin is coming on friday morning.' Lucy Aikin was a well known conversationalist.[20]

Turner's obituary in the *Gateshead Observer*, obviously written by an admirer, ends with amusing anecdotes. On one occasion, he was shown into a room where a little boy lay on the floor with the family Bible open before him looking for a psalm beginning with Q. Turner got down to help, 'and when the lady of the house entered the room, her pastor and her son were rolling on the carpet together', looking for the elusive psalm. On another occasion, he and Miss Helen Martineau came too late for a seat at a musical festival in St Mary's, Gateshead. The rector 'Mr Collinson, with a spice of that jocosity which belonged to both of them, deposited the Dissenting minister, with his fair associate, in the reading desk!'

Turner had made the acquaintance of the Reverend John Collinson, who came to Gateshead in 1810, by lending him a volume of the Fathers from his own library – he could hardly be patronised by a clergyman of the established church for lack of learning. Collinson, educated at Winchester and Oxford, wrote a number of books; his Bampton lectureship volume, *A Key to the Writings of the Principal Fathers of the Christian Church*, was published in 1813. In politics he was a conservative. Once, during the violence of a bitter strike and a time of mass ejections in May 1832, Archibald Reed, Mayor of Newcastle, had raised a force of special constables with firearms and cutlasses. They fired on the crowds of pitmen – with swan's shot, a large size – wounding several, but were eventually forced to send for a troop of Hussars and a company of infantry, which arrived with Collinson, a county magistrate, and arrested forty men. On the other hand, he had helped to found the Gateshead Dispensary and evidently did not share the animus of some against Unitarians. Elizabeth wanted to know more about the Collinsons, writing with the gay exaggeration that characterises the early letters to her friend Harriet Carr, 'I did so like the whole family, and took quite a fancy to Mrs Collinson who I do think is an angel inside and outside.' She no more considers the continuous struggles between masters and men in Tyneside than she touches seriously upon religious affairs, or mentions Dr J. Ramsay's medical practice amongst the poor of Sandgate when she reports that her 'dear Mrs Ramsay' had written to her of calling upon 'the little french bride, Mrs Wm Losh'.[21]

NOTES

1 NLPS: Moor Collection 23. i, 50, Henry Holland to WT, L Brook Street, 2 December [1826], and WT to Jane Turner, Manchester, 6 July 1822; WT, *A Sermon, Preached December 31, 1826 ... on the Lamented Death of Jane, the Wife of the Rev. W. Turner*, Newcastle, 1827; obit., *MR*, n. s. I, 1827, p. 126 (cp. 1855 in *DNB*). DWL has a presentation copy of the sermon, to Mrs S. Holland.

2 Middlebrook, *Newcastle*, p. 207; Mackenzie, *Newcastle*, I, pp. 194-5; *Oliver's New Picture*, pp. 73, 76, 126; *Losh Diaries*, II, p. 157. Photo of Westgate house in Chadwick, 1910, but not 1913.

3 When James Martineau was invited to stay with W. J. Fox, he was asked if he did 'not mind [Fox's] little girl [Eliza] sleeping in a corner of the same room' (MCO: MS Martineau 2, Coe transcripts, 13 December 1831).

4 W. Parson and W. White, *History, Directory, and Gazetteer ... of Newcastle-upon-Tyne*, I,

Leeds and Newcastle, 1827; TWA: 1787/115, Scrapbook, William Hutton to WT, Newcastle, 17 December 1831, and J. Collinson to WT, Gateshead, 6 December 1831; Chapple, 'Five early letters', pp. 10, 12; also, 'Life and liberty in Newcastle upon Tyne', *GSJ*, IX, 1995, pp. 66-9.

5 See TWA: 1787/18, Members' monthly contribution book; Oliver, *Reference*, St John's 179-83, St Nicholas' 154-6; Watson, *History*, p. 81; *Ordinary Members of the Society*, Newcastle, 1831; ECG to WT, 1 Dover Street, [6 October 1832], Chapple, 'Unofficial lives', in Parish, p. 108. I owe thanks to Margaret Norwell and Stephen Harbottle, and to Philip Yarrow and Frank Whitehead for close analysis of directories and voting lists.

6 *Obituaries of James Losh, John Bruce, Robert Hopper Williamson, and Robert Wasney*, Newcastle, 1836; *An Account of the Rejoicings, Illuminations, &c. &c. ... in Newcastle and Gateshead*, Newcastle, 1821 (both publ. by the Newcastle Typographical Society, establ. 1818); Charleton, *Newcastle Town*, p. 85.

7 Chapple, 'Five early letters', p. 10; AT to MR, Newcastle, 10 October 1835 (from photocopy). See Chapple, 'Unofficial lives', in Parish, p. 119, n. 9; Watson, *History of the NLPS*, pp. 231-2; Morell and Thackray, *Gentlemen of Science: Early Years*, pp. 278-80.

8 'Memoir of the late William Turner, of Newcastle', *CR*, n. s. XV, 1859, p. 457; NLPS: Moor Collection 49. ii, JAT to WT, Manchester, 27 May 1834; MCL: Herford, MS diary, I, p. 72; Lester Burney, *Cross Street Chapel Schools Manchester 1734-1942*, Didsbury, 1977, p. 21. Chadwick (1910, pp. 150-1) heard a similar story about WT in Newcastle.

9 For the whole text (alterations and insertions not noted) see Chapple, 'Unofficial lives', in Parish, pp. 114-16.

10 Chapple, 'Unofficial lives', in Parish, pp. 108-10, 113.

11 NLPS: Moor Collection 49. iii, JAT to WT, Manchester, 8 August 1836.

12 *Letters and Memorials*, I, p. 164. I am grateful to J. Haslem of the GL for a copy of EH's obit.; see also Joseph Stratford, *Gloucestershire Biographical Notes*, Gloucester, 1887, p. 337.

13 Messrs Small & Brough, *Catalogue of Valuable Books, Forming a Great Portion of the Library of the Rev. Wm. Turner*, Newcastle, 1842; 'Memoir of WT', *CR*, XV, 1859, p. 455. The author was evidently close to WT in Manchester (see p. 458).

14 Gordon S. Haight, *George Eliot & John Chapman, With Chapman's Diaries*, 2nd edn, New Haven, 1969, p. 174; *The Mill on the Floss*, book 4, chapter 3.

15 A plaster bust of ECS, given with a number of other items to Manchester Art Gallery in 1914, is now lost; two busts of Elizabeth were in Plymouth Grove's sale catalogue (Easson, p. 2). Manchester University possesses a marble replica, said to be by Hamo Thorneycroft and presented by Meta and Julia Gaskell (Chadwick, 1913, p. 312). Confusingly incised 'Elizabeth Gaskell' and 'D. Dunbar 1831', it is often reproduced; but cp. illustrs in Howitt, 'Stray notes', p. 610, and Leslie, 'Mrs Gaskell's house and its memories', p. 763 (both full face); Tooley, *Graphic* (London), 1 October 1910, Supplement ('in Edinburgh by Dundas, 1832'); J. A. Green, *A Bibliographical Guide to the Gaskell Collection in the Moss Side Library*, Manchester, 1911, opp. p. 30, and Chadwick, 1913, opp. p. 122. All show the whole Dunbar bust, which Green dates '1829'; it is recognisable by its decorated rather than plain pedestal. (MCL has sepia prints from four different angles.) Chadwick dates her illustr. Edinburgh, 1830, and also 1832 (p. 312), but cp. Uglow, p. 63.

16 Rupert Gunnis, *Dictionary of British Sculptors 1660-1851*, rev. edn, London, [1953]; Margaret Whinney, *Sculpture in Britain 1530-1830*, rev. John Physick, London, etc., 1988, pp. 416-22.

17 NLPS: grangerised *Reports*, 1830-32 (cp. *Losh Diaries*, II, p. 106n.). I owe thanks to the Librarian for additional information.

18 Watson, *History of the NLPS*, pp. 106-7; *Losh Diaries*, II, p. 74; Chapple, 'Five early

letters', p. 8; *Portrait*, illustr. 5. The basic strength of her character is best shown by Dunbar's bust and a late drawing by Samuel Lawrence.

19 TB review, *MR*, XIV, 1819, p. 569; Mingay, *Social History of Countryside*, pp. 72-6 (smallpox); Dermot Killingley, *Rammohun Roy in Hindu and Christian Tradition*, Newcastle upon Tyne, 1993, pp. 2, 136; Mudford, *British-Indian Relations*, pp. 112-16; *Macaulay Letters*, II, p. 47; Middlebrook, *Newcastle*, p. 167.

20 *Autobiography of Harriet Martineau*, I, p. 399 (for MW); WT to MR, Newcastle, 29 January 1812 (see Chapple, 'Unofficial lives', in Parish, pp. 108-10); G. J. Barker-Benfield, 'Mary Wollstonecraft: eighteenth-century commonwealthwoman', *JHI*, L, 1989, pp. 100-15; Knott, 'The vestry library', p. 159. In his postscript WT asks, 'Did you invite MAL?' (Marianne Lumb?).

21 Boase; *The Gateshead Observer*, 30 April and 7 May 1850 (photocopies courtesy of GCL); Manders, *History of Gateshead*, pp. 93, 137-8; Sykes, *Historical Register*, II, pp. 354-5; *Losh Diaries*, II, *passim*, but esp. pp. 109-10, 142; Chapple, 'Five early letters', pp. 4, 11.

22

Destiny

IT IS HARD to be sure just how far William Turner was expressing an idealised view of a minister's wife in his letter to Mary. His heavy stress upon her duties as a teacher and 'the management of certain public charities, as the Repository, the Lying In Charity &c' suggests that he had very practical expectations indeed, which, if it is possible to judge from Mary Robberds' memoirs, 'Recollections of a long life', suited his daughter's temperament. But the early letters by Elizabeth Stevenson are almost entirely concerned with the social life of prosperous families she had shared in Newcastle and was experiencing in the Liverpool area, together with the cultivation of her music, drawing and general reading, almost entirely light. She was presumably Unitarian in affiliation, but does not seem to have heard 'a serious call' at this stage of her life. And from the evidence, admittedly restricted, it seems highly improbable that she would ever consider any man resembling William Turner or James Currie or John Gooch Robberds as a potential husband.

The earliest letter known was addressed to a former acquaintance in Newcastle, a young lady called Anne Burnett, and mentions her mother and sisters.[1] In 1831 the Literary and Philosophical Society had five members named Burnett, two of whom belonged to Turner's congregation. George Burnett, agent, was the owner of a patent lead-shot manufacturing firm. The list of subscribers to Oliver's *Plan* places him in Gallogate. His short but warmly expressed obituary mentions that he had been a Vice-President of the Literary and Philosophical Society, 'greatly distinguished for extensive scientific attainments and kindly bearing'.[2] George Burnett junior belonged to Turner's Unitarian Tract Society in 1830, along with Emerson Charnley, John Marshall, W. A. Mitchell, Mrs Rankin, Alexander Reed and Miss Turner, and was one of those who with Turner, Collinson, Losh, Robert Stephenson and others signed a proposal to form a Natural History Society in 1829.[3]

The letter to Anne Burnett is conventional and demurely proper, thanking her for the present of a book. Newcastle was not without libraries, including one for music that announced in its 1824 catalogue, 'new publications continually added'. Turner's own vestry library contained books on 'all the principal subjects, relative to virtue and religion' rather than 'the politics and scandal of the day, or the trash of novels and romances', as he bluntly wrote in 1809, but in his congregation was John Marshall, a radical printer and bookseller, whose circulating library in 1827 had a subscription of 14s a year and contained 'over 8000 volumes in every department of science and literature'. This was as large as the library of the Literary and Philosophical Society of Newcastle. It did not exclude novels, so it is not surprising to find that Elizabeth had been able to read books by Edward Bulwer (later Bulwer-Lytton) and Susan Ferrier.[4]

She wrote to Harriet Carr that she had been reading Bulwer's novel *Paul Clifford* (a publishing event of 1830) once again and was delighted with it, as she was with all his writings, in spite of their 'alleged immorality'. In her letter of August 1831 this both neatly follows and probably accounts for the tone of a little fantasy that a dear friend had 'committed parricide, matricide and fratricide, and yet moves through life with the reputation of being a very tolerably amiable person'. *Paul Clifford*, which followed his *Pelham* and *The Disowned* of 1828, and *Devereux* of 1829, was the first of the so-called Newgate novels – largely set in the world of eighteenth-century criminals, and strongly influenced by Godwin's reformist ideas. It was an attempt to show that the law and the penal code were defective. Society rather than the criminal is at fault. Nevertheless Bulwer tells a lively and picaresque story, packed with underworld slang, quotations and allusions from a remarkable variety of sources, casuistical justification of criminals by tendentious but amusing parallels with nineteenth-century politicians, *roman-à-clef* elements (*The Asinæum*), dandiacal wit and cutting superiority. The verve of the telling is irresistible. Young Henry Solly was stirred to the depths of his soul by Bulwer's novels, inspired to 'some of the strongest and most passionate aspirations and resolves' he had ever experienced, for Bulwer's intellectual novels, whatever one thought of their morality, could hardly be called 'trash'.

Bulwer's *Eugene Aram* of 1832, which Elizabeth also read, is yet another kind of intellectual novel, very distinct from the usual run of romances. Soberly, even mystically, Bulwer investigates human character and individual psychology, conveys 'the character and tone' of its hero's mind in a book based upon the life of a notorious scholar-murderer of the previous century. But again there is a strange mingling of alien elements, like the farcical characterisation of Corporal Bunting and his cat Jacobina. (No more odd, perhaps, than the heated debates at an actual meeting of the British Association when a skull purporting to be Aram's was said to display *amativeness* so well developed that he could not have been a murderer.) If nothing else Bulwer would have introduced her to the 'multiform inconsistencies of human nature' that defeat a simplistic, rational approach to life; he would have tested the flexibility of her moral and emotional responses. In these early letters to her young Newcastle friend she was dismissive about the older books that 'we have all read hundreds of times – Such as odd volumes of Hume, Shakespeare, Tasso'.

Both girls were evidently keeping up-to-date with current works, not only the romances of the advanced, sophisticated and inimitable Bulwer, but also novels by the more straightforward and accessible Susan Ferrier. By the time she got back to Knutsford in the autumn of 1831 Elizabeth was reading the last of her three novels, *Destiny*, published anonymously in that year, after *Marriage* in 1816 and *The Inheritance* in 1824. The Edinburgh authoress was for Walter Scott one of those highly talented women whose success, he confessed in the introduction to *St Ronan's Well* (1832), had made the novel of modern life almost exclusively their own province. Elizabeth had just finished reading *Destiny* for the third time – 'and now I think I have done my duty by it'. The tone of this throwaway comment is hard to judge. Could she have met Susan Ferrier in Edinburgh?[5]

Destiny; Or, The Chief's Daughter opens strongly. Eccentric Scottish characters of the Highlands are portrayed with considerable if broad humour:

> His hands and feet were in every body's way: the former, indeed, like huge grappling irons, seized upon every thing they could possibly lay hold of; while the latter were commonly to be seen sprawling at an immeasurable distance from his body, and projecting into the very middle of the room, like two prodigious moles, or bastions.

Ferrier handles comic characters and farcical incidents well, 'with a remarkably wide range of techniques', as Wendy Craik has justly remarked. Even the less successful serious material must have had unusual resonances for Elizabeth, conventional though it was.

The central figure, a widowed Highland Chief, had a shy, repressed and delicate daughter, who had never known her mother. His speedy second marriage brought an unsatisfactory and snobbish English wife and the rivalry of a step-sister, 'an uncommonly pretty child, with a skin of dazzling whiteness, a profusion of golden ringlets, large blue eyes, a sylph-like figure, and an air of distinction'. There is even a fine young man who became a sailor on a ship 'ordered to cruize in distant seas, and in another hemisphere', with the inevitable result: 'a plank, on which were a few letters of her name, and a shattered boat, had been picked up, and all was told.' There is some parallel with William Stevenson's second marriage, if only in the eyes of one who had been an unhappy child. And had the free merchant in Calcutta ever written again to his family? Was John Stevenson still alive? Elizabeth's letter to Harriet makes nothing of all this, but it is clear that much of her Newcastle and earlier correspondence is lost.[6]

During these years she was reading a miscellany of other recent literature – J. C. Spurzheim on phrenology and 'Percy Anecdotes of Enterprize', for instance. The former, the third edition in English of whose *Phrenology* had appeared in 1826, was a pioneer in the European vogue for a new science that did not, in the event, succeed, though phrases like 'a bump of location' entered the language. Edinburgh, where a *Phrenological Journal* had been established in 1823, was a centre of argument and research. The latter belongs to a series of twenty little duodecimo volumes collected by J. C. Robertson and Thomas Byerley, published under the pseudonyms of Sholto and Reuben Percy between 1821 and 1823. The third deals with youth and enterprise, its second part being dedicated to the memory of the explorer Mungo Park. It is rather old-fashioned. Military and naval men, classical figures, Columbus, Joan of Arc and even a Royal Female Pirate (Avilda of Gothland) are included, but Sir Richard Arkwright is the sole representative of industry and commerce.

Elizabeth also refers to the *Memoirs of Count [Chamans de] Lavalette*, which appeared in two volumes in 1832, as a book she and aunt Lumb wished to read. Apparently Mrs Lumb had known both Michael Bruce and John Hely-Hutchinson, though it is not yet known exactly when and where she met them. They had been involved in one of the most romantic and sensational incidents of the allied occupation of Paris in 1815. Lavalette, who had been in charge of the postal service during Napoleon's 'hundred days', was condemned to death, but his wife took his place in the condemned cell whilst he escaped in her clothes. Bruce, Hely-Hutchinson and R. T. Wilson then helped him escape to Holland in an English uniform. They were later tried, but received derisory sentences. Sadly, the strain caused Lavalette's wife to lose her reason.[7]

A pamphlet by Edward Gibbon Wakefield, *Facts Relating to the Punishment of Death in the Metropolis* (1831), written out of the experience in Newgate of three years' imprisonment for inducing by lies and force an heiress first to accompany him to Manchester and then to marry him at Gretna Green in 1826, excited a good deal of popular attention. 'Can any good thing come from such a polluted source?', Elizabeth asks Harriet censoriously, failing to apply Bulwer's 'theoretical history' and justify Wakefield's crime, but she was writing from Woodside across the Mersey from Liverpool where Ellen, the daughter of William Turner of Pot Shrigley in Cheshire, had been at school. The Samuel Hollands would be well acquainted with the scandalous details.[8]

Her indignant reference to the compensation awarded at Winchester Assizes against William Bingham Baring, who had been accused of mistreating a Mr and Mrs Deacle during a riot – a case raised in the House of Commons in July 1831 and exciting what Macaulay called the 'low rancour' of the *Times* – also had family associations. William Bingham Baring was the shy eldest son of her dead uncle Swinton's partner, who became the second Lord Baring. His father had purchased a good deal of Hampshire.[9] Her remarks on Mrs Trollope's *Domestic Manner of the Americans*, a best-seller of 1832, spring from a similar source – the shipping and religious connections of the Samuel Hollands in Liverpool. She quips that Mrs Trollope's book had won her heart by abusing Americans. 'I don't mean abusing their more solid moral qualities', she hastily adds, 'but their manners, which I have always disliked.'

Liverpool's wealth and commerce had impressed a future American president, James Buchanan, who had been made welcome by its business community. 'Our national character now stands high', he noted in his diary for 4 May

1832, 'notwithstanding the efforts which have been made to traduce it.' But when Macaulay's sisters were staying with the J. Croppers at Dingle Bank in Liverpool in June 1832, he rattled off a series of comical questions, 'Have you been on board any vessels? Have you talked to any Yankees? Do you find them as agreeable as those whom Mrs. Trollope describes? Do they spit? Do they turn up their heels? Do they keep on their hats in your presence? Have either of you played Miss Clarissa to the Mr. Smith of any of Mr. Cropper's Captains?' Cropper, Benson and Co. had established the first regular packet service to America. Liverpool would be *the* place to meet Americans. It is hardly surprising to find that Hawthorne, who came to Liverpool as American consul in 1853, dined with Charles Holland and met many of Elizabeth Gaskell's acquaintances, becoming like her a good friend of the Unitarian Henry Arthur Bright.[10]

On the other hand, Mrs Trollope herself, for all her bias against the generality of Americans, went out of her way in her chapter on literature and the fine arts to praise William Ellery Channing as 'a writer too well known in England to require my testimony to his great ability'. The sale catalogue of the Gaskells' books in 1914 mentions his name again and again. J. S. Mill was another of his English admirers and Lucy Aikin corresponded with him for almost twenty years. Mrs Trollope had even been told that nearly all distinguished men of letters in America were Unitarians. The transatlantic connection through letters and publication was powerfully reinforced in Liverpool during the early decades of the century. Harvard had been Unitarian since 1805, when Henry Ware was elected Hollis Professor of Divinity in succession to a moderate Calvinist and began formal graduate instruction in divinity. The future Harvard Professors George Ticknor and Edward Everett landed in Liverpool on their way to the University of Göttingen in 1815 and met William Roscoe.[11]

A stream of visitors came to the Unitarian chapels in Paradise Street and Renshaw Street, the latter a chapel descended from the old Presbyterian body meeting at Toxteth Park, once under the pastorship of a Reverend Richard Mather, who had established an early transatlantic connection by emigrating to America. He was the father of Dr Increase Mather and grandfather of Dr Cotton Mather of Boston, Massachusetts, the man denounced so powerfully in Charles Wentworth Upham's lectures on witchcraft – a book later exploited by both Gaskell and Hawthorne. The pastor of the Boston Second Church (Unitarian), Henry Ware junior, recently appointed Professor of pulpit eloquence and pastoral care at Harvard Divinity School, came over in April 1829 and wrote home to Andrews Norton, Dexter Professor of sacred literature, about the organisation of the British and Foreign Unitarian Association. (Norton, called the 'Unitarian Pope', was the father of Charles Eliot Norton, one of Mrs Gaskell's best friends.) Ware's colleague in Boston for a short time, Ralph Waldo Emerson, visited Liverpool in 1833 and naturally went to hear William Hincks, James Martineau and John Yates preach. Yates, he thought, preached by far the best sermon he had heard in England. Emerson confided to Martineau, whose spirit was already beginning to detach itself from older forms of Unitarianism, how he had felt impelled to resign his own ministry.[12]

Renshaw Street chapel was Samuel Holland's place of worship. Hawthorne described it as neat, plain and small, with 'a kind of social and family aspect', its vestry full of old, rather mildewed theological works, its unpicturesque little yard with flat gravestones lost amongst city buildings. 'Nevertheless', he continued, 'there were perhaps more names of men generally known to the world, on these few tombstones, than in any other church-yard in Liverpool – Roscoe, Blanco White, and the Reverend William Enfield, whose name has a classical sound in my ears, because, when a little boy, I used to read his Speaker, at school.' *The Speaker* was an anthology of verse and prose for the young that remained popular for several generations.

In the early 1820s the chapel experienced the exciting ministry of George Harris, a social reformer and pacifist who had helped Radicals fly to America after Peterloo. His fierceness in controversy caused the walls of the chapel to be chalked with slogans like 'Harris kill the Devil' and 'No Hell fire', and inspired trenchant counter-sermons on the eternity of future punishment at St Andrew's church. Things then settled down. By 1831 John Hincks was minister, but he died on 5 February, and there was a four-month interregnum with the Reverend John Palmer before the congregation invited a man who had been pastor at Toxteth Park for the past two years, John Hamilton Thom. Samuel Holland was in the chair at his confirmation meeting on 29 May 1831. Thom, converted by the writings of Channing and with Martineau a propagandist for a more spiritualised and emotional faith, was to become a highly influential Unitarian minister in the next few decades. He preached William Roscoe's funeral sermon in July 1831 and started his ministry at the chapel on 6 August.[13]

Elizabeth was still in Woodside at the beginning of September. Notwithstanding her Unitarian connections and her own uncle's importance at Renshaw Street, she does not mention any American visitors, the change of ministers or anything else about the plain little chapel. The religious scene in Liverpool seems to be as unimportant to her as that of Newcastle. The five early letters to Harriet Carr are long and spontaneously written, speaking of what must have been in forefront of her mind. They are stuffed with light gossip and social detail – her attempt to purchase fine cloth in Liverpool for covering stools and astonishment when the shopman asked if she wanted it 'for *pantaloons!*', a meeting at Dr Thomas Traill's with one of the survivors of the loss of the Liverpool-Beaumaris steam-packet in a gale, the dinner-table chat about an acquaintance of Harriet Carr, Harriet Tidy (the future novelist, Mrs Harriet Ward, whose life and career so strangely paralleled Elizabeth Gaskell's), a postponed regatta. There is no indication that Dr Traill, for example, was the president of the Liverpool Institution and was vitally concerned with the progress of its Academy and exhibitions of painting. Relatively trivial matters appear to concern her far more than art, let alone

Renshaw Street chapel, its new minister, its services, its paid singers and brand-new organ.[14]

Ministers' salaries at the end of the eighteenth century tended to be lower than those in the professions and commerce – from about £30 to £100 per annum, needing to be supplemented by school or private teaching for a comfortable middle-class style of living. During the next century noncon-formist ministers in cities like Manchester might gain as much as £400 per annum from their congregations, though this was exceptional. Hanover Square chapel in Newcastle was more modest: by 1841 it provided a salary of £120. Despite gifts and other sources of income, such as his lectureship and a school when his children were young, William Turner was nothing like as well off as his friends James Losh, who prospered greatly as barrister and man of business, and George Carr the banker, still being paid £1000 a year in his early seventies. Of the seven Carrs who were in 1831 members of the Newcastle Literary and Philosophical Society only George Carr was called Esq., as were James and William Losh. Their minister and lecturer, William Turner, was nevertheless a force in their circle, as Losh's diaries very clearly indicate, and his relations welcome in good Newcastle society.

In her early letters to Harriet Carr Elizabeth hardly resembles what we know of Ann Turner at a similar age. She gives a strong impression that marriage was her preferred destiny, emphasising her own social standing and connections. 'I never knew such a week as this has been for marriages', she cried in October 1831; 'no less than three intimate friends of ours are become fiancées during this last fortnight, and what is even more extraordinary I am not one of the number.' On the slight grounds that retirement at Woodside provided no news she indulged in a lengthy account of Napoléon-Achille Murat, son of the King and Queen of Naples in the first decade of the century, where Swinton Holland's wife Anne had seen 'a great deal' of him – 'then a very fine young man of 18, or 19, and a great favourite with his uncle Napoleon'. Now an American citizen, he had come to London with his wife and Queen Hortense, visiting very few people – though her cousins had seen 'a great deal of them'.

This is rather naive. The more worldly-wise Charles Greville writes of 'a vulgar-looking, fat man with spectacles, and a mincing, rather pretty pink and white woman, his wife.' The man, he was told, was the nephew of Napoleon, the woman a granddaughter of Washington. 'What a host of associations, all confused and degraded!' was his sour comment. But other allusions in Elizabeth's letters – to names like Brandling, Headlam, Waldie, Reed and Rankin of Newcastle, or Traill and Tobin of Liverpool – prove that she moved amongst those provincial families that in an age of political and social reform could at last provide an appropriate number of members of parliament, mayors, founders of institutions and patrons of charities. She might even have known the traveller in the Orient who had discovered a rich goldmine and later became deputy-lieutenant and high sheriff of the county of Durham, John

Williamson of Whickham, the second son of R. H. Williamson.

'How did Mr John Williamson's bachelor dinners go off?', she asks Harriet in her letter of 31 October 1831. 'Has "nothing come of it", to use a *pussy* expression. Worthy sisterhood of cats – where are ye … '? He died a bachelor, but it is only natural that Elizabeth gave as much attention to balls, races, fêtes, shows and regattas where young women could see and be seen as she did to books and reading:

> Miss Tobin *is* the most beautiful by far in spite of Miss Jaques assertion that there was a younger sister more beautiful – I saw then all at the flower show, and admire the eldest far the most in spite of her melancholy, abstracted look. I wonder what you are doing tonight; I dare say if the truth were known you are talking of your dresses for the ball – how I should like to take a peep at you. I like the sound of your hair tied up on each side; it sounds a little bit like those portraits of Madame de Grignan, put as a frontispiece to the Second volume of Madame de Sévigné – eternal woman – how often I have begun both her and Sir Charles Grandison, and never finished either.[15]

The unfailing display of female beauty in society, so momentous for women's marriage chances, was finding new outlets. She affects to wish that 'the name of bazaar, like that of MacGregor might perish for ever', but it is possible that she went to the first bazaar ever held in Newcastle, on 6 October 1830, at the new music hall by permission of Richard Grainger for the benefit of infant schools. Fashionable ladies she knew well ran the various stalls, including Mrs T. E. Headlam, Mrs George Carr and the Misses Carr. 'A friend to early education', Mrs Burnett, sent a donation of two guineas. Elizabeth then lightly claimed that a ball projected in Liverpool was a more sensible way than a bazaar to do something for charity, and begged for details of a forth-coming event in Newcastle – dresses, flirtations, 'and what people's partners said to people, & what people said to people's partners.'[16]

Outside the pleasure-domes, however, ancestral voices were prophesying pestilence. In June 1831 a Central Board of Health under the chairmanship of Sir Henry Halford was set up to advise the Privy Council about Asiatic or Indian cholera then sweeping from lands where it was endemic across Russia and Europe. As early as July Lady Holland in Kensington was terrified and wished to know why a cordon of troops could not be simply placed around Glasgow, where she was convinced the disease had struck, to prevent all communication. She even wrote to Lord Lansdowne asking him to recom-mend the best cholera doctor he knew. In rural Knutsford on 20 October 1831 Elizabeth told Harriet Carr of the recovery of Canning's beautiful daughter, Lady Clanricarde, from '*real*' cholera', on the authority of two famous physicians, Sir Matthew Tierney and Sir Henry Halford, information which must have come to her through Henry Holland, a member of the Central Board of Health. Certainly cholera reached Sunderland by October, if not before.

Its symptoms were terrible. Two Newcastle doctors, Thomas Greenhow and W. R. Clancey, published small volumes on its treatment (mustard emetics, tobacco enemas, tincture of opium and the like), but its nature was unknown and its transmission unpredictable. Henry Holland's December 1831 letter to his uncle Turner is full of questions. Contagionists asserted that it was transmitted by persons or even goods and merchandise; their opponents theorised about a miasma actually generated by decaying organic refuse; a third group, called contingent contagionists, claimed that predisposing causes like filth, dirty water and human intemperance were the conditions in which a contagious disease could flourish. Eccentric thinkers went so far as to speculate about tiny animalculae invisible to the naked eye, but the cholera bacillus transmitted in contaminated food or water was not discovered till fifty years later. 'The disease spreads gradually in all directions in town and country, but without appearing like an epidemic', wrote Greville thoughtfully; 'it is scattered and uncertain; it brings to light horrible distress.'[17]

The threat hardly perturbed Elizabeth Stevenson in the autumn of 1831. She was more concerned with a promised drawing from Harriet, copying songs ('Isle of Beauty' was a great favourite) and waltzes, and teaching her cousins Mary, Bessy, Lucy and Susan Holland to dance the mazurka. Aunt Swinton and cousin Charlotte Holland had left Knutsford by 20 October, Ann Turner was on the point of leaving and two of Peter Holland's daughters were going to London to join Henry and Charles Aikin Holland in Brook Street after Christmas. She sounds resigned. She would be 'very regular, & quiet', ready to settle down with her books, writing things and 'helps to learning', which she herself puts in slightly distasteful inverted commas, far from the balls and flirtations of Newcastle, the regattas and dinners of Liverpool. 'This week is a gay one with us being our Sessions week', she wrote with light sarcasm, 'and I dare say if I went into the town I might meet two people, and if so I should return and say "How very gay Knutsford is today"!'

Her clever cousin Henry Holland, who had once been committed to a commercial career with Messrs Greaves in Liverpool, found life there intellectually deficient. Knutsford was even worse. 'I felt a reluctance to taking up the pen in an obscure country town', he wrote in his very first letter to Maria Edgeworth in 1809; and in 1819 he exclaimed with some degree of flattery, 'I cannot but cordially rejoice in everything which relieves to him [Peter Holland] & my sisters the dull, unsocial uniformity of life, in a small country town – with this feeling, I have hailed many things much less interesting to them than your visit; & with this feeling, I would beg you for all future time, not to pass near them, without recurring to them this pleasure.' He never seems to have stayed there, or in Newcastle, for long. He had a restless, efficient intellect, which demanded continuous nourishment. His ambition and sense of his own potential was strong from an early age. It led to a career on a national stage, where he could note in an offhand manner, 'I stopped Wordsworth some time ago, *sonnetizing* to himself, & probably of himself, in Berkeley Square.'

Elizabeth's aunt Swinton Holland, too, would have given her a taste of a far more sophisticated life in London. Her old schoolfellow Louisa was evidently blossoming at the house in Park Lane. Cousin Edward was planning his very grand establishment at Dumbleton in Gloucestershire. His sister Charlotte would soon marry into the same banking family, the Isaacs of Boughton near Worcester. But Elizabeth's main contacts were in these years amongst her Liverpool and Newcastle connections. That scene was to change radically, but not in a way that capitalised socially upon her grand relations in the metropolis, or in Gloucestershire and Worcestershire.[18]

In her last letter of 31 August 1831 from Woodside she had written with a mock-heroic fling that she would probably 'enlighten Manchester' with the sunshine of her countenance before the winter was over. The joke depends on the fact that factory smoke then formed a complete cloud over the town despite legislation against it, leading to the formation of a society for the preservation of ancient footpaths in 1826 to ensure public 'lungs' in the country about the town, including the area extending south towards Knutsford and Cheshire.[19]

Until recently nothing was known about Elizabeth's visits to Manchester, though it has been plausible enough to assume that she met the Reverend William Gaskell, a Warrington man, in the home of his senior colleague at Cross Street chapel, John Gooch Robberds and his wife Mary, Turner of Newcastle's daughter. But by this time they were no longer living out in the country at Greenheys beyond Chorlton-Row, as Chadwick (and the beginning of *Mary Barton*) has led everyone to believe.[20] On their marriage in 1811 they had taken a house in Mosley Street, number 42, where Robberds in the usual way kept a school for boys. His health gave way after about ten years, and in order to live economically upon a single salary he moved with his wife and two little boys, Charles and John, to the rustic district given its name from a house De Quincey's father had built there in 1791, 'Greenhay', near a hamlet called Greenhill and about a mile southwards from the city proper. But they stayed in Greenheys for no more than three years in the mid-1820s, according to Mary Robberds's later memoirs. 'Soon however a change came', she wrote, 'another little boy was born, and our friends persuaded us to remove to a larger house near the Town in Grosvenor Square.'[21]

They went to a new house on the south-eastern edge of the town, by Oxford Road, one of the long, new streets running out from St Peter's Square towards the boundary of Lancashire and over into Cheshire. Grosvenor Square was intended to be the centrepiece of a new and exclusive suburb. The building of a central feature in the Grecian style, All Saints' church, was completed by 1820. Spacious streets were laid out, intended for the houses of prosperous inhabitants, but by the following year only a short row of five substantial houses at the Ormond Street end had been completed, one of which was inhabited by an expert on smoke pollution, the scientist Robert

Angus Smith. On Oxford Road itself, a Georgian terrace looking out over the square was built in the 1820s, but the city was advancing more rapidly than expected into the fields and there was no more residential development. Like the bricks of London in Cruikshank's famous satirical engraving of 1826, Manchester was going out of town – which meant a chaos of belching kilns, noise and building materials. The Robberds moved to Grosvenor Square in the summer of 1826. In 1831 a new town hall was opened there and the district became known officially as Chorlton-upon-Medlock. The Robberds were still living in the square twenty years later, not quite as far out as the first married home of William and Elizabeth Gaskell at 1 Dover Street, the 'end house next Oxford Rd on N. side' Ward was told.[22]

There could have been an earlier meeting between Elizabeth and William through Henry Green, who had studied for the Unitarian ministry with the exciting George Harris at Renshaw Street chapel in Liverpool from 1819-22, graduated from Glasgow with William Gaskell in 1825 and preached for a year at Hanley, near Newcastle-under-Lyme. Holbrook Gaskell met him at the Liverpool house of R. Yates in the summer of 1826, together with William Turner III, still a tutor at York, and one of its prize students, Edward Higginson. Not long after, in January 1827, Green was appointed to the old dissenting chapel at Knutsford, where Elizabeth is said to have taught in the Sunday school. William could have been invited to preach there in the years before he himself was called to Cross Street in 1828.[23]

That William definitely courted Elizabeth at the Robberds's house, however, is proved by a young man's diary.[24] Edward Herford had come to live and study Greek, Latin and French with Robberds for two years in early 1830, when he was about fifteen. By this time Mary Robberds was like Harriet Martineau, dependent upon an ear trumpet – 'the trial of my life', she called it. It was nevertheless a lively household in his youthful account. In later years he was to become Manchester city coroner and, like many other dissenters as they rose in society, 'a churchman'. In those days he was a rather callow youth in his teens training for the law, who attended Cross Street chapel, read assiduously – *Eugene Aram* aroused predictable ecstacies – loved parties and entertained radical notions, disagreeing with his father and the Worthington family, 'who are all as high church and king as possible considering they go to chapel'. Mr Robberds, who had signed a protest in 1819 against the behaviour of the authorities at Peterloo, also refused to hold a special service at Cross Street on a government appointed fast day: 'If Government dictates to us when we are to worship, it may also command the "where" and the "how".'[25]

On a less exalted level, there are references to Elizabeth Stevenson in the diary from 16 January 1832. What seems to be her first appearance on page 9 is only too appropriate for a young woman like Isobel Archer – a vivid figure 'bent upon its fate – some fate or other; *which*, among the possibilities, being precisely the question', as Henry James put it:

Tonight the question was posed by Miss Stephenson What single word best expresses the qualities most desire in a woman? What would any of us if he were a woman prefer to be noted? She said loveable and Mrs R agreed with her. John and I thought 'sweet' would best express that sense. When Mr R came in to supper we asked him. He said 'Quiet'.

Mr Robberds was known for his jests as well as his rectitude. Elizabeth would be sweet and quiet enough, but she would achieve her own definition of what it meant to be lovable – where her destiny henceforth lay for many years, in clerical circles, improbable as this seemed at the time. The richer Holland cousins might have been like Henry Solly's brothers and not thought much of the match. It is possible that Elizabeth Gaskell was recalling for Mrs Browning what some of them had said or hinted about her imprudence at the time. Nevertheless, William had been appointed to the most famous Unitarian chapel in the north of England. Cross Street's ministers were expected to be special people – classically educated, intellectual, energetic in religious leadership, fully involved in charities and civic affairs. William had money of his own, inherited from his father; his immediate family were provided for by the father's will. We do not know of any particular incumbrances. And on the day after Edward Herford reported Elizabeth's question, he was able to record, 'I saw Paganini to day in King St.' Miss Stevenson was not going to visit in a cultural desert.[26]

NOTES

1 BPMH: ECS to Anne [Burnett], 'Thursday Eveng'. Now possible to date [c. June 1831], assuming only one visit to Woodside in 1831. Qu. in full, *Portrait*, pp. 11-12. Yarrow, 'Mrs. Gaskell and Newcastle', p. 141, discusses possible acquaintants at Bensham (across the Tyne): the families of Joseph Watson and Charles G. Allhusen.

2 TWA: 1787/12, WT, endpaper list, 'Minister's Book of Members'; Seed, 'The role of Unitarianism', p. 241; J. F. ed., *Obituaries of Some ... Distinguished Members of the NLPS ... 1844-1851*, Newcastle-upon-Tyne, 1857, p. 8.

3 *A List of the Members of the Newcastle Unitarian Tract Society, November, 1830*, Newcastle, [1830]; T. R. Goddard, *History of the Natural History Society of Northumberland, Durham and Newcastle upon Tyne 1829-1929*, Newcastle, pp. 32-3. A letter from G. Burnett jr to Turner about the presentation of 'a picture of the late Mr Gray' has survived: [Lead Works?], 2 April 1833 (NLPS).

4 Middlebrook, *Newcastle*, p. 154; Knott, 'The vestry library', pp. 157-8, 161; thesis, p. 311.

5 Chapple, 'Five early letters', pp. 9-10, 13, 17; Prothero and Bradley, *Arthur Penrhyn Stanley*, I, p. 206 (British Association, 1838); Solly, 'These Eighty Years', I, pp. 133-4; Bulwer, *Pelham*, ed. Jerome J. McGann, Lincoln, Neb., 1972, pp. xx-xxv. I have not read two other novels she mentions, William Massie's *Sydenham* (1830) and *Alice Paulet* (1831).

6 *Destiny*, Edinburgh, 1831, I, pp. 22-3, 46, 276-8; Wendy Craik, 'Susan Ferrier', *Scott Bicentenary Essays: Selected Papers*, ed. Alan Bell, Edinburgh and London, 1973, p. 325; *Sir Walter Scott on Novelists and Fiction*, ed. Ioan Williams, London, 1968, p. 428.

7 Chapple, 'Five early letters', pp. 3, 8, 10-11; M. D. R. Leys, *Between Two Empires: A History of French Politicians and People Between 1814 and 1848*, London, New York, Toronto, 1955, pp. 61-2, 76. For Hely-Hutchinson see *DNB. A Full Report of the Trial*, by Wilson, appeared in 1816.

8 W. Beamont, *A History of the House of Lyme*, Warrington, 1876, pp. 200-4; Axon, *Annals of Manchester*, p. 171; Slugg, *Manchester Fifty Years Ago*, p. 34; Uglow, pp. 43, 65, 630.

9 See Ziegler, *Barings*, pp. 86-8, 90-1, 118, 158; Fred Kaplan, *Thomas Carlyle: A Biography*, Cambridge, etc., 1983, pp. 443-5 (illustr.).

10 Chapple, 'Five early letters', pp. 11, 17; *James Buchanan's Mission to Russia 1831-1833, Works*, II, repr. New York, 1970, pp. 184-5; *Macaulay Letters*, II, pp. 74-5, 136; Anne H. Ehrenpreis, 'Elizabeth Gaskell and Nathaniel Hawthorne', *NHJ*, 1973, pp. 90, 93-4; Hawthorne, English *Notebooks*, pp. 36, 103; Raymona E. Hull, *Nathaniel Hawthorne: The English Experience, 1853-1864*, Pittsburg, 1980, pp. 41-4, 275, 282.

11 *Memoirs of Lucy Aikin*, ed. Le Breton, p. xxvii; Howe, *Unitarian Conscience*, pp. 4-20; David B. Tyack, *George Ticknor and the Boston Brahmins*, Cambridge, Mass., 1967, p. 44.

12 David Thom, 'Liverpool churches and chapels, etc.', *HSLCPP*, V, 1853, pp. 15-23; Ehrenpreis, 'Elizabeth Gaskell and Nathaniel Hawthorne', pp. 99-102; Carpenter, *Martineau*, pp. 71, 155-6, 163; *DAB; The Journals and Miscellaneous Notebooks of Ralph Waldo Emerson*, ed. Alfred R. Ferguson, Cambridge, Mass., IV, 1964, pp. 79-80, 236; Ralph L. Rusk, *The Life of Ralph Waldo Emerson*, New York and London, 1949, p. 196; Fryckstedt, pp. 64, 71.

13 Hawthorne, *The English Notebooks*, p. 50; McLachlan, *Warrington Academy*, p. 69; Evans, *Renshaw Street Chapel*, pp. 13-17, 20-3, 31-4; Davis, *Manchester College*, pp. 45-6.

14 Jeanette Eve, 'Elizabeth Stevenson and Harriet Carr: a note', *GSJ*, V, 1991, p. 75; *Liverpool Mercury*, 26 August 1831; *Memories of Sir Llewelyn Turner*, ed. Vincent, p. 174; Darcy, *Fine Arts in Lancashire*, pp. 36, 42, 51. See also *The Gladstone Diaries*, ed. Foot, I, *passim*, for identifications.

15 Seed, 'The role of Unitarianism', pp. 291-2; Chapple, 'Five early letters', pp. 4, 9, 11, 14; *Greville Journal*, I, pp. 118-19; Yarrow, 'Mrs. Gaskell and Newcastle', p. 142; 1850 obit. (aged sixty) in William Bourn, *Annals of the Parish of Wickham*, 1902, pp. 130-1. See also Darcy, *Fine Arts in Lancashire*, p. 131, for Sir John Tobin's important collection of illuminated MSS and his daughter Sarah's 'cultivated understanding' of art.

16 Chapple, 'Five early letters', pp. 3, 6-7; Sykes, *Historical Register*, II, pp. 282-3; Gary R. Dyer, 'The "Vanity Fair" of nineteeth-century England: commerce, women and the East in the Ladies' Bazaar', *NCL*, XLVI, 1991-92, pp. 208-9. *OED* gives 1816, 'Soho Bazaar', for the first usage in this sense. For her unexpected absence from the Grand Anti-Corn Law League Bazaar in 1841, see *Portrait*, p. 32.

17 Anthony Ashcroft, 'John Snow – Victorian Physician', in *Medicine in Northumbria*, p. 255; Morris, *Cholera 1832*, pp. 11-17, 25; Durey, *Return of the Plague*, pp. 12-18, 25, 108-19; Chapple, 'Five early letters', pp. 6, 15, 19; HH to WT, L Brook Street, 16 December [1831] (TWA 1787/115); *Macaulay Letters*, II, p. 76; *Greville Journal*, II, pp. 172, 319; R. J. W. Selleck, *James Kay-Shuttleworth: Journey of an Outsider*, Ilford, 1994, p. 62.

18 HH, *Recollections*, pp. 16-17; DCLH: HH to LA, Knutsford, 12 September 1805; HH to ME, 3 Sotheran Street, Edinburgh, 19 December [1809] (TS), London, 7 July [1819], and London, 13 May 1823.

19 H. Gaskell and W. Robson, who married William Gaskell's sister Anne, were subscribers to the 'Warrington Foot Path Protection Society' (WCL: MS 249).

20 Chadwick, 1910, p. 183. She had presumably obtained this address from Baines and Parsons, *History, Directory, and Gazetteer ... Lancaster* (1823), p. 254: 'Rev. I. G. Robberds Green heys, Chorlton row' [*sic*]. James Darbishire is also found there (p. 362).

21 Prentice, *Manchester*, pp. 289-91; Lindop, *De Quincey*, p. 4; 'Greenheys Fields', *GNL*, IX, 1990, pp. 14-16; MR, MS 'Recollections', p. 10.

22 Derek Brumhead and Terry Wyke, *A Walk Round All Saints*, Manchester Polytechnic, n. d., pp. ii-iv, 1-2, 6, 36-8 (illustr.); Pickstone, *Medicine and Industrial Society*, p. 43; Slugg, *Manchester*, repr. of Pigot's map, 1830; *London – World City*, ed. Fox, p. 285; Axon, *Annals of Manchester*, pp. 180, 185; Ward Notebook, f. 11. Addresses from MCO: Robberds 1, JGR to MR, especially 11 May 1826 (6 Spring Gardens, Manchester), 13 September 1826 (Grosvenor Square), 1 June 1831 (3 Grosvenor Square), 13 June 1846 (19 Acomb Street); also *Letters*, p. 2n. and Chapple, 'Unofficial lives', in Parish, p. 107 (but 14 Dover Street by 1836: see *Pigot & Son's Directory of Manchester and Salford*, and *Letters*, p. 16). I am grateful for the help of Janet Allan, Angus Easson and Jane Wiltshire for checking rate books and directories for me.

23 Payne, *An Ancient Chapel*, pp. 60-1 (author's annot. copy); *CF*, XIII, 1869, p. 59 (see p. 201 above); HG to Mrs T. Martineau, Prospect Hill, 25 August 1826 (JRULM: Cupboard 'A', Unitarian college MSS, Martineau letters, mostly 1820-25).

24 The new Edward Herford source (MCL: 923.4/H32) was announced by Joan Leach, *GNL*, XVII, February 1994, pp. 3-4. His shorthand is not the one used by many Unitarians: e.g., J. Rich, improved by P. Doddridge, *A Brief and Easy System of Shorthand*, London, 1799. I have treated it as a cypher.

25 Stancliffe, *John Shaw's*, p. 405; MCL cutting, 11 May 1896; MR, MS 'Recollections', p. 8; Prentice, *Manchester*, p. 166; Herford, MS diary, I, pp. 34, 42.

26 Waller, p. 45 (see p. 333 above); HJ, *Portrait of a Lady*, Preface.

23

Engagement

WILLIAM GASKELL was very much a local man. Portions of two old manuscript letters have survived. One, very fragmentary indeed – perhaps it was cut down to serve as a bookmark – is dated from London, 26 March 1757, and signed by an affectionate husband, Samuel Gaskell. It mentions good cloth at a reasonable price; Warrington was a centre of sailcloth production. A rather longer letter of advice was written to a son called William Gaskell, and dated Warrington, 1 June 1792.[1] This is incomplete, without a signature, but might well have been written by Samuel, the grandfather of Elizabeth Gaskell's husband, who was called William after his father. It could not have been from his grandmother, née Ann Woodcock, for she died in 1790. William Gaskell senior of Warrington was at Manchester College 1791-93, so he might have known William Stevenson.[2]

The letter speaks of sending William's clothes and tells him to keep cheerful, for 'being low Spirited as [*sic*] a great tendency to increase the Disorders of the Body & Health is greatly promoted by chearfullness'. This eminently sound psychology is followed by an evocation of the so-called Protestant work ethic. The Unitarian preacher Edmund Butcher's 'Be not slothful in business ... for diligence fits a man for Heaven'[3] is paralleled in breathless prose:

> I hope you'l take care to be a good boy be attentive to the discharge of every Duty & [also?] that you may go comfortably with your Business it is necessary that you keep beforehand with it & not put of any thing to the last & then you'l not need stay up late & if God is pleased to continue your life 'till you engage in Business[4] you will find that early habits of Industry will make Business go on very comfortably but if on the Contrary you accustom yourself to putting of things to the last you will not have time to dispatch them well & you<u> will feel yourself uncomfortable while you are conscious that you are neglecting & putting o<f> what is necessary to be done. I hope you will always remember that the appro-bation of God is the only foundation of true Comfort & that you will always endeavour to obtain it by a diligent discharge of Duty & that you will sincerely pray that the Divine will < ... >

Warrington was a busy manufacturing town, noted for glass manufacture and tool-making as well as sailcloth, with factories for the manufacture of wire, soap and pins within a mile of the town centre, causing all kinds of social problems. The bridewell needed repairing and there was not a proper fire-engine house. But for some it was a comfortable kind of place, old and self-satisfied. Cockles and mussels were sold on the streets, native oysters cost about 8 shillings a hundred and table beer a penny a quart. When Geraldine Jewsbury went there, she felt as if she had been transmigrated to a mite in a fat Cheshire cheese. 'Miss Jewsbury,' a man said to her, 'you see us just as we are; I and all my friends are people of ample means, and we make up our minds to enjoy life!' They did not want to be grand, she was told; comfort was the best thing money could buy.

Consciences were easy, too, with some reason. Gaskells helped found the town's first library and, as one might expect, for both Thomas Barnes and William Percival were born in Warrington, they supported Manchester College. Amongst the first annual subscribers were Samuel Gaskell of Warrington (3 guineas) and Daniel Gaskell (2), thereby becoming Trustees. Daniel's son Benjamin (10 guineas in 1810), who became a member of Parliament and a vice-president of the college, was a student of the 1796 entry, the year in which William Stevenson abandoned his tutorship. A John Gaskell of Warrington was admitted in the following year, well before William Gaskell junior, who did not begin his course until the college was at York, in 1825. The Gaskells of Lancashire display all the signs of a self-sufficient group: they supported similar causes and intermarried as much as the Hollands. Their pedigrees are as involuted.[5]

Though William Gaskell senior became a manufacturer, he seems to have taken seriously to the study of the Scriptures and the Fathers as he grew older, acquiring more theological knowledge, it was said, than most laymen. With the Reverend William Broadbent and other lay enthusiasts a Mr Gaskell of Warrington established Sunday evening lectures and several book societies. 'Any subscriber may, instead of his Subscription, introduce a book of whatever sentiments he pleases' wrote a contemporary in 1812. 'What confidence in the Truth!' In local circles William Gaskell preached Unitarianism. His last wishes within twelve hours of his death on 15 March 1819 were expressed with 'consistent and rational views of Christian doctrine', according to his obituary, signed H. G. He was nearly forty-two when he died, a family man, with a 'warm and affectionate heart, ever alive to the feeling of want or distress in others.' His grave is in the chapel yard at Warrington, buried with that of his wife Margaret, who died much later, on 12 January 1850 aged sixty-nine years. After her husband's death, she married the Reverend E. Dimock, who came as pastor to Sankey Street (later Cairo Street) in 1822.[6]

The oldest child of William Gaskell senior, sail canvas manufacturer of Warrington, was one of seven children, six of whom were living on 17 June 1818 when his father's will was drawn. A sister, Margaret, had died young two years before and a brother, John, died not long after his father's death, leaving William, Samuel, Ann, Eliza and Robert.[7] The executors were William senior's older brother Roger, partner in trade, his other partner and nephew, Thomas Biggin Gaskell (born in 1796, son of Roger by his first wife, née Ann Biggin), and his brother in law, Holbrook Gaskell of Prospect Hill within Appleton, which seems to have been in a healthy situation to the south of Warrington. Holbrook, the only surviving trustee after 1826, had married Ann, sister of William and Roger.[8]

William's wife Margaret (née Jackson or Balshaw) was left a decent £100 a year in lieu of dower (safeguarded from any future husband as usual) and the use of books and furniture during her lifetime. Family land in Warrington, certain premises and a steam-engine inherited from William's father Samuel were all to be let until William's second son Samuel, born 10 January 1807, should attain the age of twenty-one. At this point both William junior and his brother Samuel would have the option of purchase, either singly or jointly. The rest of William senior's property was to be used for the children's benefit until they reached the age of twenty-one, until which time it was expected they would live with their mother. She was to be their formal guardian with the trustees as long as she remained a widow. On majority they would share and share alike. The trustees were enjoined to use funds in their care to place the children, both male and female, in business or any suitable employment, to set themselves up or to advance themselves in any way in the world – rather nicely explained as 'by marrying, or otherwise howsoever'.

William, the oldest child, was born in Latchford near Warrington on 24 July 1805 and baptised at Sankey Street Unitarian chapel in the town centre by the Reverend William Broadbent. He received his early education from the Reverend Joseph Saul, vicar of Holy Trinity church in Warrington from 1814, a former teacher and classicist who began to keep the parochial records in Latin. His career in Warrington was unfortunate. One day in May 1820 William Beamont and Edward Gaskell were in their law office when Saul appeared in a state of extreme agitation, crying aloud in 'broken accents' – Beamont's language on such a theme is inevitably novelettish – about his 'wife and one of the officers' and brandishing a packet of letters. They suspected 'some return of his nervous complaint', perhaps a cautious lawyer's euphemism for intoxication, but the story ended in a marital separation and the suspension of Saul from his duties at Trinity Church. William Gaskell, however, had reached the age of fifteen and was old enough in that year to follow his cousin Thomas Biggin Gaskell to Glasgow University, where the fees were lower than Edinburgh's. He might well have gone by sea, for the steam-boat *Robert Bruce* had initiated regular sailings to Glasgow only the year before, the journey taking thirty hours.[9]

It was a heady time politically as well as technologically. The Glasgow rectors were famous men: Francis Jeffrey in 1820, elected by students (many of 'extreme youth') as a reformer against the will of the professors, followed by Sir James Mackintosh in 1822 and Henry Brougham in 1824. Both men beat the Tory Sir Walter Scott, each one by the casting vote of the retiring rector. William Gaskell graduated B.A. after four years, and then read for a fifth year in science and mathematics to achieve the degree of M.A. in 1825. He won prizes for Greek, mathematics and ethics. The prize in Greek, given after a *viva voce* examination, was obtained under the reign of the famous Professor Daniel Sandford, only recently tempted north from Christ Church, Oxford, to infuse vigour into the teaching.[10]

One can imagine the intellectual self-confidence it must have given this clever young man from a dissenting background, a student with men like Edmund and Sydney Potter, who became manufacturers and remained life-long friends with their minister in Manchester. They in their turn, together with the Heywoods, Percivals, Philipses, Hibberts, Gregs and other successful Unitarian families belonging to Cross Street and Mosley Street chapels, would play 'a part in social and cultural leadership out of all proportion' to their numbers, never very large in comparison with other nonconformist bodies. Tory and Anglican dominance of a town still governed by antique agencies and regulations was to be defeated under their leadership in the 1830s. The winners, as ever, then became rather less radical; not necessarily devoting themselves to bridge and women and champagne, but to reading poetry and the great quarterly reviews, translating from German and Persian, paying large sums for oil paintings and generally upholding high culture in Manchester. Unitarians were prominent in the establishment of an Institution for the Encouragement of the Fine Arts (later the Royal Manchester Institution) in 1823; a member of the chapel and a future M.P., the ubiquitous George W. Wood, became its first chairman. His Universities Admission Bill in 1834 was an attempt to prevent the exclusion of conscientious dissenters from Oxford and Cambridge.[11]

Family tradition and Warrington background did not inspire William Gaskell and his brother Samuel to take up careers in the declining business of sailcloth manufacture. Instead, Samuel went in for medicine and William became a student for the ministry at Manchester College, from 1825 to 1828, in days when it was established with about twenty-five to thirty students under the theologian Charles Wellbeloved, John Kenrick (a fine classicist who had studied in Germany) and William Turner III, in Monkgate, just outside the ancient York bar on the Scarborough road. History and literature were taught in combination. From 1826 Italian and French were available, and Spanish was added in the following year. Mathematics and science were read under Turner and later William Hincks. Turner of Newcastle was the College Visitor.[12]

It was no longer the Manchester College Belsham's old pupil William Stevenson had known in the 1790s. When it was at York, 1803-40, the proportion of lay students was much lower. They were socially more exclusive, offspring of prosperous Unitarian professional or industrial families, some of them owners of great cotton-spinning firms – Strutt, Marsland, Houldsworth and McConnel. Manchester merchants and manufacturers like James Darbishire, John and Robert Philips, Thomas Robinson, Thomas Potter, Jeremiah Withington and C. W. Wood all sent sons to York, which provided an expensive, broad and liberal education, during a course expected to be three years in length. In the upshot, many turned away from business and followed professional careers, the law especially.

Wellbeloved regarded the education of divinity students as the main purpose of the College. They normally followed a five-year course, unless they were already graduates like William Gaskell. A student-led missionary initiative of 1822, rather reluctantly acceded to by the tutors, ensured that future ministers became accustomed to preaching in the villages about York and in their home districts. John Relly Beard and James Martineau were prominent. William Gaskell's uncle Holbrook Gaskell senior heard him preach at Hatton near Prospect Hill in 1826, but was only moderately pleased, charitably putting the lack of eloquence down to the smallness of the room. However, he heard good reports of his preaching in the chapel at Warrington. William, he thought, had become much thinner at York and looked ill. He was also engaged to supply in September for the Reverend John Grundy of Cross Street chapel, absent in Beaumaris for health reasons and proposing to go on to Barmouth for a second month. A year later Holbrook was prepared to say that William had given 'two very excellent Sermons' and he was 'pleased to see his delivery is now *very much improved* ... very chaste and correct'.[13]

In Holbrook Gaskell's letter of summer 1826 he revealed that no less a man than Thomas Belsham took a great interest in William Gaskell as a student minister; he was 'exceedingly kind to him' and had invited William to travel with him to Bath. William evidently had a powerful Unitarian patron, but where would he be invited to serve as minister? The young and fervent John Hugh Worthington of Leicester, who had studied at York with James Martineau and was engaged to his sister Harriet, had been chosen co-pastor of the Reverend J. G. Robberds at Cross Street chapel in July 1825. 'That young man', wrote a friend, 'is all spirit; he lifts one up, one knows not where.' But in late 1826 he suffered 'a severe affliction both of mind and body' and died in the following July at the early age of twenty-two. Robberds wrote regretfully to his wife Mary of his 'sweet & devotional spirit'.[14]

Fifty years later William Gaskell wrote that of the 'four spheres of service' open to him after York he had chosen Cross Street chapel with some hesitation, 'for so many able ministers had filled the pulpit', but he had received sympathy and encouragement from John Gooch Robberds. What Robberds revealed to his wife Mary in a private letter at the time about William is somewhat different. Gaskell was not for him a perfect candidate:

> I am not sorry that James Turner expressed himself as he did. It will do those youngsters at York good to find that their shameful conduct, though passed over

by their tutors, with, I think, misplaced lenity, may yet be attended with inconvenient consequences to them in the estimation of the public. I take for granted
that nothing was known of the share which Gaskell had in that business by those
who invited him to preach, or I could hardly have helped understanding the
request as an insult to myself (both as connected with the institution & still more
as the brother [in-law] of one of the Tutors). I do not wish to injure a young
man's prospects, or I should have put in a caveat against him being chosen for
my colleague. I confess I should have but small hope of comfort in one who has
shown so little consideration for the feelings of those whom he was bound to
treat with respect. As far as any thing of this kind could be said in strict confidence, I should almost wish it to be said to those who have been instrumental in
procuring Gaskell's services. Perhaps you can find some opportunity of letting
Mr B. He<ywood> know my feeling on this subject. But do nothing rather than
< > any serious injury to a young man for an offence of which, I hope, he will be
wise enough soon to be heartily ashamed. -

You may set at rest any fears which either my mother or you may have about
my leaving Manchester. I am *not* looking out for any other situation. While my
people wish to keep me, they may. They will hardly appoint me a colleague whom
I should positively dislike; & with any one who would be only moderately agreeable I would rather remain where I have already received so much kindness than
take the chances of any other situation, however it might be recommended by its
offering me what I believe is best for a man's comfort & usefulness both, the sole
charge of a moderate sized congregation.

Robberds's letter, in tiny, crossed writing that could hardly contrast more
with Holbrook Gaskell's wildly flourishing hand, seems written more in studied
irritation than anger. The offence could not have been very great if the tutors
at York passed it off. There is a later story that William drove a cow up the staircase at York and tied it to the door of the Principal's room, giving him 'some
difficulty in making a dignified exit'. Robberds might have lacked the Nelsonian
blind eye cultivated by village policemen and tutors of excited youths, but was
evidently prepared to put up with Gaskell as a colleague if needs be.[15]

His comments on his own position suggest that he really wanted a quiet life,
rather than the charge of a major city congregation with all its differences and
factions. James Martineau had preached successfully at Cross Street in the
spring of 1826, and though not formally invited to fill the vacancy, was asked
to preach there again the Sunday before the election in 1828. He almost gave
in to this pressure from his supporters, but his fiancée, Helen Higginson, was
outraged. He thereupon refused. The inner history of such appointments is
probably irrecoverable, but Martineau of Norwich could in no way be
regarded as a local man. Together with associates like J. J. Tayler, J. H. Thom
and Charles Wicksteed, he would fight to re-orient Unitarian thought, to turn
it away from the narrow and rationalistic tradition of Priestley. He went on to
become a national figure in Victoria's reign. Robberds's reservations aside,
Cross Street appears to have played safe by appointing the sound if very slightly
imperfect William Gaskell rather than the charismatic disciple of Channing.[16]

It was a solid congregation of over six hundred, characterised by wealth, business standing and a good education, tightly knit by marriages, kinship and a liberal political alignment – the banking Jones and Loyd families were exceptions – mixed with a kind of social exclusiveness that newer chapels in the suburbs found objectionable. Only the other Unitarian chapel in central Manchester, Mosley Street, though rather smaller, resembled Cross Street in this respect, with Gregs, McConnels and Peter Ewart in its congregation. The prosperous were gradually leaving the old centre of Manchester. A famous letter by Richard Cobden in 1832 tells of his neighbours in Mosley Street selling their private houses to be converted into warehouses, a pattern to which he soon conformed. Residents left Mosley Street's chapel, theatre, court house, Portico Library, Athenaeum and Royal Institution behind and moved to new outer suburbs, which turned out to be far more varied in quality and fashionableness. The richest, like the Gregs, lived in detached mansions at some distance. Many of the middle class, including the ministers, lived to the south of the town, where the prevailing winds were favourable, over the Rochdale canal and the river Medlock, past the notoriously squalid slum 'Little Ireland', in a bend of the Medlock below the level of the high bank that carried Oxford Road and obscured by some of the largest factories in the town.[17]

The Cross Street congregation would have expected William Gaskell to be impressive in his ministerial role (commencing at a good basic salary of about £200 a year):

> Like the older-fashioned Unitarian Divines he wore a dress-suit, not, of course, with the white waistcoat, in his public capacity as minister, when he walked through the streets and during his Sunday services. He was a tall, erect, and very handsome man with chiselled features, bright blue eyes, snowy hair and side-whiskers; indeed when he brought his young bride to Manchester while his hair was still dark-brown, they were one of the handsomest couples in the great town.

Most of the portraits of William show him as an old man, though still tall and thin. There is an engraving in a volume of *Illustrations of Cross Street Chapel*, however, that portrays him in younger days. His hair is beginning to grey, yet the strong, thoughtful features above his white clerical stock and tie seem those of the lean-faced man with feeling in his eye that Charlotte Brontë met in his energetic middle years.[18]

His preaching was said to be 'polished and literary, but always marked by a simplicity and clarity often lacking in that of many a more famous popular preacher', an impression borne out by the fluent, controlled rhetoric of published sermons like his *Protestant Practices Inconsistent with Protestant Principles*, which he preached to the provincial meeting of 'Presbyterian and Unitarian ministers' held at Renshaw Street chapel in Liverpool on 16 June 1836. 'His own calm judgment and carefully-refined taste', wrote a colleague, 'diffused a quiet, gentle calm over his preaching.' Only very rarely did he refer to 'subjects which might be called political', such as the immorality of war. Also, as might have been expected, when the legal attempts during the 1830s and early 1840s to seize the endowments and chapels established by Trinitarian ancestors roused his sonorous ire. This important early sermon insists on 'the great principles of Christian Liberty' – maintained by the apostle Paul against Jewish rigorists, William asserted, and by contemporary Unitarians against those who would prevent free and conscientious interpretation of the Bible: 'They profess to take Jesus as their heaven-inspired Guide and Teacher; so do we.' To refuse to admit progress in doctrine and to call in 'the secular authority to legislate on matters of faith' sprang from unchristian intolerance.[19]

In comparison, the sermons of his colleague Robberds were said to have once had

> more of that finished elegance which belongs to the essay; but latterly he had purposely rendered it colloquial and even homely, more resembling that of a speaker than of a writer. We heard him once remark, that he was well aware his style had suffered from this cause; but, with true conscientiousness, he had sacrificed literary considerations to the one desire of pastoral usefulness. ... He was singularly happy in seizing upon the passing events of the day, and giving them an ingenious and instructive application. ... His religious views represented what is called the older phase of Unitarianism.

Baker's 1884 history of Cross Street chapel is effusive about Robberds but devotes no more than two lines to William Gaskell, deliberately, it appears. A private animus seems to be involved, but there is no doubt that the senior minister Robberds had recommended himself to the congregation, as their gift of £1000 shows. He was also enough of a scholar to be appointed Professor of pastoral theology and of the Hebrew and Syriac languages when Manchester College returned from York in 1840. His preaching technique must have depended upon a very deliberate set of choices. Or just possibly the apparent indolence from which his obituarist is at pains to defend him – 'a constitutional aversion to all constrained and artificial effort' – led him to rely more and more upon his powers of easy, gentlemanly extemporisation, a common *déformation professionelle* amongst men of a certain age.

He and his ministerial colleagues could hardly set themselves directly against the ethics and actions of economic individualism from which their congregations had profited so immensely. Nevertheless, Robberds maintained throughout his career that active religion was not just church-going or 'vivid flashes of devout feeling'; it should be part of life in 'the market, the exchange, the warehouse or the workshop'. The rich should regard themselves as the stewards of wealth for the benefit of all. The Unitarian clergy and laity of Manchester and Salford, William Gaskell amongst them, took the lead in many forms of humanitarian interposition, doing much practical good, gaining authority and prestige as well as a quiet conscience.[20]

It would be a mistake to underestimate the importance of all such matters to the men who attended Cross Street chapel – powerful, self-confident and highly successful, yet very aware of the contemptuous view of them and their spiritual leaders held by those who lumped all nonconformists together. The Christian Socialist J. M. F. Ludlow, a friend of Mrs Gaskell in the early 1850s, makes very cutting comments in his chaotic, unpublished, and unrestrained, autobiography about the ministers of religion who attended the anti-Corn Law conference held in Manchester in August 1841: 'The assembled ministers might number from three to four hundred black coats, men mostly stout, dirty, low-browed, unintelligent in face', eloquent in a rough sort of way, but whose 'poverty of thought & narrowness of mind' were, he asserted, 'all but incredible.' Ludlow believed there were no more than two or three Church of England clergy present, one of whom was in the chair, '& I must say that no one who judges from the dissenting minister of to-day, generally a well educated, often a highly educated man, can have any idea of the inferiority of the class fifty years ago.'

It is not likely that William Gaskell was involved in these corn-law meetings, though many of his relations and J. G. Robberds were. Ludlow could not have encountered Robberds or William Gaskell's friend and fellow-student at York, John Relly Beard, a member of the conference committee, the cultured and energetic Unitarian minister at Salford. Even so, Ludlow's social values were not exactly alien to Robberds, who, we find, reacted in a very similar way when he was amongst the Presbyterians of Scotland. He attended a service held in the church part of Dunkeld cathedral. It was, he thought, a 'decent place of worship', its interior arrangements like one of the best Unitarian chapels and an order of service much the same. But the singing was doleful and unmusical, the congregation drawled and droned. The minister was 'blithering', wore 'linen that looked as if it had been changed by being turned' and sported a 'dirty snuffy silk or cotton handkerchief.' And, Robberds wrote rather complacently to his wife Mary, 'I could not help contrasting his appearance with that of my own colleague, and thinking that Dissenters as we are, we yet outshine what I have yet seen of the Scottish establishment.' In the privacy of this correspondence, he could be rather less genial than he was as a public figure. His colleague's original offence as a student at York must have been forgotten by now.[21]

Other observers thought that William Gaskell in the pulpit looked more like a scholar and intelligent man of the world than a divine – 'as little like a clergyman as he was like a costermonger'. He obviously prepared his sermons carefully but was not tied to his script. His hands rested on either side of the pulpit and were hardly ever used; he trusted to the power of his matter and his strong, flexible voice. Only very occasionally did he rise to heights of eloquence. Nor, wrote John Evans, did he indulge in 'that warm, impassioned delivery which we deem so highly necessary in the peroration of a discourse from the pulpit.' In one respect, however, the strict logical clarity of his exposition was varied: he was said to be fond of analogies, 'often of a very appropriate character, sometimes very highly poetical, and always well sustained.'[22]

William's hymns, temperance rhymes and lectures on the poets and poetry of humble life are well documented, and Jenny Uglow has well teased out both the benefits and drawbacks of the poetic collaboration with his wife that led to her first appearance in print with *Sketches among the Poor, No 1*. This was a joint effort, published in *Blackwood's Magazine* for January 1837 but perhaps offered first to John Relly Beard's new magazine, *The Christian Teacher*, in January of the year before through Franklin Howorth: 'Received F. H. Sketches Among the Poor, No. 1'. It might have been written about the time Howorth married Elizabeth's cousin Bessy Holland, on 24 September 1835 at Knutsford parish church.[23] Robberds, too, used to compose hymns and verses for young ladies' albums, and Beard brought out *A Collection of Hymns for Private and Public Worship* of Unitarians in 1837. To avoid the usual Calvinistic or Trinitarian phraseology – Unitarians were no more than a few percent of nonconformists – they had to be specially composed, he tells us in his introduction. William's creativity was more than adequate: he contributed nearly eighty in a variety of forms, a number only matched by three other contributors. It was probably more than mechanical composition. In one of his later letters he writes of a hymn 'which came to me as I was walking home last night'.[24]

His life was not rigidly professional, however, nor was his character as reserved as it sometimes seems. The beginning of a comic poem in his small, curling, scholarly hand is to be found in a little sewn booklet, the watermark of which is dated 1828. More often than not, paper was used within a few years.[25] Byron, author of 'The Vision of Judgment', is his model rather than 'nature's sternest painter', Crabbe, or Wordsworth, 'seeing beauty':

> When Adam fell, as theologians show
>   On all his seed there fell a deadly curse
> Which makes this world no better than so so
>   And dooms them to another still much worse –
> The pains, the labour & the grievous woe
>   Suit not however my poor feeble verse;
> Suffice to say, 'tis thought that every evil
> Sprung from a chat which Eve had with the devil.
>
> Yet now & then I own I've felt inclined,
>   (No harm, I trust) to entertain a doubt
> On this same point, when pondering in my mind
>   How Adam & his spouse even throughout
> A single month could entertainment find,
>   Unless they knew the art of falling out,
> Which no where doth appear, it seems to me,
> They must have suffered sorely from ennui.

After two and half stanzas more the poem breaks off, but there is enough to show that William had a side to him that matched the high-spirited young woman he won for his bride, who gladly copied into her own commonplace book the splendidly eccentric prayer: 'And o'er an abune a' my brethren, let us no forget the poor aul Deil! He's e'en had a waifu' time o't poor soul: it's nae light matter, my friends, to lig in the nook o' Hell sae lang as he's dune, till he's as black as a heather hill, and as hard as a dried skate – '.[26]

Manchester, to which, it was claimed, strangers came 'only as a great manufacturing depôt' – the Liverpool-Manchester railway had been officially opened on 13 September 1830 – had a number of practising poets. John Rogerson and John Hewitt issued a weekly periodical containing poetry as well as prose in 1828, entitled the *Phœnix*. In 1831 the same men 'launched another frail barque, the *Falcon*', which suggests that their success was ephemeral, but Wheeler was able to select sixteen poets in 1838 for his anthology of *Manchester Poetry*. Two serious poems by William Gaskell appeared in this: 'Come and Pray', and a translation from Krummacher, 'Death and Sleep', along with poems by others who had been popular in the town – John Byrom, Maria Jane Jewsbury, Samuel Bamford and Charles Swain. It was the year in which Maria Jewsbury, already friends with the Wordsworths, was encouraged by Dorothy to go and stay with Felicia Hemans in North Wales. The community of poets transcended Manchester.[27]

John Gooch Robberds, like his junior colleague, was a lover of English literature:

> All things, to have value and beauty in his eye, must be in contact with human realities, and tinged with the colour of human affections. To this intellectual temperament must be ascribed his extreme fondness for the literature of fiction, especially when it was pure, kindly and graceful, and that happy alchemy of mind by which he could extract from its gayest and most humorous pages, some elements of a diviner wisdom to give sweetness and geniality to the earnest words of the preacher. His was peculiarly an English mind.

Robberds' obituary continues by outlining his easy-going nature, his charm as a companion, his liberal hospitality, his wit 'sportive and free at every turn, splashing right and left with indiscriminate hilarity'.[28]

There was a remarkable amount of purely social enjoyment for clerical Unitarians in Manchester. No Elders of Auchtermuchty, they. When Edward Herford went to live and study with the Robberds in the early 1830s he found himself caught up in a round of pleasure.[29] J. G. Robberds's sister Susanna had married a Manchester merchant called Samuel Alcock, a man close to the ministers of Cross Street chapel as their treasurer and chairman of trustees for many years. The Alcocks used to give parties where games like 'The Stool' were played. At one on 6 February 1832 William Gaskell was accused of knocking at people's doors and then running away. At the Nicholsons' a day or two later the young folk could dance, all the more merrily, perhaps, because dancing in public places had been forbidden to William Gaskell as a student at York just a few years before. 'Miss S and G' were there, looking very pretty. Edward, not quite seventeen years of age, was smitten by William Gaskell's sister, then aged nineteen: 'I think I almost love Miss Gaskell, she has such a good figure and a very sweet good tempered face.' He danced with Elizabeth as well and was clearly in his element: 'I may sum up the pleasure of the evening by saying that there was "Good music, pretty girls, excellent supper and capital port wine"- What would a man have more'! Eliza Gaskell turned out to be witty, too. At chapel on Sunday she quipped that it was 'so cold we could not talk for *chattering*'.

A week or so later he met more pretty girls, one with a very charming name, Georgiana Chappell, danced new quadrilles and enjoyed another party at the Alcocks. There Elizabeth was the chief contriver of a charade on the word 'fortune', she herself taking the part of a teacher of elocution. Mr Aspland, who, Edward thought, had 'an extraordinary genius for acting words', played a man with a terrible lisp; young John Robberds played the Reverend Mr Bumpkin, who could not pronounce his r's – 'Wuin seize thee wuthless king &c'. Aspland, as the hero, made extravagant speeches to his 'adorable Sophonisba', but was unable to prevent himself from bursting into song at critical moments, supposedly afflicted by a tune he could not get out of his head. In expressing the whole word, Elizabeth pretended to be a Miss Voilex, who told Lord Squander that she fastened down the carpet with diamond pins, had a husband who used racehorses to shoot at and made 'candle papers of £50 notes and the like'.[30]

Robert Brook Aspland, son of the minister of the Gravel Pit meeting at Hackney and a student at York, had graduated in 1826 and been, according to Holbrook Gaskell, 'ordained, or inducted or settled or whatever is the fashionable phraseology of the day' at Crook's Lane, Chester, in August. William Gaskell had attended and approved of the service. 'Ordination appears to be the Mania of York' was his uncle's sarcastic phrase. It was William Turner who, as College Visitor, encouraged 'the dying rite of ordination', with very limited success, it would seem. More pertinently in this context, aspiring ministers at York were given lessons in elocution by professional actors from Covent Garden or Drury Lane, and evidently had no hesitation in displaying their talent in secular contexts.[31]

By the end of February Edward was at a party in the house of the Reverend J. J. Tayler, the new minister of Mosley Street chapel, flirting a little with Miss Aspland and bracing himself for yet another round of parties. There was a kind of a dance at the Alcocks' in early March, where Elizabeth upset him by dancing with Mr Aspland, although he had asked her first. 'This is rather too bad', he wailed, 'I'll not stand it. She shall make an apology before I have any thing to do with her.' Soon after, on her initiative, they made it up. On 12 March there was a party at the Sydney Potters', where Elizabeth scandalously proved to be 'a good waltzer'. Edward secretly recorded that J. G. Robberds had said the next day that 'he would not want his fruit *pawed* by another person, not knowing how fond Miss Stephenson was of it.' A few years before Robberds had written to his wife about the waltzing at a large party given by the R. Potters, which made him 'feel English all over'. For foreigners, it was no worse than shaking hands, he believed. But in England, although it was pretty to look at, and Miss Crompton in particular had 'managed her part very gracefully & modestly', he could not conceive that any bachelor would wish to marry a young lady who had leaned on the arm of 'a comparative stranger' in the whirl of the dance – and been 'all but pressed to his bosom'. Robberds was behind the times. Henry Winkworth had been shocked at his first sight of waltzing back in 1816, at a ball given for the Allies in London to celebrate the conclusion of peace.[32]

Unitarian circles in Manchester were repeating in their private way the public gaieties Elizabeth's friends were enjoying in Newcastle. In March 1832 the Mayoress gave a supper and fancy dress ball that continued till six in the morning at the Mansion House, decorated with variegated lamps without, flowers and evergreens within, a truly magnificent occasion for five or six hundred guests, amongst them Miss Headlam, Miss Jaques, Miss Reed and Miss M. A. Reed, the Misses Losh, Miss Rankin and the two Misses Carr, who appropriately wore Russian costume. John William Williamson of Durham wore 'Persian dress, actually made in Persia, richly ornamented with jewels of great value'. A few days later, the ball was repeated in the Assembly Rooms. After Elizabeth had asked Harriet how the 'second serving up' of the fancy dresses had gone off, she glided naturally into exclaiming what a year it had been for weddings and proceeded to enumerate those of her Wedgwood and Holland relations. And towards the end of her letter she was agog to know if it was true that '*one* of the Miss Carrs' was to be married to Matthew Anderson.[33] In fact, she had herself become engaged.

On Tuesday 13 March 1832, young John Robberds told Herford, Elizabeth was behaving shyly, 'very much afraid of anyone looking' at her. On Wednesday William Gaskell took her out for a walk and they spent a long time together in the study that evening. When William came down at about nine o'clock he looked sheepish. 'I suppose it is all settled now', wrote Edward;

> Miss Stephenson could hardly have thought when Miss Worthington asked her in her note whether she was among the list of persons going to be married that it would so soon be so. Let the pretty creatures amuse themselves. Let every Jack have his Jill. I suppose I shall have mine some time if Miss Blank will consent.

In the privacy of his diary Edward was disconcerted to recall that he had once told Elizabeth, before he knew 'how she was interested', that applications for service in Cross Street could be prevented by giving out that William would preach. He continues with some gossip:

I was told by Cha[rles] Hall to-day that the reason why Miss Stephenson was come to Manch[ester] was that she was sent here by her parent to keep her out of the way of a [?] man to whom she was attached. John tells me it is a [?], tho' not without foundation, that there was a [?] man at Knutsford who persecuted her very much with his attentions in consequence of her tak[in]g her for some one she knew and moving to him in the street one day.

His ignorance of the fact that Elizabeth was an orphan does not inspire too much confidence. On the other hand, some things fell under his own observation, however jejune his language:

> It is Capital fun to see the two pigeons together. The *he* is so very tender, he comes at 10 o'clock in the morning – dines there with her, teas there with her, sups there with her and – I was going to say *goes to bed there with her* but it is not come to that yet, tho' I think that at the rate they are going at it will soon advance to that desirable consummation.[34]
>
> Tuesday [20 March] Mr G. here again today. He is absolutely going with her tomorrow to Knutsford. Tonight Mr Robberds & John & I were talking of their being so constantly together. Mr R. said that he must enforce Mr Sadler's Bill against them 'that they must only work ten hours of the day instead of staying 12.' I thought that [?] would not like that at all for that would prevent them from doing any *night work*.

On March 16 Michael Sadler, leader of High Tory paternalists, the opponent of Malthus ('the prolificness of human beings … varies inversely as their number', Sadler maintained) and defender of the poor laws, saw the second reading of his bill that proposed to limit the hours worked by children under nine years of age. He was representative of a broad current of thought which, Harold Perkin states, may be best traced in the columns of *Blackwood's* during the 1820s, which included the writings of John Galt and 'William Stevenson, a Treasury official'. But a few days after the second reading the Reform Bill was passed by the Commons, leading to a great struggle with the Lords, the resignation of Lord Grey and his cabinet, and then his recall by a reluctant William IV (for Greville, 'one of the silliest old gentlemen in his dominions') with a promise to create enough peers to pass the bill that summer. In May there was a steady demand for gold from the Bank of England. Soldiers were kept booted and saddled by day and night. Edward Herford, who had just left the Robberds' after two happy years in April and been presented with a four-volume Livy by them, very naturally tended to fill his pages with news of meetings and demonstrations in this 'season of great alarm and anxiety'.[35]

But not to the exclusion of everything else: 'Wednesday … The "pretty creatures" went to Knutsford this afternoon by Ruffley.'

NOTES

1 JS&PH, LUBL: both fragments lightly edited; Crowe, *Warrington Ancient and Modern*, p. 125. SG died aged eighty on 6 March 1813, his wife aged fifty-six on 22 July 1790 (Bulmer, *Unitarian Chapel, Cairo Street*, p. 41).

2 Irvine, p. 95n.; MCO: *Roll of Students*, adm. 5 Sept 1791 for Commerce, left June 1793; manufacturer, d. 1819. There are other possible William Gaskells, but the second fragment probably came down through Marianne Gaskell, who married her cousin Thurstan Holland.

3 *Sermons, For the Use of Families* (1798; 3rd edn, 1819), qu. Hilton, *Age of Atonement*, p. 116n.

4 William, first son of Samuel and Ann Gaskell, b. 24 January 1762, d. 15 December 1776, just before he became fifteen. The William of the letter was their fifth child, b. 28 March 1777 and therefore not long past fifteen. See Bulmer, *Unitarian Chapel, Cairo Street*, pp. vi, 41.

5 Crowe, *Warrington Ancient and Modern*, pp. 126-33, 136, 153-4, 171; Carter, 'William Beamont', pp. 5-6; GEJ to Jane Welsh Carlyle, Warrington, [1845], *Jewsbury Letters*, p. 168; MCO: Harrison, *Sermon at Cross Street*, p. 17; Davis, *Manchester College*, p. 59; MS 'Students admitted', no. 128; Wykes, 'Sons and subscribers', p. 56; *Report of the College*, 31 August 1810. I am grateful to John Cantrell and the staff of WCL for valuable assistance.

6 WG obit., *MR*, XIV, 1819, pp. 194-5; Bulmer, *Unitarian Chapel, Cairo Street*, p. 42; SCA: SLPS 52/12, T. A. Ward to Joseph Hunter, Sheffield, 9 March 1812; Arthur Mounfield, *Early Warrington Nonconformity*, Warrington, 1922, p. 150. I have received special assistance from G. Carter of WCL and Rachel Moffat of SCA.

7 Bulmer, *Unitarian Chapel, Cairo Street*, pp. v, 42 (Margaret); PRO: PROB 11/1624, WG's will proved 20 January 1820. It cites William (b. 24 July 1805), Samuel (b. 10 January 1807), Ann (b. 7 September 1808), Elizabeth (b. 21 September 1812), Robert (b. 30 December 1814) and John (b. 5 March 1817). John d. 4 February 1821.

8 HG's will was proved 31 March 1842; that of his wife Ann 25 August 1848. For Elizabeth Gaskell's visits with Marianne to Prospect Hill see, e.g., her diary entries of 1836 and 1838, MS, pp. 40, 75.

9 Brill, *Gaskell*, pp. 10-19; WCL: MS 285, WB's day-book and diary, 19 May 1820 (4pp. 4to account); Neal, 'Liverpool shipping in the early nineteenth century', p. 177. It was a relatively cheap journey in 1855 (*Letters*, p. 358).

10 J. D. Mackie, *The University of Glasgow 1451-1951: A Short History*, Glasgow, 1954, pp. 237, 247-56; James Coutts, *A History of the University of Glasgow*, Glasgow, 1909, pp. 343-6.

11 Slugg, *Manchester*, p. 35; Kidd, *Manchester*, pp. 65-8; H. Belloc, 'On a general election'; Seed, 'Liberal culture in Manchester', pp. 5, 8; Ruth Watts, 'Manchester College and education 1786-1853', in Smith, pp. 81-3.

12 W. B. Stephens, *Adult Education and Society in an Industrial Town: Warrington 1800-1900*, Exeter, 1980, p. 6; Watts, 'Manchester College and education', pp. 90-2.

13 Wykes, 'Sons and subscribers', pp. 59-65; Carpenter, *Martineau*, pp. 39-40; Davis, *Manchester College*, pp. 84-6; HG to Mrs T. Martineau, Prospect Hill, 25 August 1826, and 6 August 1827 (JRULM: Cupboard 'A', Unitarian college MSS.); Payne, p. 116.

14 Baker, *Memorials of a Dissenting Chapel*, p. 54; Worthington obit., *MR*, n. s. I, 1827, pp. 759-62, and *CR*, 1827, pp. 372-3; Webb, *Martineau*, pp. 49-52; MCO: JGR to MR, Dorchester, 17 July 1827.

15 Brill, p. 26; MCO: JGR to MR, Upper Clapton, 22 October 1827; Arthur W. Fox, 'The Rev. William Gaskell, M. A.', *Papers of the Manchester Literary Club*, LXIII, 1937, p. 276.

16 *Martineau*, ed. Drummond and Upton, I, pp. 50, 75; Carpenter, *Martineau*, p. 53; *Harriet Martineau Letters*, ed. Sanders, pp. 10-12; Ralph Waller, 'James Martineau: The development of his religious thought', in Smith, pp. 242-5, 251-3. See also Brill, *Gaskell*, p. 26.

17 See especially Gatrell, 'Incorporation and the pursuit of Liberal hegemony', pp. 24-9; Thackray, 'Natural knowledge in a cultural context', pp. 698-709; Seed, 'Liberal culture in Manchester', p. 4; HUL: TS, Pons, 'Housing conditions and residential patterns', pp. 30-2, 47-8, 55-60 (with maps).

18 Brill, p. 40; Fox, 'William Gaskell', p. 275-7; L. H., *Illustrations of CCC*, Manchester, 1917; J. A. V. Chapple, 'A sense of place: Elizabeth Gaskell and the Brontës', *BST*, XX, 1992, pp. 319-20 (illustr.)

19 Rev. S. A. Steinthal, *Memorial Sermon*, 1884, p. 8; WG, *Protestant Practices*, pp. 5-6, 14, 19-21; Seed, 'Liberal culture in Manchester', p. 10. Fryckstedt, pp. 74-80, analyses WG's Unitarianism. See also Webb, 'The Gaskells as Unitarians', pp. 147-52, who places him theologically with Priestley and Belsham rather than Martineau.

20 'T', Robberds obit., *CR*, n. s. X, 1854, pp. 346-8, 351; Seed, 'Liberal culture in Manchester', pp. 5, 21-2. Thomas Baker, 'an uncommonly good hater', told Alexander Gordon that 'his chief pleasure in publishing [his history] would be that he had managed to exclude every reference to Mr. Gaskell, except his bare name' (H. J. McLachlan, 'Two letters of Alexander Gordon', *TUHS*, XIX, 1987-90, p. 202).

21 CUL: Add. MS 7348/1 (qu. from draft chapter 10); *Portrait*, pp. 30, 32; JGR to MR, Dunkeld, 12 July 1835 (MCO: MSS Robberds 1, f. 5).

22 John Evans, *Lancashire Authors and Orators: A Series of Literary Sketches*, London 1850, pp. 97-9; Hopkins, p. 46 (qu. W. E. Adams, *Memoirs of a Social Atom*).

23 Uglow, pp. 99-105; Howorth marriage details from Mrs Joan Leach. In 'Les débuts littéraires de Mrs. Gaskell: réflexions sur un poème oublié', *EA*, XVII, 1964, pp. 131-3, Jean-Paul Hulin proposes 'Rich and Poor. By a Lancashire Lady', signed 'Lizzie', in *The North of England Magazine* for May 1842.

24 Brill, *Gaskell*, pp. 48-50; MCO: JGR to MR, Lyndhurst, New Forest, 14 July 1827; JRULM: UCC MSS A2¹, WG to James C. Street, 17 July 1860; G. I. T. Machin, *Politics and the Churches in Great Britain 1832-1868*, Oxford, 1977, p. 165.

25 JGS: incomplete MS, most leaves blank and three cut away, small 4to (wmk Britannia and ?'NEWEY & LAY 1828'); also a few notes and drafts by WG.

26 See Appendix E for all that is known of the commonplace book.

27 Robert E. Carlson, *The Liverpool and Manchester Railway Project 1821-1831*, Newton Abbot, 1969, p. 231; Richard Wright Procter, *Memorials of Bygone Manchester, with Glimpses of the Environs*, Manchester, 1880, pp. 167-8, 176-8; *Manchester Poetry: with an Introductory Essay*, ed. James Wheeler, London, 1838, pp. vi, 193-6; *Wordsworth Letters*, 2nd edn, III, part 1, p. 606. A note documents the influence of Wordsworth on Channing, who in 1835 sent WW 'a sermon on the evils of war'.

28 Robberds obit., *CR*, n. s. X, 1854, pp. 349-50. See also Uglow, pp. 114-16.

29 MCL: Herford, MS diary, I, pp. 15-18, 20-2, 30-4, 37-45, provides material for the paragraphs that follow.

30 Baker, *Memorials of a Dissenting Chapel*, pp. 118-19 (Alcock); Slugg, *Manchester Fifty Years Ago*, p. 165 (a Methodist, G. R. Chappell, and his 'fine family of daughters'); *Martineau*, ed. Drummond and Upton, I, p. 30; Quinlan, *Victorian Prelude*, pp. 144-5. 'Wuin', etc. from Gray's 'The Bard: A Pindaric Ode' (cf. *Portrait*, p. 6).

31 McLachlan, *Unitarian Movement*, pp. 178; *DNB*; JRULM: UCC MSS, HG to Mrs T. Martineau, Prospect Hill, 25 August 1826; Hill, 'The death of ordination', pp. 204-5.

32 MCO: JGR to MR, Manchester, 7 January 1828; *Letters and Memorials*, I, p. 6. See E. F. Burney's racy watercolour in *London – World City*, ed. Fox, opp. p. 556.

33 Sykes, *Historical Register*, II, pp. 347-51; Chapple, 'Five early letters', pp. 16-17.

34 The italicised phrase is in shorthand, though by this point in the diary, pp. 41-2, much is written in clear.

35 *Macaulay Letters*, II, pp. 117, 124; Perkin, *Origins*, pp. 241-52; *Greville Journal*, II, pp. 276, 290-314; E. A. Smith, *Reform or Revolution? A Diary of Reform in England, 1830-2*, Stroud, 1992, pp. 111-39.

24

Things dying: things reborn

THE WELL-KNOWN joint 'engagement' letter now takes up the private story.[1] On 27 March 1832 Elizabeth wrote in the highest of spirits to her future sister-in-law, Eliza Gaskell of Warrington, that William had been introduced to Mrs Lumb at Knutsford. Confined to her bed with a burst blood vessel the day after he arrived, her aunt was well enough to rally them both, 'Why Elizabeth how could this man ever take a fancy to such a little giddy thoughtless thing as you'! Were it not for the story of William and the cow at York, and his lively Byronic verses, one might think there was truth in jest. Elizabeth begged William's young sister to write again,

> and that right speedily – tell me anything that interests you – and oh! don't forget how to fight with pillows and 'farm yard noises' [as you did?] when Edward heard you laughing so plainly. I can't write a word more now, seeing I have 150 things to say to this disagreeable brother of yours – so believe me
>
> Your very loving crony.
> E. C. Stevenson.

William's half of the letter is more prim and conventional, even though he was writing to his young sister:

> Though from Mrs Lumb's unfortunate illness I was unable to see much of her, I saw sufficient to confirm the impression which I had received from Elizabeth and makes me at once admire and love her. In the short interview which I was permitted to have with her she treated me in the kindest and most affectionate manner, and expressed the great pleasure which she felt that Elizabeth had been led to form an engagement with me. I also contrived, I believe, to get into the graces of aunt A. C. [?A. H., Abigail Holland] whom upon the whole I liked very well, though she is not by any means to be compared with Mrs Lumb. I have called Mrs L's illness unfortunate – and yet in one respect I can hardly deem it so. It served to present Elizabeth to me in a still more lovely and endearing light than I had before beheld her, and did more perhaps to knit our souls together than months could have done, without it.

He does write a chattier postscript in which he mentions that 'Alma

Worthington' (probably a mistake of the copyist for Anna Worthington of Altrincham) had predicted what would happen if he and Elizabeth saw too much of each other. He also mentions that the Knutsford minister and his wife, Henry and Mary Green, who were evidently quite as sociable as their Manchester colleagues, had given 'a bit of a dance' – what else? – to celebrate the wedding of Richard and Mary Deane. William obviously knew the Greens well; he had baptised their first child, Emily, some time before, at Bolton on 10 August 1828. Emily and her two sisters, Annie and Ellen, born in 1833 and 1835 respectively, lived on to become great friends of the Gaskell family, but mention of the Deanes, even at a time of celebration, reminds us now of the terrible vulnerability of wives and young children in those days.[2]

William told young Eliza that he had been recalled to Manchester for a more ordinary reason – to take old Mrs Robberds' funeral on Thursday, that is, 29 March. He could not have promised to return to Knutsford on 28 March 1832 as Elizabeth, who was in a state of joyous confusion about mere dates, told his young sister. More significantly, neither in this joint letter nor in the two letters Elizabeth wrote to Harriet Carr during the summer of 1832 is there any other than brief allusion to the alarming public events, political and social, that encompassed their private world. This is hardly surprising in her circumstances, but at that time and place there was not only the threat of revolution but also the long-feared arrival in Britain of Asiatic cholera.

She must have heard a great deal about it. William Gaskell's brother Samuel had already been involved in fighting the epidemic, whilst studying medicine at Edinburgh. Cholera had reached the crowded tenements of that city by January 1832, and Samuel was an excellent student, in practice and well as in theory. A testimonial from his professor of clinical surgery, James Syme, dated 21 May 1832, is entirely favourable (he had obtained the first prize in what was 'at that time the largest Surgical Class in Europe'), and another in November from his lecturer on the practice of physic, Dr J. Mackintosh, praised his valuable service at the Edinburgh Cholera Hospital during the previous winter. Given that Elizabeth's miniature was painted in Edinburgh in June 1832, she might well have become acquainted with her fiancé's brother there, if she had not met him even earlier when he was training at the Manchester Royal Infirmary. It seems likely that she would have gone to Scotland with William Gaskell in order to introduce him to her stepmother.[3]

Samuel Gaskell might then have accompanied William and Elizabeth to the south again, for by July he can be shown to be practising at the cholera 'hospital' in Swan Street, Ancoats, Manchester, an old three-storey factory or workshop converted for the emergency. A subsidiary Board of Health had been established for the town back in November 1831; cholera had duly arrived in June 1832. One of his testimonials, dated 27 August 1832, indicates that his colleagues at Swan Street included Doctors Charles Philips, George Shaw and William Charles Henry, son of Henry Holland's friend, from a well-known Manchester family. Samuel was also able to be of service to another doctor destined to be famous, James Kay of the Ardwick and Ancoats Dispensary, who had already published in April the first edition of his famous and disturbing pamphlet, *The Moral and Physical Condition of the Working Classes Employed in the Cotton Manufacture in Manchester*. Kay's pamphlet, propagandist as well as indisputably documentary, awakened 'bitter animosity and fractious opposition' in some quarters, and his indefatigable efforts to investigate as well as treat disease once led a medical colleague to accuse him of interference with a patient's treatment in Swan Street. Samuel supported Kay, being prepared to affirm that he had only conversed in the ward with a woman who had previously been under his care.[4]

As biographical sources, private letters that happen to survive are both fascinating and deceptive. Hardly more than a handful of Elizabeth's are known from this period, the very end of her youth, but as far as we can tell she and William were quite naturally immersed in their own affairs, preparing for marriage after a short engagement. Yet William, like his brother, must have been continuously involved in the region's enormous problems during these years, the poverty and destitution that surrounded hospital and chapel in the centre of a fast-changing conurbation. Strikes and lockouts during a great depression of trade that lasted almost without a break in the years around 1829 had led to destructive riots at Rochdale, Macclesfield and Manchester, which were met by military force. In the first few weeks of 1830 William Cobbett gave four lectures in Manchester to large audiences, and at later reform meetings that year Richard Potter (Mrs Gaskell's 'Dicky of Wigan', who as an M.P. provided her with franks for letters) is said to have been so overcome by emotion in describing the state of the poor that he could not finish moving the motion in favour of free trade with India and China. Elizabeth Stevenson took up the reins of her Knutsford life again when distress in Manchester was high.

James Kay's pamphlet exposed in minute and graphic detail appalling conditions in Manchester's streets and houses, the moral and physical degradation of its labouring population. Not long after this Alexis de Tocqueville gave his classic description of Manchester on its collection of little hills, surmounted by thirty or forty 'palaces of industry' emitting black smoke over a ravaged landscape, where fine stone buildings were found cheek by jowl with decrepit one-story houses and repulsive cellar-dwellings. Factories and warehouses eclipsed almost everything in the town centre. 'These vast structures keep air and light out of the human habitations which they dominate; they envelop them in perpetual fog', he declared, and underlined the polarities:

> Here is the slave, there the master; there is the wealth of some, here the poverty of most; there the organised efforts of thousand produce, to the profit of one man, what society has not yet learnt to give. Here the weakness of the individual seems more feeble and helpless even than in the middle of a wilderness; here the effects, there the causes.[5]

The disease theories of doctors during an epidemic inevitably impinged upon wider concerns. Even before the arrival of cholera in Britain a new social consciousness had been forming. Private charity was regarded as necessary for the sake of all in a swiftly industrialising society, but rationally speaking, men like James Kay thought it should be highly organised, based upon systematic investigation and directed towards those who would truly benefit from it, the 'deserving poor'. Unitarians in particular were nothing if not rational. The second meeting of the British and Foreign Unitarian Association, which brought together a number of scattered societies, was held at Cross Street chapel in June 1830, following a suggestion by 'the late excellent J. H. Worthington'. It heard a number of resolutions passed at the previous meeting in London, and then added its own set, amongst which was an earnest recommendation for the establishment of 'City Missions, on a plan and for purposes similar to those detailed in the Reports of the Rev. Dr. Tuckerman, (of Boston, U.S.)'.[6]

William Gaskell was of course present on the Manchester occasion, following which 329 men dined in the Town Hall, Salford. The names of those present are a roll-call of northern ministers. They include Turner of Newcastle and Turner of Halifax, John Kenrick of York, Robberds and Gaskell of Manchester, Beard of Salford, J. Grundy and J. H. Thom of Toxteth Park, R. Smethurst of Monton, Franklin Howorth of Rochdale, John Gaskell of Dukinfield, R. B. Aspland of Chester, E. R. Dimock of Warrington, Henry Green of Knutsford, J. Ashton of Stockport and many more. There were distinguished visitors like Professor Henry Ware of Harvard, Lant Carpenter of Bristol, W. J. Fox, J. Bowring, Thomas Madge and Edward Tagart of London, and J. Martineau over from Dublin. The stewards of the dinner included no less than twenty-three laymen from Manchester – amongst them Samuel Alcock, James Darbishire, S. D. Darbishire, Francis Darbishire, R. H. Greg, James McConnel, Mark Philips, Edmund Potter, Richard Potter, Thomas Potter, John Edward Taylor, James Aspinall Turner and George William Wood, accompanied by Yateses from Liverpool, Ashtons from Hyde, William Broadbent and Holbrook Gaskell from Warrington.

The springs of their altruism were diverse. Channing's shrewd criticism of Priestley, as one who 'sought refuge in his optimism from that deep feeling of men's present miseries, that thorough sympathy with human suffering, which, I think, marks those whom God selects as the great benefactors of their race', was a sign of fundamental divisions to come in Unitarian religious temperaments.[7] But at the dinner they were united, fired by the inspirational eloquence pouring from the Reverend William J. Fox:

> A mighty change is taking place, by the diffusion of knowledge and the extension of education, among the lower classes (as they are called) of the community, which will tend to the elevation of their character, and the security of their interests. They have indeed been its lower classes. Like the strata which have been forming in the bottom of the ocean, the waves of wealth and of rank have rolled over them for ages; but the principle of knowledge in them, like the central fire

of which the geologists tell us, will heave them up to the surface (*loud cheers*), and when this redeemed land appears, we claim our portion to build thereon the temple of truth, and to sow it with the seeds of righteousness and joy (*great applause*).

'The union and energy of Unitarians will be the reformation of England', he concluded grandiloquently, 'and the reformation of England will be the regeneration of the world.'

J. G. Robberds became the first secretary of the Manchester Domestic Mission Society, J. Aspinall Turner its treasurer and key layman, and William Gaskell, still a young man, a member of the committee to which a 'minister to the poor' reported on a monthly basis. Domestic missions were set up at Spitalfields, Cripplegate, Liverpool and Bristol before the end of the decade. In the first printed *Report of the Ministry to the Poor Commenced in Manchester Jan. 1, 1833*, the 'mediator' between the rich and the poor as he termed himself, John Ashworth, detailed 3500 visits and his distribution of food, money and clothing as well as outlining the prize-fights, gaming, dram-shops and 'multitudes of females' he either encountered or heard about. He became so discouraged that he nearly gave up. The reformation of England at least hung in the balance. Fortunately Dr Tuckermann appeared in person on a visit from America, uttering 'the most sublime and eloquent passages' James Aspinall Turner had ever heard. It was Tuckerman who encouraged Mr Ashworth to continue his work amongst the poor.

Practical efforts abounded. In the 1830s several schools were established in a new building on the corner of Windmill Street and Lower Mosley Street, paid for by subscriptions, a government grant and a loan of £800 raised in bazaars and other functions by the ladies of the two central Unitarian chapels. A clothing society, a sick club, a mechanics' institute and a library were begun. As the years went by these humanitarian efforts came to involve more than an imposition upon the poor of middle-class philanthropy. Rational and practical though it was, it proved to be inadequate. Unitarian domestic missionaries found themselves mediating 'the experience of mass suffering with a directness, an immediacy and an urgency which could not be abstracted away by truths derived second-hand from Malthus or Ricardo', comments John Seed. In times of great distress even the deserving poor, they proved, could not survive.[8]

Dr James Kay became a secretary of the Manchester and Salford District Provident Society, founded in 1833. James Aspinall Turner used to visit, enquire and advise for this society in the 'Little Ireland' district off Oxford Road. Kay also joined with Mark Philips, William R. and Samuel Greg, Benjamin Heywood, Kennedys, McConnels, Thomas Potter and others to set up a Manchester statistical society in the same year. Its first project was to send an 'intelligent Irishman' out to conduct a house-to-house survey amongst the working class. They intended that social sciences, still suspect to the British

Association for the Advancement of Science, the very first meeting of which in 1831 at York had been attended by J. G. Robberds (though he did not join), should be every bit as progressive and useful as Baconian physical sciences.[9]

Back in her rustic Cheshire haven at Heathside Elizabeth wrote on 3 May 1832 to thank Harriet Carr and her family for their good wishes on her engagement to William. Her visit to Edinburgh and the painting of her picture must have followed this brief letter. Then, on 8 August, she wrote to Harriet again from aunt Lumb's – a letter of sparkling independence and subtlety – whilst 'in the middle, or rather I hope, three-quarters of the way through the bustle of wedding-gowns'. She jokes about the standard phrase, 'to learn obedience' to a husband, as something new to her, going on to say that she has 'the prettiest bonnet for the occasion that ever was'. As Jenny Uglow comments, 'in Gaskell's writing casual juxtapositions and minor details are often keys to vital issues' – but they were mostly of a highly personal and domestic kind at this stage in her life. News afloat could not be resisted. Had Harriet heard of a Mr and Mrs Boddington, struck by lightning on their wedding tour? Umbrellas served as conductors, and 'afterwards the steel in Mrs Boddington's stays, conveyed the fluid to within a straw's breadth of a vital part in her leg', in fact near the left femoral artery. Mr Boddington was rendered insensible for ten minutes.[10]

In July 1832 Edward Herford was surprised to discover that Mr Darbishire drove his wife to chapel in Manchester and then went on to his office, where he stayed until she had finished her devotions and 'Mr Gaskell his prose(y) composition'. Life was more relaxed in Knutsford. In her August letter Elizabeth told Harriet Carr that a large family party had put on a performance of Sheridan's *The Rivals*. She herself had been 'present at all the planning &c', but did not take part. Given her readiness to play charades, this might seem incredible were it not for the fact that she was away in Edinburgh that June. It might have been only by report that she knew her relations, complete amateurs, had done so well, with Lucy Holland '*great*' as Mrs Malaprop for some days afterwards. Neither taste nor fear prevented Elizabeth from making a joke about a new curse she claimed to have heard in Cheshire: '*Cholera seize thee*'. She rejoiced that the scourge had not reached Knutsford, though we find that in July the overseer of Higher Knutsford had been ordered 'to provide Lime for the Poor to whitewash the inside of their houses and also coal tar for the purpose of soaking the cloth in which the bodies of such as die of the cholera may be wrapped.' He was also instructed to inspect the dwellings of the poor and see that any filth near them was removed.[11]

There is no sign at this stage that Elizabeth would measure up to William Turner's elaborate requirements for a minister's wife, which she must have heard him expound with his usual clarity and force. She might even have read his carefully preserved 'pastoral letter' to Mary Robberds. One who should know better than almost anybody, Mary Robberds' daughter Mary Jane (Mrs Charles Herford), is very clear on the subject:

She steadily and consistently objected to her time being considered as belonging in any way to her husband's congregation for the purposes of congregational visiting, and to being looked to for that leadership in congregational work which is too often expected of 'the minister's wife;' but, at the same time, there have been few who have been more willing than she was to give time, and thought, and trouble where she felt they would be of any service; and many who, in their difficulties and troubles, have experienced her help and sympathy which none could give more tenderly, will bear witness to her thoughtful and abiding kindness.

It is, however, said that she taught in the Sunday school 'at its first home in that cellar-warehouse under the Unitarian chapel in Mosley Street'. The children came from poor districts like Ancoats, Miles Platting and Newton Heath. Later, she helped men like Thomas Wright in the rehabilitation of prisoners and she welcomed visits from the older girls of Lower Mosley Street Sunday school to her own home – on Saturday evenings for history and geography and on Sunday afternoons once a month for reading and talk. Mary Jane Herford, herself a Sunday school stalwart, was looking back upon all this after Elizabeth Gaskell's death, and was probably most aware of her attitudes in the 1850s. But in the summer of 1832, everything suggests that Elizabeth had been leading her privileged life on an island of health, pleasure and security, the vast sea of troubles of an industrialising age mirrored only emblematically in the miniature storms Turner had whipped up for his painting of Tabley mere on a windy day.[12]

On Thursday, 30 August 1832, the wedding day arrived. William and Elizabeth were married by licence in the parish church, like her parents and for the same legal reasons, by the vicar of Knutsford, Robert Clowes. Knutsford church dates from 1744, a handsome Georgian edifice in red brick with stone dressings, built at a considerable cost (£4000), a good deal of which was realised from the sale of pews to families like the Hollands. The spot where the bride and bridegroom had stood in the church was later pointed out to Mrs Chadwick. The register notes the presence of Peter Holland, his daughter Susan, Samuel Holland's daughter Catherine and William Gaskell's sister Elizabeth. Peter Holland probably gave the bride away. Aunt Lumb might have still been confined to her bed, and Henry Holland did not arrive in Knutsford till the day after the wedding, but there were many others who could have been present in the Hollands's pew. The fact that it was the youngest daughters whose names were recorded in the register suggests that a pleasant family custom has hidden the participation of relations who were probably there.

Knutsford itself had a marriage custom that was kept up for the bride and groom: white-sand flowers were sprinkled on a bed of red sand before many houses and spousal verses sung. 'When I was married', Elizabeth Gaskell wrote to Mary Howitt, 'nearly all the houses of the town were sanded'. *Looking Back at Knutsford* contains an early photograph of the church, together with one of Peter Holland's Church House taken over the graveyard between – looking like a rather less grim Haworth Parsonage. Alice Chadwick and Anne Ritchie were told that Elizabeth had been married from aunt Lumb's house, however. Mrs Chadwick also heard of a well-stocked linen press that she had given her niece and of money settled upon her as a marriage portion (perhaps from her grandfather's carefully guarded bequest). It was from Heathside, we might assume, that the couple set off on their honeymoon trip to Wales.[13]

After the wedding Kate Holland fabricated a rather laboured joke that she and Sue had pulled so hard on Sam's arms at the wedding that his shoulder had been put out. (Kate's brother Charles was to marry Samuel's sister Elizabeth.) This means that Samuel Gaskell can be added to those who had been present at the wedding ceremony on 30 August.[14] But if so, he must have returned almost immediately to Swan Street Hospital.[15]

On the morning of the following day, Friday 31st, when William and Elizabeth were off on their wedding journey to Wales, Dr Lynch admitted a child called John Brogan suffering from cholera. He died a few hours later in the afternoon. His grandfather, an Irishman called John Hayes, who had carried him to the hospital, was satisfied on the Saturday that it was a natural death, but when he saw early on Sunday morning that the coffin at the cemetery did not have the child's name chalked upon it like the seven or eight others, he became suspicious. He insisted on the lid being raised, and it was found that the child's head had been replaced by bricks, with shavings for the blood. The father and mother were distraught. Rumours of 'burking' spread, and in the afternoon riots erupted. Several thousand marched with the coffin to the hospital, broke down its gates and 'called loudly for Mr. Lynch and Mr. Gaskell, the resident medical-officers', who managed to escape over the wall at the back. Windows were smashed, beds, bedding and furniture thrown out. Some of the twenty-five patients there could not be carried out, so the mob did not set fire to the hospital but contented itself with burning the cholera van in the yard. The police were powerless at first, but the arrival of the boroughreeve and a magistrate with several troops of the 15th Hussars, added to the persuasive oratory of a Roman Catholic priest – 'not a sabre was drawn' – diverted the crowd from its intention. The coffin was then borne off into the town and finally seized by the police. The severed head was discovered in a house after enquiries by Dr Lynch and the priest.

After the infamous Burke and Hare body-snatching case in Edinburgh, the new anatomy act in the House of Commons allowing dissection of unclaimed paupers' bodies, the rattling passage of the cholera van with the sick through the streets, the denial of time for burial customs like the wake and the death carts 'moving slowly to a remote burying-ground branded with the double stigma of poverty and infection' – rough justice seemed the people's only resort.

The contrast between the swirl and surge of raw emotions and the calm deliberations of the Board of Health on Monday 3 September (insofar as they were mirrored in its cogent, succinct and beautifully engrossed set of minutes) is extreme. Newspapers both local and national reported a great deal more, with variants, and no doubt the actual discussion at the Board proceeded with the usual mixture of waffle, sarcasm, indignant denial and incisive commentary, but the official record consists of a short statement from D. Lynch jr, resident medical officer of the Swan Street Hospital, and brief interviews with John Hayes, the grandfather, and two clergymen. The Board heard that the head, now recovered, had been removed secretly at night by a Mr Robert Oldham, the newly appointed dispenser of medicines at Swan Street. John Hayes stated that he was now satisfied the death was a natural one and that he wished his grandson to be interred in St Patrick's burial ground; it need not be taken to the father's house first. The Reverend Daniel Hearne ('Revd Mr Herron' in the Board's minutes), a Catholic priest, stated that he had heard Mr Oldham confess that he had 'taken the head off for the purpose of examining it', and that 'it was his conscientious belief that Mr Lynch was perfectly ignorant of the revolting conduct of Mr Oldham' at the time. The Reverend J. Crook, another Catholic priest who used to attend the hospital several times a day, also expressed confidence in Mr Lynch. The Board then passed a number of practical resolutions, which included an application for a warrant against Oldham.

A letter from the medical staff of Commercial Street Hospital in an appendix to the minutes indicated that the Board had previously ordered that no autopsy should take place without the consent of relatives. On 4 September a similar appendix gave the text of a letter from the Swan Street medical staff after a meeting held at the Town Hall. It was ordered that it be communicated to the press. The staff had unanimously resolved

> That this Meeting feel called upon to express in the strongest terms of reprehension their censure of the unprecedented and most dangerous misconduct of the Resident Dispenser Mr Oldham. In the excited tone of public feeling, which Cholera has roused in this and other large towns, the Officers of the Swan Street Hospital had systematically foreborne the customary inspection of all those dying under their care.

The language is strong, the sense of dereliction of duty equally so. It was fortunate that blame could be limited:

> At the same time, that they feel compelled to visit the flagrant offence of Mr Oldham with their strongest censure, it becomes their duty and their pleasure to exculpate Mr Lynch and Mr Gaskell from all participation in this most unprofessional transaction and to testify their continued approbation of the zealous, active and judicious services of these meritorious officers.

The poor little lad was no longer an agonizing human loss but an item for special meetings with other fish to fry. He was interred in a leaden coffin supplied by the Board. The absconded dispenser was sought – he was never found – and a committee was appointed 'to prepare a placard explaining the unfortunate circumstances which have occurred in the case of John Brogan and stating the deep regret felt'. The Board also looked to the future and wished that the names of 'the Medical Gentlemen who are willing to continue their gratuitous services in attending on Cholera Patients and of those who are not' should be furnished.

Samuel Gaskell was not a signatory of the declaration from the Swan Street medical staff, presumably because he and Lynch were implicated in the tragic events, but the cholera epidemic was coming to an end. Stockport was reported free of cases in early September. Some weeks afterwards he became house-surgeon for eighteen months at its new Infirmary, founded in that year to deal with emergencies more frequent and continuous than cholera epidemics – the severe industrial accidents that astonished visiting strangers. The *Journal of the Royal Statistical Society* for September 1845 contained his article, 'Table of accidents brought to the Stockport Infirmary, and attended by the House-Surgeon, in the years 1833, 1834, and 1835'. This paper, read to the British Association at York in 1844, after he had been appointed resident superintendent of the Lancaster Asylum, is almost devoid of commentary in its printed form. Some figures speak for themselves, however. The ages of patients involved in factory accidents run from five to fifty upwards for men, most being ten to eighteen years old, and three to forty upwards for females, the majority being eleven to fourteen.[16]

By 16 September the whole terrible sequence of events around Swan Street had subsided into times past and gone. On this date William wrote to his 'very dear Sister' from Plas yn Penrhyn, where, he declared, 'Mrs Holland is kindness itself – and Sam I like very much – and Ann I am quite in love with'. His long letter, in crossed writing, not too easy to read sometimes, is crammed with details of travel and scenery. They had spent part of their honeymoon in 'dear little Aber', sped back to Conway in a coach with two bugles blowing all the way, sea sparkling on their left and rich-tinted hills on their right. Then they took a car south along the beautiful Conway valley to Llanwrst, over to Capel Curig, through the pass of Llanberis, where William forgot everything but his 'own Lily' in the 'wondrous wildness and rugged grandeur of the scene', and on into Caernarfon. After a night in Beddgelert and another in Tremadog, Samuel Holland's carriage came to bear them triumphantly over Madocks' embankment and up the hill to Plas yn Penrhyn with its glorious views and family welcome. At the end of this loving letter is a brief and once baffling postscript that has never been printed. It now powerfully evokes the alien context of far-away Manchester and its endless troubles: 'With my love to Sam tell him how glad I was to find he had nothing to do with the decapitation row – '[17]

'Now bless thyself; thou met'st with things dying', said the old shepherd after the shipwreck at the end of Act III of *The Winter's Tale*, 'I with things new-born.' William was honeymooning with his 'bonny wee wife'. '*My* bonny wee wife', he repeated in exultation to his sister, 'grows I do think more bonny than ever'. His words and rhythm blithely echo old lyrics, just as Elizabeth's half of the letter reminds us of the folk tradition from Thomas Percy's *Reliques*:

> You would be astonished to see our appetites, the dragon of Wantley, 'who churches ate of a Sunday, Whole dishes of people were to him, but a dish of Salmagunde' was really a delicate appetite compared to ours. If you hear of the principality of Wales being swallowed up by an earthquake, for earthquake read Revd Wm Gaskell.

Her use of his title, casually abbreviated, displays her sense that for the moment his ministerial self had been tucked away, almost forgotten as he gloried in the liberties of the newly married state.

On 5 November Herford wrote that 'last week but one' he was invited to their modest house at No. 1 Dover Street, off the Oxford Road, where he found them displaying, in a rather more temperate manner, 'evident fondness for each other'. He thought they were 'so well suited to one another – her gaiety & sprightliness will neutralise his gravity'. William's public and private personae were far more divergent than hers.[18] To William Turner Elizabeth reported that their new home was 'very countrified' for Manchester. There is no doubt that from the very beginning of their married life they were insulated from the evils that surrounded them in the shock city of the north, but works of charity would be their constant concern and they would not escape the sadness of infant deaths. Their first child, a daughter in 1833, was still-born, and two boys died as babies, one at the age of 9 months 18 days in the terrible delirium of scarlet fever.[19] As the morbid verse insisted,

> Children as young as you, as gay
> As playful and as strong,
> Are dying, dying every day,
> And so may you ere long.

Elizabeth Stevenson's family and friends lived in a world that sometimes seems incredible. In his capacity as a physician, Dr Benjamin Rush of Philadelphia believed that yellow fever could be cured by extreme measures, '*only* by *depleting* remedies'. From one newly arrived Englishman in 1794 he took 144 ounces of blood. Four of the bleedings were done in twenty-four hours; six days were sufficient for the whole twelve. Cobbett, then in America and writing under the pseudonym of Peter Porcupine, composed a mock advertisement for him: 'Wanted, by a physician, an entire new set of patients, his old ones having given him the slip; also a slower method of dispatching them than that of phlebotomy, the celerity of which does not give time *for making out a bill*. Rush was another extremist of the period, but serious bleeding of hapless patients was practised well into the nineteenth century.[20]

At least physicians believed that they were saving human life by such drastic measures. Scientists, 'experimental philosophers', could only claim to be doing this by indirect means. 'We have killed many poor robins by pouring fixable air upon them', Matthew Boulton once wrote like a fiend angelical to James Watt. The famous painting of an 'Experiment on a bird in the Air Pump' by Joseph Wright of Derby provides a permanent record of this mixture of controlled feeling and scientific enthusiasm, framed by the rational approval, silent scepticism and childish apprehension of the spectators. Mrs Barbauld's poem, 'The Mouse's Petition', which William Turner of Newcastle claimed had been twisted by her in the wires of its cage during the night before Priestley subjected it to the suffocating power of various gases, might appear to exemplify a new sensibility to suffering. It became famous, a set piece for children to memorise, but its author resisted any sentimental interpretation of her poetic plea: it was a 'petition of mercy against justice' rather than one of 'humanity against cruelty'. The poor creature 'would have suffered more as the victim of domestic economy, than of philosophical curiosity', she briskly proclaimed.[21]

By 1807, however, the young Henry Holland, training to become a doctor in Edinburgh, assisted in one painful experiment on a living dog that ended in its inevitable death from asphyxia. This made him certain that he could not face the next operation planned to take place on two rabbits, involving incisions in the trachea, a pipe with a stopcock and so on. Emotion wells up through the stilted prose of a letter to his father: 'My physiological ardour could not overcome other concomitant feelings of the mind.' A score of years later James Kay wrote his Edinburgh thesis on asphysia in warm-blooded animals, challenging the theories of the great Marie-François-Xavier Bichat by ingenious experiments on rabbits. But he too could not always maintain detachment and physiological objectivity, his latest biographer tells us, finding 'much that is deeply repugnant to the feelings in its pursuits'.

The inoculation against smallpox William Turner had so strongly campaigned for at the end of the eighteenth century turned out to be a success story of medical experimentation as far as human beings were concerned, but the sad instance of a consumptive Maria Brontë shows that between blisters applied to the side and Calvinistic doctrines administered to the soul, tubercular children might actually suffer less from the benign neglect practised by the wisest physicians and the most easy-going ministers of the gospel. Mangled victims of industrial accidents filled the graveyards, joining unfortunate patients operated on with heroic celerity by surgeons in the days before anaesthesia. The hazards of childbirth were notorious, and mothers and children who survived were still at the mercy of cholera, typhus, typhoid, whooping cough, scarlet fever and a great host of other ills that could not be cured.

After the death of her mother, Elizabeth Gaskell was lucky enough to survive the childish ailments from which none were exempt. Her flourishing and prosperous family was able to ensure that she was brought up in small towns and country places, and sent to holiday in the most pastoral areas of Wales. Even in great towns like London, Liverpool, Newcastle and Manchester she was shielded from 'contingent contagions' and apparently able to distance herself psychologically from them, just like one of her cousins. 'In a letter I had from Louisa Holland', she wrote from Woodside on 18 June 1831, 'she says it is a point of dispute as to whether Mr Wm Cayley is gone to get a wife or Cholera Morbus in St Petersburgh.' Her own joke about the latest curse in Cheshire springs from a sensibility developed under similar conditions.[22]

In childhood and youth she was both formed and protected by her family: she moved in its society, travelled with friends and relations, stayed with connections, lived and breathed in their atmosphere. This gave her as a young woman a breadth of middle-class social experience and subjected her to a considerable variety of influences, though there is no sign of religious mysticism or Romantic heights and depths. Her grandparents' home at Sandlebridge in the Cheshire countryside and the little circle of relations in Knutsford were succeeded by the companionship of fortunate young women in her Warwickshire school, diversified by visits to local gentlefolk. In her 'teens contacts with the literary society of her father in Chelsea were expanded by association with the families of successful professional men in London and Turner's coherent provincial fellowship in Newcastle-upon-Tyne. Visits to Liverpool and Wales brought her into the more precarious world of business speculations and rural industry as well as easy-going society in the wilder, 'more Welshy' places she loved so much. The contrast with the great estate purchased by Swinton Holland when she was thirteen and continuously improved by her cousin Edward as he established himself amongst the leading gentry of Gloucestershire must have been considerable, rather like that between the pretty little watering place of Beaumaris and Regency Cheltenham.

Some of her early experiences were distressing. The overlapping generations of her cousins in Knutsford, where her obvious social, intellectual and literary companions were often old enough to be her aunts, were not necessarily beneficial. She must have sensed, if she was not told, the growing desperation in the Chelsea household of her father and stepmother. She knew of the despair that came to afflict her once jolly elder brother and, as far as we know, had no certain idea of his eventual fate. She endured the death of her father and was not taken – or did not allow herself to be taken – to the bosom of the second Mrs Stevenson. Even the connection maintained with her Holland aunt and cousins in London was marred to some extent by their exceptional wealth. Sixty years later, her own daughters were able to recall what in all probability she had told them and encapsulate it in a phrase still glowing with humiliation – 'she was very beautiful in shabby dress – cousins vice versa' – just what one might expect if she had lived with aunt Lumb in 'cramped but refined poverty' and had 'a bad stepmother who ran into debt'. Their exaggeration is patent, but at its heart was the vulnerable core of their mother's lived experience.[23]

These are the personal torments of her upbringing, a private, Romantic blighting of the flower that produced all but invisible fruit when she was young. Her early formative years show no signs that, in Shelley's phrase, the pains and pleasures of her species had become her own. She existed, like her relations, in Peacock's civilised age of silver. The relaxed travel journals of her Holland cousins are examples of a literary form that she is known to have practised in her youth. Anyone would think at the time of her marriage in 1832 that she was already writing, or going to write, something like the kind of fiction produced with such ease by Katharine Thomson. The thinly disguised satiric accounts of Warwickshire society in *Constance: A Novel* could have been matched by light mockery of social life in Wales. Her letters show more than adequate abilities. What she later merely adumbrated in 'Company Manners' might have been diversified by exciting incidents like the story of Captain Barton and Kitty Holland's escape from a quicksand, or by the thrills of popular Gothic in some Welsh equivalent of Clopton House.

But Elizabeth married and came to Manchester, where the perfervid eloquence of William J. Fox in 1830 had turned his hearers' minds from the origins and history of the British and Foreign Unitarian Association to contemplation of 'the most glorious work which God has given men to do, – that of promoting the well-being of their fellow-creatures (*cheers*) ... ' William Gaskell cannot have sat unmoved. Two years later the charismatic Fox was crying, 'Let there be meadows and mountains, but there must also be streets, alleys, work-shops, and jails, to complete the scenery of the poetry of poverty.' The Gaskells' attention almost inevitably turned towards the poets and poetry of humble life, and their first effort, *Sketches among the Poor*, appeared in *Blackwood's* in 1837. Wordsworth and a romanticised Crabbe were their models. When Elizabeth at last turned to writing prose fictions in the 1840s, her own pen was destined to dwell on urban guilt and misery – *Libbie Marsh's Three Eras, Mary Barton, Lizzie Leigh, Ruth* and *North and South*, following Frances Trollope, Charlotte Elizabeth Tonna and Elizabeth Stone rather than Jane Austen, Ann Radcliffe and Katharine Thomson.[24]

We analyse with hindsight if we find the conscious origins of this initial phase of her public career during her first twenty or so years. Yet the underground streams still murmured beneath. In the course of a writing lifetime she reminds us again and again that human beings must live on and that not all facts of life are depressing. *Cranford* came bubbling up in fits and starts, and the dread voice finally past, she could produce a loving biography of her friend Charlotte Brontë and write heart-felt fictions like *Cousin Phyllis* and *Wives and Daughters*. Someone who had known her in the youthful days she recreated gave a vivid description to Anne Ritchie: 'She had a well-shaped head, regular, finely-cut features; her mien was bright and dignified, almost joyous, so my informant said, and among her many other gifts was that of delightful companionship.' The copy of her bust by David Dunbar and her portrait by William John Thomson survive to tell the same story. The flattering transformations of art and memory must be discounted, but her own best self is seen in the words she wrote on a French translation of *Round the Sofa*, presented to her youngest daughter and now in the library at Knutsford: 'Julia Bradford Gaskell from her very affectionate old mother, the distinguished Authoress'.

William was lucky to have caught her. Did he when he was wooing her ever attempt to follow the advice given in a poem by Prior, 'Let all her ways be unconfin'd / And clap your padlock – on her mind'? He would never have succeeded. In the meantime, sensibly, as a man about to be married, he reduced 'for the present' his own subscription to Manchester College from two guineas to one.[25]

NOTES

1 See *Letters*, pp. 1-2. TS, ECS and WG to EG, from Knutsford, now redated [27 and 29 March 1832]. E. Herford's MS diary, p. 46, notes Mrs Robberds' death on Monday 26 March 1832.

2 Henry Green, *Register*, transcr. W. R. Strachan, 1982; Joan Leach, 'Ruth: a subject of pain', *GNL*, VIII, August 1989, pp. 12-16; *CR*, VI, 1839, p. 630 (Anna, eldest d. of H. Worthington, esq. of Altrincham). See Appendix F for the full text of WG's letter.

3 JS&PH, LUBL: *Testimonials of SG*. See Carlyle, *Reminiscences*, ed. Campbell, p. 372, on the subject of testimonials.

4 Freeman, 'Samuel Gaskell', pp. 89-90 (SG's service at Swan Street not noticed); Thackray, 'Natural knowledge in a cultural context', p. 700 (Henrys); Pickstone, *Medicine and Industrial Society*, pp. 58-60; Selleck, *James Kay-Shuttleworth*, pp. 65-79; JRULM: SG to Dr Kay, Swan St Hospital, 15 July [1832]. Selleck emphasises that Kay's pamphlet appeared *before* cholera struck Manchester; the revised 2nd edn of November 1832 is often cited in a misleading way.

5 Prentice, *Manchester*, pp. 343-56; Alexis de Tocqueville, *Journeys to England and Ireland*, tr. George Lawrence and K. P. Mayer, ed. J. P. Mayer, London, 1958, pp. 17, 105-8; James Sambrook, *William Cobbett*, London and Boston, 1973, pp. 165, 177-8.

6 Section based upon *Report of the Proceedings*, Manchester, 1830, pp. 3-6, 15-16, kindly supplied by DWL (PP 15. 6. 6).

7 WEC to Lucy Aikin, 29 December 1831, qu. by Webb, *Harriet Martineau*, p. 82. See also Webb, 'The Unitarian background', in Smith, pp. 18-23.

8 NLPS: JAT to William Turner, Manchester, 27 May 1834; Burney, *Cross Street Chapel Schools*, pp. 14, 25-7, 89 (with illustr.); Fryckstedt, pp. 71-2; Shelston, *Industrial City*, pp. 32-64, 94-7; Seed, 'Liberal culture in Manchester', pp. 13-20, who cites Mary Carpenter, *Memoirs of Joseph Tuckermann, DD, of Boston*, 1849. I am grateful to the Reverend E. J. Raymond Cook for allowing me to consult the chapel's four bound volumes of reports (I, pp. 6-7, 12, 14-15 cited).

9 Pickstone, 'Ferriar's fever to Kay's cholera: disease and social structure in Cottonopolis', *HS*, XXII, 1984, pp. 409-10; Selleck, *Kay-Shuttleworth*, pp. 80-7; Morell and Thackray, *Gentlemen of Science: Early Years*, pp. 291-6, 399n.

10 Chapple, 'Five early letters ', pp. 16-19; Uglow, p. 77. Boddington was unidentified, but a lengthy report in *The Lancet* for 15 September 1832 (pp. 742-5) was found by pure chance. T. T. Boddington (son of Benjamin Boddington of Badger Hall) and his wife, driving in the barouche-seat of a post chariot from Tenbury to Bromyard, were struck by lightning on 13 April 1832. Faraday himself communicated with the *London and Edinburgh Philosophical Magazine*.

11 MCL: Herford, MS diary, I, p. 109; Joan Leach, 'Knutsford's poor in the 1800's', p. 29.

12 *Unitarian Herald* [ed. W. Gaskell], 17 November 1865, obit. signed M, identified by Ward in *DNB* (see *Letters*, p. 191); Joan Leach, 'Thomas Wright, the good Samaritan', *GSN*, III, p. 15. Cobden Smith, 'Mrs. Gaskell and Lower Mosley Street', p. 159, identifies her old pupils as Mrs Smethurst, Sarah Higgins (Mrs Richard Wade), Ann Royle (mother of Robert Smith), Ann Rowlands (Mrs Brown), Harriet Bates, Miss Hadfield (Mrs John Hadfield), Lizzie Fergusson (Mrs Large). Cf. MCL: BR 823. 824 P2/ 154: *Mary Barton*, 5th edn, 'To Ann Smith from her sincere friend E. C. Gaskell, May 20th 1854', presented by J. H. Pimley (son-in-law).

13 Chadwick, 1910, pp. 183-9; Ritchie, pref. *Cranford*, p. xvi; *Letters*, pp. 28-9; King, *Portrait of Knutsford*, p. 2; Goodchild *et al.*, *Looking Back at Knutsford*. For HH's belated arrival see p. 183 above.

14 See ECG to Eliza Gaskell, [Plas Penrhyn, p. m. 17 September 1832], *Letters*, p. 2. The phrasing and address, 1 Dover Street, Oxford Road, Manchester, suggest Sam Gaskell rather than Sam Holland.

15 Sources for the following account differ in details. I have mainly followed, courtesy of MCL staff, the minutes of the Manchester Board of Health, 3-6 September, and Manchester newspapers. See bibliographical appendix; also Sellek, *Kay-Shuttleworth*, p. 76.

16 Durey, *Return of the Plague*, pp. 28, 179-84; Morris, *Cholera 1832*, pp. 64-6, 110-11; SG, 'Table of accidents', *JRSS*, VIII, 1845, pp. 277-81, ref. from Pickstone, *Medicine and Industrial Society*, pp. 61, 68; JS&PH, LUBL: *Testimonials of SG*. I am here grateful to Alan Shelston for his help.

17 Details from LUBL: MSS, WG and ECG to Eliza Gaskell, Plas Penrhyn, 16 September 1832. See *Letters*, pp. 2-3, and *GSN*, IX, March 1990, pp. 5-7, for the full text of WG's half, which is often quoted inaccurately.

18 MCL: Herford, MS diary, I, p. 153.

19 See p. 325 and n. above; Sharps, 23; Chapple, 'Two unpublished Gaskell letters from Burrow Hall', pp. 67-8. ECG's sonnet, 'On visiting the grave of my stillborn little girl', Sunday, 4 [*sic*] July 1836, was printed in Knutsford Edn, I, pp. xxvi-xxvii.

20 *Letters of Benjamin Rush*, ed. Butterfield, II, pp. 750, 815 (letter of 24 September 1799), 1213-18; Sambrook, *Cobbett*, pp. 48-50.

21 Nicolson, *Joseph Wright*, I, pp. 111-14, II, plate 58; *Poems of Anna Barbauld*, ed. McCarthy and Kraft, pp. 244-5. 'Fixable air' is carbonic acid gas.

22 DCLH: HH to PH, Edinburgh, 8 February 1807; Selleck, *James Kay-Shuttleworth*, p. 41; ECG, *Life of CB*, I, pp. 72-6; Barker, *The Brontës*, pp. 134-8; Kidd, *Manchester*, pp. 47-50; Chapple, 'Five early letters', pp. 3, 19.

23 Ward Notebook, ff. 6-8.

24 *Report of the Proceedings*, p. 13; W. J. Fox, 'The poor and their poetry', *MR*, 1832, qu. Mineka, *Dissidence of Dissent*, p. 302; Pollard, p. 34; Michael Wheeler, 'Two tales of Manchester Life', *GSJ*, III, pp. 6-28; Kathleen Tillotson, *Novels of the 1840s* (1954), corr. edn, London, 1961, pp. 88-91, 123-5, 202-23.

25 Ritchie, pref. *Cranford*, p. xvi; Prior, 'An English padlock'; MCO: WG to G. H. Wood, MSS Wood 25, f. 26 [May 1832]. On 21 October [1833] he reported that he had transmitted the subscriptions of Mrs Lumb, Miss Holland and Mrs Long of Knutsford (MSS Wood 26, f. 182).

A

Stevensons of Berwick-upon-Tweed

The information in appendices A-C is not complete, nor checked in every detail against original documents, but it is more comprehensive than any other Gaskell source.

The pedigrees tipped into some copies of John Scott's 1888 *History* are not helpful for this branch of the Stevenson family. Berwick-upon-Tweed record office holds a number of essential documents: burgess rolls (B. 1; also pr. at various dates); guild enrolment books (apprentice indentures); poll books (borough archives: G. 5/6, 7); rate books, 1780-1805 (GBR. 25-27); microfilm of Berwick, Holy Trinity registers of baptisms, marriages and burials (by 'Jo: Rumney, Vicar');[1] Jean Hanson, *Parish Church of the Holy Trinity, Berwick upon Tweed: Monumental Inscriptions* (TS); marriage allegations and bonds.

Amongst other sources:

(a) [Bonner-Smith and Lewis], *Commissioned Sea Officers of the Royal Navy,* Stella Colwell, *Family Roots: Discovering the Past in the Public Record Office,* London, 1991; *IGI; DNB*; [James Good], *Directory and Concise History of Berwick-upon-Tweed,* 1806; Sharps, pp. 376-7; *Steel's Original and Correct List of the Royal Navy* (1782-1813); *The Navy List* (1814 et seq.); *Lieutenants' passing certificates* (PRO: ADM 107/4); *Returns of officers' service,* 1817 (PRO: ADM 9/7).

(b) A. W. Ward notebook at Peterhouse, Cambridge;[2] chapel register, Over Peover, Cheshire; Berwick parish church memorial tablet; notes by Mr Francis Cowe on Robert Stevenson's will (30 October 1809) and documents of 44 Bridge Street, Berwick (disentailing deed and mortgage of 1842), and correspondence with Mrs Linda A. Bankier, Archivist-in-Charge, BRO. I am most grateful to them both for expert assistance.

ECG *Elizabeth Gaskell*
dau *daughter*   B *burgess of Berwick*
b *born*   bp *baptised*   m *married*   d *died*

Joseph Stevenson[3] of Berwick, bp Berwick 11 September 1719, son of William; RN from summer 1844; B 29 January 1748 as apprentice (26 September 1735) of Gabriel Stevenson;[4] RN lieutenant's passing certificate 6 June 1853, lieutenant RN 15 June 1757 [rank of lieutenant confirmed by B, m, d records, also by son William's bp];[5] lived Hide Hill quarter of Berwick from June 1780; in *Steel's List, Corrected to February 1797*, but not later; m by licence Berwick 2 August 1769, **Isabel** [ECG note: '1st cousin once removed to the Poet'], bp Berwick 2 August 1741, dau of Joseph Thomson; she d 22 January 1806 aged sixty-four, of 'palsy' (burial register), bur Berwick parish church; he d 14 February 1799 aged eighty, bur Berwick parish church 20 February 1799. (No will found at Berwick, Durham, York, or London.)

Children of Joseph and Isabel Stevenson (née Thomson):

William, bp Berwick 26 November 1770; B 27 January 1792 as eldest son of Joseph; c. 1792 tutor at Bruges; 1793-96 tutor Manchester Academy and clergyman, Manchester [1796 burgess roll]; October 1797 began farming Saughton Mills; m by licence 1 December 1797 at Over Peover parochial chapel, Cheshire (1) **Elizabeth**, b 19 April 1771, dau of Samuel and Mary **Holland** of Sandlebridge; Elizabeth d Chelsea ?29 October, probably bur 30 October 1811 at Chelsea, King's Road burial ground; William c. 1802-6 teacher, Edinburgh [Edinburgh directories]; 20 May 1806 apptd Keeper of the Papers, Treasury; m by licence 11 April 1814 at St Luke's old parish church, Chelsea (2) **Catherine**, b Savannah 1775, dau of Alexander **Thomson** (d c. 1800), of Edinburgh, formerly of Savannah, Georgia; Scotland post-1829; living Glasgow 1855; William d Chelsea, 22 March 1829, bur 27 March 1829 aged fifty-seven [sc. 58], King's Road burial ground.

Joseph Thomson, bp Berwick 30 April 1772; B 7 November 1794 [1806 printed roll: Ship Master,[6] annotation, 'Dead'].

Dorothy, bp Berwick 20 February 1774; m ?Costorphine church October 1798 **George Landles**, master cooper of Bridge Street, Berwick (1806 directory); she d Berwick 23 February 1805 aged thirty-one; he d Berwick 23 July 1826 aged sixty-four.[7]

Robert [ECG note: 'webfooted & handed'], bp Berwick 17 April 1776; B 1798; surgeon, 44 Bridge Street, Berwick from 1807; m at Berwick 24 November 1803 **Elizabeth Wilson** [ECG pedigree: 'Marianne'], b 1779; will drawn up 30 October 1809; he d Berwick 1818; she d 1875.

John Thomson Turner, bp Berwick 21 February 1780; Lieutenant 19 February 1800 [not in *Navy Lists* after 25 June 1827]; AB, Mid, Mate *Audacious* 17 March 1793-11 December 1799; Mid *Foudroyant* 11 December 1799-19 February 1800; Lt *El Corso* 19 February 1800-26 July 1802; Lt *Sea Fencibles*, Westhaven 22 October 1803-18 June 1805; Lt *Zealous* 25 June 1805-26 December 1807.

Children of William and Elizabeth Stevenson (née Holland):

John, b Saughton Mills 27 November 1798; EIC, free mariner 1 March 1820; B 13 March 1820; c. May 1820 London, navigation, etc.; 14 June 1820 sailed from Portsmouth for Calcutta on *Lady Raffles;* November [?1820] officer, *Earl Kellie*, country ship; later on *Marianne Sophia;* a chief mate by 16 June 1823; 31 October 1824 listed as free mariner in Calcutta directory; Burmese war 1824; Calcutta 1825; London, *Catharine* 5 December [?1826]; Chelsea lodgings; sailed c. July 1827, 2nd officer *Recovery*, Portsmouth to Bombay; 30 July and 15 August [?1828] at 3 Beaufort Row; ?listed as free merchant Calcutta directory 1831, etc.

?Six children, d young;

Elizabeth Cleghorn, b 'Bell vue', Chelsea 29 September 1810; midsummer 1811 at 3 Beaufort Row; c. November 1811 Mrs Lumb's, Heathside, Knutsford; early March 1815 Edmund Sharpe's accident at ?Church House; John's letters to ECS at Knutsford: 27 December 1819, 19 March 1820, 7 May, 12 June & 29 November [?1820], 15 January 1821; c. October 1821 to Byerleys' school, Barford, and May 1824 Stratford-upon-Avon; left school, ?Dumbleton, and Knutsford by June 1826; 5 December [?1826] at 3 Beaufort Row; by c. May 1827 Knutsford (father's letter); summer 1827 'travels' and visits, ?incl. Wales and London by July 1828; John's letters to ECS at Knutsford: 30 July and 15 August [?1828]; 3 Beaufort Row by March 1829, father's death; ?Norfolk Street and by 15 June 1829 Knutsford; 10 September 1829 at Dumbleton, and to ?Cheltenham; by 4 November 1829 at ?Knutsford; visits to Essex, Newcastle-upon-Tyne and Edinburgh; by 18 June 1831 at Woodside; by 20 October 1831 at Knutsford; by 16 January 1832 visit to Manchester; c. 14 March 1832 engagement to **William Gaskell** and 21 March 1832 return to Knutsford; June 1832 Edinburgh visit; by 8 August 1832 at Knutsford; 30 August 1832 marriage at Knutsford, honeymoon in Wales.

Children of William and Catherine Stevenson (née Thomson):

William, bp London 12 June 1815; ?medical man Bridlington, d young; dead by 1859.

Catherine, b 7 December 1816, bp Chelsea 11 June 1817; m December 1833

Archibald Black; she living Dunoon 1855.

Natural child of Joseph Thomson Stevenson, possibly by a Dora [ECG pedigree]:

William Stevenson, living 1809.

Children of George and Dorothy Landles (née Stevenson):
Margaret, b 1802; m Wm Paulin B 1821; she d 1888+.
Isabella, d in infancy.

Children of Robert and Elizabeth Stevenson (née Wilson),
all living 1842:
John, b c. 1805; B 1826, attorney; ?m **Sophia Church**; d 1852.
Joseph, b Berwick 27 November, bp 17 December 1806; B 1828; London from 1831; m on 19 September 1831 **Mary Ann Craig**, b 1811; she died 11 July 1869; Durham from 1839, ordained priest; librarian and keeper of records to dean and chapter 1841; parish of Leighton Buzzard from January 1849, resigned 1862; London, Selly Park, etc.; Jesuit novice 1877, vows 1885; d Farm Street 8 February 1895; bur Fulham St Thomas.
Isabella [ECG note: 'unmar: crooked'], bp 27 July 1810; living Berwick 1827.
Elizabeth Wilson, bp 18 March 1812; m Rev. **W. M. H. Church**; she d Torquay 12 December 1853.
William Berry, b ? [ECG notes c. 1853: 'India dead – married'; 'Dr. William married a mad wife']; 18 February 1823 assistant surgeon, Bengal.
Marianne, b 1817; m **Sir Henry Manisty**, Q.C. (1808-90); she d London 1892.
Robina Dorothy [ECG note: 'widow of a surgeon'], b posth. 15 July 1818 [memorial tablet]; m (1) **Andrew Henderson** (2) **Alexander Robertson** (1805-95); she d 8 February 1898, bur Tweedmouth.

NOTES

1 Unusually, both death and burial dates appear in this register, 1797-1812.
2 It contains genealogical information (ff. 1 verso, 108) and 'an exact copy of some pencil notes [with pedigree] made by Mrs. Gaskell in the inside of an envelope (the postmark 1853), and found in Mr. Gaskell's desk' (f. 7 verso), in Meta's hand. See *Letters*, p. 272.
3 ECG pedigree: 'Captain Stevenson RN'. Spellings with *eph* and *ea* normalised to *ev*, except in quotations; similarly, *Thomson* for *Thompson*.
4 Mrs Bankier informs me that until 1783 only eldest sons of freemen were admitted by birthright; other sons had to serve a seven years' apprenticeship (often nominal) to a freeman. Joseph enrolled at the usual age of sixteen, but did not apply for the freedom until he was twenty-eight.
5 *James* Stevenson (1) was Captain RN in 1797; *James* Stevenson (2) Captain RN in 1812.
6 Said to have been Lieutenant RN, but not in Bonner-Smith and Lewis.
7 Hanson, *Monumental Inscriptions*, 385 (Chest). Buried on 28 July 1826, aged sixty-three [*sic*]; address Western Lane (Burial register).

B

Hollands of Cheshire

The main reference works are W. F. Irvine, ed. *A History of the Family of Holland of Mobberley and Knutsford in the County of Chester,... from Materials Collected by the Late Edgar Swinton Holland [1847-1896]*, pr. pr. Edinburgh, 1902, and Bernard H. Holland, *The Lancashire Hollands*, London, 1917. An important source is *The Holy Bible*, Alexander Kincaid: Edinburgh, 1762, now in the possession of Mr David C. L. Holland. On the inside cover is written 'Family Bible of Samuel Holland of Sandle-bridge. Parish of Marthall cum Warford County of Cheshire'; a printed slip bears the name of P. Holland, and 'Ann Holland 1776' is written on a flyleaf. (There is a later note to say that pictures of Samuel Holland and his wife are at Kneesworth Hall, Royston, Herts.) David Holland has also a paper written by Ann Holland (1765-1809) that gives genealogical information copied from an older letter.

The public record office in Chancery Lane holds the Protestant Dissenters' general register (RG4) of births and certificates (RG5), kept in Dr Williams's Library until 1837. The PRO also contains wills proved in the Prerogative Court of Canterbury; those proved at York are in the Borthwick Institute of Historical Research, Peaseholme Green, York. The wills of Samuel Holland (d. 1816) and his daughter Anne (d. 1809) were supplied by CRO. MSS consulted on microfilm there include: Knutsford old dissenting chapel registers of births and baptisms, marriages, deaths and burials; Over Peover parochial chapel register of marriages; Chester diocese marriage licence allegations and bonds. Knutsford dissenting chapel records do not contain all the baptisms one might have hoped for and its burial register for 1792-1821 is missing. See 'Lost Registers', *N&Q*, 13 September 1862, p. 211.

Lumb family documents are in the John Goodchild loan collection at Wakefield; Holland records in the possession of Mrs Portia Holland (LUBL loan deposit) and Mr David Holland (see the bibliographical appendix).

Printed works consulted include *CR*; Hunter, pedigree of Holland; various commercial directories. Later works include *Burke's Peerage*; Cedric II [Herbert Hulme], *Old Mobberley*, [?1909]; MCL: Hall, ed. '*Knutsford* again'; Alan Ruston, *Monthly Repository Obituaries 1806-1832*, 1985, and *Unitarian*

Obituaries from Various Denominational Journals 1784-1850, The Editor (41 Hampermill Lane, Oxhey, Watford, Herts WD1 4NS), 1990; W. R. Strachan, *Record of Graves and Inscriptions, Knutsford Chapel,* 1971, rev. 1988 (TS); W. R. Strachan, TSS of Knutsford chapel registers, 1982; Joshua Toulmin, *Memoirs of the Revd Samuel Bourn [with] Biographical Notices,* Birmingham, 1808 (W. Turner II on W. Willets); also George Pegler, 'The meeting house at Newcastle-under-Lyme', *TUHS,* V, 1930-34; Barbara and Hensleigh Wedgwood, *The Wedgwood Circle 1730-1897,* London, 1980; *DNB; IGI.*

I acknowledge especially the help of Joan Leach, Mary Thwaite and the staff of KPL.

ECG *Elizabeth Gaskell*
ODC *old dissenting chapel, Knutsford*
dau *daughter*   b *born*   bp *baptised*
m *married*   d *died*
bur *buried*   unm *never married*

John Holland of Dam Head House, Mobberley (7 December 1690- bur 24 June 1770) m 1718 **Mary,** dau of Peter and Elizabeth **Colthurst** (née Brooks); Mary bur 5 August 1757 aged sixty-five.

Children of John and Elizabeth Holland:

Rev. **John** (1720-51); **Elizabeth** (1721-82) m (1) John Norbury; m c. 1755 (2) Peter Swinton of Nether Knutsford;[1] **Peter** (1722-61) m c. March 1751 Margaret (1725-1809), dau William and Margaret Bostock; **Mary** (1725-84) m 1758 Rev. W. Turner (1714-94) of Wakefield; **Ann** (1727-69) m Thomas Holland of Manchester, brother of Philip of Bolton; **Catherine** (1728-87) m Rev. Philip Holland of Bolton (1721-89); **Thomas** (1730-51); **Abigail** (1731-living 1769) m 1762 William Coppock of Stockport; **Samuel** [see below]; **Sarah** b and d 1737).

Children of Peter, attorney of Knutsford, and Margaret (née Bostock):

John, d 2 Mar 1835 aged eighty-two or eighty-three (m Susannah, d 6 December 1836 aged seventy-eight); **Mary,** d 13 April 1796 aged forty-four (m George Checkley); **Margaret,** d 25 January 1842 aged eighty-seven; **Peter** of Liverpool, m dau of Chapman; **William,** d young; **William,** b 10 March 1761, d 8 April 1802.

Samuel Holland, from 1774 of Sandlebridge, Marthall cum Little Warford and Dogholes, Great Warford; grazier and gentleman, b 25 March 1734, youngest son of John of Dam Head House and Mary, dau of Peter (d 16 June 1741 aged seventy-two) and Elizabeth Colthurst (d 15 June 1740 aged seventy-one) of Sandlebridge;[2] m Knutsford 10 October 1763 **Ann,** b circa 1740, dau of Peter (d 6 December 1788 aged seventy-four) and Hannah **Swinton** ('a former wife', d 5 July 1771 aged sixty-two) of Cross Town and

Nether Knutsford; Ann d 1 July 1814 aged seventy-four, bur ODC 4 July 1814; Samuel d 20 or 26 (Irvine) May 1816 aged eighty-two; bur ODC.

Children of Samuel and Ann Holland (née Swinton):

Ann, b 29 Jan 1765, d unm 24 January 1809 aged forty-three; bur ODC.

Peter, b Mobberley (1851 Census) 3 June 1766; surgeon, Church House, Knutsford; m Hulme 1786 (1) **Mary**, dau of Reverend William **Willets** (1697-1779) of Newcastle-under-Lyme and his wife Catherine née Wedgwood (1726-25 August 1804); Mary d 3 October 1803 aged thirty-seven, bur ODC; Peter m Walcot church, Bath 21 Jan 1809 or December 1808 (Irvine) (2) **Mary**, b 1 Jan 1769, dau of Daniel[3] (1769-1840) or Jeremiah (Hunter, Irvine) and Esther **Whittaker** of Manchester; Mary died 5 Aug 1840, bur Knutsford St John; Peter d 10 or 19 (Irvine) June 1855; bur ODC.

Hannah, b 29 July 1767, m by licence at Over Peover 7 October 1789 **Samuel Lumb**, aged twenty-two in 1783, woolstapler of Wakefield; after separation of Leicester, later Birstall; bur Birstall 29 March 1805; 1799-1809 Hannah living Over Knutsford; by 1811 at Nether Knutsford; d 1 May 1837 aged sixty-nine; bur ODC; will proved PCC 17 August and 30 December 1837, under £2000.

Samuel, b 15 Sept 1768; merchant of Liverpool (York Street, Argyle Street, Wellington Road, Toxteth Park) and from 1832 Plas yn Penrhyn, Merionethshire; m at St Anne's Liverpool 14 September 1796 **Catherine**, b 1771, third child of John **Menzies** of Rodney Street, Liverpool; she d Caernarfon 1 September 1847 aged seventy-six; he d 28 September 1851 aged eighty-three, bur Toxteth.

Mary, b 23 Jan 1770, d unm 10 November 1812 aged forty-two, bur ODC.

Elizabeth, b 19 April 1771; m 1 December 1797 **William Stevenson** (see Appendix A).

Catharine, b 25 August 1772; July 1805–spring 1810 Trieste and Malta; later ?London; d unm 26 July 1822 aged fifty, bur ODC.

Abigail, b 12 September 1773; with Samuel Holland, Liverpool circa 1800-10; Knutsford in 1820s; d unm 26 July 1848, bur ODC; will proved PCC 30 January 1849.

Swinton Colthurst, b Sandlebridge 27 November 1777; 1793-1800 in trade Liverpool; USA to 1802, Italy to 1803; April 1803 at Trieste; m Knutsford St John 9 May 1805 **Anne**, dau of William and Catherine **Willets**; July 1805-1808 Trieste, Malta to March 1810; Newington Green, then Hackney by 1811 (Marianne Lumb's will) to 1816; Russell Square to 1819; The Priory, Roehampton and Park Lane to 1828; bought Dumbleton Hall and estate, Gloucester, June 1823; Swinton d 27 December 1827; will proved PCC 28 February 1828; Anne at 32 Norfolk Street, Park Lane 1831; d 1845.

Children of Peter and Mary Holland (née Willets):

Henry, b Knutsford 27 Oct 1788; January 1799-1803 Newcastle-upon-Tyne; 1803 Bristol; 1804-6 Glasgow University; summer 1810 Iceland; 1811 Edinburgh degree; 1816 FRS; January 1816 to Mount Street, London; 1820 to L Brook Street; m Audlem 8 September 1822 (1) **Margaret Emma,** dau James **Caldwell** of Linley Wood; she d 2 February 1830; m 20 March 1834 (2) **Saba,** b 46 George Street, Edinburgh February 1802, dau of Rev. Sydney **Smith**; she d 2 November 1866; 1837 physician extraordinary; 1852 physician in ordinary; baronet 10 May 1853; d 27 October 1873.

Mary, b 8 May 1790, d 11 May 1790.

Mary, b 1 May 1791, d 15 Feb 1792.

Mary, b 16 Oct 1792, bp 18 November 1792; 1802 in Newcastle-upon-Tyne for a year; December 1820 Liverpool visit; December 1821 Newcastle-upon-Tyne visit; ?early 1820s Lakes expedition; summer 1823 Barmouth; 1829-34 looked after M. E. Holland and children; d 11 June 1877.

Bessy, b 22 Feb 1796; 1814 London visit; ?early 1820s Lakes expedition; Christmas 1821 Manchester; summer 1823 Barmouth; September 1829 Gloucestershire visit; January 1830 refused marriage offer; m Knutsford 24 September 1835 Rev **Franklin Howorth** of Bury (1804-82), widower; spring 1849 Shottery visit; she d 16 July 1886.

Charles, b 6 Sept 1798; d 22 Apr 1799.

Lucy, b 17 Sep 1800; winter 1813-14 Newcastle-upon-Tyne; Christmas 1821 Manchester; ?early 1820s Lakes expedition; summer 1823 Barmouth; May 1826 with Swinton Hollands; late 1829 helped nurse M. E. Holland; d 24 Aug 1883.

Children of Peter and Mary Holland (née Whittaker):

Charles Aikin, b Knutsford 14 Nov 1809, bp 21 July 1810; 1821 school at Manchester and Newcastle-upon-Tyne; April 1821 Liverpool visit; c. April 1829 Liverpool solicitor's office; m Cunliffe, living 1853.

Susan, b 2 Apr 1811, m Knutsford 10 Apr 1844 **Richard T. Deane,** surgeon of Knutsford, widower; he died January 1851, aged forty-six; April 1821 Liverpool visit; September 1829 Lancaster visit; she d 10 April 1889.

Arthur, b 3 March 1813; 1821 school at ?Manchester and Newcastle-upon-Tyne; April 1821 Liverpool visit; October 1830 to Dublin; d 25 August 1833, bur 30 August ODC.

Child of Samuel and Hannah Lumb (née Holland):

Marianne, b Sandlebridge 17 October 1790, bp Wakefield 21 May 1791; d Halifax 31 March 1812, bur 4 April; will proved York 24 April 1812, under £800.

Children of Samuel Lumb and Mrs Esther Scrimsher or Skrimshaw, later Mrs Burton (d May 1816):

Sophia (Lumb) Scrimsher, bp ?Birstall 9 September 1796; c. 1816 milliner York.

Samuel, bur Birstall 11 February 1798.

Harriet, bp Birstall 3 February 1799; c. 1816 milliner York, m Jethro Carris, Easingwold; both living 1832.

Selina, bp Birstall 29 September 1800; c. 1816 Birstall.

Samuel, bp Birstall 1 June 1804, d Cotherstone June 1818.

Children of Samuel and Catherine Holland (née Menzies):

Anne, b 27 June 1797; ?early 1820s Lakes expedition; spring 1849 Shottery; April 1851 Manchester, Cheltenham by 1 September; d unm?

Charles, b 12 June 1799; 1812 to Malta; c. 1818-33 South America; m 15 November 1838 **Elizabeth**, b Warrington 21 September 1812, dau of William (d 15 March 1819 aged forty-one) and Margaret (later Mrs Dimock, d 12 January 1850 aged sixty-nine) **Gaskell** of Warrington; Elizabeth d 8 March 1892 aged eighty, bur Toxteth; Charles 1844 bought Liscard Vale; he d 5 February 1870, bur Toxteth.

Frances, b 23 September 1800; by 1847 Porthmadog, there 1856; d 1883 unm.

Menzies, b 1802; c. 1812-18 Fairfield, Lancaster and Hanau schools; d unm Leghorn ?1819 (1817 Irvine).

Samuel, b 17 October 1803; c. 1812-18 Fairfield, Lancaster and Hanau schools; 1821 to Ffestiniog; 1827-76 Plas yn Penrhyn; m January 1850 (1) **Annie** dau of Josiah **Robins** of Alesley Park, Warwickshire; she d 1877; he m 1878 (2) **Caroline June** dau Rev. J. T. **Burt** of Crowthorne; lived Maentrog and Cardeon; he d 27 December 1892; she d 1924.[4]

Catherine, b 17 November 1804; c. August 1813 to Putney; m Wales ?10 April 1838 **Richard Greaves** of Shottery by 1834; post-1849 of The Cliff, Warwick; he d 29 April 1870; she d 1 March 1886.

Children of William and Elizabeth Stevenson (née Holland):

see Appendix A

Children of Swinton Colthurst and Anne Holland (née Willets):

Edward, b Trieste 11 February 1806; Eton and 1829 B. A. Cambridge; inherited Dumbleton 1827; m ?26 April 1832 (1) **Sophia** (1813-51), dau **Elias Isaac** of Boughton, Worcs; m 1857 (2) **Frances Maria**, dau of S. **Christian** of Malta, widow of Robert Hunter; she d 1898; 1835-37 M.P East Worcs; 1855-68 M.P. for Evesham; d 4 January 1875.

Jessie, d infant.

Caroline, b Trieste 27 March 1807; d unm Knutsford 9 October 1833, bur 14 October ODC.

Charlotte, b Malta 10 August 1808; m c. April 1833 **John Whitmore Isaac** of Worcester.

Louisa, b Malta 7 February 1810; m 1857 Rev. **Richard Crofts** of Hillingdon.

Frederick, Commander, R.N., b London 6 August 1814, bp 21 May 1815; m 18 August 1846 (1) **Susan**, dau Samuel **Christian** of Malta; m (2) **Anne** (1822-1913), dau of Thomas **Denman**, 1st Baron Denman; c. 1852 purchased Ashbourne Hall; d Euston Square, London 21 July 1860.

George Henry, b Hackney 31 May 1816; m **Charlotte Dorothy**, dau of Sir Robert **Gifford**, 1st Baron Gifford; he d 1891.

Some details Ward gained from Mrs Gaskell's daughters about the Lumbs (Notebook, ff. 4-6) are not entirely accurate, but it is a unique source:

> Mrs Stevenson died within a month of Mrs G's birth – she was put in charge of a shopkeeper's wife – Mrs Withington a friend brought the baby down to Knutsford (see *Mary Barton*) to her aunt Miss Holland (Mrs S's sister) who had just [*sic*] married Mr Lumb. – Mrs Lumb only found out after her marriage that *he was out of his* wits [last six words inserted]. She then ran away from him – he lived at Wakefield in Yorks. One child Marianne [name inserted] of Mrs Lumb had jumped out of window seeing her mother come up – and become a cripple – It was to amuse and please this child that the baby E. S. was sent for to Knutsford.
>
> She looked upon Mrs Lumb as her mother.
>
> They lived in gt poverty at Knutsford – the daughter Marianne had resolved to settle all her property on her mother but she died a day or two before coming of age.

NOTES

1 As his second wife. Her younger brother had married a dau of Peter Swinton by a first wife (Irvine, p. 60).

2 See Irvine, p. 158, for Colthurst tombstones in ODC; also Payne, p. 54 or Chadwick, 1913, p. 57.

3 Family Bible. Se also Rae, *Turtle at Mr. Humble's*, pp. 67-8.

4 See *Memories of Sir Llewelyn Turner*, ed. Vincent, p. 216; *Dictionary of Welsh Biography*.

C

Turner family

The papers of Turner's Hanover Square congregation are now held by the Tyne and Wear Archives Service, Blandford Square, Newcastle-upon-Tyne. Turner's own Register of births and baptisms (TWA: 1787/9) is especially important; also, a MS copy made in 1873 of tombstone inscriptions at St Nicholas's Church, Newcastle-upon-Tyne (TWA: 1787/113, bound opp. p. 16 of George Harris, *The Christian Character*, London, 1859).

Printed works consulted include *DNB*; Boase; Hunter, pedigree of Turner-Willets; Davis, *Manchester College*; Payne, *An Ancient Chapel*, pp. 66-7; Toulmin and Pegler, cited for Holland above. I owe thanks to Stephen Harbottle for information and help.

dau *daughter*　b *born*　bp *baptised*
m *married*　d *died*　bur *buried*
unm *never married*

William Turner of Wakefield, b Preston 5 Dec 1714, only child of John Turner of Preston and Hannah, née Chorley; 1737-46 minister Allostock; health failed; 1754 started school Congleton; m 1758 **Mary**, bp Mobberley 12 January 1725, dau of John and Mary **Holland** of Dam Head House; she d 31 October 1784; from April 1761 Unitarian minister at Wakefield; d Wakefield 28 August 1794, bur Wakefield.

Children of William Turner of Wakefield and Mary (née Holland):
　William Turner, b Wakefield 20 September 1761; school at Idle and, c. 1775, Bolton; 1777-81 Warrington Academy; 1781-82 Glasgow University; minister Hanover Square Chapel, Newcastle-upon-Tyne, 25 September 1782–20 September 1841; m summer 1784 (1) **Mary**, dau of Thomas **Holland** of Manchester and Anne (sister of Samuel Holland of Sandlebridge); Mary d 16 January 1797, aged thirty-seven; m 1799 (2) **Jane**, dau of Reverend William **Willets** (1697-1779) of Newcastle-under-Lyme and

Catherine (née Wedgwood); sister of Mary, Mrs Peter Holland (m 1786) and Anne, Mrs Swinton Holland (m 1805); Jane d 25 December 1826, aged sixty-eight; William Turner d Lloyd Street, Manchester 24 April 1859.

John Turner of Mayfield, Bolton, merchant; c. 1777-80 school at Idle; m **Betty Aspinall** of Liverpool; he d 14 November 1816 aged fifty-one (*Newcastle Courant*, 23 November).

Children of William and Mary Turner:

Mary, b 24 February 1786, bp 18 June 1786, m 31 December 1811 Rev. **John Gooch Robberds** (1789-1854); lived 42 Mosley Street c. 1811-21, Greenheys three years; to Grosvenor Square summer 1826, by 1846 at 19 Acomb Street, Manchester; she d. 1869.

William, b 13 January 1788, bp 29 May 1788; 1809-27 tutor Manchester College York; Unitarian minister Halifax; d December 1853.

Thomas, b 20 June 1789, bp 8 September 1789; d 23 May 1790.

Philip-Holland, b 13 August 1790, bp 11 February 1791; d 22 September 1811.

Henry, b 4 May 1792, bp July 1795; 1817 Unitarian minister Nottingham; m June 1819 **Catharine**, dau John Cole (d 2 July 1810) and Catharine (née Holland) **Rankin**, b 21 February 1797, bp 12 March 1797; Henry d 31 January 1822.

John, b 24 March 1794, bp July 1795; d 3 May 1796.

Ann, b 21 October 1796, bp 3 February 1799; Norwich c. 1810; Clavering Place, Newcastle 1829-32; Edinburgh c. 1830-31; d Manchester 1851.

Child of John and Betty Turner:

James Aspinall, b Bolton 28 March 1797, bp 19 June 1797; m Sarah Blackmore of Manchester; 1857-65 M.P. for Manchester; d 1867.

D

Anne, Charles, Fanny and Kate Holland

Little is known about the early life of Charles Holland (born in 1799), who married William Gaskell's sister when he was thirty-nine years of age, and his three sisters, Anne, Fanny and Kate. The Merioneth Historical and Record Society's extra publication of 1953 provides a transcript of a fair-copy version of Samuel Holland's autobiography (NLW: MS 4983C) but does not print certain draft memoranda in his hand (ff. 8 verso to 13). The following lightly edited transcript of a photocopy establishes a clear text of these pages; it does not record deletions, insertions and the like:

My Father and my Sister Ann came to pay me a visit. She stayed on with me after my Father left [c. 1823?]. She was my eldest sister. She was very clever and prudent a great favourite with all who knew her. She was very fond of books. She was educated at Gettercar [Gateacre?] near Liverpool. My sister Fanny was at the same school for some time –

My sister Kate was at School at a Miss Bates in Liverpool – My Uncle Menzies who lived at Putney near London came down to Liverpool driving his gig all the way to see his father, who lived at Rodney St Liverpool. When he decided to return to London [he] asked if my Father & Mother would allow Kate to return to London with him. She was about 9 years old then [born 17 November 1804]. My parents consented so away she drove with my Uncle in his gig. He had taken a great fancy to her. She was so young that she had to be strapped on to the seat for fear she should fall – It was one of the old fashioned high gigs – and remained with them for years and was brought up with his daughters and went on with her education there –

My brother Charles who was the second in the family was educated at Nottingham. There were three girls and three boys in our family – Anne Charles Fanny Menzies Samuel and Kate –

My brother Charles when educated as my Father thought sufficiently was sent at about the age of 18 to Buenos Ayres in Sth America. He was a Clerk in Mr Robertson's office who was a London merchant.[1] After being some time in the office he decided to leave & go to Valparaso where [he] started on his own account and bought a vessel and traded up & down the coast. Mr Robertson went over to Buen. to see how things were going on and heard that my brother had gone round the coast to Valparaso. Mr Robertson went there and sent for

my brother and told him he meant to open an office there, and he would like him
to take charge of it. So Charles decided to give up his vessel and take charge of
Mr Robertson's office –

While he was sailing about with his vessel he had many adventures. There was
an Island called Chilloi [Chiloé] and he heard that they were in great straights
[*sic*] for food and clothing so he loaded his vessel with what he thought suitable
for the Island and sailed for there. When his vessel was nearing the coast he saw
Crowds of people all along the Cliff some with guns and other warlike imple-
ments. He hoisted signals from his vessel that he was friendly and when arriving
in the Bay he went ashore in the boat rowed by his own man and crowds of
people met the boat at the landing. They were afraid that the Spaniards were
come. He asked the people where the Governor lived and to show him the house.
He waited upon the Governor, and told him he was an English merchant, and
that he had landed there bringing goods that he learnt they wanted, and asked
him to allow him to trade there; he had come ashore in a boat & his vessel was
lying outside the Harbour. The Governor after having asked him many questions
gave him leave to trade. He sold all his goods to a great advantage – he returned
then to the Sth American Coast.

After a time Mr Robertson heard that there was a good opening at Lima. So
he moved Charles there and opened an office – He carried on business there for
some years. He left the office & again started on his own account – & returned
to Valparaso.

While he was at Lima a war was going on between the Spaniards and the
natives. The natives had a strong army, & Bollivar came over from [word
omitted] with his army – to assist the natives to become independant of the
Spaniards (Bollivar had made his own state independant of the Spaniards).[2]
General Mina's army the Spaniards were in great straights for clothing and other
supplies. My brother heard of this at Valparaso so he bought a quantity of
materials suitable for clothing and he loaded a number of mules with these goods
at Valparaso and went up the Country to where Mina's army was. When he
arrived he called upon Mina and stated to him who he was – an English merchant
at Val: and having heard what difficulties they were in, he had brought up mules
laden with goods. While he was stating this to the general Mina and asking him
on what spot he might fix his camp and open shop, the Soldiers had opened,
taken possession of all the goods he had. This he found to his dismay on
returning to the place where he had left his mules & all his men had run away.

After he left the General a report was taken to Mina that he was a spy and just
come to take note of the army. He returned to the General and said that he had
stated the truth and if he did not trust him keep him a prisoner and send to the
British Consul at Valparaso who wd confirm what he said – he wd learn who and
what he was. He was taken out into the camp and placed between soldiers and
was told to confess that he was a spy, but he said he was speaking the truth, he
was not a spy – he was then blindfolded and ordered to be shot, but he pleaded
again and he was then kept a close prisoner till news came from the Consul – he
was than released and returned to Val. He returned to Val: and waited upon the
English Consul settled there and stated all the circumstances to him and asked
his interference. He did interfere and got a large sum from the Spanish army to
refund to my brother – after settling his affairs there he returned to Buen:

He returned over land from Val to B – all his goods were packed on horses backs and he had quite a troop of horses & men. At one place where they had to have fresh horses, the men could not supply him with enough so a dispute arose, but he insisted on horses being procured. He eventually arrived at B – after settling his affairs there, having started a House there – he decided to return to England – but before doing so he established a house at Montevideo and left a partner there. He left Montevideo on horse back with two or three Pions (or servants) on horse back and rode from there to Paraguay – he established a House there after [a] stay there for six months or more – after this he returned to Liverpool a richer man than he started.[3] He then settled in Liverpool and carried on a very successful business as a Merchant. He lived at home with his parents for a short time at the Park, then he took lodging in Liverpool – after some years he married his cousin Miss Gaskell –

NOTES

1 In 1817 Barings commissioned a report on the trade possibilities of the river Plate from the firm of John Parish Robertson, and in 1824 made an unfortunate loan through William Parish Robertson to build a port at Buenos Aires (Ziegler, *Barings*, pp. 100-3).

2 Simón Bolívar landed to liberate Peru on 1 September 1823; the last major battle was fought in December 1824; all resistance ended in January 1825. SH perhaps mistook the name of the Spanish general; Javier Mina had been executed by this time. See David Bushnell, 'The Independence of Spanish South America', *The Cambridge History of Latin America*, III, ed. Leslie Bethell, Cambridge, etc., 1985, pp. 81, 145-6.

3 See Bushnell, 'Independence', pp. 150-3, for the financial and economic consequences of newly opened ports and the substitution of English for Spanish merchants.

E

Elizabeth Stevenson's commonplace book

This is perhaps the 'Scrapbook, for it does not pretend to the dignity of an album' she mentioned to Harriet Carr in late 1831 (*GSJ*, IV, 1990, p. 7). Its present location is unknown, but it was seen by Mrs Jane Revere Whitehill (née Coolidge), the editor of Elizabeth Gaskell's correspondence with Charles Eliot Norton in 1932. A few years ago she herself could not recall where she had seen it. Mrs Trevor Dabbs, Mrs Portia Holland and E. Holland-Martin (letter to JAVC, Overbury Court, 24 August 1979) have not been able to help. The text below is therefore taken from the typescript of Mrs Whitehill's unfinished biography, pp. 25-8, in the collection of J. G. Sharps:

> There exists, furthermore, a commonplace book which as having been compiled by Elizabeth when she was twenty-one, represents, of course, her maturer taste, but nevertheless reflects, as well, we cannot help thinking, something of the earlier directing influence of William Stevenson.
>
> The little book of selections opens with a quotation, particularly appropriate, from The Winter's Tale. 'I am littered under Mercury, who was (like me) a snapper up of unconsidered trifles.' All her life it was Elizabeth's peculiar skill to gather up the trifling and with a single gesture make it charming to consider. The passage from Shakespeare is followed by a significant mixture of choices. There are, as was to have been expected, portions of poems by Burns and by Wordsworth, and bits of Shakespearian dialogue. Likewise we find a liberal sprinkling of sentimental verses from the 'Sacred Offering' and other gift book collections of poetry so popular at the time, but then totally unlooked for, between an effusion of Robert Southey and one of Mrs Hemans', there comes, as a reminiscence perhaps of her father's teaching, a phrase from Petrarch. Possibly her father, too, was indirectly responsible for the inclusion of a number of ballads, among them the grim Scottish 'Downfall of Dalziel'. By far the most striking element in the quotations, however, is the large number of seventeenth century poems. With the writings of Ben Jonson, Lovelace, Suckling, Vaughan and George Herbert, it seems likely that Elizabeth's father was the first to make her acquainted. Still, if he drew her attention to a body of literature, both foreign and native, which ordinarily in the first quarter of the nineteenth century, was far from finding a place in the show-window of a young lady's mental adornments,

the taste with which Elizabeth made her choices must be accounted her own.

Already many of the predilections of her later time express themselves in the commonplace book. Her love of landscape has been mentioned. It was, however, landscape with the hush of serenity upon it that she wished particularly to recall and at no period of her life did the splendid or terrible aspects of nature stir her imagination. We notice that in the commonplace book there is no place for quotations from Scott or Byron or Coleridge. Likewise in the description of landscape she turned naturally towards what was gracious and smoothly flowing. We are reminded of her own apparently effortless light felicity of touch in the best prose of her later works by the long passage which she has copied out of the Compleat Angler. And here and there through the book we catch a hint of what was to be another very characteristic trait of her mind – the perception of the incongruous. One of the first quotations, for instance, was from an old Presbyterian minister who 'in his prayer for all sorts and conditions of men could not forbear, in the goodness of his heart, to include the devil himself.'

'And o'er an abune a' my brethren, let us no forget the poor aul Deil! He's e'en had a waifu' time o't poor soul: it's nae light matter, my friends, to lig in the nook o' Hell sae lang as he's dune, till he's as black as a heather hill, and as hard as a dried skate – '

The one common element of almost all the quotations indicates a lifelong preference on the part of Elizabeth Stevenson. In spite of the varieties of the subject matter nearly every one of the passages she has chosen is an expression of individual emotion. Poignant personal feeling derived from concrete experience attracts her attention in her reading as later it attracted her when she wrote. As yet she showed little originality in the themes which she selected and the pages are covered with the lyrics of deserted maidens, faithful wives and lovers who have parted from their mistresses while it is apparent that from the first Elizabeth did not escape a disproportionate interest in early death. That there was surprisingly little of the genuinely morbid in her reflections, is, however, demonstrated by some unexpected contrasts. The bland assertion that 'Love will find out the way', quoted at length from Percy's Reliques precedes Lilye's 'Cupid and Campaspe', which in turn keeps close company with the lament of Lady Jane Bothwell. The following cheerful doggerell comes almost directly after a mournful fragment of a Scotch ballad.

> Lines written in the Inn at Keswick
> In questa casa treverate
> Tout ce qu'on peut souhaiter
> Vinum, panum, carnen [carnem], pisces,
> Coaches, charges, horses' harness.

On the whole the impression gathered from the little book is of a vivacious mind, full of what the phraseology of the day termed 'sensibility' and possessing a delicate delight in the gay, the comic and the pathetic turns of emotion.

At the beginning of the commonplace book a copy of a jingle which runs,

> She hath a waye
> Anne hath a waye
> To make grief blisse Anne hath a waye, [etc.]

testifies to other influences besides her father's to which Elizabeth was susceptible. Kindly though he was, he was apt to be absorbed in his own researches and
this absorption alternating with the irritation caused by his disease and his unhappiness at home formed a combination of conditions scarcely pleasant for
Elizabeth.

F

William Gaskell's engagement letter

An inaccurate TS of this letter (*not* the original) exists in the Shorter Collection of the Brotherton Library. It has never been printed in full; what follows is a slightly edited version of the whole. With it belongs Elizabeth Stevenson to Eliza Gaskell, *Letters*, no. 1, pp. 1-2, now redated [27 March 1832]; the TS text of this is also slightly suspect.

Miss Eliza Gaskell,
Rev. E. R. Dimocks
Warrington.
Thursday Evening.

My dearest Eliza,
    I cannot think of keeping from you any longer the half of the letter, which was promised, from my better half, although I have scarcely time to make it up into a whole. Though from Mrs Lumb's unfortunate illness I was unable to see much of her, I saw sufficient to confirm the impression which I had received from Elizabeth and makes me at once admire and love her. In the short interview which I was permitted to have with her she treated me in the kindest and most affectionate manner, and expressed the great pleasure which she felt that Elizabeth had been led to form an engagement with me. I also contrived, I believe, to get into the graces of aunt A. C. [?A. H., Abigail Holland] whom upon the whole I liked very well, though she is not by any means to be compared with Mrs Lumb. I have called Mrs L's illness unfortunate – and yet in one respect I can hardly deem it so. It served to present Elizabeth to me in a still more lovely and endearing light than I had before beheld her, and did more perhaps to knit our souls together than months could have done, without it.
    You can't imagine how lonely I feel without her. I must get over to Knutsford again next week, for one day at least. I am now writing with her rings [?ring] on my fingers, in wearing of which you seem to have cautioned as the summit of impudence, and with her likeness lying before me, if likeness it can be called.[1] I had this morning the painful duty of interring Mrs Robberds and have two sermons to prepare, if I can manage it, for Sunday is of course a funeral one. Old Mrs [?Mr] R, Mrs Alcock [née Robberds] and the rest of the family are quite as

well as can be expected. I am sure you will under the circumstances excuse this
short and hurried scrawl in return for your nice kind letter and with love to all
believe me to be

Your most affectionate brother,
Wm Gaskell.

I got from Knutsford on the Wednesday afternoon. I had intended to stay till
Saturday.

While I have been away the report that I am going to be married has been, I
am told, travelling about at a wild-fire rate – and many are the congratulations I
have been obliged to receive. Alma[?Anna] Worthington was at Knutsford when
I got there but I did not see her. She sent her love and congratulations to me. It
seems she had predicted what would be the consequence, if Elizabeth and I saw
much of each other. There was a bit of a dance at Mrs Greens on Friday evening
on account of the newly-married couple (the Deans). They give another next
week and Mrs D. says she shall expect me – but I do not think I shall be at it. One
of the Miss Hollands enquired of me whether you drew, I answered 'a little',
another whether you played. I replied 'a little'. I hope to the last you will soon
enable me to reply 'Yes'. Good bye.

NOTES

1 This is unknown, since the well-known miniature was not painted until June of this year.

G

Notes and problems

STEVENSON'S ANONYMOUS FELLOW STUDENT

ABO, pp. 209-10, prints an extract from a letter by 'one of his friends and contemporaries' that begins, 'At Daventry, where I first became acquainted with Mr. Stevenson, who was then commencing his third year there ... ' Stevenson was only two years at Daventry, 1787-89, and began his third year at Northampton in 1789. If a list of Daventry students is compared with a list of students known to have transferred to Northampton, two students of the 1788 entry stand out: Samuel Rickards Esq. and Sparrow Stovin Esq. Cp. *MR*, XVII, 1822, pp. 286-7 (T. Belsham's list) and DWL: New College MS L54/3/53 (Joshua Wilson's notes and memoranda).

STEVENSON AND MANCHESTER COLLEGE

The *Roll of Students ... Entered at the Manchester Academy, 1786-1803 ... With a List of the Professors & Principal Officers*, Manchester, 1868, gives 'Rev. William Stevenson, Assistant Classical Tutor' between 1792 and 1796. V. D. Davis states that Stevenson succeeded Lewis Loyd (who left in 1792) as an assistant classical tutor and remained for four years (*Manchester College*, p. 65). There seems to be no record of Stevenson failing to complete his course at Northampton, apart from his obituary, nor of his making up any deficiency elsewhere.

The original material relating to this early period now held at Manchester College, Oxford, is not extensive. Despite the assistance of two Librarians I have found no contemporary evidence whatever to prove that Barnes actually appointed a successor to Loyd, nor is there any record of Stevenson's resignation or dismissal. The location of Davis's own papers is not known to the College.

John Unsworth, in 'Coleridge and the Manchester academy', *Charles Lamb Bulletin*, October 1980, cites Davis to the effect that Stevenson was a tutor at the College, but claims that 'other sources [unspecified] suggest that Stevenson was also a student' (p. 154). Unsworth speculates that Coleridge heard of a vacancy for a classical tutor and came to Manchester in about November 1793 (p. 156), where he met Robert Owen, John Dalton and William Winstanley. In *The Life of Robert Owen. Written by Himself,* [1857], intro. John Butt, London, 1971, p. 36, Owen states that Dalton and Winstanley were assistants under Dr Baines [*sic*], Winstanley being the brother-in-law of 'Dr. —, one of the most successful physicians in Manchester'. Owen also claims that he took part in frequent discussions on religion, morals, etc., which were eventually discouraged by Dr Barnes, who feared that his assistants would be converted from his 'orthodoxy'. Dalton, however, was a Quaker.

Joshua Wilson, in 'Documents and memoranda relating to early non-conformist academies' (DWL: New College MS L54/2/27, p. 3), makes a point of stating that Stevenson was a tutor and not a pupil at Manchester. He must have been denying some suggestion to the contrary, but I have not been able to find this. A meticulous article by W. H. Chaloner, 'Robert Owen, Peter Drinkwater, and the Early Factory System in Manchester 1788-1800', *BJRL*, XXXVII, 1955, pp. 78-102, and E. M. Fraser, 'Robert Owen in Manchester, 1787-1800', *Memoirs of the Manchester Literary and Philosophical Society*, LXXXII, 1937-38, pp. 29-41, throw no further light.

ELIZABETH'S SCHOOLFELLOWS

Considered singly, a fair number of Elizabeth's fellow pupils can be identified. 'When I was at school I think I liked Harriet Twamley very much', she once wrote to her future sister-in-law Eliza Gaskell; 'Louisa was not so clever (but a better temper;) not that we reckoned Harriet anything particular in the clever line, but she was *very* painstaking, and I never saw two sisters that loved one another more dearly.' Harriet had become a friend of the Liverpool Hollands. Mrs Gaskell was less easily pleased. Her taste warred with her sense of justice:

> Then when I saw her a year or two ago she struck me as very much gone off – I had heard of her being a great flirt in the mean time, and she seemed to me to have got a very commonplace sort of second rate cant; (such as calling Uncle Holland 'that dear sweet old gentleman' and that sort of very second-rate sweet sentimental affectation). ... But you know I only saw her once or twice then, and I had no oppy of judging. I know Fanny thinks her very much improved.

In another letter, written in 1854, she retails some unkind gossip about Effie Grey, Ruskin's bride. (Erasmus Darwin had just as unkindly classified Effie Ruskin and Elizabeth Gaskell as 'Beauty and the Beast' the year before.) Effie was much younger than Elizabeth, she said – 'still we had the bond of many mutual schoolfellows', she went on to claim. This is stretching it rather.

Effie was at Avonbank from the age of twelve in August 1840 until 1841, and from January to June 1844.[1] Similarly, a Miss Scott, 'niece of Lord Meath and afterwards Countess of Devon' – a gratifyingly aristocratic connection – can be identified as Elizabeth Ruth, daughter of the Reverend John M. Scott, but she was born about 1815 and might only just have known Elizabeth.[2]

Citing the names of pupils at the school after Elizabeth's time gives a general idea of Avonbank's continuing status, but is not especially relevant. Jessie Boucherett, for example, an important feminist who helped found the society for promoting the employment of women, is mentioned with the comment, 'It is probable that Mrs Gaskell acquired at school that independence of thought and action that characterised her in later life, and which led her to champion the cause of the Married Women's Property Bill'. Perhaps so, but Jessie, fifteen years younger than Elizabeth, was at Avonbank much later, from 1840-42. A niece of Harriet Martineau attended Avonbank, but again, she might have been younger than Elizabeth. Maria, the 'glorious niece' who was Harriet's companion, was born in 1827, her successor Jane in 1832. Their dedication to public work might be as much due to their heredity as their schooling.[3]

Contemporary evidence like Maria Byerley's letter to Wedgwood of 16 October 1822, in which she incidentally notes that the unmarried sisters have one of Fanny Parkes's children 'to educate and bring up', is preferable, though unfortunately she does not give a Christian name. Certain names of pupils who were with Elizabeth during the Avonbank years can be found in what is described as a 'beautifully bound copy in crimson and gold' of Beattie's *Minstrel* bearing an inscription to two little Edinburgh sisters, 'Elizabeth and Jessie Scott from their very affectionate friends and schoolfellows Isabella and Euphemia Scott, Emma Whitbread, Anne Longworth, Sophia Barrow and Elizabeth Stevenson. June 15. 1824'.[4]

EARLY WRITINGS

Quotation from A. W. Ward's notebook, ff. 13 verso – 16. These pencilled notes are untidily dispersed, inconsistent and sometimes illegible. Selected, ordered and lightly edited, they seem to read:

Sexton's Hero[5] query before *Mary Barton*. sent to Blackwoods 1840 – 7 or 8.

Married life

In 1844 went to Festiniog where put into rooms – Scarlet fever – Her only little boy Willie to whom she was devoted caught the fever and died there (1844).

1845 *To turn her thoughts by her husband's advice she began to write* – She had previously written two poems (one on a still born child of her own,) the other ['romantic' inserted nearby] on a stag[6] and the beginning of a short story [line leads to opposite page] just before her marriage *All unpublished.*

She seems at once to have begun Mary Barton in 1845 While writing *Mary Barton* she wrote two papers in Howitt's *Journal* (1845)? (see *Cornhill Mag*)[7] Julia G born 1846

Mary Barton

Part finished sometime in 1847 ['abt Christmas 1846' deleted]
sent to some publisher ['several publishers' wr. above] who returned it Then to Moxon ['Chapman & Hall' deleted] – no acknowledgement for some time – Mrs Gaskell settled down and declared afterwards she had forgotten all about it – when abt the beginning of 1848 (some mõs late) ['a gr' deleted] she received a letter from the publishers reader of Chapman & Hall offering £100 for the copyright. She accepted the offer Published about end of March 1849 ['by Christmas 1848/9' wr. above]. *Anonymous* Great excitement Articles in Manchester papers and London *Examiner*

[Selected from notes on opposite page:] Before this she carefully read Adam Smith's *Wealth of Nations*
first publ Oct 1848 ... by Chapman & Hall. It was offered to Moxon, but not accepted. Mrs Potter.[8]

ELIZABETH GASKELL AND THE ARISTOCRACY

A note of 1835 from William Godwin to ECG (pr. Waller, p. 27) states that 'Mrs Shelley had the audacity to take away Tomkins, Jenkins and the Minister for three days'. The reference could be to psudonymous works by Henry Brougham: Isaac Tomkins, *Thoughts Upon the Aristocracy of England*, London, 1835, and its 2nd edn, which includes 'a letter to I. Tomkins on the same subject by P. Jenkins', Newcastle, 1835. The 6th edn of Tomkins refers to 'the sensation which it has created'. It was an assertion of the lack of sense and reason in aristocratic circles and their connection with the worst of the press, combined with praise of the middle classes. *A Letter to Isaac Tomkins, Gent. ... from Mr. Peter Jenkins*, 4th edn with postscript, 1835, is a 12-page pamphlet attacking the House of Commons.

W. J. Fox wrote to Eliza Flower in May 1835 that 'Godwin was at the Gaskells' (R. and E. Garnett, *The Life of W. J. Fox*, 1910, p. 234). See Perkin, *Origins of Modern English Society*, p. 230.

NOTES

1 *Letters*, pp. 16-17, 287; K. J. Fielding, 'The sceptical Carlyles and the Unitarian Mrs Gaskell', *GSJ*, VI, 1992, pp. 46-7; Mary Lutyens, *The Ruskins and the Grays*, London, 1972, pp. 13, 17-22; Uglow, p. 461.

2 G. E. C., *The Complete Peerage*, IV, London, 1910; Hicks, *Quest of Ladies*, p. 81. She died in her hundredth year in 1914.

3 Chadwick, 1910, p. 111; Hicks, *Quest of Ladies*, p. 81; *Barbara Leigh Bodichon and the Langham Place Group*, ed. Candida Ann Lacey, New York and London, 1987, p. 223; *Harriet Martineau: Selected Letters*, ed. Valerie Sanders, Oxford, 1990, p. xxx.

4 Steuart, 'A lengthening chain', 1942, p. 10. The Steuart family retained this volume (location unknown; Chadwick had seen it by 1913, p. 81) and a pair of globes, celestial and terrestrial.

5 Pr. *Howitt's Journal*, 4 September 1847.

6 See p. 328, n. 31 above, and *Letters*, pp. 967-8, for a poem called 'Night Fancies' attributed to ECG.

7 On the opposite page there is a quotation, carefully copied in ink, from G[eorge] B[arnett] S[mith], p. 193, i.e. 'Mrs Gaskell and her novels', *CM*, XXIX, 1874, pp. 191-212.

8 Mrs Sydney Potter identified as an informant, f. 35. See Chadwick, 1910, p. 286.

Bibliographical appendix

PRINCIPAL SOURCES AND REFERENCES

Robert L. Selig, *Elizabeth Gaskell: A Reference Guide*, Boston, Mass., 1977.
Jeffrey Egan Welch, *Elizabeth Gaskell: An Annotated Bibliography, 1927-1975*, New York, 1977.
Nancy S. Weyant, *Elizabeth Gaskell: An Annotated Bibliography of English-Language Sources 1976-1991*, Metuchen, N.J. and London, 1994.

1 Berwick

(a) Early works include Robert Douglas, *Sketch of the History of the Berwick Grammar School*, Berwick, 1875 (not always reliable); John Fuller, *The History of Berwick upon Tweed*, Edinburgh, 1799; Thomas Johnstone, *The History of Berwick-upon-Tweed*, Berwick, 1817; John Scott, *Berwick-upon-Tweed: The History of the Town and Guild*, 1888 (Berwick Library copy contains pedigree sheets bound in); Frederick Sheldon, *History of Berwick-upon-Tweed*, Edinburgh, 1849; *The Memoirs of the Life, and Writings of Percival Stockdale, Containing Many Interesting Anecdotes of the Illustrious Men With Whom He Was Connected. Written by Himself*, 2 vols, London, 1809. See also Appendix A and 13 below.

(b) More recent works: Alec Clifton-Taylor, *Six More English Towns*, London, 1981; W. L. Clowes, *The Royal Navy: A History from the Earliest Times to the Present*, [London, 1898], New York, 1966; F. M. Cowe, *Berwick upon Tweed: A Short Historical Guide*, Berwick, rev. 1984; Janet Denise Cowe, 'The development of education in Berwick-upon-Tweed to 1902', M.Ed. thesis, University of Durham, 1969; Leonard Gordon, *Berwick-upon-Tweed and the East March*, London, 1985; Frank Graham, *Berwick: A Short History and Guide [incl. Tweedmouth. Spittal & Norham]*, Rothbury, 1987; R. Lamont-Brown, *The Life and Times of Berwick-upon-Tweed*, Edinburgh, 1988 (with bibliography); Michael Lewis, *A Social History of the Navy 1793-1815*, London, 1960; Iain MacIvor, *The Fortifications of Berwick-upon-Tweed*, London, 1990 (aerial photos); N. A. M. Rodger, *The Wooden World: An Anatomy of the Georgian Navy*, London, 1986.

2 Dissent and the academies

(a) Standard reference works are V. D. Davis, *A History of Manchester College, From Its Foundation in Manchester to Its Establishment in Oxford*, London, 1932; Herbert McLachlan, *English Education Under the Test Acts, Being the History of the Nonconformist Academies 1662-1820*, Manchester, 1931; *The Unitarian Movement in the Religious Life of England: Its Contribution to Thought and Learning*, London, 1934; *Warrington Academy: Its History and Influence*, CSR, n. s. CVII, 1943, and his *Essays and Addresses*, Manchester, 1950. Alan Ruston's pamphlets, *Monthly Repository Obituaries 1806-1832*, 1985, and *Unitarian Obituaries 1794-1850*, 1990 (published from 41 Hampermill Lane, Oxhey, Watford, Herts WD1 4NS) are most useful.

(b) MSS in DWL, Gordon Square, London: Samuel Newth, 'Memorials of the academical institutions sustained by the Coward Trust' [fair copy, presented 1889] (New College MSS, CT. 12/1); Joshua Wilson, 'Documents and memoranda relating to early Nonconformist academies' (3 vols, New College MSS, L54) [L54/3/47 has a pencil annotation that Stevenson was a tutor not a pupil at Daventry in 1790, which seems unlikely]; Daventry and Northampton students' essays (New College MSS, L12/15); Northampton MSS [69], Shelf 546: 7 Proceedings of the Literary Society; 8-11* *The Academical Repository*.

(c) MCO has a series of printed annual reports, the earliest of which is dated 1797. There are few early MS records: 'No. 1: Minutes of the Proceedings of the Committee'; a cash or day book; 'Students Admitted into the Manchester Academy, and into Manchester College York'. See also Martineau Letters 1, and 2 (shorthand abstracts of Harriet Martineau's correspondence, transcribed by W. S. Coe); Robberds 1 (Letters 1811-69) and 2 (transcripts); Mary Robberds (neé Turner), 'Recollections of a long life' (photocopy), presented by Barbara and Ruth Hartas Jackson.

(d) Early books consulted include John Aikin, jr, *A Description of the Country From Thirty to Forty Miles Round Manchester* (1795), repr. Newton Abbot, 1968; David Bogue and James Bennett, *A History of Dissenters 1688-1808* (1810), 2nd edn, 2 vols, 1833; Thomas Broadhurst, *Memoir of the Late Rev. Robert Smethurst, Nearly Fifty Years Minister of the Presbyterian Chapel at Monton*, pr. pr. Bath, 1847; William Charles Henry, *Memoirs of the Life and Scientific Researches of John Dalton*, London, 1854; Henry Lonsdale, *The Worthies of Cumberland: John Dalton [et al.]*, London, 1874; B. Nightingale, *Lancashire Nonconformity*, London, 1893; *The Life of Robert Owen. Written by Himself*, intro. J. Bult, London, 1971; Thomas Percival, *The Works, Literary, Moral, and Medical*, 4 vols, Manchester, 1807; John Williams, *Memorials of the Late Reverend Thomas Belsham*, London, 1833; *Roll of Students ... Entered at the Manchester Academy, 1786-1803 ... With a List of the Professors & Principal Officers*, Manchester, 1868.

(e) Later books: James D. Drummond and C. B. Upton, ed. *Life and Letters of James Martineau*, 2 vols, London, 1902; Francis E. Mineka, *The Dissidence of Dissent: 'The Monthly Repository', 1806-1838*, New York, 1972; Brian Simon, *The Two Nations and the Educational Structure 1780-1870*, London, 1974; J. W. A. Smith, *The Birth of Modern Education: The Contribution of the Dissenting Academies, 1660-1800*, London, 1955; *The Warrington Academy by Rev. William Turner*, intro. G. A. Carter, Warrington, 1957 (fronts. not a portrait of Turner, but of J. Trotter

Brockett); Michael R. Watts, *The Dissenters From the Reformation to the French Revolution*, Oxford, 1978.

(f) Articles: G. M. Ditchfield, 'The early history of Manchester College', *THSLC*, CXXIII, 1972; 'The campaign in Lancashire and Cheshire for the repeal of the test and corporation acts, 1787-1790', *THSLC*, CXXVI, 1977, and 'Manchester college and anti-slavery', in Smith; John Harland, ed., 'Manchester Academy or New College' [reprints *MM* report dated 9 August 1797] and 'Recollections of the Manchester Academy, its tutors and students, by John Moore', *CSR*, LXXII, 1867, pp. 232-41; H. L. Short, 'Presbyterians under a new name', in *The English Presbyterians: From Elizabethan Puritanism to Modern Unitarianism*, ed. C. G. Bolam et al., London, 1968; John Seed, 'Jeremiah Joyce, Unitarianism and the radical intelligensia in the 1790s', *TUHS*, XVII, 1981; D. L. Wykes, 'Sons and subscribers 1786-1840: Lay support and the College', in Smith.

3 Dissent and politics

(a) See esp. Alexander Gordon, *Historical Account of Dob Lane Chapel, Failsworth, and Its Schools*, Manchester, 1904. The MS sources Gordon mentions in his prefatory note, in particular a 'brief history' dated 23 September 1861, by Joseph Barratt, and a printed catalogue of the chapel's library dated 1803 (p. 49), are not with the chapel's records in MCL. (Gordon's papers in JRULM have not been investigated.)

Gordon also wrote an *Historical Account of Dukinfield Chapel and Its School*, Manchester, 1896. The 'original documentary sources' mentioned in the preface appear to be lost. Stevenson's letter about Smith is *not* quoted from possible sources in *MR*, 1823, *MR*, 1825 or *CR*, 1845.

(b) See G. Shaw, *Annals of Oldham*, III, [?1905], 1 January 1793, for the demonstration against Paine at Failsworth, from the *Manchester Mercury* for 8 January 1793. See also W. E. A. Axon, *Annals of Manchester*, Manchester, 1886; Edward Baines, *The History of the County Palatine and Duchy of Lancaster*, ed. James Croston, II, Manchester, 1889; Alan Kidd, *Manchester*, Keele, 1993; A. E. Musson and Eric Robinson, *Science and Technology in the Industrial Revolution*, Manchester, 1969; Percival Percival, *Failsworth Folk and Failsworth Memories* (repr. with addns from *Manchester City News*), 1901; Archibald Prentice, *Historical Sketches and Personal Recollections of Manchester ... 1792 to 1832* (1851), 3rd edn, intro. D. Read, 1970; J. T. Slugg, *Reminiscences of Manchester Fifty Years Ago*, Manchester, 1881, repr. Shannon, 1971; W. H. Thomson, *History of Manchester to 1852*, Altrincham, 1967. The violent political controversies of the early 1790s are generally discussed in Pauline Handforth's 'Manchester radical politics, 1789-1794', *TLCAS*, LXVI, 1957, pp. 87-106; E. M. Hunt, 'The anti-slave trade agitation in Manchester [1787-1792]', *TLCAS*, LXXIX, 1977, gives more detail. I must thank David Taylor of MCRL's Local Studies Unit for valuable help.

(c) Other books and theses include Alfred Owen Aldridge, *Man of Reason: The Life of Thomas Paine*, London, 1960, and John Keane, *Tom Paine: A Political Life*, London, 1995; Colin Bonwick, *English Radicals and the American Revolution*, Chapel Hill, 1977; Philip Anthony Brown, *The French Revolution in English History*, Oxford, 1918, repr. 1965; Marilyn Butler, *Burke, Paine, Godwin, and the Revolution Controversy*, Cambridge, 1984, and *Romantics, Rebels and Reactionaries: English*

Literature and Its Background 1760-1830, Oxford, 1981; Donald Davie, *Dissentient Voice: The Ward-Phillips Lectures for 1980 with Some Related Pieces*, Notre Dame U.P., 1982, and *A Gathered Church: The Literature of the English Dissenting Interest, 1780-1930*, London and Henley, 1978; R. W. Davis, *Dissent in Politics 1780-1830: The Political Life of William Smith, M.P.*, London, 1971; F. W. Gibbs, *Joseph Priestley, Adventurer in Science and Champion of Truth*, London, etc., 1965; Ian Gilmour, *Riot, Risings and Revolution*, London (1992), 1993; Boyd Hilton, *The Age of Atonement: The Influence of Evangelicalism on Social and Economic Thought, 1795-1865*, Oxford, 1988; Robert Hole, *Pulpit, Politics and Public Order in England 1760-1832*, Cambridge, 1989; Anthony Lincoln, *Some Political and Social Ideas of English Dissent 1763-1800*, Cambridge, 1938; Deryck W. Lovegrove, *Established Church, Sectarian People: Itinerancy and the Transformation of English Dissent, 1780-1830*, Cambridge, 1988; Thomas Paine, *The Rights of Man*, ed. Eric Foner, London, etc., 1984; Maurice J. Quinlan, *Victorian Prelude* (1941), repr. London, 1965; Thomas Rees, *Reminiscences of Literary London from 1779-1853 ... with Extensive Additions by John Britton* (1896), repr. New York and London, 1974 (*The English Book Trade 1660-1853*, ed. Stephen Parks); John Seed, 'The role of Unitarianism in the formation of liberal culture 1775-1851: a social history', Ph. D. thesis, University of Hull, 1981; D. O. Thomas, *The Honest Mind: The Thought and Work of Richard Price*, Oxford, 1977.

(d) William Green, 'A Plan of Manchester and Salford', engraved by J. Thornton, 1794 (29" to the mile), repr. G. Faulkner, 1902, intro. C. Roeder. See *HSLCPP*, XIV, 1896.

4 Farming and Saughton Mills

(a) Reference works include James Cleghorn, 'Edinburghshire', in Macvey Napier, ed., *A Supplement to the Fourth, Fifth and Sixth Editions of the Encyclopaedia Britannica*, 6 vols, Edinburgh, 1815-24; James E. Handley, *The Agricultural Revolution in Scotland*, Glasgow, 1963; Rosalind Mitchison, *Agricultural Sir John: The Life of Sir John Sinclair of Ulbster 1754-1835*, London, 1962; J. A. Symon, *Scottish Farming Past and Present*, Edinburgh and London, 1959. The twenty-one volumes of T. C. Smout, ed., *The Statistical Account of Scotland 1791-1799 Edited by Sir John Sinclair*, rev. edn, Wakefield, 1975, contain information gathered from nine hundred educated men. Volume II, The Lothians, originally published at Edinburgh in 1795, includes an account of the parish of Corstorphine. *The New Statistical Account of Scotland*, I, Edinburgh, 1845 is also very useful.

(b) Four letters by Mrs Dorothy Landles and a letter by James Smith to [Robert] Stevenson, which contains the medical reference, are in JGS (see Sharps, p. 377n.). Other Stevensons of Berwick are mentioned, including John, mayor on seven occasions 1802-1822, and an Easter (sc. Esther), born in 1721, daughter of Gabriel.

(c) M. J. Armstrong, 'Environs of Edinburgh', *Scotch Atlas*, 1777; John Geddie, *The Fringes of Edinburgh*, London and Edinburgh, n. d.; Robert Kirkwood, 'A map of the environs of Edinburgh', 1817; Ordnance survey, Edinburghshire sheet 6, 1852 (1: 10, 560); Edinburghshire III.10, 1895 (1: 2, 500); *Royal Commission on Ancient and Historical Monuments and Constructions of Scotland*, 10th report, Edinburgh, 1929; 'Saughton the property of Charles Watson Esqr, Surveyed by John Johnston', 1795, estate map in SRO: RHP 11151 (no key known); Stenhouse

Conservation Centre, Stenhouse Mills Crescent, Edinburgh (Scottish Development Office), TS history and description.

5 Edinburgh

(a) Older works include Thomas Aitchison's *Edinburgh and Leith Directory to July 1802; Directory for the Year 1803; Supplement to the Post Office Directory, 2 September 1805*, 'Containing the Names and Residence of Persons formerly omitted and those who have changed their residence since Whitsunday last'; *Memoir of Robert Chambers with Autobiographic Reminiscences of William Chambers*, 5th edn, Edinburgh and London, 1872; Henry Cockburn, *Memorials of His Own Time* (1856), ed. Karl F. C. Miller, Chicago and London, 1974; W. J. Couper, *The Edinburgh Periodical Press*, 2 vols, Stirling, 1908; *Autobiography of Mrs. Fletcher with Letters and Other Family Memorials*, ed. [Mary Richardson], Edinburgh, 1875; Robert Forsyth, *The Beauties of Scotland*, I, London, 1805; William Smellie, *Literary and Character-istical Lives of Gregory, Kames, Hume and Smith*, Edinburgh, 1800.

(b) More recent works include *The Book of the Old Edinburgh Club*, Edinburgh, III, 1910; VIII, 1916; David Daiches, *Edinburgh*, London, 1978; Sir Alexander Grant, *The Story of the University of Edinburgh*, 2 vols, London, 1884; James Grant, *Cassell's Old and New Edinburgh: Its History, Its People, and Its Places*, III, Edinburgh, [1883]; Ray Footman and Bruce Young, *Edinburgh University: An Illustrated Memoir*, Edinburgh, 1983; A. G. Fraser, *The Building of Old College: Adam, Playfair and the University of Edinburgh*, Edinburgh, 1989; Hew Scott, *Fasti Ecclesiae Scoticanae*, new edn, II, Edinburgh, 1917; R. B. Sher, *Church and University in the Scottish Enlightenment: The Moderate Literati of Edinburgh*, Edinburgh, 1985; F. R. Tredrey, *The House of Blackwood 1814-1954: The History of a Publishing Firm*, Edinburgh and London, 1954; C. B. Watson, *Notes on the Names of Closes and Wynds of Old Edinburgh*, Edinburgh, 1923; Douglas Young, *Edinburgh in the Age of Sir Walter Scott*, Norman, Oklahoma, 1943; A. J. Youngson, *The Making of Classical Edinburgh 1750-1840*, Edinburgh, [1966].

(c) Robert Kirkwood, 'Plan of the City of Edinburgh', 1817; John Gifford *et al.*, *Edinburgh*, 1984 (Buildings of Scotland), pp. 509-10.

(d) Stevenson's letters to Macvey Napier, c. 28 May 1814 to 6 February 1816, are in the latter's correspondence, BL: Add. MS 34, 611.

6 Lauderdale, Brougham and other Whigs

(a) The Lauderdale family muniments as a whole are deposited in the SRO, but BL has a good deal of the 8th Earl's political correspondence. C. J. Fox's letters to Lauderdale are in Add. 47564. Add 58941-3 (Dropmore papers) contain an important sequence of Lauderdale's correspondence with Lord Grenville over a long period.

(b) Holland House papers in the British Library, some in temporary order only.

(c) Arthur Aspinall, *Lord Brougham and the Whig Party*, Manchester, 1927; Alan Bell, ed., *Lord Cockburn: A Bicentenary Commemoration 1779-1979*, Edinburgh, 1979, and *Sydney Smith*, Oxford, 1980; John Clive, *Scotch Reviewers: The 'Edinburgh Review', 1802-1815*, London, 1957; M. Dorothy George, *English Political*

Caricature 1793-1832: A Study of Opinion and Propaganda, Oxford, 1959; G. Fox-Strangeways, Earl of Ilchester, intro. *The Journal of the Hon. Henry Edward Fox ... 1818-1830*, London, 1923, and *The Home of the Hollands 1605-1820*, London, 1937; *The Holland House Diaries 1831-1840*, ed. Abraham D. Kriegel, London, Henley, Boston, 1977; Loren Reid, *Charles James Fox: A Man for the People*, London and Harlow, 1969. Peter Virgin devotes a chapter to Holland House in *Sydney Smith*, London, 1994.

7 London, especially Chelsea

(a) Older reference works: Alfred Beaver, *Memories of Old Chelsea: A New History of the Village of Palaces*, London, 1892; George Bryan, *Chelsea in the Olden and Present Times*, Chelsea, 1869; Thomas Faulkner, *An Historical and Topographical Description of Chelsea and Its Environs*, 2 vols, Chelsea, 1829 [1 vol., London, 1810]; Daniel Lysons, *The Environs of London: Being an Historical Account of the Towns, Villages, and Hamlets, Within Twelve Miles of That Capital: Interspersed with Biographical Anecdotes*, 2nd edn, 2 vols, London, 1810.

(b) Dr Ian Gregg owns a TS copy of the journal of Anthony Todd Thomson, 'A journal of a pleasure tour through some parts of England and Scotland, 1823' (MS location unknown); also [Katharine Thomson], *Memoir of Anthony Todd Thomson*, pr. pr. London, 1850, various obits and MSS.

(c) Recent works include Celina Fox, ed., *London – World City 1800-1840*, New Haven and London, 1992; Ralph W. Hidy, *The House of Baring in American Trade and Finance: English Merchant Bankers at Work 1763-1861*, Cambridge, Mass., 1949; London County Council, *Survey of London*, ed. Sir Laurence Gomme and Philip Norman, IV. ii, London, 1913; *Survey of London*, VII. iii, ed. Sir James Bird and Philip Norman, London, 1921; George Rudé, *Hanoverian London 1714-1808*, London, 1971; Francis Sheppard, *London 1808-1870: The Infernal Wen*, London, 1971; Philip Ziegler, *The Sixth Great Power: Barings, 1762—1929*, London, 1988.

(d) Rate books and maps were consulted in CPL. Microfilms of the records of Chelsea parish church are to be found in GLROL. See in particular registers of marriages 1812-14; baptisms 1813-29; burials 1778-1812, 1827-38; King's Road burials 1789-1863; King's Road and Sydney Street (consecrated 1812) burials, 1828-40, 1828-34.

(e) Unitarian College, Manchester MSS, now deposited in JRULM, are not yet calendared. There may be many more references to William Gaskell than those found amongst its Martineau correspondence. Cupboard A2. 1 contains seventeen letters by WG.

8 Lumb family, Wakefield and Halifax

(a) Hitherto unpublished documents in the John Goodchild loan collection (possibly the largest and most comprehensive collection of such topographical material made by an individual in this century) are in Wakefield Library headquarters, Balne Lane. It consists of MSS, books, maps, etc., relating to the Barnsley, Wakefield and Leeds area. I am most grateful to Mr Goodchild, the Wakefield archivist, for a wealth of information, advice and assistance.

The most important items are a copy of Westgate chapel registers and inscriptions; a draft and copy marriage settlement, SL to the trustees of HH, 28 August 1789 [in the draft, 'Sandall Bridge, near Knutsford' has been deleted in favour of the Marthall address; the grandfather was Peter Swinton of Nether Knutsford, deceased]; a draft and copy of SL's will, and instructions, 7 December 1789; Scholey, Marsden and Skipworth, Wakefield, Deed and two copies of a conveyance in trust (SL to R and TL) of freehold covenants relating to copyhold premises, 3 July 1795; Coward of Wakefield, Deed dated 26 August 1801, copy grant of a rent charge with necessary powers for separate maintenance and draft release, being a reconveyance to SL; Huxby & Scholey, Wakefield, Case upon the will of the late Samuel Lumb esq. for Mr [Joseph] Burrell's opinion, 22 May 1837. Wills of Lumb and Holland family members are to be found in the record offices at York, Chester and Leicester.

(b) Older works: Henry Clarkson, *Memories of Merry Wakefield*, Wakefield, 1887; Charles Milnes Gaskell, ed., *Diaries of Mrs. Anne Lumb of Silcoates, Near Wakefield in 1755 and 1757*, London 1884; Joseph Hunter, *Familiae Minorum Gentium*, Harleian society XXXVII, London, 1894; J. H. Lupton, *Wakefield Worthies; or, Biographical Sketches of Men of Note*, London, 1864; William Turner III, *Lives of Eminent Unitarians; With a Notice of Dissenting Academies*, 2 vols, London, 1840-43; William Wood, *A Sermon, Preached, Sept. 7, 1794, on Occasion of the Death of the Rev. William Turner ... To Which Are Added, Memoirs of Mr Turner's Life and Writings* [by V. F., i.e. Virgilii Filius, William Turner II], Newcastle, 1794.

(c) See also J. Mason Bass, *Westgate Chapel, Wakefield: A Short History*, [1952]; John Goodchild, *Wakefield and Wool: A Wool Trail Illustrating Some Aspects of the Textile Industries in Wakefield*, Wakefield, 1981; Pamela Rae, *Turtle at Mr Humble's: The Fortunes of a Mercantile Family England & America 1758-1837*, Otley, 1992; *Wakefield District Heritage*, compiled by Kate Taylor for Wakefield E. A. H. Y. committee, [1976]; J. W. Walker, *Wakefield, Its History and Its People*, 2nd edn, 2 vols, Wakefield, 1939, repr. 1966; R. G. Wilson, 'The Denisons and Milneses: eighteenth-century merchant landowners', *Land and Industry: The Landed Estate and the Industrial Revolution*, ed. J. T. Ward and R. G. Wilson, Newton Abbot, 1971.

(d) For York see Godfrey Higgins, *The Evidence Taken before a Committee of the House of Commons Respecting the Asylum at York; with Observations and Notes*, Doncaster, 1816; C. G. Milnes Gaskell, *Passages in the History of the York Lunatic Asylum 1772-1901*, Wakefield, 1902; and two modern works: Anne Digby, *From York Lunatic Asylum to Bootham Park Hospital*, Borthwick Paper no. 69, York, 1986; Kathleen Jones, *Lunacy, Law, and Conscience 1744-1845: The Social History of the Care of the Insane*, London, 1953.

9 Greg family

(a) Reference works include Peter Spencer, *A Portrait of Hannah Greg (née Lightbody) 1766-1828*, 2nd edn, Styal, 1985, and *Samuel Greg 1758-1834*, rev. edn, 1989; Mary B. Rose, *The Gregs of Quarry Bank Mill: The Rise and Decline of a Family Firm, 1750-1914*, Cambridge, etc., 1986; Robert D. Thornton, *James Currie, the Entire Stranger & Robert Burns*, Edinburgh and London, 1963. Also, Jack Morell and Arnold Thackray, *Gentlemen of Science: Early Years of the British Association for the Advancement of Science*, Oxford, 1981.

10 Lumb, Holland, Sharpe and Whittaker families

(a) ML to HL, [October 1811], is owned by JGS. It is fragmentary; an incomplete text, which has no address, is to be found in an associated TS headed '(Mary Anne Lumb, 1811)', underlined. Mrs Joan Leach has MS, Legh family 'Rent Book from 1799-1812'.

(b) CRO contains Peter Holland's correspondence with Sir J. F. Leicester and other MSS: DLT/c34 /109-11, EUC 9 / 4408 / 18.

(c) Information about Swinton C. Holland from family papers [JS&PH] of the late John Swinton Holland, now deposited by Mrs Portia Holland in LUBL, especially a folio MS by SCH, 'Diary and Expenses & Journal of a Voyage & Journey from Liverpool to Trieste via Hull & Toninguen in the Summer of 1805; Do of Do from Malta to Falmouth and Sandle Bridge in the Spring of 1810', and various Dumbleton estate documents.

(d) The important holdings of Mr David Holland [DCLH] include SP Box (G): Henry Holland's *Account of an Excursion into North Wales* [ap. 6½ x 8", boards, calf spine; irregularly gathered, laid paper with Crown *over* Britannia wmk; about 109 pages written upon, 7 illustrations] and 3Di (g): his MS journals, which I have only glanced through.

Three journals of tours, jointly written by Mary, Bessy and Lucy Holland (assignment of hands not always certain): 'Lakes / 2' [ap. 4⅕ x 6¾", soft cover; three gatherings in 8s, machine-made paper with *open caps & s. caps* 'John Livesey / 1821' wmk; 48 pages, 2 pencil illustrations, second pasted over 'Charles Aikin Holland from his affectionate sister Mary']; 'Journal of an (intended) expedition to Barmouth in the Year 1823' [ap. 6½ x 8", soft marbled cover, calf spine, with slip '1st Vol. / Barmouth'; irregularly gathered, paper as 'Lakes 2', 84 pages]; '3d / Tour in Wales / Barmouth &c' [slip on soft marbled cover; ap. 3½ x 6", one gathering in 16, machine-made paper, no wmk; 32 pages; dated Barmouth August 22d 1823 at front, 20 September 1823 at end]. Other journals relating to these two tours have not been found.

There are also numerous letters, HW3: MS and TS, from HH to his father (6 June 1799–20 March [1812]); 3Di (d): Maria Edgeworth (19 December [1809]–7 August [1830]; 3Di (f): Lucy Aikin (c. 30 January 1804–19 January [1833]) and (mostly) Saba Holland; and SP Box (d): Anne Marsh, née Caldwell (1791-1874), Linley Wood, TS reminiscences, wr. 1839-40.

(e) JS&PH, LUBL: ECG, MS diary, owned by Mrs R. Trevor Dabbs, pr. pr. as *My Diary* by Clement Shorter, London, 1923; description, etc., in forthcoming edn by Anita Wilson and J. A. V. Chapple, together with a similar diary kept by Edward Thurstan Holland's mother, Turner and Robberds MSS. (Now publ. as *Private Voices*, Keele, 1996.)

(f) KUL: Wedgwood Archival Accumulations contain many letters, mostly to Josiah Wedgwood (1769-1843), from Samuel Holland of Sandlebridge, his sons Peter, Samuel and Swinton Colthurst Holland and his grandson Henry Holland; draft and copy replies.

(g) The Edward Hall collection of MSS, nos 204, 205 and 207, consists mainly of letters to John William Whittaker from his family. They are held at Leigh town hall.

Hall's introduction to EHC 220, 'John William Whittaker: a Cantab's postbag', states that 'four huge, cumbersome folio volumes' were originally 'crammed with the whole of the correspondence he received between the years 1804 and 1829' (p. ii). Some of these letters, mostly those dating from 1820 onwards, are kept in the District Central Library at Blackburn (not seen: Whittaker papers, G3WHI).

Edward Hall, ed. '*Cranford* again: the Knutsford letters, 1809-1824', TS in MCRL, is an extensive selection and commentary. For practical reasons I have used it for minor references and where an original letter (incl. some of the most interesting) could not be found. The TS is amusingly uncorrected: a bank that failed was 'likely to pay 11s ub rgw oiybs' on page 137, for example. I have silently emended its text. Wherever possible, significant quotations have been transcribed afresh from photocopies of the originals. I am greatly indebted to Wigan Archives staff for help and advice.

Rae's *Turtle at Mr Humble's* is based upon mostly earlier Whittaker papers in WYA: 34d76, letters and documents preserved by Sarah Whittaker (née Buck). See 8 (c) above.

11 Knutsford

(a) P. P. Burdett's *A Survey of the County Palatine of Chester* of 1777, facs. reprint, intro. J. B. Harley and P. Laxton, *HSLCOS*, I, 1974; 14 September 1807 map in Lysons (see below). The tithe map (1847) and apportionment (1848) are in CRO: EDT 287 /1-2. Cheshire Libraries, Arts and Archives, *Township Pack No 1*, is a useful collection of maps, directories, etc. See especially Pigot & Co.'s *Commercial Directories for 1828-9*, Manchester, n. d., and *for 1834*, repr. Manchester, 1982.

(b) Older works include Green; J. H. Hanshall, *The History of the County Palatinate of Chester*, Chester, 1817-23; *Memoirs of Richard Lovell Edgeworth, Esq., Begun by Himself and Concluded by his Daughter, Maria Edgeworth*, 2 vols, London, 1820; repr. intro. Desmond Clarke, Shannon, 1969; Daniel and Samuel Lysons, *Magna Britannia Being a Concise Topographical Account of the Several Countries of Great Britain*, II. ii, County Palatine of Chester, London, 1810; George Ormerod, *History of the County Palatine and City of Chester*, 2nd edn, London, 1882; Payne; *Historical Sketches of Nonconformity in The County Palatine of Chester by Various Ministers and Laymen Within the County*, ed. [W. Urwick], London and Manchester, 1864.

(c) More recent works include Kenneth D. Brown, *A Social History of the Nonconformist Ministry in England and Wales 1800-1930*, Oxford, 1988; Marilyn Butler, *Maria Edgeworth: A Literary Biography*, Oxford, 1972; G. Stella Davis, *A History of Macclesfield*, Didsbury, 1976; K. Goodchild, P. Ikin and J. Leach, *Looking Back at Knutsford*, Timperley, 1984; Howard Hodson, *Cheshire, 1660-1780: Restoration to Industrial Revolution*, Chester, 1978; Margaret C. Jacob, *The Cultural Meaning of the Scientific Revolution*, New York, 1988; Geoffrey King, *Portrait of Knutsford*, Wilmslow, 1988; George A. Payne, *An Ancient Chapel: Brook Street Chapel, Knutsford with Allostock Chapel, Nr. Knutsford*, Banbury, 1934; Donald Read, *Peterloo: The 'Massacre' and its Background* (1958), Manchester, 1973; Raymond Richards, *Old Cheshire Churches: A Survey [and] Old Chapels*, rev. and enl. edn, Didsbury, 1973; Geoffrey Scard, *Squire and Tenant: Life in Rural Cheshire, 1760-1900*, Chester, 1981; *Victoria County History of Cheshire*; Robert Walmsley, *Peterloo: The Case Reopened*, Manchester, 1969; John K. Walton, *Lancashire: A Social History 1558-1939*, Manchester, 1987.

12 Barford, Avonbank and Byerleys

(a) The Shakespeare Birthplace Trust acts as the record office for Stratford-upon-Avon. It contains the sketchbook, [fourteen completed sketches, mostly of Stratford], of Jessie Cuthbertson Scott, a little material about Avonbank and a great number of documents relating to the Greaves family. WRO also has Greaves documents, incl. a copy of R. Greaves's will.

(b) Phyllis D. Hicks, *A Quest of Ladies: The Story of a Warwickshire School*, [Birmingham, 1949], is by far the most important source, illustrated and based upon considerable research but inadequately referenced. The important Coltman MSS have not been found, but KUL holds letters to Josiah Wedgwood used extensively: 13 – 12228-75 (MB), 12313-17 (KB), 12334-56 (FB), 12357-61 (JB) and 12362-425 (Mrs FB).

(c) Other works: *Joseph Arch: The Story of His Life Told by Himself*, ed. The Countess of Warwick, London, 1898 [ed. J. G. O'Leary, 1966, but abridged]; Pamela Horn, *Joseph Arch (1826-1919): The Farm Workers' Leader*, Kineton, 1971; William Field, *Memoirs of the Life, Writings, and Opinions of the Rev. Samuel Parr ... With Biographical Notices*, London, 1828; Warren Derry, *Dr. Parr: A Portrait of the Whig Dr. Johnson*, Oxford, 1966.

13 William, John and Elizabeth Stevenson from 1817

(a) John Stevenson MSS purchased by J. G. Sharps from a Mrs Ethel L. Smith (see Sharps, p. xii), whose husband, when alive, wrote to the *Manchester Guardian* that he possessed them (letter in MCRL). JGS believes they were received in settlement of a small debt (JGS to JAVC, 12 June 1980). Stevenson TSS came from Mr J. T. Lancaster, who was in contact with Clement Shorter when preparing an M.Litt. at Oxford. Many of these texts are duplicated or triplicated, but a full collation reveals few variants. Their interrelationships have therefore been ignored and manifest errors – e.g., Sir David Milne as 'Sir Davidill' – silently emended. All have been used in the text above.

(b) BRO contains *Guild minute books*, B1; *The Freemen's Roll of the Burgesses or Freemen of Berwick-upon-Tweed*, Berwick, 1842; 1842 disentailing deed for 44 Bridge Street; *Berwick Advertiser* (microfilm, BRO). See also 1 above.

(c) Christopher Dandeker, 'Patronage and bureaucratic control – The case of the naval officer in English society 1780-1850', *BJS*, XXIX, 1978, pp. 311-12; H. C. A. Hardy, *A Supplement to a Register of Ships ... East India Company*, 4th edn, 1835; M. Lewis, *The Navy in Transition 1814-1864*, London, 1966.

(d) NLS: *Catalogue of MSS Acquired since 1925*, III *Blackwood Papers*: letters from William Stevenson to William Blackwood (3 February 1817 to 28 December 1827) and copies of replies in the outgoing Blackwood letter books (B2, B3, B5). References are given by date; the year of the Stevenson letters is often missing, but they are usually fully dated by the recipient. A letter to Stevenson of 21 February 1826 (wet-press copy) is indexed as to James Stevenson. The Galt correspondence is catalogued in the same volume, as are the letters from B. W. Procter, dated [?1821], and W. J. Thomson, dated 22 September 1834.

(e) *Wellesley Index to Victorian Periodicals; Autobiographical Recollections of Sir John Bowring, With a Brief Memoir by Lewin B. Bowring*, London, 1877; Charles Knight, *Passages of a Working Life During Half a Century with a Prelude of Early*

Reminiscences (1864-65), 3 vols, Shannon, 1971; George L. Nesbitt, *Benthamite Reviewing: The First Twelve Years of The Westminster Review 1824-1836*, New York, 1934; Janet Percival, TS, *A Handlist of the Diffusion of Useful Knowledge Society's Correspondence and Papers*, The Library, UCL, 1978; Thomas Rees, *Reminiscences of Literary London:* see 3 above; Harold Smith, *The Society for the Diffusion of Useful Knowledge 1826-1846: A Social and Bibliographical Evaluation*, Halifax, Nova Scotia, 1974; *Sir John Bowring 1792-1872: Aspects of His Life and Career*, ed. Joyce Youings, Plymouth, 1993.

14 India and Burma

(a) The India Office Library and Records, BL, is indispensable for documentary material like ships' logs, church records, etc., and for numerous monographs and works of reference.

(b) Older works: John Crawfurd, *Journal of an Embassy from the Governor-General of India to the Court of Ava, in the Year 1827*, London, 1829; Captain F. B. Doveton, *Reminiscences of the Burmese War, in 1824-5-6 (Originally Published in the Asiatic Journal)*, London, 1852; Henry Havelock, *Memoir of the Three Campaigns of Major-General Sir Archibald Campbell's Army in Ava*, Serampore, 1828; Intelligence Branch (Division of the Chief of the Staff, Army Headquarters India), *Frontier and Overseas Expeditions from India*, Simla, 1907; H. Lister Maw, Lt RN, *Memoirs of the Early Operations of the Burmese War. Addressed to the Editor of the United Service Journal*, London, 1832; Major [J. J.] Snodgrass, *Narrative of the Burmese War, Detailing the Operations* [May 1824 to February 1826], 2nd edn, London, 1827; An Officer, etc. [T. A. Trant], *Two Years in Ava. From May 1824, to May 1826*, London, 1827; Horace Hayman Wilson, *Documents Illustrative of the Burmese War With an Introductory Sketch of the Events of the War, and An Appendix [of documents]*, Calcutta, 1827. (Hiram Cox, *Journal of a Residence in the Burham Empire*, London, 1821, relates to the end of the eighteenth century.) I have been able to draw upon the resources of HUL's South-East Asia collection.

(c) More recent works: Maung Htin Aung, *The Stricken Peacock: Anglo-Burmese Relations 1752-1948*, The Hague, 1965, and *A History of Burma*, New York and London, 1967; C. A. Bayley, *Indian Society and the Making of the British Empire*, New Cambridge History of India, II. i, Cambridge, etc., 1988; Richard M. Cooler, *British Romantic Views of the First Anglo-Burmese War 1824-1826*, Dekalb, Ill., 1977 (28 illustr. repr. from Joseph Moore, *Eighteen Views Taken at and near Rangoon*, London, [1825] and James Kershaw, *Views in the Burman Empire*, London, [1831]); Maurice-Paul Gautier, *Captain Frederick Marryat: L'homme et L'œuvre*, Montreal, Paris, Bruxelles, 1973; Gerald S. Graham, *Great Britain in the Indian Ocean: A Study of Maritime Enterprise 1810-1850*, Oxford, 1967; G. E. Harvey, *History of Burma From the Earliest Times to 10 March 1824, the Beginning of the British Conquest*, London (1925), repr. 1967; H. B. Morse, *The Chronicles of the East India Company Trading to China 1635-1834*, Oxford, 1926; C. Northcote Parkinson, *Trade in the Eastern Seas 1793-1813*, Cambridge, 1937; B. R. Pearn, *A History of Rangoon*, Rangoon, 1939 (illustr.); Dorothy Woodman, *The Making of Burma*, London, 1962.

15 Holland family, Liverpool and North Wales

(a) Autobiographical notes and memoirs of Samuel Holland III: NLW: MSS. 4983C, partly in Holland's autograph and partly in that of his wife, with deletions, interlinings, etc. (See also appendix D.) Sir William Ll. Davies, ed., *The Memoirs of Samuel Holland One of the Pioneers of the North Wales Slate Industry*, Merioneth Historical and Record Society, Extra Publications series 1, no. 1, 1953, prints most of the text with reasonable accuracy. MS 4987B is SH's journal, 1 January 1823-29 May 1824; MSS. 4984-5C, 4986B and 4543C contain numerous other Holland papers relating to his life and work. See esp. H. L. Malchow, 'Festiniog to Westminster: Samuel Holland', in *Gentleman Capitalists: The Social and Political World of the Victorian Businessman*, London, 1991.

(b) Older works include [J. Aspinall], *Liverpool a Few Years Since*, London and Liverpool, 1852; Thomas Baines, *History of the Commerce and Town of Liverpool*, London, 1852; Richard Brooke, *Liverpool As It Was During the Last Quarter of the Eighteenth Century*, Liverpool, 1853; Samuel Lewis, *A Topographical Dictionary of Wales*, 2 vols, London, 1833; Gomer Williams, *History of the Liverpool Privateers and Letters of Marque with an Account of the Liverpool Slave Trade* (1897), repr. London, 1966.

(c) More recent books: Michael Burn, *The Age of Slate*, Blaenau Ffestiniog, 1976; Robert E. Carlson, *The Liverpool and Manchester Railway Project 1821-1831*, Newton Abbot, 1969; A. H. Dodd, *The Industrial Revolution in North Wales*, 3rd edn, Cardiff, 1971; Leslie Wynne Evans, *Education in Industrial Wales 1700-1900: A Study of the Works School System in Wales During the Industrial Revolution*, Cardiff, 1971; Ivor Wynne Jones, *Eagles Do Not Catch Flies: The Story of J. W. Greaves & Sons*, Blaenau Ffestiniog, 1986; M. J. T. Lewis, *Sails on the Dwyryd: The River Transport of Ffestiniog Slate*, and with M. C. Williams, *Pioneers of Ffestiniog Slate*, Snowdonia National Park Study Centre, Plas Tan y Bwlch, 1989 and 1987; Jean Lindsay, *A History of the North Wales Slate Industry*, Newton Abbot, 1974; B. H. Tolley, 'The Liverpool campaign against the order in council and the war of 1812', in J. P. Harris, ed., *Liverpool and Merseyside: Essays in the Economic and Social History of the Port and Its Hinterland*, Liverpool, 1969; Roy Millward and Adrian Robinson, *Landscapes of North Wales*, Newton Abbot, etc., 1978.

(d) Articles: Joseph Mayer, 'On Liverpool pottery', *THSLC*, VII for 1854-55, 1858; W. A. S. McIntyre, 'The first scheme for docks at Birkenhead and the proposed canal across the Wirral', *THSLC*, CXXIV for 1972, 1973; H. McLachlan, 'A Liverpool lady's [Caroline Thornely's] journal half a century ago', *TUHS*, XI, 1955-58.

(e) Maps: F. R. Price and William Lawton, 'Birkenhead estate', January 1824; 'Plan of the township or chapelry of Birkenhead in the County of Chester', 1844. I must thank A. J. Worthington and D. N. Thompson of BCPLA for their help.

16 Turner family and Newcastle-upon-Tyne

(a) WT's MS 'Register of births and baptisms at Hanover Square chapel, Newcastle upon Tyne, 1781-1841' is now in TWA (1787/9), which also holds the congregation's registers, minutes, financial papers and correspondence, scrapbooks and Messrs Small & Brough, *Catalogue of Valuable Books, Forming a Great Portion of the Library of the Rev. William Turner*, Newcastle, 1842. TWA: 1787/113 contains the printed record of Turner's ordination (Wakefield, 1782) and a number of Turner's own publications. It does not appear to contain a more confidential 'congregational common-place-book' mentioned in a letter Turner wrote to his daughter, Mrs Mary Robberds, in 1811, though TWA: 1787/12 is the 'Minister's Book of Members', c. 1810-34.

NLPS's library contains in particular William Turner II, 'Speculations on the propriety of attempting the establishment of a literary society in Newcastle', Literary and Philosophical Society paper, 24 January 1793, and *A Short Sketch of the History of Protestant Nonconformity, and of the Society Assembling in Hanover-Square, Newcastle*, Newcastle, 1811 [with section on 'Present State']. Its *Papers Read at the Monthly Meetings, 1894-1814*, and grangerised *Reports* are invaluable. The Amelia Moor collection of NLPS contains letters to Turner of Newcastle and his father from a variety of correspondents. See also 2 (c), 8 (b) and 10 (e) above.

(b) For Turner II himself see especially George Harris, *The Christian Character, the Union of Knowledge and Benevolence, Piety and Virtue, as Illustrated in the Life and Labours of the Late Rev. William Turner*, London and Newcastle, 1859, and J. Kenrick, 'Memoir of the late Rev. William Turner', *CR*, n. s. XV, 1959, pp. 351-66, 410-24, 451-61. See also William Gaskell, *A Sermon on the Death of Rev. William Turner*, Manchester, 1959; Derek Orange, 'Rational dissent and provincial science: William Turner and the Newcastle Literary and Philosophical Society', in *Metropolis and Province: Science in British Culture, 1780-1850*, ed. Ian Inkster and Jack Morell, London, 1983.

(c) Older works consulted include Turner's own history of Warrington Academy and its students in *MR*, VIII, IX and X, 1813-15; new edn, intro. G. A. Carter, Warrington, 1957. See also the grangerised copy of Eneas Mackenzie, *A Descriptive and Historical Account of the Town and County of Newcastle-upon-Tyne, Including the Borough of Gatshead*, 3 vols, Newcastle, 1827 (NLPS); [John Baillie], *An Impartial History of the Town and County of Newcastle upon Tyne and Its Vicinity*, Newcastle, 1801; J. Collingwood Bruce, *A Hand-Book to Newcastle-upon-Tyne*, London and Newcastle, 1863; Ralph Edward and Cuthbert Ellison Carr, *The History of the Family of Carr*, 3 vols, 1833-99; R. J. Charlton, *Newcastle Town*, 1885; Henry Lonsdale, *The Worthies of Cumberland*, IV, London, 1873 (for Losh, also in *DNB Missing Persons*); Harriet Martineau, 'The Newcastle improvements', *Penny Magazine of the Society for the Diffusion of Useful Knowledge*, 14 March–9 May 1840 (six articles); Maberly Phillips, *A History of Banks, Bankers, and Banking, in Northumberland, Durham, and North Yorkshire ... From 1755-1894*, 1894 (a remarkably comprehensive work); D. B. Reid, *Report on the State of Newcastle upon Tyne and Other Towns*, 1845; B. W. Richardson, ed., *Thomas Sopwith ... With Excerpts From His Diary of Fifty-Seven Years*, London, 1891; John Sykes, *Local Records; or Historical Register of Remarkable Events*, 2 vols, Newcastle, 1833 and 1866; William Turner III, *Lives of Eminent Unitarians*, 2 vols, London, 1840-43; R. Welford, *Men of Mark Twixt Tyne and Tweed*, 3 vols, Newcastle, 1895.

(d) *A Plan of the Town and County of Newcastle upon Tyne ... Gateshead ... From an Actual Survey by Thomas Oliver* [engraved, 1830], Newcastle, 1831 (with *Reference* directory); *Oliver's New Picture of Newcastle upon Tyne* (NLPS: no title-page [c. 1831]); Town Council, *Plan: Newcastle upon Tyne 1945*, Newcastle, 1945. J. W. Carmichael and Richard Welford, *Pictures of Tyneside, or Life and Scenery on the River Tyne Sixty Years Ago*, Newcastle, 1881, contains thirty-three engravings.

(e) More recent works include Michael Durey, *The Return of the Plague: British Society and the Cholera 1831-2*, Dublin, 1979; D. Gardner-Medwin, intro. *Medicine in Northumbria: Essays in the History of Medicine in the North East of England*, Pybus Society, Newcastle, 1993; C. J. Hunt, *The Book Trade in Northumberland and Durham to 1860*, Newcastle-upon-Tyne, 1975 (P. J. Wallis, *Supplement*, 1981); A. R. Laws, *Schola Novocastrensis: A Biographical History of the Royal Free Grammar School*, II, 1700-1845, Newcastle, 1932; *The Diaries and Correspondence of James Losh*, ed. Edward Hughes, Surtees Society, CLXXI, CLXXIV, 2 vols, 1962-63; John S. MacLean, *The Newcastle & Carlisle Railway 1825-1862*, Newcastle, 1948; F. D. W. Manders, *A History of Gateshead*, Gateshead, 1973; S. Middlebrook, *Newcastle upon Tyne: Its Growth and Achievement*, Newcastle, 1950 (with maps and illustr.); 2nd edn, Wakefield, 1968, with bibliog., brings its growth up to date; also *The Advancement of Knowledge in Newcastle upon Tyne: The Literary and Philosophical Society as an Educational Pioneer*, Newcastle, 1974; R. J. Morris, *Cholera 1832: The Social Response to an Epidemic*, London, 1976; R. Spence Watson, *The History of the Literary and Philosophical Society of Newcastle upon Tyne 1793 to 1896*, London, 1897 [vol. 2, 1896-1989, by C. Parish *et al.*, Newcastle, 1980]; R. K. Webb, *Harriet Martineau: A Radical Victorian*, London, Melbourne, Toronto, 1960; Lyall Wilkes and Gordon Dodds, *Tyneside Classical: The Newcastle of Grainger, Dobson & Clayton*, London, 1964; E. M. Youngson, 'The reform movement in Northumberland and Durham, 1815-1932' (NLPS: TS, 1936).

17 Gaskell family, Warrington and Manchester

(a) For Warrington see W. Beamont, *History of Latchford*, Warrington, 1880; J. R. Bulmer, tr. & ed., *The Unitarian Chapel, Cairo Street, Warrington: Births & Baptisms, Deaths & Burials, Monumental Inscriptions*, Warrington, 1980 (TS); G. A. Carter, *Warrington Hundred: A Handbook*, Warrington, 1947; Austin M. Crowe, *Warrington Ancient and Modern: A History of the Town and Neighbourhood*, facs. edn, Warrington, 1947; Arthur Mounfield, *Early Warrington Nonconformity*, Warrington, 1922; W. B. Stephens, *Adult Education and Society in an Industrial Town: Warrington 1800-1900*, Exeter, 1980. Both Manchester and Warrington can be found in Edward Baines and W. Parson, *History, Directory, and Gazetteer of the County Palatine of Lancaster*, II, Liverpool, 1825.

(b) MCL: 923.4 H32 is the MS diary in three vols of Edward Herford (1815-96). For him see F. S. Stancliffe, *John Shaw's 1738-1938*, Manchester, 1938, and obit. cutting (MCL: f. 942. 7589. M119). My transcriptions from vol. 1 of the diary, which contains many patches of shorthand, have been lightly edited. The second volume begins in July 1838 and the third in 1857.

(c) T. J. Wyke, 'Nineteenth century Manchester: a preliminary bibliography', in *City, Class and Culture: Studies of Social Policy and Cultural Production in Victorian Manchester*, ed. A. J. Kidd and K. W. Roberts, Manchester 1985, is very useful for its breadth of reference. Valdo Pons, 'Housing conditions and residential patterns in Manchester of the 1830s and 40s' (HUL: TS, 1975) analyses contemporary accounts of the changing town.

Sir Thomas Baker, *Memories of a Dissenting Chapel*, Manchester, 1884, and John Seed, 'Unitarianism, political economy and the antinomies of liberal culture in Manchester, 1830-50', *SH*, VII, 1982, pp. 1-25, are important for Cross Street chapel, its ministers and laity. The chapel's series of reports of the Ministry to the Poor, the first of which was printed by T. Forrest of Market Street, Manchester, in 1833, have been utilised by Seed and related to ECG's fiction by Fryckstedt. DWL supplied a *Report of the Proceedings of a Meeting of the British and Foreign Unitarian Association, Held in Cross Street Chapel, Manchester, and of the Speeches Delivered at the Dinner, in the Town Hall, Salford*, T. Forrest, Manchester, 1830.

(d) Recent works include: B. C. Bloomfield, 'A handlist of the papers in the deed box of Sir J. P. Kay Shuttleworth', College of St Mark and St John occasional papers, no. 2, 1961; H. L. Freeman, 'Samuel Gaskell', in *Some Manchester Doctors: A Biographical Collection to Mark the 150th Anniversary of the Manchester Medical Society 1834-1984*, ed. Willis J. Elwood and A. Félicité Tuxford, Manchester, 1984; V. A. C. Gatrell, 'Incorporation and the pursuit of Liberal hegemony in Manchester 1790-1839', *Municipal Reform and the Industrial City*, ed. Derek Fraser, Leicester and New York, 1982; John V. Pickstone, *Medicine and Industrial Society: A History of Hospital Development in Manchester and its Region, 1752-1946*, Manchester, 1985; A. Shelston, 'Elizabeth Gaskell's Manchester', *GSJ*, III, 1989, pp. 46-67 (illustr.); Dorothy and Alan Shelston, *The Industrial City 1820-1870*, Basingstoke, 1990; Arnold Thackray, 'Natural knowledge in cultural context: the Manchester model', *AHR*, LXIX, 1974, pp. 672-709.

(e) Standard works on cholera [see 16(e) above], which are based upon Home Office Papers and newspapers from London and Liverpool, differ about details of the Swan Street Hospital riot (orphan child or not; Hare, Haze or Hayes; three or four troops of hussars, etc.). I have followed MCL's MS 'Proceedings of the Manchester Board of Health' for 3-6 September 1832, *Wheeler's Manchester Chronicle* and the *Manchester Times* for 8 September 1832, and *Manchester City News*, query no. 457, September 1890, efficiently supplied by K. M. Lapsley, Librarian, Local Studies Unit.

18 Art in Edinburgh

The longest biographical entry for W. J. Thomson is in Basil S. Long, *British Miniaturists*, London, 1929; works and addresses listed in W. D. McKay, *The Royal Scottish Academy 1826-1916*, Glasgow, 1917; and *Royal Scottish Academy Exhibitors 1826-1990*, ed. Charles Baile de Laperrière, IV; technical description in Daphne Foskett, *Collecting Miniatures*, Woodbridge, 1979. See also Theodore Bolton, *Early American Portrait Painters in Miniature*, 2 vols, New York, 1921; Michael Bryan, *Bryan's Dictionary of Painters and Engravers*, ed. G. C. Williamson, New York, 1964; W. D. McKay and Frank Rinder, *The Royal Scottish Academy 1826-1916 [with] A Historical Narrative of the Origin and Development*, Glasgow, 1917.

Index

'Who knows whether the best of men be known?'
(Sir Thomas Browne, *Urn-Burial*)

This is a selective index, with bold type numbers used to distinguish main references. Relationships given without qualification are to Elizabeth Gaskell (née Stevenson). Other basic information about many individuals is to be found in the Appendices.